MAUI

GREG ARCHER

Contents

Although every effort was made to make sure the information in this book was accurate when going to press, research was impacted by the COVID-19 pandemic and things may have changed since the time of writing. Be sure to confirm specific details, like opening hours, closures, and travel guidelines and restrictions, when making your travel plans. For more detailed information, *see p. 378.*

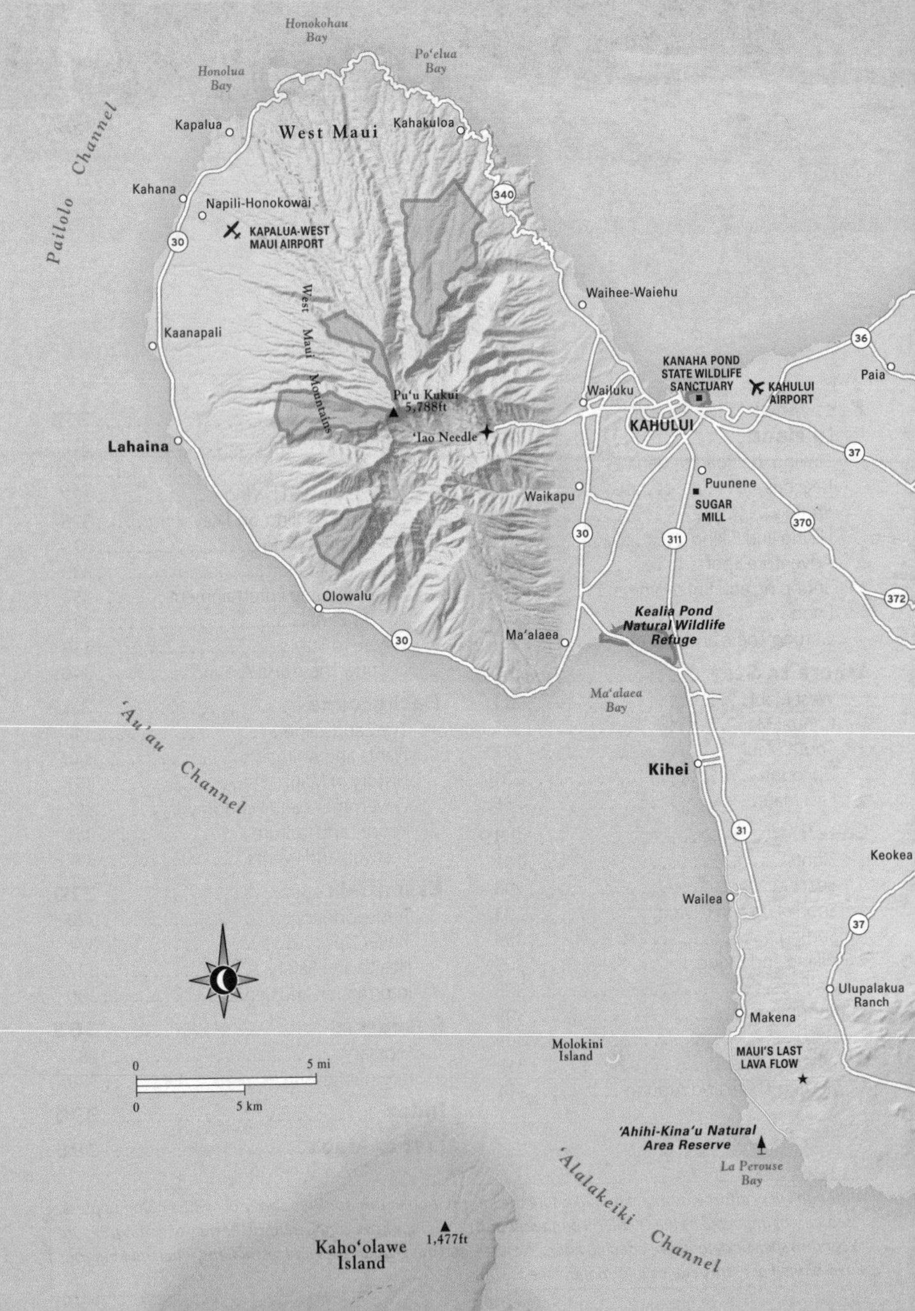
Honokohau Bay
Po'elua Bay
Honolua Bay
Pailolo Channel
Kapalua
West Maui
Kahakuloa
340
Kahana
Napili-Honokowai
KAPALUA-WEST MAUI AIRPORT
30
West Maui Mountains
Waihee-Waiehu
Kaanapali
36
KANAHA POND STATE WILDLIFE SANCTUARY
Paia
KAHULUI AIRPORT
Wailuku
Pu'u Kukui 5,788ft
KAHULUI
'Iao Needle
Lahaina
37
Puunene
Waikapu
SUGAR MILL
370
30
311
372
Olowalu
Kealia Pond Natural Wildlife Refuge
Ma'alaea
30
Ma'alaea Bay
'Au'au Channel
Kihei
31
Keokea
Wailea
37
Ulupalakua Ranch
Makena
Molokini Island
MAUI'S LAST LAVA FLOW
0
5 mi
0
5 km
'Ahihi-Kina'u Natural Area Reserve
La Perouse Bay
'Alalakeiki Channel
1,477ft
Kaho'olawe Island

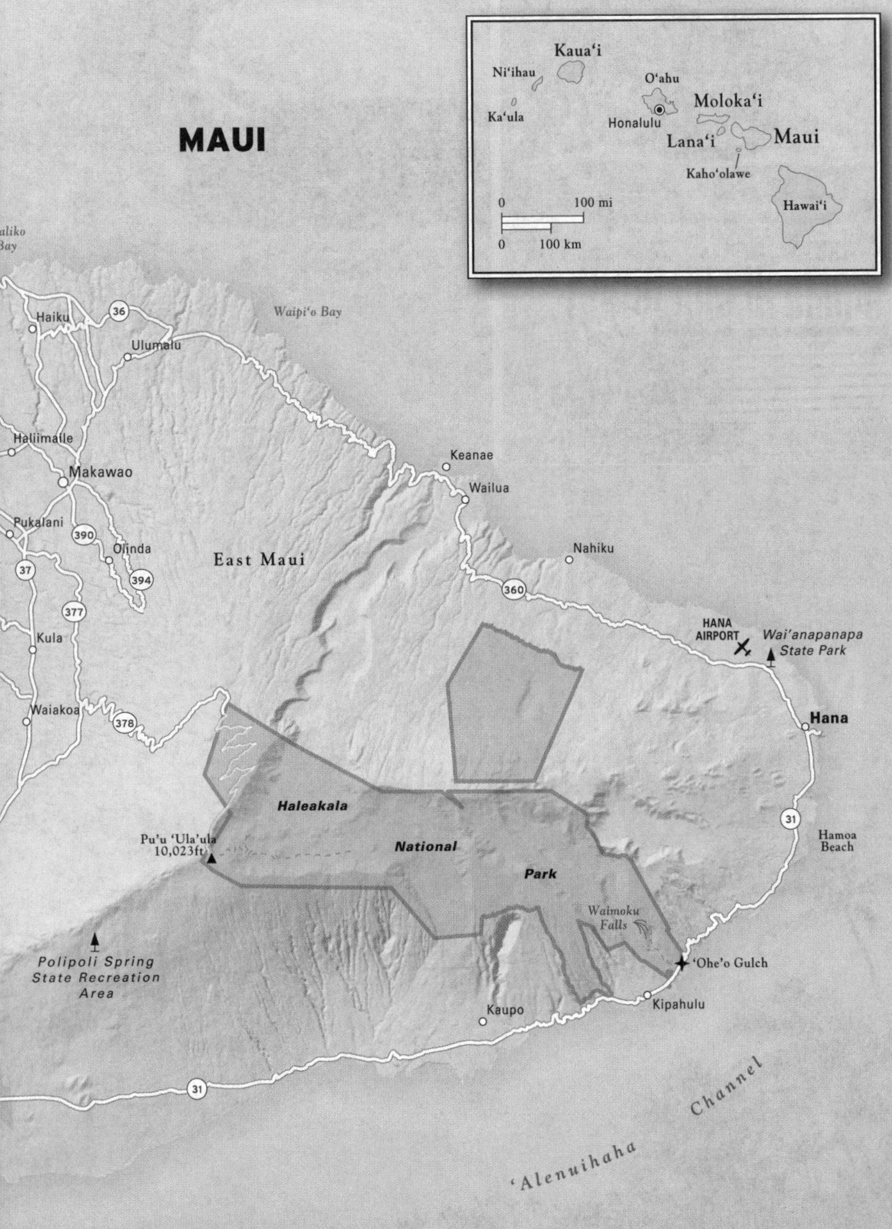
MAUI
Kaua'i
Ni'ihau
O'ahu
Moloka'i
Ka'ula
Honalulu
Lana'i
Maui
Kaho'olawe
0
100 mi
0
100 km
Hawai'i
Waipi'o Bay
Haiku
36
Ulumalu
Haliimaile
Makawao
Keanae
Wailua
Pukalani
390
Olinda
Nahiku
East Maui
37
394
360
377
Kula
HANA AIRPORT
Wai'anapanapa State Park
Waiakoa
378
Hana
Haleakala
National
Park
Pu'u 'Ula'ula 10,023ft
31
Hamoa Beach
Waimoku Falls
Polipoli Spring State Recreation Area
'Ohe'o Gulch
Kipahulu
Kaupo
31
Channel
'Alenuihaha
© MOON.COM

DISCOVER

Maui

There is a prominent Hawaiian saying about Maui: *Maui no ka oi,* "Maui is the best."

The countless stretches of golden sand are an obvious draw, but sand alone doesn't entice millions of visitors to a dot in the middle of the Pacific. Perhaps it's more than just the thought of relaxing in a lounge chair with a mai tai in hand. Maybe it's also the way the trade winds blow across a beach of black sand. Or it's the hope of a close encounter with a giant green sea turtle while snorkeling off the coast. Maybe it's the way the setting sun reflects in the waters, both fiery and calm in the same fleeting moment.

Of course, Maui's magic is also found in the endless adventures to be embraced on the island. Hike through a thick bamboo forest and find yourself at the base of a waterfall cascading down a rocky cliff. Ride your first wave and feel the thrill of the surf as you glide across a silky blue break. Or wake up at 3am and drive up a dark mountainside in the freezing cold to see the first rays of light illuminate Haleakala Crater.

No matter what drew you to the island, the secret to Maui's allure lies in the many moments that stick with you long after you've left it behind.

Clockwise from top left: Maui Wine; a diver swims near a sea turtle; waterfall near Hana; whale tail; the art of hula; sunset on Napili Bay.

11 TOP EXPERIENCES

1 **Snorkel and Dive:** Encounter the island's vibrant marinelife at offshore spots like **Honolua Bay** (pictured)—where you might see everything from a sea turtle to a spinner dolphin—and boat-accessible **Molokini Crater,** the crescent-shaped crater off Maui's south shore where more than 250 species of fish live (page 23).

2 **Drive the Road to Hana:** A journey down this lush and winding road is a tropical dream filled with **beaches, waterfalls,** and **forest trails** (page 233).

3 **Bask on the Most Beautiful Beaches:** Offering abundant beauty and water activities, the world-renowned beaches of Maui beckon (page 21).

4 Catch the Views from Haleakala: The great heights of Maui's majestic dormant volcano provide incomparable views of sunrise, sunset, and the star-studded night sky. Epic opportunities for hiking and biking also await (page 196).

5 Surf World-Class Waves: Celebrated for its surf, the island is ideal for everyone from beginners—who get the hang of it at **Lahaina Breakwall**—to big-wave adventurists, who flock to **Ho'okipa Beach Park** and **Pe'ahi,** also known as **Jaws** (pages 25 and 254).

6 **Journey to 'Iao Valley State Monument:** An atmospheric drive brings you to this historical park, where a short hike leads you to views of the much-photographed **'Iao Needle.** This spectacular landscape is so remote, it's believed the bones of Hawaiian royalty are buried in the caves (page 114).

7 **Hike:** From **volcanic landscapes** to **verdant rainforests,** Maui's varied terrain offers dramatic options for the trail-bound (page 26).

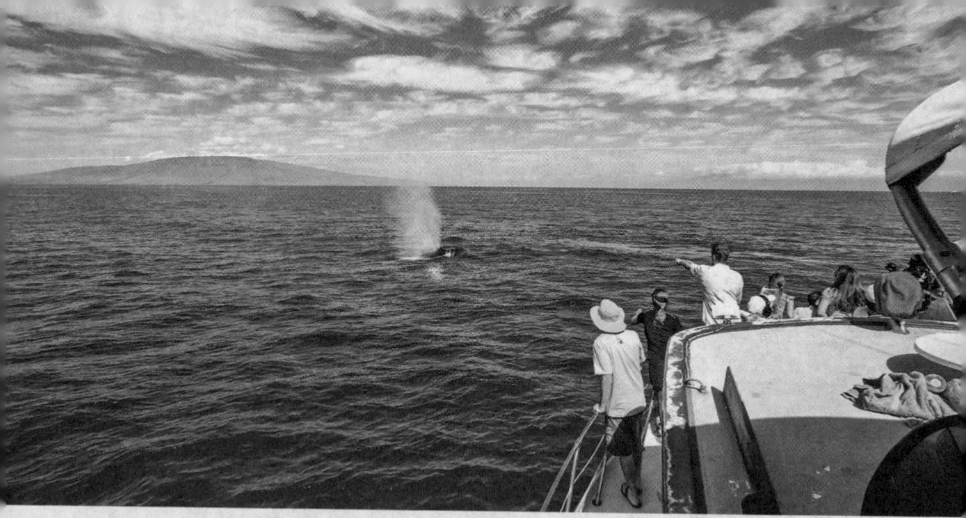

8 **Go Whale-Watching:** From December to May, these waters are home to the largest population of humpback whales in the world (page 76).

9 **Taste Your Way through Upcountry:** Sample the offerings of the island's local producers, from a **goat dairy farm** (page 202) to a **winery** (page 207) and **vodka distilleries** (pages 200 and 204).

10 **Stargaze in Upcountry:** The nighttime sky is so luminous, with the Milky Way so boldly on display, that you feel as if you're in outer space. Nothing compares to stargazing here (page 208).

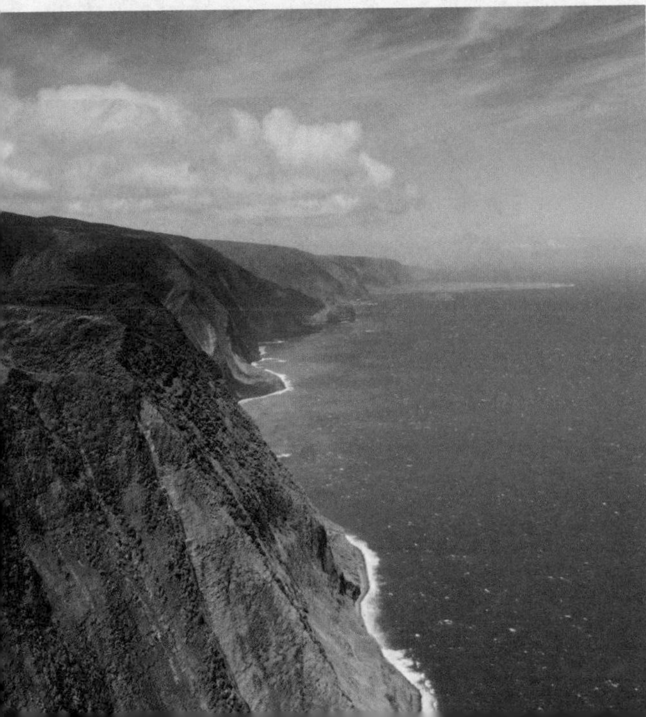

11 **Island-Hop to Lana'i or Moloka'i:** Other relaxing island getaways are just a short ferry or flight away (pages 289 and 315).

Planning Your Trip

Where to Go

Lahaina and West Maui

West Maui pulses with a unique coastal vibe. The historic town of **Lahaina** was once the capital of the Hawaiian kingdom, and it retains a port town atmosphere. Warm weather and mostly dry conditions make this region a spectacular place for outdoor adventure. Snorkel near sea turtles at **Napili Bay,** lounge on the beach in **Kapalua,** ride the zip line above **Ka'anapali,** or hike to **Nakalele Blowhole.**

Central Maui

Central Maui is the island's population center and the seat of county government. Most visitors blow through town on the way to their beachfront resort, but Central Maui has its own set of sights off the regular trail. The twisting road into **'Iao Valley** is the region's most popular attraction. **Kepaniwai Heritage Gardens** exhibits Maui's multicultural heritage, and down on the shore at **Kanaha Beach Park,** windsurfers and kitesurfers take to the waves along the stretch of Maui's North Shore.

Kihei and South Maui

From the celebrity-laden resorts of **Wailea** to the condo-dwelling snowbirds of **Kihei,** South Maui is all about worshipping the sun and enjoying the procession of beaches. **Makena** remains South Maui's most adventurous area, with snorkeling, scuba diving, hiking trails, kayaking, and some of the island's most photo-worthy beaches. Just offshore, **Molokini Crater** offers 100-foot (90-m) visibility and the chance to snorkel with up to 250 species of fish.

Ka'anapali Beach

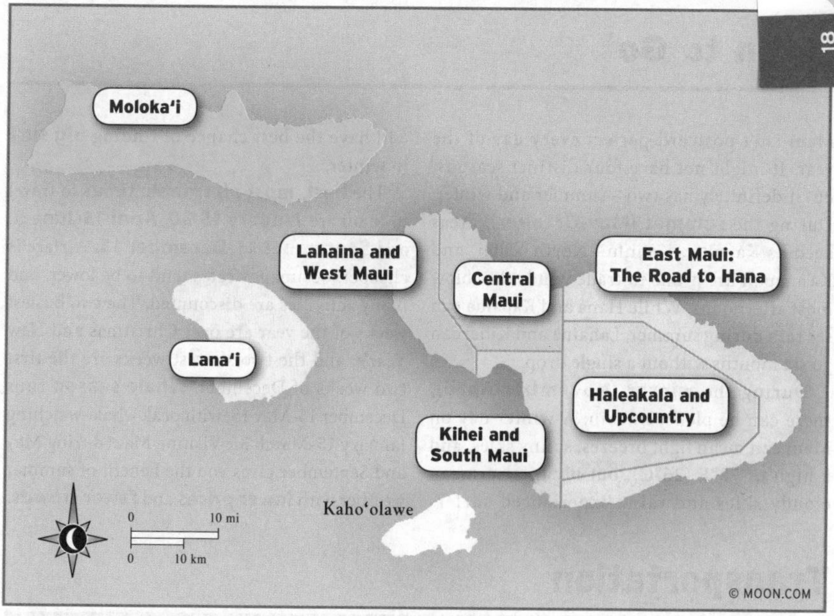

Moloka'i
Lahaina and West Maui
Central Maui
East Maui: The Road to Hana
Lana'i
Haleakala and Upcountry
Kihei and South Maui
Kaho'olawe
0 10 mi
0 10 km

Haleakala and Upcountry

Rural, laid-back, and refreshingly cool, Upcountry is Maui's most underrated zone. Agriculture and produce dominate **Kula,** and everything from vegetables to vineyards and vodka distilleries, coffee, and goat cheese can be found in this rural and relaxing enclave. **Polipoli** is the island's little-known adventure zone, where mountain biking, paragliding, and hiking take place in a forest shrouded in mist. Watch the dramatic sunrise from the frosty peak of towering **Haleakala,** the sacred volcano from which the demigod Maui famously snared the sun.

East Maui: The Road to Hana

The bohemian town of **Pa'ia** is as trendy as it is jovial. Surfers ride waves along undeveloped beaches, patrons shop in locally owned boutiques, and the town is home to some the island's best restaurants. Along the famous, twisting **Road to Hana,** tumbling waterfalls and rugged hiking trails await. The **Pools of 'Ohe'o** spill down cliffs to the sea. The hike through a bamboo forest to the base of **Waimoku Falls** is considered the island's best trek.

Lana'i

Home to 3,500 residents and one large resort, this island is a playground of outdoor adventure. Learn about the island's history at the **Lana'i Culture and Heritage Center,** and make the journey down to **Kaunolu** to see an ancient village settlement frozen in time.

Moloka'i

Taking time to explore this island offers a chance to experience the roots of native Hawaiian culture. Take a guided tour into historic **Halawa Valley,** one of the oldest settlements in Hawaii, or enjoy paddling off the sublime southern coast of **East Moloka'i.** Watch the sunset from **Papohaku Beach,** one of the state's longest and most deserted stretches of sand, or climb your way high into the mists of the **Moloka'i Forest Reserve.**

When to Go

Maui isn't postcard-perfect every day of the year. It might not have four distinct seasons, but it definitely has two—summer and winter. During the **summer (May-October),** areas such as Kapalua, Kahului, North Kihei, and Ka'anapali are prone to trade winds that blow most afternoons. While Hana and Kapalua can see rain during summer, Lahaina and Kihei can go six months without a single drop.

During the **winter (November-April),** there can be plenty of rain. A winter day on Maui can mean light breezes, sunny skies, and a high of 78°F (26°C), but it can also mean cloudy skies and rain. Experienced surfers will have the best chance of finding **big surf** in winter.

The **best, most affordable times** to travel to Maui are **January 15-30, April 15-June 5,** and **September 15-December 15.** Airfare is cheaper, occupancy rates tend to be lower, and many activities are discounted. The two busiest weeks of the year are over Christmas and New Year's, and the two slowest weeks are the first two weeks of December. **Whale season** runs December 15-May 15, with peak whale-watching January 15-March 31. Visiting Maui during May and September gives you the benefit of summer weather with **lower prices** and **fewer crowds.**

Transportation

All flights from the continental United States arrive at **Kahului Airport** (OGG). Numerous car-rental options are available, and to save money when renting a car, consider renting from an off-site operator rather than a corporate chain. The rates are often much more affordable, and you get the benefit of a local-looking car. During the peak winter season and around Christmas holidays, reserve a rental car well in advance to ensure you get the best price.

The island is most easily explored by **car,** but if you only plan to stay in the resort areas, consider using **taxis** instead. With resort parking fees and fuel for the car, it can sometimes be cheaper to take taxis than rent a car. If there's a specific place you want to visit that requires a car, you can rent one for 24 hours and drop it off when you're done.

If your schedule is flexible and you aren't in a rush, the most affordable way to travel around the island is the **Maui Bus.** You can buy a day pass for only $4, and routes service much of the island.

If you're staying in West Maui, the small **Kapalua Airport** (JHM) has daily flights to O'ahu, which can be convenient if you're hopping between islands and have a connection in Honolulu. The **Hana Airport** (HNM) has an afternoon flight that's just 20 minutes back to Kahului.

Best of Maui

Day 1

Given Hawaii's time zone, you may wake up before dawn. Take advantage by catching **sunrise at Haleakala.** Allow two hours of travel from Ka'anapali or Wailea and plan to arrive 30 minutes before sunrise. Spend an hour hiking into the crater. (Reservations are required for sunrise and can be made online up to 60 days in advance; visitors are allowed to only purchase one sunrise reservation per three-day period.) On your way down, have breakfast at **Kula Lodge** or **La Provence.** Spend the rest of the day relaxing poolside. Conversely, spend the day relaxing at poolside, and catch **sunset at Haleakala,** for a less crowded and similarly beautiful experience, possibly lingering for **stargazing.** (No reservations are required for sunset.)

Day 2

Tackle another early morning activity such as a **snorkeling tour.** Tours to **Molokini Crater** depart from Ma'alaea Harbor, while boats leave Ka'anapali Beach for **Olowalu** or **Honolua Bay.** Finish by 2pm and spend the afternoon relaxing on the beach.

Day 3

Enjoy **Lahaina,** ancient capital of the Hawaiian kingdom. Schedule a **surf lesson** or explore the town's **historic sites.** Grab lunch at **Cheeseburger in Paradise** or **Cool Cat Café.** Then head north to world-famous **Ka'anapali Beach,** where you can snorkel, cliff-jump, play in the surf, or rent a cabana. Explore the shops in **Whalers Village** and dine at **Monkeypod Kitchen.**

Day 4

Catch the 6:45am ferry to the island of **Lana'i.** Book a Jeep about two months prior to your stay and spend the morning exploring. Pick a remote beach such as **Polihua, Lopa,** or **Kaiolohia**

Kula Lodge

Molokini Crater

residents of Surfing Goat Dairy

(Shipwreck Beach). Then head back to **Lana'i City** for a plate lunch at **Blue Ginger Cafe.**

If you'd rather be **hiking,** call Rabaca's for a taxi up into town and the trailhead for the **Koloiki Ridge Trail.** Explore Lana'i City before catching a taxi down to **Hulopo'e Beach Park.** Snorkel along the reef or relax in the shade with a book. Hike around the corner to the **Pu'u Pehe Overlook,** keeping an eye out for the **spinner dolphins.** Rinse off at the beach shower, grab a drink at the **Four Seasons Resort Lana'i,** and get back to the harbor to catch the 5:30pm ferry back to Maui.

Day 5

Sleep in before grabbing a late breakfast. Those staying in West Maui should dine at **The Gazebo,** followed by a stroll along the **Kapalua Coastal Trail.** Drive to **Kahakuloa,** stopping on the way at the **Nakalele Blowhole** or the **beach at Mokulei'a Bay.** If the conditions are calm and you can't get enough snorkeling, head to **Honolua Bay.** End the day with happy hour at **The Sea House** restaurant.

If you're staying in South Maui, brunch at **Kihei Caffe** before making the drive to **Makena.** Spend the day at **Maluaka Beach,** exploring to the end of the road, and walking the length of **Big Beach** just before sunset.

Day 6

Drive to **Pa'ia** and begin the day with a stroll down **Baldwin Beach,** followed by breakfast at **Café des Amis.** Enjoy the **Road to Hana** at a leisurely pace, taking time to hike to **Twin Falls** and explore the **Ke'anae Peninsula.** Check into your accommodations in Hana and enjoy sunset from **Hamoa Beach.**

Day 7

Spend the day in rural **Upcountry.** Enjoy breakfast on the lanai at **Grandma's Coffee House,** followed by a stroll down **Thompson Road.** Drive to **Ulupalakua** for a midday wine-tasting, and then double back the way you came to the town of **Kula** and visit **Ali'i Kula Lavender,** a sprawling haven filled with 45 varieties of lavender and a gift shop. Or, head to **Surfing Goat Dairy** for an afternoon with the goats and sampling goat cheese. Since you're close, stop next door at **Ocean Vodka Organic Farm and Distillery,** Maui's famous vodka distillery. Finish the day **shopping** in **Makawao** and then dinner at **Casanova.**

Day 8

Gradually make your way toward Kahului Airport. Stop in at the **Maui Ocean Center** for one last glimpse of marinelife. Continuing on to **Wailuku,** make the short drive into **'Iao Valley State Monument** to see the famous needle. At **Kanaha Beach Park,** watch the windsurfers. Think about how you'll miss Maui—and plan your next visit.

Best Beaches

D. T. Fleming Beach Park

Fleming's offers some of the island's best **bodysurfing, beachcombing,** and **coastal hiking.** Public restrooms, showers, lifeguards, and parking make this a **family-friendly** beach. **Surfers** flock here in winter to tackle the **large swells** (page 48).

Napili Bay and Kapalua Bay

These two northwestern beaches offer **protected snorkeling** during summer. **Swim with sea turtles** at Napili and watch the sun go down from the deck of the Sea House restaurant with a drink in your hand (page 48).

Mokulei'a Bay

During summer, there are few better ways to start the day than by **snorkeling** at Mokulei'a. Tucked away at the base of the cliffs and hidden from the road, this is also a **scenic and sandy spot** for watching the **large winter surf** (page 49).

Ka'anapali Beach

Whether you're looking for **snorkeling, stand-up paddling, cliff-jumping,** or **scuba diving,** you'll find it at Ka'anapali Beach. This resort district is the see-and-be-seen shore for the island's West Side (page 49).

Keawakapu Beach

Enjoy a sunset stroll down Kihei's nicest beach, or spend your days **snorkeling, stand-up paddling,** or **basking in the sun.** Keawakapu has facilities on both ends of the beach, but despite the beach's popularity, there is always room to find your own section of shore (page 148).

Maluaka Beach

Maluaka is the **most happening beach** in Makena, where everything from **kayaking** to **snorkeling** and **stand-up paddling** is available. Public restrooms and showers make this a convenient spot for **families,** and you can walk

Big Beach at Makena State Park

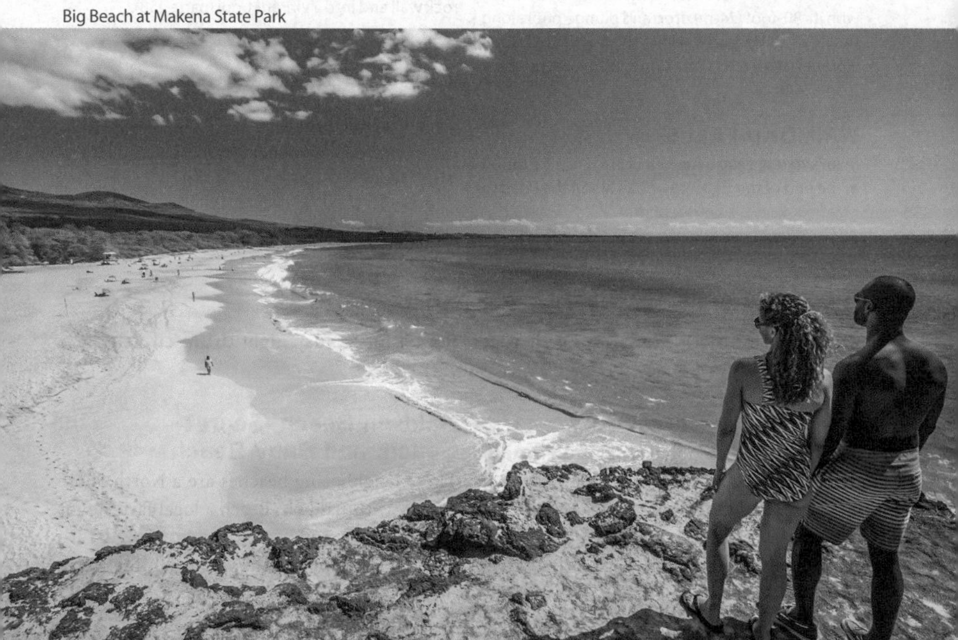

Go Chasing Waterfalls

No visit to Maui is complete without experiencing a waterfall. These stunning forces of nature should not be missed.

HONOKOHAU FALLS

Maui's tallest waterfall at 1,100 feet (335 m) is deep within the West Maui Mountains, but that doesn't mean you can't experience its beauty; the only way to do so is by air—to get there, book a flight with **Air Maui, Blue Hawaiian Helicopters, Maverick Helicopters,** or **Pacific Helicopters** (page 126).

TWIN FALLS

The **first set of waterfalls** you'll encounter along the **Road to Hana** is accessible via an easy 20-minute hike, and is particularly scenic amid its rainforest setting (page 234).

WAIKAMOI FALLS

This lovely **waterfall and swimming hole** along the Road to Hana is right off the road (page 236).

WAILUA FALLS

This side-of-the-road star captures a lot of attention with its 80-foot (24-m) drop and plunge pool along the Road to Hana. It's also in the middle of Hana's vibrant **rainforest,** making it seem otherworldly (page 244).

WAIMOKU FALLS

Maui's **most popular waterfall** can be found at the end of the **Pipiwai Trail** along the Road to Hana. A 4-mile (6.4-km) hike brings you to the base of the 400-foot (122-m) falls, rushing against a lava rock wall and into a vibrant pool (page 258).

Waimoku Falls

MOA'ULA FALLS

Visitors who embark on the **Halawa Valley Falls Cultural Hike** in **Moloka'i** are rewarded at trail's end with this multitiered wonder that cascades into a pool surrounded by rocks dotted with **ancient petroglyphs** (page 332).

down the road to historic Keawala'i Church (page 150).

Makena State Park

Wide, long, and completely **undeveloped,** aptly named **Big Beach** is a local favorite that comes alive at **sunset.** This legendary shore has a lengthy hippie history: **countercultural** visitors and nudists should visit neighboring **Little Beach** for Sunday night **drum circles** (page 151).

Baldwin Beach, Secret Beach, and Baby Beach

These neighboring beaches are a North Shore classic, with Baldwin Beach a local favorite for **bodysurfing** and **scenic jogs or strolls.** It's flanked by Baby Beach, which families with

small children will love for its **protected cove,** and Secret Beach, which draws **hippies** and **nudists** (page 248).

Hamoa Beach

If your vision of paradise involves a book, a palm tree, and the sound of waves at your feet, you'll find it at Hamoa Beach, the **nicest beach in Hana.** Travelers from James A. Michener to Mark Twain have written of the beauty of its **sandy shore** (page 250).

Hulopo'e Beach Park

This **marine reserve** on the island of Lana'i has a **sandy cove,** a **vibrant reef,** and a **palm-fringed shore.** Summer months bring good **surfing** and **bodysurfing** and easy access to **coastal hiking trails.** Public restrooms, showers, and picnic tables make this a **family-friendly** outing (page 298).

Papohaku Beach

On most days your footprints will be the only set in the sand at Papohaku, one of the longest beaches in Hawaii. This westward-facing shore offers Moloka'i's **best sunsets.** It's perfect for anyone wanting to **escape** for a little while (page 324).

Sandy Beach

Considered one of the **best swimming beaches on Moloka'i,** Sandy Beach has a protective reef offshore—perfect for snorkeling—which deflects the crashing surf. After several rocky steps on entering, the shoreline drops off and you're bathed in clear water (page 327).

Best Snorkeling and Diving

Honolua Bay

A world-renowned surf spot during winter, Honolua Bay has the island's best snorkeling during the calm, warm summer. Hawaiian **green sea turtles** are a common sight, as are **parrotfish, octopuses,** and the rare **spinner dolphin** (page 54).

Napili Bay and Kapalua Bay

Within walking distance of each other on the island's northwestern coast, these two bays offer a sandy entry and **shallow, protected conditions.** Napili has more **turtles,** while Kapalua has more fish. Summer is the best time of year for calm and flat conditions (page 57).

Pu'u Keka'a

The island's most famous snorkeling spot, also known as **Black Rock,** is one of its best. This rocky promontory on the Ka'anapali strip is a magnet for **sea turtles** and **reef fish.** Morning hours offer the calmest conditions. Keep an eye out for the dozens of **cliff-jumpers** who throw themselves off the rock (page 59).

Olowalu

Often known as **Mile Marker 14,** this historic shore along the side of the highway is great for **beginning snorkelers.** The best conditions are during the winter and earlier in the day. The outer reef is covered in **turtles** and is a playground of healthy coral (page 64).

Molokini Crater

A crescent-shaped volcanic caldera off the southern coast of Maui, Molokini Crater offers **crystal clear waters** with 100-foot (30-m) visibility most days of the year. Over a dozen snorkeling tours make the early morning pilgrimage to the crater, home to over **250 species of fish.** Companies such as **Trilogy Excursions** offer daily morning tours. For an extreme adventure, scuba divers should tackle the famous **Back Wall,** which drops straight down for several hundred feet (pages 154 and 164).

Ulua Beach and Mokapu Beach

These neighboring Wailea beaches are South Maui's most easily accessible, making them ideal for **beginning snorkelers.** The rocky point between the two beaches teems with **tropical reef fish** (page 161).

Makena Landing

The volcanic Makena coast goes by many names; **Turtle Town** is perhaps the most relevant to snorkelers. It's pockmarked with **caves** that form the perfect shelter for sea turtles. Winter months are best along this southern shore. Everyone from scuba divers to kayak tours and snorkeling boats frequents the rugged coast (page 161).

Hulopo'e Beach Park

This Lana'i marine reserve has one of the **healthiest reefs** in Maui County and fronts a beach ranked as the nation's best. Come face-to-face with multihued **parrotfish** as they snack on colorful coral, or search the shallows for the ***humuhumunukunukuapua'a,*** Hawaii's state fish (page 302).

First and Second Cathedrals

These **offshore caverns** offer the best scuba diving on Lana'i. Beams of sunlight filter through the water, mimicking stained-glass windows—First Cathedral has even been the site of underwater weddings. You'll encounter everything from **frogfish** to **lobsters** and **spinner dolphins** (page 303).

Moku Ho'oniki

Advanced scuba divers get their thrills on this Moloka'i deep-water dive. It's home to a large population of **scalloped hammerhead sharks** (page 327).

snorkeling at Molokini

green sea turtle

surfing at Pohaku Beach Park

Best Surfing

Pohaku Beach Park

A **longboarder's** dream wave, **S-Turns** is the island's most user-friendly winter break and the most accepting of visiting **beginning surfers.** The long paddle out means a **long ride.** This rolling, forgiving wave is the perfect spot for honing your skills (page 68).

D.T. Fleming Beach Park

This Kapalua beach is popular with **bodyboarders** and is best during the winter. It's less crowded than neighboring Honolua, and much more user-friendly, but is for **intermediate to advanced** surfers (page 68).

Honolua Bay

Honolua Bay is a place of local legend, with one of the **best right-hand waves** in the world during winter. If you're an **expert surfer**—and show respect to locals by waiting your turn in the lineup—you could end up snagging the **wave of a lifetime** (page 68).

Lahaina Breakwall

Crowded, shallow, and nearly always sunny, the Lahaina Breakwall is where many visitors stand up and ride their first wave. **Surf schools** dominate the inside reef, while advanced surfers hang on the outside. While most days are calm with **gentle surf,** the large south **swells of summer** are for **advanced surfers** (page 70).

Launiupoko Beach Park

Keiki (children) learn to ride their first waves here at the most happening beach park on the road to Lahaina. **Longboarders** can choose from multiple peaks, while the **gentle waves** and calm conditions make it a perfect spot for **beginners** (page 71).

McGregor Point

This is a popular spot for **advanced surfers,** with the **fastest right-hand wave in the world.** It's also an ideal arena to **study surfing techniques.** The best time to experience surfing here is afternoons, when the wind picks up (page 168).

Pa'ia Bay

Walking distance from the center of town, Pa'ia Bay is one of the island's only real beach breaks. It's best for intermediate to advanced **shortboarding** and **bodyboarding** (page 252).

Ho'okipa Beach Park

The **most popular break** on the island's North Shore is also the center of the Pa'ia **surf scene.** Small days are acceptable for **beginners** who are still learning, but during the large swells of winter, this becomes an amphitheater of towering 20-foot (6-m) surf for **experts** (page 252).

Hamoa Beach

More than just a beautiful beach, Hamoa has some of the best surf in East Maui. **Intermediate** and **advanced surfers** will find **wind swell** here any time of the year, even during summer when nowhere else on the island has waves (page 254).

Hulopo'e Beach Park

While it might not break often, Hulopo'e Beach has a **left-hand wave** on par with the best in the state—ideal for **intermediate** and **advanced surfers.** Summer is best for this south-facing shore on Lana'i. While spots on Maui can be crowded with 50 people, Hulopo'e will rarely ever have 10 (page 304).

Best Hikes

Kapalua Coastal Trail

Although just 1.75 miles, this short trail encompasses epic scenery, passing some of the most **beautiful beaches in the country** as well as offering **views of Moloka'i and Lana'i** (page 81).

Waihe'e Coastal Dunes and Wetlands Preserve

Hugging the shore of sleepy Waihe'e, this coastal track weaves its way past **ancient Hawaiian villages** along one of the island's few remaining sections of **undeveloped coast** (page 121).

Hoapili Trail

Tucked away in the "deep south," the Hoapili Trail traces the winding **footpath of royalty** across **black fields of lava.** This meandering, **rugged coastal track** is an enchanting time portal to ancient Hawaii and also passes **La Perouse,** a popular surfing spot. Mornings are best to beat the hot sun (page 175).

Sliding Sands Switchback Loop

This 12.2-mile (19.6-km) sojourn crosses the floor of **Haleakala Crater** and weaves past **cinder cones** bursting with color. Keep an eye out for **nene** geese and glistening **silversword plants.** For a real thrill, hike by the light of the full moon (page 211).

Polipoli Spring State Recreation Area

Tucked in one of the least-visited corners of Maui, Polipoli looks more like the Pacific Northwest than a Pacific island. A **network of trails** weaves through **towering redwoods.** The silence in the forest is broken only by passing pheasants (page 212).

Twin Falls

This easy-to-navigate hike along the **Road to Hana** is one of the island's most popular, and visitors traveling with children will especially appreciate the easy access to **waterfalls** and **swimming holes** (page 255).

Na'ili'ili Haele

Known as the **bamboo forest,** this rugged, slippery trail on the **Road to Hana** hides a series of

waterfalls set deep in the East Maui **rainforest.** The treacherous trail isn't for everyone, however: Hikers need to be in good physical condition (page 255).

Pipiwai Trail

If expansive **banyan trees, dark bamboo forests,** and numerous **waterfalls** aren't enough of a thrill, this 4-mile (6.4-km) trail in Kipahulu reaches a dramatic terminus at the base of 400-foot (122-m) **Waimoku Falls.** Often regarded as the island's best hike, this should be on every itinerary for a day spent in Hana (page 258).

Munro Trail

Shaded by the boughs of Cook pines, this weaving dirt track on Lana'i climbs to the **summit** of 3,370-foot (1,027-m) **Lana'ihale.** Views from this trail stretch toward Maui; on the clearest days, the summit is the only place in Hawaii where you can get a view of six islands at once (page 305).

Halawa Valley Falls Cultural Hike

More than just a hike to a **waterfall,** a trek in Halawa Valley on Moloka'i is a powerful journey to the **heart of Hawaiian culture.** Halawa Valley is one of the **oldest settlements** in the Hawaiian Islands. This valley is so **sacred** it can only be explored with a guide (page 331).

flowering silversword on Haleakala

Pipiwai Trail

Outdoor Adventures

KAYAKING OR OUTRIGGER CANOEING

Many kayak tours combine snorkeling with an upper-body workout. Those looking for a **cultural connection** should snorkel from an **outrigger canoe,** ancient craft that date back to early Polynesia. **Hawaiian Paddle Sports** can get you on the water for a private paddling tour (page 74).

WHALE-WATCHING

Few things get your heart racing faster than a 50-ton animal leaping out of the water a few feet away. **Pacific Whale Foundation** offers **whale-watching cruises** out of both Lahaina and Ma'alaea. If luck is on your side, you just might end up on a boat that gets "mugged" (page 76).

ZIP-LINING ABOVE THE TREES

From **kid-friendly** short courses to stomach-churning screamers, zip-lining has rapidly become one of the island's most popular activities. While all companies provide a thrilling experience, **Skyline Hawaii** in Ka'anapali offers some of the best views (page 85).

KITESURFING AT KITE BEACH

Kitesurfing was born here on Maui. While experienced kiters can take straight to the water, schools such as **Hawaiian Sailboard Techniques** provide lessons for visitors who are looking to pick up a new sport (page 120).

PARAGLIDING IN POLIPOLI

Paragliding is Maui's most underrated adventure option. The Polipoli flying location has ideal conditions on a **cool mountain slope** with **views** gazing out over South Maui. The instructors at **Paraglide Maui** will get you soaring (page 218).

whale-watching

STAND-UP PADDLING

Stand-up paddling (SUP) has its origins on Maui—and it's popular all over the island. While seasoned pros will endure multiple-hour **downwinders,** even renting a board for an hour is a great introduction to the sport.

MOUNTAIN BIKING MAKAWAO OR MOLOKA'I

The slopes of these islands are covered in **biking trails.** Makawao and Polipoli are the best spots on Maui, while the Moloka'i Forest Reserve is an **off-road playground.**

Best Historical and Cultural Sites

Alexander and Baldwin Sugar Museum

Within sniffing distance of the state's last **sugar mill,** this small museum takes an informative look at the island's **multicultural plantation heritage** (page 109).

Bailey House Museum

Step inside this whitewashed **missionary home** to get a glimpse into **19th-century Maui.** This museum also houses **ancient Hawaiian artifacts,** a surfboard ridden by **Duke Kahanamoku,** and one of the best bookstores for Hawaii-themed literature (page 112).

Kepaniwai Heritage Gardens

Just a few minutes before 'Iao Valley, this small park parallels **'Iao Stream** and features traditional housing of the island's **immigrant communities** (page 112).

Maui Tropical Plantation

Learn about Maui's rich **agriculture** on tram tours spotlighting Hawaii's crops before settling into lunch or dinner at the plantation's on-site **Café O'Lei at The Mill House** (page 116).

Ke'anae Peninsula

This lush peninsula offers a refreshing glimpse into **"old Hawaii."** The taro-covered promontory is one of the island's last vestiges of indigenous Hawaiian culture (page 237).

Kahanu Garden and Pi'ilanihale Heiau

This towering, 50-foot-tall (15-m) ***heiau*** is the largest remaining religious structure in all

Kepaniwai Heritage Gardens

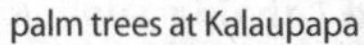

palm trees at Kalaupapa

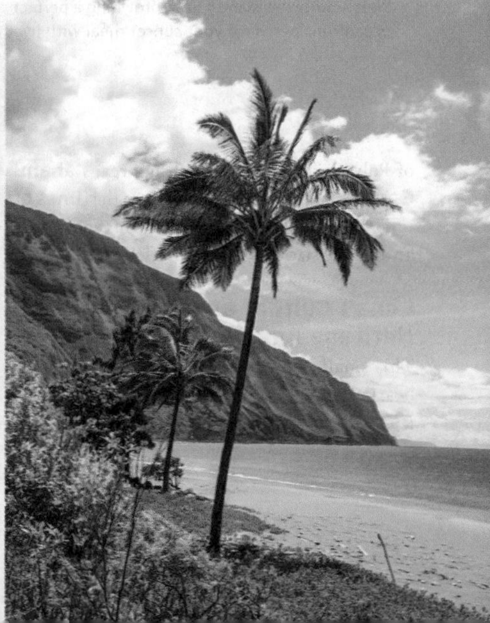

Honeymoon Hot Spots

SUNRISES AND SUNSETS

Watch the sunset from the deck of a **catamaran** with a drink in one hand and your love in the other (page 75). Skip the crowded sunrise trip and instead visit **Haleakala** for sunset (page 198). Spend the night in **Hana** to watch the sunrise from this eastern-facing shore at **Wai'anapanapa State Park,** better known as Hana's **black-sand beach** (page 241). **Pu'u Pehe,** often referred to as **Sweetheart Rock,** is visited by honeymooners who watch the sunset over the water from the panoramic overlook (page 305). A sunset dinner at **Mama's Fish House** in Pa'ia is an ideal option (page 264).

sunset at Haleakala

NATURAL WONDERS

The **Phallic Rock** is dedicated to Nanahoa, ancient Hawaiian **god of fertility.** Women traditionally visited this site in hopes of conceiving a child (page 321). Kiss beneath a waterfall on the **Road to Hana** (pages 234 and 236).

ROMANTIC UNWINDING

Nothing says "romance" better than a beachfront stroll along the **Wailea Coastal Walk** in South Maui (page 173). The **Old Lahaina Luau** in West Maui is the island's best, providing a perfect oceanfront perch for your sunset meal with live entertainment (page 92). Relax with a **couples massage** at one of the island's spas. Book a stay at peaceful **Lumeria Maui** in Upcountry and enjoy yoga sessions, an on-site farm-to-table restaurant, and starlit evenings (page 283).

of Polynesia. The surrounding area, **Kahanu Garden,** is largely unchanged from the **times of ancient Hawaii.** The stone platforms encompass an area the size of two football fields (page 239).

Lana'i Culture and Heritage Center

This small, informative cultural center in the heart of **Lana'i City** traces the **island's history** from its original inhabitants through its era as the world's **largest pineapple plantation** (page 293).

Kalaupapa Peninsula

There was a time when a visit to Kalaupapa meant you'd just been handed a **death sentence.** Today, go to this **remote peninsula** on Moloka'i to learn about the struggles of Hawaii's leprosy patients and **Father Damien,** the man who gave everything to try to save them (page 321).

Best Family Outings

Whale-Watching

Whale season is officially December-May on Maui (page 76), and while there are many charters from which to choose, **Pacific Whale Foundation** stands out for the variety of **whale-watching cruises** it offers and the expertise of its **marine biologists** (page 142). Children age six and under ride for free.

Atlantis Submarines

Submerge 100 feet (30 m) below the surface in a 48-passenger **submarine** to spot sealife and even a **shipwreck** on this family-friendly outing that educates visitors about the ocean's **diverse marinelife** (page 79).

Old Lahaina Luau

One of the best family outings on the island includes **hula lessons** for all ages, **lawn games,** a delicious **buffet,** and a memorable **stage show** that reenacts island history, set against an imminently photographable **sunset** (page 92).

Maui Ocean Center

The largest tropical reef aquarium in the western hemisphere, **Maui Ocean Center** has more than 60 permanent and seasonal exhibits including **outdoor tide pools,** a **sea turtle lagoon,** and the grand centerpiece, an **acrylic tunnel** beneath a 750,000-gallon (2.8-million-liter) **aquarium** (page 141).

Molokini Snorkeling Tour

A perfect half-day trip for the entire family—available through numerous charters—takes you just a few miles from Maui's shoreline to snorkel among the island's **colorful marinelife** at **Molokini Crater,** where the water is consistently calm and clear (page 154).

Atlantis Submarines

Live Aloha

Although millions visit Maui annually and return home without incident, every year a handful get hurt and end up in hospitals. Landowners get sued and access becomes restricted. Relations between locals and visitors have become increasingly strained. Litigation replaces handshakes, liability waivers become prolific, and warning signs stand where common sense once prevailed. Healthy respect for the island and its nature, people, and culture is essential to a meaningful vacation. Just as each local is an ambassador for Hawaii, every visitor is a representative of the tourism industry. When visitors show respect for these islands, locals take notice. Some general guidelines:

RESPECT THE LAND

In traditional Hawaiian culture, the land is sacred above all. The earth and the sea provide us with sustenance, and to disrespect the land is the ultimate offense. The concept of land ownership is foreign to traditional Hawaiian culture, which sees us as temporary stewards of the land. Pick up your *opala* (trash), stay off sensitive coral reefs, throw cigarette butts in proper receptacles, and help keep the valleys and shores as pristine as possible.

RESPECT LANDOWNERS' WISHES

Some unscrupulous travel publications encourage trespassing. As a result, far too many visitors walk across private land even when signs tell them not to. Poor behavior and lawsuits have led to restricted access for some formerly public sites. If you see a sign that says *Kapu* (Keep Out), No Trespassing, or Private Property, please respect the landowners' wishes.

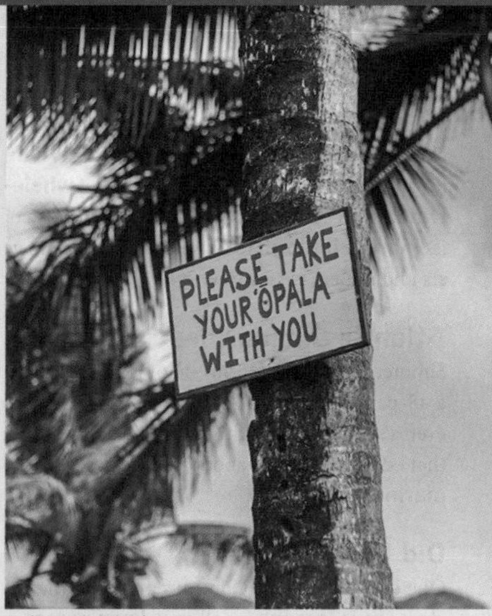

Pick up your *opala.*

RESPECT NATURE

Many visitors' injuries are a direct result of failing to respect the power of nature. Waves are stronger than in other parts of the world, and flash floods, high winds, rough seas, and slippery rocks all claim lives annually. Heed the warning signs. "If in doubt, don't go out."

RESPECT THE CULTURE

Hawaii has a culture that is unique in the world, and experiencing it is one of the best parts of visiting the islands. Tourism is the state's largest industry, but ultimately we are guests. Embrace the Hawaiian way of living and slow down for a little while.

Lahaina and West Maui

White sandy beaches, rocky coves, lush valleys, and oceanfront restaurants where the clinking glasses of mai tais and the smooth sounds of a slack-key guitar complement the setting sun—Maui is a magical place.

West Maui beaches are some of the best on the island. In winter, Honolua Bay shapes the kind of legendary right-hand point breaks that attract surfers from across the globe. In summer, this same bay offers some of the island's finest snorkeling, where bright parrotfish, shy octopuses, and curious sea turtles occupy an expansive reef.

Hot, busy, and incomparably historic, Lahaina was once the whaling capital of the Pacific as well as the capital of the Hawaiian kingdom.

Highlights

Look for ★ to find recommended sights, activities, dining, and lodging.

★ Take a short stroll to see the wave-created sculpture **Makalua-puna Point (Dragon's Teeth)**—and spectacular coastal views (page 37).

★ **Snorkel with sea turtles** in legendary **Honolua Bay** in summer, or watch as the island's best **surfers** drop into waves over 20 feet (6 m) high in winter (page 37).

★ Witness pressure transform incoming waves into a geyser at the thunderous **Nakalele Blowhole** (page 37).

★ Get your shopping, people-watching, and dining fixes by walking the length of **Front Street,** the island's most famous thoroughfare (page 40).

★ Learn the unique history of Lahaina at the **Lahaina Courthouse,** with an art gallery in the basement, old photos on the ground level, and a museum on the second story (page 41).

★ **Surf** the clear aquamarine waters at **Pohaku Beach Park**—the popular S-Turns break is perfect for beginners (page 68).

★ Feel the trade winds in your hair as you literally **sail into the sunset** off iconic **Ka'anapali Beach** (page 75).

★ Head out on a **whale-watching** expedition for an up-close encounter with humpback whales (page 76).

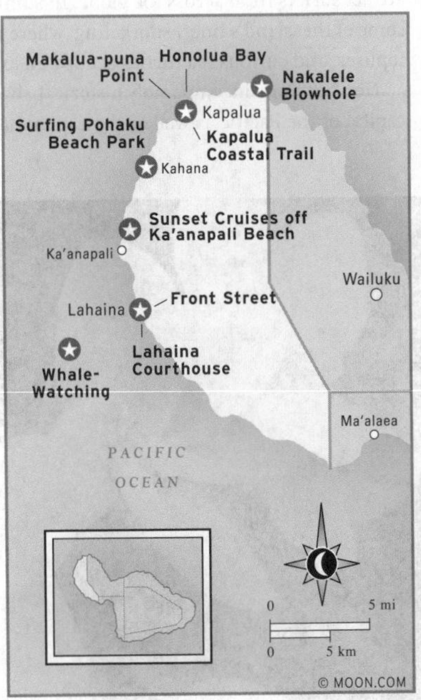

★ Spend an hour scouring the coast on the luxuriant yet rugged **Kapalua Coastal Trail,** passing some of Hawaii's most beautiful beaches along the way (page 81).

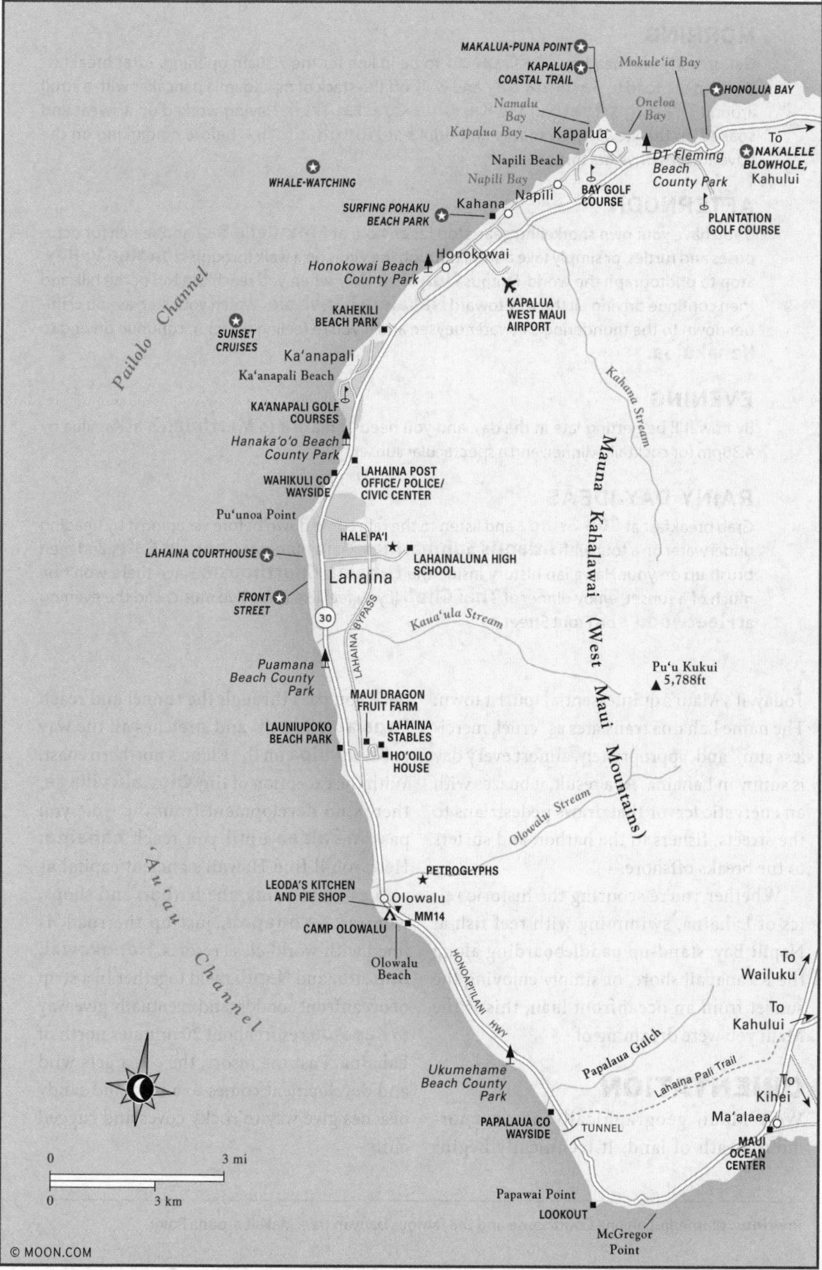
West Maui
MAKALUA-PUNA POINT
KAPALUA COASTAL TRAIL
Mokule'ia Bay
HONOLUA BAY
Namalu Bay
Oneloa Bay
Kapalua Bay
Kapalua
To NAKALELE BLOWHOLE, Kahului
Napili Beach
DT Fleming Beach County Park
Napili Bay
WHALE-WATCHING
BAY GOLF COURSE
Napili
SURFING POHAKU BEACH PARK
Kahana
PLANTATION GOLF COURSE
Honokowai
Honokowai Beach County Park
KAPALUA WEST MAUI AIRPORT
Pailolo Channel
KAHEKILI BEACH PARK
SUNSET CRUISES
Ka'anapali
Ka'anapali Beach
Kahana Stream
KA'ANAPALI GOLF COURSES
Hanaka'o'o Beach County Park
LAHAINA POST OFFICE/ POLICE/ CIVIC CENTER
WAHIKULI CO WAYSIDE
Mauna Kahalawai (West Maui Mountains)
Pu'unoa Point
HALE PA'I
LAHAINA COURTHOUSE
LAHAINALUNA HIGH SCHOOL
Lahaina
FRONT STREET
30
LAHAINA BYPASS
Kaua'ula Stream
Puamana Beach County Park
Pu'u Kukui 5,788ft
MAUI DRAGON FRUIT FARM
LAUNIUPOKO BEACH PARK
LAHAINA STABLES
HO'OILO HOUSE
Olowalu Stream
PETROGLYPHS
LEODA'S KITCHEN AND PIE SHOP
Olowalu
MM14
CAMP OLOWALU
'Au'au Channel
Olowalu Beach
HONOAPI'ILANI HWY
To Wailuku
To Kahului
Papalaua Gulch
Ukumehame Beach County Park
Lahaina Pali Trail
To Kihei
PAPALAUA CO WAYSIDE
TUNNEL
Ma'alaea
MAUI OCEAN CENTER
0
3 mi
0
3 km
Papawai Point
LOOKOUT
McGregor Point
© MOON.COM

Your Best Day in West Maui

MORNING

Get up early and head to **The Gazebo** to be in line for the 7:30am opening. After breakfast drive up the road to **Kapalua Bay** and walk off the stack of macadamia pancakes with a stroll around **Dragon's Teeth** or the **Kapalua Coastal Trail.** Having worked up a sweat and soaked up the views, grab snacks and drinks at **Honolua Store** before embarking on the adventurous drive north.

AFTERNOON

If you have your own snorkeling gear, stop for an hour at **Mokulei'a Bay** and search for octopuses and turtles, or simply take a stroll through the vines on a walk through **Honolua Valley.** Stop to photograph the world-famous **Honolua Bay** when you reach the top of the hill, and then continue driving all the way toward **Nakalele Blowhole.** Watch your step as you clamber down to the thundering saltwater geyser, and if you're feeling up for it, continue driving to **Kahakuloa.**

EVENING

By now it'll be getting late in the day, and you need to make it to **Merriman's** in Kapalua by 4:30pm for cocktails, dinner, and a spectacular sunset.

RAINY DAY IDEAS

Grab breakfast at **808 Grindz** and listen to the rain come down before escaping it by heading underwater on a tour with **Atlantis Submarines.** Get a burger at **Cool Cat Café,** and then brush up on your Hawaiian history inside the **Lahaina Courthouse.** Since there won't be much of a sunset, enjoy dinner at **Thai Chef.** If you feel like some live music, end the evening at **Fleetwood's** on Front Street.

Today, it's Maui's quintessential tourist town. The name Lahaina translates as "cruel, merciless sun," and, appropriately, almost every day is sunny in Lahaina. As a result, it buzzes with an energetic fervor that draws pedestrians to the streets, fishers to the harbor, and surfers to the breaks offshore.

Whether you're scouring the historic relics of Lahaina, swimming with reef fish at Napili Bay, stand-up paddleboarding along the Ka'anapali shore, or simply enjoying the sunset from an oceanfront luau, this is the Maui you were dreaming of.

ORIENTATION

West Maui, geographically, is an enormous swath of land. It technically begins once you pass through the tunnel and reach **Papalaua Beach,** and stretches all the way to **Kahakuloa** on the island's northern coast. With the exception of tiny **Olowalu village,** there's no development from the time you pass **Ma'alaea** until you reach **Lahaina.** Here you'll find Hawaii's ancient capital as well as restaurants, the harbor, and shops, whereas **Ka'anapali,** just up the road, is lined with world-class resorts. **Honokowai, Kahana,** and **Napili** meld together in a strip of oceanfront condos, and eventually give way to **Kapalua** resort about 20 minutes north of Lahaina. Past the resort, the coast gets wild and development comes to a halt, and sandy beaches give way to rocky coves and rugged cliffs.

Previous: plumeria; Lahaina Courthouse and the famous banyan tree; Makalua-puna Point.

PLANNING YOUR TIME

More people stay in West Maui than any other part of the island, and in many ways, it feels separated from other parts of Maui. Based here, it's easy to make simple half-day jaunts to the beach or go on tropical micro-adventures before lounging back at the resort. For other travelers who aren't based in West Maui, two full days is a good amount of time to experience the area's best sights, with one day spent in Lahaina and Ka'anapali and another exploring "up north." From Kahului Airport, it's about 40 minutes to Lahaina and an hour to Kapalua, though as the island grows, the traffic is getting particularly bad—and driving to Lahaina between 3pm and 5pm can often be bumper to bumper. Factor this in if you're trying to get to your 5pm oceanfront luau.

Sights

KAPALUA, NAPILI, AND HONOKOWAI

Exploring the island's northwestern coast is one of the island's best day trips—like a miniature Road to Hana without the waterfalls, but with far better beaches and views. If you continue all the way around the back of West Maui past the town of Kahakuloa (the road isn't limited to 4WD vehicles like your car-rental map might say, but it is far narrower, curvier, and scarier than the Road to Hana), you can combine the drive with the waterfalls of Makamaka'ole Valley in Central Maui for a full-day experience. This journey is not for the timid. Most turn back toward Kapalua once they reach Kahakuloa.

★ Makalua-puna Point (Dragon's Teeth)

For spectacular views of the northwestern coast and white-sand Oneloa Bay, take a short stroll on **Makalua-puna Point**—otherwise known as "Dragon's Teeth." The jagged rocks here have been dramatically sculpted by waves crashing on the coast, and there's a large labyrinth in the middle of the point for silently reflecting on the beauty. The trailhead is located by the small parking lot at the end of Office Road. Visit without leaving a trace; this point is sacred to native Hawaiians and access can be controversial, so tread lightly when you follow the trail out onto the windswept point.

★ Honolua Bay

Famous for its exceptional surfing and diving, **Honolua Bay** is also one of West Maui's most beautiful sights. There is a palpable magic in this bay, from the vine-laden valley that leads to the shore and the reef that's teeming with life, to the simply legendary right-hand wave that perfectly bends around the point. When visiting Honolua Bay—particularly when the surf is breaking—either stop at the overlook on the north side of the bay after climbing the short but steep hill, or drive down the bumpy dirt road that leads to the top of the bluff. To continue the Honolua adventure on foot, walk to where the dirt road ends, where a very thin trail connects with a network of coastal trails that lead to views of the coast.

★ Nakalele Blowhole

Eight miles (12.9 km) past the entrance to Kapalua, by mile marker 38, is the famous **Nakalele Blowhole.** Outside of Honolua Bay this is the most popular stop along this stretch of coast. It's about a 15-minute drive past the entrance to Kapalua if you go straight through without stopping. On the right days, the Nakalele Blowhole can jettison water upward of 100 feet (30 m) into the air. The best conditions for witnessing Nakalele are when the trade winds are blowing and there's northerly swell. In the full throes of its performance, Nakalele Blowhole is a natural saltwater geyser erupting on a windswept outcropping, and it's one of the most powerful forces of the sea you can witness on the island. Visitors in the past have been killed by standing too close to the blowhole, so pay attention to warning signs in the area.

Finding the blowhole can be a challenge for those who don't know where to look. At mile marker 38 there is a dirt pullout on the ocean side of the highway, although the trail from here that leads down toward the water will only take you as far as the decrepit old lighthouse and a marginal view of the blowhole. A better access point is 0.5 mile (0.8 km) farther down the road where a second dirt pullout serves as the trailhead for the path leading to the blowhole. Between the two parking areas are dozens of dirt-bike tracks that don't lead anywhere, so the best thing to do is park by mile marker 38.5 and make your way down from there. The trail to the blowhole is just over 0.5 mile (0.8 km) long, and the last half of the trail becomes a scramble down a moderate scree slope, which is best left to those who are steady on their feet. When you reach the bottom of the rocky trail, turn around and look behind you, facing away from blowhole. Look closely to find the **heart-shaped hole in the rocks** that's a Maui Instagram darling.

The Olivine Pools

Past the Nakalele Blowhole, by mile marker 16, the **Olivine Pools**—traditionally called Mokolea—are one of the more unique and beautiful sights on the northwestern side of the island. The coastal panoramas from here are breathtaking, and even if you don't walk down to the pools, the views alone are reason enough to stop. For most visitors, though, the goal is to swim and bathe in the shallow tide pools perfectly perched on a lava rock outcropping. On rare calm days when the wind is light and the ocean is mellow and smooth, this can be one of the most serene perches you'll find anywhere on the island. However, the ocean is treacherous here, which makes swimming in the pools risky. A good rule of thumb is to sit and watch them for a while and wait to see if any waves are crashing into them. If the ocean is calm and isn't reaching the pools, this is the safest time for swimming or wading. Visitors have died trying to reach the pools, so it is especially important to be aware of your surroundings at all times. If waves are washing into the pools, keep out. Park in the dirt area on the ocean side of the road, and follow the trail leading down toward the coast to access the pools. The trail will fork at a yellow sign that warns about the dangers of continuing. Follow the trail to the edge of the bluff and then proceed down the trail leading to the pools.

KA'ANAPALI

Pu'u Keka'a

Known to most visitors as Black Rock, **Pu'u Keka'a** is the correct name for this volcanic outcropping at the northern end of Ka'anapali Beach. Today the rock is a popular spot for snorkeling, scuba diving, and cliff-jumping, although the most popular time of day is about 20 minutes prior to sunset when a torch-wielding, shirtless member of the Sheraton staff scrambles onto the rock and lights a row of carefully placed tiki torches. Once all the torches are lit, his flaming staff is ceremoniously chucked into the water moments before he performs a swan dive off the rock. More than just a creative marketing plan, the ceremony is a reenactment of the sacred belief that this is one of the spots on the island where a person's soul leaps from this world to the next immediately following death. For a prime perch to watch the show, grab a drink at the Cliff Dive Bar inside the Sheraton Maui.

Tour of the Stars

For a truly unique Ka'anapali experience, stand on the roof of the Hyatt and stargaze through high-powered telescopes. Held at 8pm and 9pm every night, the **Tour of the Stars** (200 Nohea Kai Dr., 808/667-4727, hotel guests $25 adults and $20 children, non-guests $30) allows small groups of 14 people to

1: Makalua-puna Point **2:** Nakalele Blowhole **3:** Honolua Bay

1
2
3

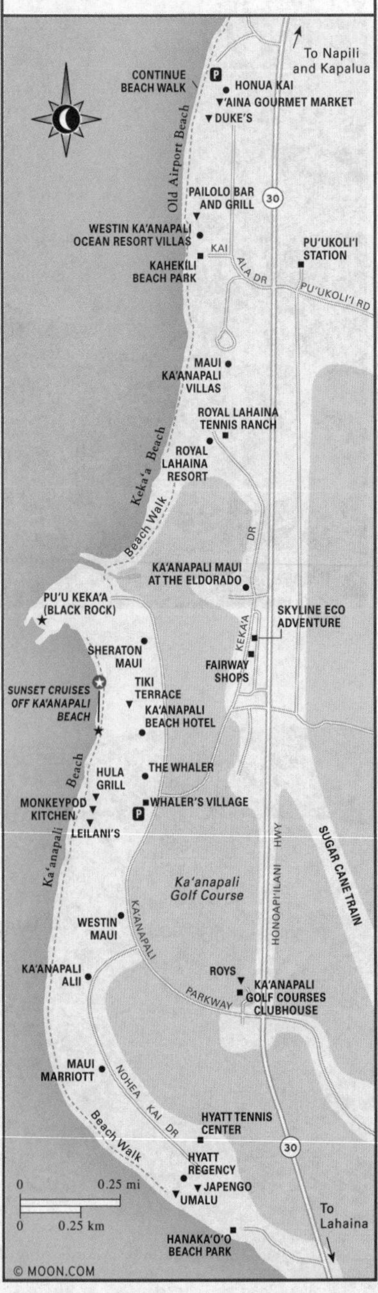

access the roof of the resort and peer through a 14-inch (36-cm) reflector telescope with the resort's director of astronomy. Make it a romantic evening by joining the nightly 10pm tour with chocolate-covered strawberries and champagne ($45 pp).

LAHAINA

From 1820 to 1845, this seaside town—which was originally called Lele—was the capital of the Hawaiian kingdom. At about the same time that the *ali'i* (nobility) and royalty were establishing their capital, fleets of New England whaling ships began anchoring in the Lahaina Roads. From 1820 to 1860, thousands of crusty whalers paddled ashore in wooden rowboats to reprovision their ships, soak their livers, and soothe their rusty loins. Answering the call to save these poor souls, Christian missionaries from New England began to arrive in the early 1820s, bolstered by the support of Queen Ka'ahumanu, who had embraced the values of Christianity. Lahaina became a battleground between drunken whalers and pious missionaries to win over the native Hawaiian populace, a Wild West of the Pacific. Today, scores of historic sites pertaining to this era are scattered around town.

Thanks to the tireless work of the Lahaina Restoration Foundation, many of the town's historic sites are well marked and accessible. Pick up a walking tour map from the Lahaina Visitors Center in the courthouse next to Lahaina Harbor or a *Mo'olelo O Lahaina* historical and cultural walking tour map from the offices of the Lahaina Restoration Foundation on the grounds of the Baldwin Missionary home.

★ Front Street

Front Street is a sight in itself that centers around shops, festive restaurants and bars, eclectic street vendors, and sublime views of Lana'i and Moloka'i, especially at sunset. Sunsets are so breathtaking on this street that **Fleetwood's,** the brainchild of musician Mick Fleetwood, often holds a sunset ceremony on the venue's rooftop bar, presided

Parking in Lahaina

If you're looking for a good way to fight with your spouse, try finding parking in Lahaina while running late for an activity. A web of narrow streets and overpriced lots, Lahaina for most visitors is an expensive source of angst and confusion when it comes to parking. But it doesn't have to be that way. Here are a few tips to help cut through the confusion.

- Parking in a paid parking lot doesn't make your car any more secure. Only a few of them are monitored. The only reason to pay for parking in Lahaina is for the convenience of being closer to where you're trying to go. There is enough free parking for everyone.
- Most street parking in Lahaina is good for three hours, and there are no parking meters. If you're only going to be a few hours, there is no need to pay for a parking lot. Free street parking can be found on Dickenson and Waine'e Streets, and there is a large, three-hour parking lot on the corner of Prison and Front Streets. The three-hour lot is heavily patrolled, however, so if you overstay, you'll likely end up with a $60 ticket.
- While there is also free street parking on Front Street, attempting to parallel park on the thoroughfare is challenging in the traffic. Save yourself the hassle and don't even try.
- If you're eating dinner in Lahaina, there is free parking at Lahaina Harbor between the courthouse and the harbor 7pm-7am daily, although you can't park in the back lot by the fishing boats because it's by permit only. On weekends and public holidays, there is free parking all day in the spaces in front of Kamehameha III School by the junction of Prison and Front Streets.
- There is also free all-day parking in the lot behind the Front Street tennis courts. The spaces when you first pull in are reserved for the cultural center, but there is a dirt parking lot in the back as well as a paved parking lot by the back tennis courts. Don't leave valuables in your car.
- Luakini Street, paralleling Front Street, is a one-way, with traffic running north to south on the south end of Dickenson, and south to north on the north end of Dickenson. Confused? Better to just avoid the street entirely.
- Allow yourself enough time. Parking may take 5 or 10 minutes, so factor this in when scheduling your day.

over by a Hawaiian *kumu* (teacher). Check the venue's website for updated information.

Listed as one of the "Great Streets in America" by the American Planning Association, it is one of the premier destinations in West Maui—the place with the most upbeat vibe. Simply walking this vivacious thoroughfare is a popular activity. Begin your experience at the famous **banyan tree** at the corner of Hotel Street, and marvel at its surreal twisty trunks and branches. Walk north and you'll find yourself in a manageable sea of curious visitors and friendly locals taking in the various street vendors selling items such as jewelry, wooden statues, and other island art. Take your time strolling farther north down the thoroughfare, which runs adjacent to the shoreline, and leisurely poke around the diverse array of art galleries and clothing shops.

★ Lahaina Courthouse

The old **Lahaina Courthouse** (648 Wharf St.) contains the most informative museum in central Lahaina. During its tenure as the town's political center, it also served as governor's office, post office, customs office, and police station, complete with a jail in the underground basement. The jail is now home to the Lahaina Arts Society's **Old Jail Gallery,** and the society has its main **Banyan Tree Gallery** on the ground floor. The **Lahaina Visitors Center** (808/667-9193, 9am-5pm daily) occupies a room on the ground floor as well. Find tourist information and brochures

Downtown Lahaina

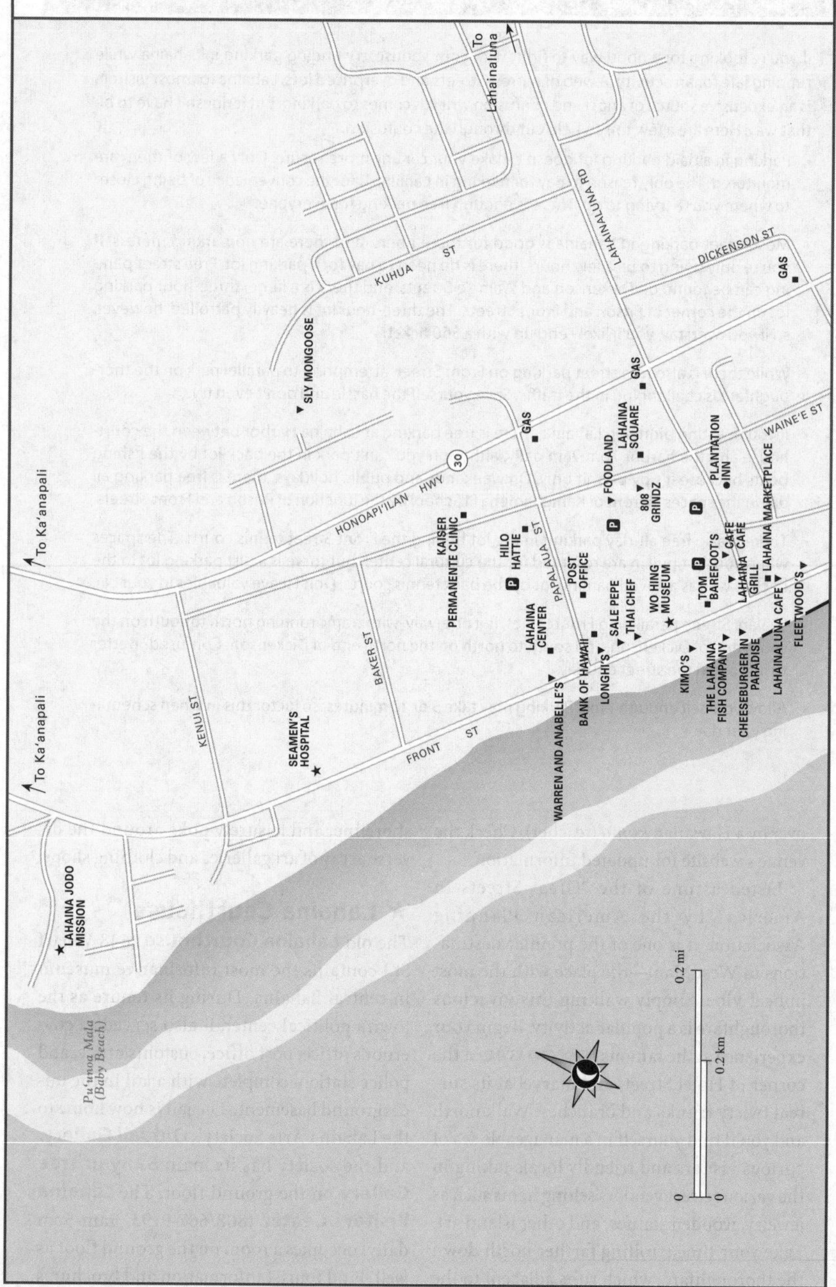
To Lahainaluna
LAHAINALUNA RD
DICKENSON ST
GAS
KUHUA ST
SLY MONGOOSE
GAS
GAS
WAINE'E ST
30
HONOAPI'ILAN HWY
KAISER PERMANENTE CLINIC
HILO HATTIE
FOODLAND
LAHAINA SQUARE
808 GRINDZ
PLANTATION INN
PAPALAUA ST
POST OFFICE
TOM BAREFOOT'S
CAFE
LAHAINA CAFE
LAHAINA MARKETPLACE
LAHAINA GRILL
FLEETWOOD'S
LAHAINA CENTER
SALE PEPE
THAI CHEF
WO HING MUSEUM
BANK OF HAWAII
LONGHI'S
KIMO'S
THE LAHAINA FISH COMPANY
CHEESEBURGER IN PARADISE
LAHAINALUNA CAFE
WARREN AND ANABELLE'S
To Ka'anapali
BAKER ST
KENUI ST
SEAMEN'S HOSPITAL
FRONT ST
To Ka'anapali
LAHAINA JODO MISSION
Pu'unoa Mala (Baby Beach)
0.2 mi
0.2 km
0
0

LAHAINA
Wahikuli County Wayside Park
FIRE STATION
LAHAINA CIVIC CENTER
POLICE STATION
POST OFFICE
HONOAPI'ILANI HWY
GARDEN GATE B&B
KANIAU RD
MAKAI INN
LOKIA ST
MALANAI ST
FLEMING ST
AINAKEA ST
KEAWE ST
HONU AND MALA
STAR NOODLE
MALA WHARF
OLD LAHAINA LUAU
SNORKEL BOB'S
LAHAINA JODO MISSION
GAS
FOODLAND FARMS
LAHAINA CANNERY MALL
FRONT STREET
FRONT ST
LAHAINALUNA RD
To Hale Pa'i and Lahainaluna High School
Lahaina Roads
Lahaina Harbor
SHAW ST
AREA OF DETAIL
HOKIOKIO PL
LAHAINA BYP
HONOAPI'ILANI HWY
0 0.5 mi
0 0.5 km
PUAMANA
To Puamana Beach County Park
© MOON.COM
SEAWALL
DICKENSON SQUARE
MARIA LANAKILA CHURCH
LAHAINA COOLERS
KOBE
SHINGON BUDDHIST TEMPLE
SUNRISE CAFE
MASTER'S READING ROOM
OUTRIGGER AINA NALU RESORT
HAUOLA STONE
LIBRARY
BALDWIN MISSIONARY HOME
BRICK PALACE SITE
PIONEER INN SHOPS
PIONEER INN
AMIGO'S
WHARF CINEMA CENTER
BANYAN TREE
COOL CAT CAFE
LAHAINA COURTHOUSE
PACIFIC WHALE FOUNDATION
HALE PA'AHAO (THE PRISON)
FORT RUINS
LOCAL BOYS WEST
KAMEHAMENA III SCHOOL
PRISON ST
(PUBLIC)
MAUI MEDICAL GROUP
LUAKINI ST
FRONT STREET
LAHAINA HONGWANJII TEMPLE
HONOAPI'ILANI HWY
EPISCOPAL CHURCH
TENNIS COURTS
(PUBLIC)
MALU'ULU O LELE PARK
WAIOLA CHURCH
KAMEHAMEHA IKI PARK
Lahaina Aquatic Center
505 FRONT ST MALL
SHAW ST
PACIFIC'O
SPANKY'S
FEAST AT LELE LUAU
Lahaina Recreation Center
LAHAINA SHORES BEACH RESORT
FRONT ST
30
OLD LAHAINA HOUSE
KAUA'ULA ST
To Ma'alaea, Kihei, and Kahului

1
2
和興會館
3
4

The Banyan Tree

This magnificent tree is the most recognizable landmark in West Maui. You can't miss it at the corner of Hotel and Front Streets because it spreads its shading boughs over almost 1 acre (0.4 ha). This tree is the **largest banyan in the state,** planted in April 1873 by Sheriff Bill Smith in commemoration of the Congregationalist Missions' golden anniversary. Every year in April a birthday party is held for the tree that draws hundreds of people to its shady confines. During most days you can find old-timers sitting here chatting, and artists gather on weekends to display their artwork under the tree's broad branches.

about the town; numerous coupon books can help save a few dollars.

In the old courtroom on the second floor, the **Lahaina Heritage Museum** (9am-4pm daily, $5 donation) displays historical objects and old photographs, and there is even the original Hawaiian flag that was lowered from the courthouse on the day it was replaced in 1898 by the American stars and stripes. On the lower level is also a small theater with informative documentaries about life in the islands. This is a must-stop for anyone with an interest in the history of Lahaina.

Fort at Lahaina

On the southwestern edge of the park containing the banyan tree are the restored coral remnants of the historic **Fort at Lahaina.** By 1825 the missionaries had convinced Hawaiian royalty that drunken sailors running amok in town was morally lamentable, so strict laws forbade native women from visiting the ships and whalers from coming ashore after nightfall. These rules, as you can imagine, proved a severe hindrance to lascivious pursuits, and riots frequently broke out between angry whalers and the missionaries. In 1827, whalers anchored offshore went so far as to lob cannonballs into the lawn of missionary William Richards's house, and it was decided by Hoapili—the governor of Maui—that a fort needed to be built to protect the town from the pent-up whalers. Hence, in 1832, a fort was constructed out of coral blocks with walls 20 feet (6 m) high and laden with cannons, the restored remnants of which are still visible today. One of the cannons from the fort is across the street at Lahaina Harbor, facing out toward the water to serve as a reminder of the "tensions" that once gripped this town.

1: Lahaina Courthouse 2: Front Street 3: Wo Hing Temple Museum 4: the banyan tree at the corner of Hotel and Front Streets

Baldwin Missionary House

On the inland side of Front Street, on the corner with Dickenson Street, you will notice the sprawling green lawn and whitewashed front of the historic **Baldwin Missionary House** (120 Dickenson St., 808/661-3262, 10am-4pm Wed.-Sat., $7 adults, $5 seniors). Established in 1834, this restored and peaceful property has stood since the days of the earliest missionaries and was the home of physician and reverend Dwight Baldwin, his wife, Charlotte, and their eight children. Baldwin was the first modern doctor and dentist in Hawaii, having studied at Harvard, and in the back of the museum are his tools. Until 1868 this building also served as a dispensary, meeting room, and boardinghouse, and Baldwin was instrumental not only in educating scores of Hawaiians but also in helping to fight the smallpox epidemic that struck the island in 1853.

Various rooms contain period furniture and artifacts indicative of missionary life in Lahaina, and coin collectors will appreciate the array of historic coins that were used as legal tender in early Hawaii, including silver bullion minted in Bolivia as early as the 1500s. Entrance to the museum also covers the Wo Hing Museum up the street, and if you purchase a $10 Passport to the Past, admission to the A&B Sugar Museum in Kahului and the Bailey House Museum in Wailuku are also included. While visiting in the daytime is educational enough, for a true glimpse of missionary life, take part in a candlelit tour 6pm-8:30pm every Friday evening.

Plantation Museum

For a look at a period of Lahaina's history that didn't have to do with whalers, missionaries, or Hawaiian royalty, idle on over to the Wharf Cinema Center and climb the stairs to the third story for a glimpse inside the informative **Plantation Museum** (685 Front St., 808/661-3262, 9am-6pm daily, free). Although it isn't much larger than a closet, there are dozens of old photos showing life during plantation times as well as a video detailing harvesting sugarcane. The Pioneer Mill was the social and economic engine of the West Side for the better part of 100 years, and the plantation days are just as much a part of Lahaina's heritage as harpoons, grog, and Bibles. A visit only takes a couple of minutes and is worthwhile.

Wo Hing Temple Museum

The **Wo Hing Temple Museum** (858 Front St., 808/661-5553, 10am-4pm daily, $7) is a small Chinese museum sandwiched between the modern commercial ventures of Front Street. Built in 1912 as a social and religious hall for Chinese workers, it's been placed on the National Register of Historic Places, showcasing Chinese immigration history on Maui as well as Chinese cultural traditions. Downstairs are displays, and upstairs is the temple altar. In the cookhouse next door, you can see film clips of Hawaii taken by Thomas Edison in 1898 and 1906. On Chinese New Year, the Wo Hing Museum is the center of the activities that play out on Front Street. The entrance fee also covers entrance to the Baldwin House.

Hale Pa'ahao

Where Luakini crosses Prison Street, turn left and walk a few yards to **Hale Pa'ahao** (187 Prison St., 808/667-1985, 10am-4pm daily, free), better known as Lahaina's old prison, one of the more historically informative sites. The peaceful courtyard inside the prison walls is a place of serenity and calm, where benches rest beneath the shade of a mango tree, but this compound once housed dozens of sailors and Hawaiians who broke the laws set out by the royals and their missionary advisors. To get an idea of an offense that would land you in the Lahaina slammer, read the list from the 1850s posted on the wall of one of the whitewashed wooden cells.

Lahaina Jodo Mission

On the northern end of Lahaina by Baby Beach and Mala Wharf, **Lahaina Jodo Mission** (99 Ala Moana St., 808/661-4304, 8am-6pm daily) is found by turning off Front Street where a sign over a building reads "Jesus Coming Soon." Turn left toward the beach and you'll immediately spot the three-tiered wooden pagoda at the end of the road. The temple bell welcomes you at the entrance gate, and a giant bronze Buddha sits exposed to the elements on a raised stone platform nearby. The largest Buddha outside Asia, this seated Amita Buddha image was dedicated in 1968 in commemoration of the centennial of the arrival of Japanese workers in Hawaii. You may stroll around, and while the buildings are closed to the public, you can climb the steps of the main building to peek into the temple. It's the perfect spot for solitary meditation if you've had enough of frenetic Lahaina. Buddha's birthday is celebrated here every April.

Hale Pa'i Printing Museum

All the way at the top of Lahainaluna Road on the grounds of Lahainaluna High School, which is the oldest high school west of the Rocky Mountains, having been founded in 1831, **Hale Pa'i Printing Museum** (980 Lahainaluna Rd., 808/667-7040, 10am-4pm

Moku'ula: The Ancient Capital of Hawaii

Until 1845, the town of Lahaina served as the royal capital of Hawaii. Generations of rulers from King Kamehameha on ruled the kingdom from this historic sun-drenched shore, and some of the most notable events in Hawaiian history were witnessed by this town.

If Lahaina was so important, you ask, where is the royal palace? Where is the seat of the monarchy? Where, exactly, was the capital? Unfortunately, when the capital was moved to Honolulu in 1845, the site of the former capital—Moku'ula—was abandoned and left to decay. Where once the home of *ali'i* and royalty existed, there is now an overgrown baseball field frequented by the island's unhoused population. If ever there were a fall from grace, it is the site of Moku'ula.

Hope was not lost for the former capital when the nonprofit group **Friends of Moku'ula** (808/661-3659) committed to restoring the nearly forgotten site, across from the area on Front Street where the 505 shopping center now stands. During the time when royalty called it home, there was a 25-acre (10-ha) *loko,* or fishpond, named Mokuhinia that was fed by the streams flowing from Mauna Kahalawai. In the middle of this pond was a small island—Moku'ula—and only the highest chiefs and Hawaiian royalty were allowed to set foot on it. Within walking distance of the ocean and framed by the mountainous backdrop, it must have been a sight to behold.

When the capital was moved, the stream was diverted to irrigate the sugar crop, and the Mokuhinia fishpond became a festering swamp of mosquitoes and bugs. Taking matters into their own hands, mill workers filled the pond with dirt in 1914. The ballfield and parking structures that stand in its place were subsequently constructed on top.

Just because Moku'ula isn't visible, however, doesn't mean that it's gone. Archaeologists estimate that the site still exists about 3 feet (1 m) below the surface, and digs have yielded artifacts that show evidence of the ancient fishpond. The Friends of Moku'ula worked diligently to raise awareness and funding for a major restoration of the former royal site. The group, whose efforts were sidetracked during the pandemic, still envision it as a historic landmark as well as an educational resource about Hawaiian culture. They hope to resume in-depth tours of Old Hawaii, which include a look at the future of Moku'ula, with the group **Maui Nei** (505 Front St., 808/661-9494).

Mon.-Wed., free) provides a phenomenally informative view into the literary past of the Hawaiian Islands. For educators and those interested in history, this is a must-stop for a look at the history of Hawaii's printed past.

In addition to the old printing press, there are a host of native Hawaiian artifacts. This small, out-of-the-way museum in the school's parking lot provides excellent insight into the development of modern Hawaii.

SOUTH OF LAHAINA

Maui Dragon Fruit Farm

The **Maui Dragon Fruit Farm** (833 Punakea Loop, 808/264-6127, www.mauidragonfruit.com, 8:30am-4pm Mon.-Sat.), in the Launiupoko subdivision, makes for a curious combination of agriculture and adventure. With the consistency of an apple but the look of an exotic poppy-seed muffin, dragon fruit is tropical and native to Central and South America, although it's most often seen in Southeast Asia. In addition to dragon fruit, various other crops are grown on this certified organic farm.

Tropical fruit tasting walking tours ($35 adults) take place at 9am, 10am, 11am, and noon Monday-Friday. Additional adventure activities include a 450-foot-long (135-m) zip line (9am, 10:30am, and noon Mon.-Fri., $119 adults, $99 children) and an enormous plastic "Aquaball" (10am, 11:30am, 2pm, and 3:30pm daily, $90 adults, $70 children) filled with water and then rolled 450 feet (135 m) downhill with you inside. Combine the farm tour, zip line, and the Aquaball ($189 adults, $169 children).

Olowalu Petroglyphs

For every 1,000 people who snorkel at

Olowalu, probably only one makes it back to the *ki'i pohaku*, the petroglyphs behind the Olowalu General Store. Hidden 0.5 mile (0.8 km) back in the recesses of Olowalu valley, the 70 rock carvings on the face of Pu'u Kilea date to nearly 300 years ago, when there was no written form of the Hawaiian language. The Olowalu valley is heavily steeped in Hawaiian history, and even though a century of sugar cultivation and the encroachment of modern development has eroded traditional village sites, a number of families living back in the valley aim to perpetuate the lifestyle of their ancestors.

To find the petroglyphs, drive on the road behind the Olowalu fruit stand at mile marker 15 and proceed on the paved segment, which runs back toward the valley. After 0.5 mile (0.8 km) are signs for the Olowalu Cultural Reserve, and when the road turns to dirt, the petroglyphs are about 200 yards (180 m) farther, on the rock face. Unfortunately, some of the petroglyphs have been vandalized, so visitors are asked to keep a respectful distance from them.

Beaches

KAPALUA, NAPILI, AND HONOKOWAI

Known to locals simply as "up north," the beaches along this stretch include tropical turquoise coves sandwiched between condos and luxurious homes. Napili and Kapalua beaches are the most popular, but past the entrance to Kapalua, the shore gets wilder and the crowds start to thin. The wind can howl in the afternoons and massive surf crashes into the coast October-April. Over the winter the shore-break often grows to 10 feet (3 m) or larger.

D. T. Fleming Beach Park

D. T. Fleming Beach Park has been named the number-one beach in the United States. Fleming's is a hybrid stretch of sand where the southern half is dominated by Ritz-Carlton resort guests and the northern half is popular with locals. This is one of the best beaches on the island for bodysurfing and bodyboarding, although the surf here can get rough and dangerous in the winter. Luckily, this is one of the only beaches on the West Side with lifeguards. There are restrooms and showers at the northern end. To access D. T. Fleming Beach Park, take Honoapi'ilani Highway (Hwy. 30) past the main entrance to Kapalua 0.9 mile (1.5 km) and turn left at the bottom of the hill. The road dead-ends in the lot.

Napili Bay and Kapalua Bay

There is a lot of debate about which beach is better: **Napili Bay** or **Kapalua Bay.** There are a couple of factors that distinguish one from the other. Although a mere 0.25 mile (0.4 km) from each other, the shore-break at Napili Bay can be larger in the winter, whereas Kapalua is more protected. The snorkeling between the two reefs is a toss-up, although Kapalua often has more fish while Napili has more sea turtles. Napili Bay is a little larger, although it can also become more crowded. If you're traveling with children, Kapalua Bay is the better bet since the water is calmer and there is easy access to beach showers and restrooms.

Your best chance for finding parking at Napili Bay is either along the side of Lower Honoapi'ilani Road between Napili Kai and the Kapalua Tennis Club, or on the south end of the beach, where there is some beach parking at the bottom of Hui Drive. The beach parking lot at Kapalua Bay fills up early. If you can't find a parking place, drop all of your beach gear by the stairs leading down to the sand and then circle back to find a parking spot along the road.

Oneloa Bay (Ironwoods)

Hidden from view from the road through

Kapalua, **Oneloa Bay** is virtually always empty. This epic expanse of shore sits right along the Kapalua Coastal Trail, although since the swimming is poor and it's out of sight, it's also out of mind. Mornings on Oneloa can be calm and still, and this is a popular spot for sunset wedding photo shoots. Oneloa is a great beach for those who just want to commune with nature and need a bit of an escape. To reach Oneloa, either park at the lot for Kapalua Bay and walk 15 minutes along the Kapalua Coastal Trail, or follow Lower Honoapi'ilani Road into Kapalua; a small beach access path and a parking lot are located across from The Ridge. While there is a small beach shower for rinsing off, the nearest public restrooms are at Kapalua Bay.

Honokowai Beach Park

The farthest point south, **Honokowai Beach Park** is a narrow stretch of sand at the northern edge of Ka'anapali. While the beach here is far from the nicest on the island—its shoreline is equally sandy and rocky—there is a large grassy park with a playground for small children, a picnic area, and a couple of shops across the street. The beach also offers some of the best views of Lana'i and Moloka'i.

Mokulei'a Bay (Slaughterhouse)

Mokulei'a Bay was once a secret, since you can't see it from the road, but has recently become so exceptionally popular it can be tough to find a place to park. Tucked at the base of dramatic cliffs, Mokulei'a offers some of the best snorkeling on the West Side. It's known to locals as Slaughterhouse Beach, but the name is less sinister than it sounds: A slaughterhouse was once located here but is now long gone. The bay is part of the Honolua Bay Marine Life Conservation District, so no fishing or spearfishing—or any other kind of slaughter—is allowed. This is also a popular beach for bodysurfing, although the surf can be treacherous during large winter swells. This beach is nearly always deserted in the early morning hours, but lately is packed by 11am. To reach Mokulei'a, travel 2.5 miles (4 km) past the entrance to Kapalua and park on the left side of the road, where you will notice a paved stairway leading down to the beach, as well as a sign that details the rules of the marine reserve.

Punalau Beach (Windmills)

Sandy, serene, and almost always empty, **Punalau** is little visited by tourists—but not for lack of beauty. The local name, Windmills, is derived from an old windmill that once stood here but has long since been destroyed. This is now a popular place for advanced surfers and ambitious beachcombers who scour the shore for flotsam and shells. The road down to the shore can often be rough, so unless you have a high-clearance vehicle, it's best to leave your car parked by the highway and make the five-minute trek on foot. Bring all of your valuables with you, and also pack a blanket or towel for lying in the sun and soaking up the silence. Since the reef is shallow and can be razor sharp, don't snorkel or swim here. This is also one of Maui's best spots to watch large winter surf, and the left break at the far southern end has been referred to as Maui's version of the Pipeline.

KA'ANAPALI

The beaches in Ka'anapali are long, wide, and lined by resorts. Much like Kapalua, however, the wind can often be a factor here in the afternoon, so it's best to get your water activities in early before the trade winds start blowing.

Ka'anapali Beach

Few stretches of Maui shore are more iconic than famous **Ka'anapali Beach.** This long, uninterrupted expanse of sand is lined from end to end with world-class resorts, has been named the number-one beach in the United States, and is the pulsing epicenter of the West Side's see-and-be-seen crowd. It should come as no surprise that the area is a constant hotbed of activity. Pick any island beach activity—surfing, snorkeling, scuba, snuba, paddleboarding, volleyball, parasailing

1
2
3
4

(summer), or whale-watching (winter)—and you'll find it on Ka'anapali Beach. A paved pathway runs the length of the beach and is popular with joggers in the morning.

The best snorkeling is found at Pu'u Keka'a (Black Rock) in front of the Sheraton at the far northern end of the beach. Most of the water sports, such as surf lessons, take place at KP Point in front of the Ka'anapali Ali'i, and the beach volleyball court is in front of the Sheraton on the north end of the beach. For bodyboarding, the best area is between Whalers Village and Pu'u Keka'a. Since the beach faces directly west, it can pick up waves any time of year. Be careful on days with big shore-break, however, and use common sense.

Another favorite activity at Ka'anapali Beach is cliff-jumping off Pu'u Keka'a. While this 20-foot (6-m) jump is popular with visitors and locals, the rock is one of the most sacred places on the island for native Hawaiians, who believe it's an entry point for a person's soul passing from this world into the next. To jump off Pu'u Keka'a is to mimic the soul at the moment of death, a legend still told during the evening torch-lighting ceremony that takes place before each sunset.

Since Ka'anapali Beach is exposed to the afternoon trade winds, the weather can often be wetter and windier than down the road in Lahaina. The morning hours are best for paddleboarding or snorkeling, and if the wind is blowing too hard by the Sheraton, you can find a pocket of calm at the southern end of the beach by the Hyatt. Also, if you plan on going for a morning swim, realize that there are two areas where large catamarans come ashore to pick up passengers, so be alert when you're in the water in front of Ka'anapali Beach Hotel or Whalers Village.

Unless you're staying at one of the resorts along the Ka'anapali strip, parking is going to be a challenge. Free public parking can be tough to come by, since most public spots are taken by 9am. There is one small public garage between the Sheraton and the Ka'anapali Beach Hotel, a lot between Whalers Village and the Westin, a handful of beach parking stalls in the front lot of the Ka'anapali Beach Hotel, and a small public lot on Nohea Kai Drive just before the Hyatt. While there's always a chance that you'll luck out and snag a spot, more often than not you'll end up having to pay to park in the garage of Whalers Village. Remember, however, that if you shop at a store or eat at a restaurant in Whalers Village, you can get the parking ticket validated.

Kahekili Beach Park (Airport Beach)

There was a time not too long ago when **Kahekili Beach Park,** named after the great king of Maui, was an undeveloped scrubland of *kiawe* (mesquite) trees that paled in comparison to Ka'anapali Beach. Over time, there has been so much development at Airport Beach (also known as Ka'anapali North Beach) that it's almost as busy as neighboring Ka'anapali. Yet Kahekili still has a family-friendly atmosphere where locals lounge on the grassy area in front of the beach pavilion or snorkel the offshore reef. The beach here is just as long as Ka'anapali Beach, although the steep grade of the shore makes it difficult for jogging. Most visitors use the boardwalk along the shore, and if you're up for a stroll, you can follow it as it weaves through the Royal Lahaina and Sheraton parking areas to meet up with the Ka'anapali beach path. There are public restrooms, and there is a large public parking lot at the Kai Ala entrance from the highway. If the lot is full, there's more parking on the north end of the beach, accessible from Lower Honoapi'ilani Road. The swimming here is much better than at Ka'anapali since there isn't as much catamaran traffic. If Ka'anapali Beach is too busy for you, you'll enjoy how Kahekili offers a world-class beach atmosphere at a slower pace.

LAHAINA

The beaches of Lahaina are the most underrated on the island. The swimming is poor

1: Napili Bay 2: D. T. Fleming Beach Park 3: sunset at Ka'anapali Beach 4: Olowalu

due to the offshore reef, but they are sunnier, less crowded, and more protected from the wind than most other beaches on Maui. If it's raining in Kapalua or Napili, or windy on Ka'anapali Beach, 90 percent of the time it's going to be sunny and calm on the beaches of Lahaina.

Makila Beach

Also known as **Breakwall, 505,** or **Shark Pit,** this is the most happening stretch of sand in Lahaina. Most visitors access the beach from Kamehameha Iki Park, and there is beach parking in a small lot or in the back of the Front Street tennis courts. This is the area where most of the surf schools set out from. There is also a beach volleyball court, which can get busy during the afternoon. Visitors are encouraged to marvel at the Polynesian voyaging canoes on display as part of the **Hui O Wa'a Kaulua Canoe Club.** Visitors rarely wander to the south end of the beach where palm trees hang over a secluded cove. Locals call this area Shark Pit for the harmless reef sharks that hang around the offshore ledge. The swimming is poor due to the offshore reef, although it provides calm water for wading with small children. There is one shower but no restroom.

Pu'unoa (Baby Beach)

On the northern end of Front Street, the beach that runs along Pu'unoa Point (known to locals as **Baby Beach**) is an oasis of tranquility where you have to ask yourself if you're still in Lahaina. Shielded from visitors by its residential location—and protected from surf by the offshore reef—the sand running along this lazy promontory is the perfect spot for sitting in a beach chair and listening to the waves. Numerous trees provide shade, and the calm waters are ideal for beachgoers with young children or those who want to tan on a raft.

Finding the beach can be a challenge, and parking can be an issue. For the access point with the largest amount of parking, turn off Front Street onto Ala Moana Street by the sign for Mala Ramp. Instead of heading down to the boat launch, proceed straight on Ala Moana until the road ends by the Jodo mission. From here you will see the beach in front of you. The best section of beach is a five-minute walk to the left along the sand. Transients sometimes hang out around this parking lot; don't leave any valuables in your car. Walking from central Lahaina, the quickest access to the nicest part of beach is to turn off Front Street onto Kai Pali Place, where you will notice a shore access path. From central Lahaina, this turn will be about three minutes after you pass the Hard Rock Café.

Wahikuli and Hanakao'o (Canoe Beach) Beach Parks

On the northern tip of Lahaina, these two beach parks are the strip of land between Front Street and Ka'anapali. **Wahikuli** is closer to Lahaina, and **Hanakao'o** is at the southern edge of the Hyatt. Of the two beaches, Wahikuli offers better swimming, although a secret about Hanakao'o is that on the days when the main stretch of Ka'anapali Beach is windy, Hanakao'o sits tucked in a cove where the wind can barely reach. Hanakao'o is also known as Canoe Beach, since this is where many of the outrigger canoe regattas are held on Saturday mornings. A beach path allows you to walk or ride bicycles from the south end of Ka'anapali through Hanakao'o, Wahikuli, and down to Front Street in Lahaina.

SOUTH OF LAHAINA

On the stretch of shore between Lahaina and Ma'alaea are a grand total of zero resorts. Paddleboards and fishing poles rule this section of coast, and even though the swimming is poor, there is one spot that offers good snorkeling. Most visitors pass these beaches without giving them another thought, but if you do decide to pull over to watch the whales, visit the beach, or photograph the sunset, don't stop in the middle of the road. If you're headed in the Lahaina direction, it's easiest to pull off on the right side of the road and wait for traffic to clear before crossing.

Puamana Beach Park

While there is a private gated community that goes by the same name, the public can visit the small **Puamana Beach Park** just south of Lahaina, off Honoapi'ilani Highway just past Hokiokio Place street. As at other beaches in the area, the swimming is poor, although the tables provide a nice setting for a picnic. For a stroll down the beach, the sandy shore fronting the condos is public property, so at low tide you can walk from the beach park to the other end of the private, gated section, although the grassy area is private. There aren't any restrooms at the beach park, but there's a refreshing shower in the parking lot with a serious nozzle.

Launiupoko Beach Park

Located at the only stoplight between Ma'alaea and Lahaina, **Launiupoko** is the most family-friendly beach park on the West Side of Maui. It has a protected wading area for small *keiki* (children), a decent sandy beach on the south end of the park, a wide, grassy picnic area, and numerous surf breaks that cater to beginner surfers and stand-up paddle surfers. This park is so popular with the weekend barbecue crowd that local families arrive before dawn to stake their claim for a birthday party with a bouncy house. There is a large parking lot as well as restrooms and showers, and since most of the parking spots are taken by 8am, there is an overflow lot on the *mauka* (mountain side) of the highway. The water is too shallow for swimming and the snorkeling is poor, but this is a good place to put your finger on the local pulse and strike up a good conversation.

Olowalu

Known to visitors as Mile Marker 14, the real name of this beach is **Olowalu,** after the village that stretches back into the valley. The snorkeling here is the best south of Lahaina, although plenty of beachgoers—particularly those with young children—come simply to wade in the calm waters. While the water may be calm, it's also shallow, and the swimming area is nonexistent during low tide. Parking is along the side of the highway, although it's easy to get stuck in the sand.

Ukumehame Beach Park

Ukumehame Beach Park is a small yet scenic beach along the shore. Look for mile marker 12 along Honoapi'ilani Highway, where you'll find a parking lot. The beach is an ideal spot for kayak launches, snorkeling, and surfing. In fact, it's one the best places for beginning surfers with its numerous surf breaks, and it earns its nickname, "Thousand Peaks." Many people bring picnic lunches or food to barbecue in the pits. While visitors have been known to spend an entire day, the best time to experience this park for snorkelers is in the morning hours when the wind is moderate.

Snorkeling

Snorkeling is the most popular activity in West Maui. Hundreds of people ply the waters of the island's western shore, flipping their fins as they chase after schools of yellow and black *manini* (convict tang). But there is always room to find your own section of reef, and the waters of West Maui teem with everything from graceful green sea turtles to the playfully named *humuhumunukunukuapua'a*—the Hawaiian state fish, whose name translates as "big lips with a nose like a pig."

Mornings are the best time of day for snorkeling. Different times of year also mean different snorkeling conditions. During the winter, places such as Honolua Bay and Napili can be dangerous due to the huge surf, so summer is the best time for exploring these reefs. Similarly, snorkeling spots on the south shore such as Olowalu can be prone to large surf during summer, although with much less frequency than the northern beaches in winter. If the surf is too big or the conditions too poor, there is probably another place that is calm and beautiful just a 20-minute drive away.

KAPALUA, NAPILI, AND HONOKOWAI

Honolua Bay

When it comes to snorkeling along Maui's shore, **Honolua Bay** is the gold standard. This wide, scenic cleft in the coast is not only a biodiverse marine reserve, it's also protected from the afternoon trade winds. Honolua Bay is one of the most sacred and revered spots on the West Side of the island, and there has been a herculean movement over the last decade to "Save Honolua" and spare the area from development. The valley, bay, and shore exude a supernatural beauty. Somewhere between the lush green foliage of the valley and the shimmering turquoise waters is a palpable magic unlike anywhere else.

As the highway morphs into a rural county road, the first glimpse of Honolua is from the paved overlook 1.8 miles (2.9 km) past the entrance to Kapalua. This is a nice place to pull over for a picture, but there are better lookouts 1 mile (1.6 km) later. Toward the bottom of the hill, parking for the shore is in a lush and shaded valley where you might encounter some merchants selling their crafts. To reach the water, find a parking spot wherever you can (all the trails along a 0.5-mi/0.8-km stretch eventually lead to the shore), grab all of your snorkeling gear, and make a short five-minute trek through a dense green understory that chirps with activity and drips with vines.

The "beach" is more a collection of boulders. Facing the water, the right side has a much larger snorkeling area and a greater concentration of marinelife. The center of the bay has a sandy bottom and is mostly devoid of marinelife, so it's best to trace the shore and snorkel around to the right. If there aren't any charter boats tied up on the right side of the bay between 9am and noon, it means that the conditions aren't good enough to bring paying snorkelers here. Also, if you see breaking waves out toward the point and there are more than 20 surfers in the water, it means that the visibility is going to be less than stellar and conditions will be dangerous. If it isn't raining on the shore but the stream on the left side of the bay is gushing with brown water, it means that it's raining farther up the mountain and

snorkeling in Honolua Bay

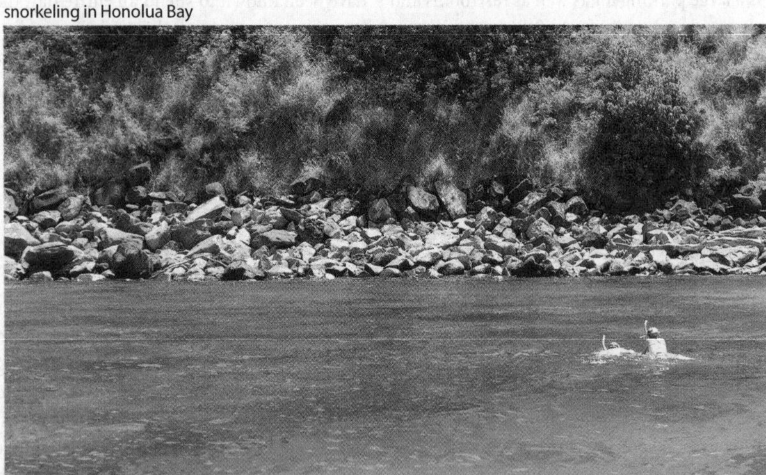

the runoff is emptying into the bay, which also makes for subpar conditions.

If, however, the sun is shining brilliantly, here's your guide to the best snorkeling area: When you enter the water from the rocky shore, swim straight out for about 20 yards (18 m) and then turn right toward the shore. You'll want to hug the shore in 5-10 feet (1.5-3 m) of water and follow it in a ring around the right side of the bay. To find Hawaiian green sea turtles, the best spot to check out is the **turtle cleaning station** on the right center of the bay. It's about 200 yards (180 m) out from the boat ramp, in line with the bend in the cliff on the right side of the bay, in about 15-20 feet (4.5-6 m) of water. Snorkeling in Honolua Bay during winter, you can dive a few feet underwater to listen for the distant song of humpback whales. Keep a keen eye out for boat traffic, as a number of catamarans make their approach through the middle of the bay.

Mokulei'a Bay

Parking for **Mokulei'a Bay** is along the highway 1.5 miles (2.4 km) past the entrance to Kapalua, and the best snorkeling is in the cove on the right side of the bay. Even though Mokulei'a is still a part of the Honolua Bay Marine Life Conservation District, the reef is completely different than at Honolua Bay, so you're likely to see different species. There's still the likelihood of seeing a sea turtle, a chance for some spotted eagle rays swimming over the sand by the end of the point, and perhaps an octopus clinging to the wall at the far end of the cove. Mokulei'a is more exposed to the afternoon trade winds, so morning hours during flat, calm days are the best time for snorkeling.

Honokowai Beach Park

Honokowai Beach Park is a fantastic area to spot sea turtles, small oval squid, and an array of colorful fish. Enter via a shallow pool between the reef's rocky shelves—and stay mindful as the jagged edges can cut skin—and venture out about 200 yards (180 m) farther to

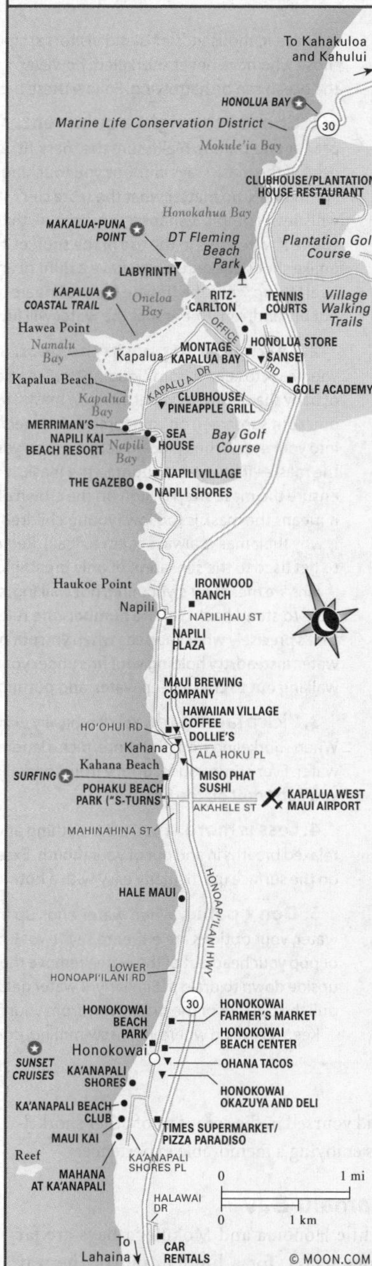

Snorkeling 101

Every year, thousands of island visitors strap on a mask for a peek at the underwater world. For those who have never snorkeled, however, the act of breathing through a tube in the middle of the ocean can be harrowing. Follow these basic snorkeling tips for a better first-time experience.

1. Choose the right equipment. Any successful snorkeling mission begins with the proper equipment. Make sure the mask fits by holding it to your face and sucking in with your nose. If the mask stays without you touching it with your hands, it means you have a good seal. For snorkels, no matter what the store clerk says, you don't have to get one with all the bells and whistles. A simple J-shaped snorkel is all that's needed, although some people like the feature where if water gets in the top of the snorkel it won't continue down toward your mouth. For fins, unlike shoes, make sure you have a tight fit around your heel instead of around your toes. If your heel lifts up while the fins are on, the fins are too big. If they feel slightly tight when you test them out on land, remember that the water will lubricate the area once you get in the ocean.

2. Learn how to put on the gear. Before getting in the water, put a defog solution in your mask to keep it from clouding up. Even better than snorkel shop gels is a homemade solution of baby shampoo and water. For new masks, use toothpaste. Also, to keep your eyes from stinging, don't put sunscreen on your forehead immediately prior to snorkeling, since it will end up running into your eyes. When placing your mask on your head, brush all of your hair back so none gets into the mask—if hair gets caught in the mask, it will break the seal and allow water to leak in. Next, ensure the mask strap is high on the crown of your head. If the mask strap is touching your ears, it means the mask is too low (young children love to put the mask strap below their ears, which is why their masks always seem to leak). Remember that your nose is inside a mask, so you need to get used to the sensation of only breathing through your mouth.

Fins are meant for swimming, not walking, so once you fall down with fins on, it's almost impossible to stand back up. The number-one rule in Hawaii is never turn your back on the ocean—that's precisely what happens when you put on your fins on the beach and back your way into the water. Instead, try holding your fins under your arm (after having put your mask on while onshore), walking out to chest-deep water, and putting your fins on once there.

3. Pick a landmark. You'll typically want to enter and leave the water from the same point. When snorkeling from the shore, pick a landmark or two to help you remain oriented while in the water. Every time you resurface from snorkeling, take a quick glance at your landmarks to ensure you don't drift off too far.

4. Less is more. If you are breathing and see fish, you're doing it correctly. Take long, slow, relaxed breaths in and out of your mouth. Excessive movement will scare away the fish. If you float on the surface (particularly easy with a flotation belt), you'll see more of them.

5. Don't panic. When water ends up in your snorkel, don't panic! To clear the snorkel of water, your options are either to say "two" loudly to shoot the water out the top of your snorkel, or pop your head out of the water, remove the snorkel from your mouth, and turn the mouthpiece upside down to drain it. Similarly, if water gets in your mask, instead of removing the whole mask, pull the bottom of the mask away from your face and let the water drain out.

Keep an eye on where you're swimming, don't overexert yourself, and most important, have fun.

find yourself in the company of other snorkelers enjoying a memorable experience.

Namalu Bay

While Honolua and Mokulei'a Bays are far from secret, for a hidden, out-of-the-way snorkeling experience in a rocky, almost Mediterranean cove, the craggy shore of **Namalu Bay** is one of West Maui's best spots. There isn't much in the way of live coral, but you can spot green sea turtles, reef fish, and the occasional eagle or manta ray. The center of the bay is about 40 feet (12 m) deep, and the areas ringing the shore are a more manageable 5-15 feet (1.5-4.5 m). As a bonus, the rocks also make for some enjoyable cliff-jumping.

Accessing the bay can be challenging, and while strong swimmers can access Namalu Bay by swimming around from Kapalua Bay, this is a long swim over deep water that's only possible when it's calm. The more practical way to reach Namalu Bay is via the dirt pathway that follows the coast. The closest public parking is at the Kapalua Bay Villas in a hidden, little-known location. To find the eight public parking spots, turn into the parking area for the Montage Hotel and make an immediate right toward the Kapalua Bay Villas. Then make a left, following the sign for beach access parking, and notice the small public parking area seemingly orphaned among the private residential lots. From here it's a short walk down to the shore and the access for the Kapalua Coastal Trail.

Now that you've found the trailhead, to find the actual snorkeling area, make your way past two brown "Trail" markers and then notice the trail goes in three different directions. The trail to the right is the Kapalua Coastal Trail; the gravel trail leading straight heads to Hawea Point, the westernmost point on the island and a great place for spotting sea turtles from shore; and the grassy trail that bends off to the left leads toward Namalu Bay. Follow the trail as it wraps to the left, past the signs that say "Proceed at your own risk." In 30 seconds you'll find yourself standing atop the cliffs overlooking hidden Namalu Bay, wondering how a place this beautiful can be so isolated and unknown.

Kapalua Bay

Kapalua Bay is a sandy cove that is a favorite for snorkeling with small children. Its relatively small size means it is easy to scour the entire bay, and you can expect to see colorful parrotfish, lots of goatfish, and even the occasional green sea turtle. Although depths rarely exceed 20 feet (6 m), the best snorkeling is found along the right side of the bay where the rocks extend out to the distant point. If you're a strong snorkeler and the conditions are calm, you can even snorkel around the northern point into neighboring Namalu Bay.

Napili Bay

A short walk from Kapalua Bay is neighboring **Napili Bay.** You can easily snorkel at both bays without even reparking your car. Napili Bay doesn't have quite as many fish as Kapalua Bay, but there is a higher likelihood of finding a green sea turtle. While many snorkelers hug the wall on the right side of the bay, there is another reef in the center of the bay that's almost exposed during low tide. About 20 yards (18 m) farther out is a second, less visited reef, and although it's deeper, at about 15-20 feet (4.5-6 m), it has the highest concentration of fish. This outer reef is far from shore, so if you're uncomfortable in the water, stay on the inside reefs and enjoy the shallower areas.

Rental Shops

In Napili, **Water Works Sports** (5315 Lower Honoapi'ilani Rd., 808/298-2446, www.waterworkssportsmaui.com, 8am-5pm daily) inside Napili Shores has snorkel rentals for $10 per day or $30 per week. They can give you tips on current conditions, and also have snorkeling gear for sale.

In Kapalua, **Snorkel Bob's** (5425 Honoapi'ilani Hwy., 808/669-9603, www.snorkelbob.com, 8am-5pm daily) offers weekly rentals ($38 adults, $25 children) and perks that include your choice of specialty masks, No Fog Goop, a net gear bag, and a free gift if you order online.

In Honokowai, locally run **All About Fish** (3600 Lower Honoapi'ilani Hwy., 808/669-1710, www.mauifish.net, 9am-5pm Mon.-Sat., noon-4pm Sun.) in the 5A Rent-A-Space mall offers affordable rentals on a full range of dive equipment. This is a good option if you're staying in a condo in Honokowai and looking for local advice on snorkeling conditions. Snorkeling gear runs $8-10 per day or up to $30 per week, and the atmosphere is relaxed.

1

2

3

Snorkeling Charters

Shoreline Snorkel (Hanakao'o Beach Park, 808/214-4743, www.shorelinesnorkel.com, 7am-9pm daily) offers exceptional tours, including a two-hour guided tour with snorkel instruction ($109). Its Three Beach Adventure ($199) showcases the best of West Maui and includes stops at three beaches—two for snorkeling, the third for lunch, with snorkel gear and drinks included (bring cash for lunch). A standout excursion is the Night Snorkel Adventure ($125), an opportunity to glimpse ocean life that few people experience. Enjoy the sparkling glow of bioluminescence, or spot octopuses and lobsters as a guide leads you from shore using LED lights.

KA'ANAPALI

Kahekili Beach Park

In the northern part of Ka'anapali, **Kahekili Beach Park** offers decent snorkeling off the park and at the far southern end of the beach. The reef extends from the shore out to about 25 feet (7.5 m) of water. Expect to see a healthy amount of herbivorous reef fish. The moderate depth and easy entry make this a user-friendly snorkeling spot during the early morning hours. At the far southern end of the beach is a rock jetty that also offers good snorkeling. The rocky promontory here is the "back" of Pu'u Keka'a (Black Rock).

Pu'u Keka'a (Black Rock)

The best snorkeling in Ka'anapali is at **Pu'u Keka'a,** better known as **Black Rock.** At the far northern end of Ka'anapali Beach in front of the Sheraton, this area offers the most consistently beautiful snorkeling conditions and a relatively easy entry. The morning hours are best, and the best chance for seeing sea turtles is during high tide, when the water comes up on the side of the rock and all the *limu* (seaweed) falls into the water. Since this is a favorite delicacy of the green sea turtles, occasionally three or four of them congregate in the shallow cove in only 5-10 feet (1.5-3 m) of water. Since the cliff is also a favorite place for cliff-jumping, steer clear of the immediate landing zone, and if you see the wind whipping up whitecaps out by the point, stay in the cove, protected from the wind and with gentler currents.

Ka'anapali Point

On the other end of Ka'anapali Beach is the reef at **Ka'anapali Point,** in front of the Marriott. It's not nearly as popular as the reef at Pu'u Keka'a but covers a larger area and isn't nearly as crowded. If Pu'u Keka'a is a flotilla of fins, take a 10-minute stroll to the southern end of the beach and try your luck at this less visited spot.

Rental Shops

Every major resort along the strip of Ka'anapali has a rental shack by the sand. Prices vary slightly among the operators, but expect to pay higher resort prices compared to what you'll find off the strip. The best deal in Ka'anapali on rental gear is at **The Snorkel Store** (2580 Keka'a Dr., 808/669-1077, www.thesnorkelstore.com, 8am-5pm daily), in the Fairway Shops by the highway. A full snorkel setup is around $20 per day or $35 per week, provided you book ahead online or fill out a coupon in the store. While here, inquire about guided tours, where a local guide takes your party snorkeling at a spot along the shore, providing individualized attention you won't find on larger boats (prices vary). It's a great option for beginner snorkelers and a nice way to find new spots.

Snorkeling Charters

A number of catamarans depart directly from Ka'anapali Beach on half-day sailing excursions along the West Maui coast. For trips to either Lana'i or Molokini Crater, you still need to go to the Lahaina or Ma'alaea harbors. For boats departing from Ka'anapali Beach, the preferred snorkeling destination is Honolua Bay. Since the surf

1: snorkelers at Mokulei'a Bay 2: the state fish, *humuhumunukunukuapua'a,* at Pu'u Keka'a (Black Rock) 3: sea turtle and snorkeler at Napili Bay

at Honolua Bay during winter can get huge, the alternate destination is Olowalu on the south shore. Most days of the year these sleek sailing yachts are able to pull right up on the sand and load passengers directly from the beach, although on days with large surf, the shore-break can be too rough, and the trip might be moved to Lahaina Harbor. If a member of your party has restricted mobility, trips out of Lahaina Harbor are a safer option.

Of the charters departing from Ka'anapali Beach, **Trilogy** (808/874-5649, www.sail-trilogy.com) loads in front of the Ka'anapali Beach Hotel and offers 7:30am snorkeling trips, making them the first boat to reach Honolua Bay. The tours from Ka'anapali are usually aboard the *Trilogy III,* a few feet smaller than other boats along the beach. The maximum capacity is about 49 people. All the food is made fresh on board. Both the Trilogy crew and the level of customer service are widely regarded as the best in the industry. Due to its slightly smaller size and its light weight, the *Trilogy III* is the fastest of the Ka'anapali sailboats. Half-day charters are $189 for adults, include all food and equipment, and usually return to the beach around 1:30pm.

On the stretch of sand in front of Whalers Village, **Teralani** (808/661-7245, www.teralani.net) has two boats that regularly make excursions along the West Maui coast. The Teralani boats are larger than Trilogy's and cap their trips at 49 people. The main snorkeling tour departs at 9:30am and returns to the beach around 2:30pm. A shorter trip departs at 11am and returns to the beach at 3pm. All food and equipment are included in the rates. Enjoy the open bar when you've finished snorkeling, with rates beginning at $199 for adults for the longer experience and $139 for the four-hour excursion.

Other catamarans departing from Ka'anapali Beach include ***Gemini*** (808/669-1700, www.geminicharters.com), which loads on the stretch of beach in front of Leilani's restaurant and is just as large as Teralani's boats. It offers a similar trip, departing at 11am and returning to the beach between 3pm and 3:30pm. Equipment, food, and an open bar are included in the tour for $139 for adults.

Hula Girl (808/665-0344, www.sailing-maui.com), which also loads on the stretch of beach in front of Leilani's restaurant, is an ornately painted boat that takes a different approach: The $108 for the five-hour tour (9:30am-2:30pm) doesn't include food, but the boat has a kitchen on board where chefs make food to order. There is also free Wi-Fi for anyone who wants to immediately upload camera footage of an encounter with a sea turtle. Scuba diving is offered for an additional cost for both certified ($69) and introductory ($80) divers.

LAHAINA

Wahikuli Beach Park

Most of Lahaina is ringed by a barrier reef, and there are surprisingly few options for decent snorkeling. One exception is **Wahikuli Beach Park,** between Ka'anapali and Lahaina, where you can find sea turtles, corals, and large schools of goat fish at a reef just a short swim offshore. For the best results, snorkel around the north end, about 10 yards (9 m) off the rocks in about 5-10 feet (1.5-3 m) of water.

Mala Wharf

In Lahaina, the best snorkeling spot is **Mala Wharf,** and since it is a functioning small-boat harbor, you have to keep an eye out for boat traffic. The reward, however, is a snorkeling site where legions of sea turtles and numerous reef sharks live under the pilings littering the ocean floor. This site is most often accessed by boat, but the easiest way to reach it from shore is to park in the public parking area and cross to where the pier meets the sand. From here, it's a kick out to where the pier drops into the water. While conditions are nice year-round, the only time you don't want to snorkel here is when the river draining into the bay is a torrent of runoff.

Don't Stand on the Reef!

At West Side snorkeling spots, signs warn against standing on the reef. While everyone knows to avoid stepping on sea urchins and sharp rocks, the signs are about harm to the reef rather than your feet.

Unlike beaches with rocky or sandy bottoms, reefs in Maui are made up of fragile corals, living animals with hard exoskeletons—just as alive as the fish swimming above them or the eels inhabiting their crevices. Corals easily die, and one of the biggest threats is the number of visitors who stand on the reefs. Many snorkelers who stop to fix their snorkel mask or readjust their hair ties don't realize they're killing the ground they're standing on.

Snorkeling areas such as Honolua Bay, Kahekili Beach Park, and Olowalu have seen the most damage in recent years. Estimates from recent studies suggest that West Maui has lost as much as 25 percent of its live coral in the last decade alone. There are other factors involved, such as sedimentation, overfishing, algal blooms, pesticide-laden runoff, and even the petroleum-based sunscreen that washes off swimmers' shoulders and ends up settling on the sensitive polyps—the latter has, in fact, led to Hawaii passing the country's first bill banning the sale and distribution of sunscreens containing oxybenzone and octinoxate. Visitors can do their part in protecting this fragile ecosystem. Adjust your snorkel mask in waist-deep water, and don't stand on the reef to take photos.

To find the parking for Mala Wharf, turn off Front Street onto Ala Moana Street, following the signs for Mala Ramp, just on the south side of the bridge from the Lahaina Cannery Mall. Once you turn, make an immediate right down toward the boat ramp, where there are restrooms, showers, and a moderate amount of parking.

Rental Shops

Lahaina Divers (143 Dickenson St., #100, 808/667-7496, www.lahainadivers.com, 9am-5pm Mon.-Sat.) is a full-service dive shop but has everything you need for snorkeling. Come if you're looking to own gear for an extended period of time. Since the staff are all divers themselves, they can give you up-to-date information on the current conditions around the West Side.

If you're just looking for cheap rental gear to get through your vacation, both **Boss Frog's** (150 Lahainaluna Rd., 808/856-4148, www.bossfrog.com, 8am-6pm daily) and **Snorkel Bob's** (1217 Front St., 808/661-4421, www.snorkelbob.com, 8am-5pm daily) provide economical rentals as low as $2.50 per day. Remember, however, that you get what you pay for, and you will be pitched activities and upsold on fancier equipment. If you aren't picky about a mask fitting perfectly or are on a budget, the offerings are fine and will get you through a couple of sessions at the beach.

For a similar operation in the center of Lahaina, check out **The Snorkel Store** (2580 Keka'a Dr., #113, 808/669-1077, www.thesnorkelstore.com, 8am-5pm daily), a small but friendly shop. There are often 2-for-1 specials on snorkeling gear if you book online, and prices can be as low as $35 per week.

Snorkeling Charters

Before sunrise, Lahaina Harbor teems with activity as fishers fuel their boats and charter captains prepare for the day. Lines form and re-form, food coolers are slung across the docks, and fresh fish is set on ice. Most snorkeling charters depart from behind the banyan tree on Front Street; a few set out from Mala Ramp on the northern edge of town. Snorkeling charters in Lahaina run the gamut from small inflatable rafts to massive two-tiered catamarans. It's important to find a tour company with the type of experience you want.

SAILBOATS

The company with the largest number of snorkeling charters from Lahaina Harbor is **Trilogy** (808/874-5649, www.sailtrilogy.com), which offers all-day cruises to Lana'i ($249 adults, $218 youth, $149 children) as well as a four-hour snorkel along the West Maui coast ($145 adults, $125 youth, $90 children). While a couple of other boat companies also travel to Lana'i to snorkel for the day, Trilogy is the only one with a commercial permit to have crew and facilities based on the island. The company has been running the trip to Lana'i for more than 45 years, and the all-day experience is far better than any other snorkel charter option.

Departing from Lahaina Harbor at 10am (during busier times of the year there can also be a 6:30am departure), the 60-foot (18-m) sailing catamarans travel to Manele Harbor on Lana'i, where passengers disembark to snorkel at Hulopo'e Bay. Since Hulopo'e faces south, during summer there are a few days with large surf, so the snorkeling can be subpar. Winter is nearly guaranteed to have pristine conditions. On the beach, Trilogy has exclusive access to the left side of Hulopo'e Bay, and it is the only company with lifeguards, beach mats, beach chairs, refreshments, beach volleyball, and all the snorkeling gear right on the beach. Also included in the rates is an optional guided van tour of Lana'i City.

The other sailing catamaran departing from Lahaina Harbor to Lana'i is ***Sail Maui*** (808/244-2087, www.sailmaui.com), a 47-foot (14-m) boat that takes just 24 passengers and is the island's fastest catamaran. The five-hour trip ($140) departs at 10:30am and docks at Manele Harbor on Lana'i. You're unsupervised while you snorkel, since the crew doesn't have permission to operate on shore, and you're given a picnic lunch to enjoy while at the beach. The trip returns to Lahaina around 4pm, and the crew might even hook an ono or a mahimahi while trolling the fishing lures under sail.

While it mostly focuses on sunset sails and sailing charters, ***Scotch Mist II*** (808/661-0386, www.scotchmistsailingcharters.com) is a 50-foot (15-m) Santa Cruz monohull that also operates four-hour sailing and snorkeling charters along the western shore of the island for $129.

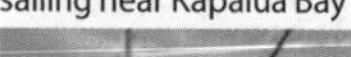

sailing near Kapalua Bay

POWERBOATS

Of the larger diesel boats that operate out of Lahaina Harbor, **Pacific Whale Foundation** (612 Front St., 808/249-8811, www.pacificwhale.org) offers the most options. Its boats are spacious and you can't beat the price: $165 for adults on the 7:30am six-hour tour to Lana'i, and each paying adult is allotted one child free of charge. Unlike other boats that dock at Manele Harbor, these cruises snorkel off the boat, with the two preferred destinations being either Kaunolu (Shark Fin Cove) or the Manele reef outside of the small boat harbor. The level of customer service on a boat this size isn't the same as on the sailing vessels, but for families who are on a budget and want to go snorkeling for the day, it's more affordable. Pacific Whale Foundation guests check in at the storefront across the street from the famous banyan tree, and loading is by the main dock at the harbor, where you wait for a crewmember to escort you to the boat.

Many of these boats go whale-watching in the winter, but during summer, **Hawaii Ocean Project** (675 Wharf St., 808/667-6165, www.hawaiioceanproject.com) has a fleet of aging but functional diesel boats that offer snorkeling charters ($139 adults, $109 children) to Lana'i and along the coast of West Maui. The cost is affordable, and trips are offered at 7am. Check the website for the most updated departure days.

For private excursions, **Captain Woody's** (808/667-2290, www.captainwoodysmaui.com) operates charters of only six people and leaves from Mala Ramp. Fishing, snorkeling, and seasonal whale-watching can all be included in these small group tours, which usually last six hours.

RAFTS

For those who don't like crowds, there are a number of rafts with small group sizes that place you closer to the water than any other type of vessel. Due to their bouncy nature, however, rafts aren't recommended for pregnant women or anyone with back problems. If you're prone to seasickness, the waters often become rough during the afternoon. Some companies swap their snorkeling charters for whale-watching during winter, however, so check ahead.

Of all the rafts, **Ultimate Snorkel Adventure** (808/667-5678, www.ultimatewhalewatch.com) is the best option, though it is best to call ahead to determine daily availability. It operates out of slip 17 of Lahaina Harbor. Group sizes are kept to 22, and this rigid inflatable is the fastest boat in Lahaina Harbor, at speeds over 35 mph (56 km/h). Snorkeling locations are chosen off the island of Lana'i based on the best conditions, and unlike some of the other options that go ashore on Lana'i, this excursion snorkels off the raft. Due to its small size, it can navigate close to the shore of Lana'i to find blowholes or follow pods of spinner dolphins hanging out by the rocks. Six-hour snorkeling trips are $175 adults, and this is a great option for a semiprivate tour with a relaxed but professional captain and crew.

Departing from Mala Ramp at 6:30am, **Maui Ocean Riders** (808/661-3586, www.mauioceanriders.com, $139 adults and children) is the only boat to circumnavigate Lana'i. Covering an astounding 70 miles (113 km) over the course of the trip, this excursion features multiple snorkeling spots and the opportunity to witness little-seen areas of Lana'i, such as the waters off Shipwreck Beach, Polihua Beach, and the snorkeling area known as Three Stone. On calm days this excursion is the best of all the rafting options. On days when the trade winds are blowing early in the morning, the ride can get rough.

For a raft that docks at Manele Harbor and spends time on Lana'i, **Maui Adventure Cruises** (808/661-5550, www.mauiadventurecruises.com) operates two trips from Lahaina Harbor, one of which allows passengers to spend more than three hours of beach time at Lana'i's Hulopo'e Bay. This excursion ($174 adults, $134 children) operates Monday, Wednesday, and Friday, docks in Manele Harbor, and allows guests to walk Hulopo'e

Bay unsupervised. Breakfast, snacks, and a deli lunch are included. Excursions depart at 7am and 9:30am from slip 11 in Lahaina Harbor. On Tuesday, Thursday, Saturday, and Sunday (Apr.-Dec.), a three-hour trip ($134 adults, $99 children) is offered, where you'll travel to Lana'i and snorkel off the boat rather than docking at the harbor.

SOUTH OF LAHAINA

The best snorkeling south of Lahaina is at **Olowalu,** otherwise known as Mile Marker 14. The reef here is a wide expanse of coral heads. The outer reef is popular with tour and dive boats, and the inside sections can teem with large parrotfish and Hawaiian green sea turtles. Directly out from the mile marker is a sand channel that leads through the shallow reef and allows access to deeper water. If you venture out from a random spot along the coast, there is a good chance you will get trapped in a maze of shallow coral heads where the water is often murky and the snorkeling is poor. If possible, get here in the morning before the winds pick up.

Scuba Diving

Scuba diving from the West Side of the island involves one of two options: Departing from a West Side harbor for an excursion to Lana'i or diving along the West Maui shore. While certified divers should seek out a dive charter, there are also a number of shore operators that offer introductory dives. For certified divers diving independently, ask at the rental shop about current conditions, and always use a dive flag. Dive spots along the northern section of the island are inaccessible during winter due to large surf. Summer is the best time for diving up north.

KAPALUA, NAPILI, AND HONOKOWAI

Dive Sites

The best shore dive in West Maui is **Honolua Bay,** although slogging all of your gear down to the water can be an exhausting undertaking. Diving from shore, launch from the center of the beach and hug the right side of the bay where the reef drops off into the sand channel. Maximum depth can reach about 40 feet (12 m), and you can expect to see green sea turtles and a wide variety of reef fish, and you may even have a rare encounter with spinner dolphins. Of the boats offering dive trips to Honolua Bay, ***Hula Girl*** (808/665-0344, www.sailingmaui.com) offers scuba diving as an add-on to the regular snorkel charter, although most dive charters head elsewhere along the West Side.

For a beginner-friendly introductory dive, **Kapalua Bay** can offer everything from a shallow dive of 25 feet (7.6 m) to a more advanced dive of 40 feet (12 m) rounding the corner toward neighboring Namalu Bay. There are showers and facilities as well as easy sandy-beach entry.

Dive Operators

Down in Honokowai, **Tiny Bubbles Scuba** (3350 Lower Honoapi'ilani Rd., 808/870-0878, www.tinybubblesscuba.com, 8am-5pm daily) operates shore dives along the West Maui coast. Under the lead of the vivacious and knowledgeable instructor Timmerz, all of the instructors for Tiny Bubbles have been diving the Maui shore for over a decade and are acquainted with the nuances of Maui diving. Introductory courses are $109, and certified divers can participate in a private guided beach dive for $89. Night dives ($109) and scooter dives ($119) are also offered. Depths on these shore dives rarely exceed 40 feet (12 m). All gear is included, and while the business is run out of the Ka'anapali Beach Club, the exact dive site is determined by the conditions.

In 2 Scuba Diving Maui Dive Co. (65 Ala Hoku Pl., 808/264-8198, www.in2scubadivingmaui.com, 7am-8pm daily) features a 1.5-hour introduction to scuba lesson ($99). One of the company's specialties is its two-hour turtle dive ($129 pp).

KA'ANAPALI

Dive Sites

The northernmost dive site in Ka'anapali and the one preferred by independent instructors is **Kahekili Beach Park.** The depth is shallow, rarely exceeding 35 feet (11 m), and the coral begins immediately. The reef parallels the shore, with the greatest diversity of life found at 15-25 feet (4.5-7.5 m). The beach is long, and the healthiest amount of coral is found right off the beach park. It is uncrowded compared to neighboring Ka'anapali Beach, and there is easier parking for lugging gear from the car. Showers and restrooms are conveniently located in the middle of the beach park.

The best dive in Ka'anapali, however, is **Pu'u Keka'a,** also known as **Black Rock.** Despite the relative ease of the dive and the fairly shallow depths, the rocky promontory draws all sorts of marinelife. Although not always guaranteed, divers frequently sight sea turtles, reef fish, eels, octopuses, and rare squid or cowries. The best way to dive Pu'u Keka'a is to do a drift dive from the southern end of Kahekili Beach Park and swim around to the front of the rock, or enter the water in front of the Sheraton, swim partway around the rock, and then double back the way you came. This is a great dive for those who have just been certified. For a real treat, consider a night dive.

To dive away from the crowds, head to the large reef at **Ka'anapali Point,** stretching from the Marriott down toward the Hyatt. The depth ranges 10-30 feet (3-9 m). You'll likely see a large number of turtles, corals, and technicolor parrotfish.

Dive Operators

The Ka'anapali resort diving scene is dominated by **Five Star Scuba** (808/667-5551), which has operations at many of the Ka'anapali resorts. Options include pool sessions, one-tank dives, certification, and night dives. A single one-tank dive for certified divers is about $89, with the exact dive location determined by where you're staying and the conditions.

Tiny Bubbles Scuba (3350 Lower Honoapi'ilani Rd., 808/870-0878, www.tinybubblesscuba.com, 8am-5pm daily) operates shore dives along the West Maui coast. The business is run out of the Ka'anapali Beach Club, but the exact dive site is determined by the conditions. Introductory courses are $109. Adventure seekers will appreciate the night dive ($109) for sightings of octopuses, eels, lobsters, crabs, shrimps, squid, and other colorful marinelife.

LAHAINA

Dive Sites

Within walking distance of southern Ka'anapali, **Hanakao'o Beach Park** is the northernmost beach in Lahaina and the site of many introductory dive classes. This is a good dive if you're practicing your skills over sand. The shallow area is also good for spotting turtles and colorful reef fish, and you can find turtles if you follow the rocks south toward Wahikuli Beach Park.

The best dive in Lahaina is **Mala Wharf,** although it's most often accessed as a boat dive. When Hurricane Iniki came storming through in 1992, the 30-foot (9-m) waves it created were strong enough to destroy the outer half of Mala Ramp. Today the collapsed pilings are still lying in 25 feet (7.5 m) of water, and the result has been decades of live coral development on what is now one of the island's best artificial reefs. The caverns of the pilings are home to numerous turtles and whitetip reef sharks, some of which can reach up to 6 feet (1.8 m). Even though the depth never exceeds 35 feet (10.5 m), this is a favorite of island dive charters due to its proximity to the harbors and wealth of marinelife.

The ***Carthaginian*** is an old whaling ship

that was scuttled in 100 feet (30 m) of water by Atlantis Submarines about 0.5 mile (0.8 km) offshore from Puamana. A couple of West Side dive charters include this deep-water dive, with a maximum depth of 100 feet (30 m), in their weekly schedule. The *Carthaginian* hasn't yet developed the same amount of live coral as neighboring Mala Ramp, and it's the deepest dive in the area. Winter dives are punctuated by whale song—and you might even spot one underwater.

Dive Operators

Lahaina Divers (143 Dickenson St., 808/667-7496, www.lahainadivers.com, 8am-5pm Mon.-Sat.) has the largest number of dive options in Lahaina. Two custom-built 46-foot (14-m) dive boats, departing from Lahaina Harbor, are the largest on Maui. Two-tank dives range $229 for dives off Lana'i to $289 for a dive off Moku Ho'oniki (Moloka'i), famous for hammerhead sharks. There are also trips to the Back Wall of Molokini Crater as well as four-tank dive trips. The full-service dive shop in Lahaina has equipment sales and rentals. Since the availability of dives varies by day, inquire ahead of time.

On the north end of Lahaina at Mala Ramp, **Extended Horizons** (94 Kupuohi St., 808/667-0611, www.extendedhorizons.com) is another reputable operation that offers tours to Lana'i and the west shore of Maui. Extended Horizons takes only six passengers, and it's the only charter boat on the island to run completely on biodiesel. Morning tours check in at 6:10am at the Mala boat ramp for dives along West Maui ($169). Other dive options include trips to Lana'i as well as night dives, beach dives, and certification classes.

A smaller operation offering scuba tours of Lana'i and beginner scuba lessons, **Dive Maui** (1223 Front St., 808/661-7333, http://goscubadivemaui.com, $124) departs from Mala Ramp aboard a rigid aluminum inflatable vessel. Group sizes are small. The shop is conveniently located within walking distance of Mala Ramp.

SOUTH OF LAHAINA

Dive Sites

Known to some operators as Turtle Reef or Turtle Point, **Olowalu** is an offshore, turtle-laden area popular with charter boats on the offshore reefs. Maximum depths are about 30 feet (9 m), and on nice days the visibility is close to 100 feet (30 m). This area is also popular with independent dive operators as a confined-water area for practicing dive skills. If you are shore-diving independently, the easiest way to get to deeper water is to enter around the mile marker 14 sign and swim in a straight line until you reach depths of 20-25 feet (6-7.5 m). When navigating your way through the coral heads, it's imperative to make sure that your gear doesn't drag across the reef, and bring a dive flag with you so that boats know you're below.

Ukumehame is a special spot accessible only by boat charter. Huge manta rays congregate here to be cleaned by reef fish that nibble algae off their wings, and the depths are a moderate 30-60 feet (9-18 m). It can't be done as a shore dive because the manta ray area is about a 25-minute surface swim from shore, and it takes trained dive instructors to determine if the water clarity is good enough for diving.

1: eagle ray at Ka'anapali **2:** paddleboarding off Ka'anapali Beach **3:** surfing at Pohaku Beach Park

1
2
3

Surfing

Surfing is more than a hobby in West Maui—it's a way of life. In Lahaina, legions of longboarders begin each morning by watching the sunrise from the water, and flotillas of surf schools operate throughout the day. Up north, Honolua is the proving ground of the island's burgeoning surfers, and whenever "The Bay" starts breaking, a palpable buzz runs through the community. Not all breaks are suitable for beginners, and only a handful of breaks are included in this guide. Practice common etiquette, and enjoy the serenity that comes with surfing one of the most beautiful spots in the world.

KAPALUA, NAPILI, AND HONOKOWAI

Winter is the best time for surfing "up north," and the waves get larger the farther north you go. With the exception of S-Turns, however, most of the breaks on the Upper West Side are for experienced surfers. Beginners will have better luck at the breaks south of Lahaina.

Surf Spots

★ POHAKU BEACH PARK

Pohaku Beach Park in Kahana is the epicenter of the West Side's longboard community. The break, commonly known as **S-Turns,** is perfect for beginners. Travel on Honoapi'ilani Highway (Hwy. 30) until you reach the intersection with Ho'ohui Street, with the McDonald's on the corner. Turn toward the ocean, and make a left once you reach the bottom of the hill. Drive for 0.25 mile (0.4 km) and find the parking lot for S-Turns on the right. From the parking lot, you can see two distinct breaks. To the right is **Mushrooms,** which can be a fun wave, but it's shallow on the inside section. To the left is S-Turns, where you'll notice a couple of A-frame peaks a long paddle offshore. Surfing at S-Turns is as much a paddle workout as a surfing workout, and you're forgiven if you need to stop to catch your breath on the way out. Beginners stay on the inside section, while more experienced surfers favor the outer peaks. Also, there have been some shark issues at S-Turns in the past, so be wary if the water is murky and no one else is out. S-Turns starts breaking on a moderate northwest swell, and on the largest of days can reach a few feet overhead.

D. T. FLEMING BEACH PARK

The surf break at **D. T. Fleming Beach Park** is at the far northern end of the beach. The wave here is a combination of a beach break and a point break, and it can get crowded with bodyboarders during weekends. This is one of the few places on the West Side that picks up wind swell, so if it's windy and there aren't waves anywhere else, check Fleming's.

HONOLUA BAY

If you're an avid surfer, **Honolua Bay** needs no introduction. The wave here is truly one of the best in the world, holding almost religious significance for the locals. Honolua is for experienced surfers, but even nonsurfers should come here during a large swell to watch the island's best pull into the gaping, barreling perfection. Honolua can become crowded, and if you paddle out and nobody recognizes you, your chances of getting a wave decrease significantly. Granted, on days when the surf is only about head high and the crowd isn't too thick, there can still be enough waves for everyone—provided you know what you're doing.

WINDMILLS

Windmills is a surf break at Punalau Beach suited to experienced surfers and an epic spot for watching the island's best. The massive left tube barrels with such ferocity it has been called Maui's Pipeline. Many professional surf films have been shot here, and the best vantage point is on the side of the road about

Waves in Hawaiian Scale

Hawaiians are weird when it comes to their waves. Not because a high surf advisory is a legitimate excuse for missing work, school, or even jury duty, but rather because Hawaiians measure the size of waves differently. Unlike places that measure the face of the waves, Hawaiian surfers measure the back of the wave. The resulting number is about half what it would be if measured elsewhere. A 6-foot (2-m) wave in California is a 3-foot (1-m) wave in Hawaii.

The history of this is foggy at best. One theory suggests that Hawaiian surfers underestimated wave size in the 1950s as a humble response to the bravado of California surfers who boasted about the size of the waves they caught. Another theory is that since Hawaiian lifeguards would be forced to work instead of surf when the waves reached a certain height, they invented a separate scale so that it would require larger waves before they had to go to work.

Whatever the reason, the practical implication is that when you're looking at a surf forecast, you need to know if it's being measured on the Hawaiian scale or by face height. On websites such as Omaui.com, the forecast is given in face height, while on Hawaiiweathertoday.com, the forecast is in the Hawaiian scale.

If you ask a local surfer what the conditions are like, you'll get a reply of either "3 feet Hawaiian" or "3 feet" (1 m), when the head-high waves are obviously larger. Australians have also adopted the Hawaiian scale system of measurement. While confusion reigns, all that matters is assessing your own ability when paddling out to the lineup.

1 mile (1.6 km) after the dirt turnoff for the bluffs at Honolua Bay.

Rental Shops

Experienced surfers will get the best selection with **808 Boards** (5425 Lower Honoapi'ilani Rd., 808/667-0808, www.808boards.com, 7:30am-5pm daily, $20-65 per day), who will pick up and drop off the board at no additional charge.

Rent a board at the **Boss Frog's** locations in Napili (5095 Napilihau St., 808/669-4949, www.bossfrog.com, 8am-5pm daily) and Kahana (4310 Lower Honoapi'ilani Rd., 808/669-6700, www.bossfrog.com, 8am-5pm daily). Rates are around $20 per day for soft-top longboards or $25 per day for fiberglass boards.

For the cheapest boards you'll find on this side of the island, little-known **Annie's A&B Rentals** (3481 Lower Honoapi'ilani Rd., 808/250-9109, 9:30am-2pm Mon.-Tues. and Fri., 9:15am-1pm Wed.-Thurs., 9:15am-4pm Sat.-Sun.) is hidden in Da Rose mall in Honokowai on the ocean side of the highway. Surfboards can be as cheap as $16 per day or $70 for the whole week.

KA'ANAPALI

Surf Spots

The only surf break in Ka'anapali is **Ka'anapali Point,** in front of the Marriott on Ka'anapali Beach. This is where the Ka'anapali surf lessons take place, although the wave here is tricky because it bends at a weird angle. Also, the inside section can be shallow and rocky, so surf school students are given booties. Ka'anapali Point can pick up both southwesterly and northeasterly swells, which means there can be surf any time of year.

Rental Shops and Schools

While the waves in Lahaina are more amenable to learning, there are still a number of operators along Ka'anapali Beach for those who would prefer to walk directly from their resort to a lesson. Since Ka'anapali gets windier than Lahaina, it's important to book the first lesson of the day for the best conditions.

Two-hour lessons ($79) can be booked at the beach shack in front of the Ka'anapali Beach Hotel. **Island Style Adventures** (808/244-6858, www.isasurfschool.com) in front of the Westin also offers two-hour lessons ($120). For rentals by Ka'anapali Point,

Surfing Etiquette

Surfing is a highlight of a visit to Lahaina, and it's important to have a basic grasp of etiquette out in the water.

- **Always wear a leash.** Errant boards in the lineup can be dangerous. Nothing ruins a session like having to swim after your board.
- **Stay out of the way of any surfer on a wave.** While this can sometimes be difficult when paddling out from shore, the best thing to do is either stop paddling so the surfer can navigate around you, or aim for a line behind the board so it ends up passing in front of you.
- **Offer a simple "hello" and a smile to your fellow surfers.** It may or may not be returned, but it's a way of signaling "friend."
- **At more advanced breaks, don't paddle directly to the peak of the wave.** Instead, wait for a while on the shoulder to let the local surfers have a turn. In more advanced lineups such as Honolua Bay and the outer reef at Breakwall, waves are earned instead of given, so it's best to keep a low profile. Share the waves. If you just got the last one, don't turn around and take the next one.
- **It's never alright to "drop in" on another surfer.** Although it might seem like a free-for-all out there, surfing etiquette dictates that the surfer closest to the breaking part of the wave has the right-of-way. To initiate a ride in front of this surfer is the worst of surfing offenses and a surefire way to get the "stink eye." As a general rule, if you're paddling for a wave and there is already someone riding that wave, and if you can see that person's face, choose a different wave.
- **Don't throw your board.** Sometimes in larger surf your board can get ripped away from you, but it's heavily frowned upon to "duck dive" a wave by throwing your board to the side and swimming under the wave. Instead, either duck dive your shortboard under the wave, or, if on a longboard, try to "turn turtle" by flipping upside down with your board and letting the wave crash over you while holding it with your hands. In the event you are riding a wave and fall, to keep the board from shooting out and hitting someone in the face, reach down and try to grab the part where your leash connects to minimize the distance it can go flying.

expect to pay $30 per hour plus $15 per additional hour. Booties are included in the price of all lessons and rentals.

LAHAINA

Lahaina and areas south have small waves breaking during most of the year, while summer has the most consistent surf. Most days will only have waves in the waist-high range, but the best swells of summer can reach overhead.

Surfing Spots

The most popular surf break in Lahaina is **Lahaina Breakwall,** between the 505 shopping center and Lahaina Harbor. This is where most of the Lahaina surf schools operate. All of the surf schools hang out in the shallow inside section, and more experienced surfers sit farther outside. The outside section at small levels can be either a left or a right, although when it gets big on a large summer swell, it can turn into a huge left that can grow to 10 feet (3 m) or more. During low tide it can get shallow enough here that you need to paddle with your fingertips and your skeg can scrape the bottom, so high tide is the optimal time for those who are concerned about falling. It shouldn't come as a surprise that this spot can get crowded, a fact of life that has earned it the moniker "Snakewall." If you're a beginner, you're better off going a few miles south to Puamana Beach Park or Guardrails.

Rental Shops and Schools

Inside the 505 shopping center, **Goofy Foot** (505 Front St., Ste. 123, 808/244-9283, www.goofyfootsurfschool.com, 7am-4pm Mon.-Sat.) has helped over 100,000 students ride their first wave since opening in 1994. Two-hour lessons are $85 per person, and the owner, Tim, often enjoys time on the water as the private surf coach for Jimmy Buffett.

One block away on Prison Street are **Royal Hawaiian** (505 Front St., Ste. 127, 808/276-7873, www.royalhawaiiansurfacademy.com, 7am-4pm daily) and **Maui Wave Riders** (133 Prison St., 808/661-0003, www.mauiwaveriders.com, 8am-2:30pm Mon.-Fri., 8am-noon Sat.). Both have been operating since the mid-1990s, and all of the instructors are competent and patient professionals guaranteed to get you up and riding. Group rates run $95 per person, and for rentals, expect to pay $25 for three hours or $35 for the whole day.

To get away from the Breakwall crowds, **Maui Surfer Girls** (808/214-0606, www.mauisurfergirls.com) is the island's premier female-only surf camp operator, although they also offer coed group lessons for $99 per person. It costs a few dollars more than in town, and lessons take place a few miles south of town along a mellow stretch of beach. At certain times of year, all-inclusive one- and two-week classes are offered to empower teenage girls through learning surfing. Lessons are offered at 8am and 10:30am daily.

SOUTH OF LAHAINA

For beginning surfers and longboarders, the mile-long (1.6-km) stretch of coast between **Puamana Beach Park** and **Launiupoko Beach Park** has numerous breaks with mellow waves for beginners. In between the two parks are peaks known as **Guardrails, Woody's,** and **Corner Pockets.** The beach parks and Guardrails have parking on the ocean side of the road, and parking for Woody's is in a dirt lot on the inland side of the highway. There can be small waves here most times of year, although summer sees the most consistent surf. If you're slightly more advanced, park in the lot for Puamana Beach Park and walk the length of shore all the way to the right along the Puamana condominium complex. At the far northern end of the beach is another break known as **Beaches or Hot Sands** that offers a fun right point that's welcoming to visitors.

Tucked right at the base of the cliffs by mile marker 11, **Grandma's** is the name of the break on the far southern end of Papalaua Beach Park. This is a playful wave that caters to beginners and longboarders.

At mile marker 12, **Ukumehame Beach Park** is another break that caters to beginners and longboarders but requires a much longer paddle than places such as Guardrails or Puamana. However, the longer effort means a longer ride. This is a favorite of island longboarders. While the beach itself is fairly long, the best waves are found directly in front of the small parking lot.

If you're experienced and prefer to ride a shortboard, the wave at **Olowalu** offers two A-frame peaks that are popular with locals and can get crowded. In a different location than the snorkeling spot of the same name, the Olowalu surf break is by mile marker 15.5.

Stand-Up Paddling

KAPALUA, NAPILI, AND HONOKOWAI

One of the best stretches of coast for paddling is the section between Kapalua Bay and Hawea Point. The sandy entry at Kapalua Bay makes it easy to launch a board into the water. Napili Bay is another popular spot for morning paddles. Never bring a stand-up paddleboard into Honolua Bay. It's heavily frowned upon by locals and you'll likely be sent back to the beach by the surfers in the water.

Rental Shops

In Napili, rent stand-up paddleboards ($20 per hour, $40 per day) from **Water Works Sports** (5315 Lower Honoapi'ilani Rd., 808/298-2446, www.waterworkssports-maui.com, 8am-5pm daily) inside the Napili Shores building. Get out early before the wind picks up.

If you'd prefer to have your boards delivered, **Bring Me A Kayak** (800/633-3580, www.bringmeakayak.com) offers stand-up paddleboard delivery to your hotel ($85 per day, depending on the type of board). Let them know before the morning you'd like to go, and they'll deliver it to the hotel lobby.

KA'ANAPALI

Sandy Ka'anapali is the perfect spot for stand-up paddling, but only during the morning hours before the wind picks up. On winter days, the water can be as smooth as glass, with dozens of whales breaching around you. Being out on the water during whale season can be an exciting adventure, but the same laws apply to stand-up paddlers as to boats: Stay 100 yards (90 m) from humpback whales—unless, of course, they swim over to you.

Rental Shops

Almost every hotel along the main strip has activity huts offering paddleboard rentals, or you can have them delivered to your hotel from either **808 Boards** (808/667-0808, www.808boards.com, 7:30am-5pm daily) or **Bring Me A Kayak** (800/633-3580, www.bringmeakayak.com, 7am-5pm daily). Rentals typically cost $45-85 per day.

LAHAINA

Lahaina is ringed by a barrier reef, which can make it shallow and dangerous for paddling. The trained instructors, however, know all the *pukas* (holes) in the reef, and by allowing them to lead the way, you'll be awarded with sweeping views of the island's West Side. When you are over the Shark Pit, there's a decent chance you'll encounter an endangered Hawaiian monk seal or a harmless whitetip reef shark. While the 505 area can be a little difficult to navigate, it has the added benefit of being protected from the wind and will usually have calm, flat conditions when Ka'anapali is rough and blustery.

If you've rented your own board, the best place in the immediate area for stand-up paddling is the stretch of shore between Puamana and Launiupoko Beach Parks, where the water isn't nearly as shallow and it's still protected from the afternoon trade winds.

Rental Shops and Schools

Stand-up paddling lessons are offered in the Lahaina Breakwall area by **Royal Hawaiian** (505 Front St., Ste. 127, 808/276-7873, www.royalhawaiiansurfacademy.com, 7am-4pm daily), **Goofy Foot** (505 Front St., Ste. 123, 808/244-9283, www.goofyfootsurfschool.com, 7am-4pm Mon.-Sat.), and **Maui Wave Riders** (133 Prison St., 808/661-0003, www.mauiwaveriders.com, 8am-2:30pm Mon.-Fri., 8am-2pm Sat.). Rather than mingling with all the surf school students, the stand-up paddling tours go the other direction from the Lahaina Breakwall down to the section of beach known as Shark Pit. For rentals, expect

Tips for Stand-Up Paddling

Stand-up paddling is very popular in Hawaii. While taking a lesson is always the best way to ensure success, here are a few tips if you'd rather rent a board and set out on your own.

- Beat the wind. **Paddle in the morning.**
- When first getting in the water, **start on your knees** to get the feeling for the board.
- When you stand up, **keep your feet shoulder-width apart.** You want to be standing in the middle of the board about where the handle is.
- A stand-up paddleboard is like a bicycle; **you need momentum for balance,** so if you stop paddling, it's like trying to balance on a bicycle without pedaling. When you first stand up from your knees, take a couple of paddles quickly to build up enough momentum so that you won't fall.
- **Use the correct side of the paddle.** Paddles are like an extension of your hand; you want to use the side of the paddle that would be your palm as opposed to the back of your hand.
- **Place one hand on top of the paddle and the other on the shaft.** To keep a straight line you must alternate paddling on both sides of your body by taking a few strokes on your left and then a few strokes on your right, much like you would in a canoe.
- **Paddle using long, full strokes.** Many first-time paddlers have a tendency to poke at the water with short strokes. Since this doesn't create much momentum, the board becomes wobbly and you're liable to fall.
- **Use a leash.** A leash is your lifeline if you fall off the board. If you are not sure which ankle to put the leash around, act as if you're going to do a cartwheel, and whichever foot you put backward is the one you should attach the leash to.
- If you are paddling where there are waves, **point your board either into the waves or away from them.** When waves hit the side of your board, there is a good chance you'll end up falling.
- **It's okay to fall.** The best thing to do is just let it happen. Most paddleboarding injuries occur when people try to save themselves from falling and end up going down awkwardly. Accept your fate and fall gracefully into the water.
- Only competent surfers should ever try to surf on their paddleboards. Large, heavy boards can become dangerous in a surf lineup if they go crashing through a crowd, and a spate of injuries related to stand-up paddlers and their large boards have created a rift in the island surfing community. Common surf etiquette is to share the waves with surfers and stay out of the way. In the event you do fall down, make sure that your board doesn't hit someone.

to pay in the $40 range for three hours to $50 for all day.

For more personalized service in an area that isn't as crowded, **Hawaiian Paddle Sports** (808/442-6436, www.hawaiianpaddlesports.com) offers lessons on beaches south of Lahaina, run by instructors who have a deep-rooted respect for the island, the environment, and Hawaiian cultural history. While they're more expensive, these tours will leave you with a deeper appreciation for the ocean. Lessons are $249 for a private lesson and $159 per person for groups of two or more.

Kayaking and Canoeing

West Maui has numerous options for both kayaking and outrigger canoeing. While kayaking isn't as hard on the shoulder muscles and allows you to hug the coast, outrigger canoeing is a culturally rich experience unique to Polynesia. The morning hours are the best time to paddle, with most operators offering an early morning tour followed by another later in the morning.

KAPALUA, NAPILI, AND HONOKOWAI

The most popular kayak trip on the Upper West Side of the island is the paddle from D. T. Fleming Beach Park to Honolua Bay. Along this stretch of coast, you pass rugged rock formations inaccessible from the road, and you'll hug this dramatic coast past Mokulei'a Bay and into Honolua. Because of the high surf during winter, these tours are only offered in summer, and all trips depart D. T. Fleming Beach Park in the early morning hours before the afternoon trade winds pick up. Snorkeling in Honolua Bay is included in the excursions, and you are likely to encounter Hawaiian green sea turtles or potentially even Hawaiian spinner dolphins.

The best company offering tours up here is **Hawaiian Paddle Sports** (808/442-6436, www.hawaiianpaddlesports.com), with group excursions for kayaking ($99 pp) and canoeing packages ($159 pp). The educational component and respect for culture are superior to other operations.

KA'ANAPALI

Off Kahekili Beach Park in front of the Westin Villas, **Maui Paddle Sports** (2780 Keka'a Dr., 808/283-9344, www.mauipaddlesports.com, 7am-7pm) offers two-hour outrigger canoe rides in a six-person outrigger ($139 pp), a memorable one-hour turtle-watching outrigger experience ($89), and a whale-watching outrigger excursion (during whale season, $139). Trips run from 7am daily. This is a convenient option if you're staying in the area off Kahekili Beach.

SOUTH OF LAHAINA

The main areas for kayaking south of Lahaina are either Olowalu (mile marker 14) or Coral Gardens, off Papalaua Beach Park (mile marker 11), where you can paddle along the rugged sea cliffs that plunge down into the sea. This is a popular area for kayaking in winter since the large surf on the northern shores makes kayaking there impossible, and these are fantastic reefs for spotting Hawaiian green sea turtles. **Kayak Olowalu** (800 Olowalu Village Rd., 808/661-0606, www.kayakolowalu.com) offers 2.5-hour tours ($65 adults).

Other Water Activities

★ SUNSET CRUISES

Few Maui activities are more iconic than a sunset sail off the West Maui coast. The feeling of the trade winds in your hair as you glide along is a sensation of freedom you can't experience on land. Watch as the setting sun paints the sky every shade of orange and pink. On most days you can make out a rainbow hovering over the lush valleys of Mauna Kahalawai.

Ka'anapali

A **sunset sail off Ka'anapali Beach** can be the most magical moment of your vacation, but there are a few things to understand to make the most of the magic.

Make sure to ask when you need to check in, as departure times for sunset sails are different in summer and winter. There's also a chance that the departure will be moved to Lahaina Harbor due to large surf on the beach. Since this isn't possible to predict until the day before, it's a good idea to double-check on the morning of your sail to confirm where the boat will be loading.

While it's fun to dress up a little, remember you'll be on a boat and outfit yourself accordingly. The Ka'anapali boats are all sailing catamarans, which are boarded from the sand, and since some days can have moderate shore-break, there's a good chance you'll end up wet from the shins down. Your shoes are collected prior to boarding (to prevent sand tracking onto the boat), so don't put too much effort into matching them with your outfit. The northerly trade winds can often be chilly, so it's a good idea to bring a light jacket. And even though the vessels are wide, spray may come over the sides. If your idea of a sunset sail is a stable platform that putts along at 3 knots (5.6 km/h), the dinner cruises from Lahaina are a better bet.

Trilogy (808/874-5649, www.sailtrilogy.com) offers sunset sails ($99) daily that feature live music and Pacific Rim pupus. Trilogy's sail isn't marketed as a booze cruise, but three premium alcoholic beverages are included in the rates, including mixed drink cocktails like the Moloka'i Mule. Unless the surf is high and they need to load from Lahaina Harbor, the

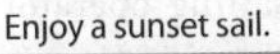
Enjoy a sunset sail.

check-in for all Trilogy tours is in front of the Ka'anapali Beach Hotel.

In front of Whalers Village, **Teralani** (808/661-7245, www.teralani.net) offers two different sails departing nightly during the busier times of year. The original sunset sail ($89 adults) includes a pupu menu as well as an open bar of beer and mixed drinks. For those who would rather dine on board, the full dinner sail ($119 adults) is 30 minutes longer.

Gemini (808/669-1700, www.geminicharters.com) similarly offers sunset sails ($83 adults) that feature a pupu menu as well as Maui Brewing Company beer and mai tais.

The most yacht-like experience departing from the beach is on the ***Hula Girl*** (808/665-0344, www.sailingmaui.com), which not only offers the newest boat but luxurious upgrades like throw pillows, free Wi-Fi, panoramic viewing from the fly-bridge, and high-tech sailing. For a full-service dinner cruise, *Hula Girl* offers cruises on Tuesday-Sunday ($90 adults) featuring upscale Pacific Rim dining options made fresh in the onboard kitchen. Standard sunset cruises ($78) offer a kids' menu and top-shelf tropical cocktails. In many ways, it's more like a floating restaurant with a cover charge.

Lahaina

DINNER CRUISES

The best dinner cruise from Lahaina is offered by **Pacific Whale Foundation** (612 Front St., 808/249-8811, www.pacificwhale.org). The power catamaran used for this charter is the nicest of the large diesel boats, and the menu includes locally sourced produce and sustainably harvested seafood. Seats are $129-139 for adults, $99 for children, free for those 2 and under. Three alcoholic beverages are included in the cruise, as is live music.

SAILBOATS

If you know what it means to "shake a reef," you'll be much happier watching the sunset aboard a small sailboat than on a large motorized platform. The fastest sailing catamaran offering sunset sails ($85 adults) from Lahaina is ***Sail Maui*** (808/244-2087, www.sailmaui.com), which provides sailing, pupus, beer, wine, and mai tais. Trips run Monday-Saturday, and maximum capacity of the cruise is just 24 people.

The newest catamaran in Lahaina Harbor is *Ocean Spirit*, part of the **Pacific Whale Foundation** (612 Front St., 808/249-8811, www.pacificwhale.org) fleet that sailed to Hawaii from St. Croix in only 42 days. The two-hour sunset sails ($119) include locally sourced pupus and three alcoholic beverages.

If you're a monohull sailor, ***Scotch Mist II*** (808/661-0386, www.scotchmistsailingcharters.com) offers evening sunset sails ($90) aboard a Santa Cruz 50-foot (15-m) racing boat, which departs from slip 2.

TOP EXPERIENCE

★ WHALE-WATCHING

Any vessel that floats is going to be offering whale-watching December 15-April 15. While whale season officially lasts until May 15, whales aren't encountered with enough regularity after mid-April to guarantee sightings. The peak of the season is January-March, and simply being out on the water turns any trip into a whale-watching expedition.

Most snorkeling and sailing operators offer whale-watching during winter, with most boats carrying whale naturalists well-versed in the study of these gentle giants. Since most prices are about the same, the choice ultimately comes down to what sort of vessel best suits your comfort level. Small rafts from Lahaina Harbor place you the closest to the water. Sailboats also offer whale-watching trips from both Lahaina Harbor and Ka'anapali Beach. The large 149-passenger diesel boats in Lahaina provide the most affordable rates, but you'll be sharing the vessel with over 100 other people and won't get 360-degree views.

The nonprofit **Pacific Whale Foundation** is noted for its ocean advocacy, and its whale-watching tours are recommended (page 142).

Whale-Watching FAQ

If whale-watching is high on your list of Maui experiences, time your visit during the peak of whale season. Officially, whale season on Maui runs December 15-May 15, during which time the waters of Maui County house the largest population of humpback whales found anywhere in the world. But the first sighting is typically mid-October, and whales can linger through the end of May. Best whale-watching is the peak season, the 10-week span of January 15-March 31. Whale-watching tours usually operate December 15-April 20, after which time there's no guarantee of spotting whales. Boats often advertise "whale searches" rather than whale-watching at the beginning and end of the season, which is a way of saying you probably won't encounter whales, but your money will gladly be accepted. During the peak of the season, anyone setting out on a charter is guaranteed to see whales. Commonly asked whale-watching questions:

Q: What kind of whales are around Maui?
A: Although there are rarely seen species such as pilot whales and false killer whales that inhabit the waters off Maui year-round, 99 percent of the time you will see North Pacific humpback whales.

Q: Where are these whales from?
A: They were born here in the warm protected waters of Hawaii. The humpbacks then migrate 3,000 miles (4,830 km) to their summer feeding grounds in Alaska, where they gorge themselves on small fish and krill, and return again in the winter to mate and give birth.

Q: Why don't the whales mate in Alaska?
A: Since baby humpbacks are born with minimal amounts of fat, the water is too cold in Alaska.

Q: Do the whales eat at all in Hawaii?
A: No. While there's no evidence to suggest that whales wouldn't eat if given the opportunity, the waters off Maui don't contain the same amount of zooplankton and marine organisms that humpback whales feed on. Adults go for months at a time without eating, losing up to one-third of their body weight.

Q: How much do humpback whales weigh?
A: At birth, humpback whales are 10-12 feet (3-3.6 m) long and weigh about a ton. Full-grown adults weight about 1 ton per foot (3 tons per m), which means that a 45-foot (13.7-m) humpback weighs about 90,000 pounds (40,800 kg).

Q: Are males or females bigger?
A: Females are a little bit larger than males, which is known as reverse sexual dimorphism, a technical way of saying "I need to give birth to a 2,000-pound (900-kg) animal, so I need to be bigger than you."

Q: How quickly do whales swim?
A: Although they can sprint up to about 20 mph (32 km/h), on average humpback whales travel at a steady rate of 3-5 mph (5-8 km/h).

Q: How long does it take them to get to Alaska?
A: Whales spend 6-8 weeks migrating between Alaska and the Hawaiian Islands.

Q: Are whales more active in the morning?
A: No. Since whales only take short "cat naps," there isn't a set time of day when they are asleep. Mornings are often best for whale-watching because the water is calmer and whales are easier to spot.

Q: What is "getting mugged"?
A: "Getting mugged" refers to the fact that all boats are required to maintain a 100-yard (90-m) distance from humpback whales. Should the whales decide to approach the boat, it is out of your hands. You need to wait until the whale loses interest. This can take 45 minutes or more.

1
2

Departures are out of Lahaina and Ma'alea Harbors.

SUBMARINE

If riding a submarine is on your bucket list, **Atlantis Submarines** (Slip 18, 808/667-6005, www.atlantisadventures.com/maui, 9am-2pm daily) operates regular charters ($124 adults, $38 children) from Lahaina Harbor to the *Carthaginian*, a sunken whaling ship in 100 feet (30 m) of water. Check-in is at the Atlantis shop inside the Pioneer Inn. Trips last two hours.

For those who are a little nervous about descending completely underwater and want to see fish without snorkeling, ***Reef Dancer*** (Slip 6, 808/667-2133, www.mauiglassbottomboat.com) is a yellow "semi-sub" that remains partially submerged for its journey along the coast. While there is an above-deck portion of the sub that never goes underwater, passengers are seated in an underwater cabin that offers 360-degree views of the underwater world. All of the boat staff double as scuba divers who can point out anything that might be living along the reef such as eels, octopuses, turtles, or urchins. This is a great way for young children, elderly visitors, and nonswimmers to enjoy Maui's reef system without having to get their hair wet. Sixty-minute tours ($45 adults, $20 children) run three times each morning, with a longer 90-minute tour ($65 adults, $25 children) departing Lahaina Harbor at 2:15pm daily.

FISHING

In no place is Lahaina's port town heritage more evident than at dingy yet lovable Lahaina Harbor. The smell of fish carcasses still wafts on the breeze, and shirtless, tanned, sweat-covered sailors casually sip beer as they lay the fresh catch on ice. Some days you can buy fresh mahimahi or ono straight from the folks who caught it, or, if you'd rather take your shot at reeling one in yourself, there are a slew of sportfishing boats ready to get you on the water.

The charters that have the best chance of catching fish are those that leave early and stay out for a full day. These are more expensive, but during a full-day charter you're able to troll around the buoys on the far side of Lana'i or Kaho'olawe. On half-day charters, you're confined to shallower water where the fish aren't biting as much, particularly during the winter. On virtually all charters you need to provide your own food and drinks. Don't bring bananas on board, since it is considered bad luck. Most boats will let you keep what you catch so you can cook it the same night.

Of all the boats in the harbor, ***Start Me Up*** (Slip 12, 808/667-2774, www.sportfishingmaui.com) has the best reputation. Prices range from $149 per person for two hours to $299 per person for an eight-hour charter. Catch a 500-pound (225-kg) marlin, and your trip is free!

A company with a sterling reputation is **Die Hard Sport Fishing** (808/344-5051, www.diehardsportfishing.com), run by the legendary Captain Fuzzy. Rates for these charters vary but expect to pay up to $375 per person for full-day, eight-hour charters.

Down at the south end of the harbor, away from many of the other boats, **Luckey Strike** (808/661-4606, www.luckeystrike.com) has two different boats and operates on the premise that using live bait for smaller fish is better. Captain Tad Luckey has been fishing these waters for over 30 years, and as with most captains in the harbor, he has an enviable and well-earned amount of local knowledge to put into every trip.

PARASAILING

Parasailing isn't possible December 15-May 15. Since the waters off West Maui are part of the Hawaiian Islands Humpback Whale National Marine Sanctuary, all "thrill craft," such as high-speed parasailing boats, are outlawed during the time of year when the whales are nursing their calves. During the summer or fall, however, parasailing is a peaceful

1: Atlantis Submarines excursion **2:** whale tail

adventure option for gazing at West Maui from hundreds of feet above the turquoise waters. It's one of the best views you'll find on the island.

Ka'anapali

UFO Parasail (2435 Kaanapali Pkwy., 800/359-4836, www.ufoparasail.net) is one of the two operators departing from Ka'anapali Beach, in front of Leilani's restaurant. Only eight people are on the boat at a time, which means that your overall time on the water is only a little over an hour. Of that hour, your personal flight time lasts 10-12 minutes, depending on the length of your line (you'll end up being 400-500 ft/120-150 m off the water). The staff and captains who run these tours do hundreds of trips over the course of the season, and from a safety and efficiency standpoint, the crew has it down to a science. Taking off and landing on the boat are a dry entry and exit, and you will be blown away by the serenity you experience up in the air. Prices begin at $129 (for observers $79). You must weigh at least 130 pounds (59 kg) to fly alone, and trips usually start around 8am.

In front of the Hyatt, **West Maui Parasail** (675 Wharf St. Slip 15, 808/661-4060, www.westmauiparasail.com) offers similar tours at $111 for 1,200 feet (365 m). If you aren't staying in the Ka'anapali resort area, a perk of going with West Maui Parasail is that free, convenient parking can be found in the Hanakao'o Beach Park area just a three-minute walk from the Hyatt.

Lahaina

The only parasailing operation in Lahaina is **West Maui Parasail** (675 Wharf St. Slip 15, 808/661-4060, www.westmauiparasail.com). The prices are the same as at the Ka'anapali operation, but a benefit of parasailing from Lahaina is that the water is consistently calmer and glassier than in neighboring Ka'anapali.

JET SKIING

Just like parasailing, Jet Skiing is only possible May 16-December 14. During summer, the island's only Jet Ski operation is **Maui Watersports** (808/667-2001, www.mauiwatersports.com) in Ka'anapali, just south of the Hyatt. Even though the area is relatively protected from the wind, morning hours are still the best for the calmest conditions. Rates are $79 for a 30-minute ride and $119 for a full hour, although you can save money by booking online.

WAKEBOARDING

Captain Ryan at **Wake Maui** (888/347-4790, www.wakemaui.com) offers wakeboarding trips in the flat water between Lahaina and Ka'anapali. Wake Maui provides the only service of its kind, where a six-passenger ski boat is equipped with all the wake toys for a fun day on the water. Since Maui's winds can often be extreme, however, wakeboarding charters usually depart early to capitalize on glassy conditions. Other toys include waterskiing and wakesurfing equipment, or you can simply charter the boat ($600 for 2 hours, $900 for 3 hours) to go whale-watching in winter.

SPEARFISHING

To take snorkeling to the next level and maybe take home dinner, **Maui Spearfishing Academy** (808/446-0352, www.mauispearfishing.com, $189) teaches visitors how to spearfish and eradicate invasive species, and can teach you the technique behind holding your breath to spear-dive and target the right fish.

Hiking and Biking

HIKING

There aren't nearly as many hiking trails on the West Side of the island as you might expect. Much of the access in West Maui is blocked by private land or lack of proper trails. Also, since much of West Maui sits in the lee of Mauna Kahalawai, there aren't any accessible waterfalls, as there are in East Maui. Nevertheless, the hiking options in West Maui offer their own sort of beauty, from stunning coastal treks to grueling ridge-line hikes.

Kapalua, Napili, and Honokowai

★ KAPALUA COASTAL TRAIL

Even though it's only 1.75 miles (2.8 km) long, the **Kapalua Coastal Trail** might just be the best coastal walk in Hawaii. The trail is book-ended on each side by beaches that have each been named the number-one beach in the United States: Kapalua Bay and D. T. Fleming Beach Park. It also affords grand views of both Moloka'i and Lana'i. While most walkers, joggers, and hikers begin the trail at Kapalua Bay, you can also access the trail from other junctions at the Kapalua Bay Villas, Oneloa Bay, the Ritz-Carlton, and D. T. Fleming Beach Park.

What makes the Kapalua Coastal Trail legendary are the various environments it passes through. If you begin at Kapalua Bay, the trail starts as a paved walkway paralleling the beach and weaves its way through ultra-luxurious residences. At the top of a short hill, the paved walkway reaches a junction by the Kapalua Bay Villas, where the path suddenly switches to dirt. Signs point to the continuation of the trail, and a spur trail leads straight out toward Hawea Point, a protected reserve that is home to the island's largest colony of *'ua'u kani* (wedge-tailed shearwaters). If you follow the grass trail to the left of the three-way junction, it connects with the trail to Namalu Bay—the rocky Mediterranean cove hidden in the craggy recesses.

Continuing along the main Kapalua Coastal Trail leads over a short rocky section before emerging at a smooth boardwalk along Oneloa Bay. The boardwalk here was constructed as a means of protecting the sensitive dunes of Kapalua, and in the morning Oneloa is one of the most gloriously empty beaches you'll find on Maui. At the end of the boardwalk, the trail leads up a flight of stairs and eventually connects with Lower Honoapi'ilani Road. From here, take a left and follow the sidewalk as it connects with the trail running in front of the Ritz-Carlton before finishing at the water's edge at D. T. Fleming Beach Park. For a side trip, hike out parallel to the golf course to **Makalua-puna Point**—otherwise known as Dragon's Teeth (page 37).

VILLAGE WALKING TRAILS

The **village walking trails** are the next most popular hikes in the Kapalua resort area. Weaving their way up the mountain-side through the cool and forested uplands are the 1.25-mile (2-km) Cardio Loop or the 3.6-mile (5.8-km) Lake Loop, an uphill, butt-burning workout popular with local joggers. More than just a great morning workout, there are also sections of the trail that offer sweeping views looking out toward Moloka'i and the area around Honolua Bay. To find the access point for the trails, park in the lot for the Kapalua Village Center (between Sansei restaurant and the Kapalua Golf Academy) and follow a paved cart path winding its way down toward an underpass, where you will find the trailhead for both loops.

MAHANA RIDGE TRAIL

The **Mahana Ridge Trail** is the longest continuous trail in the Kapalua resort area and the best option for serious hikers. Though you

1
2
3

can access the Mahana Ridge Trail from the village trails, a less confusing and more scenic trailhead is in the parking lot of D. T. Fleming Beach Park along the access road from the highway. The trailhead is a little hard to find, so look for the thin trail leading up the inland side of the road about 20 yards (18 m) back from the parking lot. This trail climbs up the ridge for nearly 6 miles (9.6 km), all the way to the Maunalei Arboretum, and is a proper hiking trail with narrow sections, moderate uphills, and sweeping views of the coast. It is an out-and-back trip, and maps are available online at www.kapalua.com.

MAUNALEI ARBORETUM TRAIL

To climb even farther up the mountainside, follow the **Maunalei Arboretum Trail** as it winds its way through a forest planted by the great D. T. Fleming. The manager of Honolua Ranch during the 1920s, Fleming forested the mountainside with numerous plant species from across the globe in an effort to preserve the watershed. Today, over 85 years after the arboretum was established, hikers can still climb the ridges of this historic upland and be immersed in a forest of wild banyan trees as well as coffee, guava, and bo trees. Trails in the arboretum range from short 0.5-mile (0.8-km) loops to a moderate 2.5-mile (4-km) round-trip that winds down Honolua Ridge. To reach the trails, you have to hike 6 miles (9.6 km) up the scenic Mahana Ridge Trail.

OHAI TRAIL

The 1.2-mile (1.9-km) **Ohai Trail** awards hikers with panoramic vistas of the island's North Shore. This area is often windy, and the way in which the wind drowns out all other sounds makes it a peaceful respite on the northern coast. The Ohai trailhead is 10 miles (16 km) past the entrance to Kapalua, by mile marker 41, between the Nakalele Blowhole and Olivine Pools. Along the moderate, winding trail are a few placards with information on the island's native coastal plants. This is also a great perch to watch for tropical seabirds soaring on the afternoon breeze. There isn't any readily available water on this stretch of coast, so be sure to pack a water bottle with you. There is sometimes a vendor selling drinks in front of Nakalele Blowhole, or a food truck (Mon.-Sat.) parked by Kahakuloa.

1: parasailing 2: Kapalua Coastal Trail 3: mountain views from the Maunalei Arboretum Trail

Ka'anapali

KA'ANAPALI BOARDWALK

The southern terminus of the 3-mile-long (4.8-km) **Ka'anapali Boardwalk** is in front of the Hyatt resort, and the easiest public beach parking is at Hanakao'o Beach Park along the highway between Ka'anapali and Lahaina. From here the boardwalk runs north all the way to the Sheraton, about 1.5 miles (2.4 km), although if you follow the paved walkway through the lower level of the Sheraton and through the parking lot, you will notice the trail re-forms and starts skirting the golf course. The walkway then runs through the Royal Lahaina resort and the parking lot of adjoining hotels. Following the Beach Walk signs, you eventually join another boardwalk that runs all the way down to the Honua Kai resort.

South of Lahaina

LAHAINA PALI TRAIL

Hot, dry, and with incomparable views, the **Lahaina Pali Trail** is a walk back in time to days when reaching Lahaina wasn't quite so easy. This 5-mile (8-km), three-hour (one-way) hike is the most strenuous trek in West Maui, as the zigzagging trail climbs 1,600 vertical feet (490 m) before reaching a crest by the Kaheawa Wind Farm. While torturous on both your legs and your thirst, the reward for the uphill slog is panoramic views over the central valley and dozens of humpback whales off the coast during winter.

Tracing its way over a part of the island that receives less than 10 inches (25 cm) of rainfall annually, this trail was originally constructed about 400 years ago during the reign of Pi'ilani, who envisioned a footpath wrapping around the island. When a dirt road was constructed along the coast in 1911, the trail fell into disrepair. Nevertheless, hikers still encounter evidence of ancient activity, such as stone shelters and rock walls. It's surreal to imagine that only 100 years ago this was the preferred route to reach Lahaina. To get the most out of this hike, pick up the hiking guide that the Na Ala Hele trail system has published, titled *Tales from the Trail.* It provides an interactive historical tour aligned with markers along the trail. Copies are available at the Department of Land and Natural Resources building in Wailuku (54 High St.), or, if you have a smartphone, download it as a PDF (www.mauiguidebook.com/hikes/lahaina-pali-trail).

The downside of this trail is that since it's a one-way hike, it can take some logistical planning. The Ukumehame trailhead on the Lahaina side is at mile marker 10.5, about 0.5 mile (0.8 km) past the tunnel in a small dirt parking lot on the inland side of the highway. If you depart from the Ukumehame trailhead, the path ascends moderately and offers pristine views of the coral reefs below. After the trail levels out at 1,600 feet (490 m), when you reach the crest by the wind farm, it descends steeply and sharply to the opposite trailhead between Ma'alaea and the junction of Honoapi'ilani Highway (Hwy. 30) and North Kihei Road. Your four options for the return route are to leave a car at the opposite trailhead, hike back the way you came, hitchhike back to the original trailhead, or turn back the way you came once you reach the wind farm (which is the shortest and most practical option).

If you plan on only hiking half the trail, setting out from the Ma'alaea trailhead offers better views of the valley and Kealia Pond, whereas departing from the Ukumehame trailhead offers better views of the coast and whale-watching opportunities. For the intrepid and those equipped with headlamps, the Ukumehame side is the best sunset perch on the West Side. Since there is absolutely no shade on this hike and it can get brutally hot, it's imperative to avoid the middle of the day and to pack more water than you would normally need. You'll be passing over rocky, rugged terrain, so wear closed-toe shoes.

BIKING

Whether you're going for a 60-mile (100-km) ride around the West Maui Mountains or a leisurely ride down Front Street on a beach cruiser, biking on the West Side of the island means cycling on roadways. For serious cyclists looking to rent a road bike, **West Maui Cycles** (1087 Limahana Pl., 808/661-9005, www.westmauicycles.com, 10am-5pm Mon.-Sat., 10am-4pm Sun.), in the industrial park of Lahaina, is the best bike shop on the West Side. Mountain bikes and high-performance road bikes range $60 per day to $280 per week; basic beach cruisers are $20 per day.

Closer to the center of Lahaina, **Maui Bike Rentals/Boss Frog's** (156 Lahainaluna Rd., 808/661-1345, www.bossfrog.com, 8am-5pm daily) also offers beach cruisers ($30 per day, $90 per week) and high-performance road bikes ($50 per day). While this location is closer to town and more convenient, diehard cyclists will appreciate the passion for the sport found at West Maui Cycles.

Adventure Sports

Even though water sports dominate the recreation options on the island's West Side, there are still a number of places where you can get a thrill on the land or over the water.

ZIP-LINING

The largest zip-lining tour in West Maui is **Skyline Hawaii** (2580 Keka'a Dr., 808/427-2771, www.skylinehawaii.com, 7am-6pm Mon.-Sat., from $169), a company that was the first zip-line operator on Maui. Each of the eight zip lines has a historical, environmental, or cultural connection explained by the guides, and the main draw is the view toward Lana'i and Moloka'i across the royal-blue channels. These tours are so popular they run eight times a day, with the earliest starting from the Fairway Shops office at 8am daily. The benefit of an early tour is that temperatures are still cool and winds are calm, although there can sometimes be some lingering morning showers, and the dirt roads can be muddy from this moisture. Try to get on the 8am or 9am tour, although there is never a bad time to be up here zip-lining. Children must be 10 years of age for the Ka'anapali course, closed-toe shoes are required, and the maximum weight is 260 pounds (118 kg).

Up north, **Kapalua Ziplines** (500 Office Rd., 808/756-9147, www.kapaluaziplines.com, 7am-3pm Mon.-Fri.) has a seven-line course that differs from Skyline in Ka'anapali in that all the lines are tandem. You can zip next to your loved one and watch them grimace with glee as you soar up to 2,100 feet (640 m) across the Kapalua mountainside. You'll walk over one of Hawaii's longest suspension bridges and ride an ATV to the summit. Tours (from $199) are offered five times per day. Since the tours can sometimes be canceled due to wind, try to go early in the morning.

ATV RIDES

The best ATV ride on the West Side of the island is with **Kahoma Ranch** (808/667-1978), to get dirty and rip across dirt roads on your own ATV ($214) or a shared ATV ($149). At the end, when you're all hot and sweaty, you can take a plunge down one of three different waterslides. Tour participants are awarded with views looking out at the island of Lana'i and back into Kahoma Valley. The tour area is closed to the public, so this is the only way you will see these views.

The waterslides look like little more than tarps stretched over a hole in the ground, but the speeds you can achieve are much faster than you'd expect. Children are $82, and those as young as age five can accompany a driver of legal age. Tours take place at 7:30am, 10am, 12:30pm, and 3pm daily, although the 7:30am tour doesn't include the waterslides.

Golf

KAPALUA, NAPILI, AND HONOKOWAI

For serious golfers, the name Kapalua should be synonymous with the **Kapalua Plantation Course** (2000 Plantation Club Dr., 877/527-2582, www.golfatkapalua.com). This 7,411-yard, par-73 course is the island's most famous and is the site of the Hyundai Tournament of Champions. With the course's fame come big greens fees: $359, but discounted to $329 if you are staying in the Kapalua resort. Greens fees decrease as the day wears on, as low as $209 in the late afternoon for nine holes, but expect the wind to be howling. Club rentals ($79) include two sleeves of balls, and shoe rental is $19. To find the clubhouse, travel along Honoapi'ilani Highway (Hwy. 30) for 1 mile (1.6 km) past the main entrance to Kapalua resort and make a right onto Plantation Club Drive. Continue up the hillside; the clubhouse is on the right.

The **Kapalua Bay Course** (300 Kapalua Dr., 808/669-8044, www.golfatkapalua.com) along the Kapalua shore is more forgiving at par 72 and 6,600 yards (6,035 m). While all of the holes offer resort-quality play, the highlight is hole 5, where the green is sandwiched between Oneloa Bay and D. T. Fleming Beach Park and you are surrounded by 270 degrees of brilliant blue ocean. The Bay Course is windy in the afternoon, so early mornings are best for calm conditions. Greens fees are $229, discounted to $209 for those staying in Kapalua resort. The fees decrease through the day, to as low as $149 for nine holes. To find the clubhouse, turn on Kapalua Drive from Lower Honoapi'ilani Road, across the street from Oneloa Bay (Ironwoods Beach). Travel up the road by the tennis center to the clubhouse on the right.

KA'ANAPALI

The courses in Ka'anapali are cheaper than in Kapalua and closer to most resorts. Perhaps most important, they're less prone to wind and rain, and it takes the trade winds about two hours longer to reach Ka'anapali than Kapalua. What this means is that an 8am tee time at Kapalua gets blustery around the sixth hole, whereas at Ka'anapali, you could be well into the back nine before the wind becomes a factor. The sacrifice in Ka'anapali is that the views aren't quite as nice—although they are still spectacular by normal standards—and the greens are slightly less manicured.

Of the two courses in Ka'anapali, the nicer is the **Royal Ka'anapali** (2290 Ka'anapali Pkwy., 808/661-3691, www.kaanapaligolfcourses.com), with the best views. In addition to paralleling the Pacific Ocean, this 6,700-yard, par-71 course is also the island's original course, opened in 1962. Greens fees are $255 for nonguests; those staying in Ka'anapali can play for $179. For those willing to tee off after 1pm, greens fees drop to $149.

Most of the holes on the course at **Ka'anapali Kai** (2290 Ka'anapali Pkwy., 808/661-3691, www.kaanapaligolfcourses.com) are on the inland side of the highway. The fairways aren't as nicely maintained as at the Royal, but the elevation provides classic ocean views. Greens fees are $205 for nonguests and $139 for those staying in Ka'anapali. Greens fees drop to $99 after 1pm,

Kapalua Bay Course

club rental is $55, and shoes are available for $10.

Both Ka'anapali courses check in at the same clubhouse. If you're looking for something just a little bit different, **Foot Golf** is offered on the Ka'anapali Kai course after 4pm; for $15 you play a modified course using a soccer ball and only your feet.

Spas

While the spa and massage services in this section are broken down by their geographic location, if you would rather enjoy an in-room, mobile massage, **Na Ali'i Massage** (808/250-7170, www.mymauimassage.com) will meet you anywhere on the West Side and offers rates much lower than the resorts or local massage parlors. A 60-minute massage is $100, and they offer a full range of other services, such as body scrubs, reflexology, and hand and foot treatments.

KAPALUA, NAPILI, AND HONOKOWAI

The best spa on the northwest side is the fantastically luxurious **Spa Montage** (1 Bay Dr., 808/662-6600, www.montagehotels.com, 9am-7pm daily), a wellness retreat unlike any other, incorporating state-of-the-art workout equipment with peaceful surroundings looking out toward Kapalua Bay. Inspired by the island's bounty, the award-winning spa offers highly personalized treatments using Maui-inspired products. Lounge poolside afterward. A 60-minute massage runs $215. For one of the island's best spa deals, purchase a day pass for $55, which gives you access to the facilities, including the fitness center, hydrotherapy circuits, and impossibly calming surroundings. A weeklong pass is $250, or $350 for two people.

For a spa experience outside a resort, **Zensations Spa** (3600 Lower Honoapi'ilani Rd., 808/669-0100, www.zensationsspa.com, 10am-5pm Mon.-Sat.), in the 5A Rent-A-Space mall in Honokowai, offers 60-minute massages for $99 as well as a full range of aromatherapy and facial and body treatment options. The spa is within walking distance of many Honokowai condos.

KA'ANAPALI

While nearly every resort in the Ka'anapali complex has a spa or beauty center, there are a couple that stand out. At the Westin Maui next to Whalers Village, **Heavenly Spa** (2365 Ka'anapali Pkwy., 808/661-2588, www.westinmaui.com, 9am-5pm daily) has been lauded as one of the top spas in the United States and has 50-minute massages beginning at $185. For slightly more affordable rates, the **Spa at Black Rock** (2605 Ka'anapali Pkwy., 808/667-9577, www.blackrockspa.com, 9am-5pm daily) offers 50-minute massages beginning at $145.

Shopping

Frenetic and fast-paced, Lahaina is the shopping capital of Maui. The section of Front Street between the Old Lahaina Center and The Shops at 505 shopping center is where you'll find the majority of shops. In Ka'anapali, Whalers Village is the undisputed epicenter of the shopping scene. Shopping in the northwestern corner of the island, meanwhile, is utilitarian, paling in comparison to the shops of Ka'anapali and Lahaina.

KA'ANAPALI

Whalers Village

Without a doubt, the undisputed epicenter of the Ka'anapali shopping scene is **Whalers Village** (2435 Ka'anapali Pkwy., 808/661-4567, www.whalersvillage.com, 9am-9pm daily), smack in the middle of Ka'anapali Beach between the Whaler Hotel and the Westin Maui. With three levels of restaurants, clothing boutiques, jewelry galleries, and kiosks, Whalers Village is the see-and-be-seen spot for all of your island souvenir shopping. While many of the stores are name-brand outlets you're already familiar with, there are still a handful of locally run stores. Get your parking validated, since the garage rates are expensive.

If you park in the Whalers Village garage, you can't help but walk directly past **Hilo Hattie** (808/875-4545, www.hilohattie.com), a gift and clothing shop with an impressive array of offerings, including Hawaiian chocolates. They also offer free shipping.

Sand People (808/662-8781, www.sandpeople.com) is a "coastal lifestyle emporium" featuring home decor and furnishings inspired by the ocean. This is a good place to find that whitewashed driftwood picture frame you've been searching for.

Other popular apparel favorites include **Johnny Was** (808/663-9698, www.johnnywas.com), a store specializing in creative women's resort wear, and **Alex and Ani** (808/868-2866, www.alexandani.com), a popular eco-conscious jewelry and accessories outpost that is heavy on symbolism in their work. A wide variety of pearl shops, jewelry stores, and surf outlets round out the popular mall.

LAHAINA

Front Street

Along the flat oceanfront stretch of Front Street, you'll find art galleries, surf shops, and more compressed in a nonstop strip of merchandise. Most shops are open 9am-10pm daily.

The **Wyland Gallery** (711 Front St., 808/667-2285, www.wyland.com) offers the artist's trademark array of marinelife scenes in a perfect oceanfront location. On the opposite side of the street, acclaimed photographer **Peter Lik** (712 Front St., 808/661-6623, www.lik.com) has a popular showroom of his oversize art, with the ability to transport you directly into the photograph. Other galleries of note are **Sargent's Fine Art** (802 Front St., 808/667-4030, www.sargentsfineart.com), on the corner of Lahainaluna Road; **DeRubeis Fine Art of Metal Maui** (766 Front St., 808/661-1431, www.derubeis.com); and **Martin Lawrence** (790 Front St., 808/661-1788, www.martinlawrence.com). Those with a passion for art should note that every Friday night is art night in Lahaina, when many galleries put on their finest show, featuring artist appearances or live jazz 7pm-10pm.

Chapel Hats (705 Front St., 808/359-2715) offers a very creative array of men's and women's hats. **Hale Zen** (180 Dickenson St., 808/661-4802, www.halezen.com)—a two-minute walk up Dickenson Street—is a local favorite for everything from homewares to candles, lotions, and crafts from local artists. Just across the street, by Lahaina Divers, **Goin Left** (143 Dickenson St., 808/868-3805, www.goinleft.com, noon-4pm Tues.-Sat.)

What's with All the Cheap Activity Signs?

Walking around Front Street in Lahaina, it only takes a few minutes to notice that every other shop is offering discount activities at rates that are too good to be true. A helicopter ride for $49? Bike down the volcano for $29? A luau for $9? There's got to be a catch.

Yes, there is a catch, but it doesn't mean the rates aren't real. In order to cash in on the advertised rates, you are essentially signing yourself up to endure a timeshare presentation, separate from the activity, that lasts a couple of hours. While no one plans on going to a meeting while on vacation, it could end up saving you a bundle on many of your island activities.

A word of caution, however, before you start committing to everything on the whiteboard. The activity providers (particularly the Molokini snorkeling tours) are with companies that aren't the best in their field, so comb over the particulars of the agreement (90 percent of afternoon Molokini snorkeling tours don't end up going to Molokini). Before committing to a discounted luau, find out which luau it is to see if it's one you want to attend.

Even though you might not plan on buying a timeshare, many of these closers could sell water to a fish. You could end up walking out with the most expensive luau you'll ever attend, but now you "own a piece of Maui."

offers apparel and accessories for the modern board-sports lifestyle.

For jewelry, stop into **Glass Mango Designs** (858 Front St., 808/662-8500, www.glassmango.com) for a colorful selection of "wearable art." For a shop that's stuffed with work from local artists, **Maui Memories** (658 Wharf St., 808/298-0261, www.mauiisland-memories.com, 11am-8pm daily) is across from the Banyan Tree and has island-themed clothing, accessories, and gifts from dozens of Maui artists.

The Shops at 505

The Shops at 505 Front Street, including several art shops, clothing shops, and the **Whalers General Store** for sundries, are generally open 9am-9pm daily.

Banyan Tree Market

While the Friday art nights are always festive, those who prefer lesser-known artists are encouraged to visit the fair beneath the banyan tree, held 9am-5pm on various weekends throughout the year. For a full schedule on when the art fair is on, visit www.lahainaarts.com.

Lahaina Cannery Mall

Enough visitors still frequent **Lahaina Cannery Mall** (1221 Honoapi'ilani Hwy., 808/661-5304, www.lahainacannery.com, 11am-6pm daily) to keep a few stores open. Stores of note include **Hawaiian Island Creations** (808/893-7873, www.hicshoponline.com), which has stellar island apparel and t-shirts, and **Maui Toy Works** (808/661-4766), for children's gifts.

SOUTH OF LAHAINA

Olowalu General Store

The only shopping to be found south of Lahaina is at **Olowalu General Store** (820 Olowalu Village Rd., 808/667-2883, 5am-6pm daily), where you can pick up affordable island-themed clothing that no one else will have. This store is a classically local operation where you can support the local economy.

Entertainment

West Maui is the island's entertainment hot spot, with the island's best luaus and most happening bars. You can't walk more than a few paces in Lahaina without tripping over an evening drink special. More than just booze, West Maui is also home to family entertainment options ranging from free hula performances and whale lectures to evening magic performances.

Despite the happening surroundings, however, if you're the clubbing type who likes to party into the wee hours of the morning, you're out of luck since most bars close by 11pm, and only a handful stay open later than 1am. Also, even though almost all of the nightlife options involve bars and pubs that have lively atmospheres, the options for dancing are woefully inadequate. For the most up-to-date info on the latest evening scene, pick up a free copy of the *Maui Time* newspaper or check out "The Grid" section on the website at www.mauitime.com.

KAPALUA, NAPILI, AND HONOKOWAI

Evening Shows

Can't get enough of *ki ho'alu* (slack-key guitar)? The **Masters of Slack Key** (5900 Lower Honoapi'ilani Rd., www.slackkeyshow.com, 6:30pm Wed. and Sat.) performance at the Aloha Pavilion of the Napili Kai Beach Resort is the best show you'll find on the island. Tickets can either be purchased online or when the doors first open. Prices for the show are normally $40.

Bars, Live Music, and Nightlife

The karaoke sessions at **Sansei** (600 Office Rd., 808/669-6286, www.sanseihawaii.com, 5pm-8pm Thurs.-Tues.) restaurant in the Kapalua resort are the most happening evenings on the northwestern side. This popular sushi and sake bar draws in a spirited crowd.

A short walk away at the Ritz-Carlton hotel you can find live music nightly in the **Alaloa Lounge.** It has the most consistent live music in the Kapalua resort.

In the Kahana Gateway Center, **Maui Brewing Company** (4405 Honoapi'ilani Hwy., 808/669-3474, www.mauibrewingco.com, 11:30am-10pm Tues.-Sat.) is a happening brewery-to-table venue that's packed with hop-soaked locals. Sit at the bar so you can keep your beer cold on the slab of ice that's inside the bar. Over a dozen beers are available on draft, many of which are only found at the brewery.

Dollie's Pub & Café (4310 Lower Honoapi'ilani Rd., 808/669-0266, www.dolliespizzakahana.com, 11am-10pm daily) is the West Side's de facto sports bar, where cheap beer and good pizza are served throughout the night. This is where island locals come to watch Sunday and Monday football games. Fifteen different televisions also show NBA, hockey, college sports, and whichever game you're hoping to catch.

KA'ANAPALI

Whalers Village

The center stage area at Whalers Village constantly teems with free events. Stalwarts of the entertainment schedule include lei-making classes, hula classes, arts and crafts sessions, and live music on most weekend nights. Since the schedule of events is constantly shifting, visit www.whalersvillage.com for an up-to-date calendar of current activities.

For drinks, every resort in Ka'anapali has fantastic and expensive drinks, but **Pailolo Bar & Grill** (808/667-3200) at the Westin Ka'anapali Villas is the island's only place that serves beer by the pitcher.

Luaus

There is no shortage of luaus along the Ka'anapali strip. The best on the island, the Old Lahaina Luau, is in nearby Lahaina, but there are four luaus in Ka'anapali. If the only reason you want to go to a luau is for the fire dancing, choose one in Ka'anapali. All will feature buffet food mass-produced for 100 people as well as local craft artisans, and all will offer premium seating for an added price. In my opinion it isn't worth the extra cost, since it usually means you get only slightly better seats and are first in line for the food. Most shows begin at either 5pm or 5:30pm. Ka'anapali can experience higher winds and a greater likelihood of rain than nearby Lahaina, so the chances of the luau needing to be moved inside or cancelled are higher. Most nights are gorgeous, but to guarantee calm conditions, you'll have better luck in Lahaina.

Of the numerous luaus in Ka'anapali, the best show is the **Wailele Polynesian Luau** (2365 Ka'anapali Pkwy., 808/667-2525, www.westinmaui.com, $175 adults, $80 children) at the Westin Maui resort. The fire dancers are the best, and the food is above average compared to the other options. Shows take place Tuesday and Thursday evenings as well as Sunday during busier times of the year, although the schedule varies. If you're driving to Ka'anapali, the one downside of this show is that parking can be challenging. Try to find free beach parking in the lot between Whalers Village and the entrance to the Westin. If you can't find a free spot, the most economical option is to park in the Whalers Village garage and then buy an ice cream or a quick beer after the show to get your parking validated for three hours.

Maui Nui Luau at Black Rock (2605 Ka'anapali Pkwy., 877/877-4852, www.sheratonmauiluau.com, $180 adults, $105 children) is Monday and Wednesday, as well as some Friday evenings, at the Sheraton resort. The crowds aren't quite as large as at other shows, and the grassy luau grounds are more spacious. While the food is fine and the dancers are entertaining, the best part is the atmosphere, looking out at Pu'u Keka'a and experiencing the torch-lighting ceremony. While children are welcome, it mainly caters to couples and adults.

At the far end of the beach at the southern tip of Ka'anapali, the **Drums of the Pacific** (200 Nohea Kai, 808/667-4727, www.drumsofthepacificmaui.com, Mon.-Sat., $379 for a table of two, $96 per extra adult, $96 children) takes visitors on a journey through numerous Polynesian cultures. This is Ka'anapali's largest luau, and the fire dancing and performance are on par with other shows. If you book directly on the luau website, you can sometimes get a deal of one child admission free with each paying adult.

On the northern side of Pu'u Keka'a, facing out toward the ocean, the **Myths of Maui Luau** (2780 Keka'a Dr., 877/273-7494, www.mythsofmaui.com, Sun.-Fri., $135 adults, $55 ages 6-12, free under age 6) at Royal Lahaina is a favorite option for those traveling with children. This is the island's longest-running luau (but don't confuse it with Old Lahaina Luau, which is better), and while there's no shaking the tourist kitsch, there's a palpable charm that goes along with the old-school venue. Everything over on this side of "the rock" is more laid-back than along the main Ka'anapali strip. Although the show doesn't face the beach, it's nevertheless set along a wide stretch of sand, and guests are encouraged to watch the sun go down while sipping a drink from the luau grounds. The show features a fire dance finale, and the entertainers bring children on stage for an impromptu hula lesson. The food is average, and while it isn't very Hawaiian, children enjoy the macaroni and cheese. Mai tais and Blue Hawaiians are included in the price of the ticket, but premium drinks cost extra at the bar.

Bars, Live Music, and Nightlife

Most of the bar scene in Ka'anapali plays out at the pool bars within the resorts. My favorite is the **Grotto Bar at the Hyatt** (200 Nohea Kai Dr., 808/661-1234), tucked beneath two different waterfalls. While the happy hour and dinner scene can be fun, there is not much nightlife after 10pm.

One of the more eclectic nightlife venues in Ka'anapali is **Java Jazz & Soup Nutz** (3350

Lower Honoapi'ilani Rd., 808/667-0787, www.javajazzmaui.com, 6am-10pm daily), frequented by locals and showcasing collectibles and diverse retail items (postcards, T-shirts, artwork, and coffee). It also has live entertainment nightly, with musicians taking the spotlight after sunset.

LAHAINA

Luaus

Lahaina is the best place on the island to attend a luau. It's dry and calm and has beautiful sunsets, and the island's best luau is here.

Old Lahaina Luau (1251 Front St., 800/667-1998, www.oldlahainaluau.com, daily, $145 adults, $80 children) is hands down the best on Maui. The food is the best, the luau grounds are immaculate, and everything from the show to the service runs like a well-oiled machine. Despite the fact that the luau seats 440 people, it still manages to retain an intimate atmosphere. You're greeted with a lei made of fragrant fresh flowers. Hula lessons for all ages are offered, and there are lawn games. Premium bar selections are included in the rates. There is a large *imu* (underground oven) for the pig, although it gets insanely crowded, so hang by the *imu* early to get a good view of the unearthing. The private oceanfront setting provides the perfect perch for watching the sun go down. There is ample free parking, or if you plan on having more than a couple of drinks, it's a short cab ride from Ka'anapali. A live show focuses on the history of Hawaii. For seating, choose either traditional *lauhala* mats (closest to the stage) or tables with chairs, which still provide a good view. The only places where it's hard to see the show are the seats in the far corners. Seating preference is given to those who book first. Remarkably, shows are offered seven days a week.

At the southern end of Front Street, the **Feast at Lele** (505 Front St., 808/667-5353, www.feastatlele.com, $176 adults, $103 children) is a luau on the oceanfront in the 505 shopping center. Lele is the ancient Hawaiian name for the town of Lahaina, and this show begins with dance native to Hawaiian culture. The event then migrates through various Polynesian cultures, including those of Aotearoa (New Zealand), Tahiti, and Samoa. The combination of cultures makes for a fast-paced, fiery, and heart-pumping performance capped off by everyone's favorite, Samoan fire and knife dancing. Unlike the other luaus on the island, the food features dishes from around Polynesia that reflect the show.

Old Lahaina Luau

Hula Shows

For a heavy heaping of Hawaiian cuteness, the **free *keiki* hula shows** (4pm Wed.) at the **Lahaina Cannery Mall** (1221 Honoapi'ilani Hwy., by Safeway) take place on the center stage.

Bars and Live Music

Rooted in the grog-shop days of its boisterous port-town past, Lahaina is Maui's nightlife capital. Most places close by 11pm, but that doesn't mean you can't find live music.

For free, family-friendly live music in a historic outdoor setting, the Lahaina Restoration Foundation hosts a **Hawaiian Music Series** (http://lahainarestoration.org, 6pm-7:30pm last Thurs. of every month) on the lawn of the Baldwin House (Dickenson St. and Front St.) in the center of town. Musical artists vary from month to month, but most sessions involve live music and *kanikapila* storytelling. Seating is limited at this popular event, and attendees are encouraged to bring a blanket or beach chair to enjoy the show.

The family-friendly **Friday Town Party** (www.mauifridays.com, 5pm-10pm 2nd Fri. of every month) is held between the Baldwin House and Wharf Cinema Center. Part of the Maui Fridays series, the free event features everything from live music and *keiki* competitions to silent auctions and dance performances. Various bars and restaurants feature live music, and most restaurants offer specials valid that night only.

One of the best spots for live entertainment in Lahaina is **Fleetwood's** (744 Front St., 808/669-6425, www.fleetwoodsonfrontst.com, 3pm-10pm daily), a two-story bar and restaurant that offers the only rooftop perch in Lahaina. This bar was opened by legendary rock musician Mick Fleetwood, and Mick himself has been known to jump in with the band for some impromptu percussion. Live music is offered most frequently on the rooftop bar at 5:45pm and 7:30pm Saturday-Thursday and 3:30pm, 5:45pm, and 7:30pm Friday.

Both **Cool Cat Café** (658 Front St., 808/667-0908, www.coolcatcafe.com, 10:30am-9pm daily) and **Kimo's** (845 Front St., 808/661-4811, www.kimosmaui.com, 11:30am-9pm daily) provide live music during the dinner hour seven nights a week. There isn't an official dance floor, so the atmosphere is relegated to drinks and mingling.

On Front Street, **Spanky's Riptide** (505 Front St., 808/667-2337, www.spankysmaui.com, 6:30am-midnight daily) in the 505 shopping center on the far southern end is a good place to grab a cheap goblet of PBR, play pool, and engage in conversation with a colorful cast of characters.

If you're looking to dance and socialize with a crowd of locals, **The Dirty Monkey** (844 Front St., 808/419-6268, www.thedirtymonkey.com, noon-10pm Mon., noon-midnight Tues., 10am-midnight Wed.-Sat., 6:30am-10pm Sun.) is the ticket. Karaoke Tuesdays, Whiskey Wednesdays with various entertainment, and popular DJs and live music acts fill out the week. It tends to get crowded—and loud—on weekends, but the spirit is always festive.

For a truly local experience, the legendary dive bar **Sly Mongoose** (1036 Limahana Pl., 808/661-8097, 10am-midnight daily) is in the Lahaina industrial park on the inland side of the highway, where visitors don't go. This is a no-nonsense dive where the beer is cold, the drinks are cheap, and the patrons are regular. This bar isn't within walking distance of Front Street, so you'll have to take a cab.

Magic Dinner Theater

At **Warren and Annabelle's** (900 Front St., 808/667-6244, www.warrenandannabelles.com, 5pm and 7:30pm Mon.-Sat., $86-151), any skepticism you might have had about attending a magic show on Maui will immediately be erased. Much more than a simple sleight-of-hand show, this enchanting evening revolves around the legend of Annabelle, a ghost whose swanky parlor you have the pleasure of dining in for the evening. After making your way through a secret entrance, you are welcomed into a plush lounge where the sound of piano keys accompanies the clink of oversize wine glasses.

The high level of service starts when you enter, and the refined waitstaff zip about with the air of a caffeinated butler. Settling into an overstuffed chair, guests can relax with some beverages from the bar and dine on gourmet pupus. Once dinner is through, it's on to the intimate 78-seat theater, and be warned, if you sit in the front row, you'll end up becoming a part of the show. Two parts magic and three parts comedy, this show will leave you laughing. Rates are $86 for the show only, but do yourself a favor and spend the extra $59 for the cocktails and appetizers package. Due to Maui County liquor laws, this show is only for ages 21 or older. The 7:30pm show is added during busier times of the year. Reservations are strongly recommended.

Art Night

Friday night is **Art Night in Lahaina.** In keeping with Lahaina's status as the cultural center of Maui, three dozen galleries open their doors 6:30pm-9:30pm, throw out the welcome mat, set out food and drink, provide entertainment, and usually host a well-known artist or two for this weekly party. Take your time to stroll Front Street from one gallery to the next. Stop and chat with shopkeepers, munch the goodies, sip the wine, look at the pieces on display, corner the featured artist for a comment on his or her work, and soak in the music of the strolling musicians. People dress up, but don't be afraid to come dressed casually.

Food

The number of dining options on the West Side is overwhelming. In most places you pay a premium for the location, so prices may seem high at ocean-view tables. That said, it's still possible to get a meal for under $10 per person outside the main visitor areas. While there is an overabundance of places on the West Side to sit and casually dine, there are only a handful of decent places for an affordable lunch on the run.

KAPALUA, NAPILI, KAHANA, AND HONOKOWAI

Hawaiian Regional

★ **Merriman's** (1 Bay Club Pl., 808/669-6400, www.merrimanshawaii.com, 4pm-8pm daily, prix fixe menu $120, $30 child) is one of the most scenic dining spots on the island. Arrive early to enjoy a glass of wine while watching the sunset from the oceanfront fire pit, and then enjoy a menu of farm-to-table fare, where over 90 percent of the ingredients are sourced from local farmers, fishers, and ranchers. Acclaimed chef Peter Merriman is one of the founders of the Hawaiian Regional movement, and his genius is evident in everything from the gluten-free taro cake and ahi ginger *poke* to the lobster, avocado, and tomato salad. For pairings, there are probably nations with constitutions shorter than the wine list, which features over 40 different varietals. Reservations are strongly recommended.

In Kapalua, the **Banyan Tree** (1 Ritz Carlton Dr., 808/665-7096, www.ritzcarlton.com, 5pm-8:30pm daily, $30-70) restaurant inside the Ritz Carlton delivers Hawaiian coastal cuisine with flair, with modern takes on fresh fish favorites, steak, and farm-to-table delights. Pair a glass from the extensive wine list with a pupu of ahi tuna tartare, and then treat your palate to Hawaiian cioppino, served with *tako* (octopus), mahimahi, prawns, lobster, Hua Momona Farm's tomatoes, scallions, and more. Much of the food is sourced here on the island, including herbs from the garden.

Another restaurant making waves in Kapalua is the spectacular **Cane & Canoe** (1 Bay Dr., 808/662-6681, www.montagehotels.com, 7am-11am and 5:30pm-9pm daily,

$25-38), inside the Montage Kapalua Bay looking out toward Moloka'i, with an acoustic guitar player perched beneath the trees. Order from a menu of Hawaiian regional cuisine: Kona kanpachi and Kauai shrimp, ora king salmon, and even a stellar lobster mac-and-cheese. For breakfast, order the Maui omelet with its cheddar cheese, tomato, roasted new potatoes, and caramelized Maui onion or the exquisite lobster Benedict.

For one of the island's best breakfasts and happy hours, **The Sea House** (5900 Lower Honoapi'ilani Rd., 808/669-1500, www.seahousemaui.com, 7am-9pm daily, $15-50) restaurant at Napili Kai is right on the sands of Napili Bay and is a longtime island classic. Happy hour runs 2pm-5pm with half-off pupus, and if you sit down and order at 4:30pm, you can often enjoy a sunset dinner for half price.

Overlooking the Plantation golf course, the ★ **Plantation House** (2000 Plantation Club Dr., 808/669-6299, www.cohnrestaurants.com, 8am-2pm and 4:45pm-8pm daily, $17-53) offers spectacular views with succulent food to match. Considering the luxurious venue, the more affordable breakfast and lunch menu make you feel like you're getting away with something. Breakfast is served until 2pm, and for dinner, you can pair fresh fish such as ahi and provençale with a glass from the extensive wine list.

Local Style

From the outside, you might wonder what's so special about hole-in-the-wall **Honokowai Okazuya & Deli** (3600 Lower Honoapi'ilani Rd., 808/665-0512, 11am-2:30pm and 4:30pm-8:30pm Mon.-Sat., $11-20, cash only). Even though the front door is often closed and it's in a strip mall next to the 5A Rent-A-Space, inside you'll find huge portions, great local food, and budget-friendly prices. There are a few seats inside for dining, but most visitors order takeout to enjoy back at the condo. The food rivals any on the island, and the prices can be half as much as food served with an ocean view. Try the coconut shrimp.

Japanese

Ask any local where to get sushi, and they'll tell you ★ **Sansei** (600 Office Rd., 808/669-6286, www.sanseihawaii.com, 5pm-8pm Thurs.-Tues.), a legendary outpost on the main entrance road to Kapalua resort. To maximize your Sansei experience, call ahead for reservations for 5pm. When the restaurant opens, they usually run an early-bird special for the first 30 minutes, with selected dishes half off. Sansei is known for its sushi rolls, like its spicy tuna with seaweed salad ($10-19). Large plates include the fresh catch of the day and items like shichimi seared salmon and jumbo prawns ($17-40).

If Sansei is too packed, or for a more intimate venue, **Miso Phat** (4310 Lower Honoapi'ilani Hwy., 808/669-9010, www.misophat.com, 11:30am-9pm Mon.-Fri., 3pm-9pm Sat.-Sun.) has exceptionally fresh sushi and phenomenal rolls ($10-25) in a humble Kahana location. Best of all, it's BYOB.

Italian

Taverna Maui (2000 Village Rd., 808/667-2426, www.tavernamaui.com, 2pm-10pm Mon.-Sat., 10am-10pm Sun., $18-40) has won accolades thanks, in part, to a convivial atmosphere—incorporating an open-air design and flickering tiki torches—and a bountiful menu featuring shared plates (pizza, bruschetta) and luscious entrées like a mushroom gnocchi and house-made pasta with crab as well as fresh fish, meat, and vegetables dishes. Order the mai tai from Taverna's extensive libations menu and get a boost from the 1970s-era rum, hints of hazelnut, and "secret spices."

The Pour House Italian Kitchen and Wine Bar (700 Office Rd., 808/214-5296, www.thepourhouse.com, 5pm-8:30pm daily, $22-43) prepares its pastas and other dishes using locally sourced ingredients. In addition to classics like Italian meatballs and spaghetti with clams, it serves items like a hummus of the day and garlic herb lamb chops with a white bean puree. The venue also boasts one of the most extensive wine lists west of Lahaina.

1
2
ULULANI'S
Hawaiian Shave Ice
3
4

Mexican

Maui Tacos (5095 Napilihau St., 808/665-0222, 11am-8pm daily, $8-15) stands out for its extensive menu and ample servings. Try favorites like the Hawaiian barbecue pork bowl and the venue's delicious Surf Burritos doused with special enchilada sauce and cheese. You can order a bountiful platter meal, too. Consider either the blackened fish or pineapple chicken fajitas.

Brewpubs

A visit to ★ **Maui Brewing Company** (4405 Honoapi'ilani Hwy., 808/669-3474, www.mauibrewingco.com, 11:30am-10pm Tues.-Sat., $14-22) should be at the top of every beer lover's island to-do list. This is the island's original brewpub, and while you can find a number of the beers in local supermarkets, at least a dozen more can only be found on tap when you visit. The interior is basic, but this isn't a place you come to for the decor. Even though the beer is the main draw, the Hawaiian beef burgers, sliders, and bacon mac-and-cheese with chorizo are hearty accompaniments to a rich pint of stout. There are also filling and affordable flatbreads as well as vegan and gluten-free options.

Breakfast and Lunch

★ **The Gazebo** (5315 Lower Honapi'ilani Rd., 808/669-5621, 7:30am-2pm daily, $10-18) has the island's best breakfast. This isn't a secret, however, and there is a line out the door by 6:45am. What makes this spot so popular is not only the oceanfront location, gazing out toward Moloka'i, but also the famous macadamia nut pancakes and enormously filling portions. Lunch is offered until closing at 2pm, and by then the line has shrunk. Finding parking can be challenging; try for a spot along Napili Place, or park by the Napili Bay beach access on Hui Drive and walk to the restaurant across the sand of Napili Bay. From the beach, looking toward the water, The Gazebo is on the point to the left.

Affordable, easy, and convenient, the **Honolua Store** (502 Office Rd., 808/665-9105, 6:30am-7pm daily) in Kapalua has some of the island's best deals. Breakfast runs 6am-10:30am daily, and if you're tight on cash, a filling to-go container of *loco moco* is only $7.

Coffee Shops

At the Kahana Gateway Center, **Hawaiian Village Coffee** (4405 Honoapi'ilani Hwy., 808/665-1114, 6am-noon daily) is a classic coffee shop with a strong local following and good community vibe. This is the earliest place to open on the northwest side, and the sunrise hours feature a collection of late-shift police officers refueling after a long night and sleepy-eyed locals stopping in on their way to work. Although small, the shop has a welcoming atmosphere for reading the morning paper or checking your email on the free Wi-Fi.

Natural Foods

One of the few places to pick up a healthy meal on the go is **Honokowai Farmers Market** (3636 Lower Honoapi'ilani Rd., 808/669-7004, 7am-7pm daily, $6-12), across from Honokowai Beach Park. There is a hot bar, a salad bar, a full health-conscious market, and a counter serving açaí and pitaya bowls.

KA'ANAPALI

Hawaiian Regional

Even though every resort in Ka'anapali has some sort of Hawaiian Regional option, none can hold a candle to world-famous ★ **Roy's** (2290 Ka'anapali Pkwy., 808/669-6999, www.royshawaii.com, 11am-8pm daily, $29-55). The location, inside the golf clubhouse, would be nicer if it had an ocean view, but what the restaurant lacks in decor, it makes up for in flavor. Chef Roy Yamaguchi was one of the founders of the Hawaiian Regional movement, and his mastery is evident in the *misoyaki* butterfish and honey mustard-braised short ribs. Even though there are over 30 Roy's locations around the country, every restaurant has a

1: sunset at Merriman's 2: Ululani's Hawaiian Shaved Ice 3: Honu 4: Three Pigs in Paradise sandwich at Maui Brewing Company

menu and a style unique to the venue. Dinner entrées are pricey; the lunch menu ($16-25) is more affordable. The chocolate ganache cake is a dessert favorite.

Hula Grill (2435 Ka'anapali Pkwy., 808/667-6636, www.hulagrillkaanapali.com, 10:45am-10pm daily, $29-46) in Whalers Village is a place that exudes the carefree nature of being on vacation in Hawaii. Sink your toes down into the sand of the outdoor barefoot bar, which has a better vibe than the pricier indoor dining room. There's live music in the afternoons, and the *poke* tacos and the kalua pork with pineapple flatbread are two affordable options along an otherwise expensive shore.

★ **Monkeypod Kitchen** (2435 Ka'anapali Pkwy., 808/878-6763, www.monkeypodkitchen.com, 11am-9pm daily, $15-44), also in Whalers Village, wins raves for its locale—what an ocean view—and handcrafted food, drink, and "merrimaking." The venue supports local and organic farming, ranching, and fishing and its menus are seasonal. Culinary cocktails abound. Try Ho'opono Potion, a Maestro Dobel tequila, Aperol, lime, and cucumber delight. *Poke* tacos or lobster deviled eggs make for good appetizers. Pizzas like the Hamakua wild mushroom and truffle oil or kalua pork and pineapple hit the mark. For entrées, consider seared ahi steak or the organic macadamia nut-crusted fresh fish. Burgers, tacos, and steaks round out the menu.

Across the Whalers Village walkway, **Leilani's on the Beach** (2435 Ka'anapali Pkwy., 808/661-4495, www.leilanis.com, 11am-9pm daily, $16-30) serves the best fish tacos on the island. The tacos are enormous, served Cajun style, and accompanied by a special sauce that brings it all together. Whether you dine on the casual patio or upstairs in the dining room, save room for the world-famous Hula Pie with macadamia nut ice cream and chocolate cookie crust; it's big enough to share.

At the far southern end of the Ka'anapali strip, **Japengo** (200 Nohea Kai Dr., 808/667-4909, www.japengomaui.com, 5pm-9pm daily, $25) has enormous and affordable sushi rolls that compete for best on the island. There's a great ocean view from the bar.

In front of the Honua Kai resort, **Duke's** (130 Kai Malina Pkwy., 808/662-2900, www.dukesmaui.com, 8am-9pm daily, $16-52) offers breakfasts that include banana and macadamia nut pancakes and lunches with a variety of sandwiches, burgers, and fish tacos. Dinner entrées are more expensive. Duke's sources ingredients from 20 local farms, and the Bloody Marys are always a good idea. Afternoon trade winds can make the outdoor dining frustrating, so go for breakfast before 10am or for dinner after sundown.

Natural Foods

The best gourmet natural foods market on the West Side, **'Aina Gourmet Market** (130 Kai Malina Pkwy., 808/662-2832, www.ainagourmet.com, 6:30am-9:30pm daily) is tucked away in the lobby of Honua Kai Beach Resort. 'Aina is in the same restaurant group as Pacific'O as well as O'o Farms, and this is a great place for grabbing a cup of 100 percent Maui coffee, organically raised produce, or a healthy panini made from locally sourced ingredients. There are a few tables, or enjoy your meal on the beach.

LAHAINA

Hawaiian Regional

In the 505 shopping area, ★ **Pacific'O** (505 Front St., 808/667-4341, www.pacificomaui.com, 5pm-9pm Tues.-Sat., $29-46) is one of the best venues in Lahaina for enjoying an oceanfront meal. Many of the ingredients are grown at the organic O'o Farm in Kula. The seaside patio is the perfect lunch spot for pairing a sesame fish salad with a crisp glass of white wine. Reservations are necessary for dinner, when you can feast on entrées such as whiskey *shoyu* duck, seafood risotto, or ahi fettuccine. Aside from the food, the wine list is one of the most comprehensive in West Maui.

On the far northern end of Lahaina, ★ **Honu** (1295 Front St., 808/667-9390, www.honumaui.com, 11am-9pm Mon.-Sat., $20-46) offers locally sourced food in an oceanfront setting. *Honu* is the Hawaiian name for sea turtle, and there's a strong likelihood that you'll spot a turtle coming up for a breath at some point during your meal. Chef Mark Ellman, one of the original founders of the Hawaiian Regional movement, has created a menu where butternut squash coconut soup complements main courses ranging from Maui cattle burgers to house-made ahi meatballs. The pizzas are similarly delicious. A favorite off the appetizer menu is the ahi bruschetta. The extensive craft beer selection features over 50 different microbrews—a rarity among island restaurants. If there's a wait, try sister restaurant **Mala,** next door.

In the heart of Front Street, **Kimo's** (845 Front St., 808/661-4811, www.kimosmaui.com, 11:30am-9pm daily, $25-39) has a deck looking out over the waters of the Lahaina Roadstead and moderately priced lunch items ($15-22) such as Maui Brewing Co. Bikini Blonde Lager-battered fish and chips and Hawaiian cowboy burgers. Dinner entrées in the dining room are pricier and include items like sesame crusted ahi and pork ribs with plum barbecue sauce. The staff at Kimo's are as professional as they come.

Local Style

For breakfast where all the locals go, **808 Grindz** (843 Waine'e St., 808/868-4147, www.808grindzcafe.com, 7am-2pm daily) is a hidden hole-in-the-wall by Nagasako supermarket, where an entire menu of omelets and *mocos* is only $8.08.

Eclectic

One of Lahaina's best-kept secrets is **Lahaina Coolers** (180 Dickenson St., 808/661-7082, www.lahainacoolers.com, 8am-1am daily, $18-35), a laid-back local favorite that can rival anywhere in town. All three meals are a reason to visit, particularly breakfast. The dinner menu is just as good as at more upscale places in town. There are also pizzas, pastas, and an affordable bar menu with kalua pig tacos.

Contemporary Cuisine

We'll come right out and say that ★ **Lahaina Grill** (127 Lahainaluna Rd., 808/667-5117, www.lahainagrill.com, 5pm-10pm daily, $43-65) is the best restaurant in Lahaina. Opened on Valentine's Day 1990, this restaurant continues to be one of Lahaina's most romantic evenings. The ambience, service, and extensive wine list are what you would expect of a fine-dining experience. The only thing missing from the classy bistro setting is an ocean view. The food is a combination of new American cuisine infused with Pacific Rim favorites, where meat dishes include the coveted Kona coffee-roasted rack of lamb, and seafood selections include sesame-crusted ahi fillets and crisp fried lobster crab cakes. Much of the produce is sourced locally from independent farmers. Reservations are recommended.

Japanese

Moved to a new oceanfront location in 2020, ★ **Star Noodle** (1285 Front St., 808/667-5400, www.starnoodle.com, 10:30am-10pm daily, $10-19) continues to inspire. The private setting is among the most scenic in Lahaina, and the award-winning food is some of the best you'll find on the island. Share plates like the Vietnamese crepe and miso salmon stand out. Tempura shrimp and adobo ribs are nice features on the entrée menu. Noodle lovers will appreciate the hot and sour noodles, Star *udon,* or the delicious pad thai. Sheldon Simeon, a local chef who made it to the final three on the reality show *Top Chef,* peppers the exquisite Asian-infused menu here.

Chinese

In the Fairway Shops on Highway 30, **China Bowl Asian Cuisine** (2580 Keka'a Dr., 808/661-0660, www.chinabowlmaui.com, 11am-9pm daily, $11-21) is no-frills in decor but with affordable and stellar traditionally popular dishes such as a hot and sour soup and moo shu shrimp. Some incorporate ingredients found only on Maui, like a Kula onion pork dish. Order ahead and take it back to your lodging.

Stock up in the Warehouse District

This ever-evolving **warehouse district** on **Kupuohi Street,** several miles north of Lahaina's busy Front Street, has grown in popularity and is now a go-to for services beneficial to travelers.

Conveniences include **Island Grocery Depot** (58 Kupuohi St., 808/866-5020, www.islandgrocerydepot.com, 6:30am-6pm daily), a full-service supermarket—perfect for stocking up your condo or timeshare—with more affordable prices than standard local grocers. Shops like **A Special Touch** (142 Kupuohi St., 808/661-3455, www.lahaina-maui-florist.com, 9am-3pm Mon.-Fri.) offer affordable flowers and leis for destination-wedding visitors or anyone looking to beautify their dwelling.

Several warehouse gyms cater specifically to visitors with drop-in rates. **Enjoy the Ride Maui** (118 Kupuohi St., 808/667-7772, www.enjoytheridemaui.com, drop-in $26, 5-class package $100) rocks the house with high-intensity spin classes set to upbeat music and mood lighting. **Lahaina Cross Fit** (48 Ulupono St., 309/242-3478, www.lahainacrossfit.com, drop-in $30, 7-day unlimited $95) features eight classes a day.

One dining establishment lures visitors and locals here. **Alchemy Maui** (157 Kupuohi St., 808/793-2115, http://valleyislekombucha.com, 11am-4pm Mon.-Fri., $15-24) is a popular kombucha bar and café serving fresh wraps and sandwiches (chicken, pork, lobster, pastrami, falafel, mahimahi) on house-baked bread.

Thai

The best Thai food on the West Side is at **Thai Chef** (878 Front St., 808/667-2814, www.thaichefrestaurantmaui.com, 11am-9pm daily, $14-25), a small hole-in-the-wall restaurant squirreled away in the parking lot between Longhi's and the Maui Theatre. The family-run restaurant is BYOB if you'd like to accompany your chicken pad thai with a Singha beer; beer and wine are available at Foodland across the parking lot. Vegetarians can order plenty of spicy tofu and vegetable dishes. It's not fancy, but you won't be disappointed. Takeout is available; reservations are recommended.

Italian

The culinary brainchild of a chef who arrived via Brooklyn, and before that Milan, **Sale Pepe** (878 Front St., 808/667-7667, www.salepepemaui.com, 5pm-9pm Mon.-Sat., $13-36) is one of Lahaina's best Italian restaurants. The authentic dishes use only the freshest island ingredients, and what isn't sourced from local farmers is brought all the way from Italy.

Burgers

Hands down, the best burger in Lahaina is at ★ **Cool Cat Café** (658 Front St., 808/667-0908, www.coolcatcafe.com, 10:30am-9pm daily, $10-25). Overlooking the banyan tree, the inside portion of the restaurant is decorated in 1950s decor, while the outdoor patio is livelier. Cool Cats is consistently voted as the island's best burger. All of the meat is massaged with a secret seasoning, and specialty burgers like the Bogy Burger (dressed with lettuce, tomatoes, pickles, sweet Maui onions, mayo and thousand island dressing, and topped with bacon and cheese), Luna (covered in avocado), and Don Ho (topped with pineapple) are what make it such a legendary choice. There are also fish sandwiches, blackened fish tacos, salads (get the Blue Hawaii with fresh fish piled on top), and a popular bar featuring "adult" milkshakes. It's extra to add fries to your meal (and cheaper to get a basket for the table than to add to each burger separately). This is where you'll find Lahaina Harbor boat crews spending their tips at the bar.

★ **Cheeseburger in Paradise** (811 Front St., 808/661-4855, www.cheeseburgernation.

com, 10:30am-9:30pm daily, $14-18) boasts a remarkable ocean view and affordable prices. Ono onion rings and chicken wings begin your culinary journey. For entrées, try any of the burgers, such as the famous Cheeseburger in Paradise, the original five-napkin cheeseburger featuring colby jack cheese, mayonnaise, lettuce, tomato, and onion on a grilled brioche bun. The buffalo bleu cheeseburger and steakhouse cheeseburger are terrific, too. Add caramelized onions or avocado to the package and you have yourself quite the feast. Non-burger items like the island tuna salad wrap or plant-based Beyond Burger are also bountiful.

Shave Ice

There are few things better than a cold shave ice on a hot Lahaina day, and the best shave ice in Lahaina is at **Ululani's Hawaiian Shave Ice** (790 Front St., 808/877-3700, www.ululanishawaiianshaveice.com, 11am-8pm daily). The locally owned favorite features a bevy of offerings, such as fresh liliko'i and coconut and the mouthwatering mango, pineapple, and mango habanero.

Coffee Shops

For a quick coffee on the run, **Bad Ass Coffee** (671 Front St, 800/738-8223, www.badassmaui.com, 6am-8pm daily) features 100 percent Kona brews in a laidback setting with gift items.

For a place to linger, grab breakfast, get free internet access, and sip on a proper espresso, try **Café Café** (129 Lahainaluna Rd., 808/661-0006, www.cafecafemaui.com, 7am-2pm daily). There are a few outdoor tables for sipping your macchiato, and you can also pick up organic locally sourced open-face bagel sandwiches ($5-7).

Natural Foods

To the delight of those who care about what they put in their bodies, ★ **Choice Health Bar** (1087 Limahana Pl., 808/661-7711, www.choicemaui.com, 8am-3pm daily) is devoted to the benefits of a healthy, active lifestyle. When you walk in the door (where a sign informs you this is a "bummer-free zone"), you can sense the antioxidants flowing. The smoothies use all-natural superfood ingredients (spirulina, açaí, coconut meat, and almond milk), so your body will thank you. Make your smoothie "epic" by adding superfoods such as kale and blue-green algae. A large selection of freshly made salads is available after 11am daily.

Markets

Believe it or not, the **seafood counter** at the back of **Foodland Farms** (345 Keawe St., 808/662-7088, 6am-9pm daily, $8) serves one of the island's best *poke* bowls. Order a bowl of ahi *poke*, served on a bed of brown rice, and then head down to Wahikuli Beach Park for a picnic out on the sand.

SOUTH OF LAHAINA

Sandwiches

The only restaurant between Lahaina and Ma'alaea is ★ **Leoda's Kitchen and Pie Shop** (820 Olowalu Village Rd., 808/662-3600, www.leodas.com, 10am-6pm daily, $6-18), in the Olowalu store building. Using many sustainable ingredients from local farms, this sandwich and pie shop has quickly become an island favorite. The deli sandwiches, potpies, and baked goods are so good, however, that you'll often find a line stretching out the front door. Try the veggie burger for a healthy lunch, or a savory chicken potpie.

Getting There and Around

AIR

Above Kahana is the small **Kapalua-West Maui Airport** (JHM, 4050 Honoapi'ilani Hwy., 808/665-6108), which is a convenient option for those commuting to Honolulu. The interisland fares ($85 and up one-way) are often a little higher than at the larger Kahului Airport, but when you factor in the hour of driving you save, it's worth the few extra dollars. This small airport is used principally by Mokulele Airlines, but it's also used by small commercial tour companies. Surrounded by former pineapple fields, the single airstrip is short and used by small propeller aircraft only. The check-in counters, inspection station, boarding gate, and baggage claim are only a few steps from each other.

Mokulele Airlines (808/495-4188, www.mokuleleairlines.com) has several flights a day between Kapalua and Honolulu. The earliest flight typically departs at 7:30am, and the last flight of the day is at 5:10pm. Outside those times, you'll have to go to Kahului. There are also flights to Moloka'i and Lana'i, and they vary depending on the day. It's best to check with the airline and schedule ahead.

CAR

Car Rentals

The largest car-rental providers on the West Side are in Honokowai, equidistant from Lahaina Harbor and Kapalua Airport. Here you'll find both **Avis** (11 Halawai Dr., 808/661-8760, 8am-5pm daily) and **Budget** (11 Halawai Dr., 808/661-8760, 8am-5pm daily). Provided you arrive at the harbor or Kapalua Airport during business hours, they have a shuttle that will pick you up.

In the Sheraton resort in Ka'anapali, **Enterprise** (2605 Ka'anapali Pkwy., 808/661-8804, 8am-1pm Mon.-Fri.) has a service counter and will pick you up anywhere from Lahaina Harbor to Kapalua.

TAXI

In West Maui, the best taxi options include **West Maui Taxi** (808/661-1122) and **Lahaina Taxi Service** (808/661-5959). A

Mokulele Airlines

Northwest Coast Mileage Guide

To use this mileage guide for Maui's northwestern coast, zero your trip odometer when you pass the entrance to Kapalua resort.

- 1 mile (1.6 km): D. T. Fleming Beach Park
- 1.6 miles (2.6 km): Mokulei'a Bay (Slaughterhouse Beach)
- 2.3 miles (3.7 km): Parking area for Honolua Valley and Honolua Bay snorkeling
- 2.7 miles (4.3 km): Honolua Bay Overlook and dirt access road to surf spot
- 3.7 miles (6 km): Overlook for Windmills surf spot
- 4 miles (6.4 km): Punalau Beach access road (Windmills)
- 5 miles (8 km): Honokohau Bay Overlook
- 5.8 miles (9.3 km): Honokohau Bay
- 7.4 miles (11.4 km): mile marker 38 and trail to lighthouse
- 7.9 miles (12.7 km): mile marker 38.5 and trail to Nakalele Blowhole
- 10 miles (16 km): Ohai Trail
- 12 miles (19.3 km): Olivine Pools
- 12.8 miles (20.6 km): Road becomes one lane and scary!
- 13.3 miles (21.4 km): Braddah Chics food truck ($12 garlic shrimp!)
- 13.5 miles (21.7 km): Kahakuloa Village

ride from Lahaina to Ka'anapali is about $17, and from Ka'anapali to Kapalua about $27. Going rates for a cab ride to Kahului Airport from Ka'anapali are about $100, so you might want to think twice about taking a cab to the hotel.

SHUTTLE

The free **Kapalua Shuttle** (808/665-9110) runs throughout the resort for guests on an on-demand basis 7am-11pm daily. In Ka'anapali, the **resort shuttle** offers free transportation across the resort and runs on a set schedule 9am-9pm daily. For a shuttle to the airport, **Speedi Shuttle** (877/242-5777, www.speedishuttle.com) offers shared ride services that range from around $35 per person in Lahaina to $65 per person from Ka'anapali.

MOTORCYCLE AND MOPED

If you want the wind whipping through your hair, there are a number of different motorcycle, Harley, and moped rentals scattered across the West Side. The place with the largest selection of bikes is **Aloha Motorsports** (30 Halawai Dr., 808/667-7000, www.alohamotorsports.com, 9am-5pm daily), in Honokowai, across the highway from the Honua Kai resort. The company offers free pickup and drop-off on the West Side. Rates for mopeds can be as low as $79 for 24 hours, and Harley rentals average around $239 for 24 hours. During slower times of the year there can be specials available.

If you don't need a full-on hog and just want a moped for the day, check out **West Maui Moped** (1036 Limahana Pl., 808/276-5790, 9am-5pm Mon.-Sat.), in a small warehouse district and near Maui Brewing Company. Rates are $45 per day.

BUS

The cheapest way to get around West Maui, albeit slowly, is the **Maui Bus** (808/249-2900, www.co.maui.hi.us/bus). There are four different routes in West Maui, and departures are once per hour. All trips cost $2 per person boarding, and you can buy a day pass for $4. The bus stations in Lahaina are in the back of the Wharf Cinema Center across the street from the banyan tree, and at the intersection of Front Street and Papalaua Street. To get from one side of Lahaina to the other, bus 23 makes various stops around town 8am-11pm daily.

From Napili or Kahana to Whalers Village in Ka'anapali, where you can connect with buses to Lahaina and beyond, bus 30 begins service at 5:30am daily at the Napili Kai Beach Resort and makes various stops along Lower Honoapi'ilani Road until 9pm. Bus 25 connects Whalers Village in Ka'anapali with the Wharf Cinema Center in Lahaina 6am-9pm daily, and bus 20 connects the Wharf Cinema Center with Queen Ka'ahumanu Mall in Kahului, making a stop in Ma'alaea to transfer to a bus down to Kihei.

Since a taxi from Napili to Kahului Airport costs about $120, if you need to get from Napili to the airport and don't have a car, the cheapest way is to buy a $4 day pass and take bus 30 to Whalers Village, change to bus 25 to the Wharf Cinema Center, hop on bus 20 to the Queen Ka'ahumanu Mall, and then take bus 40 to the Kahului Airport. Total transit time for this sojourn is 2 hours and 10 minutes, but for $4, who's complaining? You aren't allowed to have more luggage than you can place on your lap or under your seat.

SEA

Not many visitors access West Maui from the water, but those traveling from the island of Lana'i will arrive at Lahaina Harbor by interisland ferry. **Expeditions** (808/661-3756, www.go-lanai.com) ferry runs several times daily between Manele and Lahaina Harbors. From Lana'i, the earliest arrival time in Lahaina is 9am, and the latest is 6:15pm. When arriving in Lahaina by ferry, you'll find there are a large number of taxis waiting to get you to your resort. If you plan on renting a car, call ahead to the car-rental offices and they'll pick you up. If you are traveling from Lana'i, the car-rental offices are closed if you arrive on the last ferry of the day.

Central Maui

Central Maui is industrial, urban, and—most important—real.

The site of Kahului International Airport, Central Maui is the first part of the island most visitors encounter. It's more built up than you'd expect of "paradise," but beyond the traffic lights, box stores, and increasing lanes of asphalt, Central Maui is the beating heart of the island's cultural past. It's also rich in natural beauty, with muddy trails leading deep into the mountains and miles of sandy shore. It's home to the island's widest array of multicultural cuisine. The sport of kitesurfing was invented here on the shores of Kanaha Beach Park. While there might not be any palm-lined resorts or tropical beach bars with mai

Highlights

Look for ★ to find recommended sights, activities, dining, and lodging.

★ See a movie or live performance at the state-of-the-art **Maui Arts and Cultural Center** for one of the best nights out on Maui (page 109).

★ Peer into the daily lives of plantation laborers and learn about a bygone era at the **Alexander and Baldwin Sugar Museum** (page 109).

★ View authentic Hawaiian artifacts, a surfboard ridden by Duke Kahanamoku, and the best compilation of Hawaiiana literature on the island at the **Bailey House Museum** (page 112).

★ Sample the traditional architecture of the island's "mixed plate" community at **Kepaniwai Heritage Gardens** (page 112).

★ Enjoy the journey to **'Iao Valley State Monument,** where you can learn about King Kamehameha's decisive victory at the Battle of Kepaniwai and snap a photo of the iconic 'Iao Needle (page 114).

★ Learn about the island's rich agriculture on a tram tour at the **Maui Tropical Plantation,** where you'll also find zip-lining, a farm stand, shopping, and a phenomenal restaurant (page 116).

★ Watch the world's best **windsurfers** and **kitesurfers** zip through the air at unheralded **Kanaha Beach Park** (page 118).

★ Follow the trail of the undeveloped **Waihe'e Coastal Dunes and Wetlands Preserve** as it passes by the ruins of Kapoho fishing village and its associated *heiau* (page 121).

★ Hike above 2,500 feet (760 m) elevation to commune with the ferns and the clouds on the exceptionally scenic **Waihe'e Ridge Trail** (page 122).

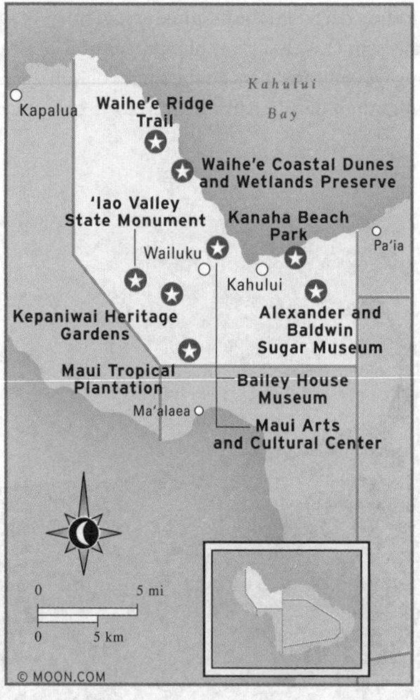

Central Maui

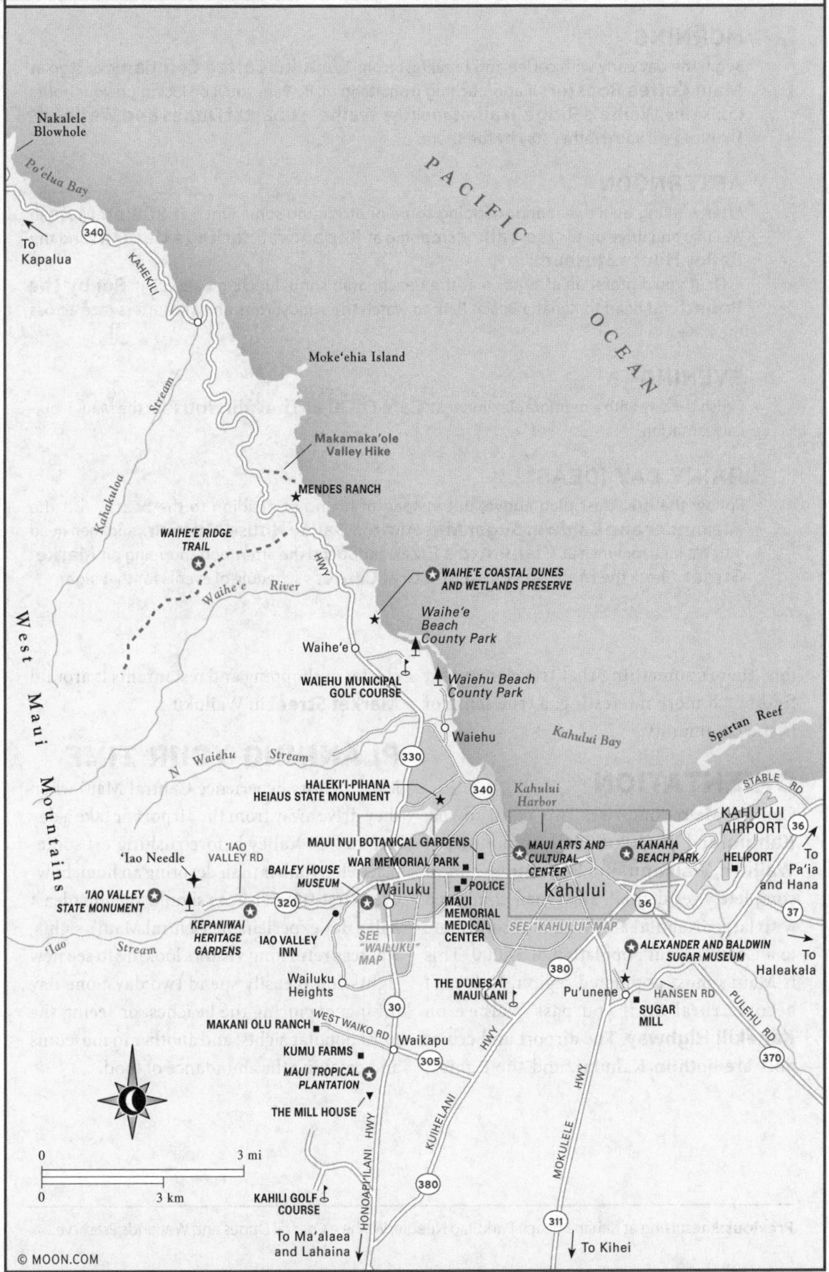

Your Best Day in Central Maui

MORNING

Begin the day early with coffee and breakfast from **Wailuku Coffee Company,** or stop at **Maui Coffee Roasters** if approaching from Kahului. By 9am you'll be lacing up your boots to hike the **Waihe'e Ridge Trail,** or stroll the **Waihe'e Coastal Dunes and Wetlands Preserve** if you'd rather stay by the shore.

AFTERNOON

After working up a sweat and snapping some photos, grab some lunch at **808 on Main** in Wailuku and drive up to **'Iao Valley,** stopping at **Kepaniwai Heritage Gardens** and the **Bailey House Museum.**

Or, if you'd prefer an afternoon at the beach, grab some lunch in Kahului at **Poi by the Pound** and head to Kanaha Beach Park to watch the windsurfers and kitesurfers race across the waves.

EVENING

Finish the day with a memorable dinner at **Café O'Lei at The Mill House** at the Maui Tropical Plantation.

RAINY DAY IDEAS

Follow the breakfast plan above, but instead of hiking or heading to the beach, visit the **Alexander and Baldwin Sugar Museum** and **Bailey House Museum,** and then head into Wailuku for lunch at **Giannotto's Pizza** and spend the afternoon shopping on **Market Street.** Check the **Maui Arts and Cultural Center**'s schedule of events for that night.

tais, there's something that travelers might find much more interesting: a true sense of island community.

ORIENTATION

Central Maui comprises two main towns: **Kahului** and **Wailuku.** The communities of **Waihe'e, Waikapu,** and **Waiehu** are almost completely residential, and when combined with larger Kahului and Wailuku, contribute to a Central Maui population of 57,000. This is Maui's most populated region. It doesn't become rural until you pass Waihe'e on **Kahekili Highway.** The airport and cruise port are both in Kahului, and the tightest cluster of shopping and restaurants is around **Market Street** in Wailuku.

PLANNING YOUR TIME

Most visitors experience Central Maui when they drive away from the airport or take a day trip to 'Iao Valley before rushing off someplace else. Rather than devoting an hour, however, first-time visitors should spend at least half a day experiencing Central Maui's sights, whereas returning visitors looking to see new sights could easily spend two days: one day hiking, exploring the beaches, or seeing the most popular sights, and another in museums and enjoying the abundance of food.

Previous: kitesurfing at Kahana Beach Park; 'Iao Needle; Waihe'e Coastal Dunes and Wetlands Preserve.

Sights

KAHULUI

★ Maui Arts and Cultural Center

One of the reasons that Maui is *no ka oi* (the best) is that it truly does have a little of everything: tropical weather, world-class beaches, and live entertainment and cultural exhibitions on par with any urban center. Though the island has multiple venues for events, none offer the professionalism of the **Maui Arts and Cultural Center** (1 Cameron Way, 808/242-7469, www.mauiarts.org).

Although it doesn't look like much from the highway, when you first step inside the Castle Theater or wander through the Schaefer Gallery, you quickly realize that this is a place you would expect to find in a metropolis. The 1,200-seat Castle Theater has three levels of seating, and the acoustics are designed in such a way that an unamplified guitar can be heard from each seat. The 250-seat McCoy Studio is a black-box theater that hosts smaller plays and theatrical events, while the 5,000-seat A&B amphitheater has drawn some of the world's biggest musical talent, from Elton John to The Eagles. The Maui Film Festival is partially held here on a screen inside the Castle Theater, and movies regularly show throughout the year. The constantly changing schedule of performances is listed on the website, and rarely is there a night there isn't something happening.

Maui Nui Botanical Gardens

For anyone with an interest in Polynesian flora or sustainable farming techniques, the **Maui Nui Botanical Gardens** (150 Kanaloa Ave., 808/249-2798, www.mnbg.org, 8am-4pm Mon.-Sat., free) is an absolute must-stop. From the moment you walk in, native trees and their informational placards are displayed, and small signs warn you to watch out for falling *ulu*, or breadfruit, which populate the treetops above.

On the self-guided walking tour, signs discuss the differences between endemic, indigenous, and introduced plant species, and a central theme is the way traditional irrigation techniques maximize the ability to farm. Freshwater was precious to Polynesian farmers, and more than 70 species of dryland *kalo,* or taro, are successfully growing in a dry coastal dunes system. Although not as expansive as the botanical gardens in Kula, the gardens espouse the Polynesian view that humans are but stewards of the land—placed here on this earth to help protect it for future generations.

★ Alexander and Baldwin Sugar Museum

There's no place on the island where you can gain a better understanding of Maui's plantation heritage than at the **Alexander and Baldwin Sugar Museum** (3957 Hansen Rd., 808/871-8058, www.sugarmuseum.com, 10am-2pm Mon.-Thurs., $7), a small worn-down building in Pu'unene. This town, which was once the beating heart of Maui's sugar industry, has been reduced to a faint pulse: A post office, a bookstore, the museum, and the old sugar mill, which closed in 2016, are all that remain. However, revitalization plans include the addition of an outdoor exhibit of sugar-harvesting equipment and a new building to house historic railway cars.

The $7 entrance fee gets you a yellow booklet called "Passport to the Past," which also includes entry to the Bailey House Museum in Wailuku, as well as Lahaina's Baldwin House Museum and Wo Hing Museum. Here in the Sugar Museum, exhibits discuss everything from sugar's Polynesian roots to historical profiles of the island's first sugar barons. Many of the businessmen who made their fortunes in sugar—Samuel Thomas Alexander and Henry Perrine Baldwin included—were the children of New England missionary

Kahului

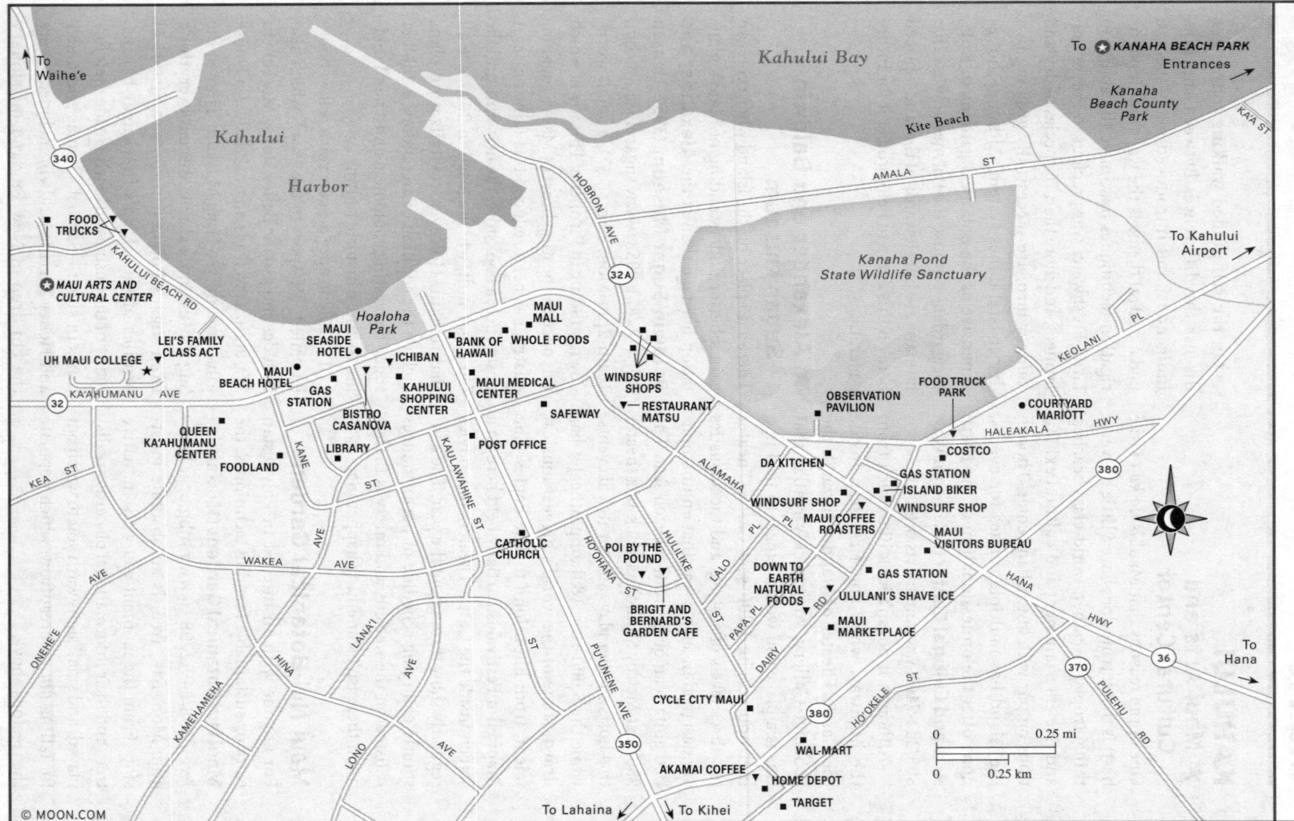
To ★ KANAHA BEACH PARK Entrances
Kanaha Beach County Park
KAA ST
To Kahului Airport
To Hana
Kite Beach
AMALA
ST
Kahului Bay
Kanaha Pond State Wildlife Sanctuary
KEOLANI
PL
HALEAKALA
HWY
380
COURTYARD MARIOTT
FOOD TRUCK PARK
COSTCO
GAS STATION
ISLAND BIKER
WINDSURF SHOP
MAUI VISITORS BUREAU
HANA
HWY
36
370
PULEHU
RD
0.25 mi
0.25 km
0
0
OBSERVATION PAVILION
DA KITCHEN
WINDSURF SHOP
MAUI COFFEE ROASTERS
GAS STATION
ULULANI'S SHAVE ICE
MAUI MARKETPLACE
HO'OKELE
ST
380
WAL-MART
HOME DEPOT
TARGET
DAIRY
RD
PAPA
PL
DOWN TO EARTH NATURAL FOODS
ALAMAHA
PL
LALO
ST
CYCLE CITY MAUI
AKAMAI COFFEE
To Kihei
RESTAURANT MATSU
HULILIKE
BRIGIT AND BERNARD'S GARDEN CAFE
POI BY THE POUND
HO'OHANA
ST
WINDSURF SHOPS
HOBRON
AVE
32A
SAFEWAY
PU'UNENE
AVE
350
To Lahaina
MAUI MALL
WHOLE FOODS
BANK OF HAWAII
MAUI MEDICAL CENTER
POST OFFICE
CATHOLIC CHURCH
ST
KAULAWAHINE
ST
ICHIBAN
KAHULUI SHOPPING CENTER
Hoaloha Park
BISTRO CASANOVA
MAUI SEASIDE HOTEL
GAS STATION
LIBRARY
ST
LANA'I
AVE
LONO
AVE
Kahului Harbor
MAUI BEACH HOTEL
KANE
AVE
WAKEA
AVE
HINA
FOODLAND
QUEEN KA'AHUMANU CENTER
KAMEHAMEHA
LEI'S FAMILY CLASS ACT
KAHULUI BEACH RD
KA'AHUMANU
AVE
MAUI ARTS AND CULTURAL CENTER
UH MAUI COLLEGE
FOOD TRUCKS
340
To Waihe'e
32
KEA
ST
ONEHE'E
AVE
© MOON.COM

Wailuku

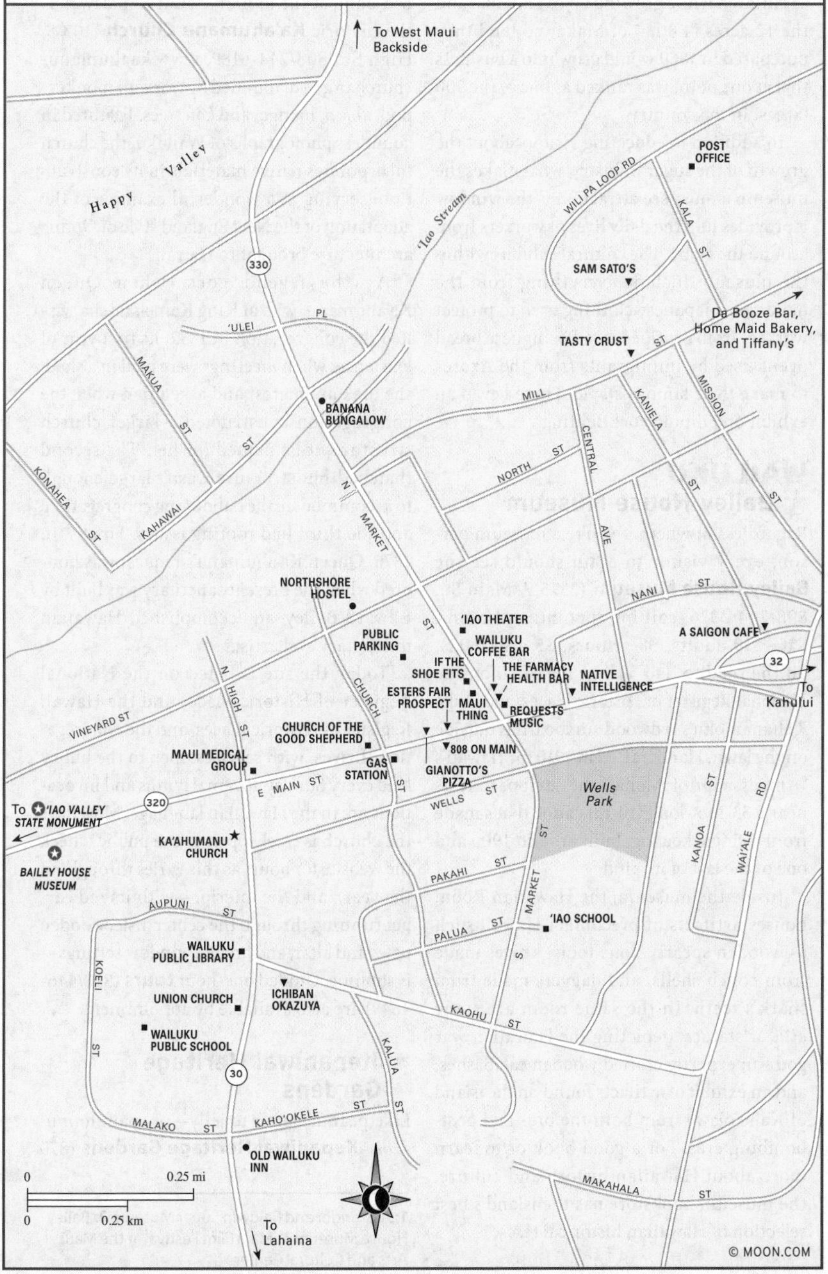

To West Maui Backside
Happy Valley
'Iao Stream
330
'ULEI PL
MAKUA ST
KONAHEA ST
KAHAWAI ST
N MARKET ST
BANANA BUNGALOW
NORTHSHORE HOSTEL
PUBLIC PARKING
'IAO THEATER
WAILUKU COFFEE BAR
IF THE SHOE FITS
THE FARMACY HEALTH BAR
NATIVE INTELLIGENCE
ESTERS FAIR PROSPECT
MAUI THING
REQUESTS MUSIC
CHURCH OF THE GOOD SHEPHERD
808 ON MAIN
GAS STATION
GIANOTTO'S PIZZA
MAUI MEDICAL GROUP
N HIGH ST
CHURCH ST
VINEYARD ST
E MAIN ST
WELLS ST
320
To 'IAO VALLEY STATE MONUMENT
BAILEY HOUSE MUSEUM
KA'AHUMANU CHURCH
Wells Park
PAKAHI ST
S MARKET ST
AUPUNI ST
PALUA ST
'IAO SCHOOL
WAILUKU PUBLIC LIBRARY
ICHIBAN OKAZUYA
UNION CHURCH
WAILUKU PUBLIC SCHOOL
KOELI ST
KAOHU ST
KALUA ST
30
MALAKO ST
KAHO'OKELE ST
OLD WAILUKU INN
To Lahaina
POST OFFICE
WILI PA LOOP RD
KALA ST
SAM SATO'S
Da Booze Bar, Home Maid Bakery, and Tiffany's
TASTY CRUST
ST
MILL ST
MISSION ST
KANIELA ST
CENTRAL AVE
NORTH ST
NANI ST
A SAIGON CAFE
32
To Kahului
KANOA ST
WAI'ALE RD
MAKAHALA ST
0 0.25 mi
0 0.25 km

families who "came to do good and stayed to do well." Alexander and Baldwin actually met as children while growing up in Lahaina, and the 12 acres (4.8 ha) of Makawao land they purchased in 1869 would grow into a business that at one point was ranked as one of the 900 largest in the country.

In addition to educating visitors about the growth of the sugar industry, what makes the museum a must-see attraction is the window it provides into the daily lives of workers from around the globe. The cultural exhibits within the museum include everything from the hand-sewn Japanese clothing used to protect workers from centipedes to Portuguese bread ovens used by immigrants from the Azores to make their famous staple. There's even an exhibit on Filipino cockfighting.

WAILUKU

★ Bailey House Museum

Regardless of whether you're a museum person, every visitor to Maui should see the **Bailey House Museum** (2375-A Main St., 808/244-3326, call for appointment Mon.-Sat., $10 adults, $8 seniors, $5 ages 7-12), on the road to 'Iao Valley. It's listed on the National Register of Historic Places, and Duke Kahanamoku's redwood surfboard is outside on the lawn. Handcrafted in 1910 for Hawaii's "Ambassador of Aloha," the surfboard rests near a 33-foot-long (10-m) canoe that's made from a single koa log, built around 1900 and one of the last of its kind.

Inside the museum, the Hawaiian Room houses artifacts of precontact Hawaii such as wooden spears, stone tools, knives made from conch shells, and daggers made from shark's teeth. In the same room are stone *ki'i*, or statues, depicting the Hawaiian war god Ku; expertly crafted wooden calabashes; and an exhibit of artifacts found on the island of Kaho'olawe from both the pre- and post-bombing eras. For a good book or to learn more about Hawaiian history and culture, the museum bookstore has the island's best selection of Hawaiian historical texts.

Ka'ahumanu Church

Just down the street from the Bailey House Museum, at the foot of Mount Kahalawai, is the historic **Ka'ahumanu Church** (103 S. High St., 808/244-5189, www.kaahumanuchurch.org), surrounded by tranquil monkeypod, *kukui*, mango, and *kou* trees. Featured in countless photographs of Wailuku, the church incorporates native materials in its construction, serving as a wonderful example of the adaptation of the New England style of Gothic architecture brought to Hawaii.

As the legend goes, when Queen Ka'ahumanu, wife of King Kamehameha, visited the congregation in 1832, its first year of existence, when meetings were held in a shed, she took an interest and asked that when the congregation constructed a larger church structure, it be named for her. The second thatched-hut structure wasn't large enough to accommodate the ballooning congregation, and the third had roofing issues. Finally, in 1876, Queen Ka'ahumanu's request was honored when the present sanctuary was built by Edward Bailey, an accomplished Hawaiian missionary and artist.

Today the site is listed on the National Register of Historic Places and the Hawaii Register of Historic Places, and the congregation thrives, with services open to the public held every Sunday at 9am. Hymns and invocations are in the Hawaiian language. Most days the church is freely open to the public (check the website for hours as this varies throughout the year), and the interior—with its red carpet running through the center aisle, wooden pews and altar, and arched window settings—is sublime. Guided one-hour **tours** (808/446-4649) are also available by appointment.

★ Kepaniwai Heritage Gardens

Like peanut butter to jelly—or spam to *musubi*—**Kepaniwai Heritage Gardens** (870

1: Alexander and Baldwin Sugar Museum **2:** Bailey House Museum **3:** Maui Film Festival at the Maui Arts and Cultural Center

ALEXANDER & BALDWIN
SUGAR
MUSEUM
Visit the
PLANTATION STORE
GIFT SHOP!
1

2

3

The Battle of Kepaniwai

Given the calming nature of Kepaniwai, it's tough to believe this narrow river canyon was the site of one of Hawaii's fiercest conflicts. Before King Kamehameha united all the islands under a single crown in 1810, opposing chiefs frequently waged battles in an effort to expand their influence. Having already conquered much of the island of Hawaii, Kamehameha sailed to Maui in 1790 with 1,200 warriors and landed at the protected waters of Kahului Bay. Though Kahekili—the reigning chief on Maui—was away on O'ahu at the time, Kamehameha met fierce opposition from the Maui warriors who, under the leadership of Kahekili's son Kalanikupule, had positioned themselves just a few miles away at the entrance to 'Iao Valley.

Using wooden spears and clubs spiked with shark's teeth, Kamehameha's forces chased Kalanikupule's warriors deep into the valley in an evenly matched battle. After two days of fighting, neither side could claim victory. It's said that on the third day of battle, Kamehameha employed two cannons he had acquired from Western explorers. The spears and stones of the Maui warriors were no match for the explosive cannons, and by the end of the third day, Kamehameha's forces had gained a hard-won victory. Over the course of the battle, not only did 'Iao Stream run red with the blood of the vanquished, but the bodies of the deceased formed a natural dam that blocked much of its flow. This dark history lives on today in the name Kepaniwai, which translates as "damming of the waters."

'Iao Valley Rd., 808/270-7232, 7am-5:30pm daily, free) goes hand in hand with a visit to 'Iao Valley. Tucked on the banks of 'Iao Stream, this simple but informative cultural park is far more interesting than it looks, as it details Maui's "mixed plate" culture. In addition to pavilions that make great picnic spots (and double as great drinking spots for locals), the park features a small monument devoted to each of the island's plantation-era immigrant communities—Japanese, Chinese, Puerto Rican, and Portuguese, each monument with a small dwelling constructed in traditional style.

Along the stream are a few places where you can swim in the shallow (and cold!) waters, although use some caution when scrambling down the bank as there aren't any official trails. Unless you're a major history buff, 30 minutes here will suffice.

TOP EXPERIENCE

★ 'Iao Valley State Monument

This is one of those Maui attractions that could turn into a dud—that is, if you focus on the destination, rather than the journey. Much like driving the Road to Hana and not stopping until you get there, traveling to **'Iao Valley State Monument** (end of 'Iao Valley Rd., 7am-6pm daily, $5 entrance, $10 parking) simply to see the park is a misguided mindset. Rather, the allure lies in leaving the streets of Wailuku behind to make the turn down 'Iao Valley Road through a thick canopy of trees. Here you'll find chickens crossing the road, rural houses, fields, and farms at the base of vertical cliffs.

Crane your neck and look skyward toward peaks that tickle the passing clouds, and embrace the feeling you've suddenly traveled 100 years back in time. When you reach the park at the end of the road, rather than hastily parking, walking, and rushing to see the 'Iao Needle, take a moment to read the history of all that's happened in the park, from the gruesome and bloody Battle of Kepaniwai to how soldiers would use the valley ridgelines to spot warriors approaching from sea.

When you do begin to hike the "trail," a walkway with 133 steps, admire the landscape that lines the edge of the stream. Once you conquer the stairs, you're met with a

1: 'Iao Stream **2:** zip-lining at the Maui Tropical Plantation **3:** Kepaniwai Heritage Gardens

1

2

3

view of **Kuka'emoku**—better known as **'Iao Needle**—rising 2,250 feet (685 m) above the distant shore. While most visitors tend to focus on and photograph the needle, what's more spectacular are the rugged ridgelines and isolated interior of the mountain, which is so inaccessible and untouched it's believed the bones of Hawaiian royalty are buried deep inside caves where they'll never be disturbed.

★ Maui Tropical Plantation

Talk about a place that's come back to life: There was a time when the **Maui Tropical Plantation** (1670 Honoapi'ilani Hwy., 808/244-7643, www.mauitropicalplantation.com, 9am-4pm Tues.-Sat., free) was a popular Maui highlight, but gradually the luster started to fade and the clientele grew old. That's changed now that new owners have set up features such as zip-line tours (page 126), a coffee shop, an ice cream stand, an art gallery, and a fresh organic farm stand. Best of all, the palate-bending Café O'Lei at The Mill House restaurant is on the property, and much of the food served is sourced right here on the farm (page 134).

The longtime draw is the **Tropical Express Tram Tour** ($25 adults, $12.50 children), otherwise known as "the train," a 40-minute ride that runs seven times 10am-4pm daily, making a loop through surrounding fields as the driver discusses the crops. While children will be excited to ride on a train (it's the island's last), adults will enjoy the informative commentary.

If it happens to be open, be sure to swing by **Kumu Farms** (808/244-4800, 9am-4pm Tues.-Sat.), to the right of the parking lot entrance. This fantastic certified-organic market is one of the island's best, where you can purchase food grown on property at a fraction of store prices. Produce is picked 25 feet (7.5 m) from the farm stand, so there isn't anywhere else on Maui with produce this fresh. The farm features cilantro, peppers, chard, eggplant, carrots, and the famous sunrise papayas that are grown at the sister store on Moloka'i. You can also purchase homemade mac nut basil pesto, or cuts of grass-fed Waikapu beef for around $6 per pound ($13 per kg). If you're staying on the West Side of the island and plan to cook in your condo, there's no better place to pick up your produce on your drive from Central Maui.

Haleki'i and Pihana Heiau

Few island visitors stop at the **Haleki'i and Pihana Heiau,** which is a shame, considering their historical importance. This site is officially classified as a Hawaii state park, but the gate to the *heiau* (temple) is no longer open for vehicular access and its condition has fallen into disrepair. Nevertheless, it's still easy to park on the street in front of the *heiau* and make the five-minute walk up the hill.

In ancient Hawaii these two *heiau* served as the religious center of the entire Wailuku *ahupua'a,* or land division. Many of Maui's ruling *ali'i* came here to either honor their deceased or commune with religious deities. It's believed that Keopuolani, the woman who would become queen, was born here at Pihana *heiau,* a site that is also believed to have been a *luakini heiau,* used for human sacrifice. Hawaiian scholars believe that one of the last human sacrifices on the island was performed here at Pihana in 1790 by King Kamehameha after his victory at the Battle of Kepaniwai. Much of Pihana *heiau* was destroyed during the 19th century when the Hawaiian monarchy converted to Christianity, but numerous walls and terraces from Haleki'i still remain.

To reach the *heiau,* travel along Waiehu Beach Road until you cross the bridge over 'Iao Stream. On the other side, make the first left onto Kuhio Place and then the first left onto Hea Place. Since the access gate to the *heiau* will likely be locked, park on the street and walk up the access road. Don't be surprised if the neighbor's dog barks—just keep walking up the hill.

Kahakuloa

Technically Kahakuloa is part of Wailuku, but this old fishing village is an entity unto itself. Lonely and remote, there are few places

The Road to Kahakuloa

If driving to Hana was the scariest thing you've ever done, you might want to take a rain check on the Road to Kahakuloa. There are sheer drop-offs with no guardrails, completely blind turns, and the occasional rockslide that will send boulders down onto the highway. The narrowest section of the road is between Mendes Ranch and Kahakuloa village, which leads many visitors to travel from Kapalua and then retreat the way they came. For a bit of adventure, however, you can drive the whole way on one of the most scenic, hair-raising drives you can take in Hawaii.

A lot of confusion surrounds the drive. Some car-rental maps show the road as for 4WD vehicles only. Others say that it's one lane. Still others say you shouldn't drive it at all. Despite the dangers, incidents are rare. The road does not require a 4WD vehicle. It's paved, although some sections can be bumpy. The road is narrow, and at some places only wide enough for one car.

Utilize these simple techniques to make what would have been a white-knuckle drive through the wilderness one of the island's best day trips:

TOP FIVE THINGS TO KNOW

1. Decide on a direction. If you're departing from West Maui and moving clockwise around the mountain, you have the benefit of being on the inside lane and away from the steep cliff faces. This is the most popular way to visit, after an outing to Nakalele Blowhole. Then again, since you are pressed against the mountainside instead of against the ocean, you run the risk of falling rocks coming down after a heavy rain. If you approach from the Wailuku direction and drive in a counterclockwise direction around the mountain, be sure the person in the passenger seat isn't afraid of heights.

2. Don't sightsee and drive at the same time. If you're driving, keep your eyes firmly glued to the road. If you want to take photos, pull over.

3. Go slow and be mindful. Drive carefully around corners and honk your horn on those you can't see around. Put the cell phone away, and turn the radio off so you can hear if anyone is honking from the other direction.

4. Take breaks. Use the gravel pullouts on the side of the road and let other cars behind you pass if you're feeling rushed or nervous.

5. Collaborate with other drivers. All drivers on this road are experiencing pretty much the same adventurous backroad as you are, and coordination is sometimes necessary to share the road wisely. If you encounter another car at a narrow spot, don't fret. One or the other of you might just have to slowly reverse to the nearest pullout to give the other car room to pass.

left in Hawaii that are quite like Kahakuloa. Many choose to get to Kahakuloa from the West Side of the island by following the road past Kapalua, Honolua Bay, and Nakalele Blowhole, but because this road is a loop, Kahakuloa can similarly be accessed from Wailuku. It will take you 30-45 minutes to reach Kahakuloa from Wailuku—and there aren't any gas stations—so be sure you have at least half a tank of gas before driving along the coast.

Following Kahekili Highway (Hwy. 340) past Mendes Ranch and Makamaka'ole Valley, the road becomes narrow and the foliage dense. The first stop is **Turnbull Studios & Sculpture** (5030 Kahekili Hwy., 808/244-0101, www.turnbullfineart.com, 10am-5pm daily), an eclectic sculpture garden with handmade crafts by local Hawaiian artists. The artist has been making sculptures at this mountainside garden for over 25 years. There are only a few parking spaces, and if it's been raining heavily, think twice before going down the short but steep driveway in a low-clearance rental car.

Farther down the road you'll reach

the **Karen Lei's Gallery at Kahakuloa** (808/244-3371, www.karenleisgallery.com, 9am-5pm daily), inside a mountaintop home overlooking Kahakuloa Valley. The gallery features more than 120 local artists and their paintings, jewelry, and crafts, and the views from the parking lot looking up the valley make it the most scenic gallery on the island.

Finally, after a few hairpin turns on a narrow one-lane road, you reach the village of Kahakuloa, accurately called "old Hawaii" and "a place that time has forgotten." The town offers visitors a unique opportunity to glimpse Hawaiian traditions, still in practice, which managed to evade modernity. If you continue driving, you'll reach Kapalua in approximately 14 miles (22.5 km).

Beaches

The little-known beaches of Central Maui are defined by wind and water sports. You won't find any tiki bars or rows of beachfront cabanas, but you will find narrow stretches of sand where the world's best boarders hang out.

KAHULUI

★ Kanaha Beach Park

Kanaha Beach Park, right next to the airport, is one of those places where you ask yourself, "How did I not know this was here?" What it lacks in visitor friendliness (it's a frequent hangout for some of the island's unhoused population), the park makes up for with vibrant energy—particularly in the afternoon. You'll find windsurfers, kitesurfers, paddleboarders, and surfers out riding the waves, and on Sunday the park is bumping with barbecues and pickup games of beach volleyball.

In the early morning, before the wind picks up, this is the perfect place for a long stroll on the string of sandy beaches, where the dramatic ridgelines of Mauna Kahalawai rise from the turquoise waters. In the afternoon, the cobalt waters become flecked with whitecaps and dozens of colorful sails as windsurfers and kitesurfers race across the water—particularly in summer, when

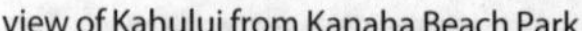

view of Kahului from Kanaha Beach Park

it's windier. The large, grassy beach park has showers and restrooms, and there's a roped-off area for swimming to cool off or wade. It's also a convenient place to hang out if you've already checked out of your hotel and are killing time before an evening flight, since it's only minutes from the airport.

To reach Kanaha from Hana Highway, make a right at the stoplight for Hobron Avenue and then another right onto Amala Place. Drive for about 1.5 miles (2.4 km). The best entrances for Kanaha Beach Park are the two at the end of the road. For a shortcut, loop through the airport, past Arrivals and Departures, and make a right onto Ka'a Street, continuing past the car-rental counters until you reach the end of the road. Turn right; the beach park is on the left.

Kite Beach

Next to Kanaha Beach Park, **Kite Beach** is the place on the island for Maui's kitesurfing crowd. The narrow strip of sand has multiple entrances—all with sand or dirt parking lots—and you can expect kitesurfers to start launching between 11am and noon.

Stable Road

To really get away from it all and just relax on an empty patch of sand, the string of beaches off **Stable Road** are a bit of a local secret. You'll find fishers casting rods and dropped tailgates with coolers, but if you walk a couple of yards down the beach, you can usually find your own patch of sand that's perfect for a chair and book. Afternoons are often windy—and don't expect any snorkeling—but a couple of spots are deep enough for swimming, and days with light wind are gorgeous. To reach Stable Road, drive on Hana Highway (Hwy. 36) in the direction of Pa'ia, and 1.4 miles (2.3 km) from the junction with Haleakala Highway (Hwy. 37), make a left onto a narrow paved road. From here, travel about 0.5 mile (0.8 km) until you see sandy parking lots on the right side.

Surfing

The majority of surfing on this side of the island takes place October-April. Some eastward-facing locations can pick up wind swell during the summer months, but it's choppy and sloppy. There are no surf schools that operate along this stretch of coast, and anyone opting to surf around here needs to be at least an intermediate surfer. On the biggest winter swells, teams of professional surfers have been known to tow-surf the outer reefs here, where waves can reach 70 feet (21 m). Thanks, but we'll be watching from shore.

SURF SPOTS

Kahului

For longboarding and stand-up paddle surfing, **Lowers** at Kanaha Beach Park (page 118) is a popular North Shore favorite. When standing on the sand, look for the lifeguard tower, which is where you'll paddle out. The wave at Kanaha breaks on an offshore reef and requires an arm-burning paddle, but a long paddle means a long ride, and the surf usually won't close out until the faces reach 10 feet (3 m). Mornings are best before the wind picks up, which is usually around 11am.

Wailuku

The most popular surf break in Wailuku is **Big Lefts** in Paukukalo. This is a long left-hand wave that can get very big on north and northeasterly swells, although it's for advanced surfers only and is heavily localized. To access the surf break, turn onto Waiehu Beach Road and then make a right on Ukali Street, following it to the end. The surf break is in front of the parking lot. Don't leave any valuables in your car, give locals the set waves, and stick to hopping the shoulder.

For a mellow longboarding wave, there's a

break in front of **Waiehu Beach Park** that usually has fewer people than neighboring Paukukalo. The wave quality isn't as good, but this is still a good wave in the early morning during any north swell. To reach Waiehu Beach Park, travel along Waiehu Beach Road before taking a right turn on Lower Waiehu Beach Road, and follow it to the parking lot at the end.

WINDSURFING

Maui is one of the world's top destinations for windsurfing, and at **Kanaha Beach Park,** the trade winds are so consistent during the summer months that they arrive like clockwork around 11am. In winter, the trade winds are a little less consistent, and waves can reach 15 feet (4.6 m) or higher.

There's strictly no windsurfing before 11am, and Kanaha is split into two main launching areas conveniently named **Uppers** and **Lowers.** Many of the windsurfing schools operate by Uppers at a cove known as Kook's Beach. Lowers is in the area by the lifeguard tower, the preferred launching point. If there are waves breaking on the reef, you'll notice a channel off the lifeguard stand where you can get past the break and out beyond the surf.

For more information on Maui windsurfing, go to www.mauiwindsurfing.net for photos, rental operators, and descriptions of the various launching sites.

KITESURFING

The best place for kitesurfing on Maui is at the aptly named **Kite Beach** (page 119), a place of hallowed ground where the sport was born. This is the beach where all kitesurfing schools operate, and just as at neighboring Kanaha, the crowd is international. Even if you aren't a kitesurfer, this is a fantastic spot to sit and watch as dozens of colorful kites zip through the gusty trade winds. Since Kite Beach is so close to Kanaha Beach Park, the unwritten rule is that kitesurfers are supposed to stay downwind (closer to Kahului Harbor) of the windsurfers to avoid high-speed entanglement. Even though this is one of the premier spots on the planet for kitesurfing, unless you're an experienced kitesurfer, lessons are imperative.

For more information about kitesurfing on Maui, check out www.kitesurfmaui.org. For a webcam of current wind and weather conditions, go to www.kitebeachcam.com.

RENTAL SHOPS

Of all the rental shops in Kahului, **HI-Tech Surf Sports** (425 Koloa St., 808/877-2111, www.surfmaui.com, 9am-6pm daily) has the largest selection of surfboards ($25 per day) and stand-up paddleboards ($35 per day), with discounts for longer rentals.

Other reputable rental spots include **Second Wind Sail Surf & Kite** (111 Hana Hwy., 808/877-7467, www.secondwindmaui.com, 10am-5pm daily) and **Kanaha Kai** (140 Hobron Ave., 808/877-7778, www.kanahakai.com, 10am-4pm Mon.-Sat.), which is the closest shop to the beach. Expect stand-up paddleboards to cost about $35 per day, and downwind boards $35-55. Windsurfing rigs are about $57-67, and kitesurf rigs about $85.

SCHOOLS AND LESSONS

When it comes to windsurfing and kitesurfing on Maui, one class isn't enough. Ideally you want to book at least a five-hour package to maximize your investment, although every school offers a single-session option if you just want to test the waters.

One of the best schools on the island is **Hawaiian Sailboard Techniques** (425 Koloa St., 808/871-5423, www.hstwindsurfing.com), inside HI-Tech Surf Sports. Founder Alan Cadiz has been teaching windsurfing on Maui since 1985, making this the longest-running outfit on the island's North Shore. Cadiz was one of the first instructors to teach the sport to others, and an instructor will accompany you on a stand-up paddleboard. Three-hour kitesurfing lessons are $299, and private windsurfing starts at $270. Stand-up paddle lessons begin at $299 for a two-hour class, and if you're experienced, ask about

Stand-Up Paddling: The Maliko Run

In the sport of downwind stand-up paddling, there's no stretch of water more legendary and hallowed than the 9-mile-long (14.5-km) Maliko Run. It's the spot where downwind racing was born, and the place where the world's best train for the professional tour.

In a "downwinder," paddlers position the wind at their backs and glide on the open ocean, connecting "bumps," or ocean swells, that pass beneath the board. When done properly, it's possible to feel like you're surfing on a wave that virtually has no end, and your mind and body are exceptionally aligned with the ocean movements beneath you. In the Maliko Run, paddlers begin at Maliko Gulch to the east of Ho'okipa Beach Park and paddle downwind to either Kahului Harbor or the beach at Kanaha Beach Park. On a typical day, paddlers will be up to a mile (1.6 km) offshore and in winds of 30 mph (48 km/h), riding on ocean swells that can range from knee-high to a couple of feet overhead. Average paddlers complete the 9-mile (14.5-km) run between Maliko and the harbor in a little under two hours, whereas the world's top paddlers can finish the course in a little over an hour—a seven-minute mile pace.

Maliko Runs are a favorite weekend activity of the island's water sports enthusiasts, and over 200 racers gather each year for the professional races, with one of the largest being the OluKai race at the end of April. A Maliko Run isn't an activity for anyone who isn't an avid stand-up paddler, but for stand-up paddling enthusiasts, this is the Holy Grail.

If you're a competent paddler and have lots of experience in the ocean, **More Watertime** (www.malikoshuttle.com) has a shuttle service ($15-18 pp; cash is preferred and exact change is encouraged) with daily runs to Maliko that leave from Kanaha and Kahului Harbor. For boards, an increasing number of Kahului shops are now renting race boards, and a couple of schools will even provide lessons where an experienced instructor can accompany you.

doing the Maliko Run along with a professional guide.

One of the largest schools is **Action Sports Maui** (808/283-7913, www.actionsportsmaui.com, 9am-5pm Mon.-Sat.), where kite foilboarding lessons range from $285 for a two-hour intro class to $1,250 for a five-day intensive training package. Windsurfing lessons range from $389 for two hours to a five-day course ($489 pp group, $975 private).

Kitesurfing School of Maui (808/873-0015, www.ksmaui.com) focuses specifically on kitesurfing, and offers a $285 three-hour semi-private package, or $1,025 for nine hours (a better option for actually learning the sport). **Aqua Sports** (808/242-8015, www.mauikiteboardinglessons.com) is right on Kite Beach and offers a $300 one-day beginner special.

Hiking and Biking

HIKING

'Iao Valley

From the winding drive back into the mountains, you would think that popular 'Iao Valley would offer some good hiking. In reality, the only hike is the paved walking trail that leads to the 'Iao Needle lookout.

If you want to swim in 'Iao Stream, the best place for accessing the swimming holes is from Kepaniwai Heritage Gardens, where short trails lead down to the refreshing—and cold—water.

★ Waihe'e Coastal Dunes and Wetlands Preserve

Here's a hike that's wildly underrated: Set on land protected by the Hawaiian Islands

West Maui's Backside

Land Trust, the 2-mile (3.2-km) trail in the **Waihe'e Coastal Dunes and Wetlands Preserve** runs the length of one of Maui's last undeveloped shorelines. Within the 277-acre (112-ha) preserve are the remains of the Kapoho fishing village as well as two different ancient *heiau*. Scholars estimate that the Waihe'e area was populated as early as AD 300-600, which is not surprising, as the freshwater streams, fertile valleys, and lush uplands provide all the natural resources to sustain life. In modern times this area was once slated for development as a golf community, although by raising funds through events such as the annual Buy Back the Beach dinner, the land trust was able to preserve this culturally rich shore and honor its history.

The trail parallels the shore and passes by a couple of abandoned houses before reaching the cultural relics at Kapoho. Expect the round-trip journey to take a little over an hour; add 30 minutes to explore the coast or ruins. To reach the trailhead, make a right on Halewaiu Place off Kahekili Highway (Hwy. 340) and follow the signs for Waiehu Golf Course. When the road makes a sharp turn to the right and starts heading toward the golf course, notice an unmarked dirt road going to the left. Park here, because around the corner is a stream crossing that's unsuitable for rental cars. Traveling on foot, the trailhead will be on the left, just uphill from the stream crossing. Avoid leaving valuables in your car.

★ Waihe'e Ridge Trail

The parking area for the **Waihe'e Ridge Trail** is at mile marker 7 of Kahekili Highway, across from Mendes Ranch. If the gate is open, which it usually is 7am-7pm daily, continue driving for another mile (1.6 km) to the upper parking area. This 2.5-mile (4-km) trail starts on a steep concrete incline, but fear not—if you can make it up this, you can make it the rest of the way. Eventually the trail levels out a bit and the concrete changes to dirt, which

1: Waihe'e Coastal Dunes and Wetlands Preserve
2: view from the Waihe'e Ridge Trail

1
2

can often lead to muddy conditions, particularly if it has recently rained. But oh, the views! This trail rises to 2,560 feet (780 m) elevation, the highest hiking trail in West Maui, and offers sweeping views into Waihe'e and Makamaka'ole Valleys. In the distance, Makamaka'ole Falls tumbles dramatically through the forest; look the other direction, and the turquoise waters of the Waihe'e shore form a dramatic backdrop. The trail continues to Lanilili summit, where you can see the northern slope of the mountain on clear days. If you start hiking before 9am, you'll usually get clear conditions. This trail takes some energy, so count on three hours for the 5-mile (8-km) trip.

Makamaka'ole Valley

There aren't many waterfalls in Central Maui that you can access, but one exception is at **Makamaka'ole Valley,** off the side of Kahekili Highway. Approaching from Wailuku, the discreet trailhead is 0.8 mile (1.3 km) past Mendes Ranch. At this point the road has climbed in elevation and narrowed in places to a single lane. You'll pass a sharp turn in the valley, and when the road starts pointing back toward the ocean, you'll notice a small dirt pullout that can accommodate four or five vehicles.

The trailhead is a very narrow but well-defined dirt pathway that heads downhill into the brush. There's also a false trailhead that departs from the same parking area but only goes for a few yards. If the trail suddenly ends, turn around and look for the other one. Once you are on the correct trail, it will wind its way downhill for about 10 minutes before arriving at a small swimming hole, where you'll find a rushing waterfall and a rope swing. Along the way you're rewarded with a dramatic view of Makamaka'ole Valley as it weaves toward the ocean below.

After the first swimming hole, the trail continues deeper into the valley toward a waterfall more dramatic than the first. You have to climb over a large boulder and move branches aside to keep following the trail, which then parallels the stream over some slippery rocks. The mosquitoes can be vicious in this shaded section, so be sure you're covered. After five minutes, the trail ends at a large banyan tree whose serpentine roots snake down a near-vertical cliff face. In order to reach the pool below, climb down using the roots of the banyan as if descending a ladder. This maneuver requires athletic ability and skill, so it should only be attempted by those who are agile and accepting of the risks. The reward, however, is a small swimming hole where you can bathe beneath a waterfall in a hidden tropical setting.

HIKING TOURS

Guided hiking tours of the Waihe'e area are available through **Unique Maui Tours** (844/550-6284, www.uniquemauitours.com). Prices start at $79 per person for custom group hikes with spectacular views, and the guides have lots of local knowledge and stories.

BIKING

The lone Central Maui mountain biking trail is in the **Kahakuloa Game Management Area,** where a 5-mile-long (8-km) 4WD road rises 1,600 vertical feet (485 m). Wear bright-colored clothing because it's also a hunting area. The turnoff from Kahekili Highway is between mile markers 40 and 41.

The **road bike ride to Kahakuloa** is one of the best on the island, where cyclists are treated to quad-burning ascents, hairpin turns through the rainforest, and sweeping views of the entire North Shore. Sharing the road with cars can be tough, considering how narrow it gets, but most cars are traveling so slowly around the tight turns that altercations are rare.

To be on a designated bike path that stays on level ground, the **North Shore Greenway** runs from the last parking lot at Kanaha Beach Park all the way to the town of Pa'ia. To reach the Kahului terminus of the bike path, follow Amala Place all the way to the end and park in the last parking lot of Kanaha Beach Park. Parts of the bike path go directly behind the airport runway. This ride is best in the morning hours before the wind picks up.

Rental Shops

Across the street from K-Mart, **Island Biker Maui** (415 Dairy Rd., 808/877-7744, www.islandbikermaui.com, 10am-5pm Mon.-Fri., 9am-3pm Sat.) offers rentals that begin at $75 per day or $250 per week. Mountain bikes and road bikes are available.

Horseback Riding and Bird-Watching

HORSEBACK RIDING

You know a ranch is the real deal when you can smell it before you see it. The family-run **Mendes Ranch** (3530 Kahekili Hwy., 808/871-5222, www.mendesranch.com, $135), on the road toward Kahakuloa, has managed 300 head of cattle since the 1940s, when it was just a homestead. Today, aside from the sweeping ocean views and trails that run along the coast, what makes Mendes such a popular option is that rather than nose-to-tail riding, you can run the horses on a 1.5-hour authentic *paniolo* (cowboy) experience of life on a working ranch. Rides depart at 9am and 12:30pm Monday-Saturday.

More centrally located is **Makani Olu Ranch** (363 W. Waiko Rd., 808/870-0663, www.makanioluranch.com), a working cattle ranch in Waikapu Valley with nearly 100 longhorn cattle. Rides accommodate four people at most, and since the entire ride is at a walking pace, this is a great option for novice riders who just want the view from the saddle.

The ride traverses Waikapu Valley and crosses Waikapu Stream, allowing you access to a part of the island you'd otherwise never see. From the lookout points, the views are back toward the central isthmus, as well as up the valley walls leading deep into the heart of the mountains. Two-hour rides are $150, and you can upgrade to a three-hour ride ($175) that includes lunch while riding through the valley. If you're nervous about getting on a horse, the Makani Olu Ranch Ride ($75) includes a one-hour lesson before heading out on the trail. Because it's located in the middle of the island, the ranch is only 25 minutes from Wailea, and 35 minutes from Ka'anapali.

BIRD-WATCHING

Kahului

Despite being smack in the middle of town, the **Kanaha Pond State Wildlife Sanctuary** houses as many as 90 species of native and migratory birds. Only five minutes from the Kahului Airport, this area was once a royal fishpond that was built in the 1700s. It provided the island's *ali'i,* or chiefs, with a consistent supply of mullet, although the dredging of Kahului Harbor in 1910 altered the natural flow of water.

Today this is where you'll spot the endangered Hawaiian stilt (*ae'o*), a slender, 16-inch (41-cm) bird with sticklike pink legs that, according to most recent population estimates, numbers around 2,000 statewide. The Hawaiian coot (*'alae ke'oke'o*), a gray-black duck-like bird that builds large floating nests, may also be seen here, and the sanctuary is open free of charge August 31-March 31. In summer, when the sanctuary is closed for nesting season, an observation pavilion is maintained on the pond's south edge, which is open year-round. To access the trails inside the sanctuary, entry is through the gates on Amala Place on the road to Kanaha Beach Park.

Wailuku

The best places for bird-watching in Wailuku are the **Waihe'e Coastal Dunes and Wetlands Preserve** (page 121), where you can spot seabirds in the low grass, and the **Waihe'e Ridge Trail** (page 122), where the song of indigenous Hawaiian forest birds might accompany your hike.

ZIP-LINE TOURS

For travelers who only go big or go home, the eight-line **Flyin Hawaiian Zipline** (1670 Honoapi'ilani Hwy., 808/463-5786, www.flyinhawaiianzipline.com, 8am-3pm Mon.-Sat., $219) covers 2.5 miles (4 km) of West Maui mountainside and finishes in a different town. The most enticing reason to book this tour is the ultra-long, cheek-clenching, three-screamer zip line that runs for more than 3,600 feet (1,100 m)—the longest on the island. The lines aren't parallel, and the height off the ground isn't as high as the fifth line at Pi'iholo, but you also get a short ATV ride at the end as they shuttle you back where you started.

In addition to views toward Haleakala, this zip-line ecotour incorporates elements of habitat restoration for Hawaii's native plants and works to remove nonnative species. The company champions sustainable, educational tourism, and the ecological element of the organization isn't just something done to appear green—it's the real deal. Expect the tour to take 4-5 hours. Small snacks are included. Riders must be 10 years old and weigh 75-250 pounds (34-113 kg). Guests meet at the Maui Tropical Plantation for a 4WD ride back into Waikapu Valley, where you suit up for your midair journey across the mountain. This tour often sells out well in advance, so reservations are a must.

If you'd rather ease into it, or are traveling with children, the most beginner-friendly zip line in the central valley is **Maui Zipline** (1670 Honoapi'ilani Hwy., 808/633-2464, www.mauizipline.com, 8am-5pm daily, $125), on the grounds of the Maui Tropical Plantation. Children as young as five and as light as 45 pounds (20 kg) can take part in this five-line adventure; children under age 11 must be joined by an adult. Because the course caters to young children, it isn't as extreme as some others, but the guides introduce educational elements to the program, such as the weather patterns of the area and lessons on plant species, making this a great option for families. Cable lengths range 300-900 feet (90-275 m), and there are two cables running parallel to each other, so you can go two at a time.

HELICOPTER RIDES

You heard it here first: Helicopter tours are the island's best splurge. They're expensive, and some people find them scary, but they are the best way to experience Maui's beauty. The majority of the island is only accessible by helicopter, and until you've seen waterfalls powerfully plunging through hidden mist-shrouded valleys or buzzed below the world's tallest sea cliffs and seen humpback whales from the air, you'll never know the breadth of beauty that Maui really has to offer. All pilots have logged thousands of flying hours and put an emphasis on safety, and when narrating the tours, most also provide information on geology, biology, and history. Morning tours are best because they offer the clear conditions necessary for visiting spots such as 1,100-foot (335-m) **Honokohau Falls,** Maui's tallest waterfall, or peering into **Haleakala Crater.**

All helicopter flights depart from the **Kahului Heliport** (0.5 mi/0.8 km from the junction of Hana Hwy. and Haleakala Hwy.), and the two most popular tour options are those combining the West Maui Mountains with Moloka'i, and East Maui (Hana) with Haleakala. Regardless of which operator you choose, inquire about getting the two front seats next to the pilot, since it's much easier to take photos. If you're really serious about photos, wear long sleeves and dark-colored clothing to avoid reflection in the window, and to get really pro, consider wearing gloves. Remember that you cannot have been scuba diving within 24 hours before the flight (although snuba is OK). All prices listed are for advance online reservations.

Air Maui (1 Keolani Pl., Hangar 110, 808/877-7005, www.airmaui.com) has a perfect safety record and has options you won't find elsewhere, including the West Maui and Moloka'i tour ($279 pp), where you tour the mountains and marvel at thundering waterfalls. There are also standard West Maui-Moloka'i and Hana-Haleakala tours, including one with a cliff-side landing on the back side of Haleakala. All helicopters are the A-Star variety, which seat up to six.

The largest operator on the island, with cheaper flights, is **Blue Hawaiian Helicopters** (1 Lelepio Pl., 808/871-8844, www.bluehawaiian.com), operating both A-Star and more expensive ECO-Star helicopters, with individual bucket seats and larger viewing windows. Options include the Waterfalls of West Maui and Molokai ($369 pp) and Hana & Haleakala ($369 pp). For a truly memorable experience, book the 1.5-hour Complete Island Maui ($449 pp), which combines a West Maui tour and a Hana & Haleakala tour, including a remote landing on the slopes of Haleakala, complete with refreshments.

Also flying ECO-Star helicopters is **Sunshine Helicopters** (107 Airport Rd., 808/871-0722, www.sunshinehelicopters.com), which charges extra for seats in front. Tours include a 45-minute Hana-Haleakala flight ($254-409 pp) and a 70-minute complete island flight with deluxe seating ($515 pp). The company also offers a jaw-dropping 55-minute tour from Maui to Moloka'i ($284-459 pp), passing by dramatic waterfalls, the world's tallest sea cliffs, and Kalaupapa Peninsula. Flights are discounted if you purchase online.

After 20 years of operating flights on the mainland, **Maverick Helicopters** (Lelepio Pl., 808/893-7999, www.maverickhelicopter.com) is the island's newest operator, with ECO-Star flights that include a 45-minute Hana-Haleakala tour ($299-349 pp), a 70-minute complete island tour ($429 pp) and the sublime Molokai Voyage ($329-359 pp).

To get really extreme and have no glare in your photos, **Pacific Helicopters** (Kahului Heliport, Hangar 109, 808/866-8165, https://pachelitours.com) can fly without the doors to enjoy the dramatic scenery with no obstructions. Private tours are extensive yet pricey, averaging $1,450 per person, depending on length.

Another Haleakala tour option is **Volcano Tours** (808/495-5500, www.volcanotours.com), offering tours of the famous dormant volcano. The 1.5-hour tours start at $487.

FLIGHTSEEING TOURS

If you're staying on Maui and want to see lava (which isn't guaranteed), the only way to see Kilauea volcano is with a flightseeing tour in an airplane. There aren't any helicopter companies from Maui that visit Kilauea volcano, although there are a couple of fixed-wing options from Kapalua and Kahului Airports. **Royal Pacific Air** (166 Kaulele Pl., 808/650-7693, www.royalpacificair.com) begins its flights at Honolulu and makes stops at Kapalua Airport (from $600 pp) and Kahului Airport ($500 pp) before continuing on to the Big Island. Staying in Ka'anapali, Napili, or Kapalua, the Kapalua Airport is only a 10-minute drive, an amazingly convenient option. In addition to active Kilauea volcano, you'll experience hidden waterfalls on the Big Island as well as Hana and Haleakala Crater. It isn't cheap but compares to the most expensive helicopter tours.

Golf

If you don't want to pay resort prices for golf but still appreciate a course that's well cared for, the three courses in Central Maui have some of the island's best deals. All have affordable restaurants with ice-cold beer. Prices listed are summer rates; expect approximately to pay $25-30 more per round in winter.

KAHULUI

The **Dunes at Maui Lani** (1333 Maui Lani Pkwy., 808/873-0422, www.dunesatmauilani.com, 6:45am-5pm daily) is a Scottish-style links course that weaves through natural sand dunes. Course designer Robert Nelson utilized the natural topography of the dunes in creating this 6,841-yard (6,255-m) course, so it includes a healthy number of bunkers. On the 18th hole, which is par 5, two pot bunkers short of the green famously challenge even those with the lowest of handicaps. The afternoon trade winds can make this course difficult, and the greens fees are priced accordingly: $99 for morning rounds, $88 after noon. Club rental is $45, and the central location makes it easy to sneak in a round before the 10-minute drive to the airport.

WAILUKU

On the hillside in Waikapu, the 6,554-yard (5,993-m) **Kahili Golf Course** (2500 Honoapi'ilani Hwy., 808/242-4653, www.kahiligolf.com, 6am-6pm daily) is one of the island's best golf values. Greens fees for visitors are $99, although if you tee off after 2pm, it drops to $59; club rentals are $35. The bicoastal views are better than at Maui Lani, although instead of links-style golf, the course is set on a gently sloping hillside. Kahili is a 35-minute drive from Ka'anapali, 25 minutes from Wailea.

If you just want to tee up the municipal course, **Waiehu Golf Course** (200 Halewaiu Rd., 808/243-7400, 6:30am-5pm Mon.-Fri., 5:30am-5pm Sat.-Sun.) is a 6,330-yard (5,788-m), par-72 course that's wildly popular with locals. Visitor greens fees are $55 weekdays, $67 weekends, although you can sneak in nine holes for only $29 if you tee off after 3pm. Cart rentals are $23 for 18 holes, and hand carts

Kahili Golf Course

are only $6. Club rentals are $25, and a couple of the holes have oceanfront tee boxes and sweeping resort-quality views.

Rental Shops

Regardless of where you're golfing, you can save on rental clubs by stopping at **Roger Dunn Golf Shop** (293 Dairy Rd., 808/873-5700, 9am-5pm Mon.-Sat., 10am-5pm Sun.), just a couple of minutes from the airport. Rental rates start at $29 per day or $80 per week—far more affordable than the $60-75 you would pay daily at some resorts.

Shopping

KAHULUI

Kahului has the island's largest amount of shopping, though it's mainly the box-store variety. The two-story **Queen Ka'ahumanu Shopping Center** (275 W. Ka'ahumanu Ave., 808/877-4325, www.queenkaahumanucenter.com, 10am-8pm Mon.-Thurs., 10am-9pm Fri.-Sat., 10am-5pm Sun.) is Kahului's largest mall, though many of the stores are large corporate chains.

Across town, the open-air **Maui Mall** (70 E. Ka'ahumanu Ave., 808/877-8952, www.mauimall.com, 7am-9pm daily) has a couple of surf shops and clothing boutiques, as well as a yoga studio, a Whole Foods, a Longs Drugs, and Asian-inspired restaurants. It's convenient for anyone visiting on a cruise ship that docks at Kahului Harbor.

For a classic Maui shopping experience, head to the Saturday **Maui Swap Meet** (310 W. Ka'ahumanu Ave., 808/244-3100, www.mauiexposition.com, 7am-1pm Sat., $0.50 adults, free under age 13) at UH Maui College, where over 200 local vendors gather to sell their foodstuffs and crafts. You can find everything from homemade jams to hand-turned koa wood bowls—often at prices much reduced from what you'd find in the stores.

Kahului also has the greatest concentration of water sports shops on the island, many of which are near the corner of Hana Highway and Dairy Road. Stop here for surf clothing, accessories, board shorts, or equipment sales. Favorites include **HI-Tech Surf Sports** (425 Koloa St., 808/877-2111, www.surfmaui.com, 9am-6pm daily), **Adventure Sports Maui** (400 Hana Hwy., 808/877-7443, www.adventuresportsusa.com, 9am-5pm Mon.-Fri., 9am-3pm Sat.), and **Maui Tropix** (261 Dairy Rd., 808/871-8726, 9am-8pm Mon.-Sat., 9am-6am Sun.), which sells the ubiquitous "Maui Built" wear.

WAILUKU

Sleepy Wailuku is turning into a hot shopping outpost. With a tight little cluster of shops, Market Street rivals Lahaina, Pa'ia, and Makawao for shopping and strolling. The difference here, however, is that many of the stores have authentic local connections—either selling products from local vendors or traditional Hawaiian crafts.

At **Native Intelligence** (1980 Main St., 808/249-2421, www.native-intel.com, 10am-5pm Mon.-Fri., 10am-4pm Sat.), visitors will find what's arguably the island's most culturally authentic store, perpetuating traditional Hawaiian culture and values, and selling everything from textbooks printed in Hawaiian to traditional lei-making supplies. You'll also find hand-carved weaponry, jewelry, and immaculate colorful feather-work, and occasional classes help introduce visitors to traditional Hawaiian culture. For anyone with an interest in traditional culture, this store is a must-visit.

For men's aloha shirts and women's clothing, **Ha Wahine** (53 Market St., 808/344-1642, 9am-3pm Thurs.-Sat.) is a clothing boutique featuring clothes made on Maui, with many featuring native designs and traditional Hawaiian patterns.

Across the street is a longtime Wailuku institution, **Request Music** (10 N. Market St., 808/244-9315, 10am-6pm Mon.-Sat.), the last holdout of true island record shops, kept alive by loyal music lovers who still want to feel the vinyl, admire the album covers, and talk with people who *really* love music. Most of the merchandise caters to the reggae and roots lifestyle, but the basement is filled with music that goes back decades.

Just a few doors down, **Sandell Artworks** (34 N. Market St., 808/249-2456, 10:30am-5pm Wed.-Sat., noon-5pm Sun.-Tues.) brings creative color and flare to funky Market Street, where paintings and prints run the gamut of characters and oddities of Maui.

At the far end of Market Street are two local water sports stores, **TriPaddle Maui** (54 N. Market St., 808/243-7235, www.tripaddlemaui.com, 9am-5pm Mon.-Fri., 9am-2pm Sat.), which specializes in accessories for outrigger paddle sports, and **Maui Sporting Goods** (92 N. Market St., 808/244-0011, 9am-6pm Mon.-Fri., 9am-5pm Sat.), the de facto fishing headquarters for most of Maui's anglers.

The string of pawn shops along Market Street always have some good deals, and at **Kama'aina Loan** (96 N. Market St., 808/242-5555, www.kamaainaloan.com, 9am-6pm Mon.-Fri., 10am-4pm Sat.-Sun.), you'll find everything from surfboards to ukuleles to ritual drums used by Nepalese shamans.

Entertainment

KAHULUI

Daytime Entertainment

There are free hula shows at the **Maui Mall** (70 E. Ka'ahumanu Ave., 808/877-8952, www.mauimall.com). Check the website for updated times. Across town, the **Queen Ka'ahumanu Shopping Center** (275 W. Ka'ahumanu Ave., 808/877-3369, www.queenkaahumanucenter.com) offers free hula shows at 10:30am Monday, followed at 12:30pm by Polynesian crafting. Similarly, a full calendar of events can be found on the website.

Evening Shows

The best option for evening entertainment in Kahului is the **Maui Arts and Cultural Center** (1 Cameron Way, 808/242-7469, www.mauiarts.org), where a constantly changing schedule of live concerts, movies, exhibits, comedy shows, and family events takes place most nights of the week. Multiple events often happen on the same evening. Check the website for a list of upcoming events.

Bars

The best bar in Kahului is **Ale House** (355 E. Kamehameha Ave., 808/877-0001, www.kahuluialehouse.com, 11am-11pm Mon.-Fri., 7am-11pm Sat.-Sun.), which has live music every night and 24 beers on draft. There are 40 TVs for watching the game, as well as ice-cold beer, surprisingly good sushi, and happy hour 3pm-6pm.

If you would rather visit a smaller bar in a darker, more intimate setting, **Koho's Grill and Bar** (275 W. Ka'ahumanu Ave., 808/877-5588, 11am-9pm Mon.-Wed., 11am-9:30pm Thurs.-Sat., 7am-9pm Sun.) inside the Queen Ka'ahumanu Shopping Center is a longtime local favorite, with daily drink specials and a casual crowd of margarita-sipping locals.

WAILUKU

Market Street is closed to vehicular traffic 5:30pm-9pm the first Friday of every month, and the area becomes a festive pedestrian thoroughfare. There's live music in Banyan Tree Park, street performers, food concessions from local restaurants, activities for children, and a beer garden for the adults. This is the original and most popular of the **Maui Friday Town Parties** (www.mauifridays.com).

Shows

A couple of times per year, theatrical shows take place inside historic **'Iao Theater** (68 N. Market St.), a Spanish mission-style theater that was opened in 1928. Listed on the National Register of Historic Places, the 'Iao is Hawaii's oldest theater and has hosted performers such as Bob Hope and Frank Sinatra over its lengthy history. For updated showtimes, visit **MauiOnStage** (www.mauionstage.com).

Bars

Brightening the cocktail scene is **Esters Fair Prospect** (2050 Main St., 808/868-0056, www.estersmaui.com, 2pm-10pm Mon.-Fri., 2pm-11pm Sat.). Inventive tropical cocktails abound here, like the Knickerbocker a la Monsieur, which pairs rum with fresh raspberry, curaçao, and lemon, or the Stirred Down Wailuku Town, which features whiskey, cocoa, sherry, and coconut oil. There are lovely views out on the patio, and the venue typically offers $3 deals for a stellar glass of wine.

Just down the street, **Tiffany's Bar and Grill** (1424 Lower Main St., 808/249-0052, www.tiffanysmaui.com, 10:30am-10pm daily, food until 9:30pm daily) is a longtime Lower Main Street institution that caters to a heavily local crowd. Karaoke is the name of the game here, and Tiffany's also has a full-service restaurant that serves surprisingly good local food.

Maui Friday Town Party in Wailuku

Food

KAHULUI

Traditional Hawaiian

Usually the only time you get Hawaiian food is when you attend a luau, but here at humble ★ **Poi by the Pound** (430 Kele St., 808/283-9381, noon-8pm Tues.-Sun., $14-25), in industrial Kahului, the kalua pig, *lau lau, poke,* and poi are just as good—if not better—than food you'd find at a luau. To go full-on local, order the Hawaiian Plate ($28), packed with Hawaiian favorites, or get the kalua pork plate or kimchee shrimp *saimin.* Fresh poi is available for purchase, and pick up a block of sweet *kulolo,* made from taro and coconut milk.

Hawaiian Regional

If hunger strikes on the way toward Lahaina, a convenient option is **Café O'Lei** (1333 Maui Lani Pkwy., 808/877-0073, 11am-8pm Tues.-Sat., $11-24) in the Dunes at Maui Lani clubhouse. There's an outdoor patio that looks out over the golf course as well as a full bar. On the menu are sandwiches, burgers, and spicy ahi nachos and fried calamari.

Local Style

★ **Tante's Island Cuisine** (100 W. Ka'ahumanu Ave., 808/277-0300, 7am-2pm daily, $11-21), in the scenic Maui Seaside Hotel, is a laid-back venue that offers traditional Hawaiian, Asian, and even American fare. Shrimp and ahi fried *poke* Benedict ($17) and paniolo steak and eggs with caramelized Maui onions ($16) are breakfast highlights. For lunch, consider *liliko'i* (passion fruit) barbecue ribs ($15) or the Hula Chicken ($15). Breakfast and lunch buffets ($19) are also available, featuring vegetable fried noodles with bay shrimp and sauteed mahimahi.

Maui Culinary Academy

To play a role in the next generation of Maui's most talented chefs, reserve a table at ★ **Leis Family Class Act** (310 W. Ka'ahumanu Ave., 808/984-3280, 11am-12:30pm Wed. and Fri.), where students of the Maui Culinary Academy gain real-world experience. The students perform all roles and serve a four-course Latin, Asian, Italian, French, or Moroccan fine-dining menu that changes each week. See the website, updated each semester, for specific menus and dates. Since it's only open twice a week, advance reservations are strongly recommended. Depending on the entrée, the prix fixe menu ranges $31-60 per person, and there's no corkage fee if you bring your own wine.

Japanese

The best Japanese in Kahului is at **Ichiban Restaurant & Sushi** (47 W. Ka'ahumanu Ave., 808/871-6977, 10:30am-2pm and 5pm-9pm Mon.-Fri., 5pm-9pm Sat., $8-14) in the Kahului Shopping Center. Rainbow rolls and heaping bowls of *udon* punctuate the menu. Cap it all off with a Kirin beer or a cup of sake.

For the Japanese restaurant equivalent of a dive bar, **Restaurant Matsu** (161 Alamaha St., 808/871-0822, 10am-3pm Mon.-Wed., 10am-6pm Thurs.-Fri., 10am-2pm Sat., $3-9) is a local favorite for affordable ramen and plate lunch. Try the flavorful *shoyu* ramen or a spam *katsu musubi,* and order at the counter before settling in for an authentic, surprisingly good meal.

Filipino

For tasty, authentic Filipino dishes, **Plantation Grindz** (70 Lono Ave., 808/873-3663, 4:30am-5pm Mon.-Sat., 5:30am-5pm Sun., $7-15) is your best option. Try chili pepper chicken, fried mahimahi, or the venue's popular baby back ribs.

German

Industrial Kahului is the last place you would expect to find a Bavarian après-ski lodge, but **Brigit and Bernard's Garden Café** (335

Hoʻohana St., 808/877-6000, www.brigitand-bernards.com, 11am-2:30pm and 5pm-9pm Mon.-Fri., 5pm-9pm Sat., $16-38) pumps out authentic, stick-to-your-ribs German fare. The vaulted A-frame ceiling is hung with colorful steins, cross-country skis, and posters of alpine ski resorts. Order a massive plate of bratwurst or schnitzel served with a huge potato *rosti* and wash it down with a Bitburger brew.

Italian

The finest restaurant in Kahului, **Bistro Casanova** (33 Lono Ave., 808/873-3650, www.bistrocasanova.com, 11am-2pm and 5pm-9pm Mon.-Fri., 5pm-9pm Sat., $14-38) livens up downtown with a fusion of Mediterranean and Italian cuisine. The tapas menu, served after 3pm, has crostini, gnocchi, and grilled calamari, and a swanky bar attracts the after-work cocktail crowd. Consider happy hour (4pm-6pm Mon.-Sat.), where draft beers are $5 and wine is $6 a glass.

For amazing pizza, check out **North Shore Pizza Company** (129 Maa St., 808/214-6830, 11am-9:30pm Mon.-Thurs., 11am-10pm Fri.-Sat., 11am-8:30pm Sun., $14-30), which offers a fantastic variety, with pizzas such as the Grizzly Pesto, Greek, and Cordon Bleu (with bleu cheese crumbles) topping our list. The popular go-to also has delicious garlic breads and wings to choose from.

Mexican

For quick and authentic Mexican food, visit **Las Piñatas** (395 Dairy Rd., 808/877-8707, www.pinatasmaui.com, 10am-8pm daily, $8-14), next to the FedEx office off Dairy Road. The Kitchen Sink burrito is so big that a growing teenager will have trouble cleaning the plate. Pair with a bottle of beer or *horchata*.

Just down the road from Las Piñatas is **Amigos** (333 Dairy Rd., 808/872-9525, www.amigosmaui.com, 9am-9pm daily, $9-12), where daily specials ($9 burritos and chimichangas) make this a cheap place to eat while in town. The main difference between Amigos and Las Piñatas is that Amigos features a small bar where you can order a margarita, get Mexican beers on draft, or cap off your *carnitas* with a shot of Patrón.

Shave Ice

If you find yourself driving to the airport and suddenly realize you never got shave ice, the most popular place in town is **Ululani's** (333 Dairy Rd., 808/877-3700, www.ululanis-shaveice.com, 10:30am-6pm daily), in a kiosk by the Wow-Wee Maui Kava Bar and Grill.

Coffee Shops

For local coffee beans, head to **Maui Coffee Roasters** (444 Hana Hwy., 808/877-2877, www.mauicoffeeroasters.com, 7am-6pm Mon.-Fri., 7am-5pm Sat., $9), the best little coffee shop in town. In the same shopping complex as Marco's Grill and Deli, Maui Coffee Roasters has an assortment of brews made from Maui, Kona, Kaua'i, and Moloka'i beans. The full breakfast and lunch menu features bagels, breakfast wraps, sandwiches, and salads, and there are multiple tables and free Wi-Fi. It's five minutes from the airport.

For a quick cup on the go, **Akamai Coffee** (100 Pakaula St., 808/575-9891, www.akamaicoffee.com, 6am-6pm Mon.-Sat.) is a drive-through coffee shop in the Home Depot parking lot that has some of the island's best coffee, despite the location. The beans are grown and roasted on Maui. To really save time, call in your order ahead of time and it's ready in 15 minutes.

Natural Foods

Vegetarians and vegans love the deli inside ★ **Down to Earth** (305 Dairy Rd., 808/877-2661, www.downtoearth.org, 6am-10pm Mon.-Sat., 7am-9pm Sun.). At only $9, the Fresh Mex burrito is both filling and affordable, and you can save time by ordering online (www.dtedeli.org). Since the grocery store is on the road between the airport and Lahaina, this is one of the few places in Kahului for a quick and healthy meal on the go.

The other option is **Broth** (340 Hana Hwy., 808/877-4950, www.aliveandwellinmaui.

com, 8am-6pm Mon.-Sat.) at Alive and Well, a health emporium. The healthy menu features local and organic fare, such as avocado toast with curried chicken or lox, a lemongrass burrito, and filling bowls (try the Mac Crack Fish Bowl or the Green Bowl). Inventive sandwiches include a fish sandwich of the day. There's also kombucha on tap and hot broths!

WAILUKU

Old-school Wailuku is quietly becoming one of Maui's best places for food. Don't expect oceanfront tiki torches like you'd find at restaurants in Lahaina, since the atmosphere here is far more "authentic," in the run-down and real local sort of way. Prices are lower because rents are lower, and the wealth of affordable international cuisine is starting to garner attention.

Hawaiian Regional

Inside the Maui Tropical Plantation, ★ **Café O'Lei at The Mill House** (1670 Honoapi'ilani Hwy., 808/270-0333, www.cafeoleirestaurants.com, 11am-8pm Tues.-Sat., $18-55) brings one of the island's most popular culinary outposts (Café O'Lei) into a tropical setting. Blending farm-to-table artistry with island favorites, standout dishes include Maui onion soup en croute ($12), slow-cooked lamb shank ($32), and a miso eggplant and root vegetable bowl ($21). Happy hour runs 3pm-5pm, when beers go for $4-5 and tossed flatbreads run an affordable $14. This is one of the most memorable dining options on the island.

Local Style

You'll probably wonder when you arrive at ★ **Sam Sato's** (1750 Wili Pa Loop, 808/244-7124, 7am-2pm Mon.-Sat., $7, cash only) if this is really the famous restaurant, hidden deep within the Wailuku mill yard in a building you can't even see from the road. This family-run institution has been offering plate lunch and *manju* pastries since the 1930s. But it's the dry noodles that make Sam Sato's legendary, served with a side of homemade broth and topped with char *siu* pork and sprouts, making an affordable and addictive meal.

Ichiban Okazuya Hawaii (2133 Kaohu St., 808/244-7276, 10am-7pm Mon.-Fri., $8) has been a popular go-to for locals for years, and while its counter-prepared meals may look basic, they taste anything but. Affordable plates like the teriyaki ahi, Korean chicken, and pork *katsu* are filling, and the fresh fish of the day offers a nice island touch with sides of noodles or kimchi. This is an ideal pit stop for lunches and snacks while on your way through Wailuku to places like 'Iao Valley or on your way back to Kahului. This authentic hole-in-the-wall is takeout only. At peak times the line can be out the door, but the staff is surprisingly fast.

Eclectic

Just half a block from Market Street is **808 on Main** (2051 Main St., 808/242-1111, www.808onmain.com, 10am-3pm Mon.-Sat.), where you can get filling paninis, sandwiches, and salads with creative culinary flare. Try the mahimahi quinoa bowl ($18) or Southern Squealer hoagie with pulled pork ($14). House favorites on the cocktail menus include a blueberry mojito and the Maui martini with Hapa Hawaiian vodka, Maui Shrub Farm ginger, and Hawaiian chili shrub. Cheers!

Thai

★ **Tiki Tiki Thai Cuisine** (395 Dairy Rd., 808/893-0026, 10am-10pm daily, $12-18) is a funky hole-in-the-wall with some excellent food in the heart of run-down Vineyard Street. It has fresh soups (thai noodle, coconut, and wonton), a variety of appetizers (pot stickers, chicken satay, crab rangoon), fried rice, and beef, fish, and pad thai dishes that are as tasty and authentic as they come. Pair your meal with a Thai iced tea.

Vietnamese

Sandwiched between a bridge and a low-income housing unit is one of Maui's most popular Vietnamese venues, ★ **A Saigon Café** (1792 Main St., 808/243-9560,

Central Maui Food Trucks

Central Maui is the island's epicenter for quirky gourmet food trucks, and the prices compare with most of the island's budget restaurants. Expect entrées to cost $8-15, and while locations can vary, here's where you can usually find them:

FOOD TRUCK PARK ACROSS FROM COSTCO

Only five minutes from the airport, this tight little cluster of food trucks (10am-4pm Mon.-Tues., 10am-8pm Wed.-Fri.), across from the Costco gas station on Haleakala Highway, has everything from fried *poke* and ahi *katsu* at local favorite **Like Poke?** to $10 plates of chicken pad thai at the **Thai Mee Up** food truck. You'll find three tacos for $5 at **Maui 8 Wonder Tacos,** and the best burgers and fries along with fresh fish sandwiches at **Dino's Gourmet Food Truck.**

KAHULUI HARBOR

In the dirt parking area across from the Maui Arts and Cultural Center you'll find **Geste Shrimp Truck** (Kahului Beach Rd., 808/298-7109, www.gesteshrimp.com, 10:30am-7:30pm Mon.-Sat., 10am-6pm Sun., cash only), where $15 gets you 12 pieces of shrimp served with crab macaroni salad and two scoops of rice. Nearby, you'll find **Lau Hee Chicken Hekka** and their local-style plate lunch of sweet salty chicken, as well as a handful of other trucks that occasionally set up shop.

11am-8:30pm daily, $9-16). It's a cultural and culinary experience that's well off the tourist radar. Opt for clay pot dishes with rice, chicken, and vegetables, or try the *pho, banh hoi,* or tasty Vietnamese soup. The portions are enormous, and the place is always packed. If locals recommend eating at "Jennifer's," this is the place they mean.

Italian

Family-owned ★ **Giannotto's Pizza** (2050 Main St., 808/244-8282, www.giannottospizza.com, 11am-8pm Mon.-Sat., $7-14) serves up homemade Italian recipes "just like Mama used to make." Next to the Wailuku Promenade, this place is as authentic as the "Joisey" accents emanating from the kitchen. Photos of mafiosi adorn the wall, and pizza by the slice is $2-4.

Diners

For a Wailuku classic that's easy on the wallet, **Tasty Crust Restaurant** (1770 Mill St., 808/244-0845, 6am-8pm Mon.-Sat., cash only) is an old-school working-class diner in a working-class part of town that has been feeding Wailuku for over 50 years. Breakfast is the time to stop by for a stack of their famous hotcakes. Not only are the banana pancakes tasty and filling, but at $5.50 they're also affordable. Best of all, breakfast is served all day, and this is a true local dining experience with local people.

Bakeries

Wailuku is the island's epicenter for bakeries, and none is more popular than **Home Maid Bakery** (1005 Lower Main St., 808/244-7015, www.homemaidbakery.com, 5am-8pm daily), which has been serving their famous *malasadas* and *manju* since 1960. Plain *malasadas* cost $0.86, cream-filled are $1.35, and both are available 5am-10am and again 4pm-10pm.

Coffee Shops

Wailuku Coffee Company (26 N. Market St., 808/495-0259, 7am-5pm Mon.-Sat., 7am-2pm Sun., $5-9) is where "the hip come to sip." For breakfast, served until noon, try a bacon, tomato, and avocado bagel served with a layer of cream cheese, and for lunch, try a chickpea veggie wrap. You'll also find fresh salads, pastries, Wi-Fi, and smoothies.

Natural Foods

For your daily fix of açaí and kale, head straight to ★ **The Farmacy Health Bar** (12 N. Market St., 10am-6pm daily, $8-12), where you can also score a dragon fruit smoothie or an açaí bowl with poi. Expect GMO-free organic ingredients and a strong community following.

Getting There and Around

CAR

Car Rentals

At the Kahului Airport, **Alamo** (844/913-0747), **Avis** (808/871-7575), **Budget** (808/871-8811), **Enterprise** (844/914-1547), **Hertz** (808/893-5200), and **Thrifty** (808/893-5200) all offer the standard corporate options for island car rentals. Other options in Kahului, which are often cheaper, include **Maui Car Rentals** (181 Dairy Rd., 800/567-4659, www.mauicarrentals.net), **Aloha Rent A Car** (190 Papa Pl., 808/877-4477, www.mauirentacar.com), and **Kimo's Rent A Car** (440 Alamaha St., 808/280-6327, www.kimosrentacar.com). Care to splurge? **SIXT Rent-a-Car Maui** (888/749-8227) offers long-term rentals and discounts midweek.

Don't get a 4WD vehicle—you won't need it. The only time you need 4WD on Maui is for Skyline Drive in Polipoli, or for peace of mind on the back road to Hana. Many visitors spend a lot of money on 4WD, often double the price of a regular car, and never end up using it. Rent a 4WD vehicle just for the day if you need it.

MOTORCYCLE

If the idea of zipping ocean-side on a groovy Yamaha is your preferred method of getting from A to B, **Maui Moto Adventures** (60 E. Wakea Ave., 808/269-9515, www.mauimotorcyclerentalsandtours.com, open 24 hours) offers rentals from the Kahului shop just minutes from Kahului Airport.

BUS

The Queen Ka'ahumanu Shopping Center is the central hub of the **Maui Bus,** and if you are connecting from one bus to another, there is a good chance that you'll end up making a stop at the mall. All segments on the bus cost $2 per person (or $4 pp for a day pass), and this is the terminus and starting point for routes heading upcountry as well as to Kihei and Lahaina.

To just get across town, buses on the Wailuku Loop (bus 1) make various stops around Wailuku and run hourly 6:30am-9:30pm daily. Similarly, buses on the Kahului Loop (bus 5) make various stops around Kahului and run hourly 6:30am-9pm daily. From Queen Ka'ahumanu to the Kahului Airport, you have to get on the Upcountry Islander bus (bus 40), which runs every 90 minutes 6:10am-9:10pm daily. For more information, a full schedule, or to see routes to other parts of the island, visit www.mauicounty.gov and navigate to "For Residents" and then "Maui Bus."

Kihei and South Maui

If one word defines South Maui, it's "beaches."

South Maui is graced with dozens of sandy stretches just waiting for your footprints.

The island's longest beach is Sugar Beach; one of its smallest is Pa'ako Cove. The sound of waves lapping against the palm-lined sand is a year-round reality in South Maui. There are enough beaches that a three-week vacation isn't enough time to possibly see them all. Because much of South Maui actually faces west, the end of each day is punctuated by a sunset that somehow outdoes the last.

It's also one of the state's hottest areas, particularly in Kihei, where the smell of coconut oil wafts on the late-morning trade winds. Mornings are for stand-up paddling and snorkeling, and afternoons are

Highlights

Look for ★ to find recommended sights, activities, dining, and lodging.

★ Surround yourself with sharks, eagle rays, and dozens of fish at the **Maui Ocean Center,** all without getting your hair wet (page 141).

★ Learn about Maui's most exciting winter visitors in an oceanfront setting by Ko'ie'ie Fishpond at the **Hawaiian Islands Humpback Whale National Marine Sanctuary Visitors Center** (page 144).

★ Go for a secluded stroll down on **Sugar Beach,** one of the longest and most scenic beaches on Maui, and watch **kitesurfers** and **windsurfers** (page 146).

★ Enjoy a peaceful getaway with a blanket and a book at the south end of **Keawakapu Beach** (page 148).

★ Go for a **snorkel** or **stand-up paddle** at **Maluaka Beach,** along Makena's historic coast (page 150).

★ Take in a glorious **sunset** along the golden shore at **Makena State Park** (page 151).

★ Immerse in crystal-clear waters at offshore **Molokini Crater**—the **snorkeling** ranks as some of the best in the state, and the **scuba diving** is some of the best in the world (pages 154 and 164).

★ Find friendly **snorkeling** conditions and an abundance of marinelife at protected **Ulua Beach and Mokapu Beach** (page 161).

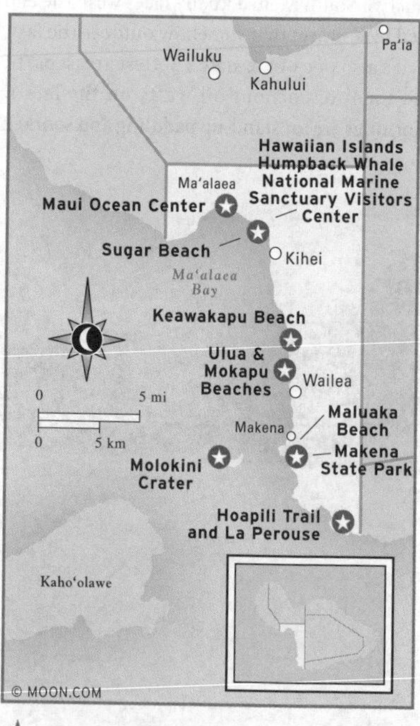

★ Hike the **Hoapili Trail,** an ancient footpath of kings that meanders through the island's most recent lava flows as well as past the popular surfing spot **La Perouse** and the remnants of an ancient fishing village (page 175).

South Maui

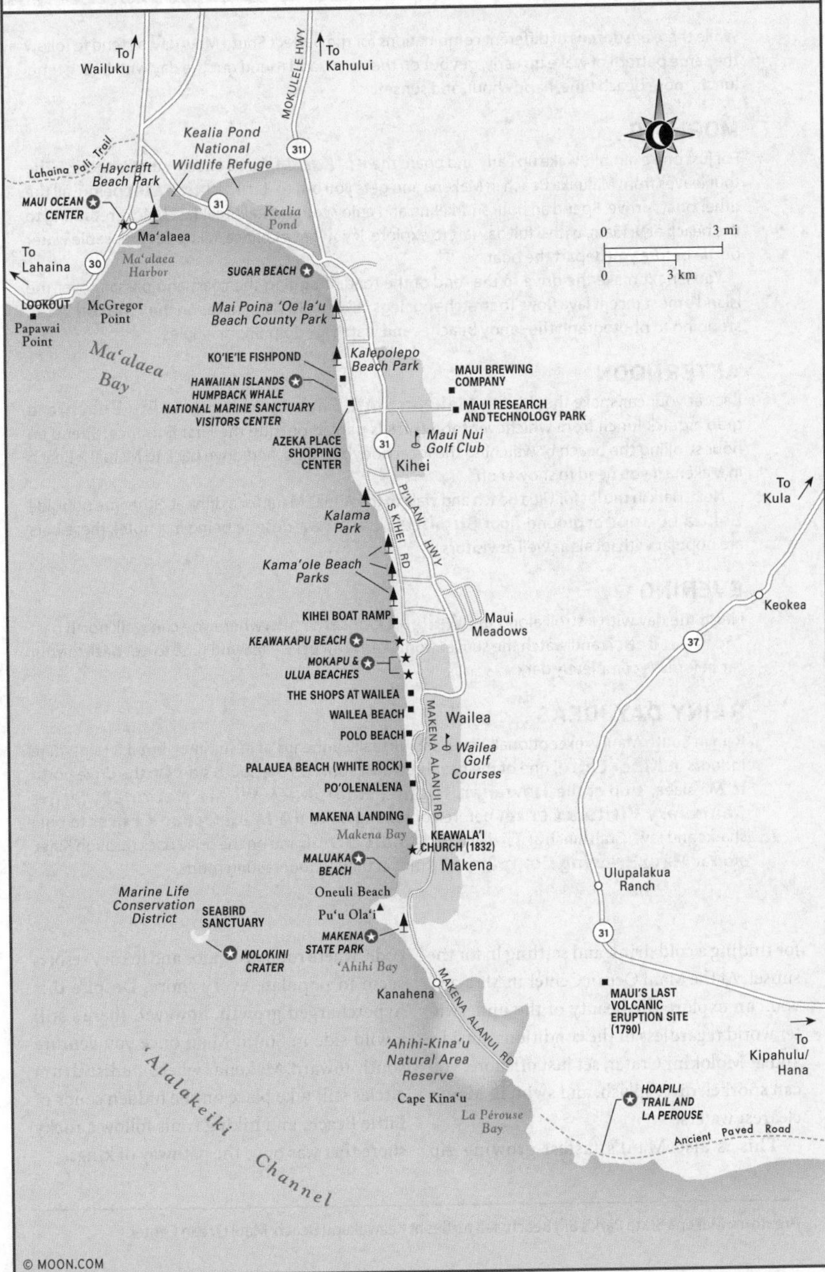
To Wailuku
To Kahului
MOKULELE HWY
311
Kealia Pond National Wildlife Refuge
Lahaina Pali Trail
Haycraft Beach Park
MAUI OCEAN CENTER
31
Kealia Pond
Ma'alaea
To Lahaina
30
Ma'alaea Harbor
SUGAR BEACH
0
3 mi
0
3 km
LOOKOUT
McGregor Point
Papawai Point
Mai Poina 'Oe la'u Beach County Park
Ma'alaea Bay
KO'IE'IE FISHPOND
Kalepolepo Beach Park
MAUI BREWING COMPANY
HAWAIIAN ISLANDS HUMPBACK WHALE NATIONAL MARINE SANCTUARY VISITORS CENTER
MAUI RESEARCH AND TECHNOLOGY PARK
AZEKA PLACE SHOPPING CENTER
Maui Nui Golf Club
Kihei
PI'ILANI HWY
S KIHEI RD
To Kula
Kalama Park
Kama'ole Beach Parks
Keokea
KIHEI BOAT RAMP
Maui Meadows
KEAWAKAPU BEACH
37
MOKAPU & ULUA BEACHES
THE SHOPS AT WAILEA
WAILEA BEACH
Wailea
POLO BEACH
MAKENA ALANUI RD
Wailea Golf Courses
PALAUEA BEACH (WHITE ROCK)
PO'OLENALENA
MAKENA LANDING
Makena Bay
KEAWALA'I CHURCH (1832)
MALUAKA BEACH
Makena
Ulupalakua Ranch
Oneuli Beach
Marine Life Conservation District
SEABIRD SANCTUARY
Pu'u Ola'i
MAKENA STATE PARK
31
MOLOKINI CRATER
'Ahihi Bay
Kanahena
MAKENA ALANUI RD
MAUI'S LAST VOLCANIC ERUPTION SITE (1790)
To Kipahulu/ Hana
'Ahihi-Kina'u Natural Area Reserve
'Alalakeiki Channel
Cape Kina'u
La Pérouse Bay
HOAPILI TRAIL AND LA PEROUSE
Ancient Paved Road
© MOON.COM

Your Best Day in South Maui

While there are dozens of different combinations for the perfect South Maui day, all tend to follow the same pattern of wake up early, get out on the water, and round out the day with beach time, lunch, more beach time, happy hour, and sunset.

MORNING

For just one example, wake up early and board the ***Kai Kanani*** for its 6:15am sunrise snorkel. The tour leaves from Maluaka Beach in Makena and gets you out to **Molokini Crater** before all the other boats arrive. Spend an hour snorkeling and enjoy continental breakfast before returning to the beach at 9:45am, with a full day left to explore. If you get a chance, fill up your reusable water bottle before you depart the boat.

You'll next make the drive to the "end of the road," hugging the coast and passing over the island's most recent lava flow. To stretch your legs, hike for 30-45 minutes on the **Hoapili Trail,** stopping to photograph the sandy beaches and watch for dolphins or whales.

AFTERNOON

Back at your car, make the drive to **Makena State Park,** better known as **Big Beach,** and grab a quick lunch from whichever food truck is parked outside the First Entrance. Spend an hour strolling the beach or watching the local bodyboarders, and drive back to Maluaka Beach in Makena if you need to shower off.

Next, park in the lot for Ulua Beach and walk to the Andaz Maui, for a drink at either the poolside **Lehua Lounge** or ground-floor **Bumbye Beach Bar;** despite being in a hotel, these bars are popular with locals as well as visitors.

EVENING

Finish the day with a stroll along the **Wailea Coastal Walk,** where you can walk north past **Mokapu Beach** and watch the sunset from **Keawakapu**—leaving time to get back to your car before it's completely dark.

RAINY DAY IDEAS

Rain in South Maui is exceptionally rare, and virtually unheard of in summer, but if it rains, dine indoors at **Kihei Caffe,** one of the best breakfast spots on the south side. On the drive north to Ma'alaea, stop at the **Hawaiian Islands Humpback Whale National Marine Sanctuary Visitors Center** before continuing on to the **Maui Ocean Center** to ogle sharks and rays. Grab lunch at **Tradewinds Mart & Deli,** and on the drive back through Kihei, stop at **Maui Brewing Company** for a pint at their indoor tasting room.

for finding a cold drink and settling in for the sunset. At the Maui Ocean Center in Ma'alaea, you can explore the beauty of the underwater world regardless of the conditions outside, and at Molokini Crater, set just offshore, you can snorkel, dive, splash, and swim in Maui's clearest waters.

This is also Maui's fastest-growing zip code, where rows of condos and luxury resorts seem to populate every shore. Despite this hypercharged growth, however, there's still a wild side in South Maui once you venture south toward Makena, where nudist drum circles still take place on the hidden sands of Little Beach, and hiking trails follow a rocky shore that was once the pathway of kings.

Previous: Makena State Park's Big Beach; sea turtles at Keawakapu Beach; Maui Ocean Center.

ORIENTATION

South Maui runs in a long, narrow column and is never far from the coast. To drive from **Ma'alaea,** the northernmost part, to the end of the road in Makena, takes approximately 30 minutes and passes through Kihei and Wailea. The high-end resorts are found in **Wailea,** whereas **Kihei** is laden with oceanfront condos and more affordable options for dining. **Makena** is where the coast gets wild and development disappears, yet it is close enough to the Wailea resorts to reach by pedaling a bike. Kihei, the commercial hub of South Maui, is sandwiched in a strip between **South Kihei Road** and **Pi'ilani Highway,** while Ma'alaea is the site of the harbor and the windy gateway to West Maui.

PLANNING YOUR TIME

South Maui could be either your base for exploring the rest of the island or a sunny, sandy strip of paradise you have no plans to leave. Exploring the wild hinterlands of Makena should take about half a day, enjoying the hiking, snorkeling, beaches, and legendary sunsets. If you aren't staying in the Wailea resort, it's still nice to spend a whole day at one of the popular beaches, strolling the Wailea Coastal Walk and dining at the fancy resort restaurants. If you are staying in Wailea, do yourself a favor and spend one day where you don't leave the resort—just pool time, beach time, and maybe a massage to enjoy the luxurious surroundings. Kihei, on the other hand, deserves two days: two mornings to try out two different beaches and two afternoons to try out two different lunch spots. Ma'alaea requires only a few hours, as the only reason to go is to visit the Maui Ocean Center or catch a boat to Molokini Crater.

Sights

MA'ALAEA

★ Maui Ocean Center

There isn't a snorkeling spot on the island where you're going to see as wide a range of marinelife as at the **Maui Ocean Center** (192 Ma'alaea Rd., 808/270-7000, www.mauioceancenter.com, 9am-5pm daily, $39 adults, $28 children), the largest tropical reef aquarium in the western hemisphere. This 3-acre (1.2-ha) marine park has more than 60 exhibits and the nation's largest collection of live tropical coral. Small children will enjoy the tide-pool exhibits and green sea turtle lagoon. Experience the 54-foot-long (16.5-m) acrylic tunnel beneath a 750,000-gallon (2.8-million-liter) aquarium filled with dozens of rays and sharks, standing in a dry space and watching a tiger shark float right over you, or contemplating how spotted eagle rays look like birds as they buzz circles just a few feet from your head. The new 139-seat 3-D dome theater has an adjacent 1,200-square-foot (111-square-m) exhibit hall that chronicles the nomadic lifestyle and other behaviors of humpback whales.

The center is deeply committed to educating visitors about the unique marine ecosystem. Did you know, for example, that nearly 25 percent of Hawaii's fish and coral species are found nowhere else on earth? The center is also a fantastic resource for learning about native Hawaiian culture, with exhibits on everything from Polynesian wayfaring to ancient Hawaiian fishponds. The center is set up to provide the animals with a realistic environment, and trained naturalists wander the grounds and give periodic talks about the various exhibits.

This is one of the island's best attractions for children as well as a rainy-day activity. Its popularity can mean crowds, however, so visit in the morning when the facility opens. There's a self-guided tour through the exhibits, and if you want to have some of them all to yourself, head directly to the last exhibit and

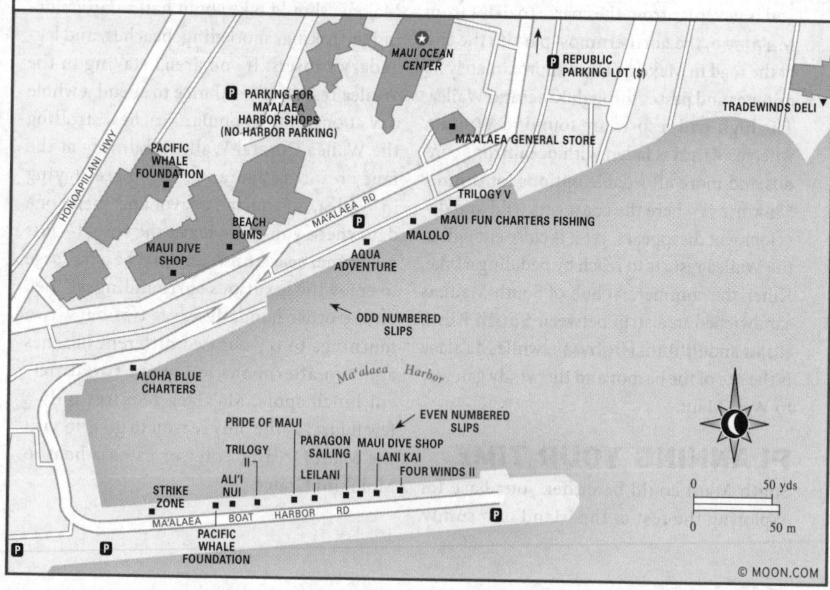

work your way backward toward the front. Expect to spend about two hours. Book online for the family pass to save up to 15 percent.

Pacific Whale Foundation Whale-Watching

After spending several months feeding off the shores of Alaska, humpback whales migrate to the shallower waters around Maui December-May to mate and give birth. This gives visitors one heck of a water show, with whale breaches, blowholing, and lobtailing. The **Pacific Whale Foundation** (300 Ma'alaea Rd., 808/249-8811, www.pacificwhale.org), a nonprofit noted for its ocean advocacy, offers a dozen unique whale-watching excursions with team members who have deep knowledge of marinelife and who make each outing festive thanks to their engaging personalities. Departures are from Ma'alaea or Lahaina Harbors with standard two-hour morning and afternoon excursions (Nov.-Apr., $59-69) that include talks by marine biologists and bar snacks.

Specialty tours include the Ultimate Whale Watch With Experts (8am Wed.-Sat., $119 adults, $69 children), a three-hour tour led by marine naturalists, with underwater hydrophones to listen for whale songs, downloadable whale photos, and lunch.

All trips guarantee a whale sighting; if whales aren't spotted, the foundation offers another trip for free. Opportunities to adopt a whale ($80) and receive updates on its status offer a way to stay abreast of these remarkable mammals. Become a Pacific Whale Foundation member ($100-500) and you'll help play a part in advancing ongoing ocean research. Added bonus: You receive at least 20 percent discounts on future excursions and events.

Kihei

Kihei's main draws are the beaches and weather, and in the morning it can seem

1: underwater marvels at the Maui Ocean Center
2: Keawala'i Congregational Church in Makena

1

2
KEAWALA'I CHURCH
FOUNDED 1832
MAKENA, MAUI

like half the town is running, snorkeling, or stand-up paddling. In ancient Hawaii, the Kihei area was called Kamaole, which translates as "barren." Even during World War II, the soft, gently sloping beaches were used by the military as practice zones for amphibious landing craft, since no one was around. Today there are a sea of snorkelers, boogie boarders, and beach umbrellas. Even with the recent growth, however, there are still a few places to get back to nature or catch a glimpse of the past.

Kealia Pond National Wildlife Refuge

The road between Ma'alaea and North Kihei passes through a large mudflat that parallels the shore. Most of this area is dry during summer, but on the inland side of the highway is the nearly 700-acre (285-ha) **Kealia Pond National Wildlife Refuge** (www.fws.gov/refuge/kealia_pond). Visit to catch a glimpse of native bird species such as the *ae'o* (Hawaiian stilt) and *'alae ke'oke'o* (Hawaiian coot). Even if you aren't an avid birder, the boardwalk off North Kihei Road is an informative place to stretch your legs and learn about the threats facing the island's species.

Ko'ie'ie Loko I'a Fishpond

Inside Kalepolepo Beach Park in North Kihei, the **Ko'ie'ie Loko I'a Fishpond** is the most prominent example of ancient Hawaiian life between Ma'alaea and Wailea. Estimated to be around 500 years old, it covered 6 acres (2.4 ha) and produced about 2,000 pounds (900 kg) of fish annually. It was formed by rocks passed by hand from the uplands to the sea, and thanks to the hard work of the **'Ao'ao O Na Loko I'a O Maui** (726 S. Kihei Rd., 808/359-1172, www.mauifishpond.com)—volunteers who have been working since 1996 to restore the ancient fishpond—it can be viewed any time by visiting Kalepolepo Beach Park. For a unique experience, contact the organization and inquire about guided cultural canoe trips. Tours have typically run at 8am Monday, Wednesday, and Friday for those who prearrange a visit.

★ Hawaiian Islands Humpback Whale National Marine Sanctuary Visitors Center

Right next door to Kalepolepo Beach Park is the **Hawaiian Islands Humpback Whale National Marine Sanctuary Visitors Center** (726 S. Kihei Rd., 808/879-2818, www.hawaiihumpbackwhale.noaa.gov, 10am-3pm Mon.-Fri.), a phenomenal educational resource for anyone with an interest in humpback whales. You can find plates of baleen, krill in a jar, and free binoculars out on the deck to view the whales in winter. There are also displays on turtles, dolphins, and teams that untangle whales, and while it's a bit out of the way in North Kihei, it's an easy stop when traveling from Ma'alaea back to Kihei or Wailea. Aside from the exhibits, the center also boasts some unique architecture: the 1940s-era coastal clapboard structure, seemingly better suited to Nantucket than North Kihei. The Ko'ie'ie Fishpond is in front of the compound, which makes this a fun and educational side trip when visiting Kalepolepo Beach.

Makena

Makena has the most evidence of ancient culture and history in South Maui. This rugged, lava-strewn shore was home to a thriving population of ancient Hawaiians, and was believed to be the most populated region in South Maui during pre-contact times. When diseases and foreign plant and animal species were introduced by European explorers, however, the combination of outside forces ravaged the indigenous population, and many of the villages in Makena were abandoned. In a fitting twist to the tale, Makena is also the landing site of the first European explorer to set foot on Maui's shore—French explorer Jean-François de Galaup, comte de Lapérouse, in 1786. Despite the amount of history in Makena, many of the archaeological and cultural remnants are either on private

Did Menehune Build the Ko'ie'ie Fishpond?

In Hawaiian lore, Menehune are the mythical little people of the Hawaiian Islands who are thought to be mysterious, mischievous, and quick in their work. While stories about Menehune abound, the most commonly told one involves the building of stone fishponds across the Hawaiian Islands. In a story similar to those found on Kaua'i and Moloka'i, Ko'ie'ie Fishpond in North Kihei is believed to have been built by Menehune in the course of a single night.

Don't pass this off as a playful legend, however; history supports the claim. It is believed by many scholars that seafaring voyagers from the Marquesas Islands populated the Hawaiian Islands around AD 400-600, and that much larger settlers from Tahiti supplanted these original small-in-stature inhabitants in 1100. As it turns out, the Tahitian word for "commoner" is *manahune,* and it's believed that the ruling Tahitian class put the Marquesans to work on building the fishponds.

As Hawaiian society progressed and the centuries wore on, it's theorized that the *manahune* remained lower-class citizens. Much of the evidence for this theory is derived from a census on the island of Kaua'i in 1820, where, in a tantalizing fusion of history and lore, 65 citizens classified themselves as being *manahune.*

So, did magical little people build Ko'ie'ie Fishpond, or did a diminutive class of indentured workers stack all the stones in the sea? Since there was no written language at the time of its construction, believed to be 1400-1500, all we are left with are the legends, the stones . . . and the Menehune Shores condominium on the shore.

land, in cordoned-off sanctuaries, or scattered along the shore in areas such as the Hoapili Trail. One site is open to visitors, and it parallels the plight of Makena's indigenous people.

Keawala'i Congregational Church

In an area of the island that's developing rapidly, there's a timeless beauty to **Keawala'i Congregational Church** (5300 Makena Rd., 808/879-5557, www.keawalai.org). Set on a palm- and *ti*-lined cove and bathed in the gentle sound of the surf, Keawala'i was founded in 1832 and constructed in 1855. The original structure was made of *pili* grass, and this Protestant church served as one of the main centers of worship in southern Maui. The grass was eventually replaced with coral, and in 1856 the church raised $70 to purchase a bell from the United States, then a different country. It took that bell almost three years to travel to Hawaii, and in February 1862 it was lifted into the belfry, where it still hangs today.

Unfortunately, in the mid-1800s, when Makena's streams began to run dry from excessive logging upslope, much of Makena's population moved elsewhere. Keawala'i slid into disrepair, and when thieves pillaged it in the years after World War II, the community opted to band together to bring the church back to life. Today, after 50 years of renovations, Keawala'i is as beautiful as at its height. United Church of Christ services are conducted in the Hawaiian language at 7:30am and 10am Sunday, although visits to the church grounds are possible any time of day.

Beaches

When it comes to beach weather, even though South Maui is dry, other elements such as the wind and clouds can greatly affect the comfort level. The closer you are to Ma'alaea, the earlier in the day it gets windy—particularly in the summer. Since the afternoon trade winds begin their march in Ma'alaea, they progressively move from north to south through Kihei, Wailea, and ultimately Makena. During trade-wind weather patterns, the "Makena cloud" forms over Haleakala and extends out toward the island of Kaho'olawe, although this doesn't normally happen until the early afternoon. Consequently, the morning hours are the best time to hit the beach. In the afternoon, the pocket of beaches in south Kihei and Wailea have the best chance of being sunny and calm. Winter months aren't as windy, and this is also when humpback whales can be seen leaping offshore. Is it any wonder so many snowbirds choose to spend the winter here?

MA'ALAEA

★ Sugar Beach

If your picture-perfect vision of Hawaii is enjoying a long, lonely stroll down an isolated beach, **Sugar Beach** is going to be your favorite spot on the island. Bordered on one side by Kealia Pond National Wildlife Refuge and the waters of Ma'alaea Bay on the other, this undeveloped strip runs for 2.5 miles (4 km) all the way to North Kihei.

There isn't any snorkeling here, although there can sometimes be waves for boogie boarding during summer. Rather, the main attraction is taking a long, quiet stroll, and since most afternoons have very fierce trade winds—perfect for windsurfers and kitesurfers—early morning is the best time to take a walk.

To access Sugar Beach, you can begin at the northern terminus at Haycraft Beach Park, the southern terminus in North Kihei, or at numerous entry points along North Kihei Road.

KIHEI

Mai Poina 'Oe Ia'u Beach Park

On summer days with northerly winds, **Mai Poina 'Oe Ia'u Beach** is known as the "Kanaha of Kihei" for the windsurfing and kitesurfing crowd. In the morning hours, before the wind comes up, this beach is a nice place for taking a stroll and wandering around the dunes, and while there isn't any swimming and snorkeling is poor, there are picnic tables and pavilions for a meal by the water, and good stand-up paddling in the morning.

Kalepolepo Beach Park

Right next to the Hawaiian Islands Humpback Whale National Marine Sanctuary, **Kalepolepo Beach Park** is Kihei's most underrated beach. What makes this little-visited enclave so special is Ko'ie'ie Fishpond (page 144), which has been masterfully restored in recent years by local volunteers. Aside from its rich historical value, the fishpond is great for families with young children since it's a protected area for swimming.

Waipuilani Beach Park

Less beach and more park, most locals know this shoreline park in central Kihei as the dog park, since it's a popular place to run the family pet. It's a popular local gathering place—particularly for watching the sunset—and is one of North Kihei's most popular beaches, even though there's hardly any sand. To reach the parking area, turn on Waipuilani Road at the corner of South Kihei Road and the Maui Sunset condo.

The Cove

Otherwise known as "the surf lesson spot," this beach at the south end of Kalama Park is known for its top-notch people-watching. The beach itself is just a small strip of sand, but it provides a front-row view for watching people surf. There's a volleyball court and shops across the street, and while it isn't Kihei's nicest beach, it's an action-packed hub of surfers, paddlers, and beachgoers soaking up rays.

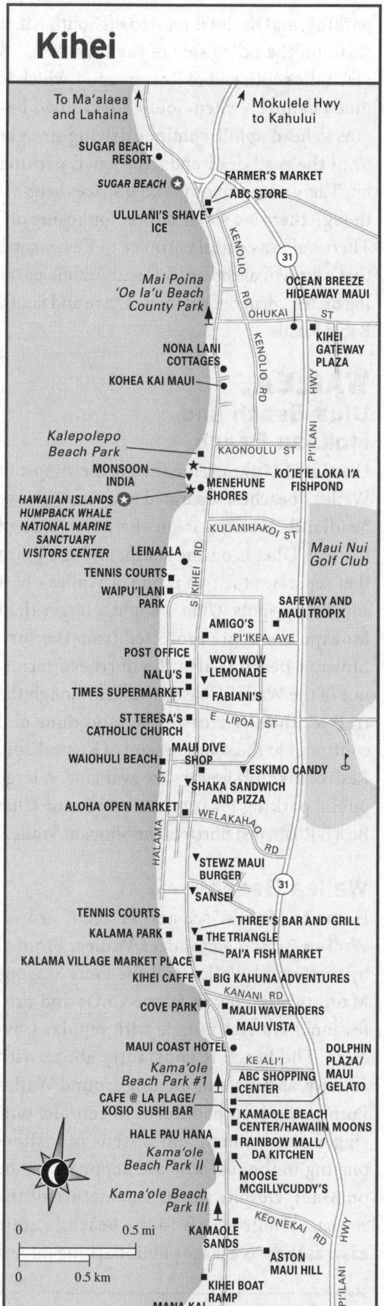

Kamaole I, II, and III

The **Kamaole Beach Parks** form the core of Kihei's beach scene. Grassy areas run parallel to the roadway, and all of the parks have showers, restrooms, picnic tables, and barbecue grills for a relaxing sunset meal. Kam I has a beach volleyball court on the north side of the park. The best way to experience these beaches is to take a stroll along the coast and link all three together. The lava rock headlands can be rough on your feet and *kiawe* (mesquite) trees drop thorns, so wear footwear if you walk all three beaches. The tide pools between Kam II and Kam III are a particularly nice place to explore, and when you reach the southern end of Kam III, there's a walking trail that runs for 0.75 mile (1.2 km) to the Kihei Boat Ramp.

Mornings are the best time for stand-up paddling and snorkeling, and by noon the wind can pick up and turn the surface to whitecaps. These are great beaches for bodysurfing almost any time of year, but sometimes waves can get dangerously large on the biggest summer swells. Kam I and Kam II have street parking, whereas larger Kam III has its own parking lot exclusively for beachgoers. Kam III is also the party spot where locals truck in horseshoes, ice chests, and bouncy houses for their three-year-old's birthday party. If you can't find parking, there's overflow parking between Kam III and the boat ramp.

Sometimes you will hear locals say they enjoy spending time at **Charley Young Beach;** this is just another name for the northern end of Kam I. It's protected from the wind when the southern section of the beach is choppy. Parking for Charley Young is along Kaiau Place, which is a small offshoot of South Kihei Road not far from the Cove Park.

★ Keawakapu Beach

Aside from Kam III, **Keawakapu** is Kihei's most popular beach. This long stretch of sand is more protected from the wind than the beaches farther north, and a small shop on the north end of the beach rents out stand-up paddleboards, kayaks, and snorkeling gear. In the morning, before the wind picks up, this beach is a bustle of snorkelers entering the water and kids splashing in the surf, and by late afternoon, it changes into the perfect perch for sunset. Snorkeling is best around the north and south headlands, and if you're feeling up for a really long stroll, you can connect with the Wailea Coastal Walk (page 173) at the southern end of the beach.

The north end of the beach has ample parking, and the lot is located off South Kihei Road on the north side of the Days Inn. To reach the south end of Keawakapu—which is much calmer—when South Kihei Road begins to head uphill, continue driving straight until the road dead-ends in a small parking lot. There aren't many parking spaces here, although there is a small shower for hosing off. There's also a central entrance to Keawakapu that's known as Sidewalks, with public parking on the corner of Kilohana Drive and South Kihei Road.

WAILEA

Ulua Beach and Mokapu Beach

Ulua and Mokapu are the northernmost of Wailea's beaches, separated by a small grassy headland. Mokapu is on the north side of the hill, Ulua is on the south, and the point that separates the two is one of Wailea's best snorkeling spots. Ulua is slightly larger than Mokapu and more protected from the surf. Mokapu Beach is also the northern terminus of the Wailea Coastal Walk, although the trail technically crosses the sand dune and continues to the southern end of Keawakapu. Restrooms and showers are available. A large public parking lot is at the bottom of Ulua Beach Road, just north of the Shops at Wailea.

Wailea Beach

Home to Maui's "see and be seen" crowd, **Wailea Beach** epitomizes Wailea. Fronted by the Grand Wailea and the Four Seasons Maui, this is a beach where CEOs and professional athletes mingle with regular travelers. The beach is constantly abuzz with activity, as there's snorkeling around Wailea Point, stand-up paddleboard rentals, outrigger canoe tours, and dozens of visitors playing in the surf who are happy to just be on Maui. Despite the private nature of the resorts, public access to the beach is quite easy, as there is a large public parking lot just

1: Sugar Beach **2:** Keawakapu Beach **3:** Kamaole Beach Park II **4:** sunset at Mokapu Beach

1
2
3
4

before the entrance to the Four Seasons. In the parking lot are public restrooms and showers.

Polo Beach

Polo Beach is the southernmost of Wailea's resort beaches, and is the southern terminus of the Wailea Coastal Walk. The cloud-white Fairmont Kea Lani dominates the shore, its Arabian spires providing a unique backdrop to the shimmering blue waters. Of all Wailea's beaches, Polo Beach is the most popular with locals due to the large public parking area being a convenient place for launching stand-up paddleboards and kayaks. There are public restrooms, showers, and one small barbecue grill. Polo Beach can also be good for boogie boarding in summer, and there is a small activity booth on the north side of the beach to rent a paddleboard or kayak. To reach Polo Beach, travel south along Wailea Alanui Drive before making a right on Kaukahi Street and following it to the end.

MAKENA AND BEYOND

Palauea Beach (White Rock)

Palauea Beach, otherwise known as **White Rock,** is a perfect spot for snorkeling, scuba diving, swimming, and lounging. Palauea translates to "lazy," and there's ample opportunity to be just that along its white sandy stretches, which are less crowded than Wailea or Polo Beaches, just north. Snorkeling is excellent around the rocky points at either end of the beach, while scuba diving is best on the south end. Boogie boarding is exceptional during south swells, and when the waters are calmer, they're ideal for wading and swimming—great for kids and adults. For decades this beach was about bonfires and guitars rather than gates and security cameras, but over the last few years, the mega-mansion sprawl has found its way to the shore. While there aren't any restrooms or showers, you can find all those amenities at Polo Beach, just a five-minute walk away. Parking for Palauea is along the side of Makena Road, and public access is at the southern end of the beach.

Po'olenalena Beach

Once frequented only by locals, **Po'olenalena Beach** can now get so busy it's tough to find a space in the potholed parking lot. There are volleyball games on Sunday afternoon, and the beach is a favorite for watching the sunset. On the north end, a small trail leads from the parking lot around a rocky point, bringing you to a cove that isn't visible from the road. There are usually about 10 percent as many people on the cove beach as on Po'olenalena. It's the perfect spot to escape with a beach chair, an umbrella, and a good book.

To find Po'olenalena, travel on Wailea Alanui Drive until you see Wailea Golf Club Drive on the left. Continue straight for one more minute to see the parking area for the beach on your right. For the public parking lot on the south end of the beach, look for the lot just before Makena Surf on the right side of the road. Barely visible and with only 10 spots, it's next to the yellow fire hydrant numbered 614.

Chang's Beach

If you're looking for a pocket of sand with exceptional snorkeling and not too many people, **Chang's Beach** will be your favorite spot in Makena. Not many make it here because it's hidden from the road. Chang's Beach is about 1.5 miles (2.4 km) past the Fairmont Kea Lani on Makena Alanui Road. Look for the small parking lot immediately past Makena Surf. If you find a spot in the parking lot *before* the Makena Surf building (the one by fire hydrant 614), walk south for 100 yards (90 m) past the gated entrance, and another parking lot with six spaces is on the right, by fire hydrant 616. From here a paved walkway leads down to the shore and the fingernail of sand.

★ Maluaka Beach

Directly in front of the Makena Beach and Golf Resort, **Maluaka Beach** is everything you've ever wanted in a beach. Locals refer to it as Prince Beach, since the hotel used to be called the Maui Prince. You'll find waters

Makena

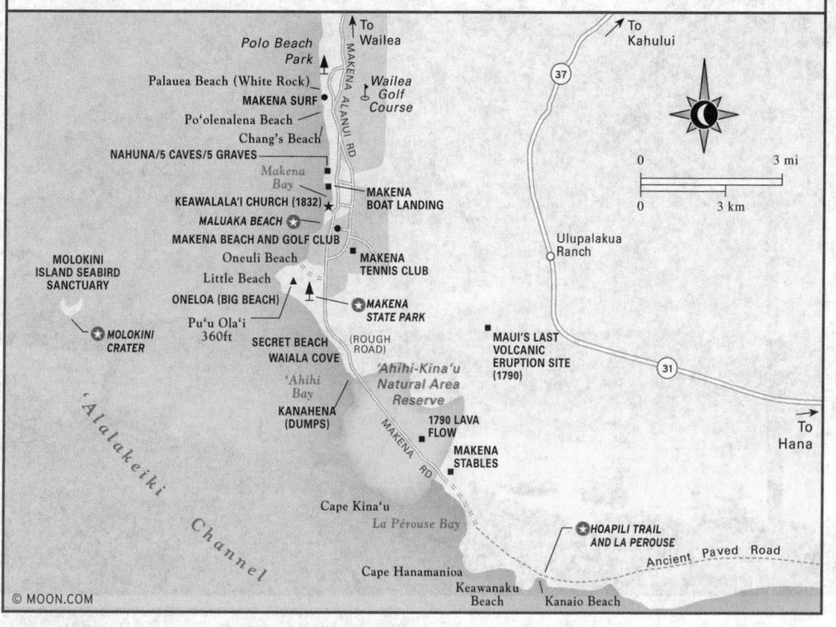

perfect for stand-up paddleboarding in the morning, good snorkeling around the north end, fun waves for boogie boarding during the summer, ample parking, restrooms and showers, and a grassy area for relaxing.

Maluaka Beach has two different entrances. On the north side, coming in on Makena Alanui, make a right on Honoiki Street, then a left onto Makena Road, to the public parking lot across from Keawala'i Church. For the south entrance, continue on Makena Alanui until you pass the entrance for the Makena Beach and Golf Resort, then continue past the turnoff for the golf and tennis club. As the road bends around to the right, you'll see a sign for Makena Keone'o'io on the right. Make a right, and follow it to the parking area.

★ Makena State Park

Among the string of golden shores, none can hold a sandy candle to **Oneloa,** or **Big Beach.** As the largest beach in Makena State Park, this mile-long (1.6-km) stretch of sand has avoided the rush of development, much of which is attributed to the grassroots movement to "Save Makena." Sunsets here are stellar.

In the early 1970s this area was a famous hippie commune where hundreds of draft-dodgers, nudists, and dropouts camped out back in the *kiawe* trees. Although Big Beach visitors have since put their pants on, the same can't be said for neighboring **Little Beach**—the island's official clothing-optional venue, just over the north side of the bluff. There's an anachronistic aura that permeates Little Beach, where simply clambering from one side to the other can transport you back to an era when life was easy and it was hip to be free. For an authentic Maui counterculture experience, check out the Little Beach Sunday night drum circle (page 184).

Before you get in the water at Makena, understand that the shore-break here is more powerful than anywhere on the island. There

1
2

should be a spinal clinic here for the number of back and neck injuries, and this isn't the place to splash in the waves with a boogie board from the ABC Store. There are lifeguard towers in case of emergency, but think twice before entering the water on days when there's any surf.

To reach Big Beach and Makena State Park, travel on Makena Alanui Road for 1 mile (1.6 km) past the entrance to the Makena Beach and Golf Resort. There are three entrances; the First and Second Entrances have large parking areas, and Third Entrance is just dirt on the side of the road. The closest parking spots are at First Entrance, and be sure not to leave any valuables in your vehicle. Despite its popularity, there still are no showers at Big Beach, and the nearest place to wash off the sand is at Maluaka Beach, 0.5 mile (0.8 km) north.

Oneuli Beach

You did it—you found a black-sand beach. The famous black-sand beach is in Hana, at Wai'anapanapa State Park, and **Oneuli Beach** in Makena State Park is dark brown and less famous. This hidden spot is a popular place for locals to kick back and fish, and there's good snorkeling at the south end of the bay only on the clearest and calmest days. The main draw, aside from the sand, is the lack of crowds, but note that the access road is potholed and bumpy. To reach Oneuli Beach, turn right off Makena Alanui Road 0.2 mile (0.3 km) past the turnoff for Maluaka Beach, and 0.2 mile (0.3 km) before the First Entrance to Big Beach.

Pa'ako Beach (Secret Cove)

If you want to go back home and tell your friends you found the "secret beach" on Maui, take the time to visit this gem. The problem is that even though **Pa'ako Beach** is also called **Secret Cove,** the tiny inlet of sand is anything but secret. Weddings take place on a daily basis, and the chances of having it to yourself are slim. To access the beach, you have to walk through a hole in a lava rock wall just south of the Third Entrance for Big Beach. Watch carefully to find the tiny opening. As you climb up and over a little hill where Big Beach ends, you will notice a lava rock wall running along the right side of the road. Next to the speed table is a blue Beach Access sign and a shoulder-width opening in the lava rock wall. If you're not sure if you're at the right spot, a telephone pole on the other side of the street has the code E2 3 written on it. The easiest access is to park at the Third Entrance for Big Beach and walk the rest of the way. As you might expect, sunsets here are as epic as they get.

Keawanaku Beach

If you're up for an epic hiking adventure to a beach hardly anyone knows about, put on your hiking boots and make the trek to **Keawanaku Beach.** The round-trip journey takes at least two hours on the Hoapili Trail (page 175).

1: Maluaka Beach **2:** Big Beach at Makena State Park

Snorkeling

MA'ALAEA

Although you'll often see little red dive flags fluttering in the wind off the harbor at **Ma'alaea Bay,** these are local spearfishers who are diving for *tako* (octopus). Don't mistake this for a nice snorkeling spot. Although Ma'alaea Bay once had a teeming reef prior to the 1990s, nearly 100 percent of it has died due to invasive species of algae. It has been a case study for what will happen to all the island's reefs if environmental dangers go unmitigated.

★ Molokini Crater

When it comes to snorkeling, what Ma'alaea is known for is the harbor that serves as the starting point for boats to **Molokini Crater,** a half-submerged volcanic caldera that rises in 300 feet (90 m) of water. Visibility here can be 100 feet (30 m) or better nearly every day of the year. Nowhere else in Hawaii is the water this consistently calm and clear. The back of Molokini Crater drops to almost 300 feet (90 m), but inside the bowl, where snorkel boats tie up, is only about 40 feet (12 m) deep, and the best snorkeling is along the rim of the crater in 15 feet (4.5 m) of water. At Molokini you have a great chance of finding colorful parrotfish, endemic reef species, octopuses, eels, and—if you're lucky—maybe a harmless whitetip reef shark. One species notably absent from Molokini, however, are Hawaiian green sea turtles—although most tour operators combine a trip to Molokini with a second snorkeling spot along the coast of Maui so that you can check turtles off your list.

Because it's so massively popular, however, Molokini is a place where it can sometimes seem like there are far more humans than fish. Avoid crowds by booking your trip for as early in the day as possible, and schedule this activity early in your trip, since you'll probably be waking up early anyway with a little bit of jet lag. Fewer fish dwell here than 20 years ago due to fish feeding, a popular activity in the 1980s, which disrupted the area's natural food chain. Since then, a handful of species took over the reef. Molokini is now a tightly controlled marine preserve, and you'll be required to fill out a form that outlines the rules for visiting.

Boats to Molokini fall into three categories: small, medium, and large. The cheaper the ticket to Molokini, the more people are going to be on the boat, which also means the more people there are going to be snorkeling with you. The larger boats, which are diesel catamarans, carry 150 people during busier months. There are three sailboat companies that carry 20-50 people. Three raft companies carry up to 24 and get you to Molokini quickly and easily. These trips can be economical, and the small group size ensures personalized service, but the tradeoff is that the food won't be as good as on larger boats, and the restroom situation can be tight. Rafts aren't recommended for anyone who is pregnant or has back or neck problems.

Nearly all boats leave for Molokini from Ma'alaea Harbor. Note that Lahaina Harbor is not a departure point for Molokini Crater. Three rafts and most scuba-diving boats leave from Kihei Boat Ramp. At Makena, the sailing catamaran *Kai Kanani* departs from Maluaka Beach; its early trip is one of the first to arrive at Molokini.

Rental Shops

The best place for renting snorkel gear in Ma'alaea is at **Maui Dive Shop** (101 Ma'alaea Harbor Rd., Slip 74, 800/542-3483, www.mauidiveshop.com, 7am-7pm daily) in the Ma'alaea Harbor Shops. There is a wide range of snorkeling equipment for rent or purchase, and you can pick up an optical mask if you normally wear prescription glasses.

What Molokini Snorkelers Need to Know

About 80 percent of the year, trade winds are so strong that Molokini Crater is filled with 4-foot (1.2-m) waves by noon, so boats **go there early in the morning.** A discount tour to Molokini that departs at 2pm, conditions permitting, is a scam, since conditions will rarely be permitting. You might get lucky, but chances are you'll end up snorkeling at a spot named Coral Gardens.

Most of the year, and every day in summer, **the ride back to Ma'alaea Harbor is very rough,** with 30-knot (56-km/h) winds and sheets of spray coming over the bow. Some people love the ride, and although it's not dangerous, others are terrified. Grab a sheltered seat toward the back of the boat and brace yourself.

The water temperature on Maui fluctuates between 73°F (23°C) in winter and 79°F (26°C) in summer—colder than the Gulf of Mexico, but still warmer than most oceans. If you go on one of the large diesel boats, you will be asked if you want to rent a wet suit. The crew receives a commission, so expect a sales pitch. **Don't rent a wet suit** unless you think you will actually need one.

Molokini Crater offers dozens of species of fish, impossibly clear water, and healthy, vibrant corals, but **there are no green sea turtles.** All the turtles are found along the southern shore, so to see some turtles, book a charter that stops along the shore.

If there is large surf along the southern shore (more frequent in summer than winter), **the water color at Turtle Town will be closer to green than blue.** If the visibility along the shore isn't what you expected, it's due to increased surf.

Even if you book an early tour to beat the afternoon trade winds, if the wind is blowing out of the north, Molokini isn't accessible. Often this wind switch can occur within minutes, so **there is a chance you'll end up snorkeling at a secondary spot,** which usually still ends up being a good trip.

Molokini Crater is a tightly controlled marine reserve. Feeding fish or stepping on coral can carry heavy penalties. **Don't feed the fish!**

Snorkeling Charters

Trilogy Excursions (Slips 62 and 99, 808/874-5649, www.sailtrilogy.com) has been the gold standard for charter boats on Maui for 45 years. Their Molokini trip ($169 adults) is pricier than the budget options, but you get what you pay for: Trilogy boats have only 40-50 passengers, snuba is available as an upgrade, and you get to enjoy a sailing catamaran to feel the breeze in your hair. The 7am trip on the *Trilogy V* departs from Slip 99, and the 8am trip is on the larger and newer *Trilogy II* from Slip 62. On Wednesday and Friday, Trilogy also offers the adults-only Captain's Sunset Dinner Sail ($145), focusing on luxury dining and drinking.

***Four Winds* Molokini Maui Snorkel Tours** (101 Maalaea Rd., 808/879-1571, www.fourwindsmaui.com) is an established enterprise with a great crew at your service. The five-hour catamaran excursion offers morning snorkel tours to Molokini ($125 adults, $95 children) and leaves the harbor at 7:30am. *Four Winds* makes Molokini its only stop, so you have plenty of time to relax and explore the crater at your own pace. The downside is that you won't get the chance to snorkel with turtles, although you do make a stop at a "turtle cleaning station" to view the turtles from above. Breakfast *and* lunch are offered. Options to delve into snuba or nab some photos from the professional photographer are also offered.

Along with *Trilogy II* and *Kai Kanani* in Makena, ***Ali'i Nui* Sailing Charters** (Slip 56, 808/875-0333, www.aliinuimaui.com) is on a sailing catamaran, but it sure feels like you're on a yacht. With sleek black-and-white trim, this 65-foot (19.8-m) catamaran is also one of the island's widest, at 36 feet (11 m), providing a more stable platform. *Ali'i Nui* is affiliated with Maui Dive Shop, and while their snorkeling excursion ($199 adults, $149 children) is more expensive than others, they also

1

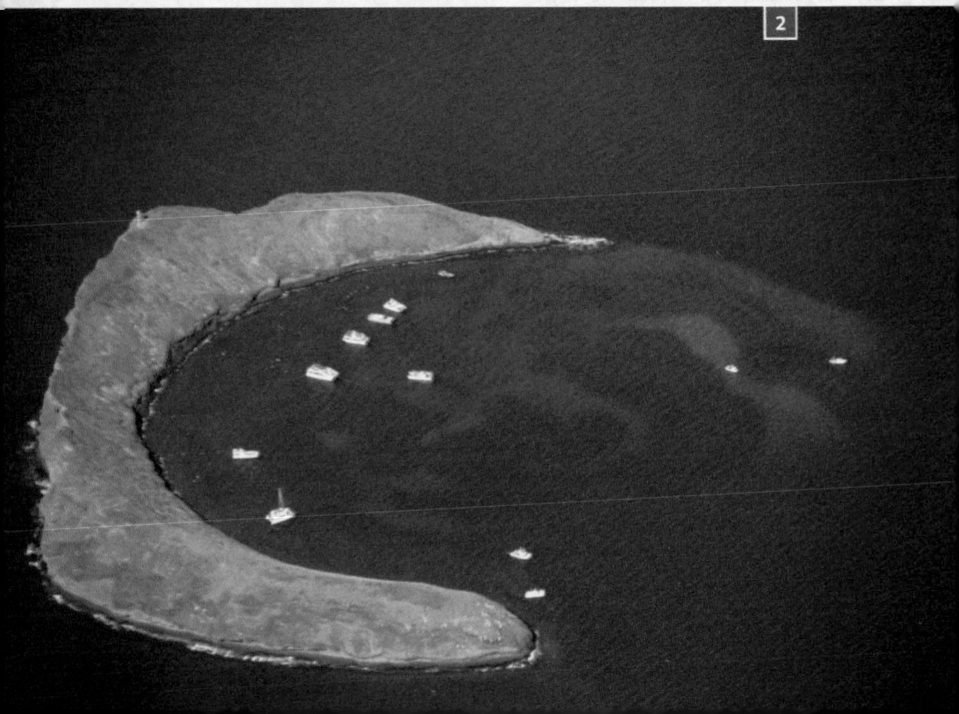

2

How to Avoid Being Eaten by a Shark

Sharks get a really bad rap, even though they're important to a healthy marine ecosystem and pose minimal danger to humans. That said, if you're still concerned about sharks in Maui when you're snorkeling, swimming, or diving (and, don't worry, you're not the only one), here are a couple of tips to minimize the minuscule chance of getting bitten:

- Stay out of the water after a heavy rain, when the water is murky and brown.
- Avoid swimming near stream mouths or river mouths that empty into the ocean.
- Avoid swimming at dawn and dusk, when sharks are slightly more active.
- Swim in a group—or at least with a buddy—if you plan to swim far offshore.
- If you encounter a shark while paddleboarding, drop to your knees, keep your eyes on the shark, and use your paddle as a weapon.

By following some basic ocean safety, you minimize the risk of an attack. If the sun is shining, the water is blue, and conditions are shallow and calm, you run a much greater risk of getting a sunburn than getting attacked by a shark.

include complimentary transportation to and from your hotel if you're staying on the west or south side of Maui. *Ali'i Nui* offers snuba—but calls it "huka"—for $65 extra, whereas other companies have switched to snuba. *Ali'i Nui* visits Molokini Tuesday, Thursday, and Saturday-Sunday during whale season (mid-Dec.-mid-Apr.). On Monday, Wednesday, and Friday mid-April-mid-December, they sail to Olowalu, or, as they call it, "Turtle Point."

The company with the largest presence in Ma'alaea Harbor is **Pacific Whale Foundation** (300 Ma'alaea Boat Harbor Rd., 808/249-8811, www.pacificwhale.org), a nonprofit organization with headquarters in the Ma'alaea Harbor Shops. Instead of checking in down at the harbor, check in at the main shop. These cruises are more economical than some of the higher-priced excursions, although on busy days you could be sharing the boat with more than 100 people. Note that the boat cruises, Pacific Whale Foundation Eco-Adventures, are a for-profit business, and the nonprofit arm of the company is funded by merchandise sales and gear rentals.

The standard Pacific Whale itinerary for trips to Molokini ($159 adults) departs at 7am and 8am daily and features two snorkeling spots. A smaller vessel, with no more than 38 passengers, is the 7:30am Molokini Wild Side Eco-Adventure ($169 adults), which is both an ecotour and snorkel excursion. May-November, when whale-watching trips aren't running, there are a greater number of options for snorkeling times and charters.

The ***Pride of Maui*** (101 Ma'alaea Boat Harbor Rd., 808/242-0955, www.prideofmaui.com) offers a five-hour excursion ($196 adults) aboard a large power catamaran that features a glass-bottom viewing area and a large top deck for sunning. Trips depart at 8am next to the U.S. Coast Guard station. This popular boat can frequently load over 100 passengers. There's also the Leilani Molokini & Turtle Town Snorkel Tour ($196 adults), which typically includes turtle sightings and explores the coral gardens of Molokini.

One of the cheapest trips to Molokini ($119 adults) is on ***Malolo*** (Slip 87, 808/661-9937, www.molokinimaui.com/malolo). The focus is on quantity, but if you're just looking for a trip to the crater, it's an affordable option. A higher-quality boat that also carries more passengers is ***Calypso*** (Slip 82, 808/661-9937, http://calypsomaui.com), whose Molokini

1: snorkelers near Molokini Crater **2:** aerial view of Molokini Crater

snorkeling trip ($149 adults) visits two spots. *Calypso* is also known for its semiformal dinner cruise ($119 adults), which features live music and often tucks around the corner of West Maui to get a good angle on the sunset and shelter from the wind. Both ships offer discounted online rates.

If you want to visit Molokini from Ma'alaea but don't want to spend a lot of time getting there, the ***Aqua Adventure*** (Slip 51, 808/573-2104, www.mauisnorkelsnuba.com) leaves at 7am and cruises at speeds much faster than the larger boats. The small number of passengers, capped at 40, is also a plus, and snuba gets people in the water. You can choose to snorkel, but if your main priority is getting to Molokini quickly to snuba dive, this trip ($171 adults) visits two snorkeling spots and offers an additional upgrade for snuba. Trips return by noon.

A similar operation that features snuba and small crowds is **Lani Kai** (Slip 76, 808/244-1979, www.mauisnorkeling.com), a trip ($141) that departs at 7am and visits two snorkeling locations. Lani Kai also has an afternoon charter ($79) that cruises the cliffs over to Coral Gardens and ties up next to *Four Winds* and *Malolo*, with the difference being there are far fewer people on the boat.

KIHEI

Mornings are the best time of day for snorkeling in Kihei, before the wind picks up. Winter mornings offer light winds, clear visibility, and calm water, and as an added bonus, if you dive down a few feet while snorkeling, you're guaranteed to hear whale song reverberating in the distance. Summer can have intermittent periods of high surf, which can affect visibility.

Snorkeling Spots

The northernmost beach in Kihei to snorkel is **Charley Young Beach,** also known as the north end of Kamaole I. There's a rocky point on the right side of the beach that offers good snorkeling, and at the southern end of the beach, the rocky points between **Kamaole I** and **Kamaole II,** and **Kamaole II** and **Kamaole III,** have colorful reef fish and turtles.

Keawakapu Beach, 0.5 mile (0.8 km) south of Kamaole III, has good snorkeling on both the north and south sides of the bay. The north end can get crowded due to the large public parking lot and bustling activity stand, and if you want to escape the crowd, either get here early, before everyone arrives, or just snorkel the outer edge of the reef in front of the Mana Kai hotel. To combine a morning snorkel with a stroll, park at the northern end of Keawakapu Beach and walk to the southern point. There are fewer crowds, it has a larger area for snorkeling, and the walk back to your car is one of the island's best beach walks.

Rental Shops

Choosing where to rent snorkels in Kihei can be overwhelming, and before you go flinging open the nearest door, it's important to understand the nature of the snorkel rental business on Maui: Most snorkel shops and activity stands in Kihei are fronts for activity sales and timeshare presentations, so expect a sales pitch for a helicopter ride or vacation rental, even if your only intention is to go snorkeling. As a general rule, if it seems too cheap, there's probably a catch.

Maui Dive Shop (1455 S. Kihei Rd., 808/879-3388, 7am-4pm daily) is a reputable option for anything related to snorkeling or diving, and **Boss Frog's** (main office 1770 S. Kihei Rd., 808/874-5225, www.bossfrog.com, 8am-5pm daily) has three locations in Kihei and some of the island's cheapest rentals. The company is heavily embedded in the activities sales market, so expect a sales pitch.

Snorkel Bob's has multiple stores in Kihei, including the Kamaole Beach Center (2411 S. Kihei Rd., 808/879-7449, www.snorkelbob.com, 8am-5pm daily), and another in the Azeka Mauka shopping center in central Kihei (1279 S. Kihei Rd., 808/875-6188, 8am-5pm daily). Snorkel Bob's is a statewide chain that also incorporates activity sales,

The Lowdown on Snuba

On many of the boats that visit Molokini Crater, you can upgrade to a snuba dive, but what exactly does that mean?

Snuba (SNOO-Bah) is the safest, easiest, and fastest way to experience what it's like to breathe underwater. It is similar to scuba diving in that you breathe through a regulator, but instead of having to wear pounds of gear, take an in-depth class, and swim with a tank on your back, on a snuba dive the air tank sits on a raft above the surface, and the only equipment you wear are a weight belt and a lightweight shoulder harness. A 10-foot-long (3-m) hose descends from the inflatable raft above you and connects to your regulator, so it's almost like snorkeling. Since snuba is more user-friendly than scuba diving, it's the perfect option if you like snorkeling but are hesitant about full-on scuba diving.

Some commonly asked questions:

Q: What is the minimum age for snuba?
A: Eight.

Q: How deep will I go?
A: Up to 20 feet (6 m); at Molokini Crater, 10 feet (3 m).

Q: How long can I stay underwater?
A: In most cases you share an air tank with another diver, and most dives last 20-25 minutes.

Q: Do I need to know how to swim?
A: Yes. Flotation devices would defeat the point of the activity.

Q: I've never snorkeled before. Can I still snuba?
A: It's helpful to have snorkeled, but not necessary. As a quick self-test, pinch your nose and breathe through your mouth for 30 seconds. If this feels awkward, you might want to pass on snuba diving.

Q: Can I fly or travel to Haleakala after a snuba dive?
A: Yes. Since you don't descend as deep as in scuba diving, your body doesn't accumulate enough nitrogen for flying to be a problem.

Q: Do I need to be in good health to snuba?
A: Although snuba is more amenable to physical limitations than scuba diving is, you still need to complete a standard medical form.

Q: If I'm congested, can I snuba dive?
A: Not unless you want to have unbearable sinus pain.

Q: My ears hurt when I dive underwater. Can I still snuba?
A: Yes. Your instructor will teach you how to equalize the air spaces in your ears so that you won't feel any pressure.

Q: How much does snuba diving cost?
A: While every operation is different, most boats offer snuba as a $59-69 upgrade.

and you're sure to see their quirky ads if you flip through any island visitors magazines. Snorkel Bob's is known for selling gear they design themselves, and a nice feature of the operation is that you can rent gear on one island and return it on another island free of charge. Packages range from $4 per day for a basic mask and snorkel rental to $48 per week for a package that includes prescription lenses and fins.

Snorkeling Boats

The great thing about the snorkeling charters from Kihei Boat Ramp is it only takes

15 minutes to reach Molokini Crater (compared to an hour from Ma'alaea Harbor). The rafts only carry about 24 people, so if you don't like crowds, these are the trips for you, unless you're pregnant or have back or neck problems.

Blue Water Rafting (808/879-7238, www.bluewaterrafting.com) meets at the boat ramp at 7am. If you've already been to Molokini and are looking for an adventure snorkel, Blue Water has a trip to the Kanaio Coast, where you can snorkel along a volcanic coast most visitors will never see. This forgotten southwestern coast is pockmarked with thundering sea caves and jagged lava formations, and there are multiple places where you can see the remnants of ancient fishing villages. The captains are geologists, historians, and marine naturalists, skilled enough to hug the coast so closely you could almost reach out and touch it. The waters in this area can be rough, however, so this isn't the best trip if you're prone to motion sickness. Book the four-hour Kanaio Coastline tour ($117 adults, $84 children) or combine it with an 11am excursion to Molokini ($181 adults, $149 children). There is no breakfast, coffee, or restroom on board, and the minimum age for children is four.

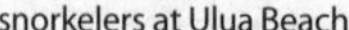

The other primary snorkeling option from Kihei Boat Ramp is **Redline Rafting** (808/698-5837, www.redlinerafting.com), which differs from Blue Water Rafting in that they go to Molokini first, even taking time to snorkel the backside of the crater in 300 feet (90 m) of water. From there they motor down toward Keone'o'io (La Perouse Bay) to snorkel and search for dolphins, and then explore the northern fringes of the rugged Kanaio Coast. Because this tour visits Molokini, it doesn't go as far south as Blue Water Rafting, although it is one of the earliest boats to the crater. Tours ($189 adults) meet at 6:30am and include breakfast, coffee, and a boat with a restroom.

Seafire (808/879-2201, www.molokinissnorkeling.com) offers a trip ($79) at 7:30am daily on its orange and silver jet-drive raft that not only looks like a Coast Guard boat but is driven by a member of the Coast Guard Reserve. Trips last for three hours, and it's one of the best budget options for reaching Molokini Crater. On the way back toward the Kihei Boat Ramp, you'll stop at a spot along the coast to look for Hawaiian green sea turtles, or maybe even stop at the wreck of the *St. Anthony*, scuttled off the Kihei coast.

snorkelers at Ulua Beach

WAILEA

★ Ulua Beach and Mokapu Beach

The best locations for snorkeling in Wailea are **Ulua Beach** and **Mokapu Beach,** listed together because the rocky point that separates them is where you'll find the most marinelife. Ulua, the southernmost, is more protected and offers a gentle, sandy entry. This is the perfect spot for beginning snorkelers. Morning hours are calm and are the best time for finding turtles. Winter months have the best visibility, and if you're staying at one of the Wailea resorts, you can reach the beaches by strolling along the Wailea Coastal Walk. If you are driving, there are two small public parking lots that fill up early; arrive before 9am. To reach the parking area, turn on Ulua Beach Road off Wailea Alanui Drive just north of the Shops at Wailea, and follow the road down to the parking lots at the end.

Wailea Point

The second most popular spot for snorkeling in Wailea is **Wailea Point,** a rocky promontory rife with green sea turtles that separates the Four Seasons and Fairmont Kea Lani. The easiest point of entry is from the south side of Wailea Beach in front of the Four Seasons, but be prepared for a five-minute swim over sand.

MAKENA AND BEYOND

While Makena offers some of the south side's best snorkeling, the entry and exit points can be a little more challenging than at Kihei or Wailea beaches. Makena is more exposed to southerly swell than the beaches to the north are, so visibility is affected and waves can sometimes crash into the lava rocks with such fury that it's the last place you want to be. Assess the conditions and your own abilities before venturing into the water.

Snorkeling Spots

The best place for beginner snorkeling in Makena is **Maluaka Beach,** in front of the Makena Beach and Golf Resort. There's a rocky point that wraps around the north end of the beach, and the entry from the sand into the water is gentle.

While Maluaka might be the easiest place to snorkel in Makena, the best snorkeling is at **Makena Landing.** The entry can be a little challenging, but once you make it out past the shallow areas, you'll be glad you made the effort. There are multiple entry and exit points for Makena Landing, the most common being the public parking area off Makena Road. To reach the parking area, drive along Makena Alanui until you reach Honoiki Street and the turn for Keawala'i Church. When you reach the bottom of Honoiki, turn right and follow the road 0.25 mile (0.4 km) until you see a parking area on the left.

Once in the water, hug the coast toward the point on the right, and when you have rounded the tip, you'll notice there is a long finger of lava underwater that extends out toward Molokini. This is what's known as the South Finger, and there's a sea cave here that houses green sea turtles. Many snorkel boat operators refer to this area as **Turtle Town,** and unless you want to share the water with 200 other snorkelers, try to be out here before 10am. If you swim north from the South Finger, you will pass over lime-green coral heads. Keep an eye out for moray eels or the strange-looking flying gurnard. Eventually you'll come to the North Finger, another underwater lava formation that houses many turtles. This finger is covered in bright-red slate-pencil urchins that the ancient Hawaiians used for red dye. Eagle rays and manta rays are sometimes seen off the deeper end of the finger.

An alternate entry point for Makena Landing is via the north side at a spot known as **Five Graves.** Parking is scarce, and the entry can be challenging, but it's a much shorter swim to reach the fingers. Instead of turning into the parking lot on Makena Road, continue driving up and over the hill. When the road drops back down to the shore, park in a dirt area on the right that can fit about five cars. On the other side of the street is a small trail. You'll know this is the right path if you see five graves in a small graveyard on the left.

The Aquarium Is Closed

Many outdated guidebooks claim the best snorkeling in South Maui is at two spots in the 'Ahihi-Kina'u Natural Area Reserve known as the Aquarium and the Fishbowl, hidden near the end of the paved road and accessible via a trail through the island's most recent lava flow.

These areas became too popular, and what was once a sensitive and protected part of the island was overrun by visitors who left trash, introduced pollutants to the water such as petroleum-based spray-on sunscreens, and destroyed sensitive ponds. It seemed the only solution for keeping troublemakers out was to keep all visitors out, so the area was closed in 2008.

The area still hasn't recovered from overuse, and you can incur a hefty fine if you're found snorkeling in this area. Sneaky visitors sometimes try to enter by sea via a long swim from La Perouse Bay, but this is dangerous. There are many other spots for good snorkeling along the island's south side.

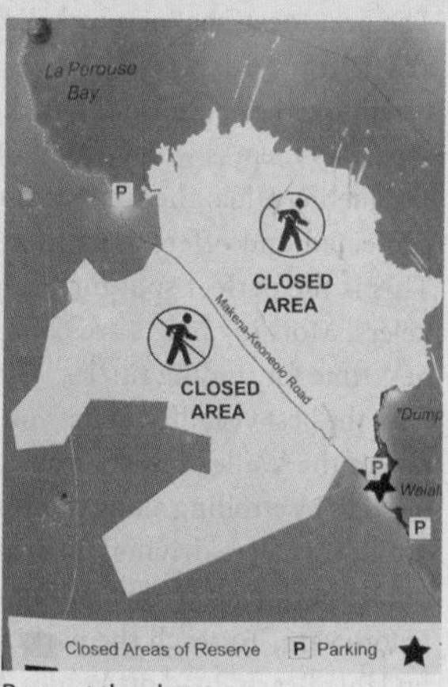

Respect the closure.

Follow this trail to the shore. The easiest place to get in and out of the water is a protected nook in the rocks on the right. Although the beach area to the left of the trail looks like it would be easier, it's shallow for a long way out, and you don't want to contend with the breaking waves. On calm days this is the quickest means of reaching the fingers. On days with surf, forget about it.

Moving south, inside **Makena State Park,** the best snorkeling is at the point that separates Big Beach from Little Beach. Park in the First Entrance to Big Beach, and turn right when you hit the sand. This leads to the far northern end of the beach, where you can enter the water to snorkel around the point. The surf can get big here in the summer, so this is only possible on a flat day. For more direct access to the reef, clamber up and over the hill to Little Beach and snorkel in the cove off the left side of the bay. If there are waves in the bay, however, it's best to go elsewhere, because this puts you in the path of oncoming boogie boarders—some of whom swim naked.

While there have been lots of complaints about the parts of 'Ahihi-Kina'u Natural Area Reserve that are closed, parts of the beautiful coast are still open, including **Waiala Cove,** a small, rocky, and mostly protected bay with crystal clear water for snorkeling. Since this area is so popular, and the road so narrow, it's common for there to be traffic jams, so rather than trying to park on the road, continue driving 0.2 mile (0.3 km) to the parking lot for Kanahena Cove. Here you'll find a gravel trail that winds its way back toward Waiala Cove. The best entry is on the northern side, just a few feet off the road. While Waiala has great snorkeling when the water is calm, if waves are breaking inside the bay, it's best to go someplace else. At **Kanahena Cove,** follow the trail from the large parking lot down to the rocky coast to snorkel the reef that's known to local surfers and divers as **Dumps.** This spot gets very busy, especially in winter, and in summer there is frequently large breaking surf that makes it too dangerous to snorkel.

The Department of Land and Natural Resources has a small office in the parking lot, offering maps of the Makena area. The staff has also erected signs with yellow fish that show the best places to snorkel (for the record, the fish is the *lauwiliwilinukunuku'oi'oi*—say that 10 times fast). To reach the Kanahena

Don't Feed the Fish!

There was a time when bread crumbs, frozen peas, and fish food were as integral to a snorkeling outing as a mask and fins. Though other places in the world still allow fish feeding for the enjoyment of snorkelers, here in Hawaii, feeding fish has had a devastating effect on the marine ecosystem—particularly on coral reefs.

Don't feed fish in the ocean for the same reason you don't feed bears in the woods: It isn't their normal diet. The next time you go snorkeling in Hawaii, in addition to looking at the colorful aquatic species, listen to what you hear underwater. The snap, crackle, and pop sounds are the reef fish feeding on algae. When herbivorous reef fish gorge themselves on the outside food you introduce into the water, they become full and stop eating the algae. Consequently, the reef's coral polyps become so overgrown that they struggle to breathe and ultimately die.

Aside from the adverse effect on the coral, larger fish species have been known to drive out the smaller fish species in areas where people feed fish. Many visitors to Molokini notice there are fewer fish than when they visited in the 1980s. This is the reason for the stringent restrictions currently in place.

If that isn't enough to deter you, remember that some fish have really sharp teeth. Many visitors have oval-shaped scars on their fingers from introducing food into the water. For your own safety and the health of the reef, don't feed the fish!

parking lot, travel 2.5 miles (4 km) past Makena Beach and Golf Resort, or about 1 mile (1.6 km) past Makena State Park. Because break-ins have been a problem, don't leave any valuables in the car.

Finally, just when you think the road will never end, the asphalt gives way to a gravel parking lot in a spot known as **Keone'o'io,** or **La Perouse Bay.** The lava field that you drive over on the way to La Perouse is the remnants of Haleakala's last eruption. The bay is named for the French explorer Jean-François de Galaup, comte de Lapérouse, who in 1786 was the first European to set foot on Maui at this very spot. As you enter the parking area, there's a stone structure memorializing this event.

The snorkeling in La Perouse Bay can be phenomenal, although there are also times when it can be a total bust. Early mornings are best, before the trade winds fill the bay with whitecaps, and summer can bring large surf, which turns the shore into a cauldron of white water. On calm days, however, the best snorkeling is found to the right of the parking lot, where you must scramble across a lava rock point to reach the protected inlet. The water here is an enchanting turquoise against the young black lava rock.

Snorkeling Boats

Kai Kanani (808/879-7218, www.kaikanani.com) is the snorkeling boat leaving from Makena, which features added amenities you would expect from a luxury yacht and top-notch captains. *Kai Kanani* departs directly from Maluaka Beach in front of the Makena Beach and Golf Resort, which, if you're staying in Makena, or even Wailea, makes it a far more convenient option for sailing to Molokini than driving to Ma'alaea Harbor.

If that weren't enough, they also offer free transportation to the beach from Wailea resorts. If Molokini was too crowded the last time you visited, *Kai Kanani*'s early morning Molokini charter ($198 adults) departs the beach at 6:15am and guarantees you're the first boat at the crater, since it only takes about 15 minutes to motor across the channel. This trip is just over two hours long, and while the second trip of the day ($229 adults) visits the crater when it's more crowded, the fact that it's nearly four hours long, as opposed to two, allows for twice the amount of snorkeling in twice the number of spots. If you're concerned about getting seasick, the journey time from Maluaka Beach to Molokini is much shorter than the journey between Molokini and Ma'alaea.

Scuba Diving

South Maui has some of the island's best shore diving, and with so many locations and so many different operators, planning your dives can be overwhelming. The information in this section will help you find the operations and locations that suit you best.

MA'ALAEA

Dive Sites

While **Molokini Crater** can be a great place to snorkel, to truly experience the crater's magic, you have to put on a tank. For experienced divers Molokini ranks among the best dive locations around the world, and for novices it's a window into a new aquatic universe. Only certified divers are allowed to dive at Molokini. If you aren't certified but want to experience it from below, sign up for a 20-minute snuba dive to depths of up to 10 feet (3 m).

What makes the crater such an exceptional dive spot is the combination of its pelagic location, where it's possible to see anything, and the multiple dive spots within the crater that cater to a wide range of ability levels. Novices will enjoy either Middle Reef or Reef's End, as depths don't usually exceed 70 feet (20 m). **Middle Reef** is home to pelagic species such as jacks and reef sharks, and the sand channel houses curious-looking garden eels. There's also a huge drop-off at the Middle Reef section where it can be easy to exceed your depth.

Similarly, at **Reef's End,** the dive traces the wall of the underwater caldera to the point where it drops off into the abyss. Since this underwater promontory sits on the fringe of the crater, this area offers the best chance of sighting bottlenose dolphins, manta rays, humpback whales, and even the occasional whale shark.

The best and most advanced dive in Molokini Crater is a drift dive of the legendary **Back Wall.** Beginning at Reef's End, divers follow the current along the back of Molokini, where a vertical wall drops 250 feet (76 m) to the ocean floor. If you use nitrox or mixed gases, this is the deepest dive available anywhere in Maui County.

Even though diving at Molokini offers a chance of seeing sharks, for a guarantee of diving with them, the most unique dive on the island is at the **Maui Ocean Center** (192 Ma'alaea Rd., 808/270-7000, www.mauioceancenter.com), where you can go diving *inside the shark tank*. As part of its Shark Dive Maui program, certified divers can spend 30-40 minutes surrounded by various species, including hammerhead and tiger sharks. The dive ($199) has a limit of four divers and is only offered on Monday, Wednesday, and Friday mornings. The cost includes the tank and the weight, although divers have to provide the rest of their gear. Although diving at an aquarium might seem like cheating, even some of Maui's most seasoned divers claim it's a great dive. More than just a novelty, this is your best opportunity to be completely surrounded by the ocean's most feared and misrepresented creatures.

One of the island's newest wreck dives is a **Helldiver** World War II airplane that was abandoned by a pilot on a training run off Sugar Beach. When the pilot ejected, his plane sank in 50 feet (15 m) of water, and for the better part of 60 years it sat forgotten in the mudflats. When a local fisher tipped off a Kihei dive instructor that there was probably something down there, the exploratory dive mission yielded a historical discovery that is now property of the U.S. military. While there isn't an overwhelming amount of marinelife here, this is a unique dive you won't find in many people's logbooks. There aren't any regularly scheduled trips to the Helldiver, but many South Maui operators periodically plan

1: exploring the contours of South Maui's shore
2: colorful fish near Molokini Crater

1

2

excursions to the site, so inquire about when the next outing might be.

Rental Operators

The only retail operator in Ma'alaea that rents out dive gear is **Maui Dive Shop** (101 Ma'alaea Harbor Rd., Slip 74, 808/875-0333, www.mauidiveshop.com, 7am-7pm daily) in the Ma'alaea Harbor Shops. Although most dive operations furnish their own gear, this is a good place to pick up equipment if you're diving at the Maui Ocean Center or need accessories.

Dive Boats

Although most Molokini dive boats depart from the Kihei Boat Ramp, two that depart from Ma'alaea Harbor are the 48-foot (14.5-m) ***Maka Koa,*** operated by Maui Dive Shop (Slip 74, 808/875-0333, www.mauidiveshop.com), as well as the 40-foot (12-m) ***Maui Diamond II*** (Slip 22, 808/879-9119, www.mauidiamond.com). Maui Dive Shop offers two-tank trips to Molokini Crater six times per week, and the second dive is either along the shore of Maui or at the *St. Anthony* wreck off Kihei. Rates for a two-tank dive are $179, and renting a buoyancy control device and a regulator is an additional $20. Snorkelers are allowed to accompany divers for $99. The trip is a good option for novice divers who want to explore in the 65-70-foot (20-21-m) range. An added perk of booking with Maui Dive Shop is that they provide transportation from your hotel to Ma'alaea Harbor. Check-in is at 6:15am at the store in the Ma'alaea Harbor Shops.

For a few dollars less, *Maui Diamond II* offers two-tank trips to Molokini and the South Maui shore ($169), and rental of a buoyancy control device and a regulator is an additional $20. If you aren't a certified diver, you have the option of partaking in a Discover Scuba Diving introductory class, where you will snorkel at Molokini and then dive with an instructor at the second spot along the shore. The cost of the snorkel and introductory dive combo ($155) includes all the equipment.

KIHEI

Dive Sites

The only real dive site in Kihei is the ***St. Anthony* wreck** off the south end of Keawakapu Beach. Maui Dive Shop offers dives to this part of a massive artificial reef system twice weekly as part of a two-tank excursion combined with Molokini.

Rental and Shore-Dive Operators

If you need to rent gear, get gear serviced, pick up tanks for a shore dive, or book a guided shore dive with an instructor, there are a number of different retail operators throughout Kihei. My top pick is **Maui Dreams** (1993 S. Kihei Rd., 808/874-5332, www.mauidreamsdiveco.com, 7am-4pm daily) in the shop across from the southern end of Kalama Park. These guys love to dive and offer a full range of excursions, including a one-tank scooter dive ($129), night dives ($139), and regular introductory dives ($149). Guided shore dives for certified divers are $89. Maui Dreams is also the only PADI Five-Star Instructor Development Center in South Maui, so these people literally instruct the instructors. You can complete your scuba certification for as little as $349 if you've already completed the E-Learning section that's found on the PADI website.

Inside the Azeka Mauka shopping center, **B&B Scuba** (1280 S. Kihei Rd., 808/875-2861, www.bbscuba.com, 7am-4pm Mon.-Sat., 7am-2pm Sun.) offers guided shore dives ($159) and scooter dives ($149) along the South Maui shore. Other operators focus on recreational diving, but B&B offers PADI certification classes and IANTD tech diving classes with trimix, nitrox, and rebreather training. They also provide gear rental and tank pumping.

Dive Boats

All dive boats in Kihei leave from Kihei Boat Ramp, just south of Kamaole III Beach. Parking is tight in the main lot, so head to the overflow lot on the right. The scene at the boat ramp in the morning can be hectic—especially in the dark. Most boats offer coffee aboard if you still need a wake-up, and most boats have private restrooms. Since a number of boats that leave from Kihei Boat Ramp don't have offices, bring a credit card or cash so you can pay on board. If you plan on diving during your time on Maui, bring your certification card.

Of all the choices in Kihei, the top pick among locals is **Mike Severn's** (808/879-6596, www.mikesevernsdiving.com), Kihei's original dive-boat operation. A number of the other operators in Kihei provide exceptional service, but it's impossible to beat Mike Severn's. An instructor might sit down with you, take out a book, and thoroughly explain the species you just saw. At Mike Severn's, the instructors wrote those books. Since Mike Severn's caters to seasoned divers, the instructors don't mandate "follow the leader," giving you the freedom to enjoy the dive at your own pace. Two-tank dives are $199. Meet at 6am at the Kihei Boat Ramp aboard the 38-foot (11.5-m) *Pilikai*.

Also among South Maui's best, **Ed Robinson's** (808/879-3584, www.mauiscuba.com) caters to advanced divers and underwater photographers. Meet at 6:30am at the Kihei Boat Ramp. Regular two-tank dives ($149) are offered Monday, Thursday, and Saturday. More advanced two-tank drift dives ($165) are offered Sunday and Friday, and a three-tank dive ($210) Tuesday. Experienced divers can join an Adventure X dive ($189) on Wednesday. Ed Robinson's has a shop in an industrial yard in central Kihei (165 Halekuai St.) that also serves as a dive museum.

Prodiver (808/875-4004, www.prodivermaui.com) is one of the last dive boats to cap its trips at 6 divers (other boats usually take 12 with 2 instructors), which guarantees a personal experience. The 34-foot (10.4-m) boat meets at 6am at Kihei Boat Ramp. Two-tank dives are $149, and it's $20 for gear rental if you didn't bring your own.

In addition to offering shore dives and rental options, **B&B Scuba** (808/875-2861, www.bbscuba.com) offers two-tank dives ($139) from Kihei Boat Ramp aboard the 40-foot (12-m) *Kilikina II*. They're out on the water by 5:45am daily, and since the goal is to beat the crowds, don't show up late. The payoff for the early wake-up is that you reach your first dive site before other boats, and if that first dive site is Molokini, there is a certain magic to the solitude most visitors never get to experience. You're usually back to the dock by 10am. The wallet-friendly cost is also a strong selling point.

WAILEA

Dive Sites

Unlike Ma'alaea or Kihei, which serve as departure points for diving elsewhere, Wailea offers shore dives with shallow depths for beginners. The entry points in Wailea are sandy and easy; the best place to enter the water is the north end of **Ulua Beach.** This is where most dive operators bring students during their certification courses, as the maximum depth is about 35 feet (10 m). Expect to see turtles, reef fish, lobsters, and perhaps a rare spotted eagle ray. There is ample parking at the bottom of Ulua Beach Road, and the concrete walkway down to the shore is convenient for hauling tanks and gear.

The next best option is **Wailea Point,** off the south side of Wailea Beach. The nearest parking lot is between the Grand Wailea and Four Seasons resorts. Expect to see more green sea turtles than you can count, since they love the lava rock caves.

MAKENA AND BEYOND

Dive Sites

In addition to being one of the best shore dives in Makena, **Nahuna,** also called **Makena Landing, 5 Caves,** and **5 Graves,** also has the greatest number of names. The general area is also referred to as **Turtle Town,** a name created by charter boat companies to sell snorkeling tours.

What makes this dive so fantastic is not only the turtles but also the possibility of seeing pelagic species like spotted eagle rays and *'awa* (milkfish). Divers are surrounded by whale song in winter, and you can also find nudibranchs, harlequin shrimp, flying gurnards, and eels. On calm days the visibility can reach 100 feet (30 m), although on days where there is a south swell, usually in summer, visibility can be reduced to 20 feet (6 m) at best.

From shore, the easiest place to enter the water is the park at Makena Landing. Once in the water, turn right and follow the coast until you reach a long finger of lava. This is what's known as the South Finger, and the depth is only about 15 feet (4.5 m). Follow the South Finger away from the shore, and halfway to the end you will notice a large cave that you can swim through from below. There are numerous turtles that hang out here, and almost always a whitetip reef shark under a ledge. Emerging on the other side of the cave, kick your way parallel to the shore for three minutes until you reach the North Finger, which is where you're sure to find Hawaiian green sea turtles.

Another nice shore dive is **Waiala Cove,** 1.5 miles (2.4 km) past the First Entrance for Big Beach. The depth goes to about 40 feet (12 m). Since this cove is protected from the wind, it offers pristine diving conditions as long as the surf isn't up. Expect to find green sea turtles and the rare spinner dolphin on the outer edge of the reef. Entry can be tricky since you have to navigate your way over slippery rocks, but you don't need to worry about boats in this cove, although it is often packed with snorkelers. Parking is 0.2 mile (0.3 km) down the road at Dumps, the Kanahena parking lot.

Surfing

If you look at a map of South Maui, you'll notice that much of it actually faces west. This means that South Maui can get waves at any time of year. The southwest swells of summer bring the best waves, but large northwest winter swells can also wrap into select areas to provide the occasional out-of-season surf. If you're a complete beginner, the only spot in South Maui you should attempt to surf is The Cove in South Kihei, but if you're an intermediate or advanced surfer, there are other spots to check out.

MA'ALAEA

Ma'alaea is one of the few spots on Maui that faces almost due south, which means that summer is the only time there will be waves.

Surf Spots

The most consistent wave in Ma'alaea is a spot known as **Off the Wall.** This is an A-frame, shifty peak that breaks directly in front of the harbor wall, and you can usually only surf here in the morning hours before the wind starts howling. To access Off the Wall, park in the dirt parking area at the end of the break wall ($0.50 per hour), and paddle to the shifty peak—which definitely beats jumping off the wall. Expect short but fun rides, and while it isn't the best break on this side of the island, it's a nice place to get wet.

Half a mile (0.8 km) up the highway in the direction of Lahaina is **McGregor Point,** the fastest right-hand point break in the world. Although McGregor's rarely gets bigger than head-high, the spot can offer a long wave and is best in the afternoon, when the wind picks up. Parking for McGregor's is in a dirt lot on the road heading toward the lighthouse. Be careful when pulling off the highway as it is a difficult turn. To get down to the shore, you have to clamber down a steep and narrow trail, which can be tough if you're surfing with a longboard. McGregor's only breaks on the biggest of south swells, but is an island classic when it does.

KIHEI

Surf Spots

The surf epicenter of Kihei is **The Cove,** at the

Top Eco-Pick for Water Sports

When it comes to water sports in South Maui, the choices can be overwhelming, with dozens of rental shops and operators to help you get out on the water. To filter through the options, my top pick for water activities on Maui is the team at **Hawaiian Paddle Sports** (808/442-6436, www.hawaiianpaddlesports.com). You'll be hard-pressed to find a company that does more to give back to the island.

Hawaiian Paddle Sports is one of only five companies on Maui certified by the Hawaii Ecotourism Association, an organization that sets stringent standards for sustainable and cultural practices. They don't use single-use plastics on their tours (think metal water bottles instead), and they don't touch or disturb marinelife, like pulling octopuses from their holes.

They're also involved in the local community, donating every year to community groups and nonprofits, and the staff is involved in island cleanups and service projects. In 2015 they became Maui's first certified B Corporation business—joining a network of over 1,500 businesses around the world dedicated to using business for environmental and social change.

In South Maui, Hawaiian Paddle Sports offers surf lessons, stand-up paddleboard tours, kayak tours, outrigger canoe tours, as well as an adventurous "Molokini Challenge" paddle to Molokini Crater and back. All tours are private, so you aren't combined with another group, and the price per person decreases with the number in your group. It tends to be more expensive than the "get 'em in, get 'em out" budget options, but as the saying goes, you get what you pay for.

- **Stand-up paddleboard tours and lessons:** $249 for 1 person, $189 pp for 2 or more
- **Surf lessons:** $249 for 1 person, $139 pp for 2 or more
- **Kayak tours:** $229 pp for 2-3 people, $189 pp for 4 people, $99 pp for a group of 10
- **Outrigger canoe tours:** $189 pp
- **"Molokini Challenge" tours:** $249 for 1 person, $229 pp for 2 or more

southern end of Kalama Park, where all of the surf schools give lessons. While the waves are gentle, the downside is that it can get crowded. On some days you'll swear you could walk on water across all the longboards crammed into the small area, but in the early morning hours, before all the surf schools show up, this is still a fun, albeit small, wave. If your goal in Hawaii is to try surfing for the first time, this is where to come.

For more advanced surfers, the best wave in Kihei is an A-frame that breaks next to the **Kihei Boat Ramp.** This is a fickle wave that needs a big southwest or west swell to start working, and you need to be cautious of the boat traffic coming in and out of the harbor area. Access can be tricky, since you're asked to not walk in the sand dune area that runs along the shore. If you're on a longboard and are up for a paddle, you could always paddle from the far southern tip of Kamaole III Beach.

Shortboarding in Kihei can be found at **Sidewalks** on the south-central end of Keawakapu Beach. This is a beach break that offers a fast wave, and the vibe here isn't nearly as localized as at the boat ramp or farther south. Nevertheless, it's still an intermediate wave that isn't suitable for longboards or beginners. Parking for Sidewalks is at the public lot on the corner of Kilohana Drive and South Kihei Road.

Rental Shops and Schools

In the area surrounding The Cove there are five or six operators crammed into the same city block. Even with the wide selection, it's best to make a reservation. Nearly all lessons take place in the morning between 8am and noon, before the trade winds fill in, and all operators offer standard two-hour lessons. If you've moved past the phase of learning how to pop up and ride straight, most operations also offer "surf safaris," where they act as your personal surf guide for the day.

The shop with the largest presence is **Maui Wave Riders** (2021 S. Kihei Rd., 808/875-4761, www.mauiwaveriders.com, 7am-3pm daily), which has a popular surf shop directly across from The Cove. The company also has a Lahaina location and has helped thousands of visitors ride their first wave. Lesson rates are $95 per person for a semiprivate lesson, and $150 for one-on-one instruction.

Closest to Kalama Village is **Big Kahuna Adventures** (1900 S. Kihei Rd., 808/875-6395, www.bigkahunaadventures.com, 7:30am-noon Mon.-Sat.), inside the Kihei Kalama Village. Lessons are the standard $95 per person in a group lesson and take place at 8am daily. Meet at the surf truck parked across the street from the shop.

Surf Shack (2960 S. Kihei Rd., 808/875-0006, www.surfshackmaui.com, 8am-5pm daily) is across the street from The Cove. Park inside the Island Surf building. Lessons are $74 per person in a group of up to six people, or $150 for a private lesson and $380 for a private lesson for four. Although they function on a smaller scale, another operation providing lessons in Kihei as well as on the West Side is **Maui Beach Boys** (808/283-7114, www.mauibeachboys.com), a company that offers $79 per person for a group lesson and $109 for a semiprivate lesson.

If you're a beginner and need a basic Soft Top longboard, head to one of the three **Boss Frog's** (www.bossfrog.com, 8am-5pm daily) around town. It's cheaper than renting from the surf schools ($25 per day), and the surf school rentals often cap the rental period at four hours, whereas Boss Frog's is open until 5pm. There are three locations in Kihei, including the stores in Dolphin Plaza (2395 S. Kihei Rd., 808/875-4477), across from Kukui Mall (1770 S. Kihei Rd., 808/874-5225), and in the Long's Shopping Center (1215 S. Kihei Rd., 808/891-0077).

If you need a pro board, you can experience great service at **Island Surfboard Rentals** (808/281-9835, www.islandsurfboardrentals.com, 7am-5pm daily), which rents longboards ($30 per day, $180 per week) and provides free delivery and pickup. Shortboards ($22 per day, $130 per week) include a leash, some wax, and inside knowledge.

WAILEA

Surf Spots

On the north side of Mokapu Beach, **Stouffer's** is a local A-frame peak for intermediate shortboarders. It can pick up southwest swells in summer and large west swells in winter. Parking is at the south lot of Keawakapu Beach or in the public parking at the bottom of Ulua Beach Road.

On the southern end of Wailea is a punchy little left on the southern end of **Polo Beach** that's good for intermediate shortboarding.

MAKENA AND BEYOND

Surf Spots

There aren't any beginner surf breaks in Makena. If you're an intermediate or advanced surfer and have always wanted to surf naked, try **Little Beach,** a left that breaks on large southern swells. To reach the wave, you need to carry your board up and over the hill that separates Little Beach from Big Beach.

Stand-Up Paddling

KIHEI

Kihei is one of the best spots on the island for stand-up paddling, and all the major surf schools also offer paddleboard services. Getting out on the water in the morning is imperative because once the trade winds pick up, it can become impossible to paddle upwind. For a truly meditative experience, rent a board the evening before and get up early for a sunrise paddle. You can always putt around by the Kamaole parks and stop at whichever beach is calling your name.

Rental Shops and Schools

Learning to stand-up paddle often takes just a single lesson. Professional instructors can give you all the pointers you need—where to stand on the board, how far apart to keep your feet, and the correct side of the paddle to use. After that you should be solid enough to paddleboard on your own.

For lessons and rentals, **Maui Stand-up Paddleboarding** (808/568-0151, www.mauistanduppaddleboarding.com) offers private lessons and guided tours ($249 for 1 person, $189 pp for 2 or more). The professional guide also brings along a GoPro and provides free photos of you and your group. They also offer rentals ($55 per day) with a minimum rental of three days, and uniquely offer inflatable Naish boards, which are convenient if you're staying upstairs or in a place without much space. Of the schools by The Cove, **Maui Wave Riders** (2021 S. Kihei Rd., 808/875-4761, www.mauiwaveriders.com, 7am-3pm daily) offers 90-minute lessons ($95 pp semiprivate, $150 pp private).

You can also try out a multisport operator such as **South Pacific Kayaks & Outfitters** (808/875-4848, www.southpacifickayaks.com, 6am-7pm daily), which offers two-hour lessons ($89 pp group, $139 semiprivate, $179 private). They also offer surf lessons, kayaking tours, hiking tours, and kitesurfing lessons.

You can also find a popular rental venue at **Maui Paddleboard Rental** (808/250-7370, http://mauipaddleboardrental.com, 7am-9pm daily), which offers stand-up paddleboard rentals for $45 per day, $175 per week.

WAILEA

When compared to neighboring services, stand-up paddleboard rentals in Wailea are egregiously expensive. Then again, you're paying for the convenience of just walking out your door and renting a board on the sand, but prepare to pay upward of $50 per hour.

If you would prefer to take part in a guided tour, **Paddle On** (888/663-0808, www.paddleonmaui.com, 6am-8pm Mon.-Sat., $139-219) offers early morning tours from Polo Beach in front of the Fairmont Kea Lani. A wonderful variety of options are available here, from Paddleboarding 101 to guided paddles down the coast. For a morning experience you'll never forget, inquire about sunrise OM tours that are as meditative as you can get.

Kayaking and Canoeing

When all factors are considered, Makena is the best area for kayaking and paddling. Not only is it far richer culturally, but it takes the wind about an hour longer to reach it than neighboring Kihei or Wailea.

KIHEI

The best outrigger canoe tour in Kihei is with **'Ao'ao O Na Loko 'Ia O Maui** (808/359-1172, www.mauifishpond.com) at Ko'ie'ie Fishpond. This cultural tour is run by a nonprofit that's working to restore the fishpond, and along with the workout you get serious culture. Learn how this fishpond was built over 500 years ago, and be a part of the cultural awakening that's helping to bring it back to life. Affordable tours ($70 adults, $40 children) are offered at 8am daily. Meet in the parking lot of the Hawaiian Islands Humpback Whale National Marine Sanctuary Visitors Center.

WAILEA

While there are a number of options for paddling tours in Wailea, the one that focuses the most on Hawaiian culture is **Hawaiian Outrigger Experience** (808/633-2800, www.hawaiianoutriggerexperience.com, 6am-8pm), operating from Wailea Beach. A play on words, the acronym HOE translates as "paddle!" in the Hawaiian language. From the moment you begin this tour, you will realize this is as much a cultural experience as it is about the water. You'll spend time snorkeling with Hawaiian green sea turtles and gain authentic cultural insight from instructors who exude the genuine spirit of aloha. Options include a 90-minute tour ($119) of paddling, snorkeling, and in winter, whale-watching.

If a full-on paddling tour is too much exertion, another activity with cultural roots is the family-operated **Maui Sailing Canoe** (808/281-9301, www.mauisailingcanoe.com, $179 adults, $129 children), which departs off Polo Beach. The distinctly red sail of the *Hina* is visible off Wailea most mornings. This is the only tour where you can harness the light breeze to slowly sail along the coast like the Polynesians who voyaged here centuries ago. Snorkeling time is also included in the tour, combined with paddling, sailing, and relaxing in the sun. With a maximum of only six people, this is a perfect adventure for families wanting to do something different.

MAKENA

The rocky shore of Makena Landing is the preferred spot of other kayak operators, most of whom also have operations elsewhere on the island. While my top pick is **Hawaiian Paddle Sports** (808/442-6436, www.hawaiianpaddlesports.com), **Aloha Kayaks Maui** (808/270-3318, www.alohakayaksmaui.com) is another operator that employs sustainable practices, and you can also choose from **Kelii's Kayak Tours** (808/874-7652, www.keliiskayak.com) as well as **South Pacific Kayaks** (808/875-4848, www.southpacifickayaks.com). Most tours are $74-85 for 2.5 hours and $95-169 for 4 hours. There are usually two tours offered per day. To kayak from Makena Landing, book the early tour to beat the wind and the crowds of snorkel boats that converge on the area later in the morning.

Fishing

MA'ALAEA

Try your luck at reeling in a trophy fish with **Strike Zone** (Slip 40, 808/879-4485, www.strikezonemaui.com), offering bottom fishing as well as sportfishing excursions. Morning charters ($188 adults) leave at 6:30am Monday, Wednesday, Friday, and Saturday, and last six hours. On Sunday, Tuesday, and Thursday, four-hour private afternoon charters ($154) are available. This boat can accommodate up to 28 passengers and is a good option for large groups.

Want to splurge? For four hours of recreational fishing ($1,100 up to 4 people), the most personalized service you'll find in Ma'alaea Harbor is **Maui Fun Charters** (Slip 97, 808/572-2345, www.mauifuncharters.com). An important difference between this boat and others is that they focus on bottom fishing instead of sportfishing, so instead of spending hours trolling in circles in hopes of catching the big one, you drift closer to shore and will catch a greater number of varied, albeit smaller, fish. If your goal is to take something home to fry up for dinner, this is your best bet.

KIHEI

To get really adventurous, **Local Fishing Knowledge** (808/385-1337, www.localfishingknowledge.com) offers kayak-fishing and fly-fishing excursions for the experienced and passionate angler. If you just want to rent a rod for casting in the surf, the "beach bum" setup is perfect for anglers on the sand.

Hiking and Biking

HIKING

Kihei

Hiking in Kihei is barefoot sandy strolls down the beach. For the island's longest uninterrupted beach walk, 5-mile-long (8-km) **Sugar Beach** runs between Kihei and Ma'alaea. You can access the beach from Haycraft Park on the Ma'alaea side, from Kenolio Park on the Kihei side, or at any of the access points along North Kihei Road.

Another popular **coastal walk** in Kihei connects the trio of Kamaole Beaches, following the trails around their headlands. Starting at Charley Young Beach on the north end of Kamaole I (parking is in a public lot on Kaiau Place), you can walk to the south end of Kamaole III along the shore and around the rocky points. Although it's always nice to feel the sand between your toes, the rocks around the headlands can be sharp, so it might be best to bring footwear.

To extend the coastal walk a little farther, there is a short 0.5-mile (0.8-km) **walking path** that parallels the coast from the southern end of Kamaole III Beach to the Kihei Boat Ramp. Along the way you will pass informative signs about the coastal dune system and the *u'au kani* seabirds that nest in the dunes. There are a few benches sprinkled along the walking path to rest or, in winter, watch for whales.

Wailea

WAILEA COASTAL WALK

If your idea of a hike means throwing on some Lululemon, talking on your iPhone, and stopping to pick up some Starbucks, then the paved 3.5-mile (5.6-km) round-trip **Wailea Coastal Walk** is going to be your favorite hike on the island. The pathway runs from Ulua Beach to Polo Beach and is undeniably gorgeous, passing a host of native coastal

1

2

plants put in to revitalize the area's natural foliage. You'll also pass the Grand Wailea, Four Seasons, Kea Lani, Marriott, Wailea Beach Villas, and Andaz Maui. To reach the "trailhead" for the walkway, park in the public lot at Ulua Beach, at the bottom of Ulua Beach Road, or in the public lot on the southern end of the trail at Polo Beach, at the bottom of Kaukahi Street. At the far northern end, the walkway becomes sand and traverses the dunes past Mokapu Beach, where it links to Keawakapu in Kihei. In front of the Marriott, you can watch whales in winter through rented binoculars ($0.50).

Makena and Beyond

★ HOAPILI TRAIL AND LA PEROUSE

Hot, barren, and in the middle of nowhere, the **Hoapili Trail** isn't as much about hiking as about stepping back in time. Although the 5.5-mile (8.9-km) round-trip trail takes about four hours, even an hour introduces you to a side of the island most visitors never see.

The trail was once an ancient Hawaiian walking path reserved for royalty. In 1824, sections of the trail were reconstructed, and the road took on a structure that remains untouched to this day. The trailhead for Hoapili (also known as the "King's Highway") is in the parking lot of the La Perouse Bay snorkeling area, 3.1 miles (5 km) past the First Entrance to Big Beach. To find the trail, drive south on Makena Alanui Road until it dead-ends.

From the La Perouse Bay parking lot, you'll see the trail paralleling the shore and weaving south along the coast. Before you set out, remember that there is no shade and the trail traverses jagged *'a'a* lava that's so sharp you'll want proper hiking boots. Since much of this hike is outside cell phone range, it's important to be prepared with food and water. Reduce the chance of overheating by starting early in the morning.

After you've followed the shoreline for 0.7 mile (1.1 km), passing a couple of pockets of sand and sometimes feral black goats, you'll see an abandoned lava rock structure off the right side of the trail. This is the popular surfing spot known as **Laps** (short for **La Perouse**), and on large south swells you can see death-defying surfers riding waves over jagged sharp lava. After the surf spot, the trail climbs for 10 minutes before arriving at a junction and veering off to the left. There is a sign informing you that you're entering the King's Highway and to respect the historic sites. The sign will also indicate that Kanaio Beach is 2 miles (3.2 km) ahead.

On the inland section of trail where the path deviates from the coast, there's a short spur trail that leads down to the lighthouse at Cape Hanamanioa, although there isn't much to see except the old weathered light. A better side trip is the short spur trail 20 minutes later that leads down to Keawanaku Beach, where you're almost guaranteed to have the beach to yourself. To find the beach, look for a short lone palm tree springing from the black lava field surrounded by a grove of *kiawe* trees, then keep an eye out for the trail down to the shore. Although rocky, the trail is noticeable, and if you find yourself asking, "Am I still on the trail?" then you probably aren't. After Keawanaku, the trail continues for 20 minutes to the coast at Kanaio Beach, a salt- and pepper-colored shore of black lava rock and sun-bleached coral. You'll notice the remnants of multiple structures, once part of an ancient fishing village.

Although Kanaio Beach is the turnaround point for most hikers, the King's Highway continues to Highway 31 on the "back road to Hana." To reach the highway, however, requires an overnight stay along the trail; camping is permitted along the shore from points east of Kanaio Beach. To travel just a little farther, however, a sandy road continues from Kanaio Beach and winds along the coast. Another 20 minutes of walking from Kanaio brings you to a shore that's

1: rocky Hoapili Trail **2:** crashing waves at La Perouse completely bathed in bleached white coral, and on the southern end of the "white beach" is an ancient Hawaiian *heiau* (temple) set out on the point that looks much the same now as it must have when it was built.

BIKING

For a casual bike ride in South Maui, it doesn't get better than renting a beach cruiser and pedaling to beach-hop, bar-hop, and coolly cruise the strip, not worrying about traffic or finding parking. For an epic half-day road biking adventure, ride from Kihei to Makena and the lava-strewn "end of the road," where you can cycle across the island's last lava flow and relax at beaches as you go.

Kihei

If you're a hard-core cyclist, head to **South Maui Cycles** (1993 S. Kihei Rd., 808/874-0068, www.southmauibicycles.com, 10am-6pm Mon.-Sat.), across the street from Kalama Park, to rent road bikes (60 per day, $250 per week). This is a full-service bicycle shop that also offers sales and repairs.

To beach-hop for a while, beach cruisers ($40 for 4 hours, $60 per day, $250 per week) are available from **Boss Frog's Bike Shop** (1770 S. Kihei Rd., 808/874-5225, www.bossfrog.com, 8am-5pm daily). There are also mountain bikes, hybrid bikes, and proper road bikes. You can also pick up a cruiser at another Boss location in the Dolphin Plaza, across from the southern end of Kamaole II Beach Park.

Golf

KIHEI

If you just want to play a relaxing round without shelling out resort prices, **Maui Nui Golf Club** (470 Lipoa Pkwy., 808/874-0777, www.mauinuigolfclub.com, 5am-5:30pm daily) is one of the island's best values. The views look out toward Molokini Crater, and while this course isn't as challenging as the Wailea Gold course, it still provides an enjoyable round. Club and equipment rentals are available from the pro shop, and there's a driving range for working on your stroke before your round. The afternoon trade winds can have a major effect on play, reflected in the greens fees for morning rounds (from $99) and afternoon tee times (as low as $69). To save a few dollars, check the website for online specials. On a winter day with light winds, you can sneak in an enjoyable twilight round after a morning at Molokini Crater. As an added bonus, your first beer at Kono's Green—the golf course's 19th hole—is the same price as the score for your round—just present your completed scorecard.

WAILEA

Without question, the **Wailea Gold** (100 Wailea Golf Club Dr., 808/875-7450, www.waileagolf.com) is the best golf course in South Maui, where the pros play when they come to town. The 7,000-yard-plus (6,400-m) course and 93 bunkers challenge even those with low handicaps. Guests at the Wailea resort complex can play a morning round from $165. The May 1-December 20 rates begin at $165-250, and sunset twilight play at 3:30pm can be as low as $149. Club rental and practice facilities are at the main Wailea clubhouse.

If the Gold course is intimidating, the **Wailea Emerald** (100 Wailea Golf Club Dr., 808/875-7450, www.waileagolf.com) is far more forgiving. The course isn't quite as long, but it is still a proper resort course with technical challenges and amenities, so you still need to bring your A-game. Greens fees are the same as the Gold course.

The **Wailea Old Blue** (100 Wailea Golf Club Dr., 808/875-7450, www.waileagolf.com) course, constructed in 1972, is Maui's second golf course after Ka'anapali. Not only

Beach Yoga

South Maui is popular for beach yoga. Nothing is quite as rejuvenating as practicing yoga on the beach, accompanied by ocean views, tropical breezes, and the sound of waves as the sensory backdrop. Standout options include:

- **Maui Beach Yoga** (808/385-6466, www.mauibeachyoga.com, $20) goes for memorable toes-in-the-sand yoga experiences, with locations that vary depending on wave and wind patterns. Options include a Group Sunrise Yoga class (around 7am Sat.) and Group Sunset class (around 5pm Mon. and Thurs.). Reservations are required and classes last an hour. Bring your own towel. You can also book a private beach yoga session.
- **Maui Yoga Path** (2960 S. Kihei Rd., 808/283-9771, http://mauiyogapath.com, $25 per class, $115 for 5-class card) holds classes on the tranquil beach in front of the Mana Kai Maui resort, near its popular Five Palms restaurant. This stretch of sand offers sweeping ocean views with glimpses of Molokini Crater. The daily one-hour Sunrise Beach Yoga class is a hit—starting times range 6am-7am during the year, so check the website. Yoga mats and props are provided, and no reservations are necessary.
- Local yoga teacher and massage therapist Johanna runs **Maui Yoga and Massage** (2450 S. Kihei Rd., 808/214-0129, www.johannawaters.com, $15) and offers one-hour yoga classes (8am Sun., Tues., and Thurs.) held on private property at Kamaole Nalu Oceanfront Resort, where expansive ocean views include the West Maui Mountains and neighboring islands such as Kaho'olawe and Lana'i. Bring a mat or rent one ($2). No reservations are necessary, but admission is on a first-come, first-served basis; arrive at least 10 minutes early. Johanna offers $5 discounts to anyone who shares a Seva tale (a story of selflessness); she shares the stories on her blog as a way to inspire people. Email info@johannawaters.com ahead of time.

is Old Blue an easier course, it's also substantially cheaper ($190 nonguests, $99 Super Twilight). In summer you can sneak in nine holes after 2pm for only $65. After you card your best round of your vacation, head down to Manoli's to celebrate at the bar.

Spas

KIHEI

There are a handful of places off South Kihei Road to get a relaxing massage. A popular choice is **808 Wellness Spa & Healing Center** (2439 S. Kihei Rd., 808/875-4325, www.808wellness.com, 9am-7pm Mon.-Fri., 9am-6pm Sat., noon-5pm Sun.), which offers a 60-minute traditional Hawaiian *lomilomi* massage ($125) as well as an aromatherapy massage ($125). Linger longer for a 90-minute massage ($165) to feel truly blissed out.

Massage Maui (145 N. Kihei Rd., 808/357-7317, www.massage-maui.com, 8am-9pm daily) is a low-key massage option that offers massages on-site ($90-190) as well as beachfront and outcall services for an additional $20 per service.

Maui Day Spa & Salon (808/879-9944, https://beautyspamaui.com, 9am-6pm Mon.-Sat.) is a low-key massage option that offers massages on-site ($85) as well as couples massages ($185).

WAILEA

When it comes to choosing South Maui's best spa, it's tough to beat a 50,000-square-foot (4,650-square-m) luxury arena that has been voted the best spa in Hawaii and among the top 10 in the United States. **Mohalu Spa Grande** (3850 Wailea Alanui Dr.,

808/875-1234, ext. 4949, www.waldorfastoria3.hilton.com, 8am-7pm daily), the palatial spa inside the Grand Wailea, completely redefines the concept of pampering. It's Hawaii's largest spa, and all guests are advised to arrive an hour early to enjoy a casual complimentary soak in the hydrotherapy baths before your treatment.

Can't decide among the Roman hot tub, Japanese *furo* baths, or honey-mango loofah exfoliation? Do them all as a package! A 50-minute massage treatment runs $190 on average, and a 100-minute *lomilomi* massage is $340. Along with an enormous selection of facials and treatment options, there's also a beauty salon and fitness center.

Down the beach at the Fairmont Kea Lani, the **Willow Stream Spa** (4100 Wailea Alanui Dr., 808/875-2229, www.fairmont.com/kea-lani-maui, 8:30am-6pm daily) has also been voted among the best in Hawaii, and they work to incorporate plants grown on property in many massages and services. During the 120-minute Natural Hawaiian Journey, pamper yourself with a clay body mask and an invigorating Hawaiian salt scrub before a therapist wraps you in a resort-grown *ti* and administers a scalp and face massage. Finish off by rinsing yourself in a rain-inspired shower, and then slink down to the pool.

As you might expect, **The Spa at Four Seasons** (808/874-8000, www.fourseasons.com, 7am-6pm daily) is just as lavish and over the top, and a nice perk here is the option of getting a massage in an oceanfront cabana. The prices are often higher than Spa Grande, but the offerings of wellness options, body treatments, and massages are no less impressive.

For guests of the Marriott, there's the **Mandara Spa** (3700 Wailea Alanui Dr., 808/891-8774, www.mandaraspa.com, 9am-4pm daily). You might also consider the 60-minute warm stone massage ($195) at **Awili Spa and Salon** (Andaz Maui, 3550 Wailea Alanui Dr., 808/243-4800, www.hyatt.com, 8:30am-6:30pm).

Wailea Healing Center (120 S. Kaukahi St., 808/205-2005, www.waileahealingcenter.com, 8am-8pm daily) is another out-of-resort option that only requires a five-minute drive yet saves almost enough money for a second round. Close to the Wailea Tennis Center, between the Shops at Wailea and the Wailea Gateway Center, this healing zone offers 60-minute massage treatments ($135) that are infused with essential oils, hot stones, and ocean views. Acupuncture, yoga classes, and crystal-bowl sound baths and meditations are also available.

Horseback Riding and Bird-Watching

HORSEBACK RIDING

Makena and Beyond

The only horseback riding in South Maui is *way* south, at the end of the road at **Makena Stables** (8299 S. Makena Rd., 808/879-0244, www.makenastables.com, 8am-6pm Mon.-Sat.), a family-run outfit that has been leading horseback riding tours since 1983. The trails meander over Ulupalakua Ranch, only accessible on a private tour. Along the way there's a good chance of spotting axis deer or wild goats that clamber across the jagged *'a'a* lava.

This is one of the few horseback riding operations on the island with the possibility of riding your horse along the shore. Not only do the views stretch out toward Kaho'olawe in the distance, but you ride directly through the island's most recent lava flow, taking time to stop at Kalua O Lapa, the volcanic vent from which Madame Pele leaked her fiery liquid. Group sizes are capped at six, and riders must be under 205 pounds (93 kg). To escape the brutal South Maui sun, take a sunset ride during the coast's most romantic hour.

BIRD-WATCHING

Kihei

If South Maui had a mascot, it would be the *kolea,* or Pacific golden plover, since it leaves its summer home in the Arctic for winter on Maui.

For exceptional bird-watching, the **Kealia Pond National Wildlife Refuge** (www.fws.gov/refuge/kealia_pond), between Ma'alaea and Kihei, is nearly 700 acres (285 ha) of open wetlands with over 30 species of birds, including the *ae'o* (Hawaiian stilt), *'alae ke'oke'o* (Hawaiian coot), and *koloa maoli* (Hawaiian duck). The greatest number of species is found in winter. There are short walking trails that leave from the visitors center (mile marker 6 on Mokulele Hwy.) into the Kealia Pond area. There's also a short boardwalk from Ma'alaea to North Kihei that parallels the shoreline and offers a number of informative placards about the island's native wildlife. The boardwalk takes about 30 minutes to walk to the end and back. It's best to approach from the Ma'alaea side of the road because there's no left turn allowed into the parking lot off North Kihei Road.

Another place to try your luck is on the beach walk between the Kihei Boat Ramp and the south end of Kamaole III Beach. The coastal dune system here is home to *'ua'u kani* (wedge-tailed shearwaters), and the fledging season is usually October-December. Although **Molokini Crater** is best known for snorkeling, few people know that the 161-foot-tall (49-m) islet is also a seabird sanctuary, home to a healthy population of *'ua'u kani* as well as soaring frigates. If you're an avid birder and are planning a trip to Molokini, bring binoculars to check out what's happening above water, not just down on the reef.

Those with an interest in Maui County's seabirds should check out the **Maui Nui Seabird Recovery Project** (www.mauinuiseabirds.org).

Makena and Beyond

The best place for bird-watching in Makena is at **Oneuli Beach** by Makena State Park. Although the chances of seeing many species of birds are slim, this coastal wetland area is home to avian species such as the *'auku'u* (black-crowned night heron), *'alae ke'oke'o* (Hawaiian coot), and *ulili* (wandering tattler).

Shopping

MA'ALAEA

Ma'alaea Harbor Shops

The handful of shops at **Ma'alaea Harbor Shops** (300 Ma'alaea Rd., 877/463-2731) have periodic craft fairs. The most popular retail outlet is **Geotrek & Red Dirt Shirt** (10am-5:30pm daily), with a surprising assortment of T-shirts dyed with 100 percent pure red island dirt and embroidered with Hawaiian-inspired themes such as sea turtles, surfboards, maps of the islands, old-school automobiles, and more.

KIHEI

North End

Up on Pi'ilani Highway, the **Kihei Gateway Plaza** is a sprawling semi-industrial compound with a smattering of clothing shops. Of the main stores in the plaza, the largest is **Maui Clothing Outlet** (362 Huku Li'i Pl., 808/875-0308, 10am-5pm daily), with an enormous selection of resort wear and island-themed clothing at discount prices. One of the sister stores in the same area is **Pretty Wahine** (362 Huku Li'i Pl., 808/879-1199, 10am-5pm daily), with women's boutique clothing options.

If you turn up Pi'ikea Avenue between the Azeka Mauka Center and the Long's Shopping Center, you'll quickly come to the **Pi'ilani Village Shopping Center** (225 Pi'ikea Ave., 11am-9pm daily), which has the most relevant shopping options in North Kihei. A big draw is the **ABC Store** (808/875-9975, 6am-10pm daily), which has the best array of snacks and last-minute groceries as well as a surprising variety of men's and women's clothing, shoes, and hats.

Central Kihei

The largest concentration of shopping in Kihei is in the **Kihei Kalama Village** (1941 S. Kihei Rd., 808/879-6610, 9am-7:30pm daily), with over 40 businesses, the most notable being **Da Beach House** (808/891-1234, www.dabeachhousemaui.com) for surf-themed apparel; **Mahina** (808/879-3453, www.mahinamaui.com) for women's apparel; **808 Clothing Company** (808/357-1988, www.808clothing.com) for island-themed T-shirts, embroidered hats, visors, and handbags; **Seasteps** (808/205-7134) for locally made products such as jewelry and Christmas ornaments; and **Sunkissed Wahine Clothing Company** (808/757-8643), featuring handmade items such as caps, shirts, embroidered pillows, lotions, and essential oils. There are also myriad kiosks and stands where you can get henna tattoos or play with a digeridoo. This shopping area is within walking distance of the Cove Park, where most of the surf rentals take place, so if part of your group is out surfing, you can wander down here for some souvenir browsing while they are on the water.

South End

In the **Kamaole Beach Center**, the main retail outlet is **Maui Clothing Company** (2463 S. Kihei Rd., 808/879-5545, www.mauiclothingcompany.com, 10am-5pm daily), specializing in high-quality beach and aloha wear. You can also shop for jewelry, footwear, and souvenirs here.

Rainbow Mall is home to **Maui Fine Art Gallery & Frame** (2439 S. Kihei Rd., 808/463-9383, www.mauiartframe.com, 10:30am-8:30pm daily), one of the few art galleries in Kihei. In addition to numerous island-themed paintings and ceramics, the frames that encompass the artwork are an art form unto themselves.

WAILEA

While all the high-end luxury resorts have a decent amount of shopping, particularly the Grand Wailea, the majority of retail on this side of the island is at the shopping centers and shops.

Shops at Wailea

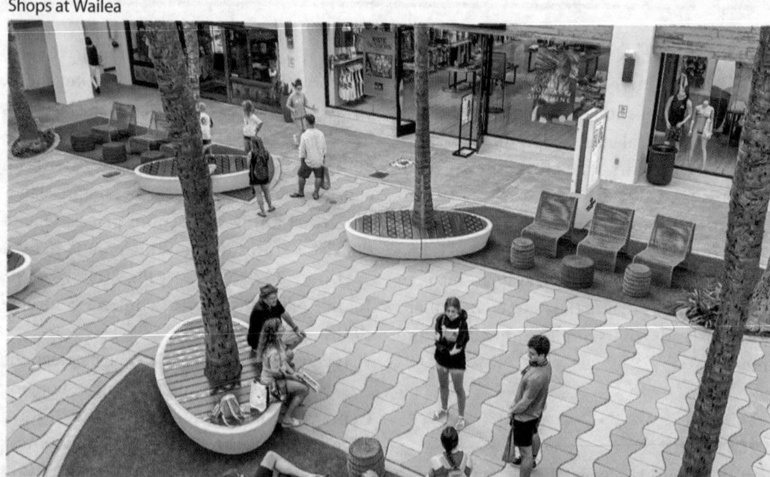

Shops at Wailea

Any longtime visitor to Maui will remember when the **Shops at Wailea** (3750 Wailea Alanui Dr., 808/891-6770, www.theshopsatwailea.com, 10am-8pm daily) were a plantation-style shopping complex with wide grassy areas and free hula shows from local *halau* (hula schools). These days, the complex has gone upscale. Inside you'll find art galleries such as **Lahaina Galleries** (808/874-8583) and **Enchantress Gallery** (808/495-4161) accompanying retail shops like **Billabong** (808/879-8330), **Honolua Surf Company** (808/891-8229), and **Crazy Shirts** (808/875-6435). For a rare, authentic souvenir, drop by **Mele Ukulele** (808/879-6353), the most established manufacturer of ukuleles on Maui. You can often spot celebrities hanging out in luxury stalwarts such as **Tiffany and Co.** (808/891-9226) and **Gucci** (808/879-1060) or in restaurants like **Lineage** (808/879-8800).

Aside from the high-end chain stores, you can also find a few island-themed shops offering unique and boutique souvenirs. At **Martin & MacArthur** (808/845-6688, www.martinandmacarthur.com), Hawaiian-made crafts and an assortment of koa woods abound. If you're in need of a fancy gift, **Na Hoku** (808/891-8040) offers unique Hawaiian-inspired jewelry.

Wailea Gateway Center

Although it doesn't have anywhere near the glitz and glamour of the Shops at Wailea, the awkwardly placed little **Wailea Gateway Center** (10 Wailea Ike Dr.) still has a couple of boutique shops worth a visit. One of those is **Sweet Paradise Chocolatier** (808/344-1040, www.chocolateonmaui.com, 11am-8pm daily), which will lure you in with the scent of rich chocolate. In addition to an ornate spread of fine chocolates, all the items are made on the island, and some of the cacao is even grown in Hawaii—the only U.S. state where cacao is currently grown.

Wailea Town Center

Although this is mostly an office complex, one retail outlet worth a mention is **Wailea Wine** (161 Wailea Ike Pl., 808/879-0555, www.waileawine.com, 10am-5pm Mon.-Sat.), with an exceptional selection of wines from across the globe and one of the largest on the island, along with gourmet culinary options.

Wailea Village

At **Wailea Village** (100 Wailea Ike Dr., 6am-6pm daily) you'll find the high-end clothing store **Waterlily** (808/868-4014, 10am-5pm Mon.-Sat.), an impressive art gallery called **Sabado** (808/242-6762, 10am-6pm daily), and other gift stores such as **Paper Garden** (808/871-5541, 10am-5pm daily) and **Bikini Market** (www.thebikinimarket.com, 10am-4pm daily).

Entertainment

KIHEI

Events

The largest and most popular event in South Maui is the **Fourth Friday** celebration, held 6pm-9pm on the fourth Friday of the month at the Azeka Mauka shopping complex. There are multiple live music performances and beer gardens scattered throughout. It's a surprisingly well organized affair that's fun for the entire family.

For an artistic event that happens most nights, **Island Art Party** (1279 S. Kihei Rd., 808/419-6020, www.islandartparty.com, $39-59) is a unique venue where you can join an instructor-led painting class while sipping a glass of wine. It's one of the island's best rainy-day activities and is for ages 16 and up.

Where the Locals Hang

Connecting with locals is one of the most enjoyable aspects of travel. Sit on a particular barstool and you might find yourself in a deep conversation about island living, sharing stories, or learning about the best day trips, dining options, and happy hours. Here are some of the top spots where locals gather in Kihei:

- **Haui's Life's A Beach** offers locals frequent incentives to visit: affordable cocktails, $2 Taco Tuesdays, karaoke nights, and live music.
- **Kahale's Local Dive Bar** dubs itself "Maui's local dive bar," and it does indeed draw lots of locals with its wide range of live music and Saturday dance nights.
- Locals convene at **Maui Brewing Company** en masse for its numerous beers on tap, island-inspired comfort food, and festive bar scene. This is hands down one of the best spots to socialize and enjoy a meal and brews with the regulars in Kihei.
- Two venues that locals tend to make weekly visits to are **Moose McGillycuddy's,** for cheap late-night drinks, and **Mulligan's on the Blue** for live entertainment on Friday and Saturday evenings. Both venues sport some of the liveliest bar scenes on the island.
- Hotels don't typically find their way onto a local's list of go-to spots, but the **Lehua Lounge** and **Bumbye Beach Bar** at Andaz Maui are the exception, thanks to the bars' friendly staff, bar bites small and large, daily entertainment poolside, and the hotel's prime location at the north end of the Wailea Coastal Walk, which draws both visitors and locals for walks or jogs. It's *Cheers,* Maui-style.
- The casual atmosphere at **Three's Bar and Grill** makes it a hit with locals, as do the two daily happy hours (3pm-6pm and 9pm-10pm) featuring discounts on both drinks—try a top-shelf mai tai—and food, including local faves like sushi rolls.
- **Nalu's South Shore Grill** always packs the house, thanks to its dynamic food menu, friendly bartenders, and local brews on tap. Visit on Wednesday or Friday after 6:30pm for live entertainment by seasoned Maui-based singers and musicians.

Live Music and Dancing

INSIDE THE TRIANGLE

The majority of Kihei's nightlife takes place at the Triangle, as in, the *Barmuda* Triangle, where you could end up getting lost for days. This collection of bars within the Kihei Kalama Village can almost seem like a tropical fraternity row, with each house on the street having a different theme party.

If you're starting your night early, check out **Haui's Life's A Beach** (1913 S. Kihei Rd., 808/891-8010, www.mauibars.com, 10am-midnight Mon.-Sat., 7am-midnight Sun.), a.k.a. **The Lab.** This rockin' beach bar has an outdoor patio that looks toward South Kihei Road and is a great place for people-watching. There's live music on weekends as well as other incentives like $2 Taco Tuesdays and karaoke Sunday through Thursday. You can also shoot some pool, watch some sports, and eavesdrop on local happenings.

The most popular club in the traditional sense of the word is the **South Shore Tiki Lounge** (1913 S. Kihei Rd., 808/874-6444, www.southshoretikilounge.com, 11am-10pm daily), where resident DJs play for a small but crowded dance floor. This place gets popular on weekends with its thumping house beats and young singles.

Across the parking lot, swap your draft beer for some cutting-edge mixology at **Vibe Bar Maui** (1913 S. Kihei Rd., 808/891-1011, 7pm-midnight daily), where martinis compete for attention with daily drink specials such as $5 lemon drop shots, $4 cocktails, and $5

Jameson. DJs spin many nights of the week, and the vibe at Vibe is super chill and fun.

For an authentic dive bar—not the fashionable kind—**Kahale's Local Dive Bar** (36 Keala Pl., 808/215-9939, http://kahales.com, 10am-10pm daily) is a working-class bar with live music, cheap drinks, Saturday dance nights, and a decidedly local atmosphere. The beer is some of the cheapest on the island, and you won't find grass skirts, convertibles, or timeshare salespeople within a respectable radius.

For a good old-fashioned touch of the *craic*, **Dog & Duck** (1913 S. Kihei Rd., 808/875-9669, 3pm-11pm Mon.-Wed., noon-midnight Thurs.-Fri., 8am-midnight Sat.-Sun.) is a small gathering place where you can throw darts, eat bangers and mash, drink Guinness, rock out to live music, or take part in the popular quiz nights. To switch up the drinking venue, right next door is **What Ales You** (808/214-6581, http://whatalesyoukihei.com, noon-9pm Tues.-Sat., noon-7pm Sun.), a small tap house with 16 beers on tap and about 20 wines on the wine list.

OUTSIDE THE TRIANGLE

At the other end of the parking lot of the Azeka Mauka shopping center is **Diamonds Ice Bar & Grill** (1279 S. Kihei Rd., 808/874-9299, www.diamondsicebar.com, 11am-midnight Mon.-Fri., 8am-midnight Sat., 7am-midnight Sun.), a small establishment tucked in the end unit that offers live music most nights. If you have a large group, there's a private VIP room. While it doesn't see the same amount of crowds as down at the Triangle, it can still be a happening place if the right band is playing.

Very popular is **Maui Brewing Company** (605 Lipoa Pkwy., 808/201-2337, www.mbcrestaurants.com, 11:30am-10pm daily). Much larger than the popular Lahaina location, this open-air warehouse restaurant and bar, along with its adjacent brewery, has become a popular go-to hangout, especially on weekends. Beyond its stellar brews, it stands out for its daily happy hour (3:30pm-5:30pm) with $1 off house beers, $3 off craft cocktails, and $10 pizzas. Logo Wear Wednesday is fun; wear the venue's logo gear and enjoy $2 off beers all day. Live music nightly rounds out the roster here. The brewery has 36 of its own beers on tap, tours (check the website for the most updated times), and Advanced Beer Tastings four times a day (12:30pm, 1:30pm, 2:30pm, and 3:30pm) Monday and Friday.

Moose McGillycuddy's (2511 S. Kihei Rd., 808/891-8600, http://moosemcgillycuddyskihei.com, 11am-10pm daily) harnesses the late-night crowd in South Kihei who are looking for cheap drink specials and an old-fashioned good time. This sports bar cranks up the music at 9pm and caters mostly to the single crowd that's looking to get a bit weird.

WAILEA

Luaus

The best luau on the island is Old Lahaina Luau in Lahaina, but if you're staying on the south end of the island and don't want to drive that far, there are two options in South Maui. My top pick is **The Grand Luau at Honua'ula** (3850 Wailea Alanui Dr., 808/875-1234, www.grandwailea.com/experiences/luau, $225 adults, $112 children) because the show focuses more on Hawaiian history than the South Pacific in general. The luau takes place on the grounds of the Grand Wailea; Honua'ula is a name given to this section of the island by the original Polynesians who migrated here centuries ago. Call in advance to check the schedule, which can vary.

Just a few steps down the coastal walkway is **Te Au Moana** (3700 Wailea Alanui Dr., 877/827-2740, www.teaumoana.com, 4:30pm Mon. and Thurs.-Sat., $225 adults, $155 children), at the Wailea Beach Marriott. Showtimes overlap with neighboring Grand Wailea. This show focuses more on the dance and mythology of greater Polynesia than on Hawaii, but it's still a highly entertaining performance, particularly if it's your first luau. The stage backs up to the shore in front of the hotel. The backdrop of the setting sun creates a panorama you would expect from a luau in paradise.

Andaz Maui puts its own spin on the luau experience with **The Feast at Mokapu** (3550 Wailea Alanui Dr., 808/573-1234, www.feastatmokapu.com, 5:30pm Sun. and Tues., $300 adults, $150 children), where food is offered family-style for more intimacy, and Polynesian values are explored.

Shows

Surprisingly there aren't that many dinner shows on Maui. If you're on a budget and looking for an inexpensive public show, the **Shops at Wailea** (3750 Wailea Alanui Dr., 808/891-6770, www.theshopsatwailea.com) usually offer free performances by famous Hawaiian artists or other live music events on a donation basis—proceeds benefit local nonprofits—during the week.

Live Music

For live entertainment after the sun goes down, the most popular place in Wailea is **Mulligan's on the Blue** (100 Kaukahi St., 808/874-1131, www.mulligansontheblue.com, 5pm-8pm Thurs., noon-8pm Fri.-Sat., 10am-8pm Sun.). This Irish pub is owned by a real Irishman, and periodic performances by award-winning local artists begin at 6pm Friday-Sunday.

At **Monkeypod Kitchen** (10 Wailea Ike Dr., 808/891-2322, www.monkeypodkitchen.com, 11am-9pm daily) restaurant in the Wailea Gateway Center, not only do they have Wailea's best *liliko'i* mai tais and beer selection, but there's also live music every day beginning at 1pm.

You can also find live music inside hotel lobbies, with one of the best being the **Lobby Lounge** (3900 Wailea Alanui Dr., 808/874-8000, 5pm-11:30pm daily) bar inside the Four Seasons Wailea, with hula dancers performing around sunset and live music each night. Just down the beach walk, at the Andaz Maui, **Lehua Lounge** (808/573-1234) has live music (except Sun. and Tues.) and a lively bar 6pm-9pm daily.

Bars

For a traditional bar scene, head to **Manoli's Pizza Company** (100 Wailea Ike Dr., 808/874-7499, www.manolispizzacompany.com, 11am-10pm daily), where, in addition to draft and bottled beers, there are 20 organic or sustainable wines. Late-night happy hour is 9pm-midnight daily, and it's within walking distance of many of the resorts.

By the clubhouse of the Wailea golf course—which requires a short drive from the resort strip—the Red Bar at **Gannon's** (100 Wailea Golf Club Dr., 808/875-8080, www.gannonsrestaurant.com, 3pm-8:30pm Tues.-Sat.) pairs the sexiest drinks in Wailea with a stunning ocean view. Choose from affordable draft beers, an extensive list of over 50 wines, and enticing cocktails made with everything from Maui's own organic Ocean Vodka to orchard guava liqueur.

At the Andaz Maui, the **Lehua Lounge** and **Bumbye Beach Bar** (3550 S. Kihei Rd., 808/573-1234, 11am-10pm daily) lure not just visitors staying at the hotel but locals as well, with friendly bar staff and bar bites like seared ahi, avocado toast, and a lobster grilled cheese. On ground level, the Bumbye Beach Bar features big-screen TVs typically tuned into a sports game. Lehua Lounge is the hotel's upper pool bar, which has particularly awe-inspiring ocean views.

Makena and Beyond

On Sunday nights, the most happening thing in Makena is the **drum circle** at sunset on Little Beach. More of a drug-infused people-watching spectacle, the event features drummers, fire dancers, hippies, nudists, and curious onlookers. It definitely isn't for everyone, but if you want a bit of counterculture or are up for enlightening conversation, climb the trail to Little Beach in the hour just before sunset. If you plan to stay late, park outside the gate of the First Entrance of Makena State Park.

Food

MA'ALAEA

Deli

For lunch on the go, **Tradewinds Mart & Deli** (20 Hauoli St., 808/242-9161, 8am-6pm Mon.-Fri., 9am-5pm Sat., 10am-4pm Sun.) has bowls of chili and rice ($6) and sandwiches ($9). This old-school store has been around for over 40 years. You'll find it tucked in the Ma'alaea Mermaid condo right next to Ma'alaea Harbor.

KIHEI

Hawaiian Regional

One of the most popular venues is ★ **Three's Bar & Grill** (1945 S. Kihei Rd., 808/879-3133, www.threesbarandgrill.com, 3pm-9pm Mon.-Tues., 11am-9pm Wed.-Sun., lunch $12-18, dinner $19-27), inside the Kihei Kalama Village. Opened by three chefs who each boast their own culinary specialty—Hawaiian, Southwestern, and Pacific Rim—the restaurant has lunch and appetizer items such as Hawaiian-style ribs and kalua pig quesadilla. Dinner menu entrées feature chicken roulade and a raw bar of sushi and *poke*. Two daily happy hours (3pm-6pm and 9pm-10pm) feature discounts on both drinks and food, including local faves like sushi rolls.

There isn't an overabundance of fine dining in Kihei, but **Sarento's on the Beach** (2980 S. Kihei Rd., 808/875-7555, www.sarentosonthebeach.com, 8am-10pm daily, $34-48), on the water at the north end of Keawakapu Beach, does the trick. You won't find a more romantic or relaxing spot in Kihei. Start off with the fish sampler or beef carpaccio before moving on to the seared Hawaiian ahi or braised veal shank with risotto. Valet parking is free, and if you show up about an hour before sunset, you'll probably get a seat with a fiery view during dessert.

Local Style

The only true local-style plate lunch in Kihei is at ★ **Da Kitchen** (1215 S. Kihei Rd., 4pm-8pm Mon.-Sat., $8-15) in South Kihei. The portions are enormous enough that you could split them and still walk away full. This hole-in-the-wall strip-mall special is one of the best deals in town. If you're looking for a place where locals eat, this is it.

Locals know **Tamura's Fine Wine & Liquors** (91 E. Lipoa St., 808/891-2420, http://tamurasfinewine.com, 10am-7pm daily) is the best spot on the island to grab a takeout container of *poke* on your way to the beach.

Seafood

In the Kihei Kalama Village, ★ **Paia Fish Market** (1913 S. Kihei Rd., 808/874-8888, www.paiafishmarket.com, 11am-9pm daily) now has a Kihei outlet for their mouthwatering fish burgers ($11-12), and it's a casual spot for grabbing some lunch after a morning of surfing at The Cove. For great fish tacos, **Coconut's Fish Café** (1279 S. Kihei Rd., 808/875-9979, www.coconutsfishcafe.com, 11am-9pm daily, $13-23) serves tacos piled high with 17 different ingredients and is a casual stop in the Azeka Mauka shopping center.

Hidden back in the central Kihei industrial yard is **Eskimo Candy** (2665 Wai Wai Pl., 808/891-8898, www.eskimocandy.com, 10:30am-4:30pm Mon.-Fri., $10-17), Kihei's best local secret for fresh seafood. Try the seafood chowder, fish-and-chips, and *poke*, featuring four different styles of seasoned ahi tuna. There are only a few tables outside for dining, and they also have wholesale rates on fish for grilling back at your condo. To find it, make the turn off South Kihei Road by Maui Dive Shop and the Avis car-rental outlet, continuing toward the end of the road; the restaurant is on the right.

Japanese

★ **Sansei** (1819 S. Kihei Rd., 808/868-0780, https://dkrestaurants.com, 4:45pm-9pm

Sun.-Mon., 5pm-9pm Tues.-Sat., $13-20) is a South Maui favorite. Award-winning dishes such as the *panko*-crusted ahi sashimi rolls and signature shrimp dynamite keep locals flocking to this nondescript spot. For a night on the town, order selected 25-percent-off menu items 5pm-5:30pm Tuesday-Saturday, when the *unagi* and rainbow rolls will leave sushi-lovers feeling like kids in a candy store.

Koiso Sushi Bar (2395 S. Kihei Rd., 808/875-8258, 5pm-9pm Tues.-Sat., $11-34) on the other hand, is a boutique sushi bar with only 15 seats that you'd expect to find in a city. The *nigiri* and sashimi are astoundingly fresh. Connoisseurs will by surprised by this hidden Kihei find.

Mexican

Eclectic decor and Mexican food make for a memorable dining experience at **Fred's Mexican Cafe** (2511 S. Kihei Rd., 808/891-8600, www.fredsmexicancafe.com, 8am-8pm Mon.-Fri., 7:30am-8pm Sat.-Sun., $11-19). On Taco Tuesdays, order seared ahi tacos ($5). Larger plates, such as the fajita platters (beef, surf and turf, veggie, chicken breast) or Cajun-stuffed enchiladas, will satisfy a hearty appetite.

On the weekend, head to **Amigos** (1215 S. Kihei Rd., 808/879-9952, www.amigosmaui.com, 8am-9pm daily, $7-22) and enjoy authentic Mexican food with everything from fresh fish tacos to plentiful burritos. Chase it all back with a margarita from the bar.

Pizza

While it may sound counterintuitive, Kihei's best pizza is at the **South Shore Tiki Lounge** (1913 S. Kihei Rd., 808/874-6444, www.southshoretikilounge.com, 11am-midnight daily, $18-27) in the Kihei Kalama Village. Pies are handcrafted with local ingredients and wheat flour; sit outside on the garden-view deck for a relaxing place to dine.

Another favorite for south shore pizza is ★ **Fabiani's Bakery and Pizza** (95 E. Lipoa St., 808/874-0888, www.fabianis.com, 2pm-8pm Sun.-Tues., 2pm-9pm Thurs.-Sat., $14-20) in central Kihei. Located in a strip mall, it's tough to find, but once you get there, you'll realize why it's a local hangout: Lunch and dinner are dominated by fresh, tasty pizzas and paninis crafted by a chef from Italy. There's also a decent wine selection, and the atmosphere inside is nicer than the exterior suggests. The fresh breakfast pastries are a local secret.

Shaka Sandwich & Pizza (1770 S. Kihei Rd., 808/874-0331, www.shakapizza.com, 10:30am-9pm daily) has been around for over 25 years and is the south side's original pizza joint. The homemade 18-inch (46-cm) Italian pies are big enough to fill two hungry teenagers, and the cheese steak supreme hoagie is a local favorite. Pizzas run $19-31, and by the slice only $3.50.

Burgers

If you just want a quick and filling burger, **Stewz Maui Burgers** (1819 S. Kihei Rd., 808/879-0497, www.stewzmauiburgers.com, noon-8pm Wed.-Sun.) in Kukui Mall is a takeout window with local grass-fed beef from Maui Cattle Company ($10).

Barbecue

For some of Maui's best barbecue and American classics, **Fat Daddy's Smokehouse** (1913 S. Kihei Rd., 808/879-8711, www.fatdaddysmaui.com, 4pm-8pm daily, $9-19) earns high marks for taste. The meatloaf is made with veal, beef, pork, and garlic, and the signature rib plate includes meat slow-cooked for five hours.

Bar and Grill

In the Azeka Mauka shopping center, ★ **Nalu's South Shore Grill** (1280 S. Kihei Rd., 808/891-8650, www.nalusmaui.com, 8am-9pm daily) is one of the most festive dining spots in Kihei, with great service and terrific atmosphere. Many of the ingredients are local or organic, and the menu includes salads and innovative fish and meat sandwiches. Try the Island Pancakes ($12) for breakfast, a seared ahi club ($15) for lunch, and the Island

Style Ribs ($22) for dinner. Order at the counter. There's live entertainment nightly by Maui-based musicians.

Brewpubs

Maui Brewing Company (605 Lipoa Pkwy., 808/201-2337, www.mauibrewingco.com, 11:30am-10pm daily, $14-24) serves 36 of their own beers on tap, and the popular open-air restaurant serves comfort food standards with island inspiration—think chicken *katsu* spaetzle, a veggie burger with macadamia nuts, and pizzas featuring Surfing Goat Dairy cheese, Kula sweet corn, and Hamakua mushrooms. Head down for happy hour 3:30pm-5:30pm daily.

Breakfast and Lunch

One of the best breakfast finds on the south side is ★ **Kihei Caffe** (1945 S. Kihei Rd., 808/879-2230, www.kiheicaffe.net, 6am-2pm daily, $9-14), which gloriously opens at 6am if you're waking up early from jet lag. The portions are enormous, and breakfast is served all day. Try a generous omelet or gargantuan breakfast burrito, and since the atmosphere can be hectic, get here early to beat the crowds.

Food Trucks

Maui's impressive food truck scene has grown considerably over the last five years, and no stay in South Maui is complete without experiencing at least one bountiful meal prepared by the innovative local chefs-proprietors helming their own operations. You will find food trucks in various parking lots throughout Kihei as well as along the roads near beaches, but there are a few areas where many can be found together.

Typically 8-10 food trucks surround covered seating in the gravel lot that makes up 1 Piikea Avenue behind the Azeka Mauka shopping center. Don't let the low-key vibe fool you. Meals here include Hawaiian, Thai, Japanese, and Greek and are substantial and expertly crafted. **Kitoko Maui** (808/214-7582, $8-15) stands out for its bento boxes and focaccia sandwiches. **Da Nani Pirates** (808/250-6671, www.dananipirates.com, $11-15) puts a fantastic culinary spin on its inventive beer-battered tacos and delicious sliders generously filled with seared ahi, pulled pork, buffalo chicken, and more.

About 2 miles (3.2 km) south down South Kihei Road, in the Kihei Kalama Village parking lot, **Horhitos Mobile Taqueria** (1975 S. Kihei Rd., 808/298-5670, $6-13) anchors the scene with its signature south-of-the-border specialties and affordable prices. Seafood tacos (mahimahi, ono, shrimp) are the biggest draw, offered with corn or flour tortillas. There's always a daily special, like a pork belly taco or a mahimahi burger. Horhitos prepares its own hot sauce daily. **South Maui Fish Co.** (1794 S. Kihei Rd., 808/419-8980, $8-16) offers fish-of-the-day specials. The best reason to stop here is the vast selection of *poke* and fish dishes that come with a bountiful side of house-made slaw. Hot dogs and chips for kids are always on hand.

Coffee Shops

The most modern coffee shop in Kihei is **Java Café** (1279 S. Kihei Rd., 808/214-6095, www.javacafemaui.com, 6am-2pm daily, $7-9), in the Azeka Mauka shopping center; 75 percent of the coffee served is grown in Hawaii. You can also buy bags of beans from coffee farms on Maui, Kaua'i, Moloka'i, and the Big Island. Flatbreads and paninis are available for lunch; there's also a large selection of breakfast bagels, pastries, and fresh juices.

For a coffee shop with a quirky French twist, **Café @ La Plage** (2395 S. Kihei Rd., 808/875-7668, www.cafealaplage.com, 7:30am-1:30pm Thurs.-Mon.) is in Dolphin Plaza across from Kam I Beach. In addition to the menu of coffee and espresso, breakfast bagels and sandwiches average $6-9.

At **Akamai Coffee Co.** (1325 S. Kihei Rd., 808/868-3251, www.akamaicoffee.com, 6am-5pm Mon.-Sat., $4-8), top-notch baristas pull espresso with nuance to create specialty coffee drinks that stand out. The coffee beans originate from Maui, and pour-overs, mochas, and lattes are served.

1
2

Natural Foods

The best natural foods market for organic, raw, or gluten-free fare is **Hawaiian Moons Natural Foods** (2411 S. Kihei Rd., 808/875-4356, www.hawaiianmoons.com, 8am-8pm daily, $5-18), in the Kamaole Beach Center across from Kamaole I. The hot bar serves up filling lunches, and the fresh juices are popular.

In the Azeka Mauka shopping center, ★ **Wow Wow Hawaiian Lemonade** (1279 S. Kihei Rd., 808/868-0466, www.wowwowhawaiianlemonade.com, 8am-4pm Wed.-Mon., $8-12) has fresh-pressed juices and açaí bowls with *haupia* or poi, topped with locally grown fruits. The local company strives to source their fruits from Hawaiian farmers and is committed to bettering the local community in addition to serving great food.

Delivery

Too tired to go out for food? A service on Maui called **Hopper Maui** (808/214-6171, www.hoppermaui.com) lets you order from one of 20 different restaurants and have it delivered to your door. You'll pay a 15 percent fee on top of your meal, which doesn't include a tip for the driver, but in terms of convenience, it's tough to beat.

WAILEA

Prices in Wailea are much higher than in other parts of the island, and double the cost in Kihei. You're often paying for master chefs, exceptional service, and unparalleled ambience in world-class resorts.

Hawaiian Regional

The first restaurant you'll encounter in Wailea approaching from Pi'ilani Highway is ★ **Monkeypod Kitchen** (10 Wailea Ike Dr., 808/891-2322, www.monkeypodkitchen.com, 11am-9pm daily, $14-37), the brainchild of renowned Maui chef Peter Merriman. Ingredients are all sourced locally, supporting sustainable farming and ensuring fresh, healthy meals. Dinner options range from hand-prepped pizzas and the popular *bulgogi* pork tacos in an Asian pear aioli to organic macadamia nut-crusted fresh fish. The craft beer list is the best in Wailea. To save a few bucks, visit during happy hour (3:30pm-5pm). There's live music daily.

At the Four Seasons, **Duo Steak and Seafood** (3900 Wailea Alanui Dr., 808/874-8000, 6am-11am and 5:30pm-9pm daily, $30-52) ranks in the upper echelon of fine island cuisine. The dinner menu is dominated by steak and seafood options such as dry-aged bone-in rib-eye filet mignon and Hawaiian snapper. For something light, try the lobster bisque. The breakfast buffet is lauded as the best in Wailea.

At the Grand Wailea, **Humuhumunukunukuapua'a** (3850 Wailea Alanui Dr., 808/875-1234, www.grandwailea.com, 7am-10am Mon.-Tues., 7am-10am and 5pm-9pm Wed.-Sun., $31-52) is not only one of the hardest restaurants to pronounce, it's also one of the most popular. Named after the state fish, "Humu" sits in a thatched-roof Polynesian structure floating on its own saltwater lagoon. Dishes include a filet mignon and lobster entrée, crispy mahimahi, and fresh ahi *poke*. The sunset view looking over the lagoon is the classic image of paradise.

Inside Wailea Beach Resort, chef Roy Yamaguchi's **Humble Market Kitchin** (3700 Wailea Alanui Dr., 808/879-4655, www.royyamaguchi.com, 7am-10pm daily, $20-45) is inspired by his family roots that trace back to Maui plantations. A breakfast standout is the "Big Guy" Omelet—a filling meal with *shoyu* pork, bacon, Portuguese sausage, and fresh Maui vegetables. Happy hour and dinner favorites include crispy calamari and *misoyaki* butterfish. Great vegetarian dishes abound here; consider the vegetable stir-fry or vegetable rigatoni pasta.

Up on the hill at Hotel Wailea, **The Restaurant at Hotel Wailea** (555 Kaukahi Rd., 808/879-2224, www.hotelwailea.com, 7am-11am and 5pm-9:30pm daily, $39-62)

1: ahi tuna tacos at Monkeypod Kitchen **2:** bacon mac and cheese at Maui Brewing Company

offers sweeping sunset views of three islands and fine dining with a twist. The culinary casual fare here reflects the best of the islands' colors, scents, and tastes. Guests can select from a three- or five-course prix fixe menu featuring seasonal ingredients sourced from farmers and fishers throughout the region. Standouts include crab pappardelle, mushroom risotto, and the bok choy-infused Kona Kanpachi with manila clams. Service is exceptional.

Seafood

In the Fairmont Kea Lani, **Nick's Fishmarket** (4100 Wailea Alanui Dr., 808/879-7224, www.nicksfishmarketmaui.com, 4:30pm-8:30pm daily, $30-50) has whitewashed walls, a vine-covered trellis, and Mediterranean ambience. Selections include seafood chowder, mahimahi, Moroccan-spiced salmon, and pan-seared ahi. Reservations are recommended.

Italian

Wailea's best pizza is at ★ **Manoli's Pizza Company** (100 Wailea Ike Dr., 808/874-7499, www.manolispizzacompany.com, 11am-10pm daily, $17-25), within walking distance from many of the hotels and across from the Shops at Wailea. It serves 14-inch (36-cm) thin-crust pizzas with organic and gluten-free options and toppings that include shrimp, pesto, kalamata olives, artichoke hearts, and feta cheese. There are salads, pasta, a selection of 20 wines, and specials at happy hour (3pm-5pm and 9pm-10pm daily).

At the luxurious Four Seasons Resort, the tables at ★ **Ferraro's Bar e Ristorante** (3900 Wailea Alanui Dr., 808/874-8000, 11am-9pm daily, $30-50) are close enough to the ocean that you can dine to the sound of the waves. Clink glasses beneath the stars and savor the authentic *cucina rustica* while listening to a live violin. Lunch is more casual, with wood-fired pizzas, and why not some pinot gris?

Markets

For a quick meal in Wailea, try **Island Gourmet Markets** (3750 Wailea Alanui Dr., 808/874-5055, www.islandgourmethawaii.com, 6am-10pm daily), inside the Shops at Wailea, where you can find breakfast ($6-8), flatbreads ($17) for a filling lunch, local favorites like mahimahi tacos ($12), and sushi and sandwiches ($7-10). There's a coffee shop inside the store as well as a decent wine selection.

Up the hill, at **The Market Maui** (10 Wailea Ike Dr., 808/879-2433, www.themarketmaui.com, 8am-4pm daily, $9-14), the offerings are a little more gourmet, with prices that are reasonable for Wailea. Recharge with gourmet cheeses, fresh breads, or plentiful sandwiches with cured meats, olives, and horseradish. The Market is inside the Wailea Gateway Center, directly under Monkeypod.

Getting There and Around

South Maui is easily navigable by car, although there are parking challenges. Anyone staying at a Wailea resort will likely pay a parking fee upward of $30 per day. Inquire whether your resort has a parking fee and factor this into the cost of the rental. When it comes to parking in Kihei, spots along the street in the Kamaole II area can be tough to find in the middle of the day, so either arrive at the beach early or be prepared to do a little walking. Parking at Ma'alaea Harbor costs $0.50 per hour, although you can find a handful of public spots on the northern side of Hauoli Street. While a car is a necessity to go exploring, those who just want to relax on the beach and make sporadic ventures elsewhere can get by with a combination of walking, shuttles, public buses, and taxis.

CAR

Car Rentals

If you've already made your way to Kihei and decide you need a rental car, there are a number of local options. One of the most popular is family-owned **Kihei Rent a Car** (96 Kio Loop, 808/879-7257, www.kiheirentacar.com), which can arrange a free pickup or drop-off at the Kahului Airport for rentals longer than five days. The rates are often better than the major corporate competitors.

If you would rather get those corporate rewards points, **Avis Car Rental** (1455 S. Kihei Rd., 808/874-4077, 9am-4pm daily) has an outlet in central Kihei next to Maui Dive Shop and Pizza Madness.

TAXI

To have someone do the driving for you and not worry about parking, directions, or sobriety, the best taxi service in Kihei is **A South Maui Taxi** (808/344-7555, www.asouthmauitaxi.com).

SHUTTLE

For a ride to the airport, contact **Roberts Hawaii** (808/539-9400, www.robertshawaii.com). Fares run $19-24 per person one-way, depending on where you're staying.

MOTORCYCLE AND MOPED

In the Azeka Mauka shopping center in North Kihei, **Hawaiian Cruisers** (1280 S. Kihei Rd., 808/446-1111, www.hawaiiancruisers.com, 9am-5pm Mon.-Sat.) offers electric bikes, mopeds, and cruisers ($35-105 per day).

Maui Scooter Shack (1794 S. Kihei Rd., 808/891-0837, www.mauiscootershack.com, 9am-5pm daily) rents mopeds ($45 per day) and motorcycles ($88-98 per day) and usually offers fair, competitive rates.

In the Kamaole Shopping Center, **Aloha Motorsports** (1975 S. Kihei Rd., 808/667-7000, www.alohamotorsports.com, 9am-5pm daily) has a wide range of three-wheeled Slingshots, Harleys, Hondas, scooters, and e-bikes ($79-219 per day).

BUS

Maui Bus operates a number of lines throughout South Maui. All rides are $2 per boarding, or you can also buy a $4 day pass if you know you'll be hopping on and off a lot. The Kihei Villager (bus 15) runs between Ma'alaea Harbor Village and Pi'ilani Shopping Center 6am-8:30pm daily with various stops in between. The Kihei Islander (bus 10) runs between Wailea Ike Drive by the Shops at Wailea and Queen Ka'ahumanu Center in Kahului 5:30am-9:30pm daily. If you are trying to get to North Kihei or Ma'alaea, you can transfer at Pi'ilani Shopping Center to the Kihei Villager (bus 15).

Haleakala and Upcountry

Upcountry is Maui's little secret that's just now starting to get out. Here's a place where the smell of eucalyptus replaces the rustle of palms, and truck-driving farmers with scuffed boots replace the pool boys with towels.

Upcountry is where you throw on a flannel shirt and go for a morning drive, perhaps stopping to relax on the porch of a small family-run coffeehouse. It's a place to go hiking through forests of pine trees or sip on Maui-made wine and watch the day begin or end over Haleakala Crater. It's seeing a Sunday polo game and wandering through Makawao's galleries and buying vegetables straight from the source at a stand on the side of the road. It's eating doughnuts at a family bakery that's been serving them for over a century or settling

Highlights

Look for ★ to find recommended sights, activities, dining, and lodging.

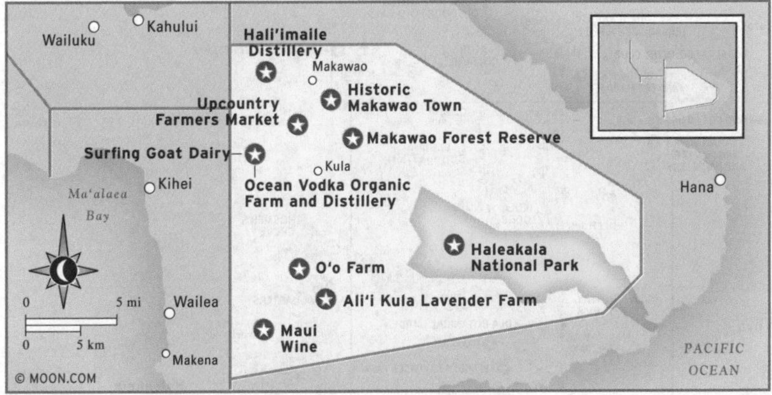

★ Watch the **sunrise** at **Haleakala National Park** and then spend the day hiking across the crater floor—or visit for **sunset** and stay for the stars, camping overnight (page 196).

★ Sample vodka made from pineapples as well as flavored whiskey and rum at **Hali'imaile Distillery** (page 200).

★ Find dozens of local farmers, bakers, fishers, and artisans offering their bounty every Saturday at the **Upcountry Farmers Market** (page 200).

★ Feast on gourmet cheese and get the chance to hand-milk a goat at **Surfing Goat Dairy** (page 202).

★ Tour **Ocean Vodka Organic Farm and Distillery** and top it off with samplings of Maui's celebrated organic vodka, with the panoramic foothills of Haleakala as a backdrop (page 204).

★ Walk through lush scenic lavender fields and enjoy mesmerizing views of the island at **Ali'i Kula Lavender Farm** (page 204).

★ Sip on Maui-made wine at aptly named **Maui Wine** and finish it off with an elk burger (page 207).

★ Enjoy a romantic, freshly cooked lunch in the middle of **O'o Farm** (page 207).

★ Hike or bike through the majestic **Makawao Forest Reserve,** filled with fragrant eucalyptus trees, blooming ginger plants, and superb island views from 2,500 feet (760 m) above sea level (page 212).

★ Discover boutiques, art galleries, and ranching history—all in two-street **Historic Makawao Town** (page 219).

Upcountry

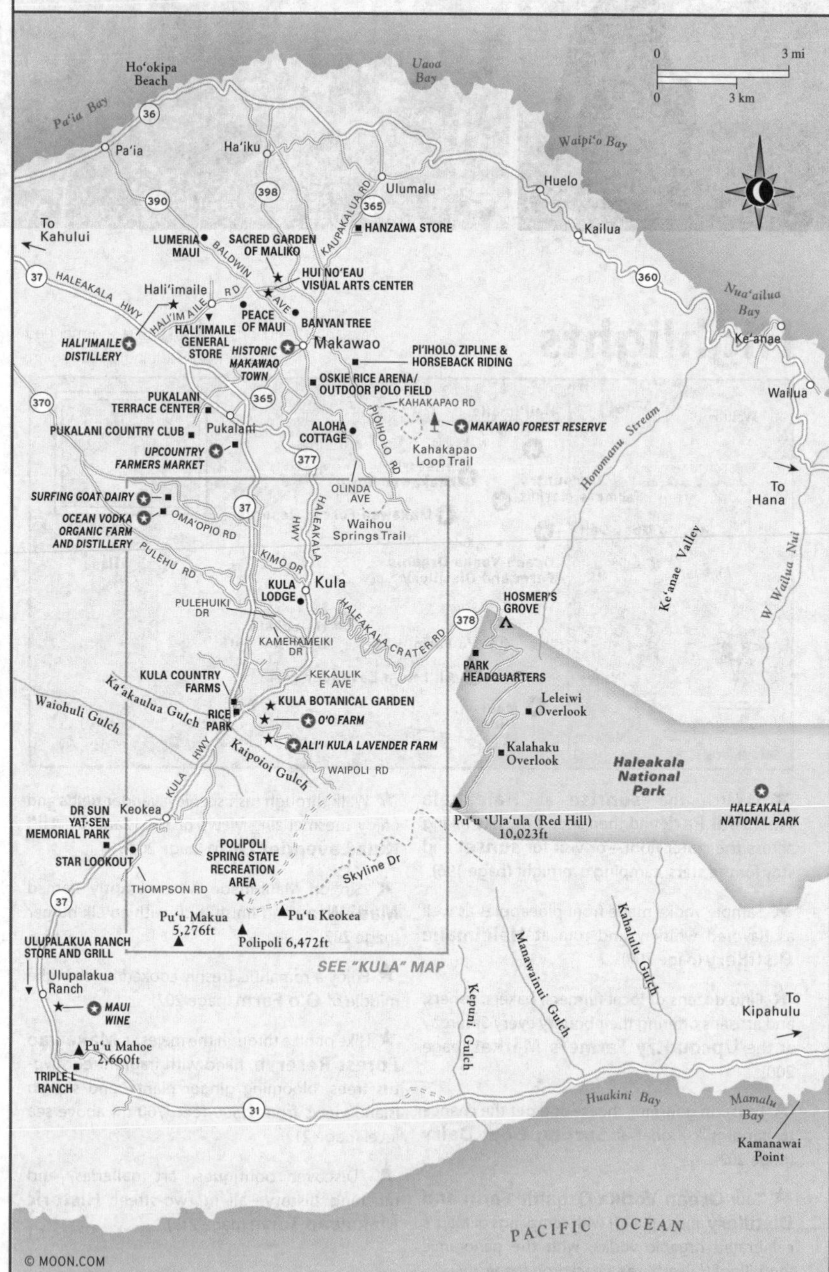
Ho'okipa Beach
Uaoa Bay
Pa'ia Bay
Pa'ia
Ha'iku
Ulumalu
Huelo
Kailua
Waipi'o Bay
KAUPAKALUA RD
HANZAWA STORE
To Kahului
LUMERIA MAUI
SACRED GARDEN OF MALIKO
HUI NO'EAU VISUAL ARTS CENTER
BALDWIN AVE
HALEAKALA HWY
Hali'imaile
HALI'IMAILE RD
HALI'IMAILE GENERAL STORE
PEACE OF MAUI
BANYAN TREE
HALI'IMAILE DISTILLERY
HISTORIC MAKAWAO TOWN
Makawao
PI'IHOLO ZIPLINE & HORSEBACK RIDING
OSKIE RICE ARENA/ OUTDOOR POLO FIELD
Nua'ailua Bay
Ke'anae
Wailua
PUKALANI TERRACE CENTER
PUKALANI COUNTRY CLUB
Pukalani
KAHAKAPAO RD
PI'IHOLO RD
MAKAWAO FOREST RESERVE
ALOHA COTTAGE
Kahakapao Loop Trail
UPCOUNTRY FARMERS MARKET
Honomanu Stream
To Hana
OLINDA AVE
SURFING GOAT DAIRY
OCEAN VODKA ORGANIC FARM AND DISTILLERY
OMA'OPIO RD
PULEHU RD
HALEAKALA HWY
Waihou Springs Trail
KIMO DR
Ke'anae Valley
W Wailua Nui
KULA LODGE
Kula
PULEHUIKI DR
HALEAKALA CRATER RD
HOSMER'S GROVE
KAMEHAMEIKI DR
KEKAULIKE AVE
PARK HEADQUARTERS
KULA COUNTRY FARMS
Ka'akaulua Gulch
Waiohuli Gulch
KULA BOTANICAL GARDEN
Leleiwi Overlook
RICE PARK
O'O FARM
ALI'I KULA LAVENDER FARM
Kalahaku Overlook
Haleakala National Park
Kaipoioi Gulch
WAIPOLI RD
KULA HWY
Keokea
HALEAKALA NATIONAL PARK
DR SUN YAT-SEN MEMORIAL PARK
Pu'u 'Ula'ula (Red Hill) 10,023ft
STAR LOOKOUT
POLIPOLI SPRING STATE RECREATION AREA
Skyline Dr
THOMPSON RD
Pu'u Makua 5,276ft
Pu'u Keokea
Polipoli 6,472ft
Kahalulu Gulch
Manawainui Gulch
ULUPALAKUA RANCH STORE AND GRILL
SEE "KULA" MAP
Ulupalakua Ranch
Kepuni Gulch
To Kipahulu
MAUI WINE
Pu'u Mahoe 2,660ft
TRIPLE L RANCH
Huakini Bay
Mamalu Bay
Kamanawai Point
PACIFIC OCEAN
0 3 mi
0 3 km
36
390
398
365
37
370
377
378
360
31
© MOON.COM

Your Best Day in Upcountry

MORNING

Begin the day in Keokea with breakfast at **Grandma's Coffee House.** Walk it off with a 30-minute stroll on neighboring **Thompson Road** before continuing on to **Ulupalakua** and a visit to **Maui Wine.**

Or start your day with a **Haleakala sunrise,** then spend an hour at the summit area hiking on **Sliding Sands Trail.** On the way back down, grab breakfast at **Kula Lodge** or **Kula Sandalwoods Café** and shop at the **Kula Market Place.** You could alternatively skip the hike (if it's a weekday) so you can make it out to **O'o Farm** for the 10:30am lunch tour.

AFTERNOON

Those who took the Haleakala-O'o Farm route can opt afterward to either go shopping in Makawao or drive out to **Maui Wine**—depending on how much energy you have after the early morning wake-up.

If you skipped sunrise, continue down the road from Maui Wine to have lunch at the **Ulupalakua Ranch Store and Grill** (try the homemade chili) before stopping for produce at **Kula Country Farms** on the drive to **Makawao** for shopping.

EVENING

Those who skipped the Haleakala sunrise might head out for the **Haleakala sunset.**

For dinner or happy hour, head to **Marlow** for exceptional wood-fired sourdough pizzas, **Polli's Mexican Restaurant** for a mango margarita, or **Casanova** at 5pm for $5 carafes of wine.

RAINY DAY IDEAS

Start with breakfast at **Kula Lodge** and a piping cup of hot chocolate, and head downstairs to look at the artwork of Curtis Wilson Cost. Drive to Makawao for an hour of shopping and have lunch at **Polli's Mexican Restaurant,** where a lively crowd often gathers whenever the rain is coming down. Drive 10 minutes to **Hali'imaile Distillery** for an hour-long tasting and tour before treating yourself to a nice dinner at **Hali'imaile General Store.**

in for a colorful sunset over bicoastal views each night. Most of all, it's slowing down and taking time to breathe the mountain air and trading the glamour of beachfront resorts for the charm of a small town.

ORIENTATION

Generally speaking, Upcountry comprises Makawao, Pukalani, Kula, Keokea, and Ulupalakua. At an elevation of 1,500-4,000 feet (460-1,220 m), it's also home to the 10,023-foot (3,055-m) summit of **Haleakala Crater.** From sea level, the 38-mile (61-km) drive to the summit is the shortest climb to 10,000 feet (3,050 m) of any paved road in the world. From Makawao or Kula, reaching the summit of Haleakala Crater is about an hour's drive, and from Ka'anapali or Wailea takes a little over two hours. The drive from Makawao to Ulupalakua takes 35 minutes, versus 10 minutes to the beach in Pa'ia or 15 minutes to Kahului Airport. **Makawao** has the greatest selection of restaurants, shops, and a defined center, whereas **Kula** is a patchwork of houses, farms, and restaurants that are fairly spread out. Tiny **Keokea** is the gateway between Kula and the winery in **Ulupalakua,** where the road continues all

Previous: historic Makawao; sunrise at Haleakala; Maui Wine.

the way around to Kaupo and the "back way" to Hana.

PLANNING YOUR TIME

While it's possible to experience Upcountry's highlights in a single day, try to spend two full days seeing the area—one day at Haleakala Crater either watching the sunrise and exploring Upcountry on the way back down, or gradually visiting Upcountry sights before heading to Haleakala for sunset. On the second day, start with horseback riding or zip-lining, and then see the sights you didn't get to see the day before. While many people drive Upcountry from the beach, there are numerous lodges and bed-and-breakfasts to base yourself on the hill. It's also possible to visit Upcountry when driving the "back road" from Hana, but by the time you get here after a full day in Hana, there's really only time for the winery.

Sights

TOP EXPERIENCE

★ HALEAKALA NATIONAL PARK

"Hale-a-ka-la," House of the Sun. Few places are more aptly named than this 10,023-foot (3,055-m) volcano. Believed to have been dormant since 1790 (the summit area has been inactive for 600 years), when measured from the seafloor, Haleakala is 30,000 feet (9,145 m) tall—surpassed only by the peaks on the Big Island as the tallest mountain on earth.

Given its size and spellbinding nature, it's little wonder the mountain is considered sacred to indigenous Hawaiians. This is where the powerful volcano goddess, Pele, crafted her colorful cinder cones, and a *wahi pana*, or sacred place, only inhabited by the gods. It's where the demigod Maui lassoed the sun to slow its path across the sky so his people could have time to grow their crops and dry their cloth in the sun. It's also a fragile ecological treasure, with more endangered species than any other national park.

Today, the most popular activity for visitors to Maui is visiting Haleakala for sunrise—but there's far more to this national park than simply the light of dawn. Over 30 miles (48 km) of hiking trails crisscross the crater, where backcountry cabins and campgrounds provide a classic wilderness experience. The sunsets and stargazing are as spectacular as viewing the crater at sunrise, and even the drive leading up to park—where the road gains 10,000 vertical feet (3,050 m) in only 38 miles (61 km)—is part of the magical, mystical experience of standing atop Haleakala.

When to Visit

The biggest question surrounding Haleakala is not if you should visit, but when. **Sunrise** is the most popular option, and everyone should experience a Haleakala sunrise at least once—reservations are required and can be made online at www.recreation.gov up to 60 days in advance (for questions, call 877/444-6777); visitors are allowed to only purchase one sunrise reservation per three-day period. Sunrise is crowded, it's tough to find parking, it requires waking up around 2am-3am, and it's often near or below freezing. But it's not the only time to visit. **Sunset** is a display nearly as colorful but without all the crowds (and no reservations required). You don't get the benefit of watching the sun emerge from the horizon, but there are often only 40 people instead of 400, and it isn't as cold. If you want to hike the crater floor, arrive at the summit in the middle of the day and time your exit for sunset.

The weather, unfortunately, can be unpredictable. Rain and even snow can fall at any

1: Haleakala National Park **2:** sunset at Haleakala

1
2

Haleakala: Sunrise or Sunset?

There's big buzz about experiencing mighty Haleakala at sunrise, but one of the lesser-known facts is how dynamic it is during sunset. Locals know this well, often declaring the sunset experience to be just as stellar—if not more so—than what you'll experience during the early morning hours. Here are some factors to consider when making your choice between sunrise and sunset.

- **Crowds:** Sunrise at Haleakala has been heavily promoted in so many travel magazines and websites that hundreds of tourists flock here for it. This has resulted in the park system requiring reservations for sunrise (which can be made online up to 60 days in advance). Not so for sunset, when crowds are considerably smaller in size—nearly 60 percent less—and views from the observation deck less obstructed.
- **Timing and parking:** To arrive in time for sunrise, you'll need to arrive before 4:30am to find a much-coveted parking spot. Depending on where you're staying on the island, this may mean setting your alarm anywhere from 2am-3am. For sunset, it's much easier to find a parking spot; you'll just need to arrive about 45-60 minutes prior to catch the best colors.
- **Position of the sun:** Watching the sun set into the ocean is particularly striking, offering a sublime color palette. Depending on cloud coverage, this time of day also offers rare and extraordinary panoramic views of Maui's south and west sides, which are in shadow around dawn.
- **Stargazing options:** If you visit Haleakala for sunset, you can stay and do some stargazing, possibly catching some shooting stars as a finale. Orion's Belt and the planets Mars and Venus will compete for attention with the Milky Way. While the stars are also visible before sunrise, with the scrambling required to find a parking space and jostling for a viewing spot, you won't be able to focus on the dark sky.

time of year, but summer typically has better conditions. Statistically, on 85 percent of mornings, it's clear enough to see the sunrise. For sunset, a good rule of thumb is that if you can't see the mountain from below, you probably shouldn't bother. On the other hand, if you can see the mountain, but not the top, the sunset will seem to float on a colorful sea of clouds. To take the guesswork out of the equation, call the National Weather Service **Hotline for Haleakala Summit** (808/944-5025, ext. 4) for an up-to-date weather forecast. You can also check out the University of Hawaii astronomy website (www.ifa.hawaii.edu/haleakalanew/weather.shtml) for up-to-the-minute weather data, including windchill, visibility, and rainfall, before heading to the summit.

Admission and Hosmer's Grove

Admission ($30 per car) to **Haleakala National Park** (www.nps.gov/hale) is good for three days and includes the Kipahulu section past Hana, home to the Pools of 'Ohe'o. If you're driving for sunrise, head straight to the summit; if you have time to explore, take the side trip to **Hosmer's Grove,** just past the park entrance (page 209).

Continuing straight past the Hosmer's Grove turnoff, you'll soon arrive at **Park Headquarters** (808/572-4400, 8am-4pm daily) at an elevation of 6,800 feet (2,075 m). Stop for information, camping permits, gifts, toilets, and a pay phone. There are some *'ahinahina* (silversword) plants outside, and sometimes nene (Hawaiian geese) frequent the area.

On the road toward the summit, **Leleiwi** (page 209) is an overlook that's a great alternative at sunrise. **Kalahaku,** on the other hand, is another overlook that's popular at sunrise but can only be accessed when traveling downhill.

Brrr...

On any given morning at the top of Haleakala there is always at least one unfortunate person shivering in a tank top. People forget that Haleakala is over 10,000 feet (3,050 m) high, which means the temperature is 30 degrees Fahrenheit (17 degrees C) colder than it is down on the beach. And, even though Haleakala is the "House of the Sun," the morning windchill—particularly in winter—can often be below freezing. Ice on the road is common in winter, and every few years the summit gets snow that stays for a couple of days. Naturally, whenever it snows on Haleakala, hundreds of locals rush to the summit to help their children build snowmen, and then, of course, immediately rush home to put the photos online.

Most mornings at Haleakala Crater are between 30°F and 50°F (-1-10°C), so consider packing pants, gloves, a hat, and a jacket. No winter clothing? Use the hotel's blankets, but be sure to return them in good condition in order to avoid fees. Temperatures rise into the 60s (15-20°C) by noon, but sunrise and sunset visitors should prepare to bundle up.

For current weather info at Haleakala summit, visit www.ifa.hawaii.edu/haleakalanew/weather.shtml or call 808/944-5025, ext. 4.

Visitors Center and Summit Observation Building

Near the end of the road is the **Visitors Center,** at 9,740 feet (2,969 m). It's about 10 miles (16 km) up the mountain from headquarters, about a 30-minute drive. This is where all of the bike tour companies bring you for sunrise, as it's the best view looking down into the crater. It's open sunrise-3pm daily and contains clear and concise displays on the geology of Haleakala. Maps and books are available, and a 30-minute ranger-guided walk takes place most days at 10am and 11am.

If you want to top out above 10,000 feet (3,050 m) and officially summit Haleakala, **Pu'u 'Ula'ula** (Red Hill) is the highest point on Maui at 10,023 feet (3,055 m). Here you'll find a glass-sided observation area that's open 24 hours daily. The view of the Big Island and coast of Maui is better than at the Visitors Center below. The lava rock ridge just in front of the parking area is the best place to watch the sunset. For perspective, it's 100 miles (160 km) from the top of Haleakala to Mauna Loa in the distance.

Close to the summit is the **Maui Space Surveillance Complex** (www.ifa.hawaii.edu/haleakala), a.k.a. Science City. It's closed to the public and highly controversial, with occasional protests over the construction of a telescope on culturally sacred land.

Camping and Cabins

To really appreciate Haleakala's beauty, you need to stay overnight. The most accessible campground is at **Hosmer's Grove,** where you don't even need a permit. There are a handful of tent sites, a few barbecue grills, a pit toilet, and running water. You can drive up to the campsites, which makes it an easy option. The campground is at 6,800 feet (2,070 m), so nights can get close to freezing. It also makes a great staging ground for driving to the summit for sunrise.

For a rugged overnight backpacking experience, there are **wilderness campsites** inside the crater at both Holua (elevation: 6,940 ft/2,115 m) and Paliku (6,380 ft/1,945 m). Camping in the crater requires a permit, which can be picked up for free from the park headquarters. Both campsites have pit toilets and nonpotable water, and although the sites are first-come, first-served, they can accommodate up to 25 people and are rarely full. Maximum stay is three nights in a 30-day period, and no more than two nights in a row at the same site. Holua is accessible by a 3.7-mile (6-km) hike down Halemau'u Trail and is set in a field of subalpine scrub brush looking toward the Ko'olau Gap. Paliku, on the other hand, requires hiking 9.2 miles (14.8 km) from the Sliding Sands Trail at the summit (or a 10.3-mi/16.6-km hike on Halemau'u Trail), and is wet, lush, surrounded by foliage, and a good place for spotting nene. This is also the preferred area for hikers opting to walk out the Kaupo Gap.

In addition to campgrounds, **backcountry cabins** ($75) are available at Holua, Kapalaoa (7,250 ft/2,210 m), as well as Paliku. Due to their popularity, however, securing reservations can be difficult. Reservations can be made up to 180 days in advance by creating a profile on www.recreation.gov and searching for Haleakala National Park (Cabin Permits). Cabins are often booked four months in advance, so if you want to include this on your trip to Maui, plan ahead and be flexible. Cabins include 12 padded berths, a wood-burning stove, and basic kitchen utilities. Pit toilets and nonpotable water are available, and all trash must be packed out.

MAKAWAO

★ Hali'imaile Distillery

When was the last time you tried vodka made from pineapples? **Hali'imaile Distillery** (883 Hali'imaile Rd., 808/758-5154, www.haliimailedistilling.com, tours 4-5 times daily beginning as early as 10am, $12) is the only place in the world you'll find the sugary spirit. The team in this Quonset hut is completely redefining cocktails, from the world's only vodka aged in French oak to Kona coffee-flavored whiskey and chocolate macadamia nut vodka. Master distiller Mark Nigbur helped pioneer the process of distilling with glass, instead of copper or steel, and he's partnered with Sammy Hagar, his wild blond doppelgänger, to create Sammy's Beach Bar Rum. Tours last 45 minutes and pass through the distillery, which is sandwiched between Hawaii's only sugar plantation and America's only pineapple plantation. Notable brands are Pau Maui Vodka and Paniolo Whiskey, and the tour is capped off by three-quarter-ounce (22-ml) pours for visitors over age 21.

Hui No'eau Visual Arts Center

About 1 mile (1.6 km) downhill from Makawao is the **Hui No'eau Visual Arts Center** (2841 Baldwin Ave., 808/572-6560, www.huinoeau.com, 9am-4pm Wed.-Sat., $2 donation), on a gorgeous 10-acre (4-ha) estate owned by the Baldwin family. The centerpiece is the neo-Spanish mansion built in 1917 and transformed in 1934 into a spectacular center for the arts. Touring the grounds is free, as is perusing the gallery, which hosts the work of local artists and has rotating exhibitions. You can pick up a self-guided tour ($6) of the property or take an hour-long guided tour ($12). History buffs should head directly to the room full of old black-and-white photographs that show what it was like to live on the estate 100 years ago.

Makawao History Museum

If you're curious how Portugal's Azores Islands are tied to Makawao's pastures, or wonder what it was like to live on a ranch in 19th-century Maui, a short visit to the **Makawao History Museum** (3643 Baldwin Ave., 808/572-2482, 10am-5pm daily, donation) is an easy way to find out. In historic Makawao town amid art galleries and boutiques, the small museum has won awards for historic preservation. Look at old black-and-white photos of early Makawao ranches and read profiles of community members who helped shape the town. The museum is completely volunteer-run and supported in part by donations. Pick up a cookbook of family recipes from Makawao's original families.

★ Upcountry Farmers Market

In Kulamalu Town Center, across from Longs Drugs, the **Upcountry Farmers Market** (55 Kiopaa St., www.upcountryfarmersmarket.com, 7am-11am Sat.) makes an ideal stop—especially if you're looking to pick up picnic items—on the way from Makawao to Upcountry sights like the Surfing Goat Dairy, Ocean Vodka Organic Farm and Distillery, and the Ali'i Kula Lavender Farm. Organic farmers, bakers, fishers, artists, and other

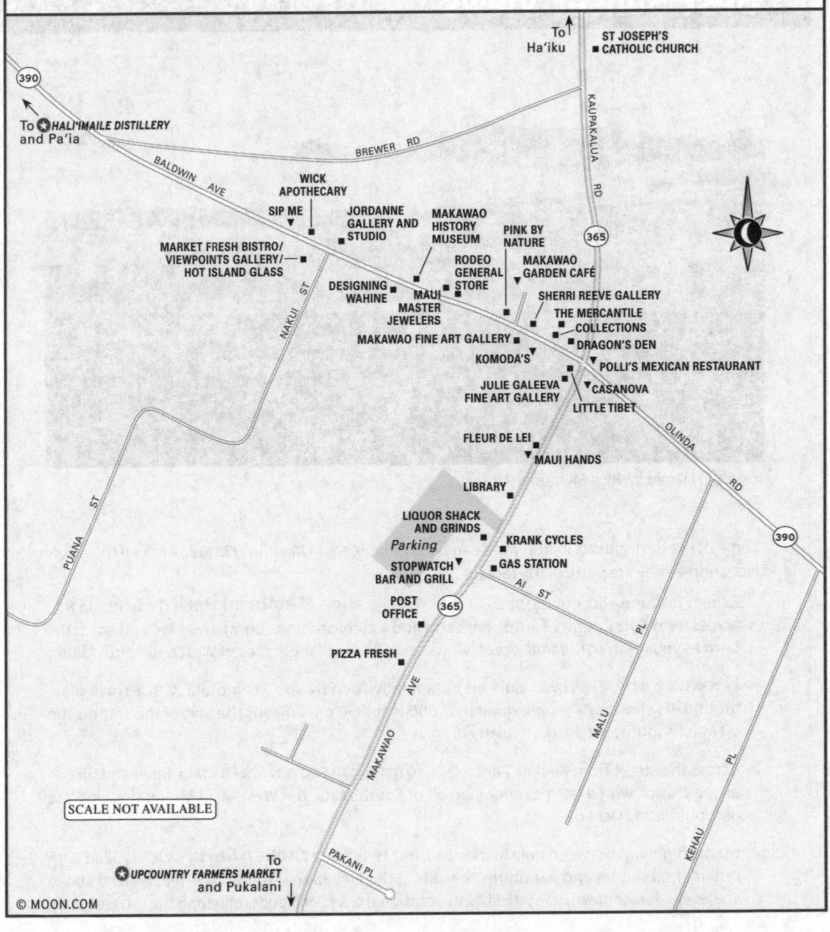

colorful locals converge weekly to showcase and sell their products and socialize; it's a quintessential people-watching hot spot. Fetch some fresh produce, artisanal breads, homemade jellies, pastries, and other locally made products, including woodcrafts and jewelry that make a nice Maui-made souvenir. Sample various treats like freshly baked banana bread, raw nut cheeses, locally made kombucha, fresh-pressed juices, pineapples, coconuts, and much more. It's very pet-friendly.

KULA

On the slopes of Haleakala between 2,000 and 4,000 feet (610-1,220 m) elevation, Kula is the hub of Maui's rural and agricultural life. Tractors drive on two-lane roads where stands sell local produce, and flannel-clad farmers lament how deer are getting into their cabbage. For visitors, the bicoastal views are reason enough to drive here—**Harold W. Rice Memorial Park** (Lower Kula Rd., across from Kula Country Farms) is a great spot for both sunset-watching and stargazing—but so are

Along the Kula Highway: Best Sunset Views

sunset at Harold W. Rice Memorial Park

Some of the best sunsets in the world can be experienced on Maui, and in Kula—given the area's elevation—they are particularly radiant.

- Expect nothing short of glorious at **Harold W. Rice Memorial Park** (Lower Kula Rd., across from Kula Country Farms). Park and find a picnic table or bring a blanket and sit on the lawn as you relish panoramic ocean views as well as the landscapes of West and South Maui.
- **Keokea Park** (218 Lower Kula Rd.) is a family-friendly spot, complete with a small playground. Its elevation—approximately 2,800 feet (854 m)—means the rays of the setting sun off Maui's south side are particularly dramatic.
- Across the street from Keokea Park is **St. John's Episcopal Church,** a small and picturesque church with a lawn overlooking all of South Maui, the West Maui Mountains, and the glorious Pacific Ocean.
- Up the highway, between mile markers 18 and 19, is **Sun Yat Sen Park,** which is filled with ornamental statues and sculptures. Sunsets at this elevation—some 2,400 feet (730 m) above sea level—feel somewhat mystical, with occasional layers of clouds reflecting the sunset colors.

the farm tours, the winery, the shops, and the laid-back small-town vibes.

★ Surfing Goat Dairy

While it's a bit out of the way, eccentric **Surfing Goat Dairy** (3651 Omaopio Rd., 808/878-2870, www.surfinggoatdairy.com, 9am-5pm Tues.-Sat.) is a must-see. Where else are you going to get the chance to hand-milk a goat and then feast on gourmet cheese? Three miles (4.8 km) down Omaopio Road off Kula Highway (Hwy. 37), a line of enormous palms provides what's probably the most regal entrance to a goat dairy anywhere. There are 30-plus flavors of gourmet goat cheese and over 25 types of goat cheese truffles. The best reason to visit is the "casual" tours ($12), which typically run every 30 minutes 10am-3pm daily. Adventurers may want to consider lending a hand to the farmers during the one-hour Evening Chore and Milking Tour ($15-20) or the Grand Dairy Tour ($39 and up),

Kula

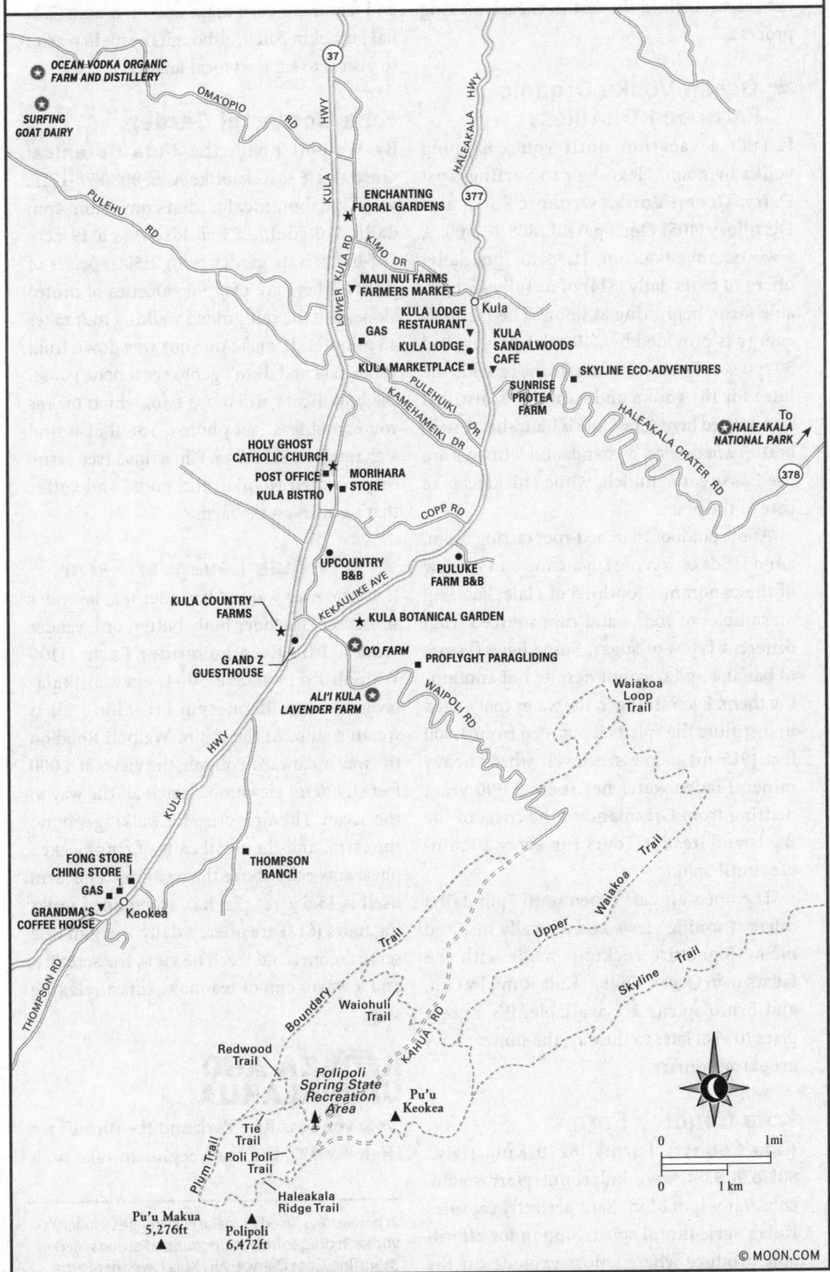
37
HWY
KULA
OCEAN VODKA ORGANIC FARM AND DISTILLERY
SURFING GOAT DAIRY
OMA'OPIO
RD
HALEAKALA
HWY
377
PULEHU
RD
ENCHANTING FLORAL GARDENS
KIMO DR
MAUI NUI FARMS FARMERS MARKET
LOWER KULA RD
Kula
KULA LODGE RESTAURANT
GAS
KULA LODGE
KULA SANDALWOODS CAFE
KULA MARKETPLACE
SKYLINE ECO-ADVENTURES
SUNRISE PROTEA FARM
PULEHUIKI
DR
KAMEHAMEIKI DR
HALEAKALA CRATER RD
To HALEAKALA NATIONAL PARK
378
HOLY GHOST CATHOLIC CHURCH
POST OFFICE
MORIHARA STORE
KULA BISTRO
COPP RD
UPCOUNTRY B&B
PULUKE FARM B&B
KEKAULIKE AVE
KULA COUNTRY FARMS
KULA BOTANICAL GARDEN
O'O FARM
G AND Z GUESTHOUSE
PROFLYGHT PARAGLIDING
WAIPOLI RD
ALI'I KULA LAVENDER FARM
Waiakoa Loop Trail
KULA
HWY
THOMPSON RANCH
FONG STORE
CHING STORE
GAS
GRANDMA'S COFFEE HOUSE
Keokea
THOMPSON RD
Upper Waiakoa Trail
Boundary Trail
Skyline Trail
Waiohuli Trail
KAHUA RD
Redwood Trail
Polipoli Spring State Recreation Area
Pu'u Keokea
Tie Trail
Poli Poli Trail
Plum Trail
Haleakala Ridge Trail
Pu'u Makua 5,276ft
Polipoli 6,472ft
0 1mi
0 1 km
© MOON.COM

which runs just over two hours, where you learn about care for the goats and uncover the secrets behind the farm's cheese-making process.

★ Ocean Vodka Organic Farm and Distillery

It isn't a vacation until you're sipping vodka by noon. Next door to Surfing Goat Dairy, **Ocean Vodka Organic Farm and Distillery** (4051 Omaopio Rd., 808/877-0009, www.oceanvodka.com, 11:30am-7pm daily) offers 10 tours daily ($14) of its fully sustainable farm, beginning at noon. The facility's energy is provided by 240 solar panels, and 30 types of Polynesian sugarcane provide the juice for the vodka and rum that's distilled and bottled here. The cane is hand-harvested, bottles are labeled by hand, and leftovers are used as organic mulch, while chickens take care of the pests.

At the outdoor thatched-roof tasting room, amid fields of waving sugarcane and in view of the panoramic foothills of Haleakala, sip on samples of vodka and rum sourced from different types of sugar. Some have flavors of banana and coconut despite not containing them. Even stranger, the water that's used in distilling the spirits is sourced from 3,000 feet (915 m) below sea level, where heavy mineral-laden water has spent 2,000 years drifting from Greenland to the coast of the Big Island (really). Tours run every 30 minutes until 5pm.

The open-air café (open until 7pm daily) offers stunning views and a locally inspired menu. Signature cocktails made with the farm's own Ocean Vodka, Kula Rum, Fy Gin, and Brum spirits are available. It's a great place to visit later in the day; the sunset views are extraordinary.

Kula Country Farms

Kula Country Farms (6240 Kula Hwy., 808/878-8381, www.kulacountryfarmsmaui.com, 9am-4pm Mon.-Sat.) perfectly captures Kula's agricultural spirit. Stop in for affordable produce where colors explode off the shelves. Buy a healthy snack to enjoy with the ocean view. In October the farm gets festive and features a corn maze and an 8-acre (3.2-ha) pumpkin patch, although the main reason to visit is to support local farmers.

Kula Botanical Garden

By Waipoli Road, the **Kula Botanical Gardens** (638 Kekaulike Ave., 808/878-1715, www.kulabotanicalgarden.com, 9am-4pm daily, $10 adults, $3 children) is a 19-acre (7.7-ha) private garden with 2,500 species of plants. There are over 90 varieties of protea alone, and the self-guided walking tour takes 45 minutes. If you're on your way down from Haleakala and didn't get to see a nene goose, the botanical garden has two, which means you can at least get photos. You'll also find a chameleon exhibit, a Christmas tree farm, three carved wooden tiki gods, and coffee that's grown on the farm.

★ Ali'i Kula Lavender Farm

If you've ever wanted lavender tea, lavender sunscreen, lavender body butter, or lavender scones, **Ali'i Kula Lavender Farm** (1100 Waipoli Rd., 808/878-3004, www.aliikula-lavender.com, 10am-4pm Fri.-Mon., $3) is worth a stop. At the top of Waipoli Road on the way up toward Polipoli, the views at 4,000 feet (1,220 m) elevation stretch all the way to the ocean. The air is crisp for walking around the farm, and the shrill calls of ring-necked pheasants echo above the pastures. The farm itself is 13.5 acres (5.5 ha), and guided walking tours ($12) are offered daily. A small café serves scones and tea. The view, the serenity, and a warm cup of tea make this a relaxing stop.

KEOKEA AND ULUPALAKUA

Once you pass Rice Park and the turnoff for Highway 377, the road begins to take on a

1: pineapples, used to make Hali'imaile Distillery's vodka **2:** dragonfruit at Upcountry Farmers Market **3:** Surfing Goat Dairy **4:** Ali'i Kula Lavender Farm

1
Dragonfruit
$7 sm. $10 med $15
Dole
2
3
4

different feel. The elevation slowly drops, the jacaranda trees provide shade over the road, and the views of South Maui begin to open up before you. Life is slow up here, in this hangout of artists, farmers, and lifelong ranchers. You'll know you've reached the community of Keokea when you see **Keokea Park** on the left, a small field that also has a playground and public restrooms; it's a great spot for sunset watching and stargazing. Picturesque **St. John's Episcopal Church** is just across the highway from the park, and also a perfect perch for panoramic views of the island and ocean at sunset.

Across from Grandma's Coffee House is the turnoff for **Thompson Road,** a one-lane pasture-lined country road that offers one of the island's best views and a leisurely spot for a stroll. By mile marker 18, on the way to Ulupalakua, is the small **Sun Yat Sen Park,** named for the revolutionary who helped found modern China. Sun Mei—Sun Yat-sen's brother—immigrated to Hawaii in 1871 to work as a rice farmer on O'ahu. He moved to Maui and opened a shop, eventually starting a ranch in Keokea that sprawled over 3,900 acres (1,580 ha). He was soon known as the "King of Kula," and with the wealth he'd amassed from his business ventures, Sun Mei paid to have his younger brother educated on O'ahu. Despite the fact that he spoke no English when he arrived from China, Sun Yat-sen eventually graduated with the highest scholarly distinction.

After finishing medical school back in China, and having witnessed modern governments on his many travels abroad, Sun Yat-sen envisioned modern China free of imperial rule. Back in Hawaii in 1894, he formed the Hsing Chung Hui, or Revive China Society, which aimed to further China's prosperity through the development of modern governance. When a revolution in Guangzhou failed spectacularly in 1895, Sun Yat-sen's family fled China to the ranch in Keokea. Forced into exile, Sun Yat-sen spent 16 years in Japan, London, and Hawaii, during which time he staged nine more revolutions—all of them massive failures. Through each failed attempt he regrouped here in Keokea, though the successive failures, funded by Sun Mei, eventually left the businessman bankrupt and forced him off the island.

Despite the failures, Sun Yat-sen had successfully sown the seeds of revolution, and having kept the movement financially alive from this ranch in Keokea, Sun Yat-sen watched as his fellow revolutionaries finally

luscious wine samples at Maui Wine

overthrew the Qing Dynasty in October 1911. Immediately returning to China from exile, he was elected on December 29 as the provisional president of the new Republic of China.

★ Maui Wine

Yes, there is actually a winery on Maui, and yes, it's actually good. Once considered an island novelty that only served pineapple wine, **Maui Wine** (14815 Pi'ilani Hwy., 808/878-6058, www.mauiwine.com, 11am-5pm Tues.-Sun.), like a fine wine, is getting better by the year. There are three varieties of pineapple wine, but there's also grenache, malbec, syrah, viognier, and chenin blanc. Aside from the wine and complimentary tastings, what makes the winery a must-see is its history and beauty.

The tasting room bar is 18 feet (5.5 m) long and made from a single mango tree. The guest cottage where King Kalakaua stayed when he visited the ranch in 1874 is now the tasting room. There's a small historical room attached to the tasting area that details the history of the ranch (allegedly Kalakaua had too much cheer and wagered Molokini while gambling), and free tours trace the ranch's progression from potatoes to sugarcane to wine. Wondering about the cannon sitting in the yard? It was fired to greet King Kalakaua as part of his regal arrival. Today, that heritage is carried on with the "King's Visit"—a private tasting, booked in advance, that pairs the fine estate wines with meat and produce sourced from the ranch and prepared by a private chef.

TOURS

Makawao

If you think pineapples grow underground or on trees, you should probably spend a couple of hours on the **Maui Pineapple Tour** (883 Hali'imaile Rd., 808/665-5491, www.mauipineappletours.com, 8am-4pm Mon.-Fri., $75). Learn why Maui's pineapples are sweet and taste like golden candy. Everyone gets a free pineapple, and you can eat Maui gold in the fields until your gums tingle. Bring a camera for the sweeping views, and don't forget the sunscreen. Check the website for tour times and availability. The minimum age is five, and the pineapple tour conveniently aligns with distillery tours next door.

For customized private tours of the island, **Open Eye Tours** (808/280-5299, www.openeyetours.com) offers extensive, memorable full-day tours that emphasize Hawaiian culture, beginning at $999 per person.

For a food, history, and walking tour through the heart of Makawao town, **Local Tastes of Maui** (808/446-1190, www.localtastesofmaui.com, 9:30am-11:30am daily, $50) offers tours of Makawao (Thurs.) as well as Pa'ia, Lahaina, and Kihei. Portions of proceeds are donated to local animal welfare organizations.

Kula

★ O'O FARM

For a romantic Maui luncheon in the middle of a farm, where you can sip wine beneath a vine-covered trellis and dine on fish or chicken prepared by a chef in an outdoor kitchen, check out the **O'o Farm Gourmet Luncheon Tour** (651 Waipoli Rd., 808/667-4341, www.oofarm.mybigcommerce.com, 10:30am-1:30pm Mon.-Fri., $94 adults, $47 children), where visitors take a tour around the 8-acre (3.2-ha) farm and choose from 60 different crops while picking a salad in the fields.

The air up here is misty and cool, at least when the clouds roll in, and there's nothing like a cup of French-pressed coffee. The first hour is spent touring the farm and meeting the on-site chef, who arrives at the farm at sunrise to source ingredients from the fields. Much of the produce used travels a total of 400 feet (120 m). Instead of a farm-to-table restaurant, the table has been brought to the farm. The wine is BYOB, and there's also a **"Seed to Cup" Coffee Tour** with coffee grown on the farm (8:30am-11:30am Mon.-Fri., $94 adults, $47 children).

TOP EXPERIENCE

Stargazing in Upcountry

stars at Haleakala

Come nightfall, the sky in Upcountry is so luminous and the Milky Way so valiantly on display—thanks to the lack of light pollution and elevation—that you may feel like you're in outer space. The best time for stargazing is during the new moon or before the moon rises.

Locals and visitors in the know often drive up and down the lightly trafficked rural Kula Highway at night, which has several safe pullouts for brief stops to stargaze, as well as other exceptional locales that allow you to linger longer. **Harold W. Rice Memorial Park,** across from Kula Country Farms on Lower Kula Road, is an ideal place to bring a blanket, lie down, and witness the star show. Farther up Kula Highway at **Keokea Park,** you'll find an open field to lie on—prime stargazing real estate with a broader sky view, perfect for spotting shooting stars. Both are also prime sunset-watching spots, so come early with a picnic dinner and stay for nightfall.

If you don't want to venture too far up in elevation, stay in Makawao and visit the grounds at **Lumeria Maui,** a wellness retreat with grounds that are open to the public. Find space near the giant Buddha statue on the central lawn for a near-spiritual experience.

If you'd like a **guided tour** of the night sky in Upcountry, you can book the impressive six-hour stargazing tour that includes sunset on **Haleakala** offered by **Maui Stargazing,** which also includes access to the largest portable telescope on Haleakala.

MAUI STARGAZING

Maui Stargazing (808/298-8254, www.mauistargazing.com, reservations required, $195-225) offers an unforgettable sunset and stargazing tour lasting six hours, up to six times weekly. Limited to 11 people, the tour meets at Kula Lodge (15200 Haleakala Hwy.), where you'll set out for the Haleakala summit. Following sunset viewing, you'll be treated to an educational laser-guided survey of the constellations, visible planets, nebulae, star clusters, the Milky Way, and more, plus 1-1.5 hours of guided telescope time through the largest portable telescope on Haleakala.

The tour provides winter jackets and snowboard pants; it gets cold 10,000 feet (3,050 m) up at night! Note that no scuba diving is allowed within 24 hours of your tour to avoid decompression sickness.

Hiking and Biking

HIKING

Haleakala National Park

Thanks to the colorful cinder cones and trails that crunch underfoot, anyone who hikes across Haleakala Crater will swear they could be on the moon. Covering a total of 19 square miles (49 square km), the crater basin is a vast wilderness with 30 miles (48 km) of trails. It's a place of adventure, mythology, and silence—and home to Maui's best hiking. If you love the outdoors, no trip to Maui is complete without a spending a day on the crater floor.

Hikers need to be prepared, however, as temperatures can range 30-80°F (-1-27°C) over the course of a single day. The hiking is at high elevation, 7,000-10,000 feet (2,135-3,050 m), and hiking back up generally takes twice as long as the hike down. **Hike Maui** (808/201-3485, www.hikemaui.com, $220) is the only company that offers commercially guided hiking tours, which typically run seven hours. Should you go on your own, here's a rundown of the most popular hikes, listed from shortest to longest. All distances are round-trip.

PA KA'OAO (0.4 MI/0.6 KM)

If you don't feel like watching the sunrise with 200 other people, huff your way up this five-minute trail that leaves from the Visitors Center parking lot. The view from the top looks down toward the crater, and it's better than from the parking lot. Bring a flashlight if you're walking the trail before sunrise.

LELEIWI OVERLOOK (0.5 MI/0.8 KM)

Running late for sunrise? Consider hiking to **Leleiwi Overlook** (8,840 ft/2,695 m). Located by mile marker 17.5, Leleiwi has smaller crowds and is usually warmer. The view looks down on the crater floor and the sheer multihued cliffs, although since the lookout faces east, it isn't as good for sunset.

HOSMER'S GROVE NATURE TRAIL (0.5 MI/0.8 KM)

Unlike other trails in the park, the **Hosmer's Grove Nature Trail** is at the park's lower boundary just after you enter the park. The short trail loops through a dense grove of trees, planted in 1910 as part of an unsuccessful experiment to test the viability of the lumber industry. Surrounded by sweet-smelling pine and fir, grab a fleece and go for a stroll through the 20-plus species of trees, listening for forest birds that flit around in the treetops. To reach the trailhead, make a left on the road pointing toward the campground immediately after entering the park. The walk, over mostly level ground, should take 30 minutes. To extend the trip, hike the **Supply Trail** for 2.3 miles (3.7 km) to where it meets with the crater rim.

HALEMAU'U TRAIL (SWITCHBACK TRAIL) (7.5 MI/12 KM)

Beginning from an altitude of only 7,990 feet (2,435 m), the first 1.1 miles (1.8 km) of this trail meander through scrub brush before bringing you to the edge of a 1,000-foot (300-m) cliff. The view down into the Ko'olau Gap is better here than from the summit, and although the trail is well defined, the drop-offs can be a bit disconcerting. After 3.7 miles (6 km)—and a 1,000-foot (300-m) drop—the trail passes Holua Cabin, where you can turn around. Tack on another mile (1.6 km) by continuing to Silversword Loop, a section of the crater known for its numerous *'ahinahina*, or endangered silversword plants.

KEONEHE'EHE'E TRAIL (SLIDING SANDS TRAIL) (8 MI/12.9 KM)

Starting at the summit visitors center at 9,800 feet (2,990 m), Keonehe'ehe'e descends 2,500 vertical feet (760 m) to the crater floor below. This trail is barren, windswept, without shade, and a stunning conduit to the cinder

Haleakala National Park

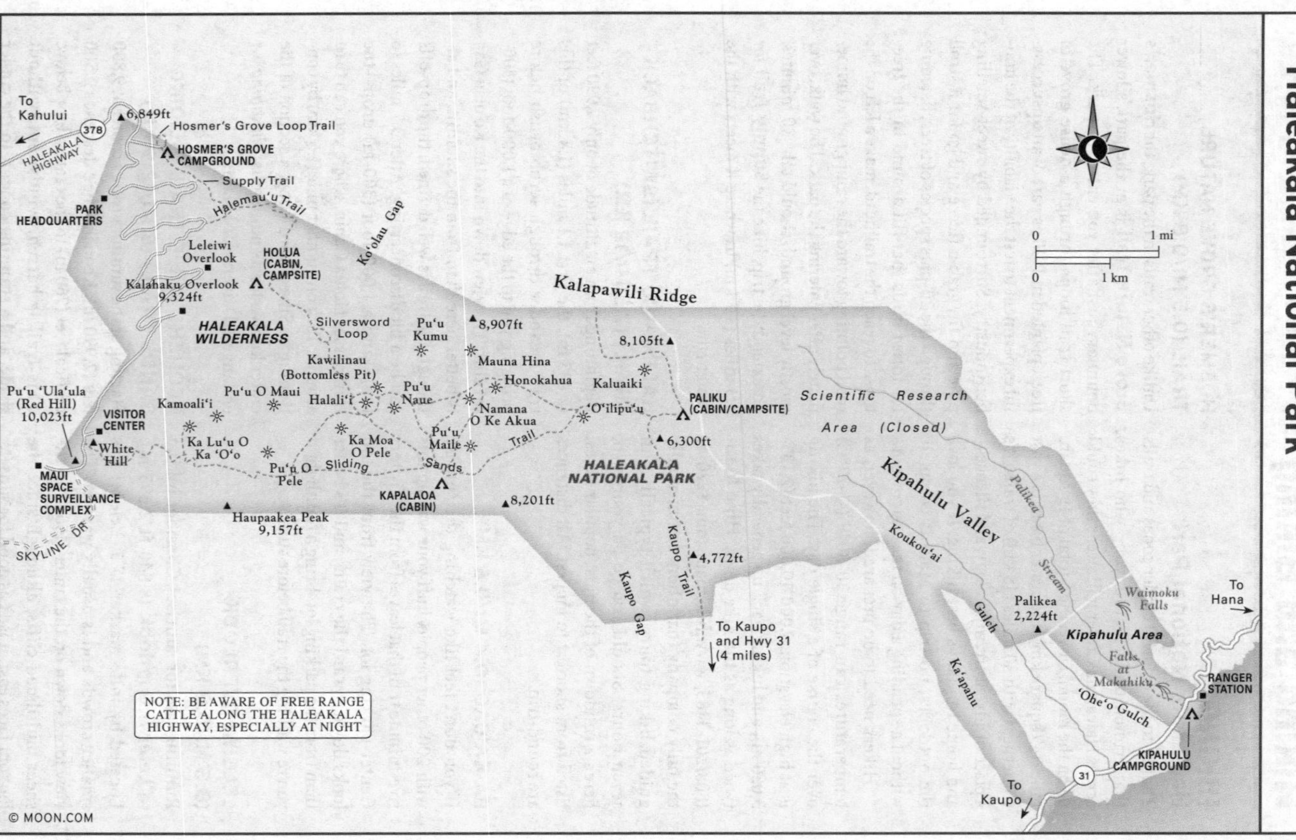

Polipoli: The Last Frontier

While no official statistics are kept, there's a good chance that **Polipoli Spring State Recreation Area** is Maui's least visited corner. Even a place as desolate as Kaupo sees more people. High above the protea farms, the lavender farm, the disc golf course, and even the paragliding school, Polipoli is almost an afterthought, so far removed from the rest of the island that most visitors don't even know it's there.

This isolation makes Polipoli an enchanting place. Set between 5,300 and 7,100 feet (1,615-2,165 m) elevation, there are sweeping views down to the shore, and trails completely enveloped in trees and thick mists. Bathed in the scent of redwood and pine (yes, there are redwoods on Maui), it's a magical, spooky, and refreshing place.

This 10-acre (4 ha) recreational area of the Kula Forest Reserve was extensively logged during the 1930s by the Civilian Conservation Corps (CCC). A large clearing at 7,000 feet (2,135 m) is nicknamed "The Ballpark," where corps members would gather on their lunch break to play high-altitude baseball. Today Polipoli is frequented by hikers and hunters looking for wild boars, goats, and pheasants. This is also the island's premier mountain biking destination, where a forested woodland of downhill and single-track provides a ride akin to Oregon or Northern California.

Mornings offer the clearest views for hiking in Polipoli, and for anyone wanting to hit the trails early, there's a small campground ($12) and a rustic cabin ($90) that can accommodate up to 10 people (no electricity). Both are reachable along the steep, switchbacking Waipoli Road, 9.7 miles (15.6 km) uphill from Kekaulike Highway (Hwy. 377). The last 4 miles (6.4 km) are unpaved and require a 4WD vehicle. For cabin reservations, contact the **Division of State Parks** (54 S. High St., Ste. 101, Wailuku, 808/984-8109, 8am-3:30pm Mon.-Fri.). Make campground reservations online at www.hawaiistateparks.org.

cones. You can turn around anytime you want to hike out. Continuing to Kapalaoa Cabin adds 3.5 miles (5.6 km) round-trip.

SLIDING SANDS SWITCHBACK LOOP (12.2 MI/19.6 KM)

If you're in good shape and have a full day to devote to exploring the crater, this is hands-down the best day hike in the summit area. Park at the Halemau'u trailhead, then hitch a ride to the top, where you'll hike down to the crater floor on the Sliding Sands Trail. Follow the signs toward Holua Cabin and the Halemau'u Trail, where a leg-burning, switchbacking, 1,000-foot (300-m) climb leads back to the car.

If you really want an island adventure that you'll never forget, consider hiking the trail at night in the light of a full moon. For this night hike, bring a backpack of extra clothing, carry extra water and a flashlight, and dress for windchill that can drop below freezing any time of year.

KAUPO GAP

Of all the hikes in Haleakala Crater, none are more legendary, or more extreme, than "shooting" the Kaupo Gap, a two-day trip, with a stay at Paliku campground, that drops 9,500 vertical feet (2,900 m) over 17.5 miles (28 km). Permits are required for camping at Paliku, in the crater's remotest corner, 9.2 miles (14.8 km) from the Sliding Sands trailhead.

On the second day of the hike, you'll descend from Paliku outside the national park boundary, and legally continue across private land until you reach Kaupo Store. Along the trail, keep an eye out for goats and deer that roam the windswept grasslands. When you finally finish the hike in Kaupo, it's best if you've prearranged a ride. If not, you may have to convince the rare passerby to shuttle your sweaty body all the way to the other side of the island. Despite the logistical challenges and the grueling backcountry terrain, this is a unique and memorable hike.

Polipoli Spring State Recreation Area

For a place to escape and commune with the serenity of nature, channel your inner Emerson or Thoreau, and meditate up in the mists, get a 4WD vehicle and head to **Polipoli Spring State Recreation Area**, an out-of-the-way forested spot with some of the island's best hiking. Trails pass through old-growth redwoods, eucalyptus, ash, and pines. Be sure to wear bright colors, since hunters are frequently in the area.

After ascending the switchbacking, pasture-lined road that continues up from the lavender farm, the first hike is the **Waiakoa Loop Trail**, which begins by the hunters check-in station. The trailhead technically doesn't begin for 0.75 mile (1.2 km) down the hunting access road, but if you don't have a 4WD vehicle, it's better to park at the hunters station and walk to the trailhead. Once you're here, a 3-mile (4.8-km) loop with a moderate elevation change of 400 feet (120 m) passes through lowland brush and pines.

Farther up the road, just past the cattle guard where the road eventually turns to dirt, you'll find the trailhead for the **Boundary Trail**, a 4.4-mile (7-km) (one-way) trail that descends to the lower fence line. This trail offers sweeping views of South Maui, and since it's 1,000 vertical feet (300 m) lower than other trails, it won't leave you as winded. It can either be done as an out-and-back hike or combined with other trails as a loop. The shortest loop is up the **Lower Waiohuli Trail**, which intersects the Boundary Trail at the 2.6-mile (4.2-km) mark. Turning left on the Lower Waiohuli Trail, it's 1.4 miles (2.3 km) back uphill to the main road, then a 2.5-mile (4-km) trek back along the dirt road to your car.

If 7 miles (11.3 km) seems too far, most of the shorter walks in Polipoli begin and end at the campground. While some are only a mile (1.6 km) long, the best hike in the park for first-time visitors is the 5.3-mile (8.5 km) loop trail formed by connecting the **Haleakala Ridge Trail, Polipoli Trail, Redwood Trail,** and **Plum Trail**. Driving all the way to the campground requires a 4WD vehicle.

It's possible to hike all the way from Polipoli to the summit of Haleakala. Follow the 6.8-mile (10.9-km) dirt road, known as **Skyline Drive**, a "back entrance" to Haleakala National Park. If it has snowed recently atop Haleakala and the rangers have closed the road, this is an alternative way to hike into the park and be the only person there. Even on regular days, however, Skyline is a strenuous hike providing panoramic views down the mountain's southwest rift zone. Though Haleakala has been dormant for more than 220 years, volcanologists claim that when the mountain erupts again, magma will cover the barren landscape that's visible from this trail. To reach the trailhead for Skyline Drive, turn left at the fork that leads down to the campground from the main dirt road. From here, the road continues climbing and begins to double back toward the north, along the way passing the trailhead for the 1.8-mile (2.9-km) **Mamane Trail**. Eventually you'll reach a locked gate at an area known as the Ballpark (7,000 ft/2,135 m). From here it's a 3,000-vertical-foot (915-m) switchbacking trail to the summit. Pack plenty of water and warm clothing, and be aware of the challenges of hiking at altitude.

Makawao

★ MAKAWAO FOREST RESERVE

Oregon meets Maui: That's how the **Makawao Forest Reserve** (www.dlnr.hawaii.gov) is best described. Lush and green and perched 2,500 feet (760 m) above sea level, this magical hamlet with flowering ginger plants and fragrant eucalyptus trees encompasses nearly 2,100 stunning acres (850 ha). It's one of Upcountry's most prominent destinations, ideal for sightseeing or more adventurous outings, thanks to miles

1: hiking the Sliding Sands Trail at Haleakala
2: biking above the clouds on Haleakala

1
2

of crisscrossing trails to entice hikers and bikers. There are phenomenal views of the island and ocean, and the reserve is a perfect place to take a break from the sun and warmer temperatures at sea level. Trails can be wet from occasional rain, so plan accordingly with proper footwear. A trail directory and trail maps are available on-site.

In the heart of the reserve, the **Kahakapao Loop Trail** is popular with families walking their dogs and mountain bikers. This verdant, easy-to-follow 5.7-mile (9.2-km) loop weaves through eucalyptus, pines, ferns, and wild ginger, and the air is cool at just over 3,000 feet (915 m) elevation. To reach the trailhead from Makawao, follow Makawao Avenue toward Ha'iku for 0.3 mile (0.5 km) before turning right on Pi'iholo Road. After 1.5 miles (2.4 km), just past the Pi'iholo zip-line tours, take a left at the fork in the road and follow it for 0.5 mile (0.8 km). Here you'll make a right onto Kahakapao Road and drive 1.5 miles (2.4 km) on a narrow uphill until you reach a metal gate (open 7am-7pm daily). From the gate, a steep asphalt road continues for another 0.5 mile (0.8 km) to a gravel parking lot.

WAIHOU SPRING FOREST RESERVE

If you don't feel like dealing with throngs of bikers, head to the **Waihou Spring Trail,** toward the top of Olinda Road. This 2-mile (3.2-km) trail is open to hikers only and doesn't have as steep an elevation gain as at Kahakapao. It's uniquely situated among an experimental planting of pine trees, and while the wooded trail is nice enough for walking, the treat is at the end, where a steep switchback leads to a hidden gulch. Here you'll find a 30-foot (9-m) vertical rock face with tunnels bored through, and if you have a flashlight, you can climb in the tunnels and follow them for a short distance. To reach the trailhead for Waihou Spring, go to Makawao's only intersection and follow Olinda Road uphill for 5 very curvy miles (8 km).

BIKING DOWN HALEAKALA

You've seen the brochures, you've heard the hype; here's the deal with cycling down Haleakala Volcano:

It's imperative to be confident and competent on a bicycle. It is marketed as beginner-friendly, but in reality, dozens of people are seriously injured each year. In almost all cases it's because they took their eyes off the road or were riding too fast.

That said, watching the day begin from Haleakala Crater and the crisp air in your face as you weave through cow-speckled pastures is magical. Visit the shops of Makawao town and finish the ride close to the beach. A wide range of operators have different options, and the key to an enjoyable trip is choosing carefully. Decide whether you want to include sunrise at Haleakala Crater. This means waking up early, with pickups at 2am. After watching the sunrise, it's back in the van for the drive down to 6,500 feet (1,980 m), where all the tours begin the cycling portion, outside the national park. If you opt for a tour that doesn't include sunrise, you'll be driven to this spot, usually arriving about 10am. The next option is whether to ride with a guide. The benefit is safety, but it means you have to follow the pace of the group. For independent-minded travelers, it's probably best to choose a company that lets you ride on your own.

The third option to consider is where the tour ends: in Upper Kula with a zip-line combo, or all the way to the beach. It's possible to ride from the summit to the beach with your own car and bike. **Krank Cycles** (1120 Makawao Ave., 808/572-2299, www.krankmaui.com, 10am-5pm daily) and **Bike Maui** (810 Ha'iku Rd., Ste. 120, 808/575-9575, www.bikemaui.com, 8:30am-3:30pm Mon.-Sat.) offer independent rentals, although **Maui Sunriders Bike Co.** (71 Baldwin Ave., 866/579-8970, www.mauisunriders.com, 8am-4pm daily) is the most convenient, as their shop is near the beach.

With those options in mind, here are some of our top picks:

Tips for Biking the Volcano

- If you go with a tour, you can't ride from the summit. To **bike from the summit,** you have to provide your own bicycle and transportation.
- Seeing the **sunrise isn't guaranteed:** 15 percent of the time the crater is clouded in. Variations in the weather aren't seasonal, so all you can do is hope for the best.
- If you want to spend more than 15 minutes at Haleakala after sunrise, **save sunrise for a separate trip** and book a midmorning bike ride. The trip will be cheaper, and you'll be able to hike and explore the crater without having to rush back to the van.
- Be prepared to wake up *really* early for a **sunrise tour.** Companies collect guests from the farthest hotels first, so if you're staying in Makena or Kapalua, expect to meet your driver as early as 1:45am.Try to book this excursion early in your trip, when you're still jet-lagged and waking up early.
- If you're on a **budget,** opt for a **midmorning tour.** It isn't as cold, you don't have to wake up as early, it isn't as crowded, and the trips are substantially cheaper. Companies charge more for the sunrise tours because they're popular.
- Remember that you're **sharing the road** with cars. There are no bike lanes, so be sure to keep your eyes on the road at all times.
- Pack **closed-toe shoes, long pants,** a **rain jacket,** and **warm clothing.** Early morning temperatures often dip below freezing at the summit. Although many tour companies provide rain gear, the more protection you have against the elements, the better.
- Don't expect to get any **sleep** in the van ride up. The road switchbacks incessantly, and drivers entertain the riders with island history and jokes.
- If you're skittish, go with a **guided group.** To go it alone, choose an independent company so you can ride without a guide.
- Don't schedule your bike ride for the day after scuba diving; **decompression sickness** can kill.

Maui Easy Riders (808/344-9489, www.mauieasyriders.com, $200) is a small operation run by two brothers, both named Billy (really). Group size is small, only eight people, and tours begin at 9am in the parking lot of Pa'ia Bay. The ride begins at 6,600 feet (2,010 m), just above where other companies begin, and the 25-mile (40-km) ride to the beach is longer than any other company. This guided tour makes a stop in Makawao for 30 minutes of exploring on foot, and at the end you can literally jump off your bike and into the waves.

Other providers include **Mountain Riders** (800/706-7700, www.mountainriders.com) and **Cruiser Phil's** (808/893-2332, www.cruiserphils.com).

For an independent ride, **Maui Sunriders Bike Co.** (71 Baldwin Ave., 808/579-8970, www.mauisunriders.com, 8am-4pm daily) has morning tours ($99) that start and end at their shop in Pa'ia. Visitors can explore Pa'ia once the ride is over. Other independent tours include **Bike Maui** (810 Ha'iku Rd., Ste. 120, 808/575-9575, www.bikemaui.com, 8:30am-3:30pm daily), offering a sunrise tour ($220).

MOUNTAIN BIKING

The mountain biking on Maui is really good. The two main areas Upcountry are the **Makawao Forest Reserve,** about 15 minutes above Makawao, and **Polipoli,** above Kula. Thanks to the team at Krank Cycles, the Makawao Forest Reserve has recently undergone over $500,000 in trail work, which means Makawao has some of the best trails in Hawaii. With 16 miles (26 km) of trail in total, there are terrain parks, single-track, 2-mile (3.2-km) climbs, and even a 30-foot (9-m) banked wooden wall you'd expect to find in a place like Whistler. The "Pineapple Express" is 2 miles (3.2 km) of downhill, and the west loop on the Kahakapao Trail is the most popular trail for climbing.

Polipoli, on the other hand, offers rugged downhill mountain biking, with a network of trails that switchback through redwoods, lava flows, and wide-open plains. You'll need a 4WD vehicle to reach some trailheads, and forget about visiting after a rain, since you'll get stuck in the mud. For a classic climb and single-track descent, park where the **Mamane Trail** meets the road toward the campground. Start by riding in the direction of the campground and turn uphill at the fork, where you'll climb along the spine of the mountain before the 2-mile (3.2-km) Mamane Trail drop.

For the island's longest off-road descent, the chance to bike from 10,000 feet (3,050 m), have someone drive you to Haleakala for the start of **Skyline Drive.** The unpaved road begins by Science City and switchbacks its way across desolate cinder that looks like the surface of the moon. Watch for wild goats and hunters, and definitely wear bright clothing. After 6 miles (9.7 km), turn down the Mamane Trail for 2 fast miles (3.2 km) of single-track. For a full 7,000-foot (2,135-m) vertical descent, continue riding all the way down to Highway 37, then turn left for the 2-mile (3.2-km) ride on pavement to Grandma's Coffee House. Arrange to have your ride pick you up here.

For Upcountry bike rentals, **Krank Cycles** (1120 Makawao Ave., 808/572-2299, www.krankmaui.com, 10am-5pm daily) is in Makawao and offers daily rentals ($55-89). One day is plenty of time for the Makawao trails, but not all of the Polipoli trails, so plan accordingly. Krank is Maui's most dedicated mountain bike shop; check out their website for current trail conditions.

Horseback Riding and Bird-Watching

HORSEBACK RIDING

Upcountry is horse country, and in the rolling Upcountry pasturelands, horseback riding is a slice of authentic Upcountry life. All of Upcountry's horseback options are on working ranches, which mean you're dealing with real *paniolo* who still ranch, wrangle, and ride.

For a small-scale, intimate experience in the most beautiful pastures on Maui, **Thompson Ranch Riding Stable** (1311 Waianu Rd., 808/878-1910, www.thompsonranchmaui.com, $200-225, cash only) offers guided trail rides on their Keokea ranch. This is a family-run working cattle ranch that's far from touristy, and the ranch owners love their horses. The view here is unforgettable, with green pastures rolling down to the blue Pacific. The climb is steep, and the maximum weight for riders is 200 pounds (90 kg).

For a ranch adventure unlike any other, book the half-day lunch tour (3.5 hours, $275) with the crew at **Triple L Ranch** (15900 Pi'ilani Hwy., 808/280-7070, www.triplelranchmaui.com, 8am-6pm daily). Located 4 miles (6.4 km) past the Maui winery on the back road toward Hana, the ranch is set in windswept Kanaio, the youngest part of Maui. The cattle are all free range and roam the mountain without fences. There's no denying the magic of riding a horse to an isolated beach, even though it's rocky and lacking sand. Kanaio is laden with archaeological sites and abandoned lava-rock fishing villages. Maximum weight is 220 pounds (100 kg), and minimum age is 12. Group size is limited to two or three.

BIRD-WATCHING

Haleakala National Park

If you're an avid bird-watcher, just get in the car, drive uphill, and don't stop until you reach the entrance of **Haleakala National Park.** Given Hawaii's extreme isolation, 71 different species of birds were once endemic to the islands. Of those species, 23 have gone extinct, and dozens more are critically endangered due to mongooses, feral cats, and the gradual loss of habitat. Endangered species such as *'akohekohe* find themselves clinging to a fragile existence on Haleakala's slopes.

One of the best bird-watching places is at **Hosmer's Grove** on the moderate 0.5-mile (0.8-km) loop trail. Even if you don't see native honeycreepers (birds whose bills have adapted to extract nectar from native plant species), the treetops chirp with birdsong different from anywhere else on the planet.

While casual hikers might spot an *'i'wi* or *'apapane* (scarlet Hawaiian honeycreeper), the best way to spot rare species is to take the three-hour ranger-led **guided walks** (808/572-4400, 9am Mon., Wed., and Fri.) into the neighboring privately owned **Waikamoi Preserve.** Reservations are required. On a less frequent basis, hikes into the preserve are arranged by the **Maui Forest Bird Recovery Project** (808/573-0280, www.mauiforestbirds.org).

Moving higher up toward the summit, bird-watchers should look for two endangered species: the *'u'au* (Hawaiian petrel), which burrows in areas near the summit visitors center, and the nene (Hawaiian goose), which can be spotted along park roadways and the valley floor. The nene is Hawaii's state bird, and one of the best places to spot them is in grasslands surrounding Paliku Cabin.

horseback riding at Haleakala

Adventure Sports

PARAGLIDING

When was the last time you ran off a hill and experienced total silence? Or saw Maui from a bird's-eye view without the whir of a chopper? **Paraglide Maui** (1100 Waipoli Rd., 808/874-5433, www.paraglidemaui.com, 7am-7pm daily) is Hawaii's only paragliding school, and thanks to Maui's optimal conditions, flights are possible about 330 days per year. The launch and landing sites are perfect for learning, and nearly every flight takes place in the morning before the clouds fill in. Tandem flights drop 1,000 feet (300 m) for $115 or 3,000 feet (915 m) for $225 over the Polipoli treetops. This unforgettable island experience is highly recommended.

ZIP-LINE TOURS

Believe it or not, Upcountry is where ziplining was born in the United States. In 2002 **Skyline Eco-Adventures** (12 Kiopa'a Pl., 808/518-2860, www.skylinehawaii.com,7am-7pm daily) opened in Kula's misty uplands, the first in the country. Today, Skyline offers a five-line course best for beginners, since the length of the lines and vertical drops aren't dramatic. There's also the option to combine a zip line with a sunrise Haleakala bike tour, although the bike ride only descends 2,500 feet (760 m), so the combo is best for people who just want a sample of both activities. The course is on the road toward Haleakala at approximately 4,000 feet (1,220 m) elevation, and the lines run through misty, cloud-shrouded groves of eucalyptus and koa. Once you unhook from the final line, which is the longest and easily most thrilling, stroll through the neighboring lavender farm with a warm drink from the café.

Other Recreation

YOGA, FITNESS, SPAS, AND RETREATS

In Makawao, next to Casanova restaurant, **Mangala Yoga** (1170 Makawao Ave., 808/868-0668, www.mangalayoga.com) offers drop-in classes ($20) that include candlelight yoga, vinyasa, hot yoga, and more. There's also a $10 Power Hour class.

Lumeria Maui (1813 Baldwin Ave., 808/579-8877, www.lumeriamaui.com) is a spa, retreat center, and lodging, with beautifully landscaped grounds overlooking Maui's North Shore. The main building is the oldest wooden structure on Maui, and in its first incarnation was the original home of Fred C. Baldwin, the famous sugarcane titan. More than half of the wellness treatments offered are designed with the teachings of the islands in mind, such as a Lomi Lomi Pohaku Massage (1.5 hours, $215), which incorporates smooth warmed lava stones into the treatment. Lumeria hosts many spiritual and educational retreats during the year. The public is also welcome on the grounds. Relax on chairs or loungers on the central lawn and partake in meditation and outdoor yoga and qi gong classes ($20-25). Lumeria also has an exceptional on-site organic farm-to-table restaurant.

The Sacred Garden (460 Kaluanui Rd., 808/573-7700, www.sacredgardenmaui.com, 9am-6pm daily, donation) is several miles from downtown Makawao, alongside a rushing creek in a lush rainforest. Owner Eve Hogan infuses her popular nursery and retreat center with charm and good intentions. This is a tranquil place where you can peruse tropical plants and birds, a spiritual and self-help library, a gift shop, creative gardens, and three outdoor meditation spaces. The centerpiece is a stunning medieval labyrinth (not to be confused with a maze), set in the rainforest behind the main nursery, which guests are encouraged to wander. There's also a smaller labyrinth within the nursery. One of the most popular events is Hogan's monthly full-moon labyrinth walks amid tiki torches in the forest.

Maui Healing Retreat (505 Auli'i Dr., 808/870-3711, www.mauihealingretreat.com) offers customized wellness sessions ranging from acupuncture to massage to more avant-garde fare like a Magical Holistic Facial and Sound Healing Therapy. Prices are typically $235 for a 1.5-hour session. Book ahead for day visits. The center's location is definitely a draw, sitting on a peaceful 9 acres (3.6 ha) of agricultural land.

For one of the island's most affordable massage deals, call **Upcountry Massage Country** (7 Aewa Pl., #4, 808/572-5959, www.upcountrymassage.com for one- to two-hour soothing treatments ($85-155) for a fraction of the price of those found at the resorts. Meanwhile, **Kulala Natural Wellness Spa & Boutique** (15200 Haleakala Hwy., 808/868-8063, www.sacredgardenmaui.com, 9am-3pm Sun.-Mon., 9am-6pm Tues.-Sat., from $99) offers variety, with everything from acupuncture to deep-tissue massages.

GOLF

Perched pristinely in Upcountry on the outskirts of Makawao is **Pukalani Country Club** (360 Pukalani St., 808/572-1314, www.pukalanigolf.com, 8am-5pm Sun.-Mon., 8am-7pm Tues.-Sat.), which boasts incredible views. Visitor specials begin at $89.

Shopping

★ HISTORIC MAKAWAO TOWN

If you want to make someone from Makawao cringe, refer to Historic Makawao Town as a smaller version of Lahaina. The galleries and boutiques here are on par with, if not better than, the shops and galleries on Front Street, and you don't have the cruise ships unloading at the shore. Instead, Makawao exudes its own unique vibe, where you might find yourself standing on the creaky wooden deck of a fashionable women's clothing boutique, allowing a misty rain shower to pass while sipping a coffee or tea, or chatting with a friendly Portuguese ranch hand, chuckling at the colorful rooster that's managed to bring traffic to a halt.

It's a town of laughter, smiles, and curious moments, where a truck might pass with a goat in the back with a tailgate made out of rope, and where locals can't stroll two blocks without waving at three people they know. It's a hive of artistic, creative individuals, with a strong *paniolo* ranching heritage and hitching posts lining the wood-shingled storefronts that don't see much use anymore. Find a roadside parking spot and stroll around town.

Art Galleries

For Polynesian jewelry, visit **Maui Master Jewelers** (3655 Baldwin Ave., 808/573-5400, www.mauimasterjewelers.com, 10am-3pm Tues.-Fri., 10am-2pm Sat.), where works by over 30 local artists are on display. They are the island's leading source for New Zealand bone and jade carvings and also offer Tahitian pearl jewelry.

Sherri Reeve Gallery & Gifts (3669 Baldwin Ave., 808/572-8931, www.sreeve.com, 9am-4pm Mon.-Sat., 10am-3:30pm Sun.) showcases this ebullient Makawao artist whose distinctive floral designs grace shirts, cards, paintings, and prints. This is a worthwhile stop among the large number of galleries in town.

At **Jordanne Gallery and Studio** (3625

Baldwin Ave., 808/563-0088, www.jordannefineart.com), meet a plein-air painter who decided at the airport during a family trip to Lana'i that she wasn't getting back on the plane. With little money and no plan, her painting talents paved an unforeseen path.

In the Courtyard shopping area, **Viewpoints Gallery** (3620 Baldwin Ave., 808/572-5979, www.viewpointsgallerymaui.com, 11am-5pm Tues.-Sun.) is a large, clean space that features a rotating array of artists, predominantly painters. **Hot Island Glass** (3620 Baldwin Ave., 808/572-4527, www.hotislandglass.com, 9am-5pm daily) is the island's best-known glass studio, where you can watch artists blow glass; call ahead to check the demonstration schedule.

On a corner in the center of town, **Julie Galeeva Fine Art** (3682 Baldwin Ave., 808/573-4772, www.juliegaleeva.com, 11am-5pm Mon.-Sat.) showcases the highly textured paintings of this talented Russian-born artist and Maui resident.

Cultural Creations Maui (3660 Baldwin Ave., 808/205-7816, www.hablewitzfineart.com) features art and jewelry with "meaning" from artist Jeanette Hablewitz. Private and group art classes are also offered. Come during the day and you can catch the intuitive reader upstairs for a look into your future.

Clothing and Gifts

You know those people who casually exude the trendy essence of cool? There's a good chance they're shopping for clothes at Makawao's fashionable boutiques.

Driftwood (1152 Makawao Ave., 808/573-1152, www.driftwoodmaui.com, 10:30am-5:30pm Mon.-Sat.) is a hip boutique with exceptional women's clothing, accessories, gifts, and household items.

Fleur de Lei (1169 Makawao Ave., 808/269-8855, 10:30am-6:30pm daily) is an eco-boutique with clothing items made from organic cotton, as well as "sail bags" made from recycled windsurfing and kitesurfing sails. The store promotes fair trade and sustainable practices, and if you aren't familiar with vegan leather, stop in and ask. Find Maui-made arts and crafts such as paintings, woodwork, and jewelry at **Maui Hands** (1169 Makawao Ave., 808/572-2008, www.mauihands.com, 10am-5pm Mon.-Sat., 11am-4pm Sun.).

At **Little Tibet** (3682 Baldwin Ave., 808/573-2275, 10am-6pm Mon.-Sat., 11am-4pm Sun.), an array of colorful gemstones and crystals warrant a look. Across the street is **Dragon's Den** (3681 Baldwin Ave., 808/572-2424, https://dragonsdenhawaii.com, daily), which has been a staple in town since 1982. The popular shop features a large variety of herbs, alternative and natural medicines, and gifts.

Collections (3677 Baldwin Ave., 808/572-0781, www.collectionsmauiinc.com, 10am-5pm Mon.-Sat., 11am-4pm Sun.) has been providing men's and women's clothing and boutique home furnishings since 1975. **The Mercantile** (3673 Baldwin Ave., 808/572-1407, 10am-6pm Mon.-Sat., 11am-2pm Sun.) specializes in boutique women's clothing. **Designing Wahine Emporium** (3640 Baldwin Ave., 808/573-0990, www.designingwahine.com, 11am-5pm daily) offers something for everyone, including a selection of men's aloha shirts. For colorful women's blouses, slacks, and unique handbags, visit **Altitude** (3620 Baldwin Ave., 808/573-4733, 10am-6pm daily), a small shop full of innovative clothing designs.

Consider **Wick Apothecary & Ritual** (3619 Baldwin Ave., 10am-3pm Tues.-Sat.) for unique gift books, elixirs, candles, jewelry, specialty gift teas, and more.

KULA

Art Galleries

There's only one artist on the island who really nails Upcountry. Driving past the Kula Lodge to Haleakala, make a stop at the **Curtis Wilson Cost Gallery** (15200 Haleakala Hwy., 808/878-6544, www.costgallery.com,

1: exploring Makawao **2:** Maui Hands **3:** a longtime employee greeting visitors at Keokea Gallery

K. MATSUI STORE
BUILDING 1923
1
MAUI HANDS
2
3
GALLERY
734
SHIPS
9230

2pm-5pm daily), tucked neatly beneath the restaurant. The vibe is like a fine wine cellar filled with exceptional art. Having painted the island's rural corners for over 40 years, Cost now has the longest-running one-man gallery in Hawaii. Art can be ordered with custom koa frames or individually commissioned, and the work of his daughter, Julia Cost, is also displayed.

Worcester Glassworks (4626 Lower Kula Rd., 808/878-4000, www.worcesterglassworks.com, 10am-5pm Mon.-Sat.), by Kula Bistro restaurant, is a well-lit gallery inside a rustic studio mostly occupied by industrial machinery used in the glassblowing process. The resident glassblowers, Bill and Sally Worcester, operate this family-run studio and welcome guests "most days."

Gifts

Down the driveway from Kula Lodge is the exceptional **Kula Market Place** (15200 Haleakala Hwy., 808/878-2135, www.kulamarketplace.com, 8am-5pm Tues.-Fri., 9am-5pm Sat.-Mon.), an oasis of gifts from over 200 local artists, including jams, honey, coffee, music, and clothing. It's a great place to wander while digesting breakfast from neighboring Kula Lodge.

KEOKEA AND ULUPALAKUA

Art Gallery and Fine Furniture

Next to Grandma's Coffee House, tiny little **Keokea Gallery** (9230 Kula Hwy., 808/283-7925, 9am-3pm Tues.-Sat., 10am-2pm Sun.-Mon.) has linocut collages, handmade frames, and a collection of painted surfboards. The affable artist in residence, Sheldon, is always up for a chat, and the works here are surprisingly good considering the rural location.

To return from vacation with a desk so beautiful it will make your coworkers cry, walk to **The Kingswood Shop and Gallery** (8900 Kula Hwy., 808/878-3626, www.kingswoodshop.com, by appointment), not far from Keokea Park. The legendary woodworker Peter Naramore has exquisite pieces of koa wood furniture and exceptional heirloom antiques, and can also commission custom pieces unique to your tastes.

Clothing and Gifts

All the way out here in "deep Upcountry," the only real place for clothing and gifts is the **Ulupalakua Ranch Store** (14800 Pi'ilani Hwy., 808/878-2561, 10am-5:30pm Tues.-Sun.), open for 150 years. The store features products from a dozen local vendors, and since it is on a working ranch, you'll find Wranglers and belts rather than aloha shirts and sunscreen. Consider buying a hat or shirt to help the ranch stay afloat, which helps keep the open spaces and *paniolo* heritage alive.

Visitors to Keokea should look inside **Ching Store** (9212 Kula Hwy., 808/878-1556, 7am-5:30pm daily) and **Fong Store** (9226 Kula Hwy., 808/878-1525, 9am-6pm daily). These family-run businesses are fascinating time portals, where oversize cigarette boxes still serve as decor. Mrs. Fong will be quick to point out that this store is in the "new" location, since 1932; the original store opened in Keokea in 1908.

Food

MAKAWAO

Hawaiian Regional

The ★ **Hali'imaile General Store** (900 Hali'imaile Rd., 808/572-2666, www.hgs-maui.com, lunch 11am-2:30pm Tues.-Fri., dinner 5pm-8pm Tues.-Sat., $22-42), which serves gourmet food in an old-school roadhouse that was once a general store, is easily the island's most unlikely location for food of this caliber. Master chef Beverly Gannon—frequently voted Maui's top chef and a founder of the Hawaiian Regional cuisine movement—crafts appetizers such as sashimi Napoleon and famous crab pizza. Entrées include *paniolo* barbecue ribs and coconut seafood curry. Portions are plentiful.

Italian

★ **Marlow** (30 Kupaoa St., 808/868-3366, www.restaurantmarlow.com, 4:30pm-9pm daily, $16-27) has become an Upcountry hot spot, thanks to the wood-fired creations from chef Jeff Scheer. His dishes are inspired by Italy's best ingredients. The wood-oven sourdough pizzas are sublime, and toppings include locally sourced meats and vegetables. Enjoy an unforgettable—and fun—dining experience in this sleek, modern location just on the outskirts of Makawao.

On the corner at Makawao's only intersection, **Casanova** (1188 Makawao Ave., 808/572-0220, www.casanovamaui.com, 5pm-9pm Mon.-Fri., 10am-2pm and 5pm-9pm Sat.-Sun., $18-34) offers wood-fired pizzas and Italian classics like *linguine pescatore*. Easily Makawao's sexiest venue, it feels like a date-night place in a city. There's a great wine list, and a $20 corkage fee if you bring your own bottle. On selected nights, Casanova becomes Maui's best nightclub with theme nights and DJs. Check the website or call for updated schedules.

Mediterranean

The charming patio setting at **Satori** (3655 Makawao Ave., 808/727-9638, 11am-6pm daily, $11-22) gives you a perfect view of Baldwin Avenue, the town's main drag, and you'll experience some of the best Mediterranean food offered on the island. The hummus, prepared daily, is downright divine. Choose from light salads (mixed local greens or a special tabbouleh infused with lemon juice, rosewater, and orange blossom water) or larger combination plates with options for freshly made falafel, seasoned lamb, or roasted chicken. Portions are abundant. Chase it all back with some ginger kombucha on tap.

Mexican

Mix some mango margaritas, a seafood burrito, and a great community atmosphere, and it's obvious why ★ **Polli's Mexican Restaurant** (1202 Makawao Ave., 808/572-7808, www.pollismexicanrestaurant.com, 4pm-8pm Mon.-Thurs., 11am-8pm Fri.-Sun., $11-25) is a Makawao classic. Portions are enormous for the seafood enchilada, chicken burrito supreme, sizzling beef fajita, and "Makawowie" nachos appetizer. Polli's also offers Maui Cattle Company cheeseburgers, barbecue pork sandwiches, a heaping array of vegetarian options, and baby back ribs that fall off the bone. The festive interior is decorated with photographs from Mexico, surf photography from Hawaii, and authentic souvenirs from all over Latin America.

Cafés

A true hole-in-the-wall favorite, the **Makawao Garden Café** (3669 Baldwin Ave., 808/573-9065, www.makawaogarden-cafe.com, 11am-2:45pm Mon.-Sat., $7-12) is hidden in an alcove next to the Sherri Reeve art gallery. The café only offers outdoor seating, which means that when it rains, the restaurant closes. Laid-back and open only for

HALIIMAILE
RESTAURANT
CATERING
TAVERN
DELICATESSEN
GENERAL STORE
1
2
SATORI
SATORI
3
4
GRANDMA'S
COFFEE HOUSE
OPEN

lunch, options include a baby brie and bacon sandwich or quinoa salad with goat cheese. Cool down with a refreshing smoothie—flavored with mango or *liliko'i* (passion fruit).

Breakfast and Lunch

Freshies Makawao (3620 Baldwin Ave., 808/868-2350, www.freshiesmaui.com, 7am-3pm Tues.-Sat., 7am-noon Sun., $7-12) has a diverse breakfast and lunch menu in a courtyard setting.

Food Trucks

For something unique, consider **Makawao Marketplace** (3654 Baldwin Ave., 808/280-5516, www.makawaomarketplace.com, 8am-5pm Mon.-Sat., 11am-5pm Sun.), which hosts several food trucks—from American to Thai cuisine, coffee, and more—in a great outdoor setting.

Bakeries

To act like an Upcountry local, start your morning with a doughnut from **T. Komoda Store & Bakery** (3674 Baldwin Ave., 808/572-7261, 7am-3pm Mon.-Tues. and Thurs.-Sat.). Komoda's *defines* Upcountry, and the unmistakable aroma of its cream puffs wafts on the predawn air. There's a line out the door before 7am, and popular items like baked butter rolls sell out within hours. Spring for the classic Komoda "stick doughnut." Fittingly, this 100-year-old store operates without computers, so expect to pay cash.

For a great snack, head into **The Maui Cookie Lady** (3643 Baldwin Ave., 808/793-3172, www.themauicookielady.com, 9am-5pm Mon.-Sat., 10am-4pm Sun., $4-9), where a variety of fresh cookies are baked daily. Try the ButterRum Triple Chunker.

Coffee Shops

For a quick coffee on the go, there's a small coffee shop inside **Rodeo General Store** (3661 Baldwin Ave., 808/572-1868, 6am-8pm Mon.-Fri., 7am-8pm Sat.-Sun.) that serves organically roasted local coffee along with organic milk.

Vida by Sip Me Maui (3671 Baldwin Ave., 808/573-2340, hours vary) is Makawao's hip spot for espresso, Wi-Fi, treats, and gifts. Ninety percent of the baked goods are gluten-free. Coffee is made from organic beans roasted on Maui, and you'll find healthy organic smoothies ($8) made from local ingredients in a vibrant setting with colorful decor.

Market and Deli

If you're in the mood for a turkey or club sandwich paired with freshly squeezed juices, the deli counter inside **Rodeo General Store** (3661 Baldwin Ave., 808/572-1868, 6am-8pm Mon.-Fri., 7am-8pm Sat.-Sun., $8-15) is great for lunch on the run. The homemade chili ($4) is filling and affordable, or boost your energy with a "Green Machine"—an all-natural collection of celery, apple, parsley, cucumber, and kale thrown in the juicer.

KULA

French

A tucked-away outdoor patio in the middle of a Kula pasture, **La Provence** (3158 Lower Kula Rd., 808/878-1313, www.laprovencemaui.com, 8am-2pm and 5pm-8pm Wed.-Sun., $12-18, cash only) is a boutique French restaurant and local Kula favorite. On Lower Kula Road just past the True Value hardware store, La Provence offers flaky croissants, café au lait, and affordable filling crepes. Order a vegetable and goat cheese crepe or a tomato and avocado Benedict, accompanied by a side of Kula greens and a cluster of roasted potatoes. Weekends can be busy, so don't come if you're in a rush. There's an ATM at the hardware store if you find yourself without cash.

Italian

For Italian food paired with local favorites, ★ **Kula Bistro** (4566 Lower Kula Rd., 808/871-2960, www.kulabistro.com, 11am-8pm Mon., 7:30am-10:15am and 11am-8pm Tues.-Sun., $14-32) surpasses all others.

1: Hali'imaile General Store **2:** T. Komoda Store & Bakery's "stick doughnut" **3:** Satori **4:** Grandma's Coffee House

Welcome to Keokea, Maui's Chinatown

Ask any local for directions to Chinatown and they'll probably point you toward Honolulu. While Hawaii's capital has one of America's oldest Chinatowns, few people are aware that Maui's Chinatown is in Keokea. Don't expect swinging red lanterns or dim sum carts on the street; this Chinatown was initially founded on potatoes.

Arriving in the 1820s on ships engaged in the sandalwood trade, many of Maui's Chinese immigrants ended up working in sugar mills. Laboring hard on the fledgling plantations, Chinese farmers saved up to buy land in Keokea, which paid off when potatoes were needed to feed prospectors in the California gold rush. At one point, Kula farmers were shipping such a steady stream of potatoes to the ports of California that the area was referred to as "Nu Kaleponi"—Hawaiian for "New California."

Meanwhile, back in China, 2,000 years of imperial rule ended when the Qing Dynasty fell in 1911. The roots of the revolution can be traced to the rural slopes of sleepy Keokea and sometime resident Sun Yat-sen.

Today, local Chinese history is evident in the town's two mom-and-pop stores, Fong Store and Ching Store. The staff at either will be more than happy to talk about the area's heritage. The Chinese community has also constructed buildings in Keokea such as the Kwock Hing Society and St. Joseph's Church.

Tasting the pesto chicken flatbread or jumbo lobster ravioli, it's obvious that owner Luciano Zanon has been perfecting this cuisine since his childhood in Venice. Maui-grown coffee is served at breakfast, and lunch has kalua pork paninis and filling hamburger steak. Most ingredients are sourced locally, the desserts are baked fresh daily, and there's no corkage fee. To pick up some booze for the BYOB, Morihara Store across the street has a decent selection.

Breakfast and Lunch

The **Kula Lodge** (15200 Haleakala Hwy., 808/878-1535, www.kulalodge.com, 7am-3:30pm daily, $14-36) has been welcoming hungry patrons into its rustic interior for so long it's become synonymous with Kula dining. Inside a 1940s private home, this panoramic mountainside perch hasn't changed much since. At 3,200 feet (975 m) elevation, it's a little bit cooler, and the dark-wood interior is a perfect fit with the low temperatures and clouds. Paintings by Curtis Wilson Cost adorn the wooden entrance (his gallery is beneath the restaurant). The Lodge is a filling breakfast stop on the way down from Haleakala.

For an affordable, laid-back, and welcoming vibe, **Kula Sandalwoods Café** (15427 Haleakala Hwy., 808/878-3523, www.kulasandalwoods.com, 7:30am-3pm Mon.-Thurs., 7:30am-noon Fri.-Sun., $9-11) serves delicious meals from its hillside location. Try the Keokea omelet; at lunch, go for the kalua pig sandwich. While the outdoor lanai is nice, the cozy interior has a small fireplace with country music on the radio.

Markets

If Kula had a center, it would be at **Morihara Store** (4581 Lower Kula Rd., 808/878-2502, 6am-8pm Mon.-Wed., 6:30am-8pm Thurs.-Sat., 7:30am-8pm Sun.)—the family-run store that services most of Kula's general needs. There are basic condiments, to-go items for lunch, and beer and wine. The store is a refreshing old-school throwback to simpler times.

KEOKEA AND ULUPALAKUA

Burgers

If hunger strikes on the back road from Hana or while at the winery, head to the **Ulupalakua Ranch Store and Grill** (14800

Pi'ilani Hwy., 808/878-2561, www.ulupalakuaranch.com, 10am-5pm Tues.-Sun.)—a carnivorous carnival of ranch-grown meats eaten on the wooden front porch. The grill features venison, lamb, elk, and beef, all raised on the 20,000 acres (8,100 ha) surrounding the store. Everything is made from scratch. Try the 100 percent natural Ulupalakua burgers (from $13) or Uncle Mike's Steak Chili & Rice Bowl ($9).

The other burger spot on the back road to Hana is **Bully's Burgers** (15900 Pi'ilani Hwy., 808/878-1362, www.bullysburgers-mauistore.com, noon-7pm Tues.-Sun.) in Kanaio. This exceptionally simple roadside shack has grass-fed burgers ($12-15) made from cattle raised on Triple L Ranch. Bully's is 4 miles (6.4 km) past Maui Wine heading in the direction of Hana, and while there aren't any restrooms and the hours are irregular, the burgers don't disappoint.

Coffee Shops

While it doesn't look like much from the outside, there's a simple romance to ★ **Grandma's Coffee House** (9232 Kula Hwy., 808/878-2140, www.grandmascoffee.com, 7am-2pm daily) that makes it Maui's best coffee shop. "Grandma" started brewing her own coffee back in 1918, and locally grown beans are roasted in the kitchen using her 100-year-old roaster. The beans are still harvested and processed by four generations of her family. For breakfast, order the French toast made with homemade cinnamon bread ($10) and enjoy it out on the porch, where slack-key musicians periodically offer live music on weekend mornings. Or grab a cup of coffee to go and enjoy a stroll on Thompson Road, across the street. The only downside is that the restrooms are located at Keokea Park, a five-minute walk.

Getting There and Around

CAR

With the exception of central Makawao, where it's possible to walk between shops, Upcountry can only be visited by car. There aren't any rental agencies for cars or mopeds, and parking is free. The main road that leads to Upcountry is Highway 37, with Highway 377 forming a loop through Kula. Haleakala National Park is up Highway 378. There aren't any gas stations in Upper Kula or on Highway 378. From Kula, expect it to take about an hour to drive to the summit of Haleakala, and from Ulupalakua over to Makawao, the drive is about 30 minutes.

BUS

Some parts of Upcountry are served by the **Maui Bus** (808/871-4838, www.co.maui.hi.us/bus), with the Upcountry Islander (bus 40) connecting Upcountry with downtown, and the Kula Islander (bus 39) connecting all the way to Kula. For the Upcountry Islander, bus stops are in front of the Pukalani Community Center, the Makawao Library, and in the center of Hali'imaile. Rates are $2 per person, and the bus makes stops at the Kahului Airport as well as at Queen Ka'ahumanu Mall, where you can link up with other lines. The earliest bus leaves from Keokea at 5:56am daily and heads all the way to Kahului.

East Maui: The Road to Hana

East Maui is more than a destination. It's a different mindset.

Lush, tropical, and riddled with waterfalls, East Maui is the location of the famous Road to Hana and where Maui locals come to escape for a few days. From the windswept taro patches of the Ke'anae Peninsula to the empty pastures of Kaupo, time in East Maui ticks by at a slower place. By no means, however, does that make East Maui lazy. It's the island's adventure center, where an average day could consist of trekking to remote waterfalls, cliff-jumping in a bamboo forest, spelunking hidden caves on a black-sand beach, or bodysurfing off sandy shores.

Many who drive the legendary Road to Hana ask, "This is it?" and "Where is the rest of town?" Hana is not a destination—it's famous

Highlights

Look for ★ to find recommended sights, activities, dining, and lodging.

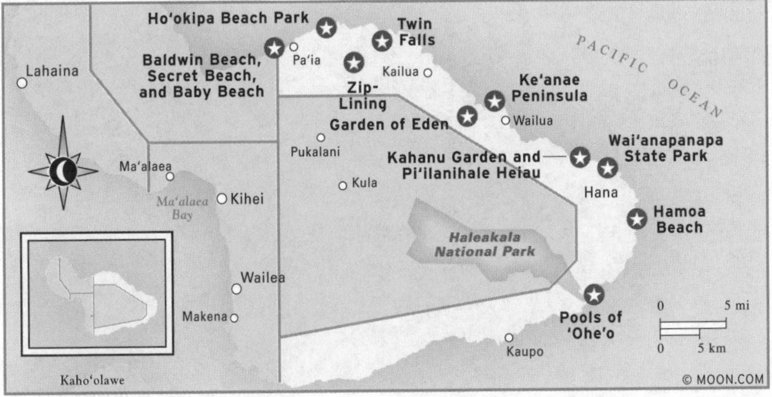

★ Explore lush botanical gardens at the **Garden of Eden,** with trails, picnic spots, waterfalls, and dramatic coastal views (page 236).

★ Glimpse into one of the last holdouts of an ancient way of life at the taro-covered **Ke'anae Peninsula** (page 237).

★ Take a journey back to ancient Hawaii at **Kahanu Garden** and gaze upon **Pi'ilanihale Heiau,** the largest *heiau* in the state (page 239).

★ Bask on the shores of a **black-sand beach,** swim inside hidden caves, and walk in the footsteps of kings at **Wai'anapanapa State Park** (page 241).

★ Swim beneath waterfalls that tumble down to the ocean at the **Pools of 'Ohe'o** (page 246).

★ Find a little bit of something for everyone—children and hippies, swimmers and bodysurfers, sunbathers and joggers—at neighboring **Baldwin Beach, Secret Beach, and Baby Beach** (page 248).

★ See giant **sea turtles** arrive just before sunset on the shore of **Ho'okipa Beach Park,** a stellar **surfing** and **windsurfing** locale as well as a picturesque spot for lounging (page 249).

★ **Surf** or **snorkel** at **Hamoa Beach,** which Mark Twain recognized as one of the most beautiful in the world (page 250).

★ Take an easy **hike** to **Twin Falls,** the first series of waterfalls on the Road to Hana (page 255).

★ Go **zip-lining** through a canopy of trees overlooking Maui's fertile North Shore (page 260).

East Maui

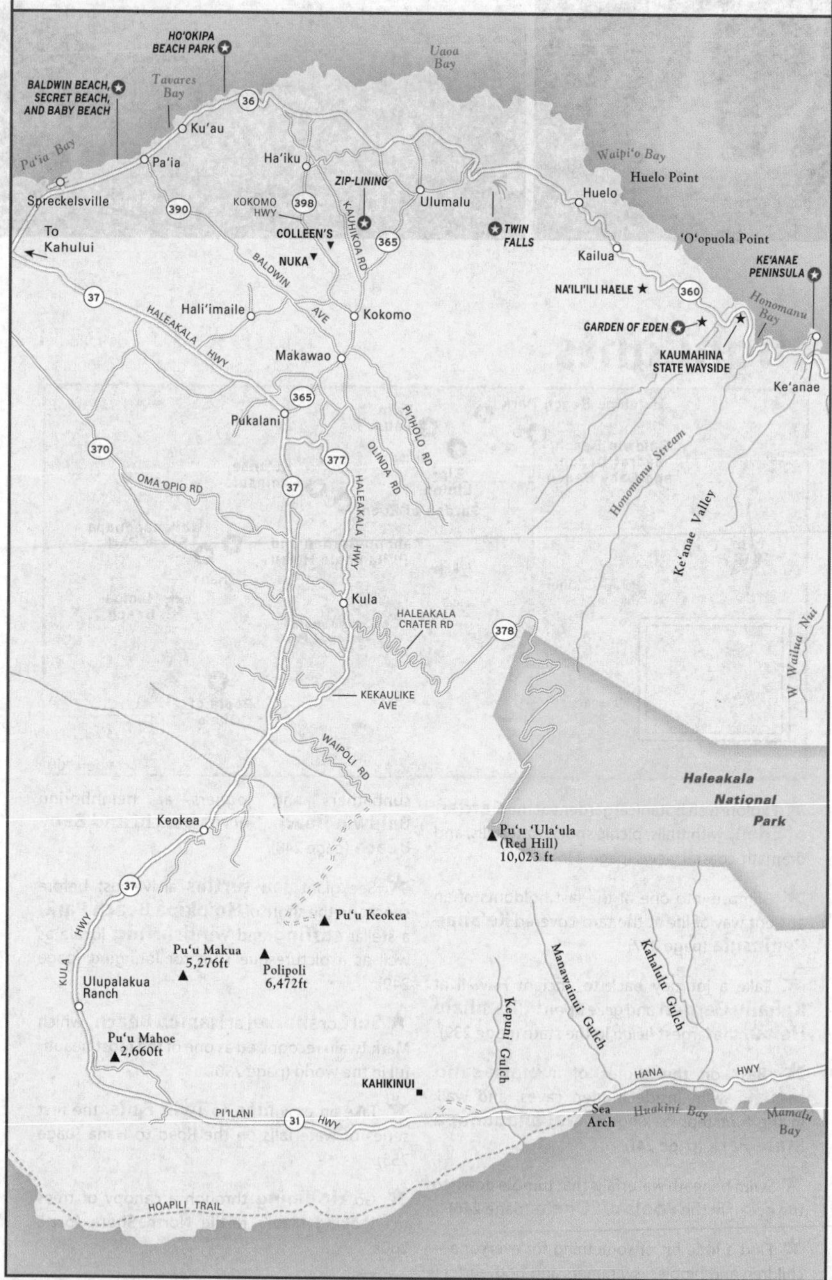
HO'OKIPA BEACH PARK
Uaoa Bay
BALDWIN BEACH, SECRET BEACH, AND BABY BEACH
Tavares Bay
36
Ku'au
Pa'ia Bay
Pa'ia
Ha'iku
Waipi'o Bay
Huelo Point
Spreckelsville
ZIP-LINING
Ulumalu
Huelo
390
KOKOMO HWY
398
KAUHIKOA RD
To Kahului
COLLEEN'S
365
TWIN FALLS
'O'opuola Point
Kailua
NUKA
BALDWIN
KE'ANAE PENINSULA
NA'ILI'ILI HAELE
37
360
Honomanu Bay
HALEAKALA HWY
Hali'imaile
AVE
Kokomo
GARDEN OF EDEN
KAUMAHINA STATE WAYSIDE
Makawao
Ke'anae
365
PI'IHOLO RD
Pukalani
370
377
OLINDA RD
Honomanu Stream
OMA'OPIO RD
37
HALEAKALA HWY
Ke'anae Valley
Kula
HALEAKALA CRATER RD
378
W Wailua Nui
KEKAULIKE AVE
WAIPOLI RD
Haleakala National Park
Keokea
Pu'u 'Ula'ula (Red Hill) 10,023 ft
37
KULA HWY
Pu'u Keokea
Pu'u Makua 5,276ft
Polipoli 6,472ft
Manawainui Gulch
Kahalulu Gulch
Ulupalakua Ranch
Kepuni Gulch
Pu'u Mahoe 2,660ft
HANA HWY
KAHIKINUI
PI'ILANI
31
HWY
Sea Arch
Huakini Bay
Mamalu Bay
HOAPILI TRAIL

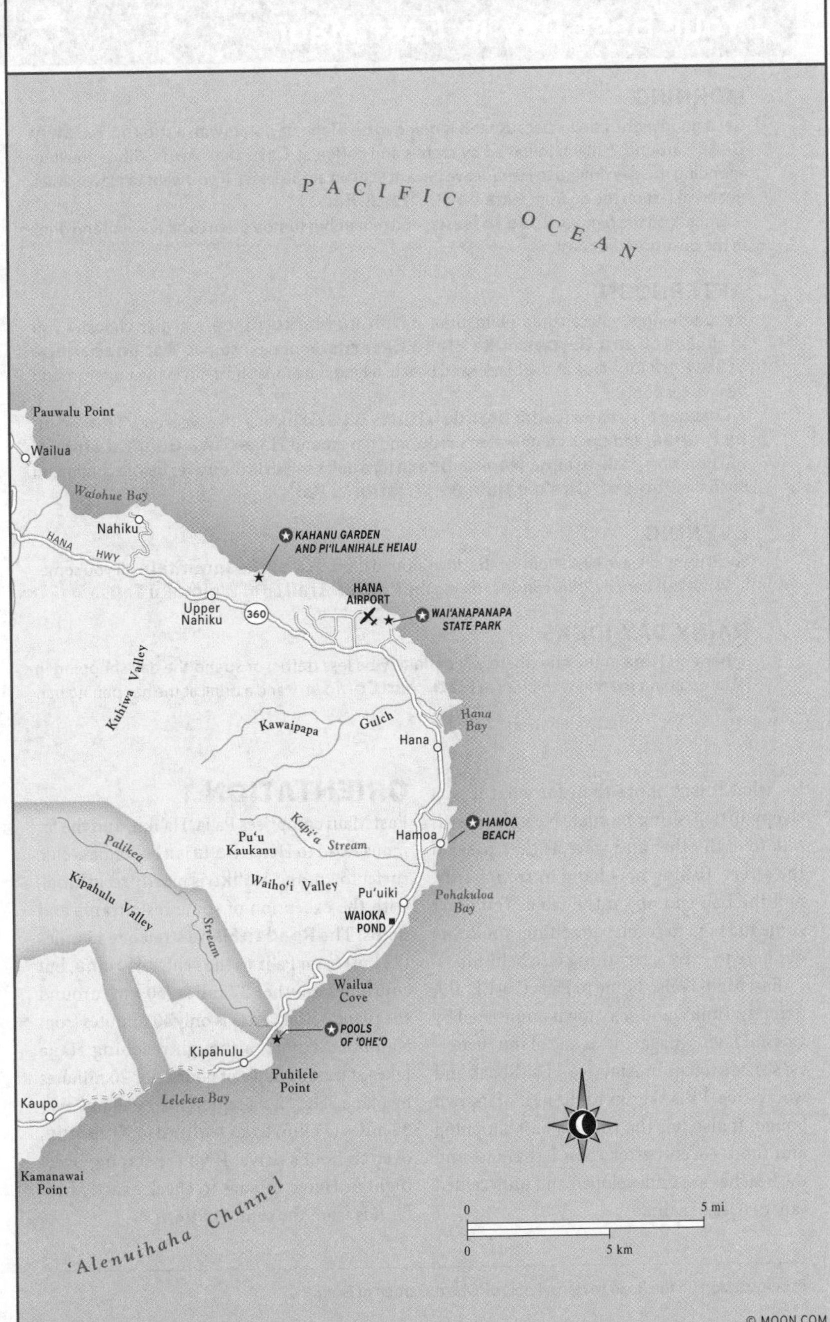
PACIFIC OCEAN
Pauwalu Point
Wailua
Waiohue Bay
Nahiku
HANA HWY
KAHANU GARDEN AND PI'ILANIHALE HEIAU
Upper Nahiku
360
HANA AIRPORT
WAI'ANAPANAPA STATE PARK
Kuhiwa Valley
Kawaipapa Gulch
Hana Bay
Hana
HAMOA BEACH
Hamoa
Kapi'a Stream
Pu'u Kaukanu
Palikea Stream
Kipahulu Valley
Waiho'i Valley
Pu'uiki
Pohakuloa Bay
WAIOKA POND
Wailua Cove
POOLS OF 'OHE'O
Kipahulu
Puhilele Point
Lelekea Bay
Kaupo
Kamanawai Point
'Alenuihaha Channel
0
5 mi
0
5 km
© MOON.COM

Your Best Day in East Maui

MORNING

Get a good night's sleep, because this is going to be a long day. Start with a stroll on **Baldwin Beach** around 7:30am, followed by crepes and coffee at **Café des Amis.** Since you'll be spending the day driving to Hana, leave Pa'ia at 9:30am at the latest. If you want to leave earlier, get breakfast on the go from **Paia Bay Coffee & Bar.**

Embark on the famous **Road to Hana,** and remember to stop often to hike, swim, and drink in the beauty of the coast.

AFTERNOON

If you're hungry, you can grab a bite to eat at **Nahiku Marketplace,** and then choose a visit to either **Kahanu Garden** or **Ka'eleku Caverns.** Your next stop is **Wai'anapanapa State Park** for a look at the black-sand beach, taking time for a short dip in the underground freshwater pools.

Continue to Hana for food at **Braddah Hutts BBQ Grill,** or if it's a weekend, **Thai Food by Pranee,** and stock up on water, snacks, and gas around **Hasegawa General Store.** If you have time, make a stop at **Hamoa Beach** for a quick splash in the waves before continuing on to the **Pools of 'Ohe'o** at **Haleakala National Park.**

EVENING

You'll want to leave by 4:30pm for the drive around the **back of the mountain.** (If you somehow made it here by 2pm, consider hiking the **Pipiwai Trail** up to **Waimoku Falls.**)

RAINY DAY IDEAS

Either visit Hana in the rain (there will definitely be less traffic) or spend the day shopping in Pa'ia, escaping the rain with pizza at **Flatbread Company** and a drink at the happening bar.

for what it isn't more than for what it is, a sleepy little fishing hamlet. Neighbors still talk to each other and wave as they pass on the street, fishing nets hang in front yards, and the fish end up on the table. You don't come to Hana to reach something; you come out here to leave everything else behind.

East Maui is also home to Pa'ia (Pa-EE-ah), a trendy, funky, and sexy town nominated by *Coastal Living* magazine as one of the "happiest seaside towns in America." Laid-back and worry-free, Pa'ia skanks to the beat of its own bongo. It also has the island's best shopping and food—even better than Lahaina—and the beaches are undeveloped and unheralded sanctuaries of calm.

ORIENTATION

East Maui comprises Pa'ia, Ha'iku, and the famous Road to Hana. **Pa'ia** is a bohemian-chic surfer town, and **Ha'iku** is mostly residential, with the exception of some restaurants and B&Bs. The **Road to Hana** stretches 45 miles (72 km) from Pa'ia to the center of **Hana,** but continues another 37 miles (60 km) around the island's back. Pa'ia is only 10 minutes from Kahului Airport, although reaching Hana takes at least a couple of hours—or 20 minutes by plane. The Hana region is spread out over 22 miles (35 km) from **Nahiku** to **Kipahulu,** over an hour's drive. If you're staying overnight in Hana, be sure to check exactly how far it is from the center of town.

Previous: sign on the Road to Hana; Pools of 'Ohe'o; Garden of Eden.

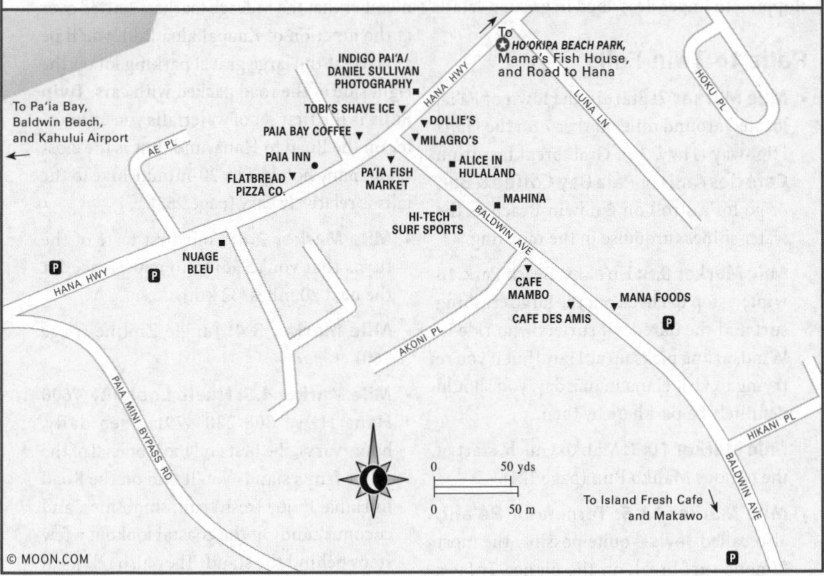

PLANNING YOUR TIME

The biggest mistake you can make on Maui is skimping on your time in Hana. Ideally, Hana is worth three full days. Choosing to spend a couple of nights here allows more time for exploring. If you only have a day, devote the entirety to driving the Road to Hana so you can see it without feeling rushed. Pa'ia is a nice place for breakfast on the way. If you have the time, visit Pa'ia separately from Hana; it's worthy of at least half a day.

Driving the Road to Hana

TOP EXPERIENCE

Ah, yes, the Road to Hana—the most loved and loathed section of the island divides visitors into two camps: those who swear it's heaven on earth and those who swear never to drive it again. Most people who don't enjoy the trip didn't know what they were getting themselves into. Three words will make or break your trip: Don't rush Hana.

Devote a full day to the experience at minimum. You're visiting one of the most beautiful places on earth; two or three days are even better. Don't expect to breeze through and see it quickly, and don't expect to be back on the other side of the island to make dinner reservations. Staying in Ka'anapali or Wailea, it will take you 3.5 hours just to reach the Pools of 'Ohe'o (a.k.a. the Seven Sacred Pools). That's not including stops, and the stops are what make the journey worthwhile.

No one should endure a journey to Hana without knowing exactly where the next waterfall, hiking trail, ATM, food cart, or restroom is going to be. Since sights can spring up in an instant—and making a U-turn isn't possible—be prepared. A mile-by-mile rundown of what you'll see along the side of the road follows, with specific sights and places worth stopping to linger described in greater detail.

Pa'ia to Twin Falls

- **Mile Marker 7:** Start in the town of Pa'ia, located around mile marker 7 on the Hana Highway (Hwy. 36). Grab breakfast from **Café des Amis** or **Paia Bay Coffee & Bar,** or go for a stroll on Baldwin Beach as the water shines turquoise in the morning.
- **Mile Marker 8.8:** Ho'okipa Beach Park. In winter, stop to check out the large crashing surf and the daredevil surfers who ride it. Windsurfing picks up at 11am, but if you're trying to visit Hana in one day, you should definitely be past here by then.
- **Mile Marker 10.3:** Maliko Gulch, start of the famous Maliko Run (page 121).
- **Mile Marker 13.5:** Turnoff for **Pe'ahi,** also called **Jaws**—quite possibly the most famous surf break on the planet. If Jaws is breaking, there will be dozens of cars parked along the side of the highway. The best thing to do is park near the highway and hitch a ride to the bottom of the hill. The viewing area is from a coastal bluff at the bottom of a 4WD road, and the chances of hitching a ride increase tenfold if you barter a six-pack of beer.
- **Mile Marker 14.5:** If you haven't already stopped for breakfast, you have another chance at **Jaws Country Store,** which offers numerous prepared options. You can also pick up a sandwich to go and stock up on snacks and drinks for the ride.
- Begin Highway 360.
- **Mile Marker 0:** Note the change in mile markers at the junction of Hana Highway and Kaupakalua Road.
- **Mile Marker 0.3:** Congratulations, your first waterfall! Just joking. They get much better than this.
- **Mile Marker 2:** Twin Falls and Wailele Farm Stand.

Twin Falls

When you round the hill by mile marker 2 (remember that the mileage markers started over at the junction of Kaupakalua Rd.), you'll be amazed at the large gravel parking lot on the right side of the road packed with cars. **Twin Falls** is the first set of waterfalls you encounter on the Road to Hana, and thus is the closest to many hotels. The 20-minute hike to the falls is relatively easy (page 255).

- **Mile Marker 2.8:** Your first taste of the turns that you're going to experience for the next 20 miles (32 km).
- **Mile Marker 3.4:** Jungle Zipline (page 260).
- **Mile Marker 4.5: Huelo Lookout** (7600 Hana Hwy., 808/280-4791, open daily, hours vary), the first and most official of the many fruits stands you'll find on the Road to Hana. Enjoy fresh fruit, smoothies, and coconut candy at the coastal lookout a few steps behind the stand. They also sell local arts and crafts.
- **Mile Marker 4.9:** Your first narrow bridge crossing.
- **Mile Marker 6.5:** Na'ili'ili Haele (Bamboo Forest), one of the most popular hikes in East Maui. Thundering waterfalls spill through a dense bamboo forest. Slippery rocks and flash-flood conditions have been known to cause injuries here (page 255).
- **Mile Marker 6.7:** Rainbow eucalyptus trees.

Rainbow Eucalyptus Trees

Just past the trailhead for the Na'ili'ili Haele hike is a grove of rainbow eucalyptus trees, silently rising from the green pasturelands. One of the most photographed sights on the Road to Hana, these trees have bark that drips with pastel red, pink, orange, green, and gray, the strokes running the length of each narrow tree.

1: rainbow eucalyptus trees **2:** waterfalls on the Road to Hana **3:** Garden of Eden

1
2
3

Unlike trees with cork-like bark, rainbow eucalyptus has a smooth, hard exterior constantly in regrowth. As a section of tree undergoes exfoliation and sheds a section of bark, the young exposed wood has a deep green hue. As the new bark ages in the sun, the wood changes from green to blue to purple to orange, eventually dying again to reveal the green growth below, starting the cycle anew. Parking can be found either at the trailhead for the Na'ili'ili Haele hike (mile marker 6.5) or at a small pullout for a hunting road, 100 yards (91 m) past the trees.

- **Mile Marker 8.1:** First scenic view of a valley looking out toward the ocean.
- **Mile Marker 8.5:** Sweeping view of dense swaths of bamboo crawling their way up the eastern flank of the mountain.
- **Mile Marker 9.5: Waikamoi Ridge Trail.** This small picnic area provides a relaxing place to stretch your legs or enjoy a roadside snack, although there are no restrooms or other facilities. There's a short loop trail that gains 200 vertical feet (60 m) in the surrounding forest (page 257).
- **Mile Marker 10:** Waikamoi Falls, the first roadside waterfall and swimming hole.

Waikamoi Falls

Simple, elegant, and easily accessible, Waikamoi Falls is a convenient place to take a dip. A small trail leads down to the pool, and a second waterfall is accessible above the first pool by wading across the streambed. The only inconvenience here is the lack of parking.

- **Mile Marker 10.5:** The Garden of Eden botanical garden and Coconut Café food cart.

★ Garden of Eden

Up the road 0.5 mile (0.8 km) from Waikamoi Falls is the enticing **Garden of Eden** (808/572-9899, www.mauigardenofeden.com, 8am-4pm daily, $20 adults, $10 children), an ornately manicured 26-acre (10.5-ha) rainforest utopia with trails winding through the property. In 1991, Alan Bradbury, the state's first ISA-certified arborist, began clearing the hillside and replanting native trees. It was truly a labor of love: After two decades of work, the Garden of Eden now has more than 600 individually labeled plants, and visitors are often welcomed by a flock of ducks or a muster of peacocks. Walk down to the farthest reaches of the arboretum toward the unique overlooks—several raised and covered wooden platforms, flanked by *'ohi'a* trees—which offer dazzling ocean views as well as views of the Upper and Lower Puohokamoa Falls, the latter of which cascades dramatically over a 200-foot (60-m) cliff below the Road to Hana. The garden also collaborates with Rappel Maui to offer visitors opportunities to rappel the falls.

This also makes a great picnic spot; bring a packed lunch and nosh at the picnic tables overlooking the falls or Keopuka Rock, also known as Jurassic Rock for its appearance in the opening sequence of the 1993 film *Jurassic Park*.

- **Mile Marker 11.5: Haipua'ena Falls.** Parking can be limited, and it's on the Hana side of the bridge. A short trail leads down to a pool that's nice for a refreshing dip, but you don't need to spend more than 20 minutes.
- **Mile Marker 12.2: Kaumahina State Wayside Park.** Finally—restrooms. This is the first place you'll find any official facilities.
- **Mile Marker 14:** Honomanu Bay.

Honomanu Bay

Honomanu Bay is a gorgeous gray-sand beach in a valley that's accessible by 4WD. If you have a low-clearance vehicle, find a parking space at the top of the road and visit the beach on foot. It's a rocky beach, so bring proper footwear. Swimming is subpar—wading in the water is fine—but the area attracts fishers, a small local surf crowd, and spectators. Honomanu Bay doesn't have any facilities, but it warrants a picnic lunch or visit if only to

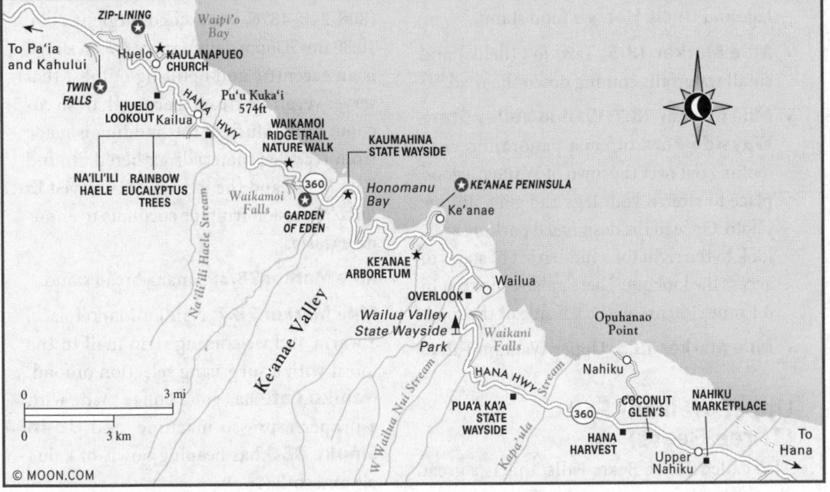

capture postcard snapshots of the bay itself and vibrant vegetation surrounding it.

- **Mile Marker 16.5: Ke'anae Arboretum.** A great spot to stretch your legs and enjoy a free walk in the forest. A 30-minute paved, wheelchair-accessible trail winds back into the lush landscape. After 10 minutes of walking, the paved trail becomes dirt as you pass a fence. If you make a left once inside the boundary and head toward Pi'ina'au Stream, you'll find a small hidden swimming hole. Reaching it requires a scramble down the rocks.
- **Mile Marker 16.6:** Turnoff for Ke'anae village.

★ Ke'anae Peninsula

When you turn off the highway at mile marker 16.6, you pass through a portal to a way of life that many forgot once existed. The peninsula is a mosaic of green taro fields, vital to the livelihood of Ke'anae. Taro, also known as *kalo,* isn't just a crop, it's a representation of indigenous Hawaiian heritage. In Hawaiian mythology, a child named Haloa was stillborn and, upon being buried, turned into a taro plant. Haloa's brother became the ancestor of the Hawaiian people.

Indigenous Hawaiians thus have a blood relationship to the plant that provides them with sustenance. It's a staple of the Aloha 'Aina movement currently sweeping the state, that we humans are but stewards of the land, placed on this earth to protect it—ensuring its health as we would our own family's, and protecting it for future generations.

In addition to the taro fields, you can watch the powerful surf crash onto the rugged volcanic shore. There aren't any beaches on the Ke'anae Peninsula, and you'll often encounter locals fishing. Stop in at **Aunty Sandy's** (808/248-7448, 8:30am-2:30pm daily) for a warm loaf of banana bread.

- **Mile Marker 17:** Ke'anae Overlook.
- **Mile Marker 17.3:** Store and ATM. The accurately named **Halfway to Hana** (www.halfwaytohanamaui.com, 8am-4:30pm daily, $3-8, cash only) is between the Ke'anae Overlook and the turnoff for Wailua. It's basically a hot-dog, sandwich, and shave-ice stand with an ATM around the corner, making it the closest thing to a

store around Ke'anae. Ask about the freshly baked banana bread.

- **Mile Marker 18:** Turnoff for Wailua village and **Uncle Harry's** food stand.
- **Mile Marker 18.5:** Taro *lo'i* (fields) and small waterfalls coming down the road.
- **Mile Marker 18.7: Wailua Valley State Wayside Park** offers a panoramic vista looking out over the town of Wailua, a good place to stretch your legs and get a unique photo. Once in the designated parking area, look to the right for a hidden set of stairs to access the lookout. There's also a lookout in 0.1 mile (160 m) on the left side of the road.
- **Mile Marker 19.6:** Upper Waikani Falls.

Upper Waikani Falls (Three Bears)

Also called Three Bears Falls, this is a great place for a photo op or a swim. There is a narrow rough trail, about 150 yards (137 m), on the Hana side of the bridge. Most people stop, take snapshots, and move on, but if you want to linger a while longer, drive about 0.1 mile (160 m) beyond the falls, turn left, and park in the designated parking area, then walk back in the direction you came. The trail starts with a slightly sharp drop-off from the bridge, but you can breathe more freely after those first few precarious steps because it gets flatter. The scene at the falls is downright dreamlike, with water cascading into a swimming hole with remarkably clear water, ideal for a dip.

- **Mile Marker 21:** Wailuaiki Falls.
- **Mile Marker 22.6:** Pua'a Ka'a State Wayside Park has restrooms and a small picnic pavilion on the *mauka* (mountain) side of the highway looking out over the stream. A short three-minute walk leads from the road up the stream to an underrated swimming pool and waterfall.
- **Mile Marker 24.1:** Painted Little Green Shack.
- **Mile Marker 25:** Pullout for view of Makapipi Falls. Look down from the top of the bridge!
- **Mile Marker 27.5: Coconut Glen's** (808/248-4876, www.coconutglens.com, 10:30am-5:30pm daily), an ice cream stand, is an eccentric and uplifting outpost that serves vegan ice cream made with fresh coconut milk. Much of the building is made from recycled materials gathered around East Maui, and the ice cream is served in *liliko'i* (passion fruit) or coconuts to eliminate waste.
- **Mile Marker 28.3:** Banana bread stand.
- **Mile Marker 28.7:** Nahiku Marketplace, a warm and welcoming strip mall in the forest with a surprising selection of food. **Nahiku Café** has good coffee made with a proper espresso machine, and **Up in Smoke BBQ** has heaping bowls of kalua pig and chili ($6-9).
- **Mile Marker 29.7:** View of the Hana Airport.
- **Mile Marker 31:** Turnoff for Ka'eleku Caverns and Kahanu Garden.

Ka'eleku Caverns

As you make your way from Nahiku Marketplace, the first sights you'll encounter are a few miles before "downtown" Hana. At mile marker 31 you'll see the signs for **Ka'eleku Caverns** (808/248-7308, www.mauicave.com, 10:30am-4pm daily, $15 pp), also known as the Hana Lava Tubes. Turn down 'Ula'ino Road to visit this 2-mile (3.2-km) subterranean network of lava tubes, the 18th largest in the world and the only lava tubes on Maui that are navigable and open to the public. Cave explorers are given a flashlight to examine the stalactite-encrusted surroundings. On your way out, navigate through the maze of red *ti* leaves that create the only such maze anywhere on the planet. Walking the caverns at an average pace will take about 30 minutes. There are no garbage cans or restrooms, so pack out your trash.

Tips for Driving the Road to Hana

One of the most beautiful activities on Maui is driving the Road to Hana. Weaving 52 miles (84 km) around 600 curves and 56 one-lane bridges, it's the most loved and loathed stretch of road on the island. Here's how to plan a visit to Hana that will leave you poring over a photo album instead of searching for a divorce lawyer.

1. Hana is not a destination, but a journey. Visitors who race to the sleepy village of Hana are left saying, "This is it?" With a population of around 1,800, Hana is a place to get away from it all.

2. The Road to Hana doesn't end at Hana. The famous Road to Hana is the 52-mile (84-km) stretch between Kahului Airport and the town of Hana, but many of the natural treasures are in the 10 miles (16 km) beyond Hana town. Hamoa Beach, consistently voted one of the top beaches in the country, is a few miles past Hana, as is Waioka Pond, a hidden pool on the rocky coast. Thirty minutes beyond Hana town are the Pools of 'Ohe'o (the Seven Sacred Pools), with a series of cascading waterfalls falling directly into the Pacific.

3. Stop early and stop often. Take a break for a morning stroll or for breakfast at a tucked-away café. Pick up some snacks and watch the waves. Stop and swim in waterfalls, hike through bamboo forests, and pull off at roadside stands for banana bread or locally grown fruit. If the car behind you is on your tail, pull over and let it pass—there isn't any rush.

4. Bring a bathing suit and hiking shoes. Hana is a land of adventure: Pack the necessary wardrobe and equipment for your activity of choice.

5. Don't drive back the way you came. Car-rental contracts may tell you the road around the back of the island is for 4WD vehicles only, but that's not true. Parts are bumpy, and a few miles are dirt road, but unless there's torrential rain, the road is passable with a regular vehicle. Following the back road all the way around the island grants new views as the surroundings change from lush tropical rainforest to arid windswept lava flows.

6. Don't make dinner reservations. Too many people try to squeeze Hana into half a day or end up feeling rushed. Hana is a place to escape the rush, not add to it. If you're planning a day trip to Hana, block off the entire day, leave early (7am), and see where the day takes you.

7. If you see a sign that says *Kapu* (Keep Out), respect it. Move along and enjoy a spot more accessible to the public.

8. Don't drive home in the dark—especially going the back way. Driving on narrow one-lane roads with precipitous drop-offs is difficult enough in daylight. Leave by 4pm to ensure a well-lit journey home.

- **Mile Marker 31.2:** Only a few miles before the town of Hana, the legendary **Hana Farms Banana Bread Stand** (mile marker 31.2, 8am-7pm daily) features six different types of banana bread as well as a full range of fruits, coffee, sauces, and flavorings. There will be more fruit stands between Hana and Kipahulu, but none are like this. Stop for a coffee, banana bread (get a loaf with chocolate chips), and advice on your Hana adventure.

★ Kahanu Garden and Pi'ilanihale Heiau

On 'Ula'ino Road, the pavement gradually gives way to a potholed dirt road leading to **Kahanu Garden** (808/240-1301, www.ntbg.org, 9am-3pm Mon.-Fri., $16, free under age 12). This 464-acre (188-ha) property is in Honoma'ele, an area ceded in 1848 to Chief Kahanu by King Kamehameha III. The land has remained largely unchanged since the days of ancient Hawaii. The sprawling gardens

1
2
3

Hana and Environs

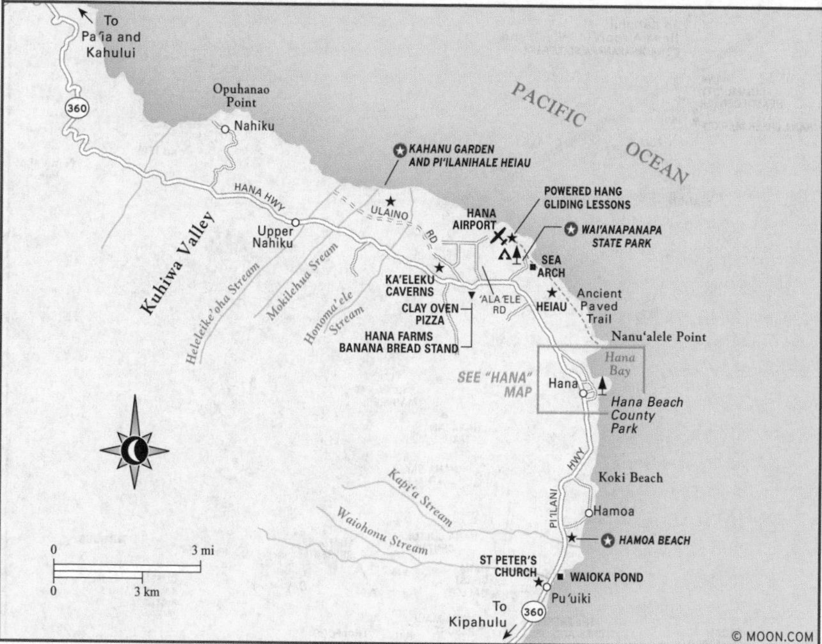

focus on species integral to Polynesian culture. You're greeted by a massive grove of *ulu* (breadfruit), and there are groves of bananas, coconuts, taro, sweet potato, sugarcane, and *'awa*. A self-guided tour details the history of the plants and the uses they had for Polynesians.

Towering **Pi'ilanihale Heiau,** a massive multitiered stone structure, is the largest remaining *heiau* (temple) in Hawaii. The walls stretch 50 feet (15 m) high in some places, and the stone platforms are the size of two football fields. Multiple archaeological surveys have determined that the temple was most likely built in stages and dates as far back as the 14th century. To learn about the *heiau* and the property, you can arrange ahead of time for an hour-long guided tour ($25 pp). To get really involved, lend a hand by volunteering (call for times and details)—you could end up pulling taro with locals at neighboring Mahele Farms.

- **Mile Marker 31.4:** Turnoff for Hana Airport and powered hang gliding lessons.
- **Mile Marker 32:** Turnoff for Wai'anapanapa State Park.

1: Pi'ilanihale Heiau 2: Kahanu Garden
3: Wai'anapanapa State Park

★ Wai'anapanapa State Park

Rugged **Wai'anapanapa State Park** is also known as "black-sand beach." At the beach overlook is one of the most iconic vistas on the drive to Hana. Take it slow on the 0.5-mile (0.8-km) road down to the park; there are often small children playing. Once you reach the park, turn left at the parking lot and follow the road to the end, where you can access the black sand of Pa'iloa Beach and its freshwater caves.

Made of crushed black lava rock, the sand is as black as Hana's night sky. Lush green foliage clings to the surrounding coast, and

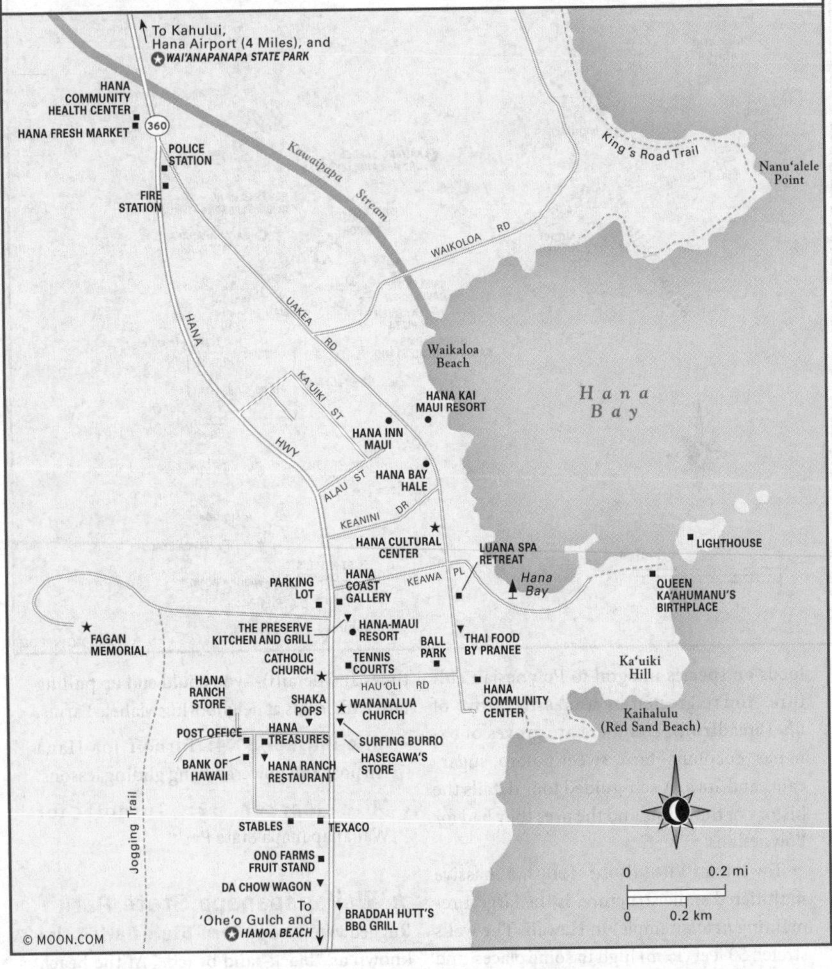

dramatic sea arches and volcanic promontories jut into the frothy sea. Since it faces almost directly east, this is a popular venue for sunrise weddings, and if you spend the night in Hana, I highly recommend getting up early to come here for sunrise.

On the main paved trail by the parking lot overlook, you'll see a trail that runs in the opposite direction of the beach; this is the beginning of a popular coastal hike. One of the more popular stops along this trail is a blowhole that erupts on days with large surf. Maintain a safe distance; people have been swept into the ocean here.

The other main draw of Wai'anapanapa is the system of freshwater caves hidden in a grotto not far from the parking area. Following the cave trail from the parking lot, you'll see a sign that details the legend of the caves. Go left at the sign and travel downhill on a short loop trail. After a three-minute walk you'll reach the cave entrance. The clear water is crisp and cold, and if you swim back in either direction, you'll find some hidden caves. Bring a waterproof light, and don't go so far that you can't find your way back!

- **Mile Marker 32.7:** Hana school.
- **Mile Marker 34:** Fork in the road; stay left. The road rejoins the main highway in 1.5 miles (2.4 km) via a right turn at the softball field in Hana town.

HANA TOWN

Before the arrival of Western explorers, Hana was a stronghold that was conquered and reconquered by the kings of Maui and the Big Island. The most strategic and historically rich spot is Ka'uiki Hill, the remnant of a cinder cone that dominates Hana Bay. It's said that the demigod Maui transformed his daughter's lover into Ka'uiki Hill and turned her into the gentle rains that bathe it to this day.

Hana was already a plantation town in 1849 when sea captain George Wilfong started producing sugar here on 60 acres (24 ha). After sugar production faded in the 1940s, San Francisco industrialist Paul Fagan bought 14,000 acres (5,670 ha) of what was to become the **Hana Ranch.** Today, Hana's population of 1,200 continues to be predominantly Hawaiian. There are far more sights in the Hana area than you can see in a single day.

Fagan Memorial

Once you finally roll in to Hana town, one of the most prominent sights is a massive cross above the village. Set on the 545-foot (166-m) summit of Pu'u O Kahaula (Lyon's Hill), the **Fagan Memorial** was constructed to honor the town's modern founder, Paul Fagan, after he died in 1960. Fagan is credited with the creation of modern Hana when he started Hana Ranch and opened the Ka'uiki Inn, which in 1946 was the island's first resort, today called the Hana-Maui Resort.

The memorial is accessible by following a steep walking path from the parking lot of the Hana-Maui Resort. Atop the summit you're treated to the best view in Hana, with a panoramic vista over Hana Bay and 'Alau Island in the distance.

Hana Cultural Center

While it might not look like much from the outside, the humble yet informative **Hana Cultural Center** (4974 Uakea Rd., 808/248-8622, www.hanaculturalcenter.org, times vary, check website, $5) provides the historical backbone for the town. Over the course of Maui's history, Hana has been a unique eastern outpost. See ancient Hawaiian artifacts excavated from the Hana region, such as stone adzes and hand-woven fishnets, and walk around the **Hana Courthouse,** listed on the National Register of Historic Places. The one-room courthouse still hosts proceedings the first Tuesday of each month, and in a testament to the island's multicultural heritage, they can take place in 24 different languages. When court isn't in session, the courthouse serves as a somber museum where Hana residents recount the morning of the 1946 tsunami, which devastated the eastern end of the island.

- **Highway 330:** Technically, Highway 360 ended at Hana Bay and Highway 330 started back at the fork in the road by the fire station. Once you drive past the center of Hana town at Hasegawa General Store and the gas station, you are on Highway 330, although the mileage markers don't start again for a couple of miles. When they do, they count down instead of up. The turnoff for **Hamoa Beach** and **Koki Beach** is at the first turnoff for Haneo'o Road, about 1.5 miles (2.4 km) past the center of Hana town, which is before the mileage markers begin again. There are two turnoffs for Haneo'o Road; take the first one, as this is the direction that local traffic naturally flows.

HANA TO KIPAHULU

- **Mile Marker 51:** Mileage markers restart.
- **Mile Marker 48:** Waioka Pond, gorgeous cliff-jumping right by the sea.

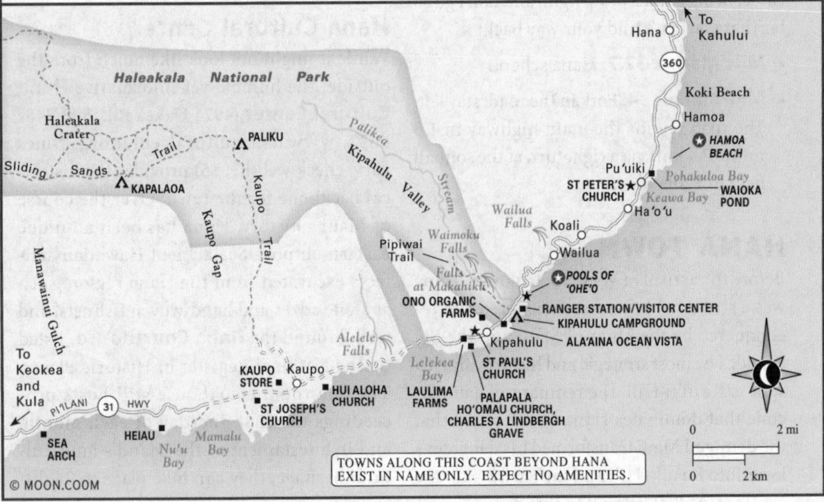

Waioka Pond (Venus Pool)

Hidden at mile marker 48, **Waioka Pond,** or **Venus Pool,** is a local favorite. You have to cross a private pasture to get to the oceanfront pool, and because it's such a popular spot, the landowners haven't yet restricted access.

The first challenge is finding a legal parking spot. Because the *mauka* side of the road is lined with residential homes, the only parking is along a fence on the *makai* (ocean side) of the road. In order for you to park legally—facing the correct direction—you have to cross the bridge past the mile marker 48 sign, pull off the road, do a U-turn, and drive back toward Hana town. Once you're facing the right way, park along the grass bordering the thin metal fence.

Once you've parked, follow the fence line toward the bridge, where you'll notice an opening in the fence. Walk through and then follow the thin dirt trail down toward the shore. Make a right through the trees at the concrete structure and you'll emerge at a cliff face looking out over a large pool. This first overlook is a popular cliff-diving spot among locals. To reach the pool without jumping, clamber down the rocks to the right. The pool is fed by both a stream and saltwater washing in from the ocean. There's a small island in the middle of the pool; swim over for a view of the rocky shore.

- **Mile Marker 47.5:** Fruit and flower stand popular with tour buses.
- **Mile Marker 46.3:** Karen Davidson Fine Art.
- **Mile Marker 45.3:** The road becomes narrow and offers dramatic views of the coast.
- **Mile Marker 45:** Laura Mango art gallery.
- **Mile Marker 44.8:** Wailua Falls.

Wailua Falls

This 80-foot (24-m) cascade may be the most photographed on Maui. The best way to experience it is to take the short trail down to the base and take a dip in the swimming pools, away from the crowds.

- **Mile Marker 43.2, 42.9:** Old bridges dating to 1910.

1: Waioka Pond **2:** Pools of 'Ohe'o

1

2

- **Mile Marker 42.1:** ʻOheʻo Stream and bridge looking over the misnamed Seven Sacred Pools.

★ Pools of ʻOheʻo

The fabled **Pools of ʻOheʻo,** inside **Haleakala National Park** (808/572-4400, www.nps.gov/hale, $30 per vehicle), are one of the island's most popular attractions. The name **Seven Sacred Pools** is the largest misnomer on the island. There are far more than seven, and there's no record in history of them having been sacred. The name likely began as a marketing ploy by hoteliers in the 1940s. The name stuck and is used to this day. The real name is ʻOheʻo (pronounced oh-HEY-oh); locals will appreciate you using it.

This part of the island is truly stunning and a highlight of visiting Maui. The first taste you'll get of the park is crossing over ʻOheʻo Gulch on a bridge at mile marker 42.1, but try not to linger too long as you'll stop traffic. The entrance to the park is 0.4 mile (0.6 km) down the road, and if you have visited Haleakala National Park within the last three days, your receipt will still gain you entry.

Once inside the park you'll notice a large parking lot next to an informative visitors center. It's the best place on this side of the island to gain an understanding of the history, culture, and unique environment of the Kipahulu region. Rangers here are the best source of information on current trail and waterfall conditions in the park.

The visitors center is also where you begin the Kuloa Point Loop Trail leading down to the famous pools. Along the 10-minute walk, you'll go through groves of *hala* trees and past a number of historic sites. Eventually the trail emerges at a staircase down to the pools and one of the most iconic vistas in Hawaii.

The three main pools are open most days for exploring and swimming, although they're closed during heavy rains and flash floods. Reaching the uppermost pools requires some rock scaling; it's worth the effort, but be careful on the slippery rocks.

- **Mile Marker 41.9:** Trailhead for Pipiwai Trail and the 400-foot (120-m) Waimoku Falls (parking for the trailhead is inside the park) (page 258).
- **Mile Marker 41.7:** Entrance to Haleakala National Park.
- **Mile Marker 41.2:** Ono Organic Farms.

Ono Organic Farms

There are numerous organic farms in Kipahulu, but the granddaddy of them all is 50-acre (20-ha) **Ono Organic Farms** (41319 Hana Hwy., 808/344-6700, www.onofarms.com, 10am-5pm daily), 0.5 mile (0.8 km) past the entrance to Haleakala National Park. You'll be blown away by the selection of exotic produce. In addition to producing 3,000 pounds (1,360 kg) of bananas *every week,* Ono also grows durians, cacao, coffee, tea, star fruit, Surinam cherries, and 60 other tropical and exotic fruits. Private tours ($375) last two hours.

The tour offers a culinary journey in certified organic and GMO-free produce directly from the land. A genuine spirit of aloha permeates the farm. It's easiest to take the tour if you're staying overnight in Hana. The driveway up to the farm is part of the adventure.

- **Mile Marker 40.9:** Hoʻonanea Farms fruit and coffee stand.
- **Mile Marker 40.8:** Turnoff for Palapala Hoʻomau Church, the final resting place of historic aviator Charles Lindbergh.
- **Mile Marker 40.6:** Laulima Farm fruit stand and kitchen, a sprawling compound growing a wealth of organic produce and a roadside kitchen.
- **Mile Marker 39.2:** Lelekea Bay.
- **Mile Marker 39:** The road begins to deteriorate and becomes narrow, with precipitous drop-offs. This is where you should turn around if you don't want to drive around the back of the island. As a point of reference, from this point it's 50 miles (81 km) to Kahului Airport via the back side, which

Understanding "The Back Road"

There's a romance to Hana's "back road."

The back road from Hana, **Highway 31,** is unlike any other stretch of road on the island. On this windswept plain, it feels like you've journeyed to the edge of the earth. Panoramic views stretch to the horizon, and the back of Haleakala opens up as it plunges from summit to sea.

At the beginning of the drive, past the Pools of 'Ohe'o, the terrain changes from a lush paradise laden with waterfalls to grasslands. Past Kaupo Store the road straightens, and the last half of the drive, between Manawainui and Kanaio, is one of the nicest stretches of pavement on the island. You may like this section of road better than the famous front section.

The biggest misconception about the Road to Hana is that the back road around Kaupo is only accessible with a 4WD vehicle, and you'll be told that driving this section of road violates your car-rental policy. Neither of these common opinions is accurate, and on almost every day of the year, the back road is passable in any vehicle, including a regular passenger car. The road is unpaved but well-graded dirt for 5 miles (8 km), and at some points it is only one lane wide and has precipitous drop-offs, but at no point is 4WD essential. The only time you would need 4WD is during a torrential rainstorm—and in that situation, you should stay off the road altogether. Your car-rental company won't penalize you because you drove out here, but if something goes wrong, they aren't going to come out and help you either. Luckily, island locals are some of the friendliest people you'll meet, and if you have problems, you won't have any trouble flagging someone down for help.

That said, preparation is key to enjoying a drive around the back side of Maui. Make sure that you have plenty of gas—at least half a tank when leaving Hana. Driving this road at night can be dangerous, and is pointless since you miss the expansive views. Keep an eye out for free-range cattle on the road. Other than Kaupo Store, there isn't anywhere to get food or water. If you're not a confident driver, the narrow sections and steep drop-offs may be too much. The road periodically closes due to construction, landslides, or flooding, so call the **Road Closure Advisory Line** (808/986-1200, ext. 2) for the latest information. Finally, no matter what your cell phone or GPS map says, there's no road from Ulupalakua back down to Kihei or Wailea.

takes about two hours without stops. If you return the way you came, it's 60 miles (97 km), about 2.5 hours without stops. While bumpier, the back road is much straighter and has less traffic.

- **Mile Marker 38.8:** Trailhead for Alelele Falls, a 60-foot (18-m) waterfall requiring a 10-minute hike (page 259).
- **Mile Marker 38.5:** Highway 31 begins.
- **Mile Marker 38.4:** The scariest section of road. If you make it past this without a heart attack, you'll be fine the rest of the way.
- **Mile Marker 37.8:** Road turns to dirt.
- **Mile Marker 36:** Surroundings morph from tropical and lush to windswept and arid. Welcome to Kaupo!
- **Mile Marker 34.6:** Kaupo Store.

Kaupo General Store

No other store on the island will amaze you quite like **Kaupo General Store** (mile marker 34.6, 10am-5pm Mon.-Sat., cash only), squirreled away inside a building constructed in 1925 in surroundings that feel like the end of the earth. Inside, find cold drinks and gourmet ice-cream bars, and stock up on water and snacks for the long, winding, beautiful drive.

- **Mile Marker 33.5:** Kaupo Gap warrants a stop for the sweeping view. At the upper rim of the gap is the 6,800-foot floor of Haleakala Crater.
- **Mile Marker 31.8:** The most amazing view of Haleakala you will see. If you thought the stretch between Kipahulu and Kaupo was desolate, you're in for a treat. The southeastern flank of Haleakala opens up into the dramatic panorama—a pristine expanse of wide-open country where visitors gawk at the desolate beauty. The road is exceptionally bumpy. After Manawainui Gulch, with its overly engineered bridge in the middle of nowhere, the road begins its gradual climb away from the coast to 3,000 feet (915 m) elevation in Keokea.
- **Mile Marker 31.1:** The gate to Nu'u Bay, a rocky beach popular for fishing and scenic coastal hiking.
- **Mile Marker 30.1:** Huakini Bay.
- **Mile Marker 29:** You survived the worst part of the road—smooth pavement begins.
- **Mile Marker 28.7:** Beautiful view of a lava-rock sea arch.
- **Mile Marker 27.3:** Manawainui Bridge and Gulch.

From this point the road climbs in elevation through the rural communities of Kahikinui and Kanaio before wrapping around to Maui Wine in Ulupalakua. If it's before 5pm, toast to your success at the winery and grab a bite at the Ulupalakua Ranch Store. The closest gas is 5.2 miles (8.4 km) down the road in Keokea.

Beaches

Beaches in East Maui are blissfully undeveloped, though due to the trade winds there isn't much snorkeling, and the water can be rough and choppy. Mornings offer the calmest conditions for a jog, a quick dip, or to commune with nature.

PA'IA

★ Baldwin Beach, Secret Beach, and Baby Beach

A lovely sequence of three beaches offers a nice diversity of options for travelers.

The long, wide, and mostly empty **Baldwin Beach** is a popular local bodysurfing spot, although the waves can get large during winter. During the afternoon, if the wind is howling, the cove on the far eastern end of Baldwin is sheltered and offers calm swimming most of the year.

Also on this far eastern end of Baldwin, closest to Pa'ia, a small trail leads around the point and connects with a spot known as **Secret Beach,** next to Pa'ia Bay. This little-known stretch of sand is often occupied by sun-worshipping nudists, affable hippies, and locals passing around the *pakalolo* (marijuana), making for a festive North Shore scene.

At the far western end of Baldwin Beach, farthest from Pa'ia, is the small cove known as **Baby Beach,** where a fringing reef creates a natural pool perfect for wading with young ones. There's less wind here before 10am. The shoreline also attracts fitness enthusiasts who appreciate a challenging jog. Instead of walking the length of Baldwin, you can also access Baby Beach by turning on Nonohe Place off Hana Highway, followed by a right on Pa'ani Place and a quick left onto Kealakai Place. There aren't any restrooms or showers, but the parking area offers scenic overlooks, and you can drive to the shower a mile (1.6 km) down the road at the main entrance.

Pa'ia Bay

The closest beach to the center of town, **Pa'ia Bay** is as active as Baldwin is calm, with a basketball court in a small park area and overflow parking for the town. The skate park at the Pa'ia Youth Center teems with area youth. Bodyboarders and surfers flock here for the waves, and a number of downhill bike companies finish tours here after descending the mountainside. There are restrooms, a beach shower, and an ever-changing cast of entertaining and colorful characters.

Kuau Cove

This beach is the scenic backdrop for **Mama's Fish House,** where many take a sunset photo. This small cove has a smattering of sand and an intriguing system of tide pools great for exploring with small children. The beach shrinks at high tide, so low tide is best for poring over the rocks to see all the slippery critters. There are a few parking spots near Mama's Fish House; the spaces with blue cones are designated as beach parking.

★ Ho'okipa Beach Park

Ho'okipa is the global epicenter of the windsurfing world as well as the go-to spot for surfers on the island's North Shore. It also has a thin, sandy beach pleasant for tanning and strolling (not so much swimming), offering ideal opportunities to appreciate and photograph Maui's rocky North Shore as well as witness the athletic skills of the surfers and windsurfers. A fringing reef creates a small pond nice for small children, and a wide range of people can usually be found hanging out on shore. Mornings are usually calm at Ho'okipa, and when the surf isn't too high, it's possible to snorkel in front of the rocks and find numerous *honu* (sea turtles). Every night in the hour before sunset, anywhere from half a dozen to 50 of them haul out on shore in front of the pavilions; this is quite a scene and attracts many onlookers. Remember that sea turtles are protected, and it's illegal to touch them. Note also that parking can be tight here—especially when the surf is up.

HANA TOWN

Pa'iloa Beach (Black-Sand Beach)

The **black-sand beach** at Wai'anapanapa State Park is the most popular beach in Hana. Just a few miles before the sleepy center of Hana and just past the turnoff for Hana Airport, dense foliage and black lava rock abut the crashing blue surf. The water along the shore is often rough, particularly in the afternoon. The beach is formed of crushed black lava rock, the result of the tumultuous wave erosion. The color of the sand is as black as the night sky.

To reach the shore, walk down a paved path from the parking lot of the state park. When you reach the bottom, you'll notice some sea caves you can explore at low tide. Since the sand is formed from lava rock, it isn't very comfortable; bring a blanket or a towel if you plan to hang out. Back at the parking lot, don't leave without checking out the freshwater caves. You can also walk the trail winding along the shore that leads to a thundering blowhole.

Hana Bay

Hana Bay is a laid-back crescent of gray sand in the middle of Hana town. Tucked in the lee of Ka'uiki Head, the working-class bay has a crumbling boat ramp where visitors end up when they "can't find Hana." It's nice enough for a picnic and a dip, but if you're looking for the nicest beach in Hana, keep driving out to Hamoa.

For a short, adventurous, and scenic hike, follow the trailhead at the end of the road as it snakes off into the trees. You'll reach a spot where it looks like the trail ends, but look across the narrow ravine and you'll see it on the other side. Follow this trail to a tiny red-sand beach, and eventually all the way to the plaque that commemorates the birthplace of Queen Ka'ahaumanu. The snorkeling can be fantastic in the morning. The best way to see it is with **Hana Bay Kayaks** (808/248-7711, www.hanabaykayaks.com).

Kaihalulu Beach (Red Sand Beach)

Before visiting **Kaihalulu,** be aware that **Red Sand Beach** is a nude beach. It can also be dangerous to access, as there are rockslides, slippery scree slopes, and sheer drop-offs. This is one of the coast's most famously scenic spots. This cavernous cove hidden in the mountainside offers decent swimming inside the rocks, and the red sand gets its color from the cinder cone.

To find the trail for Red Sand Beach, find a legal parking area on Uakea Road by the ballpark (don't park facing the wrong direction), and walk toward an open grass field where the road dead-ends by the community center. Walk across the grass field, keeping an eye on the bushes on your right for a couple of narrow trails.

Wading for a minute through waist-high grass, you'll eventually emerge at a small dirt trail that snakes down the roots of a tree. The footing can be slippery, so bare feet or closed-toe shoes are better than rubber slippers. The thin trail continues to the left up and over a bluff, where landslides can leave a lot of scree on the trail. Once at the top of the bluff, you'll be greeted with your first photo op of the stunning cove. From here it's a one-minute walk along a cliff until you emerge on the red shore.

HANA TO KIPAHULU

Koki Beach

To reach Hana's two famous beaches, travel 1.5 miles (2.4 km) past the center of town (the Hana Ballpark) and then make a left on Haneo'o Road. Going downhill, first is **Koki Beach,** a favorite hangout of local surfers. On the left side of the beach, you can scramble over rocks to reach some hidden sections of sand. Access to these smaller beaches is only possible at low tide, so most people stay on the main section of the beach. The dark-red sand is a product of a cinder cone known as Ka Iwi O Pele (The Bones of Pele). According to legend, this is where Pele, the volcano goddess, met her end. Her bones were stacked high on the shore before her spirit traveled southeast to the Big Island.

★ Hamoa Beach

Continuing along Haneo'o Road, paralleling the ocean, the snowcapped peak of Mauna Kea on the Big Island is occasionally visible in the distance. At low tide you can also see the remnants of the ancient Haneo'o Fishpond, although access is via private land. As the road rounds back to the right, you'll finally catch glimpses of **Hamoa Beach,** which Mark Twain considered one of the most beautiful in the world.

Parking is tight. Park only on the right side of the road so that traffic flows smoothly

1: Baby Beach **2:** Red Sand Beach **3:** Kuau Cove **4:** Ho'okipa Beach Park

1
2
3
4

on the left. You might have to drive past the beach before you find a space. Access to the beach is down the stone stairway. The park area at the bottom of the stairs is property of the Hana-Maui Resort, but the sandy beach is public property.

This is the best spot in Hana for a relaxing day at the beach. On the calmest of days it's possible to snorkel along the rocky coast, though most prefer to bodysurf the consistent playful shore-break. This can also be one of the best surf breaks in the area.

Surfing

Surfing in East Maui is for intermediate and advanced surfers. Ho'okipa Beach Park and Hamoa Bay can see surf at any time of year, and this stretch of coast roars to life October-April with North Pacific swells. This is some of the largest, heaviest surf on the planet. Even watching from the shore, you can feel the rush of waves large enough to shake the ground beneath you.

Pa'ia

SURF SPOTS

Although it's rarely surfed, a break in front of the lifeguard tower at **Baldwin Beach** offers fun longboarding before the afternoon wind picks up. If the surf is too large at places such as Ho'okipa or Pa'ia Bay, there is a reform on the shallow reef here that can offer a long ride.

If you rent a board in Pa'ia, the closest beach break is **Pa'ia Bay.** While the inside section is popular with bodyboarders, there is a second peak a little farther out that is better for surfing. Mornings are best before the wind blows the wave to pieces. Since the wave can be fast and steep, it's best for intermediate surfers.

The epicenter for surf on the island's North Shore will forever be **Ho'okipa Beach Park,** 3 miles (4.8 km) past the town of Pa'ia, a legendary windswept cove. For surfers, Ho'okipa has four sections: **Pavilions (Pavils), Middles, The Point,** and **Lanes.** Seen from the beach, Pavilions is the break that's the farthest to the right and can pick up wrapping wind swell even during the summer. Since it's the most consistent, it can also be the most localized, so beginners should be wary.

In the center of the beach, **Middles** is a big A-frame that breaks in deep water and can get board-shatteringly heavy during the winter. The wave can accommodate a larger crowd than Pavils, although you should still be skilled to paddle out. On the left side of the beach is the Point, a heavy right that's popular with windsurfers. Finally, Lanes is a left-hand wave that breaks in the cove to the west of Ho'okipa, but it's a long paddle.

SURFBOARD RENTALS

HI-Tech Maui (58 Baldwin Ave., 808/579-9297, www.surfmaui.com, 9am-6pm daily) offers casual board rentals ($25 per day) and has a full range of longboards, shortboards, and fun boards. It's an affordable option for playing in the waves of Pa'ia Bay or on a multiday safari to Hana.

SURF SCHOOLS

Given the advanced surf conditions of the island's North Shore, there aren't as many surf schools in East Maui as in Lahaina or Kihei. Professional longboarder **Zack Howard** (808/214-7766, www.zackhowardsurf.com) is one of the few instructors who offers lessons ($220 semi-private, $260 for 2, and $100 pp for 3 or more) to surf on Maui's North Shore. While most of his lessons are conducted at locations on the south shore on the road to Lahaina, advanced surfers can paddle out on the North Shore if the conditions are right.

1: Hamoa Beach **2:** windsurfers at Ho'okipa Beach Park **3:** a local surfer at Jaws

1

2

3

Surf Alert: Jaws

Pe'ahi, also called **Jaws,** can see 70-foot (21-m) waves, but only a few days a year October-April. The waves are created by massive storms in the North Pacific that churn between the Aleutian Islands and Japan. Since the North Pacific is calm during summer, it's only in winter that you stand a chance of seeing the large surf at Jaws.

Thanks to the wonders of surf forecasting, the massive waves can be predicted up to a week ahead of time. If Jaws is "going off," a high surf warning will be issued. The warning requires wave heights of 25 feet (7.6 m) or greater on the island's North Shore. This differs from a high surf advisory, issued when waves are 15 feet (4.5 m) or greater. If a high surf advisory is issued, there aren't going to be 70-foot (21-m) waves at Jaws.

If a high surf warning has been posted, ask a local what they've heard about the waves at Jaws—your concierge, a surf shop staffer, or any boat crew. Since island surfers watch the surf forecast like a trader watches stock futures, they'll be in the know. If Jaws is going to be breaking, get there in the morning. By the time the wind comes up in the afternoon, most of the surfers have left.

Hana

SURF SPOTS

The two main Hana surf breaks frequented by visitors are **Koki Beach** and **Hamoa Beach,** both on Haneo'o Road 1.5 miles (2.4 km) past the town of Hana. Because of its easterly location, Hana gets waves any time of the year. Since the waves are often the result of easterly wind swell, conditions can be rougher than elsewhere on the island. The steepness of the wave here is better suited for shortboards than longboards. Koki is where many of Hana's *keiki* (children) first learn how to pop up and ride.

Around the corner at Hamoa, the protected bay offers a respite from the trade winds. Koki breaks fairly close to shore, but the wave at Hamoa breaks farther out over a combination of sand, reef, and rocks. On moderate days, this is a good place for riding a longboard or a stand-up board, since the wave isn't as steep, but the largest waves are for experts. There are no lifeguards at either beach in Hana.

WINDSURFING

The world's best flock in droves to **Ho'okipa Beach Park** to combine the trade winds with waves that reach 20 feet (6 m) in winter. Don't expect to see windsurfers on a morning drive to Hana, as windsurfing is prohibited before 11am. A better bet is to see them on the drive back in the afternoon. Parking can be difficult at Ho'okipa, so if you're coming to watch the windsurfers, park up along the highway and leave the spots closer to shore for those who need to move gear.

Windsurfing Rentals

Although most of the windsurfing rental shops are in Kahului, **Simmer Hawaii** (99 Hana Hwy., 808/579-8484, www.simmerhawaii.com, 11am-6pm daily) is the closest shop to Ho'okipa and the best spot on the North Shore for windsurfing rentals and supplies.

Hiking and Biking

HIKING

Road to Hana

★ TWIN FALLS

At mile marker 2, which is 11.4 miles (18.3 km) past Pa'ia, **Twin Falls** is one of the easiest and shortest waterfall hikes in East Maui. It's also the first series of waterfalls on the Road to Hana. Much of the area is private land (respect the *Kapu*, or "Keep Out" signs on driveways), and most of the "trail" is a gravel road that is wide and easy to stroll. In a few spots the footing can be tricky, but this is a good choice for a tame walk into the rainforest. Occasionally, the trails to the upper waterfalls can be closed due to hazardous conditions. If there are signs posted that say the trails are closed, respect the landowners' wishes.

An outdoor playground peppered with waterfalls, the only downside is the crowding. During the midmorning hours, as visitors make their way toward Hana, there can be 50 cars parked along the side of the road. To visit with smaller crowds, stop on your drive back from Hana; come really early, before everyone else has arrived; or make a separate trip here in the late afternoon. Bring mosquito repellent.

Although there are myriad waterfalls at Twin Falls, two main ones are most accessible. The 1.3-mile (2-km) trail begins in the gravel parking lot and leads through a small gate in a lush and forested orchard. There are portable toilets on the right side of the trail, and visitors are encouraged to leave a donation for their maintenance and upkeep. After five minutes of walking along the gravel road, you'll hear some waterfalls off to the left. These are nice for a quick photo, but the main waterfalls are still farther down the trail.

After 10 minutes of walking, you'll come to a stream crossing that can flood during heavy rain. If the trail is closed, it will be here, and if the water appears to be rushing violently, it's best to turn around. Five minutes past the stream crossing is a three-way fork in the road; go straight. After five more minutes is another fork, where the trail to the left has a wooden plank crossing a small stream. Go straight, and after two minutes of clambering around an irrigation flume, you'll find a waterfall that has a small pool for swimming. While this waterfall is nice enough, there's a second waterfall, known as Caveman, that is far more dramatic, although it can be more difficult to reach.

To get to Caveman, turn around and go back to the fork in the trail with the wooden plank. Cross the wooden plank, ascend a small hill, take the fork to the left, and then take a right 50 yards (46 m) later. You'll be walking downhill, and a few minutes later you'll reach a concrete irrigation structure with steps leading up and over it. From here you'll begin to see the waterfall in the distance. To reach the base of the falls, wade across a stream that is usually about knee-deep. If the stream is manageable, a short scramble past it will bring you to a cavernous waterfall begging you to take your photo behind it. Since the water isn't clear enough to see the bottom, don't even think about jumping off the top.

Adjacent to the pool at Caveman is a thin trail that switchbacks up the hill, leading to more pools and waterfalls, although since it's easy to get lost back here, it's best to have a guide to venture any farther. On your way out from Caveman, after you climb up and over the irrigation structure and ascend the hill, follow the trail to the right when it forks to end up at the three-way fork in the trail you originally encountered on your walk in, ultimately making a full loop. From here it's a short walk back to the parking lot.

NA'ILI'ILI HAELE

The waterfalls of **Na'ili'ili Haele** (Bamboo Forest) are one of the highlights of the Road to Hana, but this hike has steep, slippery slopes

and stream crossings prone to flash floods. In the past few years firefighters have made hundreds of rescues. Access to the hike may soon be restricted because it has become so popular. If you decide to visit, only do so if it hasn't been raining.

At mile marker 6.5, you'll know you're approaching the trailhead by the enormous hairpin turn flanked by a rock wall. The road narrows, and parking can be difficult. You can park on the right side against the bamboo. If all these spots are taken, there are more pull-outs within 0.25 mile (0.4 km).

The correct trailhead is marked by a lone metal pole in a break in a wire fence. On the other side of the fence, the trail is narrow at first and winds downhill. After two minutes of walking is an intersection where you turn left to a steep scramble down a hill. This area can become slick, so use your hands to avoid slipping. At the bottom of the hill is a stream crossing with a wooden plank over a gap. On the other side of the stream, continue straight through a tunnel of bamboo before the path wraps around to the left and you rejoin the main trail. Make a right and follow the trail for another two minutes until you come to a major stream crossing.

It is easy to get turned around at the stream crossing because the trail ends. Across the stream is a downed tree slightly to the left. Follow the tree trunk to its base—this is the continuation of the trail. The trail parallels the water upstream. This section has some of the densest bamboo, and even when the sun is high in the sky, the thick grove blocks out the sun. A few minutes into the bamboo is a clearing off to the left. After a few more minutes is a second clearing. When you come to a third clearing on the left, you will hear the rush of a waterfall. Turn left to cross the stream again; this leads to the first waterfall, where there's a small pool.

Beyond this point the trail gets exponentially more challenging and treacherous. Should you want to continue, trace the edge of the pool to the far side of the streambed, where a thin rope dangles over a slippery rock face. This is where the trail continues; shimmy up the slick rock using the rope.

The trail flattens out and passes through more bamboo before arriving at another pool, larger and less crowded than the first. Slip off your shoes and slide in for a dip. There are additional pools and waterfalls upstream, but this is where the majority of accidents occur, so venture here only with a guide.

WAIKAMOI RIDGE TRAIL

The **Waikamoi Ridge Trail** (mile marker 9.5) provides a calming respite to stretch your legs on a 30-minute loop trail that takes you just far enough from the road that the only sounds you hear are the birds and the creak of swaying bamboo. The trail gains 200 vertical feet (60 m) and consists of two parts: the loop trail and the spur trail to the upper picnic area. Hike in a counterclockwise direction, since this is the best-maintained section of trail. The second half of the loop, heading back downhill toward the parking lot, isn't as well maintained and is a lot muddier than the platform steps on the way up.

Take the spur trail to the upper picnic area to find an open clearing to explore. The trail to the upper picnic area takes about 10 minutes and is covered in *lauhala* leaves and slippery roots. At the end of the trail is a simple picnic area where a covered pavilion provides a relaxing place for a snack and a rest. Pack mosquito repellent if you plan on stopping to eat here.

Hana Town

KING'S HIGHWAY COASTAL TRAIL

One of the few hiking options in East Maui that doesn't involve a waterfall, the 3-mile (4.8-km) **King's Highway Coastal Trail** between Wai'anapanapa State Park and the northern tip of Hana Bay is one of the few navigable remnants of the ancient King's Highway that once circled the island. Today, only scarce remnants of this ancient trail are evident, but

1: trail to Twin Falls **2:** Twin Falls **3:** Waimoku Falls **4:** Pipiwai Trail

the most prominent section is here on the coast south of Wai'anapanapa. Parking for the trailhead is in the main lot of the state park. Along the course of this 3-mile (4.8-km) trail, you'll weave around azure bays flanked by black sand, pass beneath dense groves of dry *lauhala* trees, and gaze upon lava rock arches carved from the coast by the tumultuous sea.

Wear hiking boots, as the jagged *'a'a* lava can rip rubber slippers to pieces. Carry plenty of water, as there are no facilities along the trail. As you get closer to Hana Bay, the trail becomes a little more treacherous. Most people start from the Wai'anapanapa trailhead and hike about halfway before turning back. To take the road less traveled, continue north of Wai'anapanapa past a series of smaller black-sand coves before eventually emerging near the Hana Airport. Expect to devote at least three hours to this trail round-trip from the trailhead.

For a quick and easy hike that still offers a rewarding view, the trail leading from the Hana-Maui Resort parking lot up to **Fagan's Cross** takes about 20 minutes and has a steep enough grade to offer a good leg workout. Watch for fresh guavas in the trees, as well as fresh cow pies left by the free-range cattle.

A 2-mile (3.2-km) **walking trail** leads from the trail to Fagan's Cross south toward Hamoa Beach. The track is little more than flattened grass through the pasturelands, but you'll have the coastal views all to yourself.

Kipahulu and Beyond

PIPIWAI TRAIL

Hands down, **Pipiwai Trail** is the best on Maui. It is in the upper portion of 'Ohe'o Gulch in the area known as Seven Sacred Pools. While most visitors to 'Ohe'o only pay a cursory visit to take photos, the Pipiwai Trail, which runs on the *mauka* side of the highway, is the undisputed highlight of the Kipahulu section of Haleakala National Park.

At 4 miles (6.4 km), the trail is long enough to be adventurous and short enough to be accessible, and it maintains a moderate grade. The last 0.5 mile (0.8 km) of the trail winds through bamboo so thick it blocks out the sun, and just when you think the scenery couldn't get any more tropical, the trail emerges at the base of 400-foot (120-m) **Waimoku Falls.** This two-hour expedition justifies the winding drive to get here. The best way to experience the trail is to camp overnight at the Kipahulu campground and hit the path before the throngs of day-trippers arrive.

To find the trailhead, drive 30-40 minutes past the town of Hana to mile marker 41.7, where you enter the Kipahulu section of Haleakala National Park. Parking for the trailhead is within the park boundaries. You'll have to pay the $30 park entry fee. Walk back to the road and 100 yards (90 m) toward Hana, where you'll see signs for the trailhead on the left. The trail climbs steeply up a rocky slope to a sign outlining trail distances. Much of the Pipiwai Trail parallels 'Ohe'o Gulch, and you can hear the rush of the water as you make your way uphill toward the falls. It's not safe to access the pools or waterfalls in the river. There may be days when you could get to the river by scrambling down a hillside or undefined trail, but a number of people have been swept to their deaths in flash floods. The National Park Service advises against any attempt to access the stream.

After 10 minutes on the trail is the lookout for Makahiku Falls, a 200-foot (60-m) plunge that can be anything from a trickle during drier months to a violent torrent. Past the falls, the trail begins gaining elevation for another five minutes before emerging in the shade of a beautiful banyan tree. The section between the tree and the first bridge has multiple spur trails that lead to waterfall overlooks offering views of the canyons and pools.

Ten minutes past the tree is the first of two bridges that zigzag across the stream. This is a great place to snap pictures of the waterfalls and the first bamboo forest. After crossing the second bridge, when the trail turns into stairs that climb steeply toward the bamboo, there's an opening in the railing on the left side where a path leads down to a rocky streambed. This is the Palikea Stream, and if you rock-hop up the riverbed for about 15 minutes, you'll emerge at a waterfall that is less dramatic—but also less visited—than neighboring Waimoku Falls. The waterfall here trickles down the towering canyon walls, and the pool at the bottom is occasionally used by nude bathers.

Back on the main trail, continuing up the stairs, a boardwalk leads through the densest bamboo on the island. As you emerge from the creaking cavern, five more minutes of rock-hopping brings you to the pièce de résistance, 400-foot (120-m) Waimoku Falls. This is one of the most beautiful corners of the island.

ALELELE FALLS

Few people make the short hike back to 60-foot (18-m) **Alelele Falls,** with a refreshing pool in winter that can go dry in summer. On the fabled back road about 3 miles (4.8 km) past the Pools of ʻOheʻo, the trailhead is at Alelele Bridge, at mile marker 38.8; park in one of the few parking spots available on the Kaupo side of the bridge.

If you have the energy left for a 10-minute hike through the jungle, the reward is a waterfall that offers just the right amount of seclusion. Although parking for the trailhead is on the Kaupo side of the bridge, the trailhead is back on the Kipahulu side, at the spot where the bridge begins. Follow this well-defined trail and cross the stream a couple of times, passing ancient lava-rock walls before emerging at the base of the pristine falls.

Hiking Tours

While many private adventure tours will take you hiking as part of the experience (page 268), one group that focuses specifically on hiking is **Hike Maui** (808/879-5270, www.hikemaui.com, $133-210), with knowledgeable guides who will take you hiking in a private area hidden behind Twin Falls. Group sizes are usually small. What makes these hikes worthwhile is not only being taken directly to the trailhead but also learning about the island's flora, fauna, history, and mythology from guides who love what they do.

BIKING

The town of Paʻia connects two of the most popular rides on the island: the frigid ride down Haleakala and the winding journey out toward Hana. As a cycling hub, there are a few bike shops around town.

Paʻia

One of the most comprehensive cycling experiences on Maui is at **Maui Cyclery** (99 Hana Hwy., 808/579-9009, www.gocyclingmaui.com, 10am-5pm Mon.-Sat.), a small but thorough shop in the heart of Paʻia. In addition to offering rentals (from $65 per day), parts, services, and sales, the staff offers guided tours for some of the island's best rides.

Haʻiku

In the Haʻiku Cannery, **Bike Maui** (810 Haʻiku Rd., Ste. 120, 808/575-9575, www.bikemaui.com, 8:30am-3:30pm daily) specializes in group tours making the ride down Haleakala Volcano. You can rent a bike (from $40 per day), and if you arrange your own transportation to the top, you'll be able to ride from the summit of the volcano.

Adventure Sports

★ ZIP-LINING

Most adventure sports along Maui's North Shore are in the water, but **NorthShore Zipline Company** (2065 Kauhikoa Rd., Ha'iku, 808/269-0671, www.nszipline.com, 10am-4pm Mon.-Sat., $147 pp) has seven zip lines that run through the trees of rural Ha'iku in a onetime military base. The course is family-friendly and caters mainly to first-time zippers. Children as young as five can participate as long as they're accompanied by an adult. Don't think that you won't still get a rush, however, as you can hit speeds of up to 40 mph (65 km/h) on the last line of the course, and the viewing platforms provide a unique vantage over the rural mountainside.

If you're short on time and want to combine a zip-line adventure with a day trip to Hana, **Jungle Zipline** (50 E. Waipio Rd., Ha'iku, 808/628-4947, www.junglezip.com, 7am-8pm daily), on the Road to Hana, is a great way to take a break from the car. The full course ($135) is eight lines and takes two hours. To merge this with driving the Road to Hana, opt instead for a morning tour on the abbreviated five-line course ($109). It takes about one hour, so you still have time to reach Hana. The minimum age is eight, and maximum weight is 250 pounds (113 kg).

RAPPELLING

To get all Navy SEAL on your Maui vacation, **Rappel Maui** (808/270-5100, www.rappelmaui.com, from $196) will teach you how to strap on a harness and walk down waterfalls. The company has exclusive access to waterfalls behind the Garden of Eden, and while the first descent is a dry run on a dirt hillside, eventually you're leaning backward over a waterfall with a 60-foot (18-m) drop. The guides are professional and completely committed to your safety. You could end up getting the best photo of your vacation. Weight limits are 70-250 pounds (32-113 kg). Don't look down!

HANG GLIDING IN HANA

This is the way to see the Hana coast. On an instructional lesson with **Hang Gliding Maui** (808/264-3287, www.hangglidingmaui.com), you meet your instructor, Armin, at his man-cave hangar at the Hana Airport. All flights are private, since the hang glider only has two seats, and he teaches you the basics of steering the glider as well as lift, wind speed, and direction.

This ultralight trike has wheels and a motor, so you take off down the Hana runway as you would in a regular plane, but when you reach a cruising altitude of 2,000-3,000 feet (600-900 m), you cut the engine and hang-glide back down, listening only to the wind. The view from here is life-changing, and there aren't even windows like a helicopter—just you, Armin, and the sky. Lessons are 30-minute ($240), 45-minute ($320), and one-hour ($400) flights and are offered Monday-Tuesday and Thursday-Friday.

SKYDIVING

Love the thrill of jumping out of a plane? **Maui Skydiving** (700 Alalele Rd., Hana, 808/379-7455, www.mauiskydiving.info, from $299 pp) is the island's first commercial skydive operation. The minimum age is 18, and maximum weight is 240 pounds (109 kg), with a $2 per pound ($4.40 per kg) surcharge for those over 200 pounds (91 kg).

HELICOPTER TOURS

Don't just drive the road to Hana; fly above it. **Maverick Helicopters** (Lelepio Pl., Kahului, 808/893-7999, www.maverickhelicopter.com) is one of the only operators that offers a Hana-specific tour, the superb 75-minute Hana Rainforest Experience ($299 pp) that traces Maui's North Shore with rare shoreline views

1: view from a helicopter tour **2:** walking down waterfalls at Rappel Maui **3:** Ha'iku Style Gallery

1
2
3
Hā'iku Style
CLOSED

of the towns of Pa'ia, Ha'iku, and Hana. The tour's grand opus is descending and landing in the Hana rainforest, where guests disembark and explore the grounds of a former taro plantation in the Wailua Valley. Your pilot explains the finer nuances of this remote landscape, which few people ever visit.

Air Maui (1 Keolani Pl., Hangar 110, Kahului, 808/877-7005, www.airmaui.com) covers two of Maui's most popular sights on its Hana-Haleakala tour ($229 pp), which lasts an impressive four hours and includes a cliffside landing on the back side of Haleakala, followed by a charted route over Hana's rainforest, remote valleys, and waterfalls. All helicopters seat up to six. Tours are offered twice daily, at 8am and noon.

Shopping and Entertainment

SHOPPING

Pa'ia

Once known for hippies, surf culture, and sugarcane, Pa'ia now features some of the island's trendiest boutiques and arguably the island's best shopping, with bikini shops, beachwear boutiques, and craft galleries populating the one-stoplight town.

ART GALLERIES

Maui Hands (84 Hana Hwy., 808/579-9245, www.mauihands.com, 10am-5:30pm daily) has stunning works of art from local creators and well-known artists. Many pieces reflect island culture.

At **Pueo Gallery** (96 Hana Hwy., 808/446-3974, www.pueomaui.com, 10am-6pm daily), owner/photographer Lyle Krannichfeld has curated an intimate assortment of beautiful art that pairs wonderfully with his own vibrant works. Variety—from watercolors to acrylics—abounds in this beautiful showroom.

SURF SHOPS

For surf, skate, or even snowboard wear, visit **HI-Tech Maui** (58 Baldwin Ave., 808/579-9297, www.surfmaui.com, 9am-6pm daily) and **Honolua Surf Company** (115 Hana Hwy., 808/579-9593, noon-6pm daily), both offering apparel in America's happiest surf town.

CLOTHING AND SWIMWEAR

The only genre that rivals surf gear in Pa'ia is women's clothing boutiques and bikini stores. Along Baldwin Avenue, **Alice in Hulaland** (19 Baldwin Ave., 808/579-9922, www.aliceinhulaland.com, 9am-8pm daily) offers a snarky range of clothing and accessories. On the finer end of apparel are **Nuage Bleu** (76 Hana Hwy., 808/579-9792, www.nuagebleu.com, 10am-6pm daily) and **Nectar Creations** (16 Baldwin Ave., 808/579-6063, www.nectarcreations.com, 9am-9pm daily). These are two of the more elegant and fashionable clothing boutiques.

When it comes to bikinis, sun-seekers will love **San Lorenzo Bikinis** (115 Hana Hwy., 808/873-7972, www.sanlorenzobikinis.com, 10am-7pm daily), in the center of town. The bikinis are skimpy, almost Brazilian, but that's the North Shore. Even more bikinis are at **Maui Girl** (12 Baldwin Ave., 808/579-9266, www.maui-girl.com, 11am-5pm Mon.-Sat., noon-5pm Sun.), with bikinis featured in *Sports Illustrated*'s swimsuit edition.

Sassabella Boutique (36 Baldwin Ave., 808/572-3552, noon-6pm daily) offers designer must-haves and vibrant island-based luxury fabrics.

JEWELRY AND GIFTS

While Pa'ia doesn't have as many jewelry stores as Lahaina, **Studio 22K** (161 Hana

Hwy., 808/579-8167, www.studio22k.com, noon-6pm Tues.-Sat.), on the far Hana side of town, is a small studio that specializes in handmade 22-karat-gold items with metal malleable enough to morph into all sorts of twisting shapes and designs. If sterling silver is more what you're looking for, **Oceania Maui** (96 Hana Hwy., 808/573-6597, www.oceaniamaui.com, 10am-6pm daily) has over 400 designs that are crafted on Maui.

When on Maui . . . grab an ukulele. **Mele Ukulele** (98 Hana Hwy., 808/856-0611, www.shopmeleukulele.com/maui-hawaii, 11am-6pm daily) has a wide variety of instruments and accessories, as well as island art.

By the Bay (90 Hana Hwy., 808/579-9777, www.bythebaymaui.com, 11am-6pm daily) has it all—from hand-crafted jewelry to stunning artwork. Prices are affordable and the inventory is diverse.

Ha'iku

ART GALLERIES

Treehouse Art Studios (375 W. Kuiaha Rd., www.treehouseartstudios.com, hours vary, check website) is a festive enclave where the creations of local artists are on display. It is conveniently located in the Pauwela Cannery.

A great place to stop for both art and souvenirs is **Ha'iku Style Gallery** (810 Ha'iku Rd., 808/283-1706, 10am-6pm Tues.-Sat.). There's a tremendous trove of artwork from local artists, and you'll always find something unique.

CLOTHING

Lost on Maui (3232 Luahine Pl., 808/214-5704, hours vary) is a great pit stop, featuring a wide variety of unique island wear.

GROCERY

Ha'iku Marketplace (810 Ha'iku Rd., 808/575-9291, 6am-9pm daily) is an independent grocery store. You can pick up extra snacks and drinks, and even walk out with sashimi to go.

Road to Hana

GIFTS AND SOUVENIRS

The best place for real shopping along the Road to Hana is at **Nahiku Ti Gallery** (mile marker 28.7, 808/248-8800, hours vary, usually 10am-5pm daily), a small gallery within the Nahiku Marketplace. This curious strip mall in the rainforest is already strange in that it offers legitimate food options in the middle of nowhere, and the art gallery rivals those in Ka'anapali and Wailea. While nowhere near as large as the south shore shopping venues, the gallery has a varied selection of jewelry, crafts, paintings, pottery, and a surprising collection of art.

Hana Town

ART GALLERIES

By far the most comprehensive gallery in Hana, the **Hana Coast Gallery** (5031 Hana Hwy., 808/248-8636, www.hanacoast.com, 9am-5pm daily) might be the nicest art gallery on the island. A freestanding building within the Hana-Maui Resort, the Hana Coast Gallery features fine works by Hawaiian artists. Oil paintings, ceramics, and wooden sculptures are on display in this sophisticated space, and the depth of knowledge of the staff on the intricacies of individual pieces provides an educational component to this fine-art experience.

ENTERTAINMENT

Pa'ia

LIVE MUSIC

Occasionally there is live music in the courtyard of intimate **Café des Amis** (42 Baldwin Ave., 808/579-6323, www.cdamaui.com, 1:30pm-8pm daily). Down the block at **Paia Bay Coffee & Bar** (115 Hana Hwy., 808/579-3111, www.paiabaycoffee.com, 7:30am-7pm Tues.-Sat.), live music from local artists and a fun happy hour (3pm-6pm) enliven this tropical patio setting.

Ha'iku

LIVE MUSIC

No trip to Maui is complete without at least one visit to **Temple of Peace** (575 Haiku Rd., 808/575-5220, www.templeofpeacemaui.com, 9am-5pm Mon.-Sat.). Dubbed "Maui's Healing Sanctuary," the very boho Buddhist's temple has been operating for decades. Check the website for special events. You can book a quasi-spa day here and fill it with meditation and relaxing. For a real kick, Sunday morning services are lively and filled with music and singing.

Food

PA'IA

Seafood

★ **Mama's Fish House** (799 Poho Pl., 808/579-8488, www.mamasfishhouse.com, 11am-8:30pm daily, $22-58) is synonymous with Maui fine dining. Its cult-like followers claim that if you haven't been to Mama's, you've never been to Maui. The oceanfront location and romantic ambience are unbeatable, and the fish is so fresh that the menu tells you it was caught that morning and who caught it. Call well in advance for reservations, timing your meal for sunset if possible. Lunch is an affordable alternative.

While your hotel concierge will recommend Mama's, local surfers will point you to ★ **Pa'ia Fish Market** (100 Baldwin Ave., 808/579-8030, www.paiafishmarket.com, 11am-9:30pm daily, $10-19), on the corner of the only stoplight in town. Lines stretch out the door for the popular ono and mahimahi burgers. My personal favorite is the ahi burger, paired with a Hefeweizen on draft. The fish tacos and seafood pasta are shockingly good as well.

Eclectic

Dollie's North Shore (120 Hana Hwy., 808/579-9070, 11am-6pm daily, $9-18) entertains diners with friendly service, sandwiches and burgers, appetizers, and terrific pizzas. Big-screen TVs fill the place, so there's always something lively to watch.

Paia Bay Coffee & Bar

Italian

As the name of ★ **Flatbread Company** (89 Hana Hwy., 808/579-8989, www.flatbread-company.com, 11:30am-9pm daily, $16-22) implies, you won't find any Chicago-style deep-dish pizza here. All the pizzas use organic, locally sourced ingredients and are fired in an open *kiawe* (mesquite) wood oven. Try the Pa'ia Bay Ohana, a white mushroom and caramelized organic onions delight, or Mopsy's Kalua Pork (free-range kalua pork, organic mango barbecue sauce, organic red onions, Maui pineapple, and goat cheese from Surfing Goat Dairy). On Tuesday nights, the restaurant typically hosts benefits for the local community, but the crowds are intense.

Mediterranean

The most relaxing place for a meal in Pa'ia is at ★ **Café des Amis** (42 Baldwin Ave., 808/579-6323, www.cdamaui.com, 1:30pm-8pm daily, $11-21), where you can sit in a tucked-away outdoor courtyard with Italian coffee and crepes. Lunch has exceptional Indian curries, in addition to savory crepes, and happy hour is 4pm-6pm daily.

Mexican

On the corner of Pa'ia's only stoplight, separated by the bustling crosswalk, ★ **Milagros** (3 Baldwin Ave., 808/579-8755, www.milagrosfoodcompany.com, 11am-9pm daily, $10-20) is known for Mexican fare with a funky island twist, enormous portions, and the best happy hour in town. The black-bean nachos, ahi burrito, and blackened ahi tacos are all local favorites. Get a seat at the outdoor patio, which has some of the best people-watching in Pa'ia.

Café Mambo (30 Baldwin Ave., 808/579-9021, www.cafemambomaui.com, 11am-8pm daily) creates some of the best fajitas in Pa'ia. The locally sourced burgers are another standout.

Ice Cream

Everybody needs ice cream at some point on a tropical island. **Artisan Ice Cream** (40 Baldwin Ave., 808/579-8030, www.artisan-paia.com, 1:30pm-8:30pm daily, $6-12) does the trick with its delicious offerings. The venue crafts fresh ice cream in small batches daily. Check out the soy/vegan options made with coconut cream and coconut milk. For a real treat, order the homemade *liliko'i* butter or banana macadamia nut brittle.

Coffee Shops

For a morning coffee on the way out to Hana, **Paia Bay Coffee & Bar** (115 Hana Hwy., 808/579-3111, www.paiabaycoffee.com, 7:30am-7pm Tues.-Sat., 7:30am-noon Sun.) is in a hidden courtyard behind San Lorenzo Bikinis. Walk through the bikini store to get to this local favorite, and if the store isn't open yet, there's an entrance around the back of the building. In addition to coffee, there's a filling selection of bagels and sandwiches ($6-9). It also has cocktails, beer, and wine, as well as live music.

Natural Foods

Mana Foods (49 Baldwin Ave., 808/579-8078, www.manafoodsmaui.com, 8am-8:30pm daily) is the epicenter of the island's health-conscious, with a selection of organic and natural offerings. There's a hot bar as well as a deli section where you can build your own picnic lunch for the Road to Hana, or pick up filling and affordable sandwiches ($7).

HA'IKU

The town of Ha'iku is mostly residential, and aside from tropical bed-and-breakfasts has little for visitors. The exception is food, with a couple of restaurants worth the drive.

Japanese

The best restaurant in Ha'iku is ★ **Nuka** (780 Haiku Rd., 808/575-2939, www.nuka-maui.com, 10:30am-2:30pm Mon.-Fri. and 4:30pm-10pm daily, $9-19), with hand-rolled sushi that can rival the best on Maui.

Mediterranean

Mediterranean Grill (810 Haiku Rd., 808/868-3518, noon-6pm Thurs.-Mon., $6-12) is one of the east side's best food trucks. It's a local favorite for sandwiches filled with lamb gyro, chicken, and falafel and larger plates featuring the same, with the addition of saffron basmati rice, salad with Lebanese olive oil, and grilled pita.

Diners

Colleen's (810 Haiku Rd., 808/575-9211, www.colleensinhaiku.com, 7am-9:30pm daily, $9-28) is a longtime local favorite for breakfast and a boozy brunch (Bloody Marys!), and it's the perfect spot for lunch if you've just biked down the volcano with Bike Maui next door.

Cafés

Jaws Country Store (4320 Hana Hwy., 808/419-6887, www.jawscountrystore.com, store 6am-5pm daily, café 7am-4pm daily, $8-14), about a mile (1.6 km) before Twin Falls at mile marker 14.5 on Highway 36, is a store as well as café. It's a good place to stop for breakfast—perhaps an omelet or the banana bread toast—or pick up sandwiches or snacks to go if you're driving the Road to Hana.

Coffee Shops

For a pit stop before the Road to Hana, or to chill for a while with friends, turn south on West Kuiaha Road from Highway 36 and visit **Baked On Maui** (375 W. Kuiaha Rd., 808/575-7836, 6:30am-5pm daily, $4-10). The coffee and espresso drinks are robust, and there's freshly baked bread, a full breakfast menu, and sandwiches. This is a great place to hang with the local crowd.

Wailuku Coffee Company (810 Kokomo Rd., 808/868-3229, www.wailukucoffeeco.com, 7am-2pm daily, $4-11) is one of the island's most popular coffee chains. Order a special coconut buttered latte and fresh breakfast wrap.

ROAD TO HANA

There's a myth that you won't find any food while driving the Road to Hana. Stores in Pa'ia and as far away as Ka'anapali offer "Road to Hana picnic lunches" as a means of staving off starvation, even though the longest stretch without any food options is under 7 miles (11 km). The best plan for food when driving the Road to Hana is to grab breakfast in Pa'ia at **Café des Amis** or **Paia Bay Coffee & Bar** or in Ha'iku at **Jaws Country Store** early on in the drive. You can also buy a sandwich or stock up on snacks like chips, fruits, dried fruit, trail mixes, coconut water, and a variety of juices at Jaws Country Store.

HANA

On weekdays Hana has many lunch options. Dinner options are sparse, however, and only a handful of lunch venues are open on weekends.

Hawaiian Regional

A longtime staple, the **Hana Ranch Restaurant** (5031 Hana Hwy., 808/270-5280, 7am-10am and 11am-9pm daily, $11-29) is on the mountain side of the road in the "center of town." There are filling lunch sandwiches, such as a black-bean burger and slow-roasted kalua pork. The takeout window is open 11am-4pm daily. The inside seating area stays open as one of Hana's only dinner options where you can feast on rib-eye steaks, Hawaiian barbecue pork ribs, or fresh ono fish tacos.

The dining room and bar at **Hana-Maui Resort** (5031 Hana Hwy., 808/270-5285, www.hyatt.com, 7:30am-9pm daily, $20-48) overlooks beautiful Hana Bay and features Hana-grown produce and a large variety of succulent fresh fish.

Thai

Hana isn't a place you'd expect to find mouthwatering Thai, but ★ **Thai Food by Pranee** (5050 Uakea Rd., 808/264-9942, 10:30am-5pm Mon.-Tues. and Fri.-Sat., 11am-4pm Sun., $10-12) is a culinary gem in the humblest of locations. Little more than a glorified food truck across from the Hana Ballpark, this open-air restaurant gets packed for lunch—especially since it's open on weekends. The filling portions of pad thai and green curry are worth the wait, and if the food is too spicy, you can ask them for coconut milk to bring the heat down. Parking is along Uakea Road, and be sure to park facing the correct direction, since violators are often ticketed.

Food Trucks

Lunch in Hana is defined by food trucks, the most popular of which is **Braddah Hutts BBQ Grill** (808/264-5582, 10:30am-3pm Mon.-Fri., $8-12) just past Hasegawa General Store. The smoky flavor of the kalua pig tacos is magic. Try the macaroni salad.

Another great choice is **Da Chow Wagon** (808/281-0023, 10am-4pm Mon.-Fri., $10-12), next to the gas station, which has local classics like chicken *katsu* and teriyaki beef.

For a cool treat on a hot day, pick up frozen juice on a stick from **Shaka Pops** (808/442-2926, www.shakapopsmaui.com, 11am-4pm Sun.-Fri., $4.75) across from Hasegawa General Store. The frozen treats are made here on Maui using small-batch, freshly squeezed juices.

Farmers Market

One of the best Hana lunch options is **Hana Fresh Market** (4590 Hana Hwy., 11am-3pm Mon.-Sat.), in the parking lot of the Hana Health clinic between Wai'anapanapa and the center of town. Proceeds support the Hana Health programs and services, and many of the vegetables and fresh produce are grown in a greenhouse on the property. There is an ample selection of filling lunch options ($8-12), including veggie, smoked turkey, and Italian paninis, fresh kebabs, spinach and mushroom quesadillas, wraps, and Asian turkey lettuce wraps. You can also get a tasty *poke* bowl with brown rice, and wash it all down with a fruit smoothie or a cup of Hana-grown coffee.

KIPAHULU AND BEYOND

Driving the back road to the other side of the island, the only real food option is **Kaupo Store** (mile marker 34.6, 10am-5pm Mon.-Sat., cash only) in the dusty Kaupo hinterlands. If you're planning on venturing from Hana to 'Ohe'o (Seven Sacred Pools) and then continuing around the back side of the island, stock up on water and snacks at **Hasegawa General Store** (5165 Hana Hwy., 808/248-7079, 7am-6pm daily) lest you end up marooned with no water or food.

Getting There and Around

CAR

There aren't any car-rental operators in East Maui, so plan on driving here yourself or taking a guided tour.

Gas

There are two gas stations within walking distance of each other in **Pa'ia.** Be sure you have close to a full tank for the long, winding journey out to Hana. Neither of the stations has a public restroom; the closest ones are at Pa'ia Bay.

Tucked away on a back road that visitors only end up on if they're lost, the only gas station in **Ha'iku** can be found at **Hanzawa's Variety Store** (1833 Kaupakalua Rd., 808/298-0407, 7am-7pm daily), about halfway between Hana Highway and the town of Makawao.

In all of **Hana** there is only one gas station. **Texaco** (5200 Hana Hwy., 808/270-5299, 7am-8pm daily) is across from Hasegawa General Store. It has a few auto supplies, snacks, and a telephone, although for a public restroom you're better off going down to the Hana Ballpark. Gas in Hana is expensive: $0.50 or more per gallon higher than elsewhere on the island. Fill up before leaving town, because the nearest gas station west is in Pa'ia; going south around the bottom of the island, the closest is in Keokea in Upcountry, and it isn't open in the evening.

GUIDED TOURS

Despite how much fun it is to craft your own Hana adventure, you can visit Hana as part of a private tour.

The best option is **Valley Isle Excursions** (808/871-5224, www.tourmaui.com, $224 adults, $204 children), the only guided Hana tour that's part of the Hawaii Ecotourism Association. Guides are professional, knowledgeable, and funny, and the company has gone to exceptional lengths to eliminate waste from their tours. Book online and save $10.

Temptation Tours (808/817-1234, www.temptationtours.com, from $219) offers small group tours in "limo vans" and has a number of different options for visiting Hana with a picnic lunch. One of the tours explores the recesses of Ka'eleku Caverns, and a Hana picnic tour has a similar itinerary but much nicer vans. The top choice, however, is the Hana Sky Trek ($399 pp), driving the Road to Hana and then hopping aboard a helicopter at the Hana Airport for the ride back to Kahului. During the flight you'll zip by towering waterfalls you would never see from the road, and buzz over the multihued cinder cones of Haleakala Crater.

For smaller, private, customized tours, **Awapuhi Adventures** (808/280-8779, www.awapuhiadventures.com) and **Open Eye Tours** (808/280-5299, www.openeyetours.com) provide personalized experiences that are the best and most expensive. Pono Fried, an exceptional guide at Open Eye Tours, has deep respect for the culture and can offer an educational journey unlike any other.

To include hiking, adrenaline, excitement, and adventure, **Maui Easy Riders** (808/344-9489, www.mauieasyriders.com, $185 pp) offers a half-day in Hana. A similar tour operator is **Blue Soul Maui** (808/217-9520, www.bluesoulmaui.com, $950 for 2-3 people), offering high-end customizable adventures.

BUS

The **Maui Bus** provides regular service between Pa'ia, Ha'iku, the Kahului Airport, and Queen Ka'ahumanu Center in Kahului, where you can connect with buses to anywhere else on the island. The rate is $2 per boarding or $4 for a day pass, and pickups begin in Pa'ia at 5:53am daily headed toward Ha'iku and 6:29am daily headed toward Kahului. The route also makes stops at the Ha'iku Marketplace and Ha'iku Community Center, with the final bus going from Ha'iku to Kahului departing the Ha'iku Marketplace at 9:11pm daily.

FLIGHTS

At the small Hana Airport, you can swap the nausea-inducing three-hour drive for the convenience of a 20-minute flight. Of course, you'll miss out on all the sights along the Road to Hana, but if your focus is on getting to Hana and relaxing at the resort, **Mokulele Airlines** (808/295-4188, www.mokuleleairlines.com, 7am-7pm daily) operates flights twice daily between Kahului Airport and the landing strip in Hana. Often the Hana-Maui Resort runs specials with the airfare included with a stay of three nights or more. If you fly to Hana, however, remember that there aren't any car-rental agencies here, so you'll have to arrange your own transportation from the airport before you get on the flight.

Where to Stay

With so many options, finding accommodations on Maui can be overwhelming.

Regardless of where you choose to stay, the rates listed here don't include the 14.42 percent tax added at checkout. If you're staying in a condo, be sure to read the fine print about additional cleaning fees. In large resorts, resort fees are $25-40 per day, and parking can be upward of $30 per day. Since Maui is spread out, consider spending your time in two separate lodgings instead of being tied to one area. Rates are lowest May-October, and resort room rates can double in winter.

1
2
3
4

CONDOS AND VACATION RENTALS

There are literally hundreds of independently owned condos and vacation rentals on Maui. Oftentimes these might be a better fit than a resort or a B&B. The best place to begin your search is on **VRBO** (www.vrbo.com). In West Maui, check out **Maui Travel Partners** (651/446-9868, www.mauitravelpartners.com). Another option is **Chase N' Rainbows** (808/611-6022, www.westmauicondos.com), a management company with dozens of properties. For houses in East Maui check out **Hana's Finest Rentals** (www.hanasfinestrentals.com) or **Island Style Vacations By Kim** (www.islandstylevacationsbykim.com) for Pa'ia and Ha'iku.

West Maui

KAPALUA, NAPILI, AND HONOKOWAI

Resorts

The largest and best-known resort on the northwestern side is the ★ **Ritz-Carlton Kapalua** (1 Ritz-Carlton Dr., 808/669-6200 www.ritzcarlton.com, $799-5,000), offering the amenities expected of a Ritz-Carlton. Also offered are several cultural and environmental programs, such as the acclaimed Ambassadors of the Environment. It can often be windy and wetter than in central Lahaina, but showers usually pass quickly.

Also in Kapalua is the ★ **Montage Kapalua Bay** (1 Bay Dr., 808/626-6600, www.montagehotels.com, $1,200-5,200), with 56 residences laid out like luxurious homes. It's pricey, but you'll feel like a rock star.

Condominiums

On the point between Napili and Kapalua Bays, the ★ **Napili Kai Beach Resort** (5900 Lower Honoapi'ilani Rd., 808/669-6271, www.napilikai.com, $394-831) is a West Side classic that offers individually owned condos in a family-friendly resort setting. This is a great option for families who want to stay in one place and play on the beach. There is a miniature putting course, multiple swimming pools, and a weekly mai tai party. Many of the units have recently been renovated and are the nicest they've ever been.

An affordable spot on Napili Bay, **Napili Village Hotel** (5425 Lower Honoapi'ilani, 808/669-6228, www.napilivillagehotel.com, $170-224) is the area's best value. These studios and one-bedroom apartments include air-conditioning, maid service, and full kitchens. The rooms aren't as luxurious as some of the other options on the beach, but being steps from Napili Bay, it's hard to argue with the price.

In Honokowai, the **Maui Kai** (106 Ka'anapali Shores Pl., 808/667-3500, www.mauikai.com, $359-429) is at the boundary of Honokowai and Ka'anapali, so it's possible to take a long morning stroll down the beach to the center of the Ka'anapali strip. All units have full kitchens, gas barbecues, and the convenience of being just steps from the beach. Parking and Wi-Fi are included in the rates. This is an affordable place for families who want to be near Ka'anapali without the resort rates.

Previous: pool at the Andaz Maui
1: Montage Kapalua Bay **2:** Napili Kai Beach Resort
3: the Ka'anapali resort area **4:** Pioneer Inn

KA'ANAPALI

Hotels and Resorts

As the slogan says, ★ **Ka'anapali Beach Hotel** (2525 Ka'anapali Pkwy., 808/661-0011, www.kbhmaui.com, $231-488) is Maui's "most Hawaiian hotel." A genuine feeling of aloha permeates this laid-back resort, and while it's not nearly as lavish as its neighbors, KBH occupies prime oceanfront real estate

Where to Stay in West Maui

Name	Type	Price	Features	Why Stay Here?	Best For
'Aina Nalu Lahaina	condo	$212-455	pool, kitchen	location	couples
Camp Olowalu	camping	$24-195	restrooms, oceanfront	location, affordable	budget travelers
Ho'oilo House	B&B	from $369	pool, breakfast	quiet, view	couples, honeymooners
Hyatt Regency Maui Resort and Spa	resort	$594-1,500	waterslides, oceanfront	location, pools	families
★ Ka'anapali Beach Hotel	hotel	$231-488	free hula show	location	families, couples
Lahaina Shores Beach Resort	condo	$355-585	pool, oceanfront	location	couples
Maui Kai	condo	$359-429	kitchens, oceanfront	location	families, couples
★ Montage Kapalua Bay	resort	$1,200-5,200	kitchens, oceanfront, spa, pool	full-service resort	couples, families, honeymooners, luxury-lovers

a two-minute stroll from Pu'u Keka'a (Black Rock). The open lawn is the perfect place to relax in the shade of an *ulu* tree, and while there is no hot tub, there is a swimming pool next to the popular tiki bar, a welcoming place for families. On the lawn is an outrigger sailing canoe crafted by employees of the resort, and free hula shows are held each night on the hotel's outdoor stage. Guests are made to feel like *'ohana* (family), and the rates are much more affordable.

In front of Pu'u Keka'a is the 503-room **Sheraton Maui Resort & Spa** (2605 Ka'anapali Pkwy., 808/661-0031, www.sheraton-maui.com, $597-769), the original Ka'anapali resort in the 1960s. This luxurious beach resort is tucked into the sacred cliff face, and despite being the "oldest" hotel on the strip, it has been renovated numerous times and feels brand-new. There is a large oceanfront pool, tennis courts, spacious rooms, and a spa, and a few of the rooms are on top of the legendary Ka'anapali promontory.

On the far southern end of the Ka'anapali strip is the **Hyatt Regency Maui Resort and Spa** (200 Nohea Kai Dr., 808/661-1234, www.hyatt.com, $594-1,500), with the best pool system in Ka'anapali. This is a favorite of families who want to spend the day by the pool, and the best place along the strip to grab a drink from a bar tucked behind a waterfall or ride a twisting waterslide. This southern end of the beach is also sheltered from the afternoon trade winds, although the sand in front of the resort has been steadily eroding for years.

The **Royal Lahaina** (2780 Keka'a Dr., 808/661-3611 www.royallahaina.com, $279-415), on the northern side of Pu'u Keka'a, offers rooms for tighter budgets. In addition to the oceanfront tower are a number of individual cottages scattered around the property,

Name	Type	Price	Features	Why Stay Here?	Best For
★ **Napili Kai Beach Resort**	condo	$394-831	pool, oceanfront	full amenities	families, couples
Napili Village Hotel	condo	$170-224	oceanfront	location, rates	families, couples
Pioneer Inn	hotel	$267-297	garden, pool	location	couples, budget travelers
★ **Plantation Inn**	B&B	$194-362	pool, breakfast	location, quiet, price	couples, honeymooners
★ **Puamana**	condo	$224-799	pool, oceanfront	location, quiet	families, couples
★ **Ritz-Carlton Kapalua**	resort	$799-5,000	golf, spa	full-service resort	luxury-lovers, honeymooners
Royal Lahaina	hotel	$279-415	oceanfront, tennis	location	couples
Sheraton Maui Resort & Spa	resort	$597-769	pool, oceanfront	full-service resort	families, honeymooners
Westin Ka'anapali Ocean Resort Villas	resort	$573-772	pool, oceanfront	full-service resort	families, couples

where the Ka'anapali golf course runs right through the resort. A little more laid-back than some of the glitzier resorts, this is one of Ka'anapali's best oceanfront values.

Just down the beach, the **Westin Ka'anapali Ocean Resort Villas** (6 Kai Ala Dr., 808/667-3200, www.westinkaanapali.com, $573-772) combine the luxury of an oceanfront resort with the convenient amenities of a condo. The 1,029 villas are huge and great for groups and families, and most of the villas have full kitchens and are just steps from Kahekili Beach. There's also a fascinating cultural center—the only one of its kind at any Maui resort.

LAHAINA

While there are no large resorts in Lahaina, the town's accommodations range from historic inns and modern condos to a handful of budget options.

Hotels

The **Pioneer Inn** (658 Wharf St., 808/661-3636, www.pioneerinnmaui.com, $267-297) is the oldest hotel on Maui, and it was the only hotel in West Maui until 1963. Now a Best Western hotel, the PI is across the street from Lahaina Harbor and right in the center of the action. Food, drinks, and live music are served downstairs at the popular bar.

Bed-and-Breakfasts

Couples looking for a romantic retreat will love the ★ **Plantation Inn** (174 Lahainaluna Rd., 808/667-9225, www.theplantationinn.com, $194-362), a hidden little pocket of calm that manages to retain its 19th-century charm in otherwise frantic Lahaina. On Lahainaluna Road, just a one-minute walk from Front Street, this 19-room getaway has a swimming pool, included parking and Wi-Fi, and daily maid service. Breakfast is served daily until

9:30am and features French-inspired cuisine from chef Gerard Reversade, whose acclaimed restaurant on the same property gives hotel guests a discount.

Condominiums

The best condo complex in Lahaina is ★ **Puamana** ($224-799), a 28-acre (11-ha) private community on the southern edge of town. There is a sandy beach in front of the complex good for swimming, and a luxurious pool out on a point surrounded by the ocean. There are tennis courts and a beautiful old clubhouse. It's just a 10-minute stroll to central Lahaina. The oceanfront rentals are much nicer than those along the highway, and reservations are available through various West Side rental agents, including **Puamana Vacations** (www.puamanavacations.com).

Right on the water by 505 Front Street, the **Lahaina Shores Beach Resort** (475 Front St., 808/661-4835, www.lahainashores.com, $355-585) is a six-story condo with individually owned units. This is a convenient base to take a surf lesson, stroll down the beach, access Lahaina Harbor, or walk from town.

Smack in the center of town, a block off Front Street, is the 188-room **'Aina Nalu Lahaina** (660 Waine'e St., 808/667-9766, www.outrigger.com, $212-455), a modern condo complex in a garden atmosphere that has the benefit of being right in town. Rooms are spacious and recently renovated, and a swimming pool provides a respite from the heat.

SOUTH OF LAHAINA

Bed-and-Breakfasts

In the residential community of Launiupoko, above the beach park of the same name, the **Ho'oilo House** (138 Awaiku St., 808/667-6669, www.hooilohouse.com, from $369) is one of the most luxurious B&Bs on the island's West Side. The views are toward Lana'i and offer panoramic sunsets on a nightly basis. Everything about this house, from its Thai-inspired architecture to its furnishings and outdoor garden area, says comfort and relaxation. Six suites are decorated in unique style, a continental breakfast is served daily, and guests can make use of the swimming pool and lounge area with a view over the water. Only two adults per room.

Camping

The camping spot with the nicest facilities is **Camp Olowalu** (800 Olowalu Village Rd., 808/661-4303, www.campolowalu.com), with tent spaces ($24 adults, $5 children), and "tentalows" ($140-195) that have beds and outdoor showers. There's a beautiful beach here hidden from the road that consequently isn't very crowded, and it's a convenient option for travelers on a budget who still want a little comfort.

Central Maui

WAILUKU

Bed-and-Breakfasts

The nicest place to stay in historic Wailuku is the ★ **Old Wailuku Inn at Ulupono** (2199 Kaho'okele St., 808/244-5897, www.mauiinn.com, $194-321, 2-night minimum), built in 1924 and listed on the Hawaii Register of Historic Places. The 10 rooms are filled with period furniture that evokes the feeling of Grandma's house. Although it sounds like marketing, this really is Maui's most Hawaiian bed-and-breakfast. Wi-Fi is included, and each room has a private bath. A filling gourmet breakfast is served at 8am daily. Most rooms are set up for double occupancy.

For peace and serenity in 'Iao Valley, the ★ **Iao Valley Inn** (80 'Iao Valley Rd., 808/633-6028, www.iaovalleyinn.com) is a spectacular B&B on 37 lush acres (15 ha), a true sanctuary that's just minutes outside Wailuku. There are two guest rooms ($210-320) and a separate cottage ($235-320) that can sleep up to four.

Hostels

The most affordable places to stay in Wailuku are the two hostels in the funkier, older part of town. While they are by no means a beach resort, they are practical, centrally located, and provide an affordable base for exploring the island. All non-U.S. residents must show a valid passport and a ticket off the island as a prerequisite for booking a bed.

Although it's in a less attractive part of the island, the ★ **Banana Bungalow** (310 N. Market St., 808/244-5090, www.mauihostel.com, $55-162) offers free daily tours—there isn't a more affordable way to experience Maui. And while it's expected that you leave a tip for the guides, that is the only cost for tours to Hana, Haleakala, 'Iao Valley, or Little Beach. Rooms are basic and the garden is relaxing, and if you're looking for a party scene, you'll find it here. Rates are $55 for a dorm bed, $123 for a private single, $138 for a double, and $162 for a triple. Linens are included, towels aren't, and surfers are always welcome.

Closer to the center of Wailuku is **Northshore Hostel** (2080 W. Vineyard St.,

Banana Bungalow

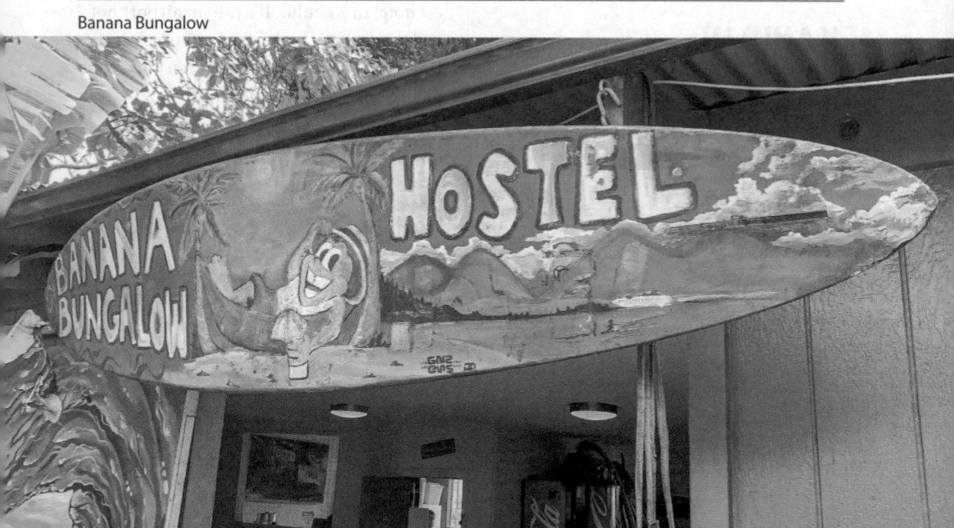

Where to Stay in Central Maui

Name	Type	Price	Features	Why Stay Here?	Best For
★ Banana Bungalow	hostel	$55-162	free tours	affordable	budget travelers
Courtyard Marriott	hotel	$474-569	modern fitness room, swimming pool	location	business travelers
★ Iao Valley Inn	B&B	$210-320	quiet, breakfast	location, affordable	couples
Maui Beach Hotel	hotel	$223-335	airport shuttle	affordable	budget travelers
Northshore Hostel	hostel	$41-112	quiet	affordable	budget travelers
★ Old Wailuku Inn at Ulupono	B&B	$194-321	breakfast, quiet	historic	couples

808/986-8095, $41-112). The rooms are clean, and breakfast, Wi-Fi, airport transfers, shuttles to Kanaha Beach, and linens are all included. There aren't any private baths and rates begin at $41 per person for a shared room and $112 for something more private. It's also within walking distance of Market Street and Wailuku's best restaurants and shops.

KAHULUI

Hotels

A hotel with the name **Maui Beach Hotel** (170 Ka'ahumanu Ave., 808/877-0051, www.mauibeachhotel.net, $223-335) sounds like the epitome of paradise, but here the beach is on the inside of Kahului Harbor, and you're in an industrial part of town. Still, it's a convenient spot just minutes from the airport, and there's an airport shuttle included in the rates.

The **Courtyard Marriott** (532 Keolani Pl., 808/871-1800, $474-569) is the newest and nicest hotel in Kahului. It's just an airport hotel, and the rates are high for an uninspiring view. Nevertheless, the hotel is modern and conveniently located near the airport.

South Maui

South Maui is the island's sunniest area and one of the most popular places for visitors. Ma'alaea and Kihei are dominated by condos, with few hotels or cottages. Wailea offers the island's most luxurious resorts and some moderately priced condos.

MA'ALAEA

Condominiums

The only accommodations in Ma'alaea are condos, all of which are found along Hauoli Street. The benefits of staying in Ma'alaea include the central location within walking distance of Ma'alaea Harbor, the ability to cook your own meals, and some of the most affordable ocean views on the island. **Aloha Island Rentals** (808/280-8226, www.igo-maui.com) has an office at 33 Church Street and manages more than 100 units. All units are fully furnished with complete kitchens, TVs, phones, and a lanai, and each property has a pool and laundry facilities. Rates range $335-535 mid-December-mid-April but drop significantly in summer and fall. Many of the condos have a three-night minimum, or longer during the Christmas holidays. For month-long stays, rates are typically reduced by 10 percent.

KIHEI

Hotels

On the northern edge of South Kihei is the **Maui Coast Hotel** (2259 S. Kihei Rd., 808/874-6284, www.mauicoasthotel.com, $360-512), a 265-room high-rise that is a three-minute walk from the beach. You'll find tennis courts, a fitness room, and a swimming pool. Rooms have air-conditioning. Parking, Wi-Fi, and a resort shuttle around the South Kihei and Wailea area are included.

The most affordable hotel option in South Kihei is the **Days Inn** (2980 S. Kihei Rd., 844/275-2969, www.wyndhamhotels.com/days-inn, $311-417), on the north end of Keawakapu Beach. Rooms are small, there is air-conditioning and a small fridge, and while it might be basic, it's tough to argue with the price, considering the location. Wi-Fi, parking, and outdoor grills are included. Oceanfront suites can reach $417.

In North Kihei, across from Mai Poina 'Oe Ia'u Beach Park, is the **Kohea Kai Maui** (551 S. Kihei Rd., 808/879-1261, www.choicehotels.com, $342-500), featuring 16 rooms in a small and quiet setting. A sundeck with a hot tub is on the roof, there are kitchenettes in the rooms, and laundry facilities are available on-site.

Cottages

On the southern end of Kihei, the ★ **Maui Mango Cottages** (45 Kilohana Dr., phone number provided at booking, www.mauimangocottages.com) are just steps from Keawakapu Beach. The two-bedroom cottage ($195) sleeps 4-5, and the three-bedroom cottage ($295) can accommodate 6. This is as close to Wailea as you can get for these rates. Wailea Beach Walk is a 10-minute stroll from the front door. The cottages have kitchens, and in summer, mangoes dangle from the trees.

On the north end of Kihei, **Nona Lani Cottages** (455 S. Kihei Rd., 808/879-2497 www.nonalanicottages.com, $223-409) has eight cottages in a garden setting. The property is a refreshing throwback to simpler times, and it is across the street from Kalepolepo Beach in North Kihei.

Bed-and-Breakfasts

In North Kihei, the **Ocean Breeze Hideaway** (808/879-0657, www.hawaiibednbreakfast.com, $149-325) is a comfortable and affordable bed-and-breakfast just minutes from Sugar Beach. Included are Wi-Fi, breakfast each morning, and organic fruits in the garden.

Where to Stay in South Maui

Name	Type	Price	Features	Why Stay Here?	Best For
Aloha Island Rentals	condo	$335-535	pool, kitchen, oceanfront	location, amenities	couples, families
★ Andaz Maui	hotel	$829-$2,579	pool, oceanfront	location, amenities	couples, families
Aston Maui Hill	condo	$399-999	pool, kitchen	location, amenities	couples, families
Days Inn	hotel	$311-417	oceanfront, barbecue	affordable, location	budget travelers
Fairmont Kea Lani	resort	$709-2,100	pool, oceanfront	romantic, luxury	families, couples, honeymooners
Four Seasons Resort	resort	$1,070-10,000+	pools, spa, oceanfront	romantic, luxury	couples, honeymooners, luxury-lovers
★ Grand Wailea	resort	$788-2,429	waterslides, spa, oceanfront	romantic, luxury, pools	families, couples, honeymooners
Hale Pau Hana	condo	$310-482	oceanfront, kitchen	location, amenities	couples, families
★ Hotel Wailea	hotel	$466-2,000	pool, spa, amenities	boutique, romantic	couples, luxury-lovers

Condominiums

One of the several condos at the far north end of Kihei is **Maui Sugar Beach Condos** (145 N. Kihei Rd., 808/879-7765, www.mauisugarbeachcondos.com, $210-340), an oceanfront building with individually owned units as well as a swimming pool, spa, and sundries shop. The beach outside is great for a long walk, but afternoons are windy.

Right on the sands of Kamaole II, the **Hale Pau Hana** (2480 S. Kihei Rd., 800/367-6036, www.thehalepauhana.com, $310-482) is one of the best options for condos on the water. Parking and internet access are included, as are grilling facilities, a full kitchen, a swimming pool, and a private lanai in each room. Rates vary by season. This is a good location in a happening part of town.

Within walking distance of Kamaole III, Kihei Boat Ramp, and Keawakapu Beach is the **Aston Maui Hill** (2881 S. Kihei Rd., 808/879-6321, www.aquaaston.com, $399-999), an upbeat condo with a Spanish motif. This quality condo resort is high on a hill and a nice alternative to expensive Wailea. There is a tennis court, swimming pool, putting green, and Wi-Fi, and each room comes equipped with a kitchen. Parking is free and there's no resort fee.

Closer to the water, the eight-story **Mana Kai Maui** (2960 S. Kihei Rd., 808/879-1561, www.manakaimaui.com, $410-760) offers the nicest resort accommodations in South Kihei. This 50-unit complex is on the north end of Keawakapu Beach and offers snorkeling and water activities right out the front

Name	Type	Price	Features	Why Stay Here?	Best For
Kohea Kai Maui	hotel	$342-500	pool, kitchen, oceanfront	location, ocean views	couples, extended stays
Mana Kai Maui	condo	$410-760	kitchen, oceanfront	location, water sports	couples, families
Maui Coast Hotel	hotel	$360-512	pool, fitness center, shuttle	amenities	couples, business travel
★ **Maui Mango Cottages**	cottages	$195-295	kitchen, gardens	location, amenities	couples, families
Maui Sugar Beach Condos	condo	$210-340	pool, kitchen	location	couples, families
Nona Lani Cottages	cottages	$223-409	gardens, kitchenette	quiet, affordable, location	couples
Ocean Breeze Hideaway	B&B	$149-325	gardens, breakfast	quiet, affordable	couples
Wailea Beach Marriott	resort	$789-1,999	pool, spa, luau	oceanfront, watersports	families, couples
★ **Wailea Ekolu Village**	condo	$261-425	kitchen, amenities	location, affordable	couples, families

door. The Five Palms restaurant is one of Kihei's best, and there are full kitchens in the units. Rates can begin at $410 for a standard hotel room and up to $760 for suites with private balconies.

WAILEA

Hotels and Resorts

Wailea hotels are expensive, fancy, and meant to provide indulgence. The northernmost and oldest of the Wailea resorts is the **Wailea Beach Marriott** (3700 Wailea Alanui Dr., 808/879-1922, www.marriott.com, $789-1,999), a 497-room oceanfront property that has been extensively restored. Families will enjoy the large system of pools, and the snorkeling and sand of Ulua Beach is a few steps away. Parking is $40 per day, internet is included in the $35-per-day resort fee, and rates begin around $610 during the slow seasons.

Not far from the Marriott is ★ **Andaz Maui** (3550 Wailea Alanui Dr., 808/573-11234, www.hyatt.com, $829-2,579). This opulent, modern resort fronts the beach and boasts two remarkable pool bars and live music. Grab a lounger on the lawn overlooking the ocean and bliss out. Everything at Andaz, from the service to the dining, stands out.

Directly in front of Wailea Beach are two of Wailea's largest resorts, the sprawling pink ★ **Grand Wailea** (3850 Wailea Alanui Dr., 808/875-1234, www.grandwailea.com, $788-2,429) and the ultra-luxurious **Four Seasons Resort** (3900 Wailea Alanui Dr., 808/874-8000, www.fourseasons.com, $1,070-10,000+).

1

2

While both resorts offer the highest quality, the Grand Wailea is famous for its pool system and the largest corporate art collection in Hawaii. Families will enjoy navigating the waterslides, rope swings, lazy river, and water elevator. In recent years the resort has instituted numerous cultural programs. Next door at the Four Seasons, the pool scene is much more reserved, but the cream villas looking out over the water redefine island luxury. Rooms are expensive and amenities lavish.

Around the southern end of Wailea Point are the twirling white spires of the **Fairmont Kea Lani** (4100 Wailea Alanui Dr., 808/875-4100, www.fairmont.com, $709-2,100), on the sands of Polo Beach. There's no shortage of eye candy here. From your poolside perch, enjoy stunning ocean views, especially at sunset. Anybody seeking romantic luxury will be enamored of the hotel's extravagance and attention to detail. From the minute you step on the property, it's as if you've entered a royal experience.

For a boutique hotel experience rather than an oceanfront mega-resort, the ★ **Hotel Wailea** (555 Kaukahi St., 866/970-4167, www.hotelwailea.com, $466-2,000) is a stunning Relais & Châteaux property. The hillside location provides sunset views from the comfort of a private lanai, and there's a wine social each evening around the exclusive pool. Watch whales jump while you walk on the treadmill, and with only 72 suites on 16 acres (6.5 ha), there's a peaceful garden feel. While it isn't oceanfront, there's a free resort shuttle down to the beach, a three-minute drive.

Condominiums

To be walking distance from the beaches of Wailea without the hefty price tag, look into some of the affordably priced condos on the northern edge of the resort. The ★ **Wailea Ekolu Village** (866/901-0982, www.destinationhotels.com, $261-425) offers one- and two-bedroom condos with included parking and internet, and kitchens. You can often get hefty discounts with advance reservations.

Upcountry

Upcountry is completely free of resorts, different from most Maui experiences. Peace and tranquility replace mai tais and swimming pools, and the cool mountain area is a refreshing change from the sunbaked shores below. Most accommodations are 20 minutes from the beach, although most are also conveniently located within an hour of Haleakala Volcano. Rustic, cool, and blissfully laid-back, Upcountry is where visitors come to relax, although if you plan to scuba dive, you probably shouldn't stay here since many of the accommodations are over 3,000 feet (915 m) elevation. Aside from these listings, there are many accommodations in Upcountry that are small and privately owned, so **VRBO** (www.vrbo.com) and **AirBNB** (www.airbnb.com) are good places to check.

MAKAWAO

Cottages

In the forest above Makawao town are the intimate ★ **Aloha Cottage and Thai Tree House** (808/573-8555, $239-259), two peaceful spots down a quiet country lane off rural Olinda Road. The only neighbors are the horses in the pastures beyond the distant fence. On a 5-acre (2-ha) estate, the Aloha Cottage has a panoramic view from the deck of the octagonal structure. Use the two-person hot tub on the cool Olinda nights, and wake each morning to birdsong from the surrounding forest. Rates vary depending on length of stay, and there is a $100 cleaning fee.

1: pool at the Grand Wailea **2:** Fairmont Kea Lani

Where to Stay in Upcountry

Name	Type	Price	Features	Why Stay Here?	Best For
★ Aloha Cottage and Thai Tree House	cottage	$239-259	hot tub, kitchen, lanai	quiet, peaceful, romantic	couples
Banyan Bed and Breakfast	B&B	$165-225	kitchen, breakfast	quiet, location	couples
G and Z Upcountry Bed and Breakfast	B&B	$149	kitchenette, breakfast	quiet, affordable	budget travelers, couples
★ Hale Ho'okipa Inn	B&B	$145-188	breakfast, garden	quiet, historic	couples
★ Kula Lodge	cottage	$313-384	fireplace, lanai	location, romantic, quiet	couples, hikers
Kula Sandalwoods	cottage	$275-295	lanai, views	quiet, location, retreat	couples
★ Lumeria Maui	retreat	$449-509	yoga classes, garden courtyard	meditative retreat	solo travelers, couples, groups
★ Peace of Maui	inn	$115-255	kitchen	affordable	budget travelers
Polipoli Spring State Recreation Area	camping	$18-100	none	quiet, wilderness	budget travelers, adventure travelers
The Sacred Garden	retreat	from $145	forest setting, labyrinth	meditative retreat	solo travelers, small groups, couples
★ Star Lookout	cottage	$275	kitchen, views	location, quiet, romantic	couples

Bed-and-Breakfasts

Built in 1924 and used by a Portuguese family to raise 13 children, the five-bedroom plantation house ★ **Hale Ho'okipa Inn** (32 Pakani Pl., 808/572-6698, www.maui-bed-and-breakfast.com, $145-188) has been turned into a lovely B&B with bedrooms ($145-168) and a two-bedroom suite ($188) within walking distance of Makawao town. While improvements have been made, it still has the feel of an old-fashioned country home, and the accommodating owners provide tips and insight into Maui life. Organic fruits from the garden are served.

Down the hill 0.5 mile (0.8 km) from Makawao town, the **Banyan Bed and Breakfast** (3265 Baldwin Ave., 808/866-6225, www.bed-breakfast-maui.com, $165-225) is an old plantation bungalow with adjoining cottages that provides laid-back accommodations in a country setting. The complex is shaded by a monkeypod and banyan, with swings hanging from the wide boughs to complete the rural feel. All cottages and suites have kitchens or kitchenettes, breakfast is included, and Makawao town is a short walk away. A variety of group retreats take place here annually.

Down near the intersection of Hali'imaile Road and Baldwin Avenue is the guesthouse ★ **Peace of Maui** (1290 Hali'imaile Rd., 808/572-5045, www.peaceofmaui.com, rooms $115-255), centrally located between Makawao and Pa'ia. Peace of Maui overlooks the pineapple fields, and while the rooms aren't extravagant, they are clean and affordable. Rooms in the main lodge share a kitchen and baths. For a private bath, rent the two-bedroom cottage, which also provides access to the jetted tub.

Retreats

★ **Lumeria Maui** (1813 Baldwin Ave., 808/579-8877, www.lumeriamaui.com, $449-509) is a luxurious, holistic retreat center between Makawao and Pa'ia. Housed in a brilliantly restored plantation building and with its own organic garden, Lumeria focuses on educational vacation experiences with rejuvenation and wellness. All 24 rooms are decorated differently, and Asian accents punctuate the courtyard. Lumeria is popular for yoga retreats, and there are regularly scheduled classes and workshops.

The Sacred Garden (560 Kaluanui Rd., 808/573-7700, www.sacredgardenmaui.com, from $145) offers personalized private and small group retreats in a lush Upcountry forest setting with outdoor meditation spaces. The grounds include a studio cottage and a five-bedroom log house, which Jimi Hendrix reportedly slept in during the filming of *Rainbow Bridge*. The lodging is adjacent to the property's stunning garden center, which hosts a large outdoor labyrinth near a creek.

KULA

Cottages

The ★ **Kula Lodge** (15200 Haleakala Hwy., 808/878-1535, www.kulalodge.com, $313-384) is Upcountry's most popular option. On Highway 377 at 3,200 feet (975 m) elevation, the air is crisp, cool, and more comfortable than on the coast. There are five detached chalets, and all feature private lanais and electric fireplaces. The rustic yet comfortable setting makes a perfect base for visiting Haleakala Crater.

Just up the road, the **Kula Sandalwoods** (15427 Haleakala Hwy., 808/878-3523, www.

Kula Lodge

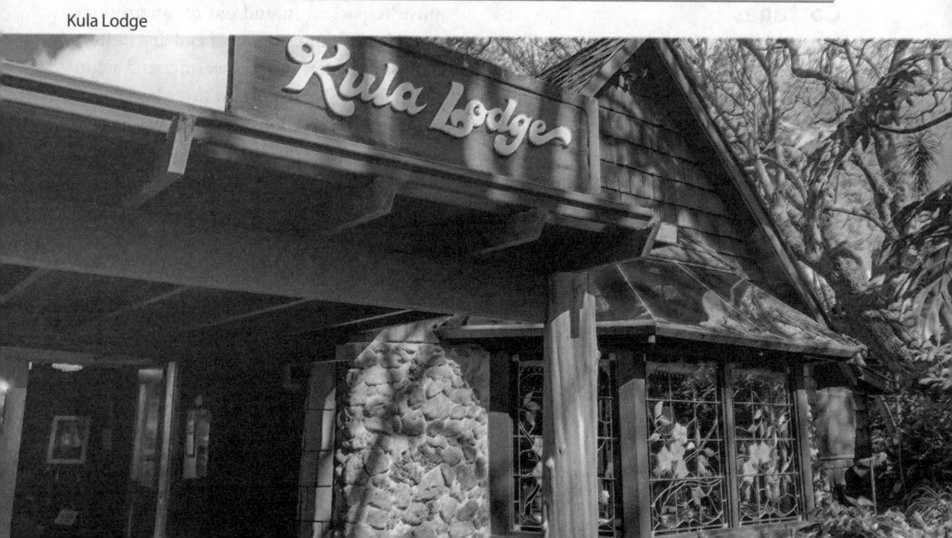

kulasandalwoods.com, $275-295) is another Kula classic that is far more laid-back than its popular neighbor. These stand-alone cottages are on a hillside and offer sweeping views of the island's central valley. Wi-Fi and morning coffee are included; the cottages are otherwise free of appliances. The summit of Haleakala is only a 45-minute drive from this location at 3,300 feet (1,000 m) elevation.

Bed-and-Breakfasts

Out by the Kula Country Farms stand, where Highway 377 meets Highway 37, **G and Z Upcountry Bed and Breakfast** (60 Kekaulike Ave., 808/224-6824, www.gandzmaui.com, $149) is on a beautiful 6-acre (2.4-ha) farm with exceptionally welcoming owners. John and Marsha have lived on Maui since the 1960s and can tell you every tidbit about the island. The B&B has a separate entrance, a king bed, and a queen sofa bed. There's a barbecue grill on the private lanai you can use while watching the sunset. Upcountry fruit is served with each morning's breakfast, and Haleakala Crater is under an hour away. There is a $25-per-child surcharge up to a maximum of two children.

KEOKEA AND ULUPALAKUA

Cottages

For rural tranquility in a cool Upcountry setting, the ★ **Star Lookout** (622 Thompson Rd., 907/250-2364, www.starlookout.com, $275, 2-night minimum) is on Thompson Road just minutes from Grandma's Coffee House. This single cottage is a ranch-style retreat with views over the Keokea pastureland to the South Maui shore. From the "Star Bed," fall asleep gazing out at the stars through the enormous picture window. Advance reservations are required as it's Upcountry's most desirable spot.

Camping

The rugged can camp in **Polipoli Spring State Recreation Area** (permits 808/984-8109 or www.dlnr.hawaii.gov, $18). The dirt road to the campground requires a 4WD vehicle. You can also book a backcountry wilderness cabin ($100); permits are issued by phone.

HALEAKALA NATIONAL PARK

Spending a night in Haleakala Crater is a unique adventure on Maui. Cold, arid, and beneath a blanket of stars, it's a backcountry trip you'd never expect on a tropical island. The warmest and most accessible campsite is **Hosmer's Grove,** at 6,800 feet (2,070 m) elevation as you enter the park. No permit is necessary for camping at Hosmer's Grove, and you can drive to the campground. Barbecues and toilets are available.

For the three backcountry campsites, you have to obtain a free permit and watch a short safety video at **Park Headquarters** (808/572-4400, 8am-4pm daily). All gear must be packed in and out on an arduous trail. **Holua** campsite is cold and dry, **Paliku** campsite is a few degrees warmer and set in a lush forest. There are also three backcountry cabins (reservations: www.recreation.gov, $75) with basic cooking facilities and bunk beds. Reservations for cabins are required about six months in advance.

East Maui

PA'IA AND HA'IKU

Inns

In the center of town, the ★ **Pa'ia Inn** (93 Hana Hwy., 808/579-6000, www.paiainn.com, $299-1,999) is a trendy and chic boutique hotel steps from the beaches of Pa'ia. The decor has a dark-wood Balinese tone, and each individually designed room offers a luxurious private getaway in the middle of Pa'ia's bustle.

Right on Kuau Cove, ★ **The Inn at Mama's Fish House** (799 Poho Pl., 800/860-4852, www.mamasfishhouse.com, adults only, $395-850) is an impossibly romantic boutique hotel in one of the North Shore's best settings. The suites, studios, and cottages feature amenities such as full kitchens, maid service, and 15 percent off at the restaurant. The real perk, however, is the location, as there's nothing like staying where people lust over the dinner.

Bed-and-Breakfasts

Up in Ha'iku, **Maui Tradewinds** (4320 Une Pl., 808/573-0066, www.mauitradewinds.com, from $279) is only 10 minutes' drive to the beaches in Pa'ia but is secluded, quiet, and has sweeping views of the island's North Shore. Rates decrease with the length of stay, and there is a $100 cleaning fee.

Vacation Rentals

Tucked away in Spreckelsville and within walking distance of Baby Beach, **Sprecks Plantation House** (phone number provided at booking, www.sprecksplantationhouse.com, $140-220) is an affordable option on the outskirts of trendy Pa'ia. Rooms are basic, very clean, and arranged in a single-level apartment style. Windsurfers can even ride a bike to Kanaha and Kite Beach in under 20 minutes.

Retreats

Hale Akua Garden Farm & Eco-Retreat Center (110 Door of Faith Rd., 808/572-9300, www.haleakua.org, $402-960) is less than a mile (1.6 km) from Twin Falls, near the start of the Road to Hana's winding route. The lush rainforest setting, which overlooks the vibrant Hana coast and nearby waterfalls, is ideal for walks and self-reflection. Group retreats—whose themes might range from couples intimacy to nonviolent communication—are scheduled in advance; check the website for dates. Solo retreats are also encouraged. If your room doesn't include a kitchen, there is access to one in the main clubhouse, adjacent to a dreamy saltwater pool, hot tub, and outdoor massage area.

Hostels

A short walk above Pa'ia, the **Aloha Surf Hostel** (221 Baldwin Ave., 808/868-0117, www.alohasurfhostel.com) offers dorm rooms ($49) or private rooms ($129-164). There is a communal kitchen and Wi-Fi is included, and the hostel offers free daily tours.

ROAD TO HANA

Vacation Rentals

In Huelo you'll find the ★ **Huelo Point Lookout** (800/871-8645, www.mauivacationrentals.com, $270-425), a collection of five vacation rentals in a lush and heavenly section of the island, not for the resort-loving crowd. These five separate vacation rentals provide sweeping views of the Huelo coast and are a place to escape from it all. There is no beach outside your door, but there is a blanket of stars every night and outdoor hot tubs from which to enjoy them. Those traveling with a group could also book the entire Lookout House, which features a large kitchen and an outdoor hot tub ($3,150-4,158 per week).

Where to Stay in East Maui

Name	Type	Price	Features	Why Stay Here?	Best For
Ala'aina Ocean Vista	B&B	$248-258	gardens, hot tub, barbecue	quiet, peaceful	couples
Aloha Surf Hostel	hostel	$49-164	kitchen	affordable, location	budget travelers
★ **Bamboo Inn**	B&B	$245-335	ocean-view lanai, breakfast	location, romantic	couples
Haleakala National Park: Kipahulu	camping	$25	pit toilets, barbecue	location, affordable	budget travelers
Hale Akua Garden Farm & Eco-Retreat Center	retreat	$402-960	ocean views, saltwater pool, hot tub	meditative retreat	solo travelers, groups
Hana Inn	inn	$175-196	kitchen	location, affordable	budget travelers
Hana Kai Maui Resort	condo	$365-465	kitchen, lanai, oceanfront	location, quiet	couples

HANA

The east end of the island is another place where booking engines like **VRBO** (www.vrbo.com) display many privately owned options that don't have formal websites.

Resorts

★ **Hana-Maui Resort** (5031 Hana Hwy., 808/400-1234, www.hyatt.com, $584-1,264), the nicest place in Hana, is a luxurious compound featuring dynamic ocean views from many of its rooms. It's right in the center of town and was the island's first resort hotel when it opened in 1946. Since that time it has continued as the island's best resort in various iterations. Amenities include tennis courts, a swimming pool, a fitness center, spa, several restaurants, and meeting rooms. The resort has Wi-Fi but no TVs, as you're supposed to unwind, relax, untether, and breathe.

Inns

Formerly Joe's Rentals, the budget-friendly and basic **Hana Inn** (4870 Uakea Rd., 808/248-7033, www.hanainn.com, $175-196) is close to Hana Bay and walking distance from the center of town. This home has been split into eight guest rooms, with shared or private bath. There's kitchen access, a communal TV room, and daily towel change, but if a little dirt and the occasional bug bother you, you might want to look elsewhere.

Bed-and-Breakfasts

Closer to town, the funky, ultra-relaxing ★ **Bamboo Inn** (808/248-7718, www.bambooinn.com, $245-335) offers three oceanfront rooms that look out over the water toward Waikoloa Beach. A thatched-roof hut serves as the centerpiece for the property. The owner, John, is a wealth of information on Hana history and culture, and this is a

Name	Type	Price	Features	Why Stay Here?	Best For
★ Hana-Maui Resort	hotel	$584-$1,264	ocean views	location, romantic	couples, families
Hana Retreat Ala Kukui	retreat	$310-1,500	ocean views, meeting rooms	meditative retreat	solo travelers, groups
★ Huelo Point Lookout	vacation rental	$270-425	hot tub, ocean view	location, quiet, peaceful	couples
★ The Inn at Mama's Fish House	inn	$395-850	kitchens, oceanfront	location, romantic	couples, honeymooners
Maui Tradewinds	B&B	from $279	lanai, kitchen	quiet, romantic	couples, honeymooners
★ Pa'ia Inn	inn	$299-1,999	oceanfront, gardens	location, boutique	couples
Sprecks Plantation House	vacation rental	$140-220	kitchenette	affordable, location	budget travelers, couples

modern, soothing place to fall asleep to the crash of the waves. Wi-Fi is available in the courtyard, and breakfast is included.

Condominiums

The **Hana Kai Maui Resort** (4865 Uakea Rd., 800/346-2772, www.hanakaimaui.com, $365-465) is the only condo in Hana. The 18 rental units are well maintained and offer a lot for the price, especially considering the condo is near the sands of Hana Bay.

Retreats

Hana Retreat Ala Kukui (4224 Hana Hwy., 808/248-7841, www.alakukui.org, $310-1,500) rests on a sloping hillside in Hana, overlooking the majestic eastern shoreline. Solo and group retreats happen here, and with no Wi-Fi and limited cell service, visitors have the opportunity to regroup without distractions. What stands out is that the property encourages visitors to learn about Hawaiian cultural practices from local *kumus* (teachers) on-site. In addition to many open-land spaces on the property, there are several meeting rooms available for groups.

KIPAHULU

Bed-and-Breakfasts

One of the best parts of staying in Kipahulu is waking in the morning and having the Pools of 'Ohe'o virtually all to yourself. One of the most peaceful accommodations in this area is the **Ala'aina Ocean Vista** (808/248-7824, www.hanabedandbreakfast.com, $248-258, plus $63 cleaning fee), a tropical bed-and-breakfast on 4 lush acres (1.6 ha) that is the exact opposite of the Ka'anapali resort experience. Birds chirp in the nearby treetops, there is a barbecue area for those who want to cook their own dinner, and a large assortment of various fruit trees sustain the daily breakfast. The bamboo forest of the Pipiwai Trail is only a short walk away. This is a romantic getaway

Kipahulu Campground

set out in the country for those who just want to unwind. Directions to the location are provided at booking.

Camping

Some of Maui's best camping is in the **Kipahulu Campground** ($25 per vehicle) of Haleakala National Park. There are few things better than falling asleep to the sound of crashing surf, then waking in the morning to walk to the pools before anyone else has arrived. There are pit toilets at the campground and grassy campsites. The best sites are hidden beneath *lauhala* trees on the trail leading toward the pools. Rates for camping also cover the entrance fee to the national park. If you didn't pack camping gear, contact **Hana Camp Gear** (800/332-4022, www.hanacampgear.wordpress.com), or consider heading to Hana in an old VW camper bus you can rent at **Aloha Campers** (855/671-1122, www.mauicamperrental.com, from $89).

Lana'i

It's hard to find an outdoor playground more

stunning than Lana'i, home to a mere 3,500 residents and crisscrossed by just 30 miles (48 km) of paved roads.

The late 1980s saw this island's cash crop transition from the world's largest pineapple plantation to high-end tourism. With the construction of the luxurious Four Seasons Resort, the island instantly became one of Hawaii's most exclusive getaways. In 2012, Oracle CEO Larry Ellison purchased 98 percent of the island, and while a range of projects, including a winery, a college, and a tennis center, has been discussed for the tiny island, as of yet the largest change has been the spectacular renovations of the Four Seasons Resort, comprised of two

Highlights

Look for ★ to find recommended sights, activities, dining, and lodging.

★ View everything from wooden spears used in ancient battles to old photographs of Lana'i's plantation days at the **Lana'i Culture and Heritage Center** (page 293).

★ Take in an otherworldly landscape at **Keahiakawelo (Garden of the Gods),** dotted with red boulders that appear to have fallen from the sky (page 293).

★ Get an idea of what life on Lana'i must have been like a century ago at **Keomoku Village,** a coastal ghost town with a haunting abandoned church (page 293).

★ Visit **Kaunolu Village,** a complex that was once the home of King Kamehameha I, virtually untouched since the 19th century (page 296).

★ Snap a photo at picturesque **Hulopo'e Beach Park,** which has the island's best **snorkeling** when the ocean is calm and its best **surf** on a southern swell (page 298).

★ Escape to what feels like the end of the earth at **Polihua Beach** on the island's northern coast—this is the place to make the only set of footprints in the sand (page 301).

★ Hike the 12.8-mile (20.6-km) **Munro Trail,** which winds to the island's 3,370-foot (1,027-m) summit (page 305).

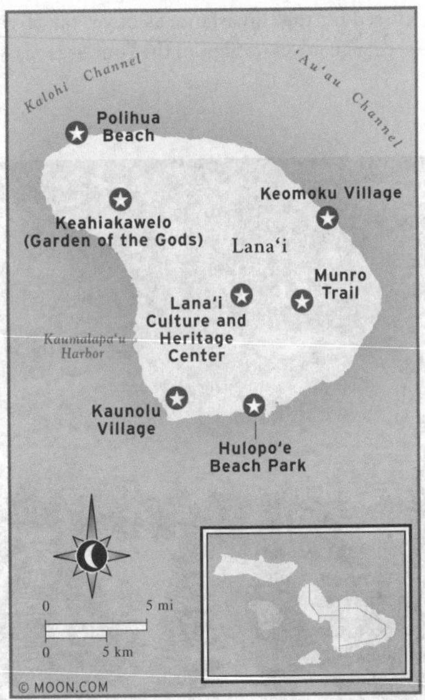

Lana'i

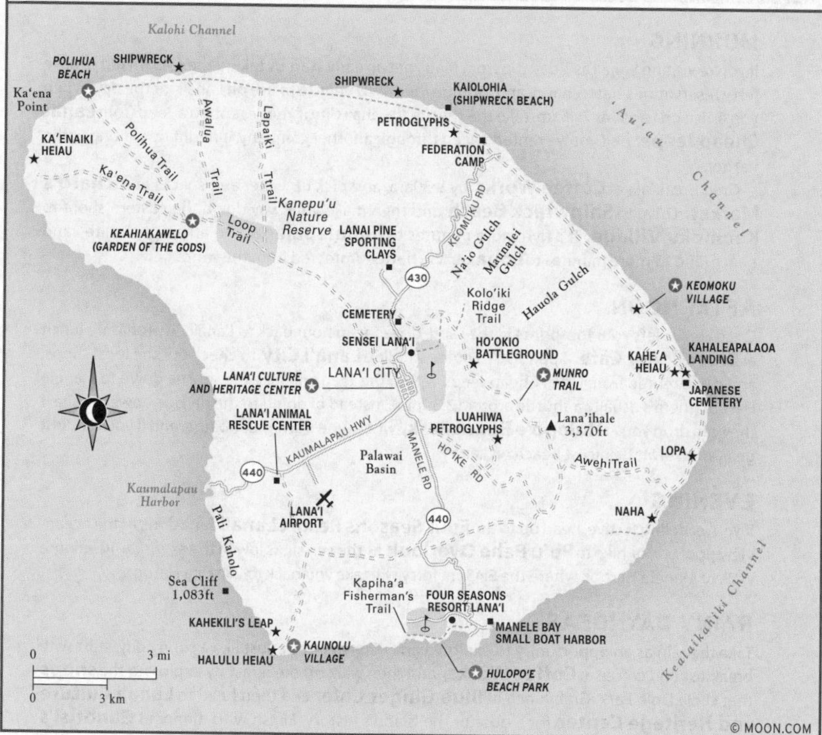

hotels, one on the Manele waterfront and one inland called Sensei Lana'i.

Resort life aside, visitors come to enjoy the snorkeling at Hulopo'e Beach Park, and the plantation-era charm of cozy Lana'i City—the island's only town. Choose to explore a little deeper, however, with morning hikes on pine-shrouded mountain trails, off-roading through otherworldly moonscapes, and surfing empty waves along an empty beach.

Lana'i is an island of unparalleled luxury, but it's also about 4WD trucks with deer skulls mounted to the bumper, aging Filipino plantation workers "talking story" in Dole Park, and petroglyphs scattered across rock faces that predate any of the island's modern history. It's a tight-knit community where townsfolk greet each other with first names and a smile.

ORIENTATION

The island's only town, **Lana'i City,** is in the middle of the island at about 1,700 feet (520 m) elevation, 20 minutes from **Manele Harbor** and the **Four Seasons Resort Lana'i** and about 10 minutes from the **Lana'i Airport.** The inland wellness resort **Sensei Lana'i,** located less than 1 mile (1.6 km) northeast of Lana'i City, is also about 10 minutes from the airport. **Hulopo'e Beach Park** is a 10-minute walk from the harbor, and with the

Previous: Lana'i countryside; Hulopo'e Beach Park; Keahiakawelo (Garden of the Gods).

Your Best Day on Lana'i

MORNING

If you're visiting Lana'i as a day trip from Maui, get an early start by taking the 6:45am ferry. Make ferry reservations beforehand, and arrange for a 4WD vehicle to use on Lana'i for the day. When you arrive on Lana'i at 7:45am, take the shuttle to Lana'i City if you're renting a Jeep from **Lanai Cheap Jeeps,** or if you've rented a Jeep through another company, it might be waiting at the harbor.

Grab breakfast at **Coffee Works** by 8:30am, and pick up water and snacks at **Richard's Market.** Drive to **Shipwreck Beach** and then make your way down the eastern shore to **Keomoku Village.** It's five more minutes to **Kahalepalaoa** and an empty white-sand beach, and 15 more minutes to **Lopa** beach, better protected from the wind.

AFTERNOON

Once you've left your footprints in the sand, drive for an hour back to Lana'i City for a late lunch at **Blue Ginger Cafe.** Spend 30 minutes strolling **Lana'i City** to check out the local shops, and if you rented from Lanai Cheap Jeeps, return the Jeep and take the shuttle down to Manele Harbor (there's usually a shuttle around 3:30pm). Instead of going to the harbor, however, see if they can drop you at **Hulopo'e Beach Park,** where you'll swim, sunbathe, and if you brought gear, snorkel at the nicest beach on Lana'i.

EVENING

If you're feeling festive, head up to the **Four Seasons Resort Lana'i** for a drink at the ocean-view pool bar, or hike to **Pu'u Pehe Overlook** as the sun sinks low in the sky. It's a 10-minute walk to Manele Harbor, where the 6:45pm ferry will take you back to Lahaina Harbor.

RAINY DAY IDEAS

Take the rain as an opportunity to explore Lana'i City in depth. Just like a sunny day, start with breakfast and coffee at **Coffee Works,** and then walk off breakfast by exploring the **shops** that circle Dole Park. Grab lunch at **Blue Ginger Cafe,** and then head to **Lana'i Culture and Heritage Center** for a dose of the island's history. Finish with dinner at **Ganotisi's Pacific Rim Cuisine.**

exception of the restaurants and shops at the Four Seasons Resort Lana'i, all of the island's stores and facilities are in Lana'i City. The rest of the island is a network of dirt roads perfect for off-road exploring, with many sights 45 minutes to an hour outside Lana'i City.

PLANNING YOUR TIME

Most people visit Lana'i as a day trip from Maui. If you take the 6:45am ferry from Lahaina Harbor, you have 8-10 hours to explore the island before catching the ferry back. You'll have enough time to visit Hulopo'e Beach and do some snorkeling, hiking, and sunbathing, as well as time to rent a Jeep and explore the island's east shore. (Book the Jeep about two months prior to your stay.) If you spend a couple of nights on Lana'i, you'll have enough time to explore the island's remote and isolated spots and still be able to relax and enjoy the island's slow pace.

Sights

★ LANA'I CULTURE AND HERITAGE CENTER

There's no better place to learn about the history of Lana'i than at the **Lana'i Culture and Heritage Center** (730 Lana'i Ave., 808/565-7177, www.lanaichc.org, hours vary, check website for updates, free). In a building adjacent to the Hotel Lana'i, the exceptionally informative little museum features displays pertaining to the days of ancient Hawaii through the end of the Dole plantation. Black-and-white photos from Lana'i's ranching days are joined by stone adzes, poi pounders, and a 10-foot (3-m) *'ihe pololu* wooden spear used as a weapon similar to a jousting lance. More than just a collection of historical photos and artifacts, the center also highlights how the culture of Lana'i has been influenced by historic events.

KANEPU'U PRESERVE

Six miles (9.7 km) down Polihua Road, just before reaching Keahiakawelo (Garden of the Gods), **Kanepu'u Preserve** is the only remaining dryland forest of its kind in Hawaii. Thanks to a fence erected in 1918 by Lana'i Ranch manager George Munro, this 590-acre (240 ha) preserve is home to 48 species of native Hawaiian plants that covered most of the island prior to the arrival of the invasive *kiawe* (mesquite) tree and root-destroying goats and sheep. Managed by The Nature Conservancy, the preserve features a short, self-guided trail where visitors can see native hardwoods such as *lama* (Hawaiian ebony) and *olopua* (Hawaiian olive). The trail only takes about 15 minutes to walk, and it makes a nice stop before exploring the Garden of the Gods.

★ KEAHIAKAWELO (GARDEN OF THE GODS)

Although we've successfully put a rover on Mars, **Keahiakawelo** is the closest most of us will ever get to walking on the red planet. Despite being only 7 miles (11.3 km) from the pine-lined streets of Lana'i City, the Garden of the Gods looks like a moonscape. Erosion created ravines and rock spires in deep reds, purples, and sulfuric yellows. The best time to visit this dry, dusty, and often windswept area is at sunset, when the rich palette of color is enhanced by the afternoon light.

Keahiakawelo is almost completely devoid of vegetation, but the strangest part of the panorama is the expanse of boulders that tumble over the barren hillside. It's unclear how they got here, but the ancient Hawaiians had a number of theories. According to legend, the rocks were dropped by gods as they tended their heavenly gardens, providing the site's English name, Garden of the Gods.

Keahiakawelo remains a must-see for its consuming sense of seclusion. The road here can be rutted and rough, and a 4WD vehicle is needed if you're visiting after a heavy rain. To reach the site, take a left just after the Sensei Lana'i resort and travel 7 miles (11.3 km) on Polihua Road, taking the right at the fork after the Stables at Koele.

KA'ENA IKI HEIAU

On the dusty stretch of road between Keahiakawelo and Polihua Beach, a side road branches off to the left and leads to the island's westernmost promontory, Ka'ena Point. The deep waters off Ka'ena make this a favorite among islanders for fishing. The main reason to venture down Ka'ena Trail, however, is to see **Ka'ena Iki Heiau,** a large stone platform constructed in the 17th century and the largest remaining *heiau* (temple) on Lana'i. It doesn't take long to explore the area around the *heiau*, but it makes a nice side trip.

★ KEOMOKU VILLAGE

There isn't much to see in the abandoned village of **Keomoku,** but driving through

& HERITAGE CENTER
1
2
3
4

The Myth of the "Private Island"

A pesky myth needs to be dispelled: Lana'i is not a private island. It's true that the island has historically had only one main landowner, and today 98 percent of the island is owned by Oracle CEO Larry Ellison. However, the state of Hawaii retains ownership of certain parcels, such as the Manele Small Boat Harbor, and many local families own their own homes. You do not need to ask permission from the primary landowner to come here. There is a public airport and regular ferry service, and there are 3,500 full-time residents.

Imagine that you live in a neighborhood where there are 100 homes and you somehow manage to buy 98 of them. You still live in a neighborhood that's in a U.S. state and subject to its laws. Even on a mostly private island, you can't just do whatever you want. There are police officers, firefighters, a public school, a county council member, and myriad laws that apply. Under Hawaii state law, all shores from the ocean up to the line of vegetation are for public use. Consequently there is no such thing as a private beach in Hawaii. On this "private island," anyone can freely walk the shore.

this coastal ghost town provides a feeling of Lana'i's recent past. It also makes a great stop if you are heading out to the beach at Lopa.

Before the arrival of Europeans, it's believed there were thousands of indigenous Hawaiians living along Lana'i's eastern shore. *Heiau* were constructed as places of worship, and petroglyphs such as those found at Kaiolohia depict basic scenes from this ancient time. By the time Frederick Hayselden chose Keomoku as the site for his Maunalei Sugar Company in 1899, however, the island's population had dwindled to fewer than 200. Water was routed from Maunalei Valley, a locomotive was installed to move cargo, and Keomoku bustled like any other Hawaiian plantation town. Problems arose when the water turned brackish, and the supply at Maunalei quickly dried up.

In one of the state's shortest-lived sugar ventures, the Maunalei Sugar Company closed in 1901 after only two years in operation. Indigenous Hawaiians living in the area attribute the company's demise to the stones from ancient *heiau* being used in constructing the plantation. This, it would seem, did not sit well with Hawaiian deities. In 1951 the last resident of Keomoku—Daniel Kaopuiki—begrudgingly moved his family into the uplands, and Keomoku, once the pulse of the island of Lana'i, was officially abandoned.

Keomoku remains abandoned, and there are a couple of places where you can see the remnants of its past. Driving the sandy 4WD road through the former plantation town is a tour through Lana'i's history. Simple beachfront fishing shacks dot the sandy road, their yards ringed with fishing nets.

The number-one attraction in Keomoku is **Ka Lanakila Church,** 5.5 miles (8.9 km) from where the pavement ends on Keomoku Highway. The hauntingly beautiful wooden structure was constructed in 1903 to house a Hawaiian-speaking congregation. Abandoned for years, the church is currently in the process of being restored, and special sermons are still intermittently conducted in Hawaiian throughout the year.

Behind the church, a small trail leads for 10 minutes to remains of the Maunalei Sugar Mill, and across the street, a trail passes through the coconut grove to the wooden Lahaina passenger boat that has sat in the mud for more than a century. A small shrine 1.5 miles (2.4 km) past the church honors the Japanese field laborers who died on Lana'i in the few short years of the sugar plantation's existence, and 0.5 mile (0.8 km) beyond the shrine is the abandoned pier at Kahalepalaoa, which offers good fishing and sweeping views of neighboring Maui.

1: Lana'i Culture and Heritage Center **2:** a resident of the Lana'i Cat Sanctuary **3:** Ka Lanakila Church **4:** rugged Keahiakawelo

LUAHIWA PETROGLYPHS

The good thing about the **Luahiwa Petroglyphs** is they are only 10 minutes from Lana'i City and accessible with a regular car. The bad part is they have been permanently scarred by modern graffiti, and they no longer resemble the rock art they once were. There are nearly 1,000 drawings at Luahiwa, and stepping from one rock to another reveals different tales emblazoned on the out-of-place boulder formations. While 95 percent of the drawings date before Western contact, some etchings, such as those featuring horses, suggest that the petroglyphs are a multigenerational canvas that records Lana'i's varied history.

To reach the Luahiwa Petroglyphs, head south on Manele Road from Lana'i City as if you're driving down toward Hulopo'e Beach Park. After 1.5 miles (2.4 km), turn left at a small building on the left side of the road. When you find a locked gate, proceed to the dirt road that immediately parallels it on the left side. Head down this road for 0.7 mile (1.1 km) until you reach a Y-junction, at which point you go left again. After 0.3 mile (0.5 km), make an extreme right turn, almost doubling back the way you came, up onto a higher road. If you're unsure if this is the correct turn, look for a rock just after the intersection that has the name "Luahiwa Petroglyphs" emblazoned on it facing the opposite direction. Proceed for 0.4 mile (0.6 km) on the upper road until you reach another rock that says "Luahiwa," and park in the small dirt pullout. The petroglyphs are on the large boulders at the base of the hill, and a 30-second scramble through the bushes will bring you face-to-face with the ancient rock carvings.

★ KAUNOLU VILLAGE

Kaunolu is difficult to reach, but it is a historically significant place, and its isolation has kept it undeveloped and virtually untouched. Follow Highway 440 south from Lana'i City. Just past the airport turnoff is a large boulder inscribed with "Kaunolu." Turn left on the smooth, dusty road, accessible to any vehicle provided it hasn't rained heavily. After 2 miles (3.2 km) is a historical marker and another sign pointing toward Kaunolu. Make a right down this road, which is steep, eroded, and rough. Lanai Cheap Jeeps allows its Jeeps to go to the top of the road but not all the way to the bottom. To reach the bottom, you can chance it with the Jeep and hope for the best, procure a private vehicle that has no restrictions, or drive until the road gets too rough and then get out and walk, which is probably the best option. It's 3 miles (4.8 km) from here to the shore.

At the bottom of the road is a Y-junction. The road to the left leads to a set of fishing shacks used by locals who come to drink beer and fish, but turn right instead. The road abruptly ends at a wooden picnic table beneath a tree, marking the entrance to Kaunolu. This shore was home to a thriving population from the 15th century until it was abandoned in the late 19th century. Notice that except for the wind and the waves, Kaunolu is completely silent.

The sandy ravine fronting the beach is the only successful canoe launch between here and Hulopo'e. To reach the remains of the ancient canoe *hale* (house), look for a trail that leads down the hill from where the road ends. After a rocky scramble to the dry riverbed, follow the trail toward the water, passing some petroglyphs. An interpretive placard points out the canoe *hale*. This is the base of the Halulu *heiau*, a place of worship and of immense cultural significance to indigenous Hawaiians. It's also the best-preserved *heiau* on Lana'i.

The trail bends to the right as it climbs up from the rocks, eventually crossing a footbridge toward the top of the *heiau*. Up the short hill is a Y-junction. Go left to find petroglyphs in the rocks, or go right to a viewpoint of the Kaholo Pali sea cliffs, the highest on Lana'i, with some over 1,000 feet (300 m). A notch in the cliff here is labeled Kahekili's Leap. Kahekili was a fearless warrior chief from the late 18th century, with half his body tattooed black, eyelids and tongue included.

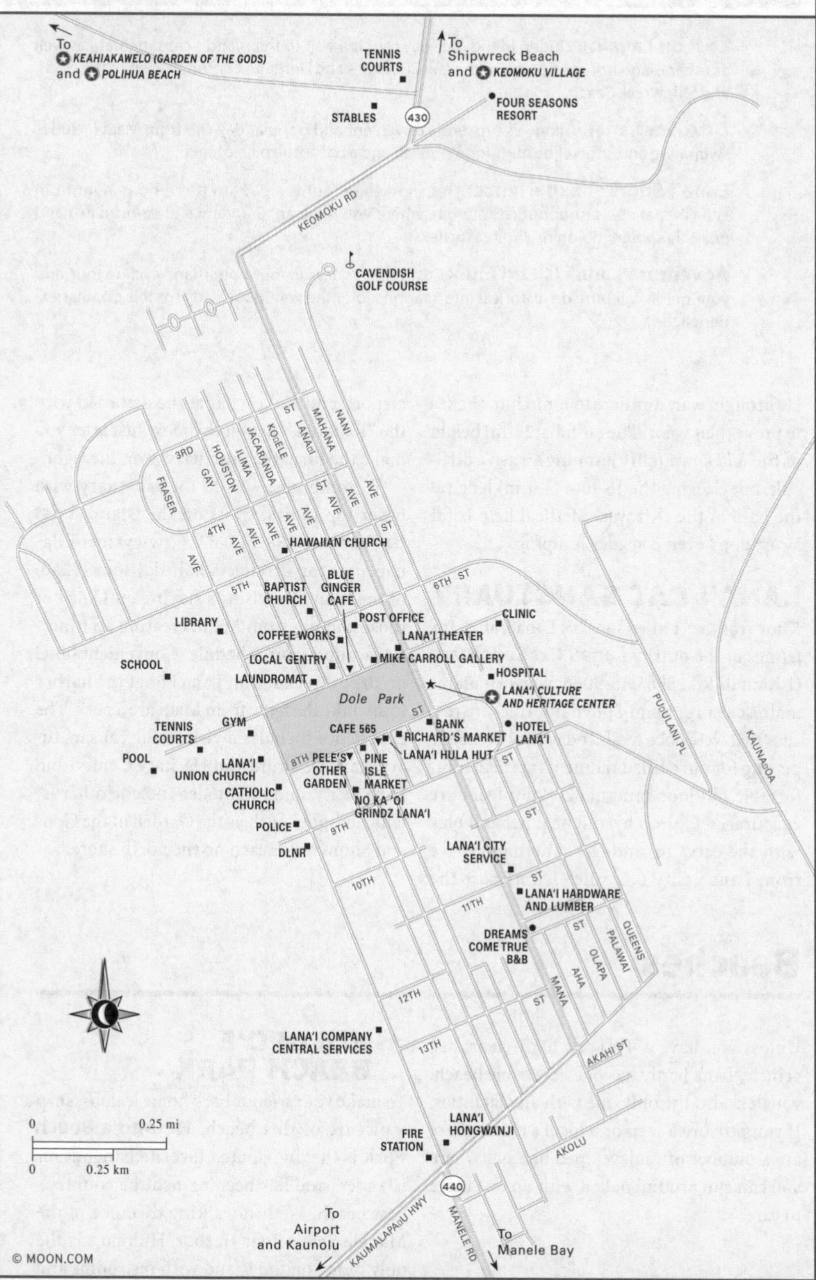
Lana'i City
To
KEAHIAKAWELO (GARDEN OF THE GODS)
and POLIHUA BEACH
TENNIS COURTS
To
Shipwreck Beach
and KEOMOKU VILLAGE
STABLES
430
FOUR SEASONS RESORT
KEOMOKU RD
CAVENDISH GOLF COURSE
3RD
FRASER
GAY
HOUSTON
ILIMA
JACARANDA
KOʻELE
LANAʻI
MAHANA
NANI
ST
AVE
4TH
5TH
6TH ST
HAWAIIAN CHURCH
BAPTIST CHURCH
BLUE GINGER CAFE
LIBRARY
POST OFFICE
CLINIC
COFFEE WORKS
LANA'I THEATER
SCHOOL
LOCAL GENTRY
MIKE CARROLL GALLERY
LAUNDROMAT
HOSPITAL
LANA'I CULTURE AND HERITAGE CENTER
Dole Park
GYM
TENNIS COURTS
CAFE 565
BANK
RICHARD'S MARKET
HOTEL LANA'I
POOL
LANA'I UNION CHURCH
8TH
PELE'S OTHER GARDEN
PINE ISLE MARKET
LANA'I HULA HUT
CATHOLIC CHURCH
NO KA 'OI GRINDZ LANA'I
POLICE
9TH
DLNR
LANA'I CITY SERVICE
10TH
LANA'I HARDWARE AND LUMBER
11TH
DREAMS COME TRUE B&B
PUʻULANI PL
KAUNAʻOA
QUEENS
PALAWAI
OLAPA
AHA
MANA
12TH
13TH
LANA'I COMPANY CENTRAL SERVICES
AKAHI ST
LANA'I HONGWANJI
FIRE STATION
AKOLU
440
0 0.25 mi
0 0.25 km
To Airport and Kaunolu
KAUMALAPAʻU HWY
MANELE RD
To Manele Bay
© MOON.COM

Best Tours of Lana'i

- **Lost on Lana'i:** Included in this half-day tour is a visit to the island's cat sanctuary as well as other island hot spots, such as the Lana'i Culture and Heritage Center, Garden of the Gods, and Shipwreck Beach.
- **Discover Lanai:** Trilogy Excursions' convenient and popular day trip from Maui includes swimming and snorkeling at Hulopo'e Beach and a barbecue picnic lunch.
- **Lana'i Snorkel Experience:** This snorkeling tour is a two- to three-hour jaunt from Lana'i's Manele Harbor out to Kaunolu, where you'll see an abundance of colorful fish and possibly spinner dolphins and sea turtles.
- **Adventure Lana'i Island Club:** Customize your own four-hour island cycling tour, and your guide will provide historical information along the way. Book early for this popular experience.

He brought warriors here to jump into the sea to prove their valor. The 80-foot (24-m) height of the *lele kawa* (cliff jumping) wasn't difficult, but clearing the 15-foot (4.5-m) ledge at the base of the cliff was. Medical help is far away; don't even consider jumping.

LANA'I CAT SANCTUARY

Known as the "Little Lions" of Lana'i, all of the felines at the quirky **Lana'i Cat Sanctuary** (1 Kaupili Rd., 808/215-9066, www.lanaianimalrescue.org, 10am-3pm daily, free) are rescues that were once feral. Today they exchange petting for purr-filled moments at their comfortable outdoor sanctuary. Volunteers are encouraged to drop by and help pet and play with the cats. To find the sanctuary, drive from Lana'i City 0.6 mile (1 km) past the airport, and make a left at the dirt road with the "Kaunolu" sign on the rock. Just after you make the turn, the sanctuary is on the right.

To combine a visit to the sanctuary with other top tourist spots on the island, **Lost on Lana'i** (888/716-6336, www.lostonlanai.com) can arrange a half-day tour ($260) of the island for visitors staying on Lana'i or those coming from Maui, creating an itinerary around your schedule. Convenient hotel or airport pickups on Lana'i or at the harbor if you take the ferry from Maui are a perk. The experience includes a visit to the cat sanctuary, Lana'i Culture and Heritage Center, and Lana'i City, and might also include other island hot spots, such as the Garden of the Gods and Shipwreck Beach on the north shore.

Beaches

Unless you have a 4WD or high-clearance vehicle, Lana'i only has one accessible beach, which is also the only one with any facilities. If you procure a Jeep or a local's truck, there are a number of undeveloped beaches where you can run around naked with no one there to care.

★ HULOPO'E BEACH PARK

To make your friends back home jealous, snap a picture of this beach. **Hulopo'e Beach Park** is the undisputed favorite hangout for islanders and has been named the country's best beach. Within walking distance of the Manele Small Boat Harbor, Hulopo'e is the only beach on the island with restrooms and showers. Despite being the island's most popular, it's far from crowded. The right side of the beach is used by guests of the Four Seasons Resort Lana'i and Sensei Lana'i, who have access to the white umbrellas and lounge chairs. Similarly, guests of Trilogy Excursions' snorkel tour from Maui inhabit the left-hand side of the beach Monday-Friday, leaving the middle section of the beach for visitors to relax in the shade or bake in the sun.

Hulopo'e Bay is a marine reserve and home to one of the few reefs in Maui County that isn't in decline. The reef extends over the left side of the bay, where colorful parrotfish the size of your forearm can easily be spotted and heard nibbling on the vibrant corals. Hulopo'e is also famous for the Hawaiian spinner dolphins that regularly enter the bay. In an effort to protect the natural sleep cycles of the dolphins, swimmers are asked not to approach them. If dolphins happen to swim toward you, consider yourself lucky.

In addition to the sugary sand and perfectly placed palm trees, there are two nature trails on each side of the beach. The **Kapiha'a Fisherman's Trail** departs from the right side of the bay, and the **Trail to Pu'u Pehe Overlook** starts from the left side. There is also a fantastic system of tide pools stretching around the left point of the bay, and one is even deep enough to teach young children to snorkel. The easiest way to get to the tide pools is to use the stairway on the trail to Pu'u Pehe Overlook.

KAIOLOHIA (SHIPWRECK BEACH)

The most popular beach among island visitors after Hulopo'e is **Kaiolohia,** also called **Shipwreck Beach.** To get to Shipwreck, drive past the Sensei Lana'i resort and down Lana'i's windswept "back side" by following the switchbacking, but paved, Keomoku Highway. The views as you descend this winding road stretch all the way to neighboring Maui. A favorite pastime of island teenagers during the plantation days was to flash their headlights at family members on Maui at a prearranged time, then wait eagerly for their cousins to flash them back. (Did I mention life on Lana'i can be slow?)

Once you reach the bottom of the paved highway, a sign points left toward Shipwreck Beach. Follow the sandy road (4WD recommended) for 1.5 miles (2.4 km) before it dead-ends in a parking area. When you pass the shacks built out of driftwood and fishing floats, you've arrived.

Traditionally this area was known as Kaiolohia. The current moniker originates with the unnamed World War II Liberty ship that was intentionally grounded on the fringing reef. Numerous vessels have met their demise on this shallow stretch of coral, but this concrete oil tanker has deteriorated more slowly than most. Stoic in its haunted appearance, the ship remains firmly lodged in the reef as a warning to passing vessels of the dangers.

Because of the persistent northeasterly trade winds, Kaiolohia is rarely suitable for snorkeling or swimming. Your time is better spent combing the beach for flotsam: Japanese glass balls used as fishing floats are the beachcomber's ultimate reward. To reach the Liberty ship is about a mile's walk (1.6 km) along the sandy shore, although numerous rocks interrupt the thin strip of sand to give the appearance of multiple beaches. From here it's technically possible to walk all the way to Polihua Beach, but unless you have arranged a ride at the other side, it's a 16-mile (26-km) round-trip venture in an area with no services or shade. Walking as far as the ship gives you ample time to explore.

Make a side trip to visit the **petroglyphs** on your way back to the car. About 0.25 mile (0.4 km) after the road ends, you'll encounter the concrete base of what was once a lighthouse. If you're uncertain whether you're at the right place, check the concrete base, where names were inscribed in 1929. From the base of the lighthouse, turn directly inland and rock-hop for 300 yards (275 m) until you see a large rock with "Do not deface" written on it. A white arrow points to a trail behind the rock

1
2
3

Lana'i's Other Shipwreck Beach

Besides Shipwreck Beach, a second wreck off Lana'i, the Navy ship YO-21, is hardly ever visited. Take your 4WD vehicle 7 miles (11.3 km) out along Polihua Road to Keahiakawelo (Garden of the Gods), and make a right onto Awalua Road. This steep, eroded trail offers sweeping views across the Kalohi Channel to neighboring Moloka'i before you arrive, 3 miles (4.8 km) later, at a coastal outpost known as Awalua. Rental companies don't recommend going down this road, so if you choose to drive to Awalua, you're doing so at your own risk—stay out of the deep sand. There are multiple pullouts on the side of the road if you drive part of the way and walk to the beach. The reward is a narrow stretch of coast where you'll be the only person, and the chance to view a rusting ship that was stationed at Pearl Harbor on the morning of the Japanese bombing in 1941. Just like at the better-known Shipwreck Beach, photographing the ship and beachcombing are safer options than trying to swim.

Aside from the wrecks at Awalua and Kaiolohia, hundreds of ships have met their demise on this remote stretch of reef. In 1826 the U.S. ship *London* sank here with a large amount of gold and silver aboard, only a portion of which was ever recovered. No divers have ever come back carrying gold bullion, however, so whatever treasure may remain has been lost to the sea.

that leads to petroglyphs of dogs, humans, and a drawing known as "The Birdman."

KAHALEPALAOA

When you reach the bottom of Keomoku Highway, where the pavement ends, take a right at the fork in the road, which leads to a rugged coastal track that ranks as one of the best drives on the island. A 4WD vehicle is recommended, as the deep sand patches can drift onto the road, and depending on recent rains, the road can become rutted and rough. Nevertheless, some of Lana'i's nicest beaches are down this road, and provided there aren't enormous puddles, anyone with a Jeep or SUV should be able to navigate it.

While there are a number of small pullouts along the side of the road leading to narrow windswept beaches, the first beach of any size is **Kahalepalaoa,** 7.5 miles (12 km) from where the pavement ended. The name translates to "House of the Whale Ivory"; whale bones are believed to have washed ashore and were then used to build a dwelling. In more recent times this spot was also the site of a Club Med-style day resort named Club Lana'i. The booze-fueled excursion from Maui no longer operates, but the coconut grove that once housed the venue marks the start of a long white-sand beach that's perfect for casual strolling.

LOPA

Just over 1 mile (1.6 km) past Kahalepalaoa is **Lopa,** a protected stretch of sand that is the nicest on Lana'i's back side. Although the beach isn't that different from Kahalepalaoa, Lopa faces south, so it's more protected from the northeasterly trade winds, which makes reading a book in a beach chair infinitely more enjoyable. Lopa is a popular camping spot for locals, and a couple of picnic tables have been placed beneath the thorn-riddled *kiawe* grove lining the beach. Although the swimming and snorkeling are poor compared to Hulopo'e Beach Park, Lopa is the perfect place for longboard surfing or paddling along the shore in a kayak (if you brought one). The chances of encountering anyone else on Lopa are higher on the weekend, when locals come to camp and fish, but as at many of Lana'i's beaches, if there happens to be anyone else, it's considered crowded.

★ POLIHUA BEACH

Polihua is so remote that even Lana'i residents consider it "out there." A vast,

1: Hulopo'e Bay **2:** sea stack at Pu'u Pehe Overlook **3:** Polihua Beach windswept, and often completely empty stretch of sand, Polihua is utterly unrivaled in its seclusion. If you've ever fantasized about placing the only set of footprints on a deserted beach, this is the place to do it. The name Polihua derives from a Hawaiian term for "eggs in the bosom," a reference to the green sea turtles that haul out on the sand to bury eggs on the isolated shore.

The strong currents at Polihua make the water unsafe for swimming, and oftentimes the afternoon trade winds turn the entire beach into a curtain of blowing sand. The morning hours are best for a relaxing stroll through the sand dunes, and by sunset the winds have usually died down enough to watch the sun sink behind the northwest horizon. With views that stretch across the Kalohi Channel toward Moloka'i, this is one of the last beaches in Hawaii where it's still possible to feel alone.

A 4WD vehicle is imperative to reach Polihua. Travel 7 miles (11.3 km) from Lana'i City on Polihua Road to Keahiakawelo. Continue on the same road for another 25 minutes as it switchbacks down the rutted dirt track before reaching its terminus a few yards short of the beach. There are no services, so if you visit Polihua, remember to bring water and food, and to pack out everything you brought with you.

Snorkeling and Diving

SNORKELING

When it comes to snorkeling, **Hulopo'e Beach Park** easily trumps any other place on the island for the health of the reef, clarity of the water, and variety of fish. Thanks to its protected status as a marine preserve, the reef is in better shape than other places on the island, and snorkelers will revel in the large schools of *manini* (convict tang) and vibrant *uhu* (parrotfish) that flit around the shallow reef. The best snorkeling in the bay is on the left side of the beach. Since Hulopo'e faces south, it can be prone to large surf and shore-break April-October. The shore-break can make entry and exit to the water a little challenging, and the visibility won't be as good as on days that are calmer.

Nevertheless, even a mediocre day at Hulopo'e is better than a good day at many other places. The reef never gets deeper than 25 feet (7.6 m). Occasionally Hawaiian spinner dolphins venture into the bay, although they usually hang out over the sand on the right, closer to the hotel.

Not far from Hulopo'e but equally as gorgeous is the vibrant reef at **Manele Bay.** Don't confuse this with snorkeling in Manele Harbor; that would be disgusting. The reef at Manele Bay is on the opposite side of the break wall between the harbor and the cliffs. Entry from shore can be tricky, since you have to come off the rocks, but if you follow the driveway of the harbor all the way to the far end, there is a little opening in the rocks where it's possible to make a graceful entry. Schools of tropical reef fish gather in abundance, and the spinner dolphins sometimes hang out in this area as well. Although Manele Bay is 0.25 mile (0.4 km) from Hulopo'e Beach, it's still part of the marine preserve, so the same rules apply: Don't stand on the coral, and don't feed the fish. It's best not to touch anything at all.

There isn't anywhere on Lana'i to rent snorkeling equipment for the day, so your best bet is to bring your own. The snorkeling equipment at Hulopo'e Beach is only for Trilogy's day guests who come from Maui, and the gear at the Four Seasons beach kiosk is exclusively for guests of the Four Seasons Resort Lana'i and Sensei Lana'i.

To explore the island's remoter reefs, only accessible by boat, **Trilogy Excursions** (808/874-5649, www.sailtrilogy.com, 8am-4pm, $189 pp) provides a snorkel charter operating on Lana'i. The 3.5-hour snorkeling and sailing excursion usually heads around the southwestern coast to the towering sea cliffs of Kaunolu, also known as Shark Fin Cove due to the dorsal fin-shaped rock in the middle of the bay. There can occasionally be other boats from Maui here, but more often than not this trip provides the opportunity to snorkel the waters of the historic fishing village with only a handful of others. Given that Kaunolu is exposed to the deeper waters offshore, snorkelers intermittently see pelagic species such as spinner dolphins, bottlenose dolphins, eagle rays, manta rays, and whale sharks. If there's wind on the way back to Manele, the crew will hoist the sails, and since bookings are sporadic due to the low numbers on Lana'i, call the Maui office ahead of time to inquire about a charter.

If you're day-tripping from Maui, Trilogy Excursions also offers an eight-hour sailboat tour called **Discover Lanai** ($249 adults, $218 ages 13-17, $149 ages 3-12, free under age 3) twice daily (6:30am and 10am), including swimming and snorkeling at Hulopo'e Beach and a plantation-style barbecue picnic. It operates out of both Lahaina and Ma'alaea Harbors.

Lana'i Ocean Sports (808/866-8256, www.lanaioceansports.com) offers the **Lana'i Snorkel Experience** daily (noon, $169-179) for Four Seasons Resort Lana'i and Sensei Lana'i guests only and departs from the Manele Small Boat Harbor. Shuttle service is offered from the Four Seasons. The snorkeling tour lasts 2-3 hours and heads to Kaunolu. Guides provide information on the marinelife, which includes spinner dolphins, sea turtles, and a plethora of colorful fish. The tour includes a picnic lunch and refreshments on the way back to the harbor.

SCUBA DIVING

Lana'i has some of the best diving in the state, with 14 named dive sites along the southwestern coast. The most famous are **First** and **Second Cathedrals.** At First Cathedral, just offshore from Manele Harbor, the cavern entrance is at 58 feet (18 m). Inside, beams of sunlight filter down through the ceiling like light passing through a stained-glass window. There have even been a few underwater weddings here.

The best way to exit the cathedral is via a hole in the wall known locally as The Shotgun, where divers place their hands on the sides of the cathedral and allow the current to wash through a narrow opening. In addition to the

snorkeling off the coast of Lana'i

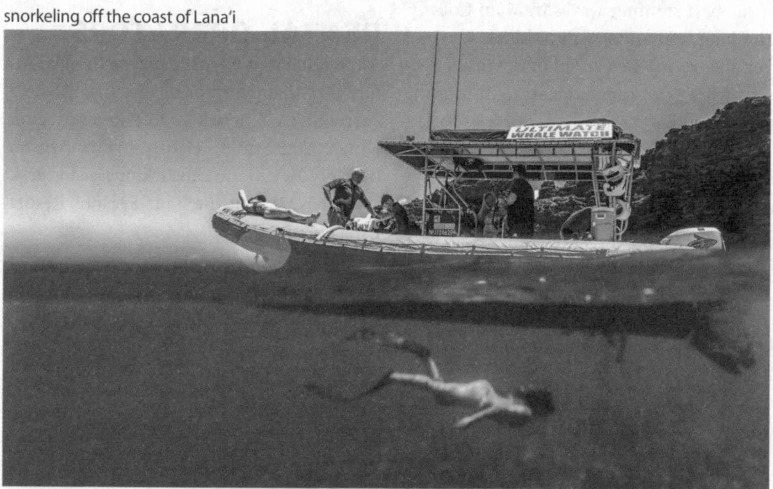

main cathedral, there are a number of other swim-throughs and arches where you can catch a glimpse of spiny lobsters, frogfish, colorful parrotfish, and if you're lucky, a pod of spinner dolphins passing overhead.

Down the coast at Second Cathedral, the underwater dome is about the same size but intersected by so many openings it looks like Swiss cheese. Divers can pass in and out of the cathedral from a variety of different entry points. The highlight is a rare black coral tree that dangles from the cathedral ceiling. Large schools of *ta'ape* (blue-striped snapper) congregate on the back side of the cathedral, and you can swim through a school that numbers in the hundreds. Visibility at both of these sites regularly reaches 80-120 feet (24-37 m), and the water can be so clear that you see most of the dive site standing on the pontoon of the boat.

The most affordable way to dive off Lana'i is with a boat from Maui. The island's only dive operator, **Trilogy Excursions** (808/874-5649, www.sailtrilogy.com), only offers private charters with high prices, mainly as an amenity for guests of the Four Seasons Resort Lana'i and Sensei Lana'i. Check with dive operators in Lahaina about the best way to dive off Lana'i.

Surfing

SURF SPOTS

Hulopo'e Beach Park

Hulopo'e Beach is the island's most popular surf spot. Since it faces south, it's exposed to southerly swells, which means April-October are the best for finding surf. This left point break can be challenging, however, and it's not for beginners. The wave breaks over a shallow coral reef and the takeoff can be steep, although when Hulopo'e is firing, it can be one of the best summer waves in Maui County. The long lefthander will hold its size 2-12 feet (0.6-3.7 m). Be careful of the inside section, which can carry you straight into the shore-break.

Lopa

Lopa is the island's preeminent beginner wave, and just because it's user-friendly doesn't mean that it can't be a great ride. A beach break with multiple peaks, the waves at Lopa aren't usually as steep and are better suited for longboards and nose-riding. Winter months can be flat, but on summer days there's almost always something to ride. You'll have to bring your own board and provide your own transportation. To reach Lopa, take Keomoku Highway to where the paved road ends, then take a right and proceed for 9 miles (14.5 km).

RENTAL OPERATORS

Although things might change in the near future now that the resort is open again, there currently isn't anywhere to rent a board on Lana'i. You can either bring your own on the ferry, or call the Lana'i Ambassador desk (808/565-2388) at the Four Seasons Resort Lana'i to inquire.

Hiking and Biking

HIKING

★ Munro Trail

Munro Trail doesn't look like anywhere else on Lana'i, or in Hawaii. This 12.8-mile (20.6 km) dirt road is more like the Pacific Northwest than the tropics. Wandering around the stands of Cook pines is one of Lana'i's most iconic adventures. Get up early, throw on a light jacket, and head into the uplands, where the smell of eucalyptus wafts through an understory of ironwoods and pines. For clear skies and dry conditions, it's best to hike Munro Trail in the morning hours before enveloping clouds blow in on the trades.

To reach Munro Trail, travel past the Sensei Lana'i resort on Keomoku Highway until you reach a sign for Cemetery Road, where you make a right just before the first mile marker. On Cemetery Road, the pavement turns to dirt and then branches off to the left, bringing you to the start of the trail. Technically Munro Trail is a single-lane dirt road navigable by anyone with a 4WD vehicle. But rental companies don't allow their Jeeps on the steep and potentially muddy track. Park at the trailhead and make the 5.5-mile (8.9-km) (one-way) hike to the summit, stopping at lookouts along the way.

The first lookout, starting from Cemetery Road, is **Koloiki Ridge,** about 2.5 miles (4 km) into the trail. A small red-and-white sign on the left side of the trail points the way to the ridge, and after a brief 0.25-mile (0.4-km) jaunt, you are rewarded with grandiose views back into Maunalei Gulch and out to the islands of Maui and Moloka'i. This lookout is also accessible as part of the **Koloiki Ridge Trail** hike, which starts behind the Sensei Lana'i resort.

Back on the main trail, continue for a couple of miles beneath a shroud of forest until you pass some communication towers. Just past the towers is **Ho'okio Gulch,** a place that forever transformed Lana'i. In 1778 Kahekili, ruler of Lana'i and Maui, was besieged by Kalaniopu'u, a powerful chief from the Big Island whose army featured a fearless young warrior named Kamehameha. In the battle at Ho'okio, Kahekili and his warriors attempted to defend the island from the invading warriors by slinging stones down from the hilltop and hiding in crevasses carved into the cliff face. Ultimately, Kahekili and his men were defeated, and the ensuing occupation of Lana'i by Kalaniopu'u and his army drove the resource-strapped island into famine, which decimated much of the population. It's said that the spirits of those who perished in the battle still reside in the cool forests and keep watch over the eroded gulches and canyons.

Finally, after you've climbed an uphill section of trail, 5.5 miles (8.9 km) from the end of Cemetery Road you'll find the 3,370-foot (1,027-m) summit of Lana'ihale, or The Hale, as it's known to locals. This is the only point in Hawaii where it's possible to see five other islands on the clearest days, and during winter even the snowcapped peaks of Mauna Kea and Mauna Loa on the Big Island can be seen, over 100 miles (161 km) southeast. If you continue the length of the trail, it descends for 7 miles (11.3 km) down the southern side of the ridge, past turnoffs for the Awehi and Naha trails, and eventually emerges in the remains of old pineapple fields at Highway 440 (Manele Rd.).

Pu'u Pehe Overlook

This often photographed sea stack is an iconic symbol of Lana'i and one of the most scenic places on the island. It's not possible to climb onto Pu'u Pehe (also known as Sweetheart Rock), but the **Pu'u Pehe Overlook Trail** offers hikers a sweeping panorama of the rock and the surrounding coast. To reach the overlook, take the dirt road at the south end of Hulopo'e Beach Park (the side opposite the resort) and follow it for 100 yards (90 m) until it

Lana'i on Horseback

Lana'i is steeped in its ranching heritage. The island was once a huge sheep and cattle ranch where *paniolos* roamed the terrain on horseback. Cattle no longer roam, but the island's ranching heritage lives on at the **Stables at Koele** (1 Keomoku Hwy.), where local guides who are authentic *paniolos* offer guided trail rides (1.5 hours, $150 pp) through the Lana'i City hinterlands. Keep an eye out for axis deer or mouflon sheep as you ride at your own pace on excursions geared to your skill level. The knowledgeable guides fortify the excursion with tales of the island's history. Rides are booked through the Adventure Center desk at the Four Seasons Resort Lana'i (808/565-2000).

reaches a set of stairs leading down to the tide pools. From here the road becomes a trail that wraps left across the headland before reaching a hidden sandy cove popular with bodyboarders and nudist sunbathers. To get down to this sandy cove, known as Shark's Bay, requires a scramble through a chute in the rocky cliff that involves some risk.

To reach the overlook, carefully follow the edge of the cliff until it reaches a promontory about 100 feet (30 m) above the shimmering reef below. Aside from the sweeping vista, it's also possible to get a good view from here of the *heiau* that stands atop Pu'u Pehe, an archaeological site that is a mystery given that it's nearly impossible to access the top of the rock.

Kapiha'a Fisherman's Trail

The **Kapiha'a Fisherman's Trail** begins on the side of Hulopo'e Beach in front of the Four Seasons Resort Lana'i and meanders past the mega-mansions on the point. Well-marked by a natural stone walkway, this 1.5-mile (2.4-km) trail hugs the rocky coast as it weaves its way through the ancient village of Kapiha'a. Little remains of the village today, but various historical markers point out the location of *heiau* still visible in the area.

Even though this trail catches the coastal breezes off the surrounding water, there is little shade. Given the rugged nature of the path, wear closed-toe shoes. After the trail reaches a dramatic terminus atop sea cliffs on the back nine of the golf course, an easier return route is to follow the cart path back to the golf clubhouse.

Koloiki Ridge Trail

An offshoot of the Munro Trail, the **Koloiki Ridge Trail** is a 5-mile (8-km) out-and-back hike that begins directly behind the Sensei Lana'i resort. On a nice day, this is the perfect way to spend two or three hours. Walking the trail is like taking a historical tour through Lana'i's past.

To reach the trailhead, go to the main entrance of the Sensei Lana'i resort and then follow the service road toward the golf clubhouse. Once you reach the main clubhouse, another paved service road running behind the fairway ultimately leads to the trailhead. Along the initial paved section of trail, you'll encounter white-and-red signs on the trail as part of an interpretive map available at the hotel's concierge desk.

Once the dirt trail begins, you'll find yourself walking beneath a canopy of ironwood trees and Cook pines that predate the luxury hotels. Planted in 1912 by the botanist George Munro, the pines were used as a means of securing water by trapping moisture from the passing clouds, and even today they still play a major role in providing water for the island's residents.

Making a right at the red-and-white sign marked "10" places you directly on the Munro Trail. About 0.5 mile (0.8 km) down Munro Trail at sign number 17, an arrow points the way down to the dramatic Koloiki Ridge. Once out from beneath the canopy of trees,

1: hikers along the Munro Trail **2:** horseback riding **3:** shoreline view on the hike to Pu'u Pehe Overlook **4:** Koloiki Ridge Trail

you'll notice that the ridge is flanked on both sides by dramatic gulches. From this often windy vantage point at the end of the trail, the islands of Moloka'i and Maui appear on the horizon beyond the deep blue Pailolo Channel. When facing the islands, on the left side of the ridge is Naio Gulch, a dry rock-strewn canyon where you can occasionally catch a glimpse of the island's elusive mouflon sheep. On the right is Maunalei Gulch, a deep cleft in the island that once had the island's only free-flowing stream. If you look closely on the valley floor, you can still see an old service road leading to a pump house. Water from Maunalei once fed the island's sugar plantation.

BIKING

Unless you brought your own bicycle over on the ferry, the best option for biking on Lana'i is with **Adventure Lana'i Island Club** (808/565-7373, www.adventurelanaiisland-club.com), which will deliver a mountain bike to you at the harbor once you disembark from the ferry, or to your accommodations on the island ($39 per day). The company also offers guide-led customizable tours (4 hours, $159), which might include a visit to Keahiakawelo (Garden of the Gods) or some ancient petroglyphs. Given the popularity of these tours, book 3-4 months in advance.

Golf

Unless you're a guest of the Four Seasons Resort Lana'i or Sensei Lana'i or have a Hawaii ID, you can't golf at the famous Jack Nicklaus-designed **Manele Golf Course** (1 Challenge Dr., 808/565-4000, $325 guests, $495 nonguests). If you are able to play, prepare for a round with sweeping ocean views and tee shots over the water, and a 19th-hole clubhouse where you can often see dolphins splashing in the bay.

Another course on Lana'i is open to everyone. More of the no-shirt, no-shoes, beer-a-hole type of course, the nine-hole **Cavendish Golf Course** is suited for recreational golfers who want a quick practice round. Best of all, the course is free. Constructed in 1947 as a recreational option for island pineapple workers, the Cavendish still operates as a place for islanders to practice their game and casually unwind. Although the fairways and tee boxes can be speckled with crabgrass and patches of dirt, the greens are still properly maintained. There are no carts or cart paths, so you get a workout walking the course's moderate elevation changes. To reach the first tee box for the Cavendish course, make a right as if going to the Koele golf clubhouse off Keomoku Highway. Just after the turn is an open field on the right side of the road with a small flag fluttering in the distance. Welcome to the Cavendish. You'll have to supply your own clubs, balls, tees, and beer.

Shopping

Lana'i is the only Hawaiian Island where you could visit every store on the island without having to move the car. With the exception of the small stores within the Four Seasons Resort Lana'i, every shop is within walking distance of the parking area around Dole Park.

CLOTHING AND SOUVENIRS

The only gas station on the island, the **Lana'i Plantation Store** (1036 Lana'i Ave., 808/565-7227, 7am-7pm daily) offers a great selection of island souvenirs and clothing along with the usual snacks and beverages.

By Dole Park, the **Lana'i Hula Hut** (418 8th St., 808/565-9170, 10am-6pm Mon.-Sat.) sells everything from hand-painted ceramic ornaments to women's jewelry and wind chimes. The Balinese woodwork gives an exotic feel to the interior. Facing the park, **The Local Gentry** (363 7th St., 808/565-9130, 10am-6pm Mon.-Fri., 10am-5pm Sat., 10am-2pm Sun.) offers a larger men's selection as well as a full range of women's clothing and Olu Kai shoes.

In the Four Seasons Resort Lana'i, Makakae, Pilina, and Mua Loa offer high-end apparel and luxury boutiques that are curated by Seaside Luxe.

ART AND JEWELRY

The most prominent gallery on the island is **Mike Carroll Gallery** (443 7th St., 808/565-7122, www.mikecarrollgallery.com, 10am-5pm Mon.-Sat., 10am-6pm Sun.), between Canoes restaurant and the Lana'i City theater. There's a good chance that you'll find Mike painting right in the store. Many of his pieces focus on the simple yet captivating beauty of Lana'i. He is an in-demand artist who is constantly crafting original works. The gallery will occasionally feature visiting artists who come to relax and hone their craft in this charming plantation-style studio.

For a look at local artwork, visit the **Lana'i Art Center** (339 7th St., 808/565-7503, www.lanaiart.org, 10am-4pm Mon.-Sat.) to see just how much talent exists on an island of only 3,500 people. Fine photography and handmade jewelry accompany paintings and woodwork. A portion of this nonprofit's proceeds fund local art programs for Lana'i's youth. This gallery is a worthwhile stop after the Saturday farmers market or while walking off a Blue Ginger cheeseburger.

Food

HAWAIIAN/PACIFIC RIM

The fanciest meal in Lana'i City is at ★ **Ganotisi's Pacific Rim Cuisine** (831B Houston St., 808/565-7120, 6pm-8pm Mon., 10am-2pm and 6pm-8pm Tues.-Sat., $15-29). The fare is more expensive than at hole-in-the-wall plate-lunch stands, but when the waiter serves a plate of miso-marinated sea bass with mushroom potato hash, cost seems less important. Ganotisi's has the island's most comprehensive wine list. Reservations are strongly recommended, particularly on Friday evenings, when the live jazz band performs.

LOCAL STYLE

While the exterior might not look like much, at ★ **Blue Ginger Cafe** (409 7th St., 808/565-6363, www.bluegingercafelanai.com, 7am-2pm daily, $5-14, cash only) the swinging screen door and funky plantation-style appearance are all part of the hole-in-the-wall charm. Breakfast is heaping *loco moco* plates of fried eggs, hamburger meat, rice, and gravy, and the homemade hamburger patties are the lunchtime draw that has kept patrons coming in from Dole Park since 1991. It's a true local hideout.

No Ka 'Oi Grindz Lana'i (335 9th St., 808/565-9413, 9am-1pm daily, $6-11) is a popular low-key venue that serves bountiful breakfasts, plate lunches—which is the thing to get here—and a lunch buffet. The folks behind the counter are some of the friendliest you'll encounter on the island, and the vibe is upbeat. Try the sweet potato or kimchi fries as sides.

BISTRO

Pele's Other Garden (811 Houston St., 808/565-9628, www.pelesothergarden.com, breakfast and lunch 11am-2pm Mon.-Fri., dinner 4:30pm-7:30pm Mon.-Sat., $9-22) is the hangout of anyone hankering for a good sandwich or a cold draft beer. The bistro also whips up healthy and affordable food options, ranging from avocado and feta wraps to pizza and chicken parmesan.

RESORT RESTAURANTS

Four Seasons Resort Lana'i

If you've only made it as far as the pool by lunch and have no intention of leaving the **Four Seasons Resort Lana'i** (1 Manele Bay Rd., 808/565-2000, www.fourseasons.com/lanai), order some food poolside from **Malibu Farm** (808/565-2092, 11am-5pm and 5:30pm-9:30pm daily, $16-32), where you can get a vegan chopped salad, classic Hawaiian pupus, craft beers, and fresh local pineapples. For slightly lower prices and a view of the bay, **Views** (808/565-2230, 11am-3pm Tues.-Sun., $20) restaurant at the golf clubhouse has burgers, sandwiches, and local beer.

For dinner, **Nobu Lana'i** (808/565-2832, 5:30pm-9:30pm daily, $35) has a sushi selection from famed chef Nobu Matsuhisa.

★ **One Forty** (808/565-2000, 6:30am-11am and 5:30pm-9pm daily, $40-67) has exceptional plates of Hawaiian Regional cuisine. The ahi *poke* appetizer served with dinner can compete with the best in the islands, and the hand-cut steaks and plates of fresh fish are the best that you'll find on Lana'i. For breakfast, start your day with Morning Tacos filled with local venison ($25).

Sensei Lana'i

At the wellness resort **Sensei Lana'i** (1 Keomoku Hwy., 808/565-4500, www.fourseasons.com/sensei) is **Sensei by Nobu** (808/565-4500, 6am-11am, noon-4pm, and 5:30pm-9pm daily, $25-65), a fine-dining restaurant set in a glass pavilion amid gardens. Representing a collaboration between chef Nobu Matsuhisa and resort cofounder and physician David Agus, the menu offers an array of health-conscious meals that feature everything from Hana-grown produce and fresh fish to vegan and vegetarian meals.

QUICK BITES

For a quick and easy grab-and-go option, **Lana'i City Service** (1036 Lana'i Ave., 808/565-7227, 6am-10pm daily) has a soup-and-sandwich bar as well as enormous shave ice.

Lana'i Nightlife

Don't visit Lana'i for the nightlife. Evening is that inconvenient stretch of darkness that brings outdoor adventure to a halt. There are no nightclubs or dinner shows, and aside from the hotels, there is only one place you can even get a beer (Pele's Other Garden). Nevertheless, there is still a semblance of activity on certain nights of the week—just don't expect it to stretch past 10pm. On Wednesday, the party is at **Pele's Other Garden** (811 Houston St., 808/565-9628, www.pelesothergarden.com), with live music rocking the bistro in the evening. On Friday, head to **Ganotisi's Pacific Rim Cuisine** (831B Houston St., 808/565-7120), where the live jazz band provides the best entertainment in town.

COFFEE SHOPS

Even sleepy Lana'i City needs help waking up in the morning, and **Coffee Works** (604 Ilima Ave., 808/565-6962, www.coffeeworkshawaii.com, hours vary, typically 7am-2pm daily) is the island's only full-time java establishment. Breakfast bagels and lunch sandwiches accompany the usual range of coffee offerings, and the outdoor porch is a great place for watching the mellow town slowly spring to life.

MARKETS

Even though it's no longer a sprawling pineapple plantation, the red dirt of Lana'i still manages to produce some locally grown crops. The **Lana'i City Farmer's Market** (Dole Park behind Richard's Market, 8am-1pm Sat.) is the best place for fresh items such as corn, papaya, and pineapple. It's a great weekend activity in the island's only town.

Richard's Market (434 8th St., 808/565-3781, 6am-10pm daily), located in the heart of town, is ideal for picking up fresh fruit, produce, snacks, frozen goods, and beverages.

Where to Stay

While Lana'i is home to two of the most luxurious resorts in the state, there are a handful of more affordable options if you want to stay in the town. Lately, almost every vacation rental option on Lana'i has gone on **VRBO** (www.vrbo.com), the first place to check to find a little plantation home on the hill. There are still a few you can book directly by phone or through their own sites.

HOTELS

Small and historic ★ **Hotel Lana'i** (828 Lana'i Ave., 808/565-7211, www.hotellanai.com, $265-710) is in the center of tranquil Lana'i City. This was the island's first hotel, built in 1923 for visiting guests of the ruling Dole Pineapple Company. While you won't find the same amenities as at the resorts, the 10 rooms of this plantation-style building retain a historical feel without sacrificing comfort. The best rooms are those with their own private lanai, and there is also a cottage removed from the main building. Wi-Fi and breakfast are both complimentary, and shuttle service to the harbor ($15 pp) is available, as are complimentary shuttles from the airport.

Lavish, luxurious, and delightfully over the top, the ★ **Four Seasons Resort Lana'i** (1 Manele Bay Rd., 808/565-2000, www.fourseasons.com/lanai, from $2,465) is one of Hawaii's most exclusive. Owner Larry Ellison devoted millions of dollars to major renovations when he took over from David Murdock, and the Asian decor that once dominated has been replaced by Hawaiian designs. The massive tech infusion, such as futuristic Toto toilets, makes every part of staying at the Manele resort an experience unto itself. Sit beachfront by the pool and sip on a cocktail while gazing at Hulopo'e Bay as spinner dolphins splash in the distance and pool staff clean your sunglasses. You'll feel like a celebrity.

Perched among expansive Lana'i valleys that overlook the ocean is **Sensei Lana'i, A Four Seasons Resort** (1 Keomoku Hwy., 808/565-4500, www.fourseasons.com/sensei, $880-1,280). At this sister resort to the Four Seasons Resort Lana'i, you will experience unmatched luxury with a customized retreat and wellness experience, including everything from yoga and meditation to exploring the property's gardens or relaxing poolside. Culinary innovation is provided by revered Japanese chef Nobu Matsuhisa; however, guests can also design their own health-conscious meals. You're meant to feel spoiled here.

1
2
HOTEL LANAI
3
KEAHIKAWELO
(GARDEN OF THE GODS)
KAIOLOHIA
(SHIPWRECK BEACH)
KEOMOKU

Where to Stay on Lana'i

Name	Type	Price	Features	Why Stay Here?	Best For
Dreams Come True	B&B	$179	kitchen	affordable, location	couples, budget travelers
★ **Four Seasons Resort Lana'i**	resort	from $2,465	pool, golf, oceanfront	luxury, romantic	couples, honeymooners, luxury-lovers
★ **Hotel Lana'i**	hotel	$265-710	lanai, breakfast	romantic, location, historic	couples
Hulopo'e Beach Park	camping	$80 per night	restrooms, water, oceanfront	location, affordable	budget travelers, groups, families
Sensei Lana'i, A Four Seasons Resort	resort	$880-1,280	wellness experiences, pool, gardens	luxury, rejuvenation	health-conscious travelers

BED-AND-BREAKFASTS

The **Dreams Come True** (808/565-6961 www.dreamscometruelanai.com, $179) guesthouse has four rooms. The house dates to 1925 and has been renovated with hardwood floors and Italian marble in the baths. The local owners have a wealth of island knowledge. Breakfast is included in the rates, as is internet access.

CAMPING

The island's only official campground is at **Hulopo'e Beach Park** (reservations: info@lanaibeachpark.com, $80 per night with a 3-day maximum), and it's more expensive than you'd expect for camping. You do get to wake up steps from one of the nicest beaches in the country, and it's still cheaper than any room in town. The campground is within walking distance of the ferry dock, and having a cooler with wheels is a big help for carrying supplies.

1: pool at the Four Seasons Resort Lana'i **2:** dusk at Hotel Lana'i **3:** directions, Lana'i style

Getting There and Around

GETTING THERE

Air

Flying to Lana'i requires a jump from neighboring Honolulu. **Hawaiian Airlines** (800/367-5320, www.hawaiianairlines.com) operates turboprop planes with 25-minute flights from Honolulu (HNL) that run a couple of times per day.

Ferry

Traveling from Maui, the easiest and most practical way to get to Lana'i is the **Expeditions Ferry** (808/661-3756, www.go-lanai.com, one-way $30 adults, $20 children), which runs four times daily between Lahaina and Manele Harbors. Travel time is usually about an hour, and during whale season (Dec.-Apr.), you can frequently spot humpback whales from the outdoor seating of the upper deck. Although you can buy tickets at the harbor kiosk in Lahaina the morning of your journey, make reservations ahead of time, particularly for the early morning trip. Don't be late; this is one ferry that doesn't wait around.

GETTING AROUND

If you're staying at the Four Seasons Resort Lana'i or Sensei Lana'i, there is a complimentary shuttle service to Lana'i City, the airport, and the harbor. If you're staying at Hotel Lana'i, there's a complimentary shuttle from the airport and a shuttle to the harbor for $15. If you're staying elsewhere or visiting for the day, you'll have to rent a vehicle or take a cab.

Car

CAR RENTALS

There are two main go-to agencies for car rentals on the island: **Lanai Cheap Jeeps** (418 8th St., 808/489-2296, www.lanaicheapjeeps.com, 7am-7pm daily) has rentals from $285 per day, and **808 Day Trip** (10 Manele Rd., 808/649-0664, www.808daytrip.com, 6am-11pm daily) offers economy cars and SUVs, and even provides delivery. Rates fluctuate but typically begin at $129 per day.

GAS

There is only one station on the entire island: **Lana'i City Service** (1036 Lana'i Ave., 808/565-7227, 6am-10pm daily) supplies fuel for all 3,500 residents. Don't worry about the price; you're better off just not looking, as it's often $1 to $1.50 more per gallon than on Maui. Then again, with only 30 miles (48 km) of paved roads, it isn't uncommon for a tank of gas to last a month or more.

Taxi

The island's only taxi service is **Rabaca's Limousine Service** (808/559-0230), which connects the airport, harbor, and Lana'i City ($10 pp).

Lahaina-Lana'i Ferry Schedule

DEPART LAHAINA HARBOR (MAUI)

- 6:45am
- 9:45am
- 1pm
- 4pm

DEPART MANELE HARBOR (LANA'I)

- 8:15am
- 11:15am
- 2:30pm
- 5:30pm

Moloka'i

Visitors often mistake Moloka'i's lack of typical

resort activities for a lack of things to do.

But the protected vibe is incomparably relaxed and epitomizes "old Hawaii," where you find yourself talking to strangers as you would with an old friend. Moloka'i is a step back to simpler times when life was slower. That doesn't mean it's boring. Imagine surfing perfect waves off an empty white-sand beach, hiking through rainforests to thundering falls in Hawaii's original settlement, or tattooing the sand with a string of footprints on a sunset stroll.

Moloka'i is Hawaii's most "Hawaiian" island in that it has the highest percentage of ethnic Hawaiians and is one of the last places you might hear Hawaiian spoken on the street. It's a place where culture

Highlights

Look for ★ to find recommended sights, activities, dining, and lodging.

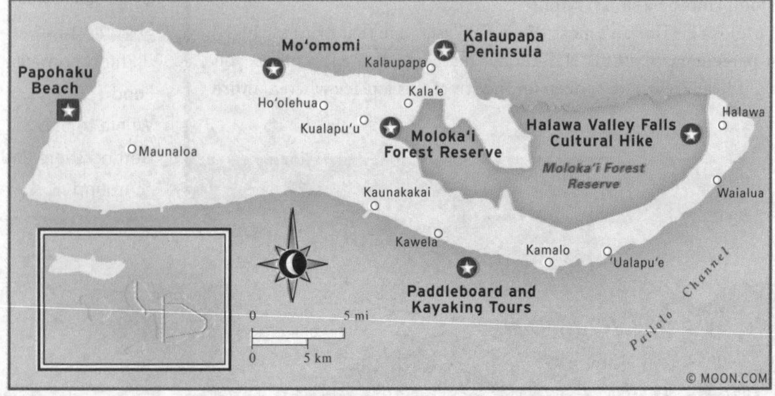

★ Visit **Moloka'i Forest Reserve,** one of the few places in the state with an ecosystem identical to what the Polynesians first found over 1,500 years ago (page 317).

★ See the **Kalaupapa Peninsula** on an air tour—the former leper colony fuses some of Moloka'i's darkest moments with its most dramatic surroundings (page 321).

★ Watch a fiery **sunset** at **Papohaku Beach,** 3 miles (4.8 km) long and virtually deserted (page 324).

★ Stroll along the beach at wild and secluded **Mo'omomi,** which feels like Moloka'i's lost coast (page 326).

★ Enjoy a downwind paddle off the island's southern coast on **paddleboard and kayaking tours** (page 329).

★ Travel to the roots of Hawaiian culture on the **Halawa Valley Falls Cultural Hike** and swim at the base of a waterfall (page 331).

and ancient tradition are preferred over modern progress.

ORIENTATION

Though the airport is in Ho'olehua, **Kaunakakai** is the island's main town and the hub of everyday life. It's the location of the island's only gas stations and the bulk of the restaurants, and also the Hotel Moloka'i, the island's largest. The western shore is about 30 minutes away and is best for beaches and sunsets. Eastern Moloka'i has oceanfront cottages and lush **Halawa Valley.** Central Moloka'i, near **Kualapu'u,** has a handful of sights and a restaurant, and it's on the way to the misty uplands and **Kalaupapa Trail.**

PLANNING YOUR TIME

In general, 4-5 days is plenty of time to properly visit the island, though you can visit most of the island's highlights in a very efficient two days. (In the past, a day trip to the island from Maui via ferry may have sufficed; however, ferry service to Moloka'i has been suspended indefinitely.) When scheduling your trip, plan on one day for Halawa Valley and East Moloka'i, and a second day for Kalaupapa. A third day could be spent at the west-end beaches or hiking Mo'omomi or the Bog, and a fourth and fifth day provide nice buffers if activities are canceled by rain.

To visit Moloka'i in two days, head to the west end to catch the sunset after a morning in Kalaupapa, and the next day go hiking in Halawa Valley before dinner at Hiro's Ohana Grill. By staying in the vicinity of Kaunakakai, most places are within a 30-minute drive, and an hour to Halawa Valley.

Sights

People who claim that there isn't a lot to do on Moloka'i have more than likely never visited. Sure, Moloka'i is a place to decompress and generally kick back and relax, but in addition to the hiking, biking, snorkeling, diving, surfing, and eating, there are also traditional sightseeing and activities.

KAUNAKAKAI

Kapuaiwa Coconut Grove

Planted in 1860 by King Kamehameha V, the **Kapuaiwa Coconut Grove** once sported over 1,000 waving palms. It makes a beautiful picture from the road.

Moloka'i Plumerias

Have you ever wanted to make your own lei and be surrounded by the scent of plumeria? Just west of town on Highway 460, as the road starts heading uphill, is **Moloka'i Plumerias** (808/553-3391, www.molokaiplumerias.com), where you can tour the property (8am-noon Mon.-Fri., $25), pick your own flowers, and make a plumeria lei. Tours require advance reservations.

TOPSIDE

★ Moloka'i Forest Reserve

As you head west from Kaunakakai, slowly gaining elevation, the turnoff for the **Moloka'i Forest Reserve** is just before mile marker 4. Turn right before the bridge, and after a few hundred yards you'll pass the Homelani Cemetery, where red-dirt Maunahui Road winds its way into the mountains. Your car-rental agency will tell you that this road is impassable except in a 4WD vehicle, and that's true if it has rained recently. The road is rough even when it's dry and requires at least a high-clearance truck or jeep.

Previous: Halawa Bay; Halawa Valley; beach at Kalaupapa.

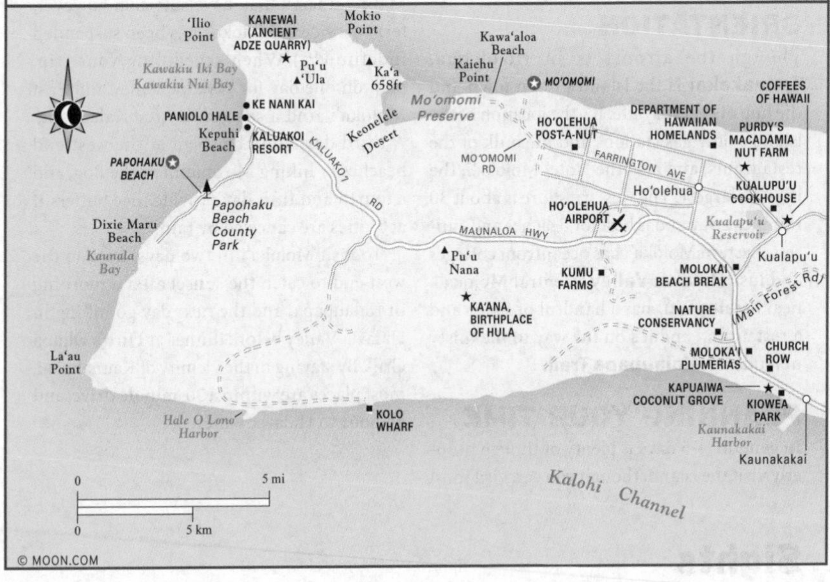

Follow the rutted road up into the hills into a deep forest of *'ohi'a*, pine, eucalyptus, and giant ferns planted in the early 1900s. The cool, pleasant air carries the rich earthy smells of the forest. At 5.5 miles (8.9 km) you enter the Moloka'i Forest Reserve, where nearly 98 percent of the plant species are indigenous to Moloka'i.

After 9 miles (14.5 km) is the **Sandalwood Measuring Pit,** a depression in the ground in the shape of a ship's hull. Now bordered by a green pipe fence, it's not worth the drive out here in itself. Hawaiian chiefs had the pit dug to measure the amount of sandalwood necessary to fill the hold of a ship, and traded the aromatic wood to Yankee captains for whiskey, guns, and tools. The traders carried the wood to China, where they made huge profits. The trade was so lucrative that the male population of entire villages were forced into the hills to collect it. It took only a few years to denude the mountains of their copious stands of sandalwood, which is even more incredible when you consider that all the work was done by hand.

One mile (1.6 km) after the Sandalwood Pit is the **Waikolu Overlook,** a precipitous 3,700-foot (1,130-m) drop that's frequently lined with waterfalls. Waikolu Overlook is as far as most vehicles can go. Continuing farther is the **Kamakou Preserve** and the hike to **Pepe'opae Bog** (page 330). The road is so bad that the only way forward is to park at Waikolu and walk.

Purdy's Na Hua O Ka 'Aina Farm (Macadamia Nut Farm)

A popular visitor stop is **Purdy's Na Hua O Ka 'Aina Farm** (808/567-6601, www.molokai-aloha.com/macnuts, 9:30am-3:30pm Mon.-Fri., 10am-2pm Sat., Sun. and holidays by appointment) behind the public high school on Lihi Pali Avenue. This is the island's only macadamia nut farm, where you'll learn everything you wanted to know about macadamias. An informal tour led by the jovial owner teaches you how to crack open the hard nut,

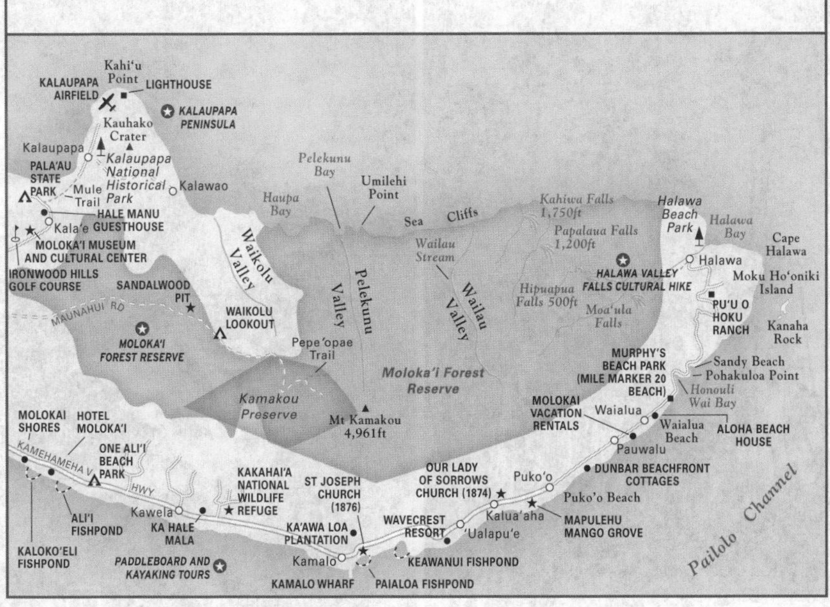

how the nuts are grown, and how to pick out the good ones. There are no pesticides, herbicides, or other chemicals used in this 50-tree grove. While samples are included with the free tour, a small gift shop sells everything from macadamia-nut honey to mac nut-themed clothing.

Kumu Farms

The place for the island's best healthy organic produce is **Kumu Farms** (551 Hua Ai Rd., 808/351-3326, www.kumufarms.com, 9am-4pm Tues.-Fri., free). Despite the recent explosion of farm-to-table cuisine, this working farm has been growing crops since 1981 and is the best place on the island to pick up fresh veggies straight from the *kumu*, or source.

Visitors can peruse the outdoor market for certified organic and non-GMO produce and glean some expert culinary advice from recipes and cookbooks around the shop. Five minutes west of the airport on Hua Ai Road, an easy turn from Highway 460, this rapidly expanding farm now produces over 20,000 pounds (9,070 kg) of papaya every week. Pick up a bag of frozen basil and macadamia-nut pesto for a homemade pasta dinner.

Ho'olehua Post-A-Nut

Never have kids loved going to the post office more than in Ho'olehua. A simple one-room building on arid homesteading land, the **Ho'olehua Post Office** (69-2 Pu'u Pila Ave., 808/567-6144, 8:30am-noon and 12:30pm-4pm Mon.-Fri.) is home to the popular Post-A-Nut, where you can decorate a coconut and ship it anywhere in the world. Postmaster Gary has shipped coconuts to Kathmandu, Namibia, Kyrgyzstan, and Antarctica (twice). Rates to the U.S. mainland run $10-15.

Moloka'i Museum and Cultural Center

Two miles (3.2 km) north of Kualapu'u, off Highway 470, is the **Moloka'i Museum and Cultural Center** (808/567-6436, 10am-1pm Mon.-Fri., 10am-2pm Sat., $5 adults, $1 students), a simple museum focused on the

1
2
3

Rainy Day Ideas

Grab a warm drink from **Coffees of Hawaii** and sit on the covered front porch before heading to the **Post-a-Nut** in Ho'olehua to mail yourself a coconut. Pick up souvenirs at the strip of stores on Ala Malama Avenue, Kaunakakai's main thoroughfare, and strike up conversation while listening to live music at **Hiro's Ohana Grill.** Sometimes if it's raining in town, it is sunny on the west end of the island for tanning or watching the sunset, so ask a local if they know what the weather is like out west.

history of Kalaupapa. There's a small exhibit on Hawaiian artifacts as well as a basic gift shop, but most informative are the documentary videos and old newspaper articles about life on the Kalaupapa Peninsula. On the same grounds, behind the museum, is the **R. W. Meyer Sugar Mill,** constructed in 1878 during the island's short-lived sugar era.

Pala'au State Park

Above the residential town of Kala'e and past the mule barn, Highway 470 eventually dead-ends in the parking lot of **Pala'au State Park.** The park offers decent camping, and there are public restrooms at the parking lot, but no potable water and only basic facilities. The air is noticeably cooler than at the shore, and by midmorning the northeasterly trade winds are usually blowing.

To reach **Kalaupapa Overlook,** follow the paved path at the edge of the parking lot until it reaches a terminus at a low rock wall at the edge of a cliff. From this vantage point are unobstructed views of the town of Kalaupapa, the former leper settlement that still houses a handful of patients. Unless you obtained a permit to hike down, this is the closest to Kalaupapa that you can get.

Back at the parking lot, an unpaved trail leads 200 yards (180 m) through a cool canopy of trees before emerging at a sacred spot named **Ka Ule O Nanahoa,** also called **Phallic Rock** for reasons that are immediately apparent. According to legend, Nanahoa, the male god of fertility, once lived nearby in the forests surrounding Pala'au. One day, when Nanahoa sat to admire a beautiful young woman looking at her reflection in a pool, Kawahua, Nanahoa's wife, became so jealous that she attacked the young woman by yanking on her hair. Nanahoa was outraged in turn and struck his wife, who rolled over a nearby cliff before turning to stone. Nanahoa also turned to stone, in the shape of an erect penis, and sits here today.

1: Kapuaiwa Coconut Grove **2:** plumeria lei
3: Waikolu Overlook

★ KALAUPAPA PENINSULA

This isolated peninsula is where people with leprosy were sent to die. The story goes deeper than that, and touring the **Kalaupapa Peninsula,** now the **Kalaupapa National Historical Park,** is one of the most powerful and scenic adventures you can experience in Hawaii.

The peninsula is currently only accessible via aircraft. The Pali Trail to Kalaupapa was closed indefinitely in 2018 due to a landslide, so hiking isn't possible, and the once-popular mule ride down has been suspended indefinitely. **Mokulele Airlines** (808/495-4188, www.mokuleleairlines.com) offers air tours from the Moloka'i airport to the Kalaupapa airstrip (prices vary), providing historical background information; check with the airline as tour times shift seasonally.

Be sure to check the **National Park Service website** (www.nps.gov) or **Kalaupapa Rare Adventure/Kekaula Tours** (808/567-6088, www.muleride.com), which had offered land tours (from $209) in

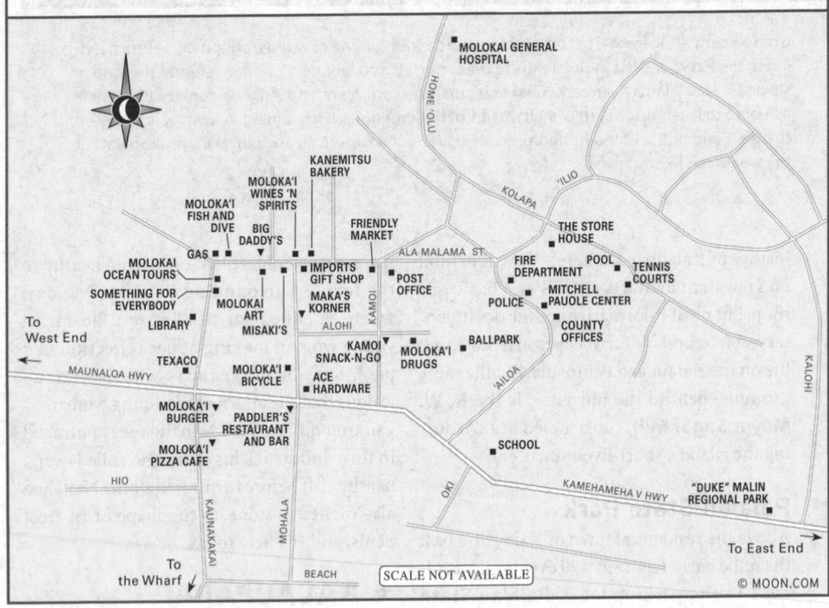

the past, for updates. Land tours require a permit and guide. Guides share Kalaupapa's history and discuss its uncertain future, and take you to sights like the Kalawao lookout and St. Philomena Church.

WEST MOLOKA'I

The only sights in West Moloka'i are the fiery sunsets and the procession of isolated beaches that line the western coast.

In 1897 a group of wealthy Honolulu businesspeople purchased 70,000 acres (28,300 ha) of land in the western half of Moloka'i and named it Moloka'i Ranch. It attempted a number of ventures until finally succumbing in 2008 to public pressure over proposed development. Closing the ranch's hospitality operations eliminated 120 jobs, and the area has yet to recover.

Over the years the ranch supported sugarcane, pineapples, sweet potatoes, wheat, cattle, safari tours, a luxury lodge, an 18-hole golf course, a movie theater, and rustic accommodations on Kaupoa Beach, colloquially known as "tentalows." With ranch operations mostly on hold, the small residential town of **Maunaloa** is all that remains. Occasionally there are still rodeos in town. The ranch may rise again, but for the time being it's an abandoned hinterland of isolated ghost-town confusion.

EAST MOLOKA'I

Since the arrival of the Polynesians, eastern Moloka'i has supported most of the island's population. The mountains provide the water, farmland, and pigs, and the ocean provides fish that have been sustainably managed for over 1,000 years. Many of the residents maintain this subsistence-based lifestyle, where the people are stewards of the land that nourishes them.

Many of the historic sites in this area have limited access because they are on private land. Sites that landowners have not opened to visitors, such as 'Ili'iliopae, the largest *heiau* (temple) on the island, are not included here. Nevertheless, a day trip to the east end of the island is easily Moloka'i's best road trip, with views toward Maui and humble historical sights. The white-sand beaches are nice for a picnic or a quick dip to cool off, and the road to Halawa rivals Maui's Road to Hana when it comes to magnificent views.

Ali'i Fishpond

Driving east from Kaunakakai, you'll come to **Ali'i Fishpond** at mile marker 3, just before One Ali'i Beach Park. It's an illuminating glimpse into early aquaculture. The 35-acre (14-ha) fishpond was originally constructed with lava rocks carried by hand 10 miles (16 km) over the adjacent mountain. The rocks were erected in a semicircle, creating a protective seawater fishpond. At the time of use, a gate would open to allow fish to swim into the pond until they grew too big and could not swim out. Having fallen into disrepair, the Ali'i Fishpond has been painstakingly brought back to life by Ka Honua Momona (www.kahonuamomona.org), a nonprofit organization dedicated to sustainable land practices on Moloka'i. If you pull in to the parking lot and staff members are working on the property, they will happily show you around. Workers are usually here in the morning before the wind picks up, and if no one is around, it's best to admire the fishpond from a distance.

View from the Heights

Since the coastal road doesn't have great views, drive up to the **Kawela Plantation** to get a panoramic photo of the fringing reef and coast. Just a few minutes east of One Ali'i Beach Park, turn *mauka* (toward the mountain) into the Kawela Plantation I development, drive past rows of plumeria trees, and make the first left. From here, follow the steep hill until it dead-ends in a cul-de-sac. This is the best view of the southern coast until mile marker 20.

St. Joseph's Church

Driving along Highway 450, **St. Joseph's Church** (www.damienchurchmolokai.org/wp) is around mile marker 10. Although Father Damien is famous for reaching out to the patients of Kalaupapa, he would also frequently make the arduous trek over the mountains to the southern coast where, in 1876, he constructed St. Joseph's Church. A statue of Damien stands outside this small, recently restored building. To look inside, check the doors; they are often unlocked.

In an effort to convert Hawaiians to Christianity, it's believed that Father Damien purposely chose this spot in Kamalo to provide an alternative to the Puili *heiau*, which lies just inland.

Pu'u O Hoku Ranch

Past mile marker 20 and Waialua and Murphy's Beaches, the road narrows and runs near the sea. Honk your horn as you come around tight corners, and if you feel queasy from the drive, there's a sandy cove past mile marker 21 where you can rest. This far out on the island is very rural, and often you'll encounter groups of residents just hanging out and fishing. Be sure you have more than a quarter tank of gas if you plan to venture farther, as there are no facilities as you continue east.

Once Highway 450 starts gaining in elevation, the sweeping pasturelands of **Pu'u O Hoku Ranch** (808/558-8109, www.puuohoku.com) come into view. This 14,000-acre (5,670-ha) working ranch and farm dominates the eastern tip of the island. You've driven so far north and east that it's possible to see Maui's northern coast. There's a basic store at the ranch headquarters that sells its own products, such as organic honey, dried banana fingers, kale, chard, eggplant, cherry tomatoes, and sweet apple bananas. The ranch is also one of the only places that produces and sells *'awa,* a traditional Polynesian medicinal and painkilling drink, and it also sells ranch-raised beef and venison. Driving through the ranch, watch for nene geese in the pastures and on the road. The ranch also has a number of lodging options to get away from it all.

Halawa Valley

At the end of Highway 450, after utopian plantation homes, single-lane turns, and the ranchland's windswept bluffs, **Halawa Valley** suddenly appears when you reach a hairpin turn. At the lookout, you can snap a shot of Moa'ula Falls, toward the back of the valley. This is the best possible view of the falls unless you take a Halawa Valley guided hike (page 331).

Halawa is believed to be Hawaii's first settlement, circa AD 650, with some evidence suggesting settlement as early as AD 300. This is the "old Hawaii," where mythology, nature, and residents commune in a way not found in modern society. The handful of residents who still inhabit this valley live a subsistence lifestyle that parallels their ancestors. Electricity is scarce, there's no cell phone reception, and taro *lo'i* (fields) weave their way up the verdant valley floor. Aside from swimming at the sandy beach or joining the guided hike, there is little to do in Halawa but snap photos and enjoy the beauty.

Beaches

If having a beach to yourself seems like your kind of afternoon, then pack a beach chair and a good book. Moloka'i's beaches are meant for sunbathing rather than snorkeling or swimming, as northwesterly swells bring large surf in winter and a reef lines the southern coast. You won't find beachside tiki bars or activity agents—in Moloka'i it's just you, the sand, the vast blue Pacific, and a fiery sunset each night.

WEST MOLOKA'I

The west end of Moloka'i has the island's best beaches, usually spared the relentless trade winds that buffet the eastern coast. Summer months are best for swimming, with the exception of Papohaku, which is always dangerous. In winter, surf turns the western coast into a cauldron of white water. The empty shores are always good for sunbathing, and the sunsets are the best on the island.

★ Papohaku Beach

At 3 miles (4.8 km) long and nearly 100 yards (90 m) wide, **Papohaku Beach** is easily Moloka'i's most scenic and popular. Six people is considered a crowd, and while parts of the beach are dotted with homes, the majority of Papohaku is undeveloped with empty sand for strolling. Swimming is a terrible idea, as the rip currents and undertow are overwhelming year-round. Instead, take a morning jog or watch the sunset over the lights of Honolulu, 32 miles (52 km) away.

To get here, follow Highway 460 toward the town of Maunaloa, and take a right on Kaluakoi Road. Follow Kaluakoi to sea level until it wraps around to the left. The beach park has multiple entrances on the right side of the road. For extended stays, **camping** is possible at Papohaku if you obtain a permit from the County Parks Department (808/553-3204).

Kepuhi Beach

Kepuhi Beach fronts the Kaluakoi Villas and the abandoned Sheraton resort. It's an ideal beach for swimming during the summer, and the sunset each night is the kind that ends up on your Christmas card. To reach Kepuhi Beach, follow the signs for Kaluakoi Villas off Kaluakoi Road. Public beach parking is available.

Kapukahehu (Dixie Maru)

Named after a fishing boat that sank near the

1: Papohaku Beach **2:** Ali'i Fishpond **3:** sunset at Kaunakakai **4:** heading for a surf session

1
2
3
4

bay, **Dixie's** is at the southern end of the road. From Papohaku Beach Park, follow Kaluakoi Road until it reaches Pohakuloa, turn *makai* (toward the sea), and follow it to the end of the cul-de-sac. The narrow alleyway that looks like a driveway is the beach access, and there's a small parking area about 100 yards (90 m) down. For an even smaller, more hidden beach, there's a small trail through the *kiawe* (mesquite) trees that eventually leads over a fence. Follow this trail for 10 minutes, and it will bring you to sandy **Kaunala Beach,** frequented by surfers, nudists, and locals, but you'll often have it all to yourself.

Kawakiu and Pohaku Mauliuli Beach

Between Kepuhi and 'Ilio, a number of hidden, sandy coves provide splendid isolation. To reach **Kawakiu Beach,** follow the signs to the Paniolo Hale condominium complex from Kaluakoi Road by making a right on Kaka'ako and then turning left down Lio Place, following the pavement to the end. A rudimentary sign here points the way to the beach, and when the dirt road ends in a parking lot, it's a short walk to the shore. If you don't have a high-clearance or 4WD vehicle, consider parking near the end of the pavement and walking along the dirt road. While the first beach is nice, it's nothing compared to Kawakiu, so continue north by scrambling over some rocks until you arrive at **Pohaku Mauliuli.** From here, a dirt road runs along the bluff and leads to Kawakiu. If the tide is low and the surf is calm, walk along the shore. The protected cove is idyllic in summer, tumultuous in winter, and almost always empty. If you prefer to bathe in the buff, this is the place to do it. Bring lots of water as well as proper footwear for lava rocks and thorns.

★ Mo'omomi

If you crave adventure, head to **Mo'omomi.** You'll need a 4WD vehicle to get to this coast, which is pristine. Its seclusion is revered and in some cases protected by local indigenous Hawaiians. Mo'omomi is currently open to visitors, but it's imperative to be respectful and keep on established trails. In the past, access has ranged from total freedom to discussion of erecting a gate. Contact the **Department of Hawaiian Home Lands** (600 Maunaloa Hwy., 808/560-6104) to inquire about current restrictions. The western portions of Mo'omomi are run by The Nature Conservancy, and visitors are asked to stay out of the dunes because of the fragile ecosystem.

To reach the Mo'omomi pavilion from Ho'olehua, follow Farrington Avenue until the road becomes dirt, and keep right at the fork. Once parked, walking along the shore leads to a series of underwhelming beaches, but once you get back on the dirt road, the beauty of windswept **Kawa'aloa Beach** opens up before you. Swimming is only possible in summer, as large north swells create dangerous rip currents the rest of the year. The best activity at Kawa'aloa is strolling. For a unique way to visit, contact **The Nature Conservancy** (808/553-5236, www.nature.org), which hosts monthly hikes March-October.

EAST MOLOKA'I

The eastern beaches are the most popular among residents, and morning hours offer the calmest conditions before the trade winds arrive. Like a South Pacific postcard, white-sand coves ringed by lazy palms are dotted by colorful fishing boats, and more than anywhere else on the island, there's a sense of enveloping calm. The swimming and snorkeling are best at high tide, the beachcombing and sunbathing are better at low tide, and everything is better before the afternoon wind.

Puko'o Beach

Just east of the Mana'e Goods & Grindz, by mile marker 16, a small beach access sign points down a dirt driveway to hidden **Puko'o Beach.** You'll find water that's calm, clear, protected, and good for swimming. It's a good spot for enjoying a casual plate lunch or taking a dip to cool off.

Waialua Beach

Waialua Beach is a narrow ribbon of sand 18.5 miles (30 km) east of Kaunakakai, with some of the island's best swimming. As with other beaches in the area, the wind gains in strength throughout the day, and at high tide the sand almost disappears completely. Be sure to watch for coral heads exposed at low tide.

Kumimi Beach

Also known as Twenty-Mile Beach or Murphy's Beach, **Kumimi Beach** is by mile marker 20 on Highway 450 and is the last stretch of sand before the road narrows to one lane. This is arguably East Moloka'i's most popular beach and has sweeping, spectacular views. It also has wide sand and is a nice spot for snorkeling, and in the afternoon hours you might see kitesurfers running laps down the coast.

Sandy Beach

Simple and small, **Sandy Beach** is past mile marker 21 on the winding drive toward Halawa. You'll have just enough room to put down a towel, but the beach stands out on the island for its deeper ocean bottom, allowing for easier movement without having to walk over rocks or reefs. Protected from the surf by an offshore reef, this is one of the best swimming beaches on Moloka'i. Waters here are also crystal clear, unlike the murkier waters of many other beaches on the island, making this a fun snorkeling spot. You might share space here with kids wading in the shallows or locals selling bananas out of the back of a truck.

Halawa Bay

After weaving 10 miles (16 km) over the rocky coast and down through the lush eastern valleys, the two beaches that form **Halawa Bay** are like gold at the end of a rainbow. At the terminus of Highway 450, Kama'alaea Bay is the more protected beach on the far side of the stream. This is the best option for swimming and escaping the wind. Kawili Beach, at the bottom of the cliff, is more exposed to the currents and the trade winds. It's a surreal feeling to hang out on the shores of a place considered one of the oldest settlements in Hawaii. The only facilities are two portable toilets and a single trashcan by the pavilion at the end of the road.

Snorkeling and Diving

Don't tell anybody, but Moloka'i has some of the best snorkeling and diving in Hawaii. With the exception of a few protected areas, Moloka'i's dive and snorkel spots can only be accessed by boat. **Dixie Maru Beach** on the west shore and **Kumimi Beach** on the east shore usually have calm conditions and are the only two bays to snorkel from shore. The island's southern shore is home to Hawaii's longest fringing reef, and dive outfitters have 40 named spots along its outer edge. **Moku Ho'oniki,** off the eastern tip, is known for hammerhead sharks and occasionally some larger pelagic species, from tiger sharks to whales.

CHARTERS, TOURS, AND RENTAL SHOPS

With an office right on a corner on Kaunakakai's main thoroughfare, literally inside the gas station, **Moloka'i Fish and Dive** (53 Ala Malama Ave., 808/553-5926, www.molokaifishanddive.com, hours vary, usually 6am-7:30pm Mon.-Thurs., 6am-8pm Fri.-Sat., 6am-7pm Sun.) offers three-hour snorkeling trips ($99 pp) and scuba trips ($179) to the reef. This shop is the only **PADI** operation on the island and can accommodate a variety of snorkel and dive excursions. Prices and open hours can vary, so call for rates and availability.

For snorkeling only, **Moloka'i Ocean**

Tours (40 Ala Malama Ave., Ste. 107, 808/298-3055, www.molokaioceantours.com, hours vary, typically 9am-6pm Mon.-Sat., 9am-noon Sun.) can accommodate up to six passengers on the 40-foot (12-m) catamaran *Manu Ele'ele* for snorkeling excursions to Kaunakakai ($85 pp). This boat visits the south shore's fringing reef, and trips usually leave around 7:30am. Rent full snorkel sets ($10 per day, $35 per week). If the downstairs office is closed, check upstairs at the sister shop, **Something For Everybody** (40 Ala Malama Ave., Ste. 201, 808/553-3299, www.allthingsmolokai.com, 10am-5pm Mon.-Sat.) for rentals and more info.

Surfing, Paddling, and Kayaking

WEST MOLOKA'I

Remote and empty, West Moloka'i is best in winter when the swells that send waves to O'ahu come crashing onto this coast. The difference is that there aren't 200 people vying for the same wave, and traffic on the highway is nonexistent. While the quality isn't as good as O'ahu's, the surf in western Moloka'i can be heavy, and only experienced surfers should paddle out on big-wave days.

The best-known and consequently most crowded spot on this end of the island is **Sheraton's** at Kepuhi Beach, named after the defunct resort that fronts the beach. Access is sandy and easy, but be wary of occasional shallow boulders while paddling out. The wave is on the left side of the beach, and on better days can be an A-frame that holds to 10 feet (3 m). Sheraton's is a decent spot for intermediate surfers if it's small, and only for experts if it's pumping.

If Sheraton's is too big, drive south to **Dixie Maru,** where a right point break wraps into the bay at sizes half of Sheraton's. If Dixie's is crowded, meaning more than three people, or if you're up for a little adventure, a goat trail leads back into the *kiawe* trees and to **Kaunala Beach,** where another right break bends in toward the shore. The takeoff can be a little difficult since you sit off the rocks, but it's a fun wave to get a few turns in when Sheraton's is all closed out.

On the southern end of the island, the beaches around **Hale O Lono** harbor are able to pick up swells any time of year and can often be heavy in winter. The wind can be fierce in the afternoon, and the murky conditions conjure fears of toothy predators, but there's a 95 percent chance you'll have the waves to yourself. If the wind is down, the waves are up, and the water is clear, the beaches off Hale O Lono can offer some of the most adventurous surf on Moloka'i. Follow the 7-mile (11-km) dirt road from Maunaloa town straight downhill to the shore. A 4WD vehicle is recommended.

KAUNAKAKAI

Since Kaunakakai faces directly south, the best waves are from May through September. Despite the fact that the area boasts miles of shoreline, the majority is blocked by the fringing reef, which makes paddling out virtually impossible. Nevertheless, locals still flock to **Kaunakakai Wharf** during the big swells of summer. Expect a long paddle, since you have to get out past the reef to get to the waves, but the long paddle is rewarded by Moloka'i's best summer wave. Expect a very local crowd, as well as lots of "spongers" (bodyboarders).

EAST MOLOKA'I

The only place for beginners to surf in East Moloka'i is **Waialua Beach,** where gentle rollers provide enough push to practice getting up on two feet. While the waves can be fun, it can be shallow at low tide. More advanced surfers can ride waves at **Halawa,** which can be powerful and barreling on the largest swells of winter. If a group of locals paddles out, head back to shore.

Rental Shops and Tour Operators

If you don't bring a board from Maui (airlines only allow boards up to 6 ft/1.8 m), the best place to rent is **Moloka'i Ocean Tours** (40 Ala Malama Ave., Ste. 107, 808/298-3055, www.molokaioceantours.com, hours vary, typically 9am-6pm Mon.-Sat., 9am-noon Sun.). Prices begin from $30 per day, with weekly specials.

★ Paddleboard and Kayaking Tours

Inside Hotel Moloka'i, the desk staff for **Moloka'i Outdoors** (808/553-4477, www.molokaioutdoors.com, hours vary, typically 8am-10am and 3pm-5pm daily) can line you up with stand-up paddleboard or kayak tours (beginning at 6:45am Mon. and Wed.-Fri.); tours range $55-99 and meet at Hotel Molokai. Tours of the island's southeastern coast that range 5-8 miles (8-13 km) are memorable, with visits to the island's fringing reef—the longest of its kind in the United States. You'll paddle by fishponds, oceanfront homesteads, and colorful sections of reef, and gain fascinating insight on sustainable practices and Moloka'i's rural way of life.

Hiking and Biking

Even for Maui residents, Moloka'i's hiking trails are shrouded in mystery. Often the trails require a 4WD vehicle to access or permission from private landowners, although there are still a number that are accessible to the public.

HIKING

Topside

Bathed in the scent of eucalyptus and pine, the "topside" of central Moloka'i feels like the mountains. With trails ranging 1,500-4,000 feet (460-1,220 m) in elevation, the air is cooler, and once you enter the **Kamakou Preserve,** the weather turns wetter and the surroundings more lush. Songs of native *i'iwi* birds ring from the treetops while mist hangs in the silence of deeply carved valleys.

KALAUPAPA OVERLOOK

The easiest walk is the 1,500-foot (460 m) paved walkway to the **Kalaupapa Overlook,** which starts at the end of the road in Pala'au State Park. Take Highway 470 all the way until it dead-ends in a parking lot. There are basic restrooms here but no potable water. Be prepared for high winds that can blow your hat off, and get your camera ready for the best views of the Kalaupapa Peninsula.

KALAUPAPA TRAIL

Note that the Pali Trail to Kalaupapa was closed indefinitely in 2018 due to a landslide, so hiking down isn't possible until it reopens. The isolated Kalaupapa Peninsula, a former leper colony, is part of Kalaupapa National Historical Park; be sure to check the **National Park Service website** (www.nps.gov) for updates on restrictions and access.

For good reason, the **Kalaupapa Trail** (Mon.-Sat.) is the most popular hike on Moloka'i. It descends 1,700 vertical feet (520 m) over the course of 3.2 miles (5.2 km) and 26 switchbacks. There are photo-worthy views of the sea cliffs and the gorgeous, empty white-sand beach at the bottom. This trail was hand-cut into the mountain in 1886 by Portuguese immigrant Manuel Farinha to establish a land connection with the residents living topside. Remember that everything that goes down must come back up: Expect the hike down to take 1.5 hours, and close to 2 hours for the return.

Once restrictions are lifted, check with **Kalaupapa Rare Adventure/Kekaula Tours** (808/567-6088, www.muleride.com), which had arranged permits and tours in the past. Be sure to bring rain gear and a good pair of shoes, and while there's a small store in Kalaupapa where you can restock on water and snacks, it's best to pack enough food and water that you don't have to rely on the store.

PEPE'OPAE BOG

Constantly shrouded in cloud cover and dripping in every color of green imaginable, if ever there were a place to visualize Hawaii before the arrival of humans, it is **Pepe'opae Bog.** Ninety-eight percent of the plant species here are indigenous to Moloka'i, and 219 of the species are found nowhere else on earth. Following Highway 460 from Kaunakakai, make a right before the bridge at the Homelani Cemetery sign and follow the dirt road for 10 miles (16 km) to the parking area at Waikolu Overlook.

Making it to Waikolu Overlook in a regular vehicle requires high clearance and the best road conditions, and you will get stuck if you go any farther. With a 4WD vehicle, you can drive another 2.6 miles (4.2 km) to the trailhead, but this is precarious at best and requires advanced driving skills. The best option is to park at Waikolu and hike.

From the road, follow the signs for Pepe'opae Bog. Once the trail begins, stay on the metal boardwalk. If you step off, expect to sink shin-deep into the soggy moss and mud. The boardwalk runs for 1.5 miles (2.4 km) through some of the most pristine rainforest left in the state. Hikers who make it to the end are rewarded with a view into **Pelekunu Valley,** plunging 4,000 feet (1,220 m) through the uninhabited, untouched wilderness below. Hikers can attempt the climb on their own, and **The Nature Conservancy** (808/553-5236, www.nature.org) leads hikes into Pepe'opae once per month March-October; advance reservations are required.

PU'U KOLEKOLE

On the same 4WD road leading to the Pepe'opae trailhead, hikers who take the fork to the right will reach the start of the **Pu'u Kolekole Trail,** a 2-mile (3.2-km) hike to the 3,951-foot (1,204-m) summit of Pu'u Kolekole. The view overlooks the southern shore and fringing reef, the island's best view of the southern coast.

West Moloka'i

Given western Moloka'i's lack of mountains, and that the land is privately owned, all the hikes on this side of the island follow the isolated coast.

KAWAKIU AND 'ILIO POINT

A nice walk from the condo complexes of Kaluakoi follows either the coast or a dusty dirt road to the secluded beauty of **Kawakiu Beach.** From Maunaloa Highway (Hwy. 460), take the Kaluakoi Road exit and follow it to the bottom of the hill before making a right on Kaka'ako Road. A left on Lio Place leads to the Paniolo Hale parking lot, where you can follow the signs for the beach, crossing over the fairway of the old golf course before you reach the shore. Make a right, and it's 45 minutes of walking along the coast to Kawakiu.

If the tide or surf is too high to walk along the coast, turn inland past **Pohaku Mauliuli Beach** (Make Horse Beach). After a few minutes, you'll be on a dirt road that leads north and deposits you at Kawakiu. About 100 yards (90 m) before the road drops onto the sand at Kawakiu, there's an ancient Hawaiian *heiau* out on the rocky point. To continue on to **'Ilio Point,** follow the coast for another 30 minutes, where you'll eventually encounter an old U.S. Coast Guard LORAN station and refreshingly little else. Be sure to bring plenty of water, and let someone know where you're going beforehand, since this area is exceptionally remote.

MO'OMOMI COASTAL TRAIL

Hikers with a 4WD vehicle can visit **Mo'omomi** (page 326), where a coastal trail

Don't Change Moloka'i

Nowhere in the islands do the war drums against development beat louder than in Moloka'i, often with regard to development around the island's beaches. It's a complex and sensitive issue, but a popular bumper sticker on the island describes local sentiment: "Moloka'i: not for sale. Just visit. Our lifestyle and economy depend on it." Some visitors assume residents of Moloka'i are anti-tourism, but Moloka'i vendors know tourism is integral to the struggling island economy.

But a glance across the Pailolo Channel to the resorts of Ka'anapali demonstrates what Moloka'i wants to avoid becoming. Most of the island is majority indigenous Hawaiian, and in many ways it is the last holdout of ancient Hawaiian culture. With development comes modernization and loss of culture, as seen in countless indigenous societies across the globe.

The concept of land ownership has never existed in traditional Hawaiian culture. We are stewards of the land, not its owners. Given this belief, Moloka'i residents don't instantly buy in to Western concepts of property rights, real estate, and development. The people of Moloka'i are happy to welcome visitors to share their culture and aloha, but not outsiders who want to put up housing developments, wind farms, or piers to accommodate cruise ships. As another popular bumper sticker says, "Don't change Moloka'i; let it change you," which is really all that needs to be said.

connects a string of beaches with a windswept series of dunes. Each month, March-October, **The Nature Conservancy** (808/553-5236, www.nature.org) leads guided hikes through the area, and while the trail is open year-round, due to the fragile ecosystem, it's imperative that hikers stay on the trail to protect the natural surroundings.

★ Halawa Valley Falls Cultural Hike

You heard it here first: The **Halawa Valley Falls Cultural Hike** (808/542-1855, www.halawavalleymolokai.com, $70, $45 under age 12) is the best activity in Hawaii for those interested in Hawaiian culture. This hike is about more than walking through a rainforest to a beautiful waterfall; it's an educational experience and a journey back in time, where you are welcomed into one of Hawaii's most sacred valleys.

You'll pass numerous *heiau*, the temples that have sat here silently for centuries, and crush *kukui* nuts straight from the trees to feel the healing oils. Depending on the season, your guide might pick *liliko'i* (passion fruit) or guava from the trees to share as a snack on the trail, and if it begins to rain back in the valley, just grab an enormous elephant ear leaf as a natural umbrella. You'll learn about taro and how it's cultivated, learn how residents hunt pigs with knives, and hear stories of the 1946 tsunami from the last remaining resident. At the end of the hike is **Moa'ula Falls,** a multitiered 250-foot (76-m) waterfall that spills toward a plunge pool, where the rocks are dotted with ancient petroglyphs. This is the real Hawaii, and if you schedule the hike, bring along a *ho'okupu,* or offering—pieces of fruit or items you'd use around the house.

To book the trip, phone and leave a message, or book through the **Moloka'i Outdoors** (808/553-4477, www.molokai-outdoors.com) desk in Hotel Moloka'i or through **Moloka'i Fish and Dive** (53 Ala Malama Ave., 808/553-5926, www.molokaifishanddive.com, 6am-7:30pm Mon.-Thurs., 6am-8pm Fri.-Sat., 6am-7pm Sun.). You can also just show up around 9am at the pavilion at the end of the road and hope for a last-minute spot (usually $60 pp). Be sure to pack mosquito repellent, water, snacks, and clothes that can get wet and muddy.

BIKING

The best mountain biking in Moloka'i is on the roads of the Moloka'i Forest Reserve, and road cyclists enjoy miles of open road with minimal traffic. The ride east from Kaunakakai to Halawa Valley is comparable to Maui's ride to Kahakuloa.

In central Kaunakakai, **Moloka'i Bicycle** (80 Mohala St., 808/553-3931, www.maui-molokaibicycle.com, 3pm-6pm Wed., 9am-2pm Sat.) caters to every bike need: rentals (one-day $35 plus $20 per day thereafter, $135 per week), parts, and advice on good rides. They can arrange free pickups and drop-offs from a number of Moloka'i hotels, and $25-30 pickups from the airport and hotels such as Wavecrest and Kaluakoi.

people enjoying a waterfall in Halawa Valley

Other Recreation

BIRD-WATCHING

Many of Hawaii's original bird species are extinct, but there are a number of rare species that cling to existence on Moloka'i. The last known sightings of the *oloma'o* (Moloka'i thrush), for example, as well as the *kakawahie* (Moloka'i creeper), were both in the forests of **Kamakou Preserve,** a rugged and wet mountain area that requires a 4WD vehicle to access. **The Nature Conservancy** (808/553-5236, www.nature.org) leads trips into the preserve once per month March-October.

During the fall and winter, it's common to see *kolea* (Pacific golden plover) scuttling across the shore and grassy areas of the island. These birds migrate to the Arctic Circle during summer before returning to Hawaii for the winter. Once the *kolea* are seen in the islands, locals know that the humpback whales aren't far behind.

FISHING

Fish are central to Moloka'i's culture, and it's the only island where fishing is sustainably managed around the Hawaiian lunar calendar. Fishing is a way of life on the island, and aside from the fishponds along the southern coast, many houses have traditional fishing nets hanging and drying in the yard. Offshore, the Penguin Banks between Moloka'i and O'ahu are some of Hawaii's best fishing grounds, although fishing near shore is good as well. As a general rule, the earlier you depart, the better your chances for success.

Charters

The best place in Kaunakakai for buying fishing accessories is **Moloka'i Fish and Dive** (53 Ala Malama Ave., 808/553-5926, www.molokaifishanddive.com, 6am-7:30pm Mon.-Thurs., 6am-8pm Fri.-Sat., 6am-7pm Sun.), which also operates several trips ($695 for 4 hours, $895 for 6 hours) on the 38-foot (12-m) Delta cruiser *The Coral Queen*.

To throw out some lines with one of Hawaii's best fishers, book a charter with Captain Mike Holmes of **Fun Hogs Fishing** (808/336-0047, www.molokaifishing.com), an avid canoe racer and sailor. Aboard the 27-foot (8-m) *AHI,* Holmes takes guests trolling for blue-water game fish such as mahimahi, ono, ahi, and marlin on four-hour charters ($450) or very reasonably priced full-day eight-hour charters ($750). Fun Hogs can also arrange seasonal whale-watching trips ($75 adults), private snorkeling charters, or any other sort of outing for six or fewer passengers.

Also based at Kaunakakai is Captain Joe Reich of **Alyce C. Sportfishing** (808/558-8377, www.alycecsportfishing.com), who similarly offers half-day, three-quarter-day, and full-day charters aboard his 31-foot (9-m) cruiser. Call for rates, and expect fresh fish for dinner.

For a unique Moloka'i shore-based adventure, **Moloka'i Ocean Tours** (40 Ala Malama Ave., Ste. 107, 808/298-3055, www.molokaioceantours.com, hours vary, typically 9am-6pm Mon.-Sat., 9am-noon Sun.) offers several memorable tours aboard *Alele*—from snorkeling in sparkling blue waters (with visibility to the bottom of the ocean) and majestic sunset cruises to whale-watching December-March. You can also book standard deep-sea charters ($650).

Shopping and Entertainment

SHOPPING

If your idea of vacation is spending time at the mall, you won't find the experience here. Most shops on Moloka'i are utilitarian general stores, some with worthy souvenirs.

Kaunakakai

Shopping in Kaunakakai, you don't have to go very far: All the stores are on the same street. You can park on Ala Malama Avenue and walk to every shop in town.

Imports Gift Shop (82 Ala Malama Ave., 808/553-5734, hours vary, typically 9am-6pm Mon.-Sat., 9am-1pm Sun.) offers a small selection of imported gifts and locally made items in addition to clothing, souvenirs, and snacks.

Moloka'i Art from the Heart (64 Ala Malama Ave., 877/305-1750, www.molokaigallery.com, 10am-5pm Mon.-Fri., 9am-2pm Sat.) is a consignment boutique where 136 local artists are able to showcase and sell their products. Find anything from sarongs to CDs to original paintings. It's a great stop to support the local community.

By the gas station at the end of the road, **Moloka'i Fish and Dive** (61 Ala Malama Ave., 808/553-5926, www.molokaifishanddive.com, 6am-7:30pm Mon.-Thurs., 6am-8pm Fri.-Sat., 6am-7pm Sun.) provides basic gear for the beach as well as camouflage hunting clothing, stickers, souvenirs, and a surf shop.

Toward the wharf, upstairs from the American Savings Bank, **Something For Everybody** (40 Ala Malama Ave., Ste. 201, 808/553-3332, www.allthingsmolokai.com, 10am-5pm Mon.-Fri., 9am-5pm Sat.) is where you'll find *na mea Moloka'i*, "all things Moloka'i," from clothing and stickers to custom-made hats as well as fantastic advice about the island.

Topside

In Kualapu'u, the gift shop **Coffees of Hawaii** (1630 Farrington Ave., 808/567-9490, 7am-3pm Mon.-Fri.) has aloha shirts, coffee, island-themed gifts, and staff who can explain the history of coffee on the island.

West Moloka'i

With the 2008 closing of Moloka'i Ranch, a lot of Maunaloa businesses closed too, so options for shopping are limited.

A Maunaloa staple since 1980, the **Big Wind Kite Factory** (120 Maunaloa Hwy., 808/553-2364, www.bigwindkites.com, 10am-2pm Mon.-Sat.) is an eclectic hodgepodge of handmade kites and woodwork from Bali. As the only store left in the town, by process of elimination, it's worth a look. The owner, Jonathan, will give free factory tours of where the kites are made, help you fly a kite in the park, or even make a kite for any children you may have with you. The store has the largest collection of books found on the island. It's possible to visit repeatedly and still find something new. Look for the rainbow stairs in what is left of central Maunaloa.

ENTERTAINMENT

Kaunakakai

LIVE MUSIC

Paddler's Restaurant and Bar (10 Mohala St., 808/553-3300, www.paddlersrestaurant.com, 11am-8pm Tues.-Sat.) has dancing and live music most evenings. Rolling Rock draft beer is $3 all day, and you'll find evening drink specials and football on the TV. Check the website for an up-to-date schedule on entertainment.

Local music groups can usually be found at Hotel Moloka'i's **Hiro's Ohana Grill** (1300 Kamehameha V Hwy., 808/658-1757, www.hotelmolokai.com) 5:30pm-8:30pm Tuesday-Sunday. The bar scene is lively.

Food

Food on Moloka'i is mostly "local style," meaning stick-to-the-ribs plate lunches, but recent years have seen a welcome increase in culinary diversity. The options are sparse outside Kaunakakai, so be sure you have a plan for food if you venture away from town.

KAUNAKAKAI

Hawaiian Regional

The island's only restaurant to serve resort-quality food is ★ **Hiro's Ohana Grill** (1300 Kamehameha V Hwy., 808/658-1757, www.hotelmolokai.com, 11:30am-2pm and 5:30pm-8:30pm daily, $10-40), which also has Moloka'i's only restaurant tables with an oceanfront view. The restaurant's star attraction is chef Woody's fresh *poke* and a rotating menu of seasonal fresh seafood, surf and turf, and boneless short ribs. Another menu favorite is crab-stuffed mushrooms. For lunch, feast on a fresh fish burger or a hamburger steak plate. Since it's the island's only spot with a hotel liquor license, you can order a cocktail from the oceanfront bar.

Local Style

★ **Kanemitsu Bakery** (79 Ala Malama Ave., 808/553-5855, 6am-2pm Sat.-Tues., 6am-noon Wed.-Fri., $6-10, cash only) isn't just a restaurant; it's a Moloka'i institution that has served baked goods and bread since 1922. Breakfast and lunch are plate-lunch fare, but what catapults the bakery to legendary status is **Hot Bread Lane** (hours vary so call ahead), where their famous hot bread is served from a window in a dingy, dimly lit alley out back. The experience feels illicit, trading cash for gargantuan loaves of cream cheese- and strawberry-filled bread. Other flavors include cinnamon and butter, or a blueberry with cream cheese. Loaves ($7-8) are big enough for two or three people.

★ **Paddler's Restaurant and Bar** (10 Mohala St., 808/553-3300, www.paddlersrestaurant.com, 11am-8pm Tues.-Sat., $12-23) has some of the best burgers, plate lunches, and pasta dishes on the island. In summer, it's the place to be for the canoe races. Paddler's is also the closest thing to a sports bar on the island, with multiple TVs, ice-cold beer on tap, and a happy hour (2pm-5pm daily), plus $3 Rolling Rocks all day. Order from the window inside, and grab a seat on the patio.

For a quick plate lunch at a local favorite, check out **Maka's Korner** (35 Mohala Pl., 808/553-8058, 7am-9pm Mon.-Fri., 8am-1pm Sat.-Sun., $7-10), where you'll find hamburger steak, teriyaki chicken, and heaping bowls of *saimin*.

Filipino

Big Daddy's (67 Ala Malama Ave., no phone, 9am-5pm daily, under $9), along the main Ala Malama Avenue strip, serves a variety of inexpensive Filipino food and Hawaiian fare, in addition to the eggs and omelets for breakfast and local-style plate lunches. Next door is Big Daddy's Market, for a limited selection of groceries, some prepared foods, and a few true Filipino delicacies such as *balut*.

Pizza

The de facto Moloka'i pizza spot is **Moloka'i Pizza Café** (15 Kaunakakai Pl., 808/553-3288, 11am-10pm Mon.-Thurs., 11am-11pm Fri.-Sat., $12-26, cash only). Pizzas are served either whole or by the slice ($3), and there's also a decent selection of pasta dishes as well as rides and games for the kids.

Burgers

Even sleepy Kaunakakai has a takeout burger joint, and the patties at **Moloka'i Burger** (20 Kamehameha V Hwy., 808/553-3533, http://molokaiburger.com, 7am-5pm Mon.-Sat., $8-20) don't disappoint. Little more than a drive-through shed next to Moloka'i Pizza Café, this place has budget burgers big enough to fill you up. For a local treat, skip the bun and spring for a *loco moco,* a hamburger patty served with two eggs, white rice, and gravy.

Ice Cream

To step back in time to the days of dessert at the general store, **Kamoi Snack-n-Go** (28 Kamoi St., 808/553-3742, 10am-6pm daily) has tubs of ice cream like succulent Kona mud pie, which you can get in a waffle cone. There are fresh chocolate chip cookies baked daily, as well as free Wi-Fi, an assortment of gifts, and the old-school charm of a drugstore counter.

Coffee Shops

Hula Bean Coffee (35 Mohala St., 808/553-5183, 6:30am-5pm Mon.-Sat., 8am-5pm Sun.) serves Moloka'i's earliest cup of coffee, beginning at 6:30am Monday-Saturday. It stands out as the only place to get chai tea lattes on the island.

Natural Foods

If you simply can't handle another plate lunch and need healthy fare, head to **The Store House** (145 Ala Malama Ave., 6am-3pm Sun.-Fri., $8-15) for mango or strawberry tropical bowls ($6) topped with almonds, granola, coconut, banana, and honey. You'll also find kale and protein smoothies ($7.50) as well as salads, kombucha, and BLT sandwiches. This small spot is family run, and the fresh food is an oasis in a town of rice and mac salad.

Markets

If you're in town on a Saturday morning, the **Farmers Market** (7am-noon Sat.) is held on the sidewalk in front of the banks, and it is as much a social event as a shopping experience for fresh, locally grown food. Don't be surprised if you find fisherfolk selling their catch from the back of a truck.

Friendly Market (90 Ala Malama Ave., 808/553-5595, 8am-6pm Mon.-Sat.) stays open later than most places in town and is a great spot to pick up picnic supplies for a beach day. If the Friendly Market doesn't have what you need, **Misaki's Groceries and Dry Goods** (78 Ala Malama Ave., no phone, hours vary), a few doors down, should be able to fill the gap.

TOPSIDE

Local Style

A longtime Moloka'i classic, ★ **Kualapu'u Cookhouse** (102 Farrington Ave., 808/567-9655, hours vary so call ahead, $9-15, cash only) is a swinging-screen-door plate-lunch institution where life moves slowly. Order inside at the counter and sit outside on the open-air lanai. You'll get your food when it's ready—no sooner, no later, no worries. Try the chicken *katsu* or *loco moco.*

Coffee Shops

For a morning or afternoon pick-me-up, **Coffees of Hawaii** (1630 Farrington Ave., 808/567-9490, 7am-3pm Mon.-Fri.) is a happening spot to grab a coffee, mocha, or glazed guava pretzel. The coffee is grown and processed right across the street. Try the Moloka'i Mule Skinner, the island's signature blend.

WEST MOLOKA'I

Since the Moloka'i Ranch shuttered its operations, there are no restaurants on this side of the island. **Maunaloa General Store** (200 Maunaloa Hwy., 808/552-2346, 10am-5pm Mon.-Fri., 9am-2pm Sat., 9am-noon Sun.) has basic grocery items to put together a picnic for the beach. If you're hanging out on the beach in Kaluakoi and need an overpriced snack, there's a **sundry store** (typically 9am-5pm daily) in the otherwise abandoned resort.

EAST MOLOKA'I

The only restaurant on the east end is ★ **Mana'e Goods & Grindz** (mile marker 16, Hwy. 450, 808/558-8498, 8am-3pm Thurs.-Tues., $7-11), where a takeout window serves everything from chicken *katsu* to freshly made fruit smoothies. If the banana pancakes happen to be on the menu, don't even hesitate—just order them.

1: local musicians at Hiro's Ohana Grill **2:** Paddler's Restaurant and Bar **3:** Kualapu'u Cookhouse

1
2

3
Kualapu'u
Cookhouse
Molokai's Eating Landmark

Where to Stay

Moloka'i is gloriously free of resorts, and no building on the island is taller than a palm tree. The closest thing you'll find to a resort is laid-back Hotel Moloka'i, which has a concierge, an oceanfront restaurant, a bar, and daily maid service. Most of the island's accommodations are condos, and both **Moloka'i Vacation Properties** (800/658-1717, www.realestateonmolokai.net) and **Friendly Isle Realty** (808/553-3666, www.alohamolokairealty.com) have a wide selection of options. Like elsewhere in the islands, check **VRBO** (www.vrbo.com) for deals on privately owned condos.

WEST MOLOKA'I

Staying in West Moloka'i means you're really far from everything—except beaches and sunsets. The weather has a tendency to be drier, but it's a 25-minute drive to Kaunakakai and the closest restaurant or gas. While the abandoned Sheraton complex is endlessly creepy, there are still a large number of condo units in the surrounding vicinity of Kaluakoi, as well as a handful of privately owned condos that are closer to Dixie Maru Beach.

The **Paniolo Hale** (100 Lio Pl., 800/552-2631, www.paniolohale.org, $150-295) is steps from the shore with sublime views. A two- to three-night minimum stay is required, and some units have longer minimum stays.

CENTRAL MOLOKA'I

Near Kaunakakai, ★ **Hotel Moloka'i** (1300 Kamehameha V Hwy., 877/553-5347, www.hotelmolokai.com, $132-300) is on the water and offers A-frame rooms in a resort-style setting, with a swimming pool, activities desk, included Wi-Fi, and live entertainment every night. The rooms, refurbished numerous times, have fridges and microwaves. This is a convenient, comfortable, and relaxing option. Rates vary by room size and season, and the hotel is home to the island's only oceanfront restaurant and bar.

EAST MOLOKA'I

Along this eastern section of the island are the bulk of vacation rentals, cottages, and B&Bs. Afternoons are punctuated by brisk trade winds, and the setting is more tropical than arid West Moloka'i.

Bed-and-Breakfasts

Ka Hale Mala (808/553-9009, www.bnbmolokai.com, $80, with breakfast $90, cash only) is less than 5 miles (8 km) east of Kaunakakai on Kamakana Place, on the ground floor of a family house set amid a tropical garden. There is a large living room, a full kitchen, a full bath, a separate bedroom, and a laundry room, plus use of snorkel gear.

Condominiums

The largest condo on the east end of the island is the **Wavecrest Resort** (855/201-4087, $125-230), at mile marker 13, with individually owned units. General amenities include a swimming pool, a tennis court, laundry facilities, and a nicely manicured 5-acre (2-ha) setting. One- and two-bedroom units have full kitchens and look across the Pailolo Channel toward Maui. There is a front desk (7:30am-1:30pm Mon.-Fri.).

Vacation Rentals

The two neat and trim two-bedroom **Dunbar Beachfront Cottages** (808/336-0761, www.molokaibeachfrontcottages.com, cash only) are on a secluded section of beach, each with a full kitchen, living room, laundry, and deck. These are quiet surroundings but you still have TV and free Wi-Fi. Cottages can sleep up to four. Rates are $240 with a three-night minimum, plus a $125 cleaning fee.

At the far eastern end of the island high on the eastern hillside is 14,000-acre (5,670-ha) ★ **Pu'u O Hoku Ranch** (808/558-8109, www.puuohoku.com, from $275). The lodge

Where to Stay on Moloka'i

Name	Type	Price	Features	Why Stay Here?	Best For
Dunbar Beachfront Cottages	vacation rental	$240	oceanfront, kitchen	location, quiet	couples
★ **Hotel Moloka'i**	hotel	$132-300	kitchenette, pool, breakfast	modern, activities desk	couples, families
Ka Hale Mala	B&B	$80-90	gardens, kitchen	quiet, affordable	budget travelers, couples, solo travelers
Pala'au State Park	camping	$18	restrooms, pavilion	affordable, location	budget travelers
Paniolo Hale	condo	$150-295	oceanfront, kitchen	location, quiet	couples, families
Papohaku Beach Park	camping	$10-20	toilets, water	oceanfront, quiet	budget travelers
★ **Pu'u O Hoku Ranch**	cottages	from $275	kitchen, views	quiet, retreat	couples, honeymooners, families
Waikolu	camping	$18	toilets, picnic tables	quiet, nearby hiking	budget travelers, adventure travelers
Wavecrest Resort	condo	$125-230	pool, tennis, amenities	oceanfront, modern	couples, families

and three cottages are some of the best and remotest on the island. This is a working ranch that's minutes away from the shore at Halawa Bay. Wi-Fi is available in a few spots, but most accommodations are "unplugged." Check in at the ranch office along the highway at mile marker 25, where there is a small sundries store that sells basic food and gift items. The two-bedroom Sunrise Cottage has a full kitchen and a covered lanai and sleeps up to four. The larger, four-bedroom Grove Cottage (call for rates) can sleep up to eight. From this cottage there are ocean views to Maui with amazing whale-watching in winter. Five miles (8 km) closer to Kaunakakai along the main highway, the one-bedroom Sugar Mill cottage sleeps four, has a full kitchen, and is walking distance from one of the island's nicest beaches.

CAMPING

There are a couple of campgrounds scattered across Moloka'i for travelers on a budget.

The **Papohaku Campground** (808/553-3204, $10 pp Mon.-Thurs., $20 pp Fri.-Sun.) at Papohaku Beach in West Moloka'i requires a permit from the Department of Parks and Recreation office (90 Ailoa St., 808/553-3204, hours vary daily, so call ahead) in Kaunakakai, inside the Mitchell Pauole Center.

For the **Waikolu Campground,** near the Pepe'opae Bog, and the **Pala'au Campground,** within walking distance of the trailhead for the hike to Kalaupapa and accessible only with a 4WD vehicle, obtain permits online at least seven days in advance from the Hawaii Department of Land and Natural Resources (www.camping.ehawaii.gov, $18 for up to 6 people).

Getting There and Around

GETTING THERE

Air

When flying to Moloka'i, don't expect a big plane or a smooth ride. The small aircraft are vulnerable to the brisk trade winds, although the flights are scenic. Often flights from Maui, which take 30 minutes, provide views of Moloka'i's dramatic northern sea cliffs as well as aerial views of the Kalaupapa Peninsula. From Maui, sit on the left side of the aircraft for the best chance of waterfall and coastal views.

The largest planes are with **Hawaiian Airlines** (800/367-5320, www.hawaiianairlines.com), with 37-seat aircraft and multiple flights per day from both Kahului and Honolulu.

Mokulele Airlines (808/567-6381 or 866/260-7070, www.mokuleleairlines.com) offers direct flights from Honolulu and Kahului; any other city will require a connecting flight. Be sure to check the baggage restrictions, since there isn't much space on the planes.

MOLOKA'I AIRPORT

The **Moloka'i Airport** (MKK, 3980 Airport Loop, 808/567-9660) at Ho'olehua is a small open-air facility where you still walk out on the runway to board your plane. There's a single coffee shop (6am-6:30pm daily), and the only car-rental operator, **Alamo** (808/567-6381, www.alamo.com, 7am-7pm daily), has offices across the street.

GETTING AROUND

Car

CAR RENTALS

The only car-rental agency with a booth at the airport is **Alamo** (808/567-6381, www.alamo.com, 7am-7pm daily), which has a large fleet of cars and 4WD Jeeps. If you rent from Alamo, don't lose your key—they don't have extras. For an affordable cruiser, check out **Molokai Car Rental** (3980 Airport Loop, 808/553-3535, www.molokaicars.com), a casual locally owned company that can deliver the car to the airport. They don't have 4WD vehicles, but ask about their room-and-car package at Hotel Moloka'i. The only place besides Alamo to get a 4WD vehicle, **Moloka'i Outdoors** (808/663-8700, www.molokaioutdoors.com) occasionally rents SUVs for stays of three days or longer.

GAS

There are only two gas stations on the island, right next to each other in Kaunakakai. Be sure you have at least half a tank of fuel before heading out on a day trip to Halawa or Papohaku. **Texaco Kaunakakai** (20 Mauna Loa Hwy., 5:30am-7pm Mon.-Sat., 7am-7pm Sun.) has longer hours and more supplies, though it costs at least $1.50 more per gallon than on Maui.

Taxi

The best option for taxis on Moloka'i is **Hele Mai Taxi** (808/336-0967, www.molokaitaxi.com), also offering private tours of the island. Expect to pay about $40 from the airport to Hotel Moloka'i to Kalaupapa Trail.

Shuttle Bus

On a budget, the **MEO public shuttle bus** (www.meoinc.org) operates three routes across the island—but you need to be flexible with your schedule, and there's no service on weekends. Shuttle stops include Hotel Moloka'i and in front of Misaki's Market in central Kaunakakai. The Maunaloa shuttle stops at the airport, and the shuttle typically runs six times Monday-Friday to Maunaloa, and eight times Monday-Friday to Puko'o in East Moloka'i. Along the routes the driver will usually let you get off wherever you want.

Although it's free, donations to keep the shuttle going are accepted. For schedules visit the website.

Tours

Moloka'i Outdoors (808/553-4477, www.molokaioutdoors.com) offers Island Tour packages (prices vary) from Halawa Lookout all the way to Papohaku Beach. Operating three times per week, these tours cover the island in an air-conditioned van and usually carry a small group of only 4-8.

Moloka'i Day Tours (808/895-1673, www.molokaidaytours.com) offers an impressive day-long tour (9am-5pm, $125 pp) that begins at the Moloka'i Museum and Cultural Center and includes guided stops at some of the island's most iconic spots, including Kapuaiwa Coconut Grove and Purdy's Macadamia Nut Farm. Lunch is included.

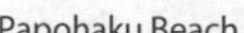

Papohaku Beach

Background

The Landscape

GEOGRAPHY

Maui is 727 square miles (1,880 square km), making it the second-largest island in Hawaii. There are 120 miles (195 km) of coastline. At its widest point, the island is 26 miles (42 km) from north to south and 48 miles (77 km) from east to west.

Known as the "Valley Isle," Maui is the product of two volcanoes—Haleakala and the older Mauna Kahalawai—that merged together into a central isthmus to form the island we know today. At 10,023 feet (3,055 m) above sea level, Haleakala is estimated to be

The Tsunami Siren

If you are visiting Maui on the first workday of the month, don't be alarmed when you hear a loud siren around noon. This is the island's tsunami warning system. The sirens are systematically tested once a month. The loud wailing will last about 30 seconds, after which the regular peace and tranquility will resume. If you hear the tsunami siren at any other time, ask your hotel about potential tsunami evacuations, which have occurred five times since 2011.

about 750,000 years old, making it half as old as Mauna Kahalawai, otherwise known as the West Maui Mountains, which have stood for 1.5 million years. In looking at the two mountains, it's evident that Mauna Kahalawai—with its deeply eroded valleys and dramatically carved peaks—has been exposed to the forces of nature longer than smooth Haleakala. Haleakala's aging is visible in the ravines of Kipahulu, the Kaupo Gap, and the cleft in the mountainside towering above Ke'anae.

Although the islands of Maui, Lana'i, Moloka'i, and Kaho'olawe are four separate landmasses today, all were once connected in an island known as Maui Nui (Great Maui). This massive island was larger than the modern-day Big Island, and it's estimated that the islands were joined until as recently as 20,000 years ago when sea levels were lower as a result of an ice age.

If you look at a map of Hawaii, you will notice that the islands align northwest to southeast. The islands were formed by volcanoes over a consistent hot spot in the mantle of the earth. The tectonic plate in the crust containing the islands drifts northwest at 3-5 inches (7.5-13 cm) per year, essentially creating an "island conveyer belt." Over the course of millions of years, islands bubble up from the ocean floor and drift off the hot spot. Their cores then become extinct volcanoes and they drift northwest, steadily eroding until they become shorter, smaller, and more dramatically sculpted. This explains why the Big Island of Hawaii, which has 500 new acres (200 ha) of land in its most recent eruption, is the largest island with the tallest mountains, and why Maui, next in the chain, is the second largest with the second-tallest mountain. Kaua'i is the oldest in the chain at four million years, and of the 132 islands that make up the state of Hawaii, tiny Midway and Kure atolls are the northwestern reaches.

A seamount known as Lo'ihi is believed to be the next Hawaiian island in the long Pacific chain. Researchers estimate that the island of Lo'ihi will surface southeast of the Big Island in 10,000 years.

Rivers, Lakes, Streams

Maui has no navigable rivers, but there are hundreds of streams. Two of the largest are **Palikea Stream,** which runs through Kipahulu Valley, forming 'Ohe'o Gulch, and **'Iao Stream,** which has sculpted the amazing monoliths in 'Iao Valley. The two largest natural bodies of water are the 41-acre (17-ha) **Kanaha Pond** on the outskirts of Kahului and 500-acre (200-ha) **Kealia Pond** on the southern shore of the isthmus. Be aware that streams and rivulets can quickly turn from trickles to torrents, causing flash floods in valleys that were nearly dry only minutes before.

NATURAL DISASTERS

Maui has experienced a number of events that remain fresh in recent memory, the most dramatic being the 1946 **tsunami** that swept entire villages away along the flank of East Maui and flooded much of Halawa Valley on the eastern tip of Moloka'i. More recently, the tsunami that struck Japan in 2011 also caused a big mess on Maui. There was no loss of life,

Previous: a performer telling a Hawaiian story through hula.

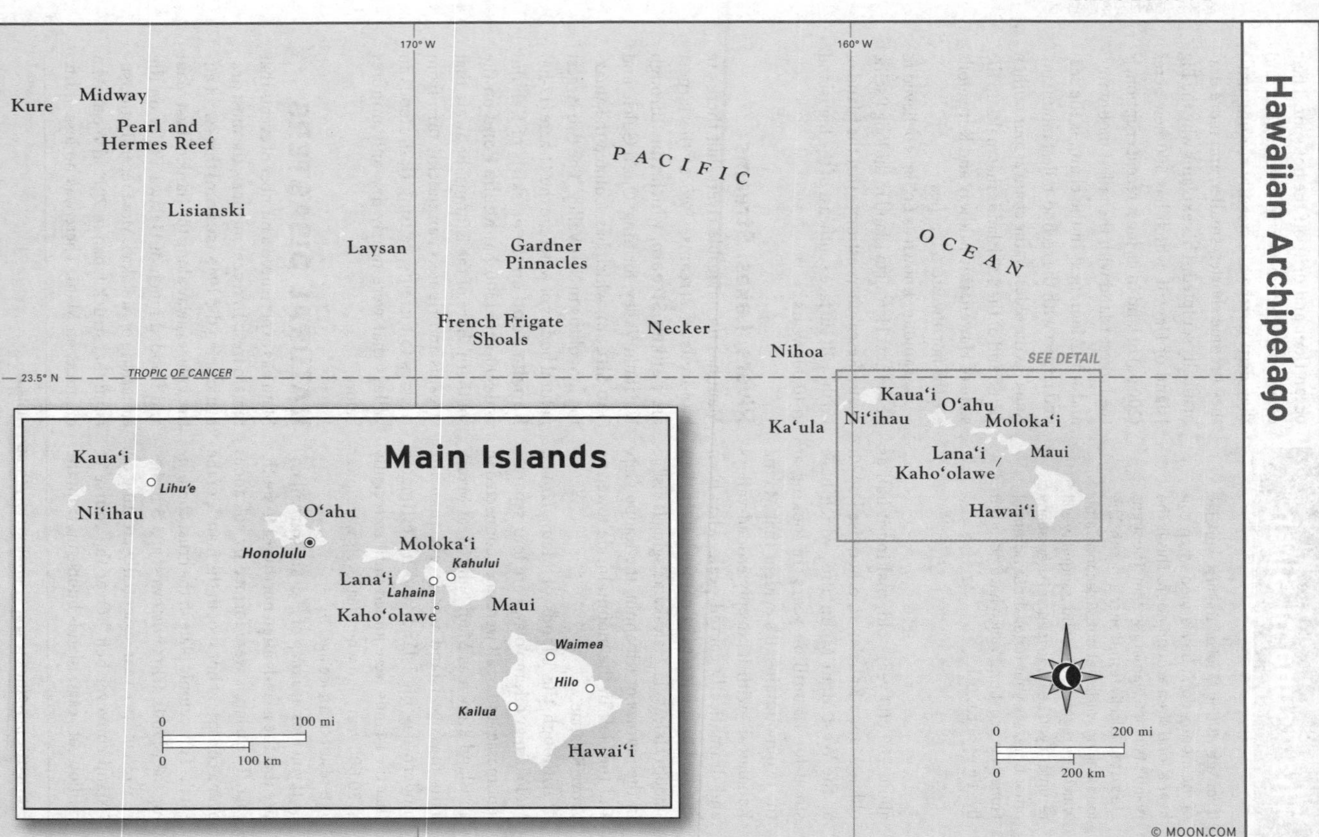
Hawaiian Archipelago
170° W
160° W
Kure
Midway
Pearl and
Hermes Reef
PACIFIC
OCEAN
Lisianski
Laysan
Gardner
Pinnacles
French Frigate
Shoals
Necker
Nihoa
SEE DETAIL
23.5° N
TROPIC OF CANCER
Kaua'i
O'ahu
Ni'ihau
Moloka'i
Ka'ula
Lana'i
Maui
Kaho'olawe
Hawai'i
Main Islands
Kaua'i
Lihu'e
Ni'ihau
O'ahu
Honolulu
Moloka'i
Kahului
Lana'i
Lahaina
Maui
Kaho'olawe
Waimea
Hilo
Kailua
Hawai'i
0
100 mi
0
100 km
0
200 mi
0
200 km
© MOON.COM

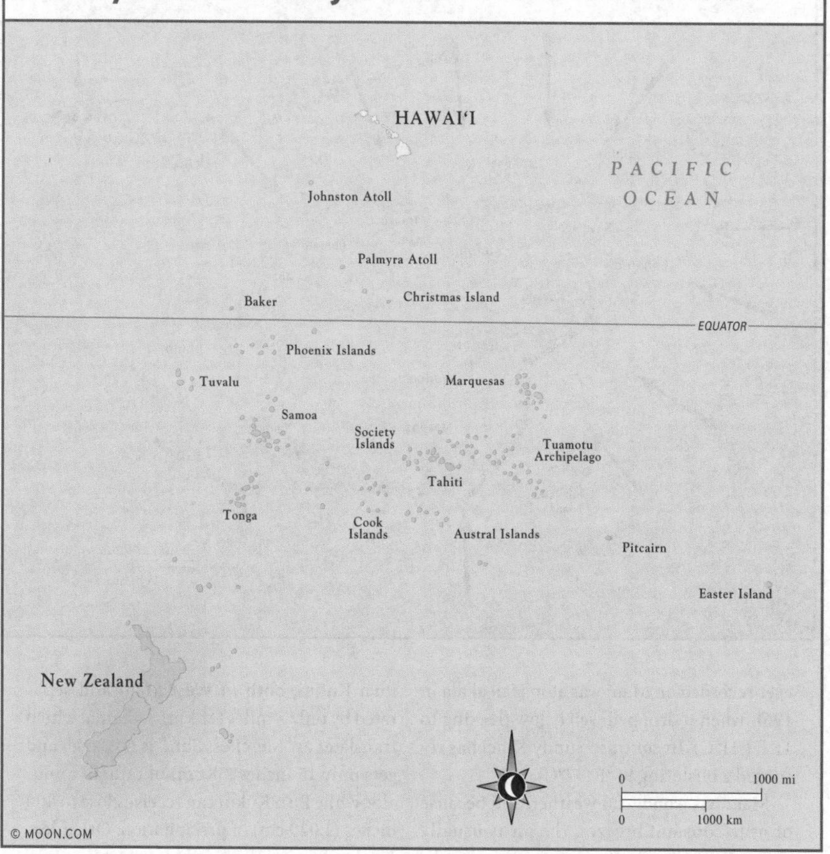

but Lahaina Harbor completely drained, and the returning water was strong enough to sink numerous boats and destroy the docks at many of the island's harbors. At Manele Harbor on Lana'i, the end of the ferry dock was finally repaired in 2016.

The last **hurricane** to affect Maui was Hurricane Iniki in 1992, and while Maui avoided the billions in damage the storm caused on Kaua'i, waves destroyed the pier at Mala and sank numerous boats. Hurricane Iwa in 1982 crept close to the islands, although Maui is outside the hurricane belt, usually spared direct hits.

Although **earthquakes** are rare, a large temblor in October 2006 caused enough damage to close the back road to Hana for almost two years due to landslides and structural damage to bridges.

CLIMATE

Maui, Lana'i, and Moloka'i have weather similar to the rest of the Hawaiian Islands. The weather on Maui depends more on where you are than on the season, and the average daily temperature along the coast is about 78°F (26°C) in summer and about 72°F (22°C) in winter. On Haleakala summit, the average is 43-50°F (6-10°C), although snow can fall in rare winter storms. The lowest temperature

Maui Ocean Conditions

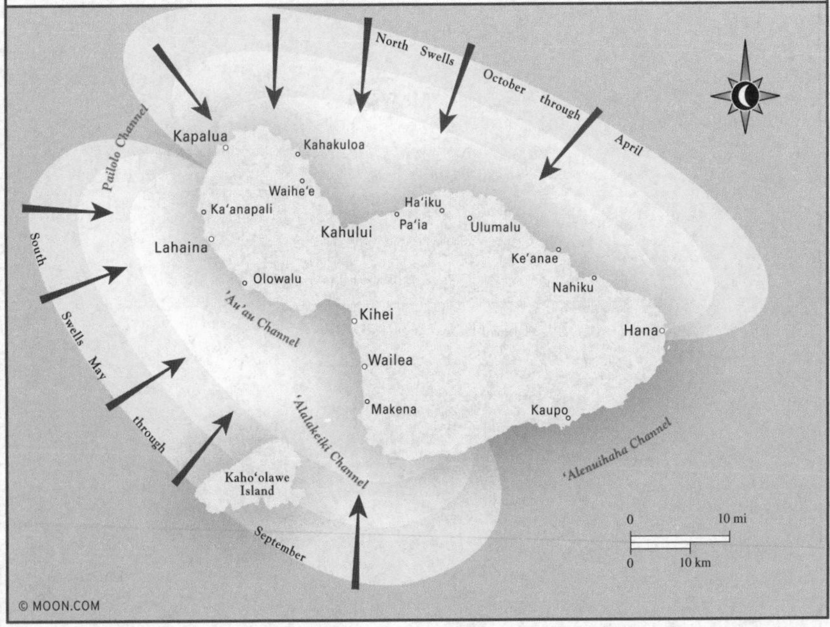

ever recorded on Maui was atop Haleakala in 1961, when it dropped well below freezing to 11°F (-11°C). In contrast, sunny Kihei has recorded a blistering 98°F (37°C).

Maui has wonderful weather, and because of near-constant breezes, the air is usually clear and clean. Traffic and weather conditions never create smog, although on days when the winds blow from the south, a volcanic haze, known as "vog," drifts up from the volcano on the Big Island.

On Lana'i, the average summer temperature along the coast is about 80°F (27°C), while the average winter temperature is about 70°F (21°C). It can be as much as 10 degrees Fahrenheit (5 degrees C) cooler in Lana'i City, in the cooler uplands.

Precipitation

It's raining somewhere on Maui every day while other areas experience drought. A dramatic example is comparing Lahaina with Pu'u Kukui, both in West Maui and separated by only 7 miles (11 km). Lahaina, which translates as "Merciless Sun," is hot, arid, and gets only 15 inches (38 cm) of rainfall annually, while Pu'u Kukui can receive close to 400 inches (1,020 cm) of precipitation. Other leeward towns get a comparable amount of rain as Lahaina, but as you move upcountry and around the north coast, the rains become more frequent. In Hana, rainfall is about five times as much as on the leeward side, averaging more than 80 inches (200 cm) per year.

The Trade Winds

Temperatures in the 50th state are both constant and moderate because of the trade winds, a breeze from the northeast that blows at 10-25 mph (16-40 km/h). These breezes are so prevalent that the northeast sides of the islands are always referred to as **windward,** regardless of where the wind happens to be blowing on any given day. You can count on

Microclimates

The weather on Maui can be confusing. Often it can be raining at your hotel but sunny 2 miles (3 km) down the road, and the wind can be blowing 30 knots (56 km/h) at one beach but completely still at another.

On the mainland, frontal storm systems can stretch for thousands of miles, but weather on Maui is regulated by microclimates. Since the trade winds blow from a northeasterly direction, towns on the northern or eastern coasts are on the windward side of the island and are prone to more wind and rain. Towns on the southern and western shores are in the lee of the steep mountains and are consequently drier and calmer. This explains why parts of the island such as Kapalua, Napili, and Hana are wetter and drier than Lahaina or Kihei. Conversely, during the hot summer months when Lahaina can swelter in 90°F (32°C) heat, the northern areas of Napili and Kapalua can be 10 degrees Fahrenheit (5 degrees C) cooler and blessed with cooling breezes.

Many visitors only check the weather forecast on sites such as Weather.com, which only displays the forecast for the Kahului Airport, on the windier and wetter windward side of Maui. Consequently the forecast will almost always call for showers. Don't be discouraged: Chances are resort areas such as Wailea, Kihei, Lahaina, or Ka'anapali are experiencing a completely different, often sunnier, forecast. For a more accurate weather forecast, see local weather sites such as www.mauiweathertoday.com, which breaks down the island's forecasts by microclimates.

Microclimates don't vary from each other all the time. October-April, Maui can be affected by large cold fronts in the same way that the mainland is. If a large cold front in the North Pacific, which will eventually drop snow and rain on the U.S. West Coast, decides to swing south, the front can move across the islands and bring heavy rain everywhere. While these fronts often dissipate over Kaua'i and O'ahu before reaching Maui, occasionally the front will envelop the entire state and bring up to a week of rain.

For locals, this is what's known as "winter." The island might not get snow (except atop Haleakala), but Maui is still prone to winter storms that bring a lot of rain. No one wants to have a week of rain on their vacation, but a "normal" winter day in Hawaii can be 78°F (26°C) and sunny, or 74°F (23°C) and rainy—but at least it's warm.

If you're staying in Kapalua, Napili, or Ka'anapali and it's windy and rainy at your hotel, don't assume it's raining everywhere. If you're planning a vacation in winter, particularly January-February, cross your fingers that you'll enjoy some midwinter sun.

the trades an average of 300 days per year, rarely missing a day during summer and occurring half the time in winter. Although usually calm in the morning, they pick up during the heat of the afternoon and weaken at night.

Kona Winds

Kona means "leeward" in Hawaiian, and when the trades stop blowing, these southerly winds often take over. To residents of Hawaii, *kona wind* is a euphemism for bad weather because it brings in hot, sticky air. Luckily, kona winds are most common October-April, when they appear roughly half the time. The temperatures drop slightly during the winter, so these hot winds are tolerable, and even useful for moderating the temperature.

A kona storm is another matter. These subtropical low-pressure storms develop west of the Hawaiian Islands, and as they move east, draw winds from the south. Usually occurring only in winter, they can cause heavy rainfall and considerable damage, often continuing for the better part of a week. For locals, this is "winter."

Plants and Animals

Anyone who loves a mystery will be intrigued by the speculation about how plants and animals first came to Hawaii. More than 2,000 miles (3,220 km) from any continent, Hawaii is isolated from the normal ecological spread of plants and animals. Even the most tenacious flora and fauna would have trouble crossing the mighty Pacific. Those that made it by chance would find a totally foreign ecosystem where they had to adapt or perish. Survivors evolved quickly, and many plants and birds became so specialized that they were limited not only to specific islands in the chain but to habitats that frequently consisted of a single isolated valley. After traveling so far and adapting to a niche, they didn't budge again.

Before settlement, Hawaii had no fruits, vegetables, coconut palms, edible land animals, conifers, mangroves, or banyans. The early Polynesians brought 27 varieties of plants they needed for food and other purposes. About 90 percent of the plants on the Hawaiian Islands today were introduced after Captain Cook first set foot here. Tropical flowers, wild and vibrant as we know them today, were relatively few. In a land where thousands of orchids now brighten every corner, there were only four native varieties, the fewest in any of the 50 states. Today, the indigenous plants and animals have the highest rate of extinction anywhere on earth. By the beginning of the 21st century, native plants growing below 1,500 feet (460 m) in elevation were almost completely extinct or totally displaced by introduced species. The land and its life have been greatly transformed by humans and agriculture.

PLANTS

Introduced Species

The majority of flora considered exotic was introduced either by the original Polynesians or by later settlers of European origin. The Polynesians who colonized Hawaii brought foodstuffs, including coconuts, bananas, taro, breadfruit, sweet potatoes, yams, and sugarcane. Non-Hawaiian settlers brought mangoes, papayas, passion fruit, pineapples, and the other tropical fruits and vegetables. The flowers, including protea, plumeria, anthuriums, orchids, heliconia, ginger, and most hibiscus species, have come from every continent on earth.

Native Trees

Koa and *'ohi'a* are two indigenous trees still seen on Maui. Both have been greatly depleted by the foraging of introduced cattle and goats and through logging and forest fires. The **koa,** a form of acacia, is Hawaii's finest native tree. It can grow to more than 70 feet (21 m) and has a strong, straight trunk that can measure more than 10 feet (3 m) in circumference. The Hawaiians used koa as the main log for their dugout canoes, and elaborate ceremonies were performed when a log was cut and dragged to a canoe shed. Koa wood was also preferred for paddles, spears, and surfboards, and today, fine Hawaiian galleries across the islands sell koa wood bowls and crafts.

The ***'ohi'a*** is a survivor and therefore the most abundant of all the native Hawaiian trees—though a recent outbreak of *'ohi'a* disease is currently ravaging the forests. The *'ohi'a* produces a tuft-like flower—usually red, but occasionally orange, yellow, or white, the latter being rare and elusive—that resembles a pompom. The strong, hard wood was used to make canoes, poi bowls, and temple images. *'Ohi'a* logs were also used as railroad ties and shipped to the mainland from Pahoa on the Big Island. It's believed that the golden spike finally linking the rail lines spanning the U.S. East and West Coasts in Ogden, Utah, was driven into a Puna *'ohi'a* log.

1: protea **2:** silversword **3:** dolphins **4:** monk seal

1
2
3
4

'Ahinahina (Silversword)

Found on the high alpine slopes of Haleakala above the 6,000-foot (1,830-m) level, the *'ahinahina* plant is an iconic symbol for the beauty of Haleakala Crater. The plant may live for only a few years or for nearly a century, but each ends its life by sprouting a gorgeous stalk of hundreds of purplish-red flowers before withering from a majestic 6-foot (1.8-m) plant to a flat, gray skeleton. *'Ahinahina* bloom mostly in July and August, but they can bloom as early as May and as late as November. An endangered species, *'ahinahina* are completely protected.

Protea

The slopes of leeward Haleakala between 2,000 and 4,000 feet (610-1,220 m) elevation have perfect growing conditions for protea. The days are warm, the nights are cool, and the well-drained volcanic soil has the right minerals. Protea make excellent gifts that can be shipped anywhere, and although they are beautiful as fresh-cut flowers, they have the extra benefit of drying superbly: just hang them in a dark, dry, well-ventilated area. You can see protea, along with other botanical specialties, at the gardens, flower farms, and gift shops in Kula.

Lokelani Flower

Lokelani, the official flower of Maui, is pink and fragrant and originates from Asia. Brought to the islands in the early 1800s by the Spanish, it's the only nonnative flower recognized as an island flower. Lokelani are often used in leis, found in gardens, and used in ceremonies. You can see the flowers in vivid display in Upcountry at such prominent destinations as Kula Botanical Garden as well as the Garden of Eden along the Road to Hana.

ANIMALS

Birds

One of the great tragedies of natural history is the continuing demise of Hawaiian birdlife. Perhaps only 15 original species of birds remain of the more than 70 indigenous species that thrived before the coming of humans. Since the 1778 arrival of Captain Cook, 23 species have gone extinct, with 31 more in danger. Hawaii's endangered birds account for 40 percent of those officially listed as endangered or threatened by the U.S. Fish and Wildlife Service. In the last 200 years, more than four times as many birds have become extinct in Hawaii as in all of North America.

Despite the threats, a few cling to life in the remote reaches of the East Maui rainforest, with the ***'akohekohe, 'i'iwi,*** and ***'amakihi*** some of the notable varieties. While visitors aren't likely to encounter many of the island's forest birds, those interested in these fragile species should contact the **Maui Forest Bird Recovery Project** (www.mauiforestbirds.org) for more information and ways to volunteer.

Other than forest birds, two water birds found on Maui are the **Hawaiian stilt** (*ae'o*) and the **Hawaiian coot** (*'alae ke'oke'o*). The stilt is about 16 inches (40 cm) tall and lives on Maui at Kanaha and Kealia Ponds, with a black body, white belly, and distinctively pink legs.

At Haleakala Crater, the dark-rumped petrel is found around the summit visitors center about one hour after dusk May-October. The **nene goose**—the Hawaiian state bird—is a close cousin of the Canada goose and can be found in large numbers in the grass around Paliku Cabin.

Sealife

Hawaii's only two indigenous land mammals are the Hawaiian monk seal and the hoary bat; all other mammals have been introduced. While **monk seals** are sometimes sighted along island shores and reefs, the most famous mammals are the whales and dolphins that ply the waters offshore. The channels among the islands of Maui County are home to the world's largest population of **humpback whales.** These acrobatic, aerial cetaceans are a delight for winter visitors, and there are few things like the thrill of a 45-ton animal erupting out of the water before

No Land Predators

Maui can be a hiker's dream, and not just because of the scenery. Unlike other parts of the world, where bears, mountain lions, and snakes are a concern, Maui has no land predators. Remote sections of the island are home to wild boars, axis deer, and mountain goats, although all flee at the sound of human footsteps. There are centipedes and a small number of scorpions, but unless you're hiking through a compost pile, you're not likely to encounter them. When you set off on a hike, there is nothing to worry about in the way of natural predators.

your eyes. Humpbacks migrate to the islands November-May to mate, give birth, and care for their young, and during the course of their four-month stay, they don't eat anything at all.

While whales are only observed during the winter, **dolphins** are year-round residents and a common sight around the islands. There are three distinct pods of Hawaiian spinner dolphins residing along West Maui, South Maui, and the southwestern coast of Lana'i. The acrobatic spinners can complete up to seven full rotations in the air before splashing back down into the water. Larger bottlenose dolphins are also occasionally seen, while pan-tropical spotted dolphins are confined to deeper waters.

History of Maui

DISCOVERY OF THE ISLANDS

It is unknown exactly when the first Polynesians arrived in Hawaii, but the great deliberate migrations from the southern islands seem to have taken place AD 400-800, although anthropologists keep pushing the date back as new evidence appears. They arrived through an uncanny ability to sail and navigate without instruments, using the sun by day and the moon and stars by night. The first planned migrations were from the Marquesas, a group of 11 islands in eastern Polynesia, and for five centuries the Marquesans settled and lived peacefully on the new land.

It appears that in the 12th century, a deliberate exodus of warlike Tahitians arrived and subjugated the settled islanders. A Tahitian priest named Pa'ao introduced the warlike god Ku and the rigid *kapu* system of laws, forever altering the religious and social landscape. Voyages between Tahiti and Hawaii continued for about 100 years, and Tahitian customs, legends, and language became the Hawaiian way of life. Suddenly, for reasons not recorded, the voyages discontinued, and Hawaii returned to isolation.

CAPTAIN COOK

On January 18, 1778, Captain Cook's 100-foot (30-m) flagship HMS *Resolution* and its 90-foot (27-m) companion HMS *Discovery* first caught sight of the island of O'ahu. Two days later, Cook ventured ashore at the town of Waimea to reprovision his ships, and from this moment, life would never be the same for the Hawaiians. He didn't stay long in Waimea, but Cook noted in his diary that the Hawaiians looked similar to other peoples of the Pacific he had encountered, specifically those of New Zealand.

Once the seafarers were on shore, brass medals were traded for a mackerel, and Cook noted that the Hawaiians were quite enamored with the ships. Sailors immediately took to mixing with the women, bringing the first sexually transmitted diseases to the island. They would later ravage the population.

When Cook returned a year later, his impact would become much more significant. Cook had named Hawaii "the Sandwich Islands" in honor of one of his patrons, John Montague, the Earl of Sandwich. On his return voyage he spotted Maui, on November 26, 1778. After eight weeks seeking a suitable harbor, the ships bypassed the island and finally found safe anchorage at Kealakekua Bay on the Kona coast of the Big Island. Fortunately Mr. Anderson, the ship's chronicler, left a handwritten record of the strange and tragic events that followed.

When Cook landed on the Big Island it was the time of the *makahiki,* a celebration dedicated to the beloved god Lono. For a few days, as Cook circled the island, the Hawaiians circled it too, parading a structure that resembled a ship's mast: a crossbeam held overhead with two flowing white sheets of tapa. On January 16, 1779, as the Hawaiians reached Kealakekua Bay, Lono's sacred harbor, Cook's ship came into the port. Because of the timing with the *makahiki,* the Hawaiians believed Cook to be a god and welcomed him to shore with respect.

In the following weeks the Englishmen overstayed their welcome, but when they left, the *Resolution* broke down at sea. Cook returned to Kealakekua but was no longer well received. As the Hawaiians stole random items from the sailboat, the sailors became violent. When the Hawaiians stole a cutter that had been moored to a nearby buoy, Cook lost his temper—a reaction that would ultimately cost him his life. He went ashore with backup, intending to take Chief Kalaniopu'u hostage for ransom. When the violence escalated, Cook was killed. A bitter, protracted argument ensued over the return of Cook's bones (he was ceremoniously roasted to remove the bones from the flesh), and upon finally receiving the bones of their leader, Cook's men sailed back to England.

At the time of Cook's visit, Hawaii was in political turmoil. In the 1780s the islands were divided into three kingdoms: Kalaniopu'u ruled the Big Island and the Hana district of Maui; Kahekili ruled the rest of Maui, Kaho'olawe, Lana'i, and eventually O'ahu; and Kaeo ruled Kaua'i. Soon after, the great warrior Kamehameha conquered all the islands and brought them under one rule, a dynasty that would last 100 years until the Hawaiian monarchy fell forever.

With regard to Western explorers, however, it became known that Hawaii was a convenient stop on routes to the Pacific Northwest and China, leading to an influx of Westerners and increased foreign trade. Hawaii, it seemed, was no longer a secret.

THE OLOWALU MASSACRE

In 1790, as Western traders were still beginning their forays to the islands, the U.S. merchant ship *Eleanora,* commanded by Yankee captain Simon Metcalfe, was looking for a harbor after a long voyage from the Pacific Northwest. Following a day behind was the *Fair American,* a tiny ship sailed by Metcalfe's son, Thomas. While the elder Metcalfe's ship was anchored off the southern coast of Maui, some natives slipped close in their canoes and stole a small boat, killing a sailor in the process.

Upon learning that the perpetrators were from the village of Olowalu, about 5 miles (8 km) south of Lahaina, Metcalfe decided to sail there and trick the Hawaiians by first negotiating a truce and then unleashing full fury upon them. Signaling he was willing to trade, he invited canoes of innocent natives to visit his ship. In the meantime, he ordered that all cannon and muskets be readied with scatter shot. When the canoes were within hailing distance, he ordered his crew to fire at will. More than 100 people were slain, and the Hawaiians remembered this killing as "the Day of Spilled Brains." Metcalfe then sailed away to Kealakekua Bay and, in an unrelated incident, succeeded in insulting a ruling chief named Kameiamoku, who vowed to annihilate the next *haole* ship he saw.

Fate sent him the *Fair American* and young Thomas Metcalfe. The little ship was overrun by superior forces, and in the ensuing battle, the mate, Isaac Davis, so distinguished himself by open acts of bravery that his life alone was spared. Kameiamoku later turned over both Davis and the ship to Kamehameha. Meanwhile, while harbored at Kealakekua, the senior Metcalfe sent John Young to reconnoiter. Kamehameha, having learned of the capture of the *Fair American,* detained Young so he could not report, and Metcalfe, losing patience, marooned his own man and sailed off to Canton. Kamehameha quickly realized the significance of his two captives and the *Fair American* with its brace of small cannons. He appropriated the ship and made Davis and Young trusted advisers, eventually raising them to the rank of chief. They would all play a significant role in the unification of Hawaii.

KAMEHAMEHA'S UNIFICATION OF THE ISLANDS

Kamehameha was born on the Big Island of Hawaii, after a prophecy that he would become a "killer of chiefs." Because of this, other chiefs ordered the child to be killed, so his mother had to sneak off to the royal birthing stones near Moʻokini Heiau on the island's Kohala coast. After giving birth, she gave the child to a servant, who took him down the coast to raise him in solitude. As he grew and matured, Kamehameha proved himself a fierce and hardy warrior, and in due time became one of the strongest chiefs on the island.

In 1790, Kamehameha invaded Maui with the assistance of cannons from the captured *Fair American.* In the Battle of Kepaniwai at ʻIao Valley, Kamehameha killed so many commoners it's said that he dammed the stream waters with their bloody bodies. After his decisive victory on Maui, Kamehameha was drawn back to the Big Island to quell uprisings on his home island. When the king of Maui, Kahekili, sailed to the Big Island to exact revenge for the slaughter at ʻIao, he was thoroughly beaten by Kamehameha's forces at the Battle of Waimanu Valley. Demoralized and defeated, Kahekili succumbed to the rule of Kamehameha, and the battle for Maui had been won.

By the time Kamehameha had won the Big Island and Maui, Hawaii was becoming a regular stopover for ships seeking the lucrative sandalwood trade with China. In February 1791, Captain George Vancouver, who had originally sailed on Cook's ill-fated voyage, returned to Kealakekua and was greeted by a throng of 30,000. The captain at once recognized Kamehameha, who was wearing a Chinese dressing gown that he had received in tribute from another chief, who in turn had received it directly from the hands of Cook himself. Captain Vancouver became a trusted adviser of Kamehameha and told him about the Westerners' form of worship, and the captain gave him gifts of beef cattle, fowl, and breeding stock of sheep and goats. The Hawaiians were cheerful and outgoing, and they showed remorse for the earlier incident when they indicated that the remainder of Cook's bones had been buried in a temple close to Kealakekua. Young, by this time firmly entrenched in Hawaiian society, made no request to sail away with Vancouver. During the next two decades of Kamehameha's rule, the French, Russians, English, and Americans discovered the great whaling waters off Hawaii, and their increasing visits shook the ancient religion and social order of *kapu*.

Kamehameha's final victories over the other islands would come later, with a decisive conflict in 1794 on the island of Oʻahu. Kamehameha and 16,000 of his troops pushed Kalanikupule—the leader of Oʻahu—back into the mountains of Nuʻuanu to the edge of towering cliffs that form the backdrop of Honolulu. After fierce fighting, Kamehameha's men drove Kalanikupule's warriors over the cliffs, and with the dramatic victory, Kamehameha now took control of Oʻahu. In 1796 Kamehameha put down a revolt on Hawaii, and Kaumualiʻi, the king of

Kaua'i, recognizing his strength, gave up the island rather than suffer attack. For the first time in history, Kamehameha became the sole ruler of all of the islands in Hawaii.

Under Kamehameha, social order was medieval, with *ali'i* (nobility) owing their military allegiance to the king and the serf-like *maka'ainana* paying tribute and working the lands.

The great king ruled until his death on May 8, 1819. Hawaii knew a peaceful rule under Kamehameha. After years on Maui, he returned to his home in Kona on the Big Island where he eventually died. To this day, his burial place is unknown. His son, Liholiho, gained the kingdom (and would become Kamehameha II), although Kamehameha's wife Ka'ahumanu had a strong influence and power.

NO MORE *KAPU*

As Ka'ahumanu used her strength to counsel Kamehameha's son and successor, Liholiho, she knew that the old ways would not carry Hawaii into the future. In November 1819 she inspired Liholiho to eliminate the *kapu* system of laws that had so rigidly dominated Hawaiian society. Men eating with women had been prohibited under *kapu*, as was women eating certain foods, such as bananas and particular fish. To exhibit the end of the *kapu* system, Ka'ahumanu and Liholiho ate together in public, thereby shattering these important taboos and marking the demise of the old ways. As the first morsels passed Ka'ahumanu's lips, the ancient gods of Hawaii tumbled. Throughout the land, revered *heiau* were burned and abandoned and idols knocked to the ground. Now the people had nothing but their weakened inner selves to rely on. Nothing and no one could answer their prayers; their spiritual lives were in shambles.

MISSIONARIES AND WHALERS

The year 1819 was of the utmost significance in Hawaiian history. It marked the death of Kamehameha, the overthrow of the ancient *kapu* system, the arrival of the first whaler in Lahaina, and the departure of Calvinist missionaries from New England, determined to convert the heathen islands. With the *kapu* system and all of the ancient gods abandoned (except for the fire goddess Pele of Kilauea), a great void existed in the souls of the Hawaiians.

Missionaries

Into this spiritual vortex sailed the brig *Thaddeus* on April 4, 1820. Coming ashore in Kailua-Kona, the Reverends Bingham and Thurston were granted a one-year trial missionary period by King Liholiho. They established themselves on the Big Island and O'ahu and from there began the transformation of Hawaii. By 1824 the new faith had such a foothold that Chieftess Keopuolani, the first wife of Kamehameha and mother of Kamehameha II, climbed to the fire pit atop Kilauea and defied the volcano goddess Pele. This was even more striking than the previous breaking of the food *kapu* because the strength of Pele could be seen. Keopuolani ate forbidden *'ohelo* berries and cried out, "Jehovah is my God."

The year 1824 also marked the death of Keopuolani, who was given a Christian burial. She had set the standard by accepting Christianity, and several of the *ali'i* had followed the queen's lead. Liholiho had sailed off to England, where he and his wife contracted measles and died. During these years, Ka'ahumanu allied herself with Reverend Richards, pastor of the first mission in the islands, and together they wrote Hawaii's first code of laws based on the Ten Commandments. Foremost was the condemnation of murder, theft, brawling, and the desecration of the Sabbath by work or play. The early missionaries had the best of intentions, but they were blinded by the single-mindedness that was also their greatest ally. *Anything* indigenous was felt to be inferior, and they set about wiping out all traces of the old ways. In their rampage they reduced the

Hawaiian culture to ashes—more so than the diseases brought in by the whalers.

Whalers

A good share of the common sailors of the early 19th century came from the lowest levels of the Western world. Many a lecherous drunkard had awoken from a stupor and found himself on the pitching deck of a ship, discovering to his dismay that he had been "pressed into naval service." These sailors were uneducated and lawless. Their present situation was dim, their future hopeless, and they would live to be 30 if they were lucky and didn't die from scurvy or a thousand other miserable fates. They snatched brief pleasure in every port and jumped ship at any opportunity, especially in an easy berth such as Lahaina. In exchange for aloha they gave drunkenness, sloth, and insidious death by disease. By the 1850s the population of native Hawaiians had tumbled from the estimated 300,000 reported by Captain Cook in 1778 to barely 60,000. Common conditions such as colds, flu, sexually transmitted diseases, and sometimes smallpox and cholera decimated the Hawaiians, who had no natural immunity to these foreign ailments.

Two Worlds Collide

The 1820s were a time of confusion for the Hawaiians. When Kamehameha II died, the kingdom passed to Kauikeaouli (Kamehameha III), who made his residence in Lahaina. The young king was only nine years old when the title passed to him. His childhood was during the cusp of the change from old ways to new, and he was often pulled in two directions by vastly differing beliefs. Since he was royal born, he was bound by age-old Hawaiian tradition to mate and produce an heir with the highest-ranking *ali'i* in the kingdom. This mate happened to be his younger sister, Princess Nahi'ena'ena. To the old Hawaiian advisers, this arrangement was perfectly acceptable. To the influential missionaries, incest was an unimaginable abomination. The young king could not stand the mental pressure imposed by conflicting worlds, and he became a teenage alcoholic too royal to be restrained.

Meanwhile, Nahi'ena'ena was under even more pressure because she was a favorite of the missionaries, having been baptized into the church at age 12. At times she was a pious Christian, at others she drank all night. As the prince and princess grew into their late teens, they became even more attached to each other, and whenever possible, they lived together in a grass house built for the princess by her father.

In 1832 the great Ka'ahumanu died, leaving the king on his own, and in 1833 Kamehameha III fell into total drunken confusion, one night attempting suicide. After this episode he seemed to straighten up a bit and mostly kept a low profile. In 1836, Princess Nahi'ena'ena was convinced by the missionaries to take a husband, and though she married Leleiohoku, a chief from the Big Island, she continued to sleep with her brother. It's uncertain who fathered the child, but Nahi'ena'ena gave birth to a baby boy in September 1836, though the young prince survived for only a few hours and Nahi'ena'ena never recovered. She died in December 1836 and was laid to rest in Lahaina. After the death of his sister, Kamehameha III became a sober and righteous ruler, and he governed longer than any other king until his death in 1854.

Missionaries Take Over

In 1823 the first mission was established in Lahaina, and within a few years many of the notable *ali'i* had been converted to Christianity. Construction began on Waine'e Church in 1828, while a struggle brewed between missionaries and whalers centering on public drunkenness and the servicing of sailors by indigenous women. The missionaries placed a curfew on sailors and prohibited local women from boarding ships. The sailors were outraged. In 1825 the crew of the *Daniel* attacked the home of Reverend Richards, and in 1827, sailors from the whaler *John Palmer* fired their cannon at his house, prompting the construction of the Lahaina fort.

The Hawaiian Written Word

Prior to the arrival of the missionaries, the Hawaiian language—like all other Polynesian languages—had no written form. All information was passed along orally through song, chant, or dance. The missionaries, however, found it difficult to convert Hawaiians to Christianity without the ability to read, write, or create a Hawaiian-language Bible, so they took on the task of creating a Hawaiian orthography and establishing a written form of the language.

With a 12-letter alphabet in place (14 if the *okina* and *kahako* characters are included), the island's first printing press was shipped from Honolulu and housed here in Hale Pa'i in 1834. Not long after its arrival, the first printed newspaper west of the Rocky Mountains—a four-page publication called *Ka Lama Hawaii*—was printed on Valentine's Day of the same year. Along with the press came myriad other benefits of written language, such as hymn books, written laws, and a Hawaiian Constitution. In the course of a single lifetime in the 19th century, the indigenous Hawaiians went from having no form of written communication to boasting one of the highest literacy rates in the world.

The Great Mahele

In 1840, Kamehameha III instituted a constitutional monarchy, bringing about the Hawaiian Bill of Rights. The most far-reaching change was the transition to private ownership of land, although the Hawaiians did not think in terms of "owning" land. No one could *possess* land, one could only *use* land, and its ownership was a strange foreign concept. As a result, naive Hawaiians gave up their lands for a song to unscrupulous traders, and land ownership issues remain a basic and unrectified problem to this day. In 1847, Kamehameha III and his advisers separated the lands of Hawaii into three groupings: crown land (belonging to the king), government land (belonging to the chiefs), and the people's land (the largest parcels). In 1848, there were 245 *ali'i* who entered their land claims in the *Mahele Book*, ensuring their ownership. In 1850 the commoners were given title in fee simple to the lands they cultivated and lived on as tenants, not including house lots in towns. Commoners without land could buy small *kuleana* (farms) from the government for $0.50 per acre ($1.24 per ha). In 1850, foreigners were also allowed to buy land in fee simple, and the ownership of Hawaii from that day forward slipped steadily from the hands of its indigenous people.

SUGAR

While the first successful sugar plantation was on Kaua'i, Maui wasn't far behind when it came to refining the sweet stuff. Many of the successful sugar barons were sons of New England missionaries, and by the mid-1800s sugar mills were springing up from Hana to Lahaina. Labor was the main issue, however. Upon realizing their contracts amounted to indentured servitude, many of the Hawaiians refused to work. Chinese laborers were brought in, but rather than slaving for $3 a month, they often abandoned their contracts and went on to start other businesses. Japanese laborers were then tried, and they worked 10-hour days, six days a week, for $20 a month plus housing.

Eventually sugar was doing so well the industry seemed promising to foreigners who needed work. Boatloads of immigrants from Japan, Portugal, Germany, and Russia came to the islands, and their religions, foods, customs, and cultures mixed together in the multiethnic plantation communities. As the sugar industry boomed, the plantation owners became the new "chiefs" of Hawaii who would carve up the land and dispense favors. With the power of the sugar barons growing with each year, the writing was on the wall that the Hawaiian monarchy would soon be eliminated.

END OF THE MONARCHY

As with the Hawaiian people themselves, the Kamehameha dynasty was dying from within. King Kamehameha IV (Alexander Liholiho) ruled 1854-1863, and his only child died in 1862. He was succeeded by his older brother Kamehameha V (Lot Kamehameha), who ruled until 1872. With his passing, the Kamehameha line ended. William Lunalilo, elected king in 1873 by popular vote, was of royal, but not Kamehameha, lineage. He died after only a year in office and, being a bachelor, left no heirs. He was succeeded by David Kalakaua, known far and wide as the "Merrie Monarch," who made a world tour and was well received wherever he went. Kalakaua died in 1891 and was replaced by his sister, Lydia Lili'uokalani, last of the Hawaiian monarchs.

When Lili'uokalani took the throne in 1891, the native population was at a low of 40,000. When the McKinley Tariff of 1890 brought a decline in sugar profits, she made no attempt to improve the situation, and planters saw her as an obstacle to economic growth. Lorrin Thurston, a Honolulu publisher, gathered a group of 30 men and challenged the Hawaiian monarchy. Naturally, the conspirators could not have succeeded without some solid assurances from a secret contingent in the U.S. Congress as well as outgoing President Benjamin Harrison, who favored Hawaii's annexation. Marines from the *Boston* went ashore to "protect American lives," and on January 17, 1893, the Hawaiian monarchy came to an end. As for Lili'uokalani, she remained staunchly loyal to her people until her death in 1917, and her struggles are documented in *Hawaii's Story,* a powerful read detailing the history of the era.

ANNEXATION

In relinquishing the throne, Lili'uokalani surrendered not to the conspirators, but to U.S. ambassador John Stevens. She believed that the U.S. government, which had assured her of Hawaiian independence and had signed numerous friendly treaties, would be outraged by the overthrow. Indeed, incoming President Grover Cleveland was appalled at the events that had transpired in Hawaii, and he sent a delegation to the islands to research their legality, with hopes of transferring lands back to the queen. Meanwhile, when the conspirators brought the movement for annexation to Congress, it failed to pass, given the shaky ground on which it stood. Not to be deterred, they refused to reinstate Lili'uokalani, and instead continued to operate as a republic with Sanford Dole at the helm.

An unsuccessful countercoup was staged in 1895. After a cache of weapons was found in the queen's garden, Lili'uokalani was relegated to house arrest in a bedroom of 'Iolani Palace. Over the next couple of years, two more annexation movements would be offered to the U.S. Congress, although after witnessing the stiff resistance of the Hawaiian people to formal annexation (a petition of over 30,000 signatures known as the Ku'e Petition opposed joining the union), the movement failed in Congress three times.

Circumstances changed, however, when the United States was drawn into the Spanish-American War in 1898. Recognizing that Hawaii was strategically situated for fighting the Spanish in the Philippines and that Pearl Harbor would make the perfect naval port, a joint resolution of Congress was signed that deemed it acceptable to annex Hawaii as a circumstance of the impending war, known as the Newlands Resolution.

There remains great debate today over the legality of the situation. In many ways it appears that since no formal annexation treaty was signed—particularly one pertaining to international lands that are extraterritorial of immediate borders—that Hawaii technically may never have been annexed through proper and constitutional channels. Furthermore, whatever documents were in fact signed were done so as an agreement with the Republic of Hawaii, and at no point was an agreement made with the original Hawaiian Kingdom, representing more than 90 percent of the population. Even now, over 120 years later, it remains a hotly contested issue, and as time

The "Lawful Hawaiian Government"

At Ho'okipa Lookout and Maliko Gulch you will notice signs proclaiming that the land is under the jurisdiction of the "Lawful Hawaiian Government." While the issue of Hawaiian sovereignty is lengthy and complex, here are the basics about the ongoing movement.

The Kingdom of Hawaii was formed in 1810 when King Kamehameha united all the islands under a single rule, and it lasted until 1893 when the monarchy was illegally overthrown in a bloodless coup by a group of Western businesspeople. While the kingdom existed under a monarchial system of rule from 1810 to 1840, a notable change took place in 1840 when King Kamehameha III changed the system of governance to a constitutional monarchy similar to those found in modern-day Spain, Thailand, or Sweden. A congress was established, there were recognized officials, and a constitution was drafted that outlined the laws of the nation. Due to the efforts taken to create a legitimate form of government, the Kingdom of Hawaii was officially recognized by England and France in 1843, and the United States followed suit in 1846. Hawaii had embassies in dozens of countries; there was a Hawaiian embassy in Washington DC as well as consulates in New York and San Francisco.

When Western business interests overthrew Queen Lili'uokalani in 1893 and formed the Republic of Hawaii, it was governed by Sanford Dole and a motion put forth to have the United States annex the islands. It failed when President Grover Cleveland ruled through an investigation that the takeover was not performed through legal means. Another annexation attempt was put forth in 1897, but this too was shot down due to a letter of protest from Queen Lili'uokalani, who remained under house arrest, along with tens of thousands of Hawaiian signatures. Finally, with the outbreak of the Spanish-American War in 1898, U.S. congressional legislation decided that Hawaii would be occupied by U.S. military forces as a strategic military base in the Pacific. Once the war was over, the occupiers remained, and Hawaii stayed a territory to the United States despite the end of the hostilities (it would later become a state in 1959). Since Hawaii was never formally annexed by either treaty or war, however, the Hawaiian offices of government were consequently never abolished, and when Queen Lili'uokalani died in 1917, the offices sat vacant.

In 1993, President Bill Clinton signed the Apology Resolution, which basically said that the

marches on, there is growing support for the kingdom that may have never ceased to exist.

Nevertheless, as Hawaii entered the 20th century, it became largely Americanized. Hawaiian language, religion, and culture were nearly gone. Everyone dressed like Westerners and practiced Christianity, and Asians made up 75 percent of plantation workers. By 1900 everyone was encouraged to attend school, and almost 90 percent of Hawaiians were literate. Interracial marriages were accepted, and Hawaii became a true melting pot.

Pearl Harbor Attack

On December 7, 1941, the Japanese carrier *Akagi* launched the attack on O'ahu. At the end of the day, 2,325 U.S. military members and 57 civilians were dead, 188 planes were destroyed, 18 major warships were sunk or heavily damaged, and the United States was in World War II. It roared on for four years through the Nagasaki and Hiroshima bombings, and when it was over, in the hearts of a nation, Hawaii was an integral part of the United States.

Statehood

During World War II, Hawaii was placed under martial law, but no serious attempt to intern the Japanese population was made. Many Japanese-Americans went on to gain the respect of the American people through their outstanding fighting record during the war. Hawaii's own 100th Battalion became the famous 442nd Regimental Combat Team, which would be the most decorated battalion in all of World War II. When these GIs returned home, no one was going to tell them

United States was sorry for overthrowing the Hawaiian monarchy, recognizing officially that it had done so. It was at this time that sovereignty leaders realized that even though the monarchy had ceased to exist with the death of Queen Lili'uokalani, the Hawaiian framework of government established had never actually disappeared. Since the framework was still in place, it simply needed to be reinstated with new officers, citizens, and elections.

Using the old electoral processes established in the 1864 constitution, elections were held in 1999 to once again establish a congress for a kingdom that had never disappeared. Henry Noa was elected prime minister, there are now representatives to the congress from 24 districts across the state, and elections take place among the Hawaiian Kingdom citizens. In order to become a citizen of the Hawaiian Kingdom, you must swear an oath of allegiance to the kingdom and renounce your citizenship to the United States. As of July 2011, there were 400 citizens in the Hawaiian Kingdom, with 7,000 citizenship applications being processed. In addition to the elected offices, there are also a Department of Health and Department of Transportation. There is a slight chance you might see a vehicle displaying a Hawaiian Kingdom license plate on both the front and back of the car during your time on the island.

Citizens of the Hawaiian Kingdom are quick to point out, however, that they are not seceding from the United States, because the Kingdom of Hawaii was never formally ceded in the first place; after more than a century, the positions are being filled once again. This reinstated government has been officially recognized in numerous international proceedings, notably at the International Criminal Court in 2012. No U.S. government grants are involved in the funding of the nation, and you will often see *huli huli* chicken stands (especially in the Wahikuli section of Lahaina) that help raise funds for reinstating the lawful Hawaiian government.

Proponents of the Hawaiian Kingdom do not hope to seek "nation within a nation" status such as those granted to Native Americans because this would mean formally ceding the nation to the overall governance of the United States. Instead, they would prefer to continue with their sovereignty, which was never formally abolished.

that they were not loyal Americans. Many of these Americans of Japanese Ancestry (AJAs) took advantage of the GI Bill and received higher education. They also rallied grassroots support for statehood. When the vote finally occurred, approximately 132,900 voted in favor of statehood with only 7,800 votes against. Congress passed the Hawaii State Bill on March 12, 1959, and on August 21, 1959, President Eisenhower announced that Hawaii was officially the 50th state.

Government and Economy

GOVERNMENT

The government of Hawaii is limited to two levels, the state and the county, of which the islands of Maui, Moloka'i, Lana'i, and Kaho'olawe make up Maui County. Politics and government were at one time taken seriously in the Aloha State, which once consistently turned in the best national voting record per capita. For example, in the first state elections, 173,000 of 180,000 registered voters cast ballots—a whopping 94 percent of the electorate. These days, however, although there is still great voter turnout for state and local elections, Hawaii boasts one of the worst voter turnouts for national presidential elections. In the 2016 election, Hawaii saw a measly 43 percent of registered voters cast ballots. Because of Hawaii's location in the far west, when presidential elections are held, the results are often known before many in the state have time to cast their ballots. There is also a vocal minority that sees no point voting in elections for a nation they would rather not be a part of.

Hawaii is the only state to have just a single school district. A packed schoolroom in downtown Honolulu falls under the same set of guidelines as a one-room schoolhouse in West Moloka'i. Consequently, the idea of moving to a neighborhood where the schools are better isn't part of Hawaiian life.

ECONOMY

Today, tourism and the military are the two prime sources of income for Hawaii. Tourists come in anticipation of endless golden days on soothing beaches, while the military is provided with the strategic position of an unsinkable battleship. Each economic sector nets Hawaii billions annually. Also contributing to the state revenue are, in descending proportions, manufacturing, construction, and agriculture.

Tourism

Maui is the second most frequently chosen Hawaiian destination after O'ahu and welcomes more than two million visitors annually. On any given day about 40,000 visitors are enjoying the island. Maui's most popular attractions are Haleakala National Park, Lahaina town, the Maui Ocean Center, the Whalers Village Museum, 'Iao Valley, and Hana.

Agriculture

Maui generates agricultural revenue through cattle, pineapples, coffee, and flowers, along with a substantial subculture for *pakalolo* (marijuana). Cattle grazing occurs on the western and southern slopes of Haleakala, where 30,000 acres (12,140 ha) are owned by the Haleakala Ranch and more than 18,000 acres (7,280 ha) by the Ulupalakua Ranch. The upper slopes of Haleakala around Kula are a gardener's dream, where delicious onions, potatoes, and all sorts of garden vegetables are grown.

Maui's lone remaining sugar mill closed in 2016, and actions have been taken to replace the acreage with the growth of coffee beans, hemp, and other organic farming. Hali'imaile Pineapple Company grows pineapples between Pa'ia and Makawao on the lower slope of Haleakala. Since Maui's last cannery closed in 2007, the only way to buy pineapples is in the form of a whole fruit.

Meanwhile, renegade entrepreneurs grow patches of *pakalolo* wherever they can find a spot that has the right vibes and is away from the prying eyes of authorities. Deep in the West Maui Mountains and along the Hana coast are favorite areas of island growers.

Military

The small military presence on Maui comprises a tiny U.S. Army installation near Kahului, the U.S. Coast Guard facility at Ma'alaea, and an Air Force tracking station on top of Haleakala.

People and Culture

POPULATION

Hawaii is a true ethnic melting pot where more than 50 diverse groups are represented. With nearly 168,000 residents, Maui has the third-largest island population in Hawaii, with about 7,400 residents on Moloka'i and 3,100 on Lana'i. Maui's population density is 210 people per square mile (81 per square km), with Moloka'i at 27 per square mile (10 per square km) and Lana'i at 24 per square mile (9 per square km). The Kahului-Wailuku area has the island's greatest population with nearly 50,000 people, and the South Maui zip code is one of the island's largest, with nearly 29,000 residents in Kihei and Wailea. The Upcountry population is nearly 25,000, including Pa'ia and Ha'iku, and West Maui has 21,000. In East Maui about 5,000 live along the Hana Highway, although fewer than 2,000 reside in Hana itself. For Maui County, 78 percent are urban while 22 percent live rurally. The ethnic breakdown of Maui County's 163,000 people is 36 percent Caucasian, 29 percent Asian, 23 percent mixed, 11 percent Hawaiian, and 1 percent other.

PEOPLE

Hawaiians

Any study of the indigenous Hawaiians is ultimately a study in tragedy because it nearly ends in their demise. When Captain Cook first sighted Hawaii in 1778, there were an estimated 300,000 Hawaiians living in relative harmony with their ecological surroundings; within 100 years a scant 50,000 demoralized and dejected Hawaiians existed almost as wards of the state. Today, although more than 240,000 people claim varying degrees of Hawaiian blood, experts say that fewer than 1,000 are pure Hawaiian, and this might be stretching it.

It's easy to see why people of Hawaiian lineage could be bitter over what they have lost, being strangers in their own land, much like Native Americans. The good news is Hawaiians are gradually reclaiming some parcels originally lost, with many families now owning homes through the Department of Hawaiian Home Lands. The movement for independent rule is continuing to gain strength, and a Hawaiian cultural awakening continues to grow by the year.

POLYNESIAN ROOTS

The Polynesians' original stock is muddled and remains an anthropological mystery, but it's believed that they were nomadic wanderers who migrated from both the Indian subcontinent and Southeast Asia through Indonesia, where they learned to sail and navigate on protected waterways. As they migrated, they honed their sailing skills until they could take on the Pacific. As they moved, they absorbed people from other cultures and races until they had coalesced into the Polynesians.

THE CASTE SYSTEM

Hawaiian society was divided into rankings by a strict caste system determined by birth and from which there was no chance of escaping. The highest rank was the *ali'i*—the chiefs and royalty. Ranking passed from both father and mother, and custom dictated that the first mating of an *ali'i* be with a person of equal status.

A *kahuna* was a highly skilled person whose advice was sought before any major project was undertaken, such as building a house, hollowing a canoe log, or even offering a prayer.

Besides this priesthood of *kahuna*, there were other *kahuna* who were not *ali'i* but commoners. The two most important were the healers (*kahuna lapa'au*) and the black magicians (*kahuna 'ana'ana*). The *kahuna lapa'au* had a marvelous pharmacopoeia of herbs and spices that could cure more than 250 diseases common to the Hawaiians. The *kahuna 'ana'ana* could be hired to cast a love spell over a person or cause his or her untimely death.

The common people were called the *maka'ainana,* "the people of land"—the farmers, craftspeople, and fishers. The land that they lived on was controlled by the *ali'i,* but they were not bound to it. If the local *ali'i* were cruel or unfair, the *maka'ainana* had the right to leave and live on another's lands. The *maka'ainana* mostly loved their local *ali'i* much like a child loves a parent, and the feeling was reciprocal. All *maka'ainana* formed extended families called *ohana* who usually lived on the same section of land, called *ahupua'a.* Those farmers who lived inland would barter their produce with the fishers who lived on the shore, and thus all shared equally in the bounty of land and sea.

A special group called *kauwa* was an untouchable caste confined to reservations. Their origins were obviously Polynesian, but they appear to have been descendants of castaways who had survived and become perhaps the indigenous people of Hawaii before the main migrations. It was *kapu* for anyone to go onto *kauwa* lands, and doing so meant instant death. If a human sacrifice was needed, the *kahuna* would summon a *kauwa,* who had no recourse but to mutely comply. To this day, to call someone *kauwa,* which now supposedly means only "servant," is still considered a fight-provoking insult.

HAWAIIANS TODAY

Many of the Hawaiians who moved to the cities became more and more disenfranchised. Their folk society stressed openness and a giving nature but downplayed the individual and the ownership of private property. Ni'ihau, a privately owned island, is home to about 120 pure-blooded Hawaiians, representing the largest concentration of them, per capita, in the islands. The Robinson family, which owns the island, restricts visitors to invited guests only.

The second-largest concentration is on Moloka'i, where 2,700 Hawaiians, living mostly on 40-acre (16-ha) *kuleana* of Hawaiian Home Lands, make up 40 percent of that island's population. The majority of mixed-blood Hawaiians, 240,000 or so, live on O'ahu, where they are particularly active in the hotel and entertainment fields.

Chinese

Next to Yankees from New England, the Chinese are the oldest migrant group in Hawaii, and their influence has far outshone their meager numbers. They brought to Hawaii, along with their individuality, Confucianism, Taoism, and Buddhism, although many have long since become Christians. The Chinese population of 56,000 makes up only 5 percent of the state's total, but the vast majority live on O'ahu. The first Chinese were brought to Hawaii in 1852 to work on sugar plantations. They were contracted to work for $3 a month plus room and board. After working 12-hour days six days a week, the Chinese nearly always moved on when their contracts were done and started their own businesses or shops.

Japanese

The first Japanese to come to Hawaii were ambassadors sent to Washington DC by the shogun, who stopped in Honolulu on the way in 1860. A small group came eight years later to work on the plantations, and a large influx came in 1885. After a migration of Japanese farmers who were sent over because of a famine, there was a steady influx 1897-1908. By 1900 there were more than 60,000 Japanese in the islands.

Caucasians

Next to Hawaiians themselves, Caucasians have the longest history in Hawaii. They settled in earnest since the missionaries of the 1820s and were established long before any other migrant group. Caucasians have a distinction separating them from all other ethnic groups in Hawaii in that they are lumped together as one. A person can be anything from a Protestant Norwegian dockworker to a Greek Orthodox shipping tycoon, but if his

Local Custom: No Shoes in the House

One of the local customs visitors often find surprising is the removal of shoes before entering a house. Unless you're directly told otherwise, not wearing shoes inside the house is the rule. There are a few theories about where the custom came from. Some say it's common sense not to track added dirt and germs inside, while others say it's a Japanese custom relating to not following in other people's shoes (or paths, or footsteps). Whatever the origins might be, follow it if you visit a local's home. It's even usually requested by the management of vacation rentals. This rule doesn't extend to hotels or businesses, but if you notice a pile of shoes at the door of a small business, it's probably a sign that the owner prefers the no-shoes rule. If you are a fan of the custom or already practice it at home, locally made Please Remove Shoes signs and tiles can be purchased around the island.

or her skin is light, in Hawaii, he or she is a *haole.* What's more, a person could have arrived at Waikiki from Missoula, Montana, in the last 24 hours, or his or her *kama'aina* family can go back five generations, but again, if the person is Caucasian, he or she is a *haole.*

The word *haole* has a floating connotation that depends on the spirit in which it's used. It can mean everything from a derisive "honky" or "cracker" to nothing more than "white person." The exact Hawaiian meaning is clouded, although it largely has to do with the fact that when white people first arrived, they lacked any true *ha,* which means "spirit," or "breath." Europeans did not "share breath" in the same way that many Polynesian cultures would (such as the traditional greeting of pressing noses rather than hands), and this lack of "breath" lives on today in the semi-derogatory term.

Portuguese

Between 1878 and 1887, around 12,000 Portuguese came to Hawaii. Later on, 6,000 more arrived between 1906 and 1913. They were put to work on plantations and gained a reputation as good workers. Although they were European, for some reason they weren't *haole,* but somewhere in between. Nearly 27,000 Portuguese made up 11 percent of Hawaii's population by 1920. They intermarried, and the Portuguese remain an ethnic group in Hawaii today. One item they brought in that would influence local culture was the *cavaquinho,* a stringed instrument that would evolve into the ukulele.

Filipinos

The Filipinos who came to Hawaii brought high hopes of amassing personal fortunes and returning home as rich heroes, but for most it was a dream that never came true. Filipinos had been U.S. nationals ever since the Spanish-American War of 1898 and as such weren't subject to immigration laws that curtailed the importation of other Asian workers. The first to arrive were 15 families in 1906, but a large number came in 1924 as strikebreakers. From the first, Filipinos were looked down on by other immigrant groups and were considered particularly uncouth by the Japanese. The value they placed on education was the lowest of any group, and even by 1930 only about half could speak rudimentary English, the majority remaining illiterate. They were billeted in the worst housing, performed the most menial jobs, and were the last hired and first fired.

One big difference between Filipinos and other groups was that the men brought no Filipino women to marry, so they clung to the idea of returning home. In 1930 there were 30,000 men and only 360 women. Many of these terribly lonely bachelors would feast and drink on weekends and engage in cockfighting on Sundays. When some did manage to find wives, their mates were inevitably part Hawaiian. Filipino workers continued

The *Shaka* and You

Chances are you'll see locals on the islands greeting each other with a hand gesture, a loose fist extending the thumb and pinkie fingers while holding down the middle three fingers. That's the *shaka,* which can mean "hello," "good-bye," and "thanks." In modern times, the *shaka* has been associated with the phrase "hang loose." But where did it originate? According to local newspapers, the hand gesture came about because of an O'ahu local who lost his three middle fingers. Other reports suggest the *shaka* has its origins in early whalers who used the gesture to signify "tails up"—a whale's tail spotted in the water. Now it's your turn. Get your hand into formation, oscillate it a bit, and you're all set, brah.

to be imported, although sporadically, until 1946, so even today there are a few old Filipino bachelors who never managed to get home.

Other Groups

About 10 percent of Hawaii's population is a conglomerate of small ethnic groups. Of these, one of the largest and fastest growing is Korean, with 23,000 individuals. About 30,000 residents consider themselves Puerto Rican, and 22,000 residents identify as Black. Another fast-growing group is Samoans, with 16,000 currently settled in Hawaii and more on the way. Other lesser-represented ethnic groups include 3,500 Native Americans, 4,000 Tongans, 7,000 other Pacific Islanders, and 8,000 Vietnamese.

FOOD

Although modern Hawaiian food is extremely meat-based, traditionally Hawaiians were nearly vegetarian, reserving meat for celebrations rather than daily meals. Traditional Hawaiian food can still be found, but a lot of it now is simply considered "local food" and blended with food from other cultures.

For ancient Hawaiians, the ocean was a great source of food, and they cultivated successful land crops such as taro, sweet potatoes, breadfruit, and sugarcane. They raised pigs and chickens for celebratory meals, although they wouldn't make use of the eggs.

The taro root was the staple crop, and it was the first thing they got going when settling the island. Taro would mostly be pounded into poi, which is another staple often eaten with other foods. Women avoided the starch while pregnant in hopes of avoiding growing a large baby.

Today, **Hawaiian regional cuisine** draws upon the influences of Japanese, Filipino, Tahitian, Chinese, and Portuguese cuisines. Island dishes include a variety of ingredients such as fresh fish, pork, Spam (which the U.S. military introduced to the islands during World War II), onions, sweet potatoes, yams, taro, coconut, pineapple, rice, and soy sauce. An island favorite, ahi *poke* is a dish served at many delis and supermarkets and enjoyed as a snack or a meal; it consists of raw yellowfin tuna mixed with soy sauce, onions, seaweed, and other flavors. *Lau lau* is a luau food that is served as a small package of meat, fish, or vegetables all wrapped in *ti* leaves and then baked or steamed. Usually served as a dessert, *haupia* is a custard-like substance made from coconut.

The essence of **local-style food** is found in the form of **plate lunch,** which originated in the 19th century as a midday meal for plantation workers. This hearty meal typically features white rice, macaroni salad, and a choice of protein, such as Hawaiian pulled pork.

THE ARTS

Since everything in old Hawaii had to be fashioned by hand, almost every object was either a genuine work of art or the product of a highly refined craft. With the "civilizing" of the indigenous population, most of the old ways disappeared, including the old arts and crafts. Most authentic Hawaiian art by master craftspeople exists only in museums. But with the resurgence of connecting to Hawaiian roots as part of the Hawaiian Renaissance, many old arts are being revitalized, and their legacy lives on in a number of proficient artists.

Hula

The hula is more than an ethnic dance; it's the soul of Hawaii expressed in motion. It began as a form of worship during religious ceremonies and was danced only by highly trained men. As time went on, however, women were allowed to learn the hula, and today both genders perform the dance equally.

During the 19th century, the hula almost vanished because the missionaries considered it vile and heathen. King Kalakaua saved it during the late 1800s by forming his own troupe and encouraging the dancers to learn the old hula. Many of the original dances had been forgotten, but some were retained and are performed to this day.

Hula is art in swaying motion, and the true form is studied rigorously and taken seriously. Today, hula *halau* (schools) are active on every island, teaching hula and keeping the old ways and culture alive. Ancient hula is called *hula kahiko,* and modern renditions are known as *hula auana.* Performers still spend years perfecting their techniques. They show off their accomplishments during the fierce competition of the Merrie Monarch Festival in Hilo every April.

Canoes

The most respected artisans in old Hawaii were the canoe makers. With little more than a stone adze and a pump drill, they built sleek and seaworthy canoes that could carry 200 people and last for generations. The main hull was usually a gigantic koa log, and the gunwale planks were minutely drilled and sewn to the sides with sennit rope. Apprenticeships lasted for years, and a young man knew that he had graduated when one day he was nonchalantly asked to sit down and eat with the master builders. Small family-size canoes with outriggers were used for fishing and perhaps carried a spear rack; large oceangoing double-hulled canoes were used for migration and warfare. On these, the giant logs had been adzed to about 2 inches (5 cm) thick. A mainsail woven from pandanus was mounted on a central platform, and the boat was steered by two long paddles. The hull was dyed with plant juices and charcoal. The entire village helped launch such a canoe.

Carving

Wood was one of the primary materials used by Hawaiian craftspeople. They almost exclusively relied on koa because of its density, strength, and natural luster. It was turned into canoes, wood ware, calabashes, and furniture used by the *ali'i.* Temple idols were another major product of wood carving. A variety of stone artifacts were also turned out, including poi pounders, mirrors, fish sinkers, and small idols.

Weaving

Hawaiians became the best basket makers and mat weavers in all of Polynesia. *Ulana* (woven mats) were made from *lauhala* (pandanus) leaves. Once the leaf was split, the spine was removed and the fibers stored in large rolls. When needed these would be soaked, pounded, and then fashioned into various floor coverings and sleeping mats. Intricate geometric patterns were woven in, and the edges were rolled and well fashioned. Coconut palms were not used to make mats in old Hawaii, but a wide variety of basketry was fashioned from the aerial root *'ie'ie.*

Featherwork

This highly refined art was practiced only on the islands of Tahiti, New Zealand, and Hawaii, but the fashioning of feather helmets and idols was unique to Hawaii. Favorite colors were red and yellow, which came only in limited supply from a small number of birds such as the *'o'o, 'i'iwi, mamo,* and *'apapane.* Professional bird hunters in old Hawaii paid their taxes to the *ali'i* in prized feathers.

The Mystical Labyrinths of Maui

It's fitting that there are labyrinths on a magical island in the middle of the Pacific Ocean. Not to be confused with mazes, a labyrinth is an ancient symbol built to represent a path to clarity and wholeness. Circular in design, it has an inner pathway that leads toward its center. Labyrinth walkers are asked to contemplate a question before making their way toward the middle—where pausing for contemplation and reflection is encouraged—and then just as purposefully retracing their steps back out. Think of it as a walking meditation.

WEST MAUI

The most vivid island labyrinth is the **Kapalua Labyrinth,** near popular attraction Makaluapuna Point (Dragon's Teeth) in West Maui. It occupies an ocean-side perch and has mesmerizing views of Lana'i and Moloka'i. To find it, head north on Office Road from Highway 30 in Kapalua, pass the Ritz-Carlton entrance, and park in the lot in front of the Steeple House chapel. Follow the signs to Dragon's Teeth, walk another 100 yards (91 m) beyond it, and you'll find the labyrinth.

UPCOUNTRY

The most prominent two labyrinths on Maui are at **The Sacred Garden** in Makawao. The main labyrinth is near a creek, while a smaller one is within a forest nursery. Owned and operated by Eve Hogan (a.k.a. "The Labyrinth Lady"), The Sacred Garden hosts a monthly full moon labyrinth event, complete with harp music and a brief lecture by Hogan on the history and mystique of labyrinths. Afterward, Hogan leads guests on a labyrinth walk surrounded by torches underneath the moonlight.

Nearby at **Lumeria Maui,** a stunning outdoor labyrinth made of lava rocks sits on the property behind a giant Buddha statue, with views overlooking the island's North Shore. A smaller labyrinth is in the parking lot of **St. John's Episcopal Church,** which offers panoramic views in a tranquil setting.

The feathers were fastened to a woven net of *olona* cord and made into helmets, idols, and beautiful flowing capes and cloaks. These resplendent garments were made and worn only by men, especially during battle, when a fine cloak became a great trophy of war. Featherwork was also employed in the making of *kahili* and lei, which were highly prized by the *ali'i* women.

Lei Making

Any flower or blossom can be strung into a lei, but the most common are orchids or the lovely-smelling plumeria. Lei, like babies, are all beautiful, but special lei are highly prized by those who know what to look for. Of the different stringing styles, the most common is *kui*—stringing the flower through the middle or side. Most "airport-quality" lei are of this type. The *humuhumu* style, reserved for making flat lei, is made by sewing flowers and ferns to a *ti*, banana, or sometimes *hala* leaf. A *humuhumu* lei makes an excellent hatband. *Wili* is the winding together of greenery, ferns, and flowers into short, bouquet-type lengths. The most traditional form is *hili*, which requires no stringing at all but involves braiding fragrant ferns and leaves such as *maile*. If flowers are interwoven, the *hili* becomes the *haku* style, the most difficult and most beautiful type of lei.

Tapa Cloth

Tapa, cloth made from tree bark, was common throughout Polynesia and was a woman's art. A few trees such as the *wauke* and *mamaki* produced the best cloth, but a variety of other types of bark could be used. First, the raw bark was pounded into a feltlike pulp and beaten together to form strips (the beaters had distinctive patterns that helped make the cloth supple). The cloth was decorated by stamping (a form of block printing) and dyed with natural colors from plants and sea animals in shades of gray, purple, pink, and red. They were even painted with natural brushes made from pandanus fruit, with an overall gray color made from charcoal. The tapa cloth was sewn together to make bed coverings, and fragrant flowers and herbs were either sewn or pounded in to produce a permanent fragrance.

Festivals and Events

For such a small island, there is always something happening on Maui. From sporting events to film festivals and rodeos to wine festivals, Maui is a flurry of community fervor. Dates are rarely constant, however, so check local listings and websites for up-to-date information.

For other events of all sorts throughout the state, visit the calendar of events listing on the Hawaii Visitors Bureau (HVB) website (www.calendar.gohawaii.com), or check out the weekly schedule of events on the *Maui Time* website (www.mauitime.com/calendar), or the fantastic daily calendar of events that's featured on Maui Now (www.mauinow.com/events).

MAUI

February

Chinese New Year (www.visitlahaina.com) celebrations are held in the evening along Front Street in Lahaina and include a lion dance, martial arts demonstrations, live music, food, and, of course, firecrackers.

For artists, the **Maui Open Studios** (www.mauiopenstudios.com) takes place during each weekend in February, showcasing the talent of the island's local art community.

The **Maui Whale Festival** (www.mauiwhalefestival.org) is sponsored by the Pacific Whale Foundation and features live music, festivals, fun runs, and community activities through the month of February. The annual **World Whale Day** takes place at Kihei's Kalama Park and is the largest event of the festival.

Seeing as February is the peak of whale season, it only makes sense that another event, **Whales Tales** (www.whaletrust.org), is held during the busy month. The event at the Ritz-Carlton Kapalua resort supports local whale research teams such as the Whale Trust, Center for Whale Studies, and Hawaii Whale Research Foundation.

March

March 26 is **Prince Kuhio Day,** a public state holiday observed in remembrance of Prince Kuhio, heir to the throne of the Hawaiian monarchy.

April

The **East Maui Taro Festival** (www.tarofestival.org) is celebrated in Hana with traditional ceremonies, music, food markets, symposia, demonstrations, and exhibitions to honor one of the island's most basic food sources and the resurgence of Hawaiian cultural traditions.

In Lahaina, April 20-24 is the approximate date of the **Banyan Tree Birthday** (www.visitlahaina.com) celebration for the town's famous banyan tree.

Toward the end of the month, the **Celebration of the Arts** (www.celebrationofthearts.org) at the Ritz-Carlton hotel in Kapalua begins its monthly spotlight (through December) on various indigenous art forms and cultural traditions. It's an absolute must-visit if you are in town.

Upcountry, the **Haiku Ho'olaulea and Flower Fest** (www.haikuhoolaulea.org) is held at the Ha'iku Community Center with live music, auctions, "talk story" sessions, vendors, and a welcoming atmosphere that defines this rural town.

TGIF

Maui Friday Town Parties (www.mauifridays.com) take place every Friday night 6pm-9pm, rotating regularly between the towns of Wailuku (1st Fri., Main St.), Lahaina (2nd Fri., Front St.), Makawao (3rd Fri., Baldwin Ave.), and Kihei (4th Fri., Azeka Shopping Center, 1279 S. Kihei Rd.), and, on the rare fifth Friday, Lana'i (Dole Park, Lana'i Ave and 7th St.). These are great free community events featuring live music, food vendors, and other merchants. Get your groove on, dance in the street, sample local foods, people-watch, and purchase some jewelry or art to take home.

May

May 1 is **Lei Day** in Hawaii. There are usually large lei day celebrations held in Wailea and various other places around the island.

At Whalers Village in Ka'anapali, the **Maui Onion Festival** (www.kaanapaliresort.com) celebrates everything about the Maui onion with food vendors, craft booths, recipe contests, chef demonstrations, and live entertainment.

Upcountry in Makawao, the **Seabury Hall Craft Fair** (www.seaburyhall.org) is held on the Saturday before Mother's Day and features Hawaiian craft vendors from across the state. With live music, food booths, and hundreds of artists, it's the perfect place to pick up a gift for mom.

At the Maui Arts and Cultural Center, the **Maui Brewers Fest** (www.mauiarts.org) celebrates the culture of craft brewing and the love of good beer.

June

One of the largest events in West Maui, the **Kapalua Wine & Food Festival** (www.kapaluawineandfoodfestival.com) takes place over four days in June and is considered the longest-running food and wine event in the United States. Established in 1981 by the Kapalua Wine Society, a nonprofit whose mission is to educate and boost appreciation for wine, the event takes place on the grounds of the luxurious Kapalua Resort and features master sommeliers, seasoned chefs from around the globe, and events such as cooking demonstrations, lectures, themed food tastings, bountiful brunches, and plenty of wine from renowned wineries. Pricing ranges $100-300 for various events, although true foodies can splurge on a festival pass for $1,250-1,400. You can't beat the extraordinary variety of cuisines and wines offered at this oceanfront setting.

The annual **Upcountry Fair** at the Eddie Tam Center, Makawao, is an old-fashioned farm fair right in the heart of Maui's *paniolo* country. Crafts, food, and competitions are all part of the fair, as are the county 4-H championship and auctions.

June 11 is **King Kamehameha Day** in Lahaina. Festivities include a parade through town, crafts, and lots of food and entertainment.

The annual **Slack-Key Guitar Festival** (www.slackkeyfestival.com) at the Maui Arts and Cultural Center in Kahului features some of Hawaii's best musicians.

The **International Windsurfing Tour,** a professional windsailing competition for men and women, is held at Kanaha Beach, and is part of the summer-long Maui Race Series.

The **Maui Film Festival** (www.mauifilmfestival.com) typically unfolds over a span of 10 days in June, so check the schedule and consider attending screenings, some of which are held outside under the stars. Note: In recent years, the festival has added events during November and December, too.

July

Over the July 4 weekend, head for the coolness of Makawao for the annual **Makawao Rodeo.** *Paniolo* are an old and important tradition in Hawaiian life. Held at the Oskie Rice

Arena, this old-time Upcountry rodeo can't be beat for fun and entertainment. It's accompanied by the Paniolo Parade through town.

October

The **Maui County Fair** (www.mauifair.com) at the Wailuku War Memorial Complex brings out the kid in everyone. An old-fashioned fair with Western and homespun flavor, this popular event caters to more than 100,000 people every year and offers rides, booths, exhibits, and games, plus plenty of music and food.

In Lahaina, the **Lahaina Plantation Days** (www.lahainarestoration.org) is hosted by the Lahaina Restoration Foundation and features live music, food booths, and movies held under the smokestack.

November

Each year the Ka'anapali Beach Hotel hosts **Hula O Na Keiki,** the state's only children's solo and partner hula contest. Two days of competition make this an entertaining event for everyone.

December

The **Holiday Lighting of the Banyan Tree** takes place in Lahaina, as well as decorating the Old Courthouse for Christmas.

MOLOKA'I

While there are numerous smaller festivals that take place on Moloka'i, the following are some of the larger annual events. For specific dates and more information, visit www.molokaievents.com.

January

The **Ka Moloka'i Makahiki Festival** is held for one day each January to celebrate the *makahiki*, a traditional time following the harvest when wars would cease in favor of arts, crafts, competition, and merriment. This tradition is carried on today at the Mitchell Pauole Center in Kauanakai.

May

The **Moloka'i Ka Hula Piko** (www.kahulapiko.com) festival is perhaps the largest annual event on the island and celebrates the history of the hula at its legendary birthplace in West Moloka'i.

September

Moloka'i is well known for its outrigger canoe races, when the island buzzes with visitors from across the Pacific. The **Pailolo Challenge** (www.facebook.com/pailolo) features paddlers who race from Maui to Kauanakakai, and the **Na Wahine O Ke Kai** features all-women paddle crews who race from Hale O Lono Harbor to the neighboring island of O'ahu.

October

More famous than the Pailolo is the **Moloka'i Hoe** (www.molokaihoe.com) outrigger canoe race, in which paddlers race from West Moloka'i to O'ahu. More than 1,000 paddlers compete in the event. It's an exciting time to be visiting West Moloka'i.

LANA'I

Many events on Lana'i are small in scope and akin to a community potluck. However, the biggest event of the year on the island is the **Annual Lana'i Pineapple Festival** (www.lanaipineapplefestival.com) in July at Dole Park. Ranked among the top 10 specialty food festivals by *USA Today* in 2014, the event features vendor exhibits, games, arts and crafts, live entertainment, an annual food fight, and fireworks after sunset.

Essentials

Transportation

GETTING THERE

Air

You'll likely land at the **Kahului Airport** (OGG, 1 Keolani Pl., 808/872-3830, www.airports.hawaii.gov/ogg), which is 30-45 minutes by car from the resort areas of Wailea and Ka'anapali. Kahului has direct flights to a host of mainland cities and a handful of international destinations, and most major carriers serve it.

Other than Kahului, there are two small airstrips, in Kapalua and in Hana. They have no direct flights to the mainland, but there are seven

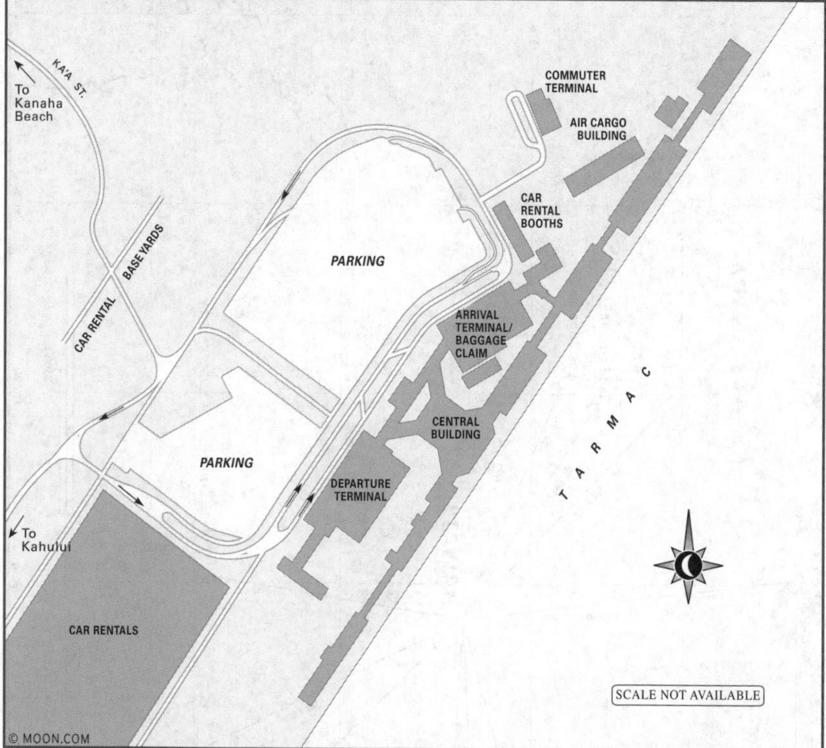

flights per day from the **Kapalua Airport** (JHM, 4050 Honoapi'ilani Hwy., 808/665-6108, www.hawaii.gov/jhm) to Honolulu on neighboring O'ahu.

GETTING AROUND

Car

CAR RENTALS

Rental cars are the easiest way to get around and explore the island. One of the airport's massive reconstruction projects relocated most major car rentals on-site. However, there are also a number of locally owned companies that can provide better rates and more "authentic"-looking cars. A shiny new rental car is nice to drive around in, but the downside is that rentals are car thieves' preferred target. Having a car that looks like a local's can potentially save you the cost of a break-in.

Most local car-rental companies offer free transportation to the airport if arranged ahead of time. Check **Maui Windsurfing Vans** (180 E. Waikea Ave., 808/877-0090, www.mauivans.com), **Kimo's Rent a Car** (440 Alamaha St., 808/280-6327, www.kimosrentacar.com), **Kihei Rent a Car** (96 Kio Loop, 808/879-7257, www.kiheirentacar.com), and **Manaloha Rent a Car** (200 Waiehu

Previous: aerial view of Kapalua.

Pacific Crossroads

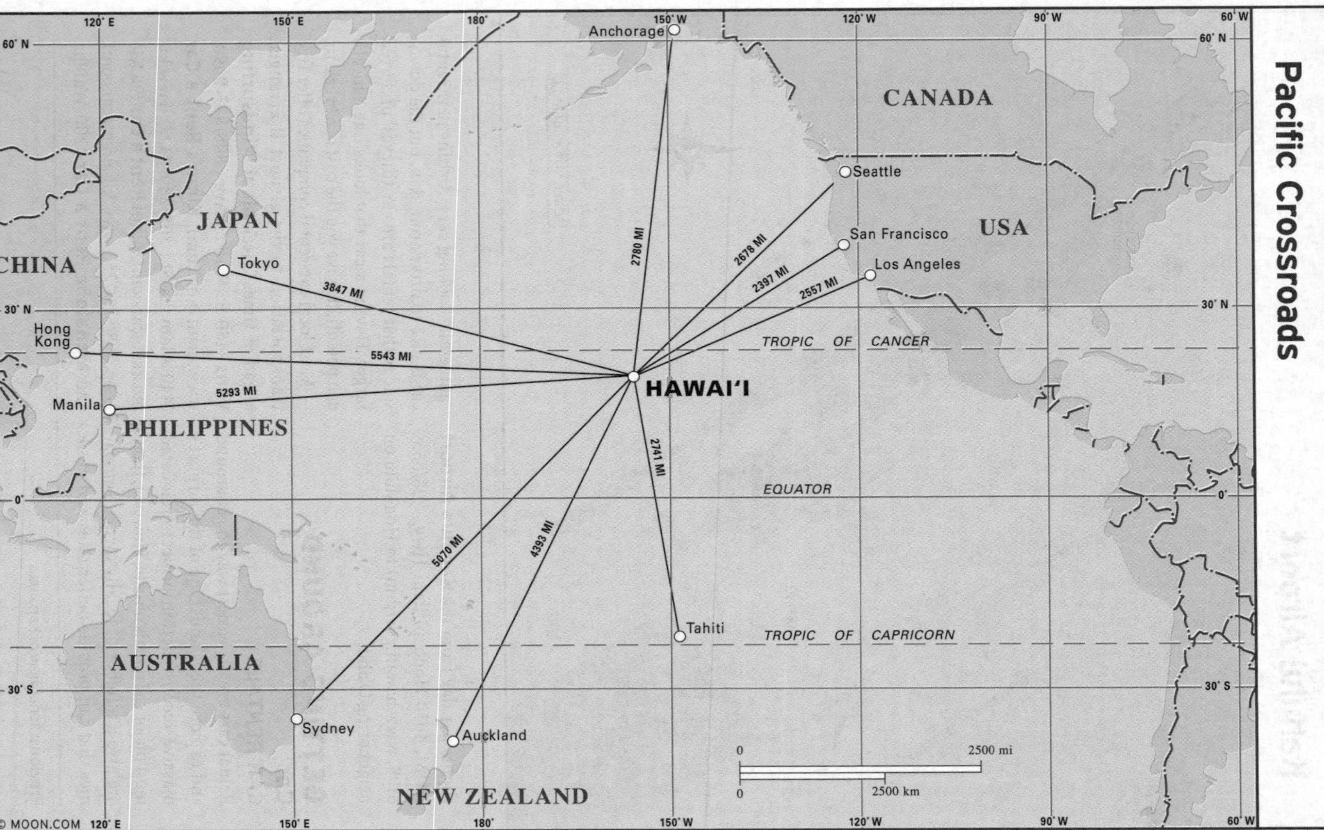

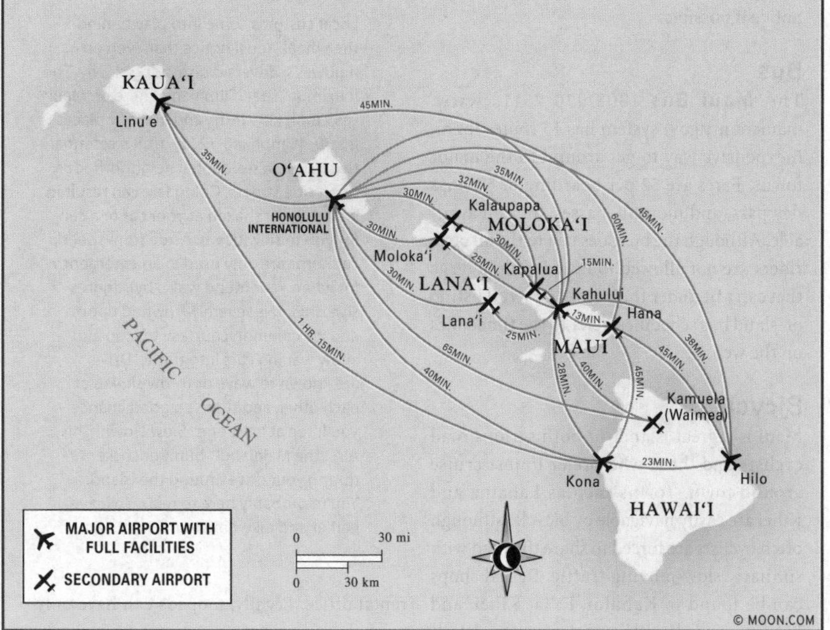

Beach Rd., 808/283-8779, www.manaloharentacar.net).

Book far ahead if you're traveling during the peak season, and know that drivers who are under 25 will often incur extra fees. To save some money, only rent a 4WD vehicle for the days you'll need it rather than for the duration of your trip.

Taxi

More than two dozen taxi companies operate island-wide service on Maui, and besides providing normal taxi service, they will also run tours all over the island. Taxis are expensive and metered by the distance traveled. From Kahului Airport, the fare to Lahaina should be roughly $70, and $85-90 to Ka'anapali, $100-125 to Kapalua, and $60-65 to Wailea. Expect $5-10 in and around Kahului, and about $15 to the hostels in Wailuku. Any taxi may drop off at the airport, but only those with permits may pick up there.

Those in need of a taxi can call **West Maui Taxi** (808/661-1122, www.westmauitaxi.com), **Kihei Taxi** (808/298-1877, www.kiheitaxi.com), or **Taxi of Wailea** (808/797-3950, www.wailea-taxi.com).

Shuttle

Robert's Hawaii (866/539-9400, www.robertshawaii.com) connects the Kahului Airport to virtually anywhere on the island and operates daily during flight arrival and departure times. With this door-to-door service, pickup can be either from the airport or from any hotel or condo if you're going to the airport. **Executive Airport Transportation** (808/669-2300) offers virtually the same service to and from the airport and to points around the island for marginally better rates, which average $60-65 per person from

Kahului to Ka'anapali. Although these companies will pick you up as soon as they can, they prefer several hours' or even 24 hours' notice if possible.

Bus

The **Maui Bus** (808/270-7511, www.mauicounty.gov) system has 13 routes for an inexpensive way to get around to the major towns. Fares are $2 per boarding or $4 for a day pass, and monthly passes are also available. Although the bus does run to the airport, riders are not allowed to board with luggage that can't fit under their seat. For a full listing of island bus schedules, refer to the timetables on the website.

Bicycle

Maui is a great island for both serious road cyclists and those who prefer to just cruise around town. Towns such as Lahaina and Kihei are easily navigable by bicycle, although often cyclists are forced to share the road with similarly slow-moving traffic. Rental shops can be found in Kahului, Pa'ia, Kihei, and Lahaina, and all will have island maps detailing the best rides.

Scooter

Scooters are great for running around town. Most rental operators will ask for a cash or credit card deposit. You must be at least 18 years old, have a valid driver's license, and often stay within a certain distance from your rental office. Legally, mopeds can have only one rider.

On the West Side of the island, you can get scooters from **Aloha Motorsports** (30 Halawai Dr., 808/667-7000, www.alohamotorsports.com), among other providers. In Kihei, **Maui Scooter Shack** (1794 S. Kihei Rd., 808/891-0837, www.mauiscootershack.com) offers scooter rentals and guided tours.

Drive with Aloha

Local customs come into play behind the wheel. You'll notice that even on highways, drivers cruise along slowly. The maximum speed limit anywhere on Maui is 55 mph (89 km/h), and in many places it's 30-45 mph (48-72 km/h). It's essential to go slow in residential neighborhoods or on side streets. Going fast can result in an angry fist shaken at your car or a call for you to slow down. Aside from speed, car horns are only used in an emergency (or when your friend walks by), aggressive driving is severely frowned upon, and it's common courtesy to stop and allow waiting cars into traffic. Drivers are known to wave or throw *shakas* at each other, and there's a good chance you'll see at least one "Slow Down! This Ain't the Mainland!" bumper sticker during your drive around the island. You're probably here to relax, so leave earlier and take time to enjoy the ride.

Travel Tips

ACCESS FOR TRAVELERS WITH DISABILITIES

A person with a disability can have a wonderful time in Hawaii; all that's needed is a little planning. Make as many arrangements ahead of time as possible: Tell the transportation companies and hotels the nature of your disability so they can make prearrangements to accommodate you. Bring your medical records and notify medical establishments of your arrival if you'll need their services. Travel with a friend or make arrangements for an aide upon arrival. Bring your own wheelchair if possible and let airlines know if it is battery-powered. Boarding interisland carriers sometimes requires steps. Wheelchairs are boarded early on special lifts, but they must know in advance that you're coming. Most hotels and restaurants easily accommodate people with disabilities, but call ahead to make sure.

Information

The state Commission on Persons with Disabilities was designed to aid disabled people. It is an invaluable source of information and distributes self-help booklets, published jointly by the Disability and Communication Access Board and the Hawaii Centers for Independent Living. Any person with disabilities heading to Hawaii should write first or visit the office of the **Hawaii Centers for Independent Living** (414 Kuwili St., Ste. 102, Honolulu, HI 96817, 808/522-5400). Additional information is available on the **Disability and Communication Access Board website** (www.hawaii.gov/health).

TRAVELING WITH CHILDREN

Traveling with children on Maui can be a memorable experience. Consider the kind of trip you want and book activities accordingly. Other than the beach, one of the best sites on the island for kids is the **Maui Ocean Center,** full of hands-on activities and educational experiences. To sneak away for a romantic dinner, the best service on the island for a short-term sitter is **The Nanny Connection** (808/875-4777, www.thenannyconnection.com), where professional sitting staff will meet you at your hotel and take care of children in your absence.

LGBTQ

Gay and lesbian travelers are welcome throughout Hawaii. While acceptance is part of the general state of mind, Maui has a smaller gay and lesbian community in terms of nightclubs, bars, and other gathering places than O'ahu does, for example. In 2011, Hawaii was the seventh state to legalize civil unions for same-sex couples, well before national marriage equality was established.

The first Sunday of the month, LGBTQ locals and visitors converge at **Nalu's South Shore Grill** (10:30am) in Kihei for brunch and socializing. On the second Saturday of the month, LGBTQ hikers—although everyone is welcome—head into nature; check out the **Maui LGBT Hiking Group** on Facebook for details. **Aloha Maui Pride** (www.alohamauipride.org) offers a concise calendar of upcoming events, including the annual **Pride festival** in early October, as well as general LGBTQ information.

Pride Guide Hawaii (www.gogayhawaii.com) has detailed listings of dining, nightlife, and lodging options. Another source is the **International Gay and Lesbian Travel Association** (954/630-1637, www.iglta.org), which can connect you with gay-friendly organizations and tours.

PEOPLE OF COLOR

Like the rest of Hawaii, Maui is a melting pot with a diverse population. Of the nearly 168,000 Maui County residents, 34.9 percent identify as white (30.1 percent non-Hispanic white), 29 percent Asian, 24.2 percent two or more races, 11.6 percent Hispanic, 10.6 percent Hawaiian or Pacific Islander, 0.8 percent Black or African American, and 0.6 percent American Indian or Alaskan Native. In 2020, there were four crimes related to race in the entire state, with one anti-white crime reported on Maui.

The **African Americans on Maui Association** (www.africanamericansonmaui.com) offers unique resources for the local population and presents cultural exhibits, arts, and programs related to the African American experience. Similarly, the **African American Heritage Foundation of Maui** strives to increase awareness of African American culture and contributions; check its Facebook page (www.facebook.com/AAHFMAUI) for information and events.

Tune into 88.5 FM at noon on Friday for ***The Latino Connection,*** hosted by a Maui local. The program's intention is to connect Maui's Spanish-speaking community and often includes a roundup of local events.

Maui for Free

Maui can be expensive, but it doesn't have to be. A number of Maui activities don't cost a thing:

- A morning stroll on the Kapalua Coastal Trail or Baldwin Beach
- Bodysurfing at D. T. Fleming Beach Park
- Watching the sunset at Haleakala and staying to watch the stars come out
- Free hula performances at the Lahaina Cannery Mall
- Hiking in Polipoli, Makena, or Hana
- Any ocean swim or even swimming beneath a waterfall on the Road to Hana
- Free evening entertainment at Whalers Village
- Watching the surfers at Lahaina or Honolua Bay or windsurfers at Kanaha Beach Park or Ho'okipa Beach Park
- Whale-watching from the Pali Lookout between Ma'alaea and Lahaina
- Attending a Maui Friday Town Party, a free event that rotates weekly from town to town

The **Japanese Cultural Society of Maui** (www.jcsmaui.org) seeks to perpetuate Japanese culture on the island and offers listings of a variety of cultural events.

CLOTHING-OPTIONAL BEACHES

Little Beach in Makena in South Maui is one of the most popular clothing-optional beaches and attracts a decent-size crowd. Access it by parking in Lot 1 of Makena State Beach and heading right once you get to the main beach. It's a modest 0.5-mile (0.8-km) hike to get here, but worth the effort.

Secret Beach on the North Shore is relatively secluded, situated between Pa'ia Bay and Baldwin Beach. Access this tranquil haven by parking at Pa'ia Bay and walking through a small wooded area on the west end.

OPPORTUNITIES FOR VOLUNTEER WORK

West Maui: Honokowai Valley

Spend a Saturday with **Maui Cultural Lands** (808/276-5593, www.mauiculturallands.org) in the magical Honokowai Valley for one of the best volunteering experiences on the island. Away from the highway in a valley forgotten by time, the remains of an ancient Hawaiian village are slowly being brought back to life. The structures, including rock walls and *lo'i,* are over 600 years old. The village was abandoned in the 1800s when the water was diverted to grow sugarcane. Today, spending a morning volunteering in Honokowai Valley is one of the most culturally authentic and meaningful experiences you can have in West Maui. In most cases, groups meet at 9:15am Saturday at the bottom of Pu'ukoli Road across from Kahekili Beach Park.

Central Maui

Volunteer for the **Hawaii Land Trust** (808/744-2462, www.hilt.org/protected-lands/maui) and you can join a trusted guide for the day in exotic places such as the Waihe'e Coastal Dunes and Wetlands Preserve. Expect an informative day that begins early in the morning and includes planting *hala* trees or supporting coastal cleanup by gathering easy-to-pick-up runaway nets and more.

Upcountry: Haleakala

For the chance to stay in a wilderness cabin inside Haleakala Crater, volunteer with **Friends of Haleakala** (www.fhnp.org) on one of their monthly service trips. The majority of these backpacking trips are free, and a few cost $15. During the three-day trip you'll clean the cabins and remove invasive species. You'll need to pack your own sleeping bag as well as food, water, and supplies, and participants are required to be physically fit and comfortable hiking at altitude. Space is limited, so check the website for trip dates and ways you can volunteer.

Health and Safety

Every year Hawaii ranks among the healthiest states. People here live longer than those anywhere else in the country, with an average life span of about 80 years. Lifestyle, heredity, and diet help with these figures, but Hawaii is still an oasis in the middle of the ocean, and germs just have a tougher time getting here. There are no cases of malaria, cholera, or yellow fever, and because of strict quarantine laws, rabies is nonexistent.

Due to the perfect weather, the soothing negative ionization from the sea, and the carefree lifestyle, everyone seems to feel better in the islands. Hawaii is just what the doctor ordered: a beautiful, natural health spa. The food and water are perfectly safe, and the air quality is the best in the country.

On the other hand, tooth decay, perhaps because of the wide use of sugar and the enzymes present in certain tropical fruits, is 30 percent above the national average. Obesity and related heart problems, as well as hard-drug use—especially crystal meth, or "ice"—are prevalent among native Hawaiians.

WATER SAFETY

Hawaii has a sad claim to fame: More people drown here than anywhere else in the world. Moreover, there are dozens of scuba, snorkeling, and boarding accidents yearly, with broken necks and backs or other injuries. These statistics shouldn't keep you out of the water. The best remedy is to avoid situations you can't handle, and ask lifeguards or beach attendants about conditions and follow their advice. If local people refuse to go in, there's a good reason. Even experts can get in trouble in Hawaiian waters, and while some beaches are calm and gentle, others can be frothing giants.

While beachcombing and especially when walking out on rocks, never turn your back to the ocean. Always be aware of what is going on with the water. Undertows (the water drawing back into the sea) can knock you off your feet and pull you into the shore-break. Observe the water carefully before you go in. Study it for rocks, breakers, and reefs. Look for ocean currents, especially those within reefs that can cause riptides when the water washes out a channel. Note where others are swimming or snorkeling, and go there. Don't swim alone, if possible, and obey all warning signs. When snorkeling, come ashore before you get tired.

When the wind comes up, get out. Stay out of the water during periods of high surf. High surf often creates riptides, powerful currents that can drag you out to sea. Mostly they peter out not far from shore, and you can often see their choppy waters on the surface. If you get caught in a "rip," don't fight by swimming directly against it; you'll only exhaust yourself. Swim diagonally across it, while letting it carry you, and try to stay parallel to the shore until you are out of the strong pull.

When bodysurfing, never ride straight in with your hands out in front you. This is the number one cause of broken necks in Hawaii. Instead, ride the wave at a 45-degree angle, and try to kick out the back of the wave instead of letting it slam you into the sand. Remember, waves come in sets, and little ones

Coronavirus and Maui

At the time of writing in early 2022, the coronavirus pandemic had significantly impacted the United States, including Hawaii, and the situation was constantly changing. Be mindful of the evolving situation when planning your trip.

BEFORE YOU GO

- Check local websites (listed below) for updated **local restrictions** and the **overall health status** of destinations in this area.
- If you plan to fly, check with your airline as well as the **Centers for Disease Control and Prevention** (www.cdc.gov) for updated **recommendations** and **requirements.**

RESOURCES

- **State of Hawaii:** Hawaii State Department of Health (https://health.hawaii.gov), Safe Travels Hawaii (https://hawaiicovid19.com/travel), Hawaii State Parks (https://dlnr.hawaii.gov/dsp)
- **Maui:** Maui County (www.mauicounty.gov), Maui Nui Strong (www.mauinuistrong.net)
- **National Park Service:** Haleakala National Park (www.nps.gov/hale)

can be followed by giants, so watch for a while before jumping in. Standard procedure is to duck under a breaking wave. You can survive even thunderous oceans using this technique. Don't try to swim through a heavy froth, and never turn your back and let it smash you.

Sharks and Marinelife

Some visitors fear that the moment their feet can no longer touch the sand they will be immediately attacked by **sharks.** The reality is that the chances of even seeing a large shark are remarkably slim, and since Hawaiian sharks have plenty of fish, they don't usually bother with unsavory humans. Still, try to avoid the mouths of rivers, murky water, and swimming around dawn and dusk.

Portuguese men-of-war and other jellyfish put out long, floating tentacles that sting if they touch you. It seems that many floating jellyfish are blown into shore by winds on the 8th, 9th, and 10th days after the full moon. Don't wash a sting off with freshwater—this will only aggravate it. Hot saltwater will take away the sting, as will alcohol, aftershave lotion, or meat tenderizer. After rinsing, soak with a wet towel. Antihistamines may also bring relief. Expect to start to feel better in about half an hour.

Coral can give you a nasty cut and is known for causing infections because it's a living organism. Wash the cut immediately and apply an antiseptic. Keep it clean and covered, and watch for infection. With coral cuts, it's best to have a professional look at it.

Poisonous **sea urchins** found in tide pools and shallow reefs can be beautiful creatures, but if you step on them, their spines will enter your foot, break off, and burn like blazes. This is known to locals as *wana* (vah-na). Soaking a couple of times in vinegar for half an hour or so should stop the burning, or if that's not possible, the Hawaiian solution is urine. It might seem gross, but it should put the fire out. Don't worry—the spines will die in a few days, and there are generally no long-term effects.

Hawaiian reefs also have their share of **moray eels.** These creatures are ferocious in appearance but will never initiate an attack. You'll have to poke around in their holes while snorkeling or scuba diving to provoke them. Sometimes this is inadvertent on the diver's part, so be careful where you stick your hands while underwater.

Present in streams, ponds, and muddy soil, **leptospirosis** is a freshwater-borne bacteria, deposited by the urine of infected animals. From 2 to 20 days after the bacteria enter the body, there will be a sudden onset of fever accompanied by chills, sweats, headache, and sometimes vomiting and diarrhea. Preventive measures include staying out of freshwater sources and mud where cattle and other animals wade and drink, not swimming in freshwater if you have an open cut, and not drinking stream water. Leptospirosis may be fatal in some cases if left untreated.

SAFETY IN THE OUTDOORS

Hiking

Other than bodysurfing and swimming, the most common way that visitors end up hurt or in trouble is taking unnecessary risks while hiking. Remember that wet rocks are slippery, and that stream crossings can be dangerous since flash floods can occur without warning. Stay away from the tops of waterfalls, where something as unpredictable as a gust of wind can send you one step farther than you had originally planned. If you are doing any cliff-jumping, be sure you've scouted the landing zone for rocks and that it's been verified as safe by someone in the know. When hiking along the sea, remember that large surf can unpredictably crash onto the shore, so keep a safe distance from turbid seas and slippery rocks.

While elastic bandages and disinfectants are great for cuts and scrapes, the most important thing to pack with you before heading out on an adventure is a dose of common sense; don't go out in conditions with which you're unfamiliar, and never push yourself outside your comfort zone when wandering off on your own. As the motto says, "If in doubt, don't go out." Remember that the moment you set foot on a trail—in the mountains, the rainforest, or along the shore—every action is a direct result of choices you made. It isn't the fault of the landowner that wet rocks on the property are slippery, so be prepared to accept personal responsibility for keeping yourself safe while exploring.

Sun

Many can't wait to strip down and lie on the sand, but the tropical sun will burn you to a crisp if you aren't diligent about sunscreen. Burning rays come through more easily in Hawaii because of the sun's angle, and you don't feel them as much because there's always a cool breeze. The worst part of the day is 11am to 3pm. Even though Maui is at about 21 degrees north latitude, not even close to the equator, it's still hundreds of miles south of sunny Southern California.

While spray-on sunscreens might be convenient, they stain the decks of boats, end up in your neighbor's mouth, and can ignite your skin if you stand next to an open flame (yikes!). The best, albeit most expensive, option is a sunscreen that isn't petroleum-based so that the chemicals don't wash off in the water and damage the coral. The best local sunscreen is **Doc Martin's,** developed by a local dermatologist and surfer to be highly water-resistant and great for covering your face.

Be aware of dehydration. The sun and wind sap your energy and your store of liquid. Bottled water in various sizes is readily available in all parts of Hawaii, or better yet, carry a reusable water bottle.

INSECTS

While Hawaii isn't infested with a wide variety of bugs, it does have its share. **Mosquitoes** are a particular nuisance in the rainforests. Be prepared, and bring a natural repellent such as citronella oil, available in most health food stores on the islands, or a commercial product available in grocery and drugstores. Campers will be happy to have mosquito coils to burn at night.

Bees and **wasps** tend to be found on the drier parts of the island—South Maui, West

Maui, and even Haleakala. **Cockroaches** are a common sight in Hawaii and are nothing to worry about.

While you aren't likely to encounter too many **spiders** while on vacation, brown spindly cane spiders can grow to be about the size of your hand, although their bite isn't dangerous. Also considered harmless is the yellow garden spider, which you might see in a captivating web. Two known venomous spiders on the island are the female western black widow and brown violin, but the chances of getting bitten are slim; if it does happen, wash the area thoroughly. Symptoms vary but typically result in inflammation or a rash.

Perhaps the most dangerous island critters are the fearsome-looking **centipedes,** which wiggle their way into dark places, particularly after the grass is mowed or the neighboring field harvested. Centipedes can deliver a nasty bite, causing inflammation, soreness, and some redness; juveniles pack more venom than adults. The best way to deal with them is with the old rubber slipper. If you get stung, meat tenderizer has been known to ease the discomfort.

HAOLE ROT

A peculiar skin condition caused by the sun and damp towels is referred to locally as *haole* rot because it supposedly affects only people of European descent, but you'll notice some dark-skinned folks with the same condition. Basically, the skin becomes mottled with white spots that refuse to tan. You get a blotchy effect, mostly on the shoulders and back. Dermatologists have a name for it, and they'll give you a prescription with a high price tag to cure it. It's common knowledge throughout the islands, however, that Selsun Blue shampoo has an ingredient that stops the white mottling effect. Just rub the lather over the affected areas, and it should clear up.

MEDICAL SERVICES

Hospital

Between central Kahului and central Wailuku, **Maui Memorial Medical Center** (221 Mahalani St., 808/244-9056) is the only full-service hospital on the island.

Medical Clinics

Several clinics dot the island. In South Maui, visit **Minit Medical Urgent Care Clinic** (808/667-6161) in any of its three locations (270 Dairy Rd., Ste. 239, Kahului; 1325 S. Kihei Rd., Ste. 103, Kihei; 305 Keawe St., Ste. 507, Lahaina) or **Kihei-Wailea Medical Center** (808/874-8100) in the Pi'ilani Village Shopping Center. **Kaiser Permanente** has clinics in Lahaina (910 Waine'e, 808/243-6800), Wailuku (80 Mahalani St., 808/243-6800), and Kihei (1279 S. Kihei Rd., 808/243-6000). In West Maui, **Urgent Care West Maui** (808/667-9721, www.westmauidoctors.com, 8am-6pm Mon.-Sat., 8am-1pm Sun.) is in the Ka'anapali Fairway Shops, and in Hana, **Hana Health** (808/248-8294) is along the highway as you enter town.

Information and Services

VISITOR INFORMATION

Free Travel Literature

Free travel literature is loaded with tips, discounts, maps, happenings, and more. Found at the airport arrival lounge and on some street stands, they include the narrow-format *This Week Maui, Maui Gold, Maui Magazine, Maui Beach and Activity Guide, Maui Activities and Attractions*, and the magazine-style *Maui Drive Guide*, with excellent maps and tips, provided free by many car-rental agencies. A great resource for activities is *101 Things to Do in Maui;* it also has money-saving coupons.

Book Online

If you want to save some serious cash when booking activities on Maui, virtually every activity operator on the island offers discounts for booking directly online. Oftentimes these discounts are in the range of 10-15 percent, which saves them money in the long run since concierge commissions can be as high as 30 percent (really). Granted, concierges work hard to earn that commission by educating themselves on exactly which activity will be right for you and your family, but if you've already decided on the activity you want, bust out that laptop and save some money by making your own reservation. Be sure to read the fine print: Sometimes the deal is only valid if booked at least seven days in advance.

Visitors Bureaus

The **Hawaii Visitors and Convention Bureau** (HVCB, www.hvcb.org) is a top-notch organization providing help and information to Hawaii's visitors. Anyone contemplating a trip to Hawaii should visit a nearby office or check out its website for specific information that might be helpful or required.

The best information on Maui is dispensed by the **Maui Visitors Bureau** (427 Ala Makani St., Kahului, 808/244-3530, www.gohawaii.com). Additional online information pertaining to Maui County can be found at the official **County of Maui website** (www.mauicounty.gov).

Weather Reports and Surfing Conditions

Remember that Maui has microclimates with weather unlike that on the mainland. To check what the weather is going to be in a certain part of the island, refrain from using large national websites such as Weather.com and instead opt for a local site more in tune with the island nuances. For weather, the best site around is www.mauiweathertoday.com by Glenn James, which offers both weather and surf conditions, with surf heights in the Hawaiian scale.

Consumer Protection

If you encounter problems with accommodations, bad service, or downright rip-offs, try the following: **Maui Chamber of Commerce** (62 N. Market St. #302, Wailuku, 808/244-0081, www.mauichamber.com), the state **Office of Consumer Protection** (808/243-4648, www.hawaii.gov), or the **Better Business Bureau** (808/244-0081).

MONEY

Currency

Only U.S. currency (the dollar) is accepted in Hawai'i.

Credit Cards

Credit cards are accepted for virtually all business transactions on Maui. Almost every form of lodging, shop, restaurant, and amusement takes them, although a handful of local mom-and-pop shops only accept cash.

COMMUNICATIONS AND MEDIA

Telephone

The telephone system on the main islands is modern and comparable to any system on the mainland. For landlines, any phone call to a number on that island is a local call; it's long-distance when dialing to another island or beyond the state. Cell (mobile) phone reception is good throughout Hawaii. Like anywhere, however, there are pockets where reception is poor or nonexistent.

For directory assistance, dial 1-411 (local), 1-555-1212 (interisland), 1-area code/555-1212 (mainland), 1-800/555-1212 (toll-free). The area code for all of Hawaii is 808.

WEIGHTS AND MEASURES

Hawaii, like the rest of the United States, employs the U.S. system of measurements. Dry weights are in ounces and pounds; liquid measures are in ounces, quarts, and gallons; and distances are measured in inches, feet, yards, and miles. The metric system is known but not in general use.

Electricity

The same electric system is in use in Hawaii as on the U.S. mainland. The system functions on 110 volts, 60 hertz alternating current (AC); type A (two-pin) and type B (three-pin) plugs are used. Appliances from Japan will work, but there is some danger that they will burn out, while those requiring the normal European 220 volts, with other types of plugs, will not work.

Time Zones

There is no daylight saving time in Hawaii. In winter, Hawaii is 2 hours earlier than the West Coast's Pacific standard time, 4 hours earlier than central standard time, 5 hours earlier than eastern standard time, and 11 hours earlier than Germany. During the mainland's daylight savings time, Hawaii is 3 hours earlier than Pacific daylight time, and 6 hours earlier than eastern standard time.

Because Hawaii is just east of the International Date Line, it is almost a full day behind Asian and Pacific cities. Hawaii is 19 hours earlier than Japan, 18 hours earlier than Singapore, 21 hours earlier than Sydney, and 23 hours earlier than New Zealand and Fiji.

Resources

Glossary

HAWAIIAN

There was once a time when it was illegal to speak Hawaiian. The language was relegated to the home, children were punished for speaking it in school, and a census performed in 1983 determined there were only 50 island youths who could speak their native tongue. It wasn't until 1978 that the language began a monumental comeback as part of a greater movement known as the Hawaiian Renaissance, and today, Hawaiian is fluently spoken by nearly 25,000 people, not counting the tens of thousands of residents who pepper their daily speech with Hawaiian loan words.

While English is the official language of tourism and daily life, the following list provides a basic vocabulary of words you are likely to hear. You might even discover some Hawaiian words that are so perfectly expressive they'll become regular parts of your vocabulary.

'a'a: rough clinker lava; *'a'a* has become the geological term to describe this type of lava found anywhere in the world.

'ae: yes

ahupua'a: pie-shaped land divisions running from mountain to sea that were governed by *konohiki,* local *ali'i* who owed their allegiance to a reigning chief

aikane: friend; pal; buddy

'aina: land; the binding spirit to all Hawaiians. Love of the land is paramount in traditional Hawaiian beliefs.

akamai: smart; clever; wise

akua: a god, or divine

ali'i: a Hawaiian chief or noble

aloha: the most common greeting in the islands; can mean both hello and good-bye, welcome and farewell. It can also mean romantic love, affection, or best wishes.

anuenue: rainbow

'a'ole: no

'aumakua: a personal or family god, often an ancestral spirit

auwe: alas; ouch! When a great chief or loved one died, it was a traditional wail of mourning.

halakahiki: pineapple

halau: school, as in hula school

hale: house or building; often combined with other words to name a specific place, such as Haleakala (House of the Sun)

hana: work; combined with *pau* means end of work or quitting time

hanai: literally "to feed." Part of the true aloha spirit. A *hanai* is a permanent guest, or an adopted family member, usually an old person or a child. This is an enduring cultural phenomenon in Hawaii, in which a child from one family (perhaps that of a brother or sister, and quite often one's grandchild) is raised as one's own without formal adoption.

haole: a word that at one time meant foreigner, but which now means a white person

hapa: half, as in a mixed-blooded person being referred to as *hapa haole*

hapai: pregnant; used by all ethnic groups when a *keiki* is on the way

haupia: a coconut custard dessert often served at a luau

he'enalu: surfing

heiau: A platform made of skillfully fitted

Hawaiian Language Pronunciation Guide

The Hawaiian language can appear baffling. Seemingly chaotic chains of vowels blend to create extremely long words. Confronted with the task of pronouncing words like *Honoapi'ilani* (a.k.a. Hwy. 30) or *Kealaikahiki*, many give up.

Vowels are not pronounced like those in English but as in Spanish: "aw, eh, ee, oh, ooh." Take the word *la* (sun), pronounced phonetically as "law," as opposed to "lah." The word *ala* (which means "road" or "path") is pronounced as "aw-law."

Much like in German, long words are easier to understand as several smaller words run together. Take, for example, *Haleakala*, Maui's famous mountain. Break it into smaller words: *hale a ka la*, phonetically "haw-lay-aw-kaw-LAW." Broken down, the meaning of the name is also easier to parse. *Hale* means "house," *a* means "of," *ka* means "the," and *la* means "sun," so, "House of the Sun."

Honoapi'ilani breaks down to *hono a Pi'ilani: hono* (bay) *a* (of) *Pi'ilani* (an ancient king of Maui), or completely, "the bays of Pi'ilani." This is a fitting name for the highway, seeing as Pi'ilani once created a footpath around much of the island as a way of connecting all the parts of his domain.

Kealaikahiki breaks down to *ke ala i kahiki: ke* (the) *ala* (road) *i* (to) *kahiki* (Tahiti), or completely, "the road to Tahiti." The "k" and "t" sounds are interchangeable in many Polynesian languages, and lacking a "t" in modern Hawaiian, the "k" is substituted. The name refers to the channel between Lana'i and Kaho'olawe, which points south, so it makes sense that "the road to Tahiti" is the direction canoes would head when journeying back to their ancestral homeland.

rocks, upon which temporary structures were built as temples and offerings made to the gods

hono: bay, as in Honolulu (Sheltered Bay)

honu: green sea turtle; endangered

ho'olaule'a: any happy event, but especially a family outing or picnic

huhu: angry; irritated

hui: a group; meeting; society; often used to refer to Chinese businesspeople or family members who pool their money to get businesses started

hukilau: traditional shore fish-gathering in which everyone lends a hand to *huki* (pull) the huge net

hula: indigenous Hawaiian dance in which the rhythm of the islands is captured by swaying hips and stories told by lyrically moving hands. A *hula halau* is a hula group or school.

huli huli: barbecue, as in *huli huli* chicken

imu: underground oven filled with hot rocks and used for baking. The main cooking method featured at a luau, used to steam-bake pork and other succulent dishes. The tending of the *imu* was traditionally for men only.

ipo: sweetheart; lover; girlfriend or boyfriend

kahuna: priest; sorcerer; doctor; skillful person. In old Hawaii *kahuna* had tremendous power, which they used for both good and evil. The *kahuna ana'ana* was a feared individual who practiced black magic and could pray a person to death, while the *kahuna lapa'au* was a medical practitioner bringing aid and comfort to the people.

kai: the sea. Many businesses and hotels employ *kai* as part of their names.

kalua: roasted underground in an *imu*. A favorite island food is *kalua* pork.

kama'aina: a child of the land; an old-timer; a longtime island resident of any ethnic background; a resident of Hawaii or native son or daughter. Hotels and airlines often offer discounts called "*kama'aina* rates" to anyone who can prove island residency.

kanaka: man or commoner; later used to distinguish a Hawaiian from other races

kane: man, but used to signify a relationship such as husband or boyfriend. Written on a restroom door, it means "men's room."

kapu: forbidden; taboo; keep out; do not touch

Understanding the *Okina*

Notice what appears to be a backward apostrophe in the middle of Hawaiian words such as Lana'i and Ka'anapali. This character is the *okina,* used to indicate pronunciation. To a linguist the *okina* denotes a glottal stop, meaning the voice stops briefly between two vowel sounds. An example in English is the hyphen in "uh-oh." *Lana'i* is pronounced "lah-NA-ee," the final *a* and the *i* each pronounced distinctly. Incorrect pronunciation would be to blend the two final vowels together as "lah-nai," which in the Hawaiian language means "a porch," written *lanai.*

Similarly, *Ka'anapali* is correctly pronounced with two distinct *a's*, phonetically "kah-ah-naw-PAW-lee." Incorrect pronunciation would be to blend the vowels together as "KAW-nah-paw-lee," or the dreaded "Ka-NAH-poli." The *okina* points out that the vowels are pronounced individually and not blended. *Lahaina*, written with no *okina,* is correctly pronounced with the blended vowels as "law-HIGH-nah."

kaukau: slang word meaning food or chow. Some of the best food in Hawaii comes from the *kaukau* wagons, trucks that sell plate lunches and other morsels.

keiki: child or children; used by all ethnic groups. "Have you hugged your *keiki* today?"

kiawe: an algaroba or mesquite tree from South America commonly found in Hawaii along the shore. It grows nasty long thorns that can easily puncture a tire. Legend has it that the trees were introduced to the islands by a misguided missionary who hoped the thorns would coerce Hawaiians into wearing shoes. Actually, they are good for fuel, as fodder for hogs and cattle, and for reforestation, none of which you'll appreciate if you step on one of the thorns or flatten a tire.

kokua: help. "Your *kokua* is needed to keep Hawaii free from litter."

kolohe: rascal

kona wind: a muggy subtropical wind that blows from the south and hits the leeward side of the islands. It usually brings sticky hot weather and is one of the few times when air-conditioning will be appreciated.

ko'olau: windward side of the island

kukui: a candlenut tree whose pods are polished and then strung together to make a beautiful lei. Traditionally the oil-rich nuts were strung on the rib of a coconut leaf and used as a candle.

kuleana: home site; the old homestead; small farms. Especially used to describe the small spreads on Hawaiian Home Lands on Moloka'i.

Kumulipo: ancient Hawaiian genealogical chant that records the pantheon of gods, creation, and the beginning of humankind

kupuna: a grandparent or old-timer; usually means someone who has gained wisdom. The statewide school system now invites *kupuna* to talk to the children about the old ways and methods.

la: the sun. Often combined with other words to be more descriptive, such as Lahaina (Merciless Sun) or Haleakala (House of the Sun).

lanai: veranda or porch. You'll pay more for a hotel room if it has a lanai with an ocean view.

lani: sky or the heavens

lauhala: traditional Hawaiian weaving of mats, hats, etc., from the prepared fronds of the pandanus (screw pine)

lei: a traditional garland of flowers or vines. One of Hawaii's most beautiful customs. Given at any auspicious occasion, but especially when arriving or leaving Hawaii.

lele: the stone altar at a *heiau*

limu: edible seaweed of various types. Gathered from the shore, it makes an excellent salad. It's used to garnish many island dishes and is a favorite at luau.

lolo: crazy, as in *lolo buggah* (stupid or crazy guy)

lomilomi: traditional Hawaiian massage; also, raw salmon made into a vinegared salad with chopped onion and spices

lua: the toilet; the bathroom

luakini: a human-sacrifice temple. Introduced to Hawaii in the 13th century at Waha'ula Heiau on the Big Island.

luau: a Hawaiian feast featuring poi, *imu*-baked pork, and other traditional foods. Good ones provide gastronomic delights.

luna: foreman or overseer in the plantation fields. They were often on horseback and were renowned for either their fairness or their cruelty. Representing the middle class, they served as a buffer between plantation workers and white plantation owners.

mahalo: thank you. *Mahalo nui* means "big thanks" or "thank you very much."

mahele: division. The Great Mahele of 1848 changed Hawaii forever when the traditional common lands were broken up into privately owned plots.

mahimahi: a favorite eating fish. Often called "dolphin," but mahimahi is a true fish, not a cetacean.

mahu: similar to transvestite or transgendered person; often used derisively

maile: a fragrant vine used in traditional lei. It looks ordinary but smells delightful.

maka'ainana: a commoner; a person "belonging" to the *'aina* (land), who supported the *ali'i* by fishing and farming and as a warrior

makai: toward the sea; used by islanders when giving directions

make: dead; deceased

malihini: what you are if you have just arrived: a newcomer; a tenderfoot; a recent arrival

malo: the native Hawaiian loincloth. Not worn except at festivals or pageants

mana: power from the spirit world; innate energy of all things animate or inanimate; the grace of god. Mana could be passed on from one person to another, or even stolen. Great care was taken to protect the *ali'i* from having their mana defiled. Commoners were required to lie flat on the ground and cover their faces whenever a great *ali'i* approached. *Kahuna* were often employed in the regaining or transference of mana.

manini: small; stingy; tight

mauka: toward the mountains; used by islanders when giving directions

mauna: mountain. Often combined with other words to be more descriptive, such as Mauna Kea (White Mountain).

mele: a song or chant in the Hawaiian oral tradition that records the history and genealogies of the *ali'i*

Menehune: the legendary "little people" of Hawaii. Like leprechauns, they are said to shun humans and possess magical powers.

moa: chicken; fowl

moana: the ocean; the sea

moe: sleep

mo'olelo: ancient tales kept alive by the oral tradition and recited only by day

nani: beautiful

nui: big; great; large; as in *mahalo nui* (thank you very much)

'ohana: a family; the fundamental social division; extended family. Now often used to denote a social organization with grassroots overtones.

oli: chant not done to a musical accompaniment

'ono: delicious; delightful; the best.

'opihi: a shellfish or limpet that clings to rocks and is gathered as one of the islands' favorite pupu. Custom dictates that you never remove all of the *'opihi* from a rock; some are always left to grow for future generations.

'opu: belly; stomach

pahoehoe: smooth, ropy lava that looks like burned pancake batter. It is now the geological term used to describe this type of lava found anywhere in the world.

pakalolo: "crazy smoke"; marijuana

pake: a Chinese person. Modified from the Chinese word meaning "uncle." Can be derisive, depending on the way it's used.

pali: a cliff; precipice. Hawaii's geology makes them quite common. The most famous are the *pali* of O'ahu, where a major battle was fought.

paniolo: a Hawaiian cowboy. Derived from Spanish. The first cowboys brought to Hawaii during the early 19th century were Mexicans from California.

pau: finished; done; completed. Often combined into *pau hana,* which means the end of work or quitting time.

pilau: stink; bad smell

pilikia: trouble of any kind, big or small; bad times

poi: a glutinous paste made from the pounded corm of taro, which ferments slightly and has a light sour taste. Purplish in color, it's a staple at luau, where it is called one-, two-, or three-finger poi, depending on its thickness.

pono: righteous or excellent

pua: flower

puka: a hole of any size. *Puka* is commonly used by island residents, whether talking about a pinhole in a rubber boat or a tunnel through a mountain.

pupu: an appetizer; a snack; hors d'oeuvres; can be anything from cheese and crackers to sushi. Often, bars or nightclubs offer complimentary pupu.

pupule: crazy; nuts; out of your mind

pu'u: hill, as in Pu'u 'Ula'ula (Red Hill)

tapa: a traditional paper cloth made from beaten bark. Intricate designs were stamped in using beaters, and natural dyes added color. The tradition was lost for many years but is now making a comeback, and provides some of the most beautiful folk art in the islands. Also called *kappa.*

taro: the staple of old Hawaii. A plant with a distinctive broad leaf that produces a starchy root. It was brought by the first Polynesians and was grown on magnificently irrigated plantations. According to the oral tradition, the life-giving properties of taro hold mystical significance for Hawaiians, since it was created by the gods at about the same time as humans.

ti: a broad-leafed plant that was used for many purposes, from plates to hula skirts. Especially used to wrap religious offerings presented at the *heiau.*

tutu: grandmother; granny; older woman. Used by all as a term of respect and endearment.

ukulele: *uku* means "flea" and *lele* means "jumping," so "jumping flea," the way the Hawaiians perceived the quick finger movements used on the banjo-like Portuguese folk instrument called a *cavaquinho*

wahine: young woman; female; girl; wife. Used by all ethnic groups. When written on a restroom door, it means "women's room."

wai: freshwater; drinking water

wela: hot.

wiki: quickly; fast; in a hurry. Often seen as *wiki wiki* (very fast), as in Wiki Wiki Messenger Service

USEFUL PHRASES

Aloha kakahiaka Good morning

Aloha ahiahi Good afternoon

E komo mai Welcome

Mahalo nui loa Thank you very much

PIDGIN

More so than Hawaiian, Pidgin is the language spoken around the islands. A mix of words from English, Hawaiian, and a host of other languages, it has a lilt, cadence, and grammar entirely its own. Even though it uses a lot of English, to nonresidents, Pidgin can be completely undecipherable. It can take years to fully understand Pidgin, but for the *keiki* who were raised here it is a natural native tongue. While you probably won't become fluent, here are some basic phrases to get by.

an' den and then? big deal; so what's next?

auntie respected elderly woman

bumbye Later; after a while

blalah from *brother,* but refers to a large, heavy-set, good-natured Hawaiian man

brah brother; pal. All the bros in Hawaii are brahs. Used to call someone's attention. One of the most common words even among people who are not acquainted. After a fill-up at a gas station, a person would say "Tanks, brah."

chicken skin goose bumps

choke lots of something

cockaroach steal; rip off

da kine a catchall word of many meanings that epitomizes the essence of Pidgin. *Da kine* is a euphemism for Pidgin and is substituted whenever the speaker is at a loss for a word or just wants to generalize.

geev um Give it to them; Give them hell; Go for it. Can be used as an encouragement. If a surfer is riding a great wave, the people on the beach might yell, "Geev um, brah!"

grinds food

hana hou again. Especially after a concert, the audience shouts "hana hou" (one more!).

hele on Let's get going.

howzit? as in "Howzit, brah?" What's happening? How's it going? The most common greeting, used in place of the more formal "How do you do?"

lesgo Let's go! Do it!

li'dis an' li'dat like this or that

lolo stupid, crazy

mo' bettah a better way of doing something.

pakalolo "crazy smoke," meaning marijuana

pau finished; done; over and done with. A Hawaiian word. *Pau hana* means end of work or quitting time. Once used by plantation workers, now used by everyone

rubbah sleepah rubber slippers, sandals, flip-flops. Referring to slippers as "sandals" is only something that mainlanders would do.

seestah sister, female

shaka hand wave where only the thumb and baby finger stick out, meaning "Thank you, all right!"

shoots whatever, sure, in agreement. Example: "What, you like go Makena today?" "Shoots!"

stink eye basically, frowning at someone; using facial expression to show displeasure. Hard looks. What you'll get if you give local people a hard time.

talk story spinning yarns; shooting the breeze; throwing the bull; a rap session. If you're lucky enough to be around to hear *kupuna* (elders) talk story, you can hear some fantastic tales in the tradition of old Hawaii.

tanks, brah thanks, thank you

to da max all the way

wea stay? literally, "where stay," to ask a location. Examples: "Wea the car stay?," "Wea you stay?," or the glorious "Wea you stay going?" (Where are you going?)

We go Let's go! Usually used in conjunction with *shoots*, as in "Shoots we go!"

Internet Resources

African Americans on Maui Association (AAOMA)
www.africanamericansonmaui.com

An outstanding regional resource for authentic African American historical information. It also includes events listings.

Aloha Maui Pride
www.alohamauipride.org

This site offers general LGBTQ information as well as a concise calendar of upcoming events, including the annual Pride festival in October.

Hawaiian Kingdom Government
www.hawaiiankingdom.org

Site of one of the organizations of native Hawaiians advocating for sovereignty and independence.

Hawaiian Music Island
www.mele.com

Check out the Hawaiian music scene at one of the largest music websites focusing on Hawaiian music, books, and videos related to Hawaiian music and culture, with concert schedules, Hawaiian music awards, and links to music companies and musicians.

Hawaii Ecotourism Association
www.hawaiiecotourism.org

Lists goals, members, and activities, and provides links to member organizations and related ecotourism groups.

Hawaii Museums
www.hawaiimuseums.org

This site is dedicated to the promotion of museums and cultural attractions in the state, with links to member sites on each of the islands.

Hawaii Visitors and Convention Bureau
www.gohawaii.com

The official site of the state-run tourism organization has information about all of the major Hawaiian Islands: transportation, accommodations, eating, activities, shopping, Hawaiian products, an events calendar, a travel planner and resource guide for a host of topics, as well as information about meetings, conventions, and the organization.

Hawaii Visitors Bureau Calendar of Events
www.gohawaii.com/trip-planning/events-festivals

Events listings for events of all sorts happening throughout the state. Information can be accessed by island, date, or type.

Maui County
www.mauicounty.gov

Includes information on city government, the county-sponsored bus system, disability access, and a calendar of events.

Maui Information Guide
www.mauiinformationguide.com

A large, informative, and modern website that offers insights into everything from activities and trip planning to helpful tips and safety guidelines.

Maui News
www.mauinews.com

Website of Maui's largest newspaper. It has a concentration of news coverage about Maui, but also covers major news from the neighboring islands.

Office of Hawaiian Affairs
www.oha.org

Official site for the state-mandated organization that deals with indigenous Hawaii-related affairs.

State Foundation of Culture and the Arts
www.sfca.hawaii.gov

This site of the State Foundation of Culture and the Arts features a calendar of arts and cultural events, activities, and programs held throughout the state.

University of Hawaii Press
www.uhpress.hawaii.edu

This University of Hawaii Press website has the best overall list of titles for books published on Hawaiian themes and topics.

Index

F

GH

IJ

K

L

M

NO

P

QRS

T

UV

WXYZ

List of Maps

Photo Credits

All images © Greg Archer except: Title page photo: HTA / Tor Johnson; page 2 © Greg Nunes | unsplash.com; page 3 © Hawaii Tourism Authority (HTA) /Tor Johnson; page 6 © (top right) Jeannette Howard; (bottom) Stealthc4 | Dreamstime.com; page 7 © (top) HTA / Tor Johnson; (bottom left) HTA / Kuni Nakai; (bottom right) Jeannette Howard; page 8 © Ivansabo | Dreamstime.com; page 10 © (top) HTA / Tor Johnson; (bottom) HTA / Tor Johnson; page 11 © (top) HTA / Tor Johnson; (bottom) Anton Repponen | Unsplash.com; page 12 © HTA / Tor Johnson; page 13 © MNStudio | Dreamstime.com; page 14 © (top) HTA / Tor Johnson; page 15 © (top) Laglider | Dreamstime.com; (bottom) Eugene Kalenkovich | Dreamstime.com; page 16 © (bottom) Jeff Whyte | Dreamstime.com; page 19 © HTA / Ron Garnett; page 21 © (bottom) HTA / Tor Johnson; page 24 © HTA / Blake Bronstad; Gilney Lima | Dreamstime.com; page 25 © (top) Jeannette Howard; page 27 © Roninphotography | Dreamstime.com; Jeannette Howard; page 29 © HTA; HTA / Dana Edmunds; page 31 © (bottom) Atlantis Submarine; page 33 © Bbeckphoto | Dreamstime.com; page 34 © (top left) Mike7777777 | Dreamstime.com; page 39 © (top left) HTA / Max Wanger; (top right) MNStudio | Dreamstime.com; (bottom) Kyle Ellison; page 44 © (top) HTA / Tor Johnson; (left middle) HTA / Tor Johnson; (right middle) HTA / Tor Johnson; (bottom) HTA / Tor Johnson; page 50 © (top) Eugene Kalenkovich | Dreamstime.com; (left middle) Artboardman39 | Dreamstime.com; (right middle) Jeannette Howard; (bottom) HTA/Dana Edmunds; page 54 © Kyle Ellison; page 58 © (top left) Kyle Ellison; (top right) Underwatermaui | Dreamstime.com; (bottom) Jeannette Howard; page 62 © Jeannette Howard; page 67 © (top left) Gilney Lima | Dreamstime.com; (top right) Kyle Ellison; (bottom) Jeannette Howard; page 75 © Gilney Lima | Dreamstime.com; page 78 © (top) Atlantis Submarine; (bottom) Idreamphotos | Dreamstime.com; page 82 © (top left) Kyle Ellison; (bottom) Kyle Ellison; page 86 © HTA / Tor Johnson; page 92 © Jeannette Howard; page 96 © (top) Jeannette Howard; (bottom) Maui Brewing Co.; page 102 © Ralf Broskvar | Dreamstime.com; page 105 © Creatista | Dreamstime.com; page 106 © (top right) HTA / Heather Goodman; page 113 © (top left) Igokapil | Dreamstime.com; (top right) Kyle Ellison; (bottom) HTA / Maui Film Festival / Randy Jay Braun; page 115 © (top left) HTA / Tor Johnson; (top right) HTA / Dana Edmunds; page 118 © Pikappa | Dreamstime.com; page 123 © (top) Kyle Ellison; (bottom) Mike7777777 | Dreamstime.com; page 131 © HTA / Tor Johnson; page 137 © Peteleclerc | Dreamstime.com; page 138 © (top left) Jeannette Howard; (top right) HTA / Tor Johnson; page 143 © (top) HTA / Daeja Fallas; (bottom) Mike7777777 | Dreamstime.com; page 149 © (top) Stan Jones | Dreamstime.com; page 152 © (top) Mike7777777 | Dreamstime.com; (bottom) HTA / Tor Johnson; page 156 © (top) HTA / Blake Bronstad; (bottom) Marco Pitacco | Dreamstime.com; page 162 © Kyle Ellison; page 165 © (top) Kyle Ellison; (bottom) Greg Amptman | Dreamstime.com; page 174 © (bottom) Manuel Balesteri | Dreamstime.com; page 188 © (bottom) Maui Brewing Co.; page 193 © (top left) HTA / Maui Wine; page 197 © (top) Elise St.Clair | unsplash.com; page 205 © (top left) Amy Vosters | unsplash.com; (top right) Marissa Rodriguez | unsplash.com; (bottom left) HTA / Deaja Fallas; (bottom right) Scott Griessel | Dreamstime.com; page 206 © HTA / Maui Wine; page 208 © Evan Austen | Dreamstime.com; page 213 © (top) MNStudio | Dreamstime.com; (bottom) Reinout Van Wagtendonk | Dreamstime.com; page 217 © Maomaotou | Dreamstime.com; page 221 © (top left) HTA / Tommy Lundberg; page 224 © (top) Dana Edmunds | unsplash.com; (left middle) Kyle Ellison; page 228 © Christopher Bellette | Dreamstime.com; page 229 © (top left) Garyhartz | Dreamstime.com; (top right) Digital94086 | Dreamstime.com; page 235 © (top left) Gilney Lima | Dreamstime.com; (top right) Jeannette Howard; (bottom) Irina88w | Dreamstime.com; page 240 © (top left) HTA / Tor Johnson; (top right) National Tropical Botanical Garden; (bottom) Pierre Leclerc | Dreamstime.com; page 245 © (top) aulacobleigh | Dreamstime.com; (bottom) Nathan Ziemanski | Unsplash.com; page 247 © Kyle Ellison; page 251© (left middle) Pierre Leclerc | Dreamstime.com; (bottom) George Cole | Dreamstime.com; page 253 © (top left) Jeannette Howard; (top right) Gavril Margittai | Dreamstime.com; (bottom) HTA | Anton Repponen; page 256 © (top left) Gavril Margittai | Dreamstime.com; (top right) Pierre Leclerc | Dreamstime.com; (bottom left) Idreamphotos | Dreamstime.com; (bottom right) HTA / Tor Johnson; page 261 © (top left) HTA / Blake Bronstad; (top right) HTA / Tommy Lundberg; page 270 © (top left) HTA / Montage Kapalua Bay; (top right) Roodboy | Dreamstime.com; (bottom left) HTA / Tor Johnson; (bottom right) Mariusz Prusaczyk | Dreamstime.com; page 280 © (top) EQRoy | Shutterstock.com; page 288 © Kyle Ellison; page 289 © HTA / Pierce M Myers Photography; page 290 © (top left) HTA / Heather Goodman; (top right) HTA / Heather Goodman; page 294 © (top) HTA / Pierce M

Myers Photography; (left middle) KnelsenPhoto | Shutterstock.com; (right middle) Kyle Ellison; (bottom) HTA / Dana Edmunds; page 300 © (top left) HTA / Heather Goodman; (top right) Christopher Eng Wong | Dreamstime.com; (bottom) HTA / Pirece M. Myers Photography; page 303 © Ultimate Whale Watch; page 306 © (top left) HTA / Lanai Hospitality Partners; (top right) HTA / Heather Goodman; (bottom left) HTA / Heather Goodman; (bottom right) HTA / Blake Bronstad; page 312 © (top left) HTA/ Blake Bronstad; (top right) HTA / Lanai Hospitality Partners; (bottom) Kyle Ellison; page 315 © Fischinger | Dreamstime.com; page 316 © (top left) William Lee Bowman | Dreamstime.com; (top right) Kyle Ellison; page 320 © Kyle Ellison; (top right) HTA / Dana Edmunds; (bottom) Aga Monka | Shutterstock.com; page 325 © (top) Bob Pool | Shutterstock.com; (left middle) HTA / Heather Goodman; (right middle) HTA / Heather Goodman; page 331 © William Lee Bowman | Dreamstime; page 332 © Nickolas Warner | Shutterstock.com; page 337 © (top left) HTA / Dana Edmunds; (top right) HTA / Jason Rothenberg; (bottom) Flying2lowak | Dreamstime.com; page 341 © HTA / Dana Edmunds; page 342 © HTA/Lehua Waipa AhNee; page 349 © (top left) Rudi Strydom | unsplash.com; (top right) Jeannette Howard; (bottom left) Yale Cohen | unsplash.com; (bottom right) Jeannette Howard; page 370 © HTA

MAP SYMBOLS

Expressway	City/Town	Airport	Golf Course
Primary Road	State Capital	Airfield	Parking Area
Secondary Road	National Capital	Mountain	Archaeological Site
Unpaved Road	Highlight	Unique Natural Feature	Church
Trail	Point of Interest	Waterfall	Gas Station
Ferry	Accommodation	Park	Glacier
Railroad	Restaurant/Bar	Trailhead	Mangrove
Pedestrian Walkway	Other Location	Skiing Area	Reef
Stairs	Campground		Swamp

CONVERSION TABLES

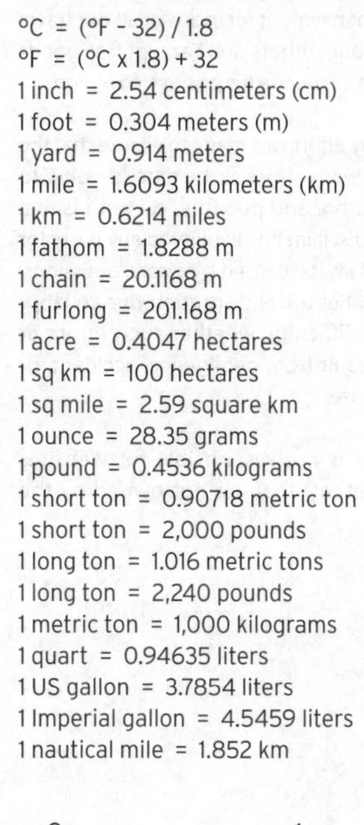

°C = (°F - 32) / 1.8
°F = (°C x 1.8) + 32
1 inch = 2.54 centimeters (cm)
1 foot = 0.304 meters (m)
1 yard = 0.914 meters
1 mile = 1.6093 kilometers (km)
1 km = 0.6214 miles
1 fathom = 1.8288 m
1 chain = 20.1168 m
1 furlong = 201.168 m
1 acre = 0.4047 hectares
1 sq km = 100 hectares
1 sq mile = 2.59 square km
1 ounce = 28.35 grams
1 pound = 0.4536 kilograms
1 short ton = 0.90718 metric ton
1 short ton = 2,000 pounds
1 long ton = 1.016 metric tons
1 long ton = 2,240 pounds
1 metric ton = 1,000 kilograms
1 quart = 0.94635 liters
1 US gallon = 3.7854 liters
1 Imperial gallon = 4.5459 liters
1 nautical mile = 1.852 km

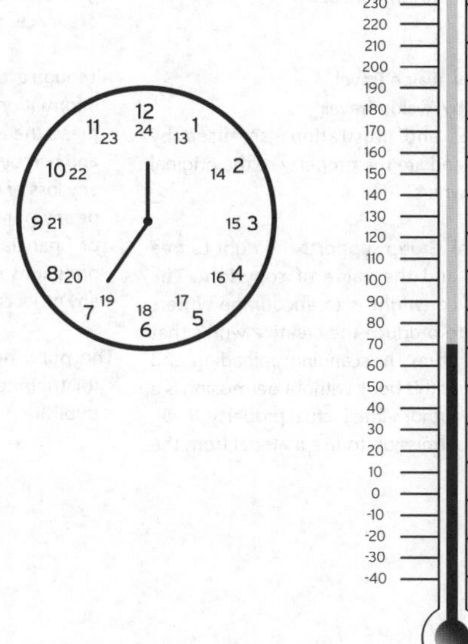

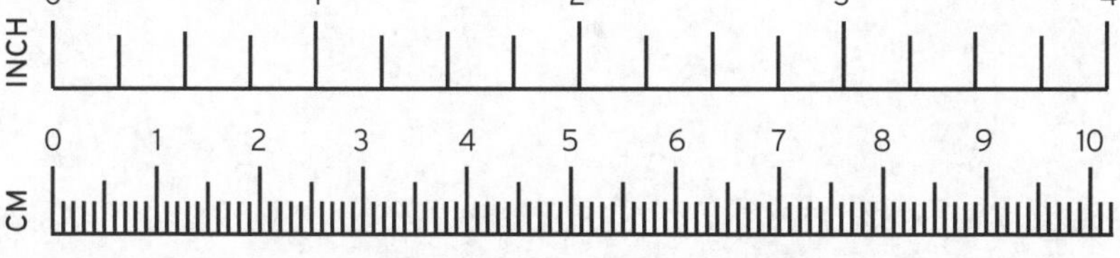

MOON MAUI
Avalon Travel
Hachette Book Group
1700 Fourth Street
Berkeley, CA 94710, USA
www.moon.com

Editor and Series Manager: Kathryn Ettinger
Acquiring Editor: Nikki Ioakimedes
Copy Editor: Ann Seifert
Graphics Coordinator: Ravina Schneider
Production Coordinator: Ravina Schneider
Cover Design: Toni Tajima
Map Editor: Albert Angulo
Cartographers: Brian Shotwell, John Culp
Indexer: Greg Jewett

ISBN-13: 978-1-64049-670-5

Printing History
1st Edition — 1986
12th Edition — November 2022
5 4 3 2 1

Front cover photo: sea turtle at sunset © Mitchell Pettigrew | Gettyimages.com
Back cover photo: Ka'anapali Beach © Tomas Del Amo | Dreamstime.com

Printed in Malaysia for Imago

All recommendations, including those for sights, activities, hotels, restaurants, and shops, are based on each author's individual judgment. We do not accept payment for inclusion in our travel guides, and our authors don't accept free goods or services in exchange for positive coverage.